AMERICAN

GOVERNMENT

AMERICAN
GOVERNMENT

Political Development and Institutional Change

CAL JILLSON
Southern Methodist University

Eighth Edition

Routledge
Taylor & Francis Group

NEW YORK AND LONDON

Editor: Jennifer Knerr
Editorial Assistant: Lillian Rand
Production Editor: Lisa Salonen
Project manager: Swales & Willis Ltd, Exeter
Copyeditor: Swales & Willis Ltd, Exeter
Proofreader: Swales & Willis Ltd, Exeter
Indexer: Sue Lightfoot

Eighth edition published 2016
by Routledge
711 Third Avenue, New York, NY 10017

And published in the UK
by Routledge
2 Park Square, Milton Park, Abingdon, Oxon OX14 4RN

Routledge is an imprint of the Taylor & Francis Group, an informa business

First edition published 1999 by Harcourt Brace College Publishers
Seventh edition published 2013 Taylor & Francis

Library of Congress Cataloging in Publication Data
A catalog for this book has been requested

ISBN: 978-1-138-78366-9 (pbk)
ISBN: 978-1-315-76855-7 (ebk)

Printed in Canada

To Jane

"Give me liberty to know, to utter, and to argue freely according to conscience, above all liberties. And though all the winds of doctrine were let loose to play upon the earth, so Truth be in the field, we do injuriously . . . to misdoubt her strength. Let her and Falsehood grapple; who ever knew Truth put to the worse, in a free and open endeavor."

John Milton, *Aeropagitica*, 1644

BRIEF CONTENTS

CONTENTS

SPECIAL FEATURES

THE CONSTITUTION TODAY

PRO & CON

LET'S COMPARE

TABLES

FIGURES

PREFACE

American politics is not as simple as it looks. This has probably always been true, but it has never been truer than it is today. Whether you are president, pundit, scholar, or student, you have to decide what to make of Islamic fundamentalism, Russian democracy, global free trade, and Iran's pursuit of nuclear weapons. Closer to home you have to decide what to make of gay marriage, the fear that social security might go broke, and judicial activism.

On the other hand, how difficult can it be for a college professor to introduce a college student to American politics? After all, politics and government are all around us: in the newspapers that we read, on the evening news that we watch, and in the high school history and civics courses that we all took—some more recently than others. We all have a general feel for American politics.

But for most students, even those who have been out in the world for a while between high school and college, information about politics and government comes in bits and pieces having little structure and less meaning. How do the pieces of American politics fit together, from public opinion and political participation, to constitutional limitations and political institutions, to the enactment of particular laws, policies, and programs? This book offers a systematic introduction to American government and politics for college and university students.

In my experience, students have three broad reactions to the initial description of virtually any aspect of the American political system. Whether the discussion is of the electoral process, the committee system in Congress, or the rules governing eligibility for food stamps, the preeminent and continuing question that students bring to the discussion is: How does it work? Answering this question—the descriptive question—is usually the easy part. Halfway through the answer, the student's brow begins to knit and that quizzical look that teachers know so well comes over the student's face, and he or she asks: Why do we do it that way? The teacher's answer, of course, is couched in terms of how things came to be this way—the historical explanation—and then, almost inevitably, and often immediately, students want to know about potential alternatives—the normative concern—isn't there a better way to do this?

My goal in this book is to provide solid descriptive and historical answers to the first two questions and open and encourage discussion among students and between students and their teachers of the broader issues involved. Historical development and institutional change are the organizing themes of this book. History regularly empties ideas and institutions of their initial meanings and refills them with different, although never wholly different, meanings more relevant to the new day. Freedom, equality, and democracy did not mean the same thing to Thomas Jefferson as they came to mean to Abraham Lincoln or Franklin Roosevelt. They did not mean exactly the same thing to George W. Bush that they meant to his predecessors. Moreover, the presidency that Barack Obama occupies is simply not the same office that Roosevelt, Lincoln, or Jefferson occupied.

On the assumption that it is hard to know where you are going if you do not know where you have been, each chapter of this text opens with a discussion of the origins and development of the subject of the chapter, whether that be individual rights and liberties, the electoral system, the presidency, or America's place in the world. Once we know how some aspect of American politics stands today and how it got that way, we are in position to begin a discussion of what alternatives might look like. A truly useful text should show where we have been, where we are today, and where we seem to be headed.

I have chosen to write the brief American government text that you have before you rather than a book twice its size, because faculty know too much that is fascinating and students have too many interesting questions for any book to try to anticipate and address them all. What I have tried to do is to describe how the American political system works, how it came to work that way, and what the general range of possibilities, both for continuity and for change, seem to be. Where the conversation goes from there is up to students and their teachers, as it should be.

To students, I hope to say more than that politics is important, that it will affect your lives, time and again, continuously, and in important ways. I hope to provide a sense of how politics works so that when an issue arises about which you care deeply you will not feel helpless. Politics is not just a spectator sport. Rather, it is a sport in which all who turn out make the team and all who come to practice get to start—not always with the varsity, to be sure, but politics is a game that we are all entitled to play. To faculty teaching American government, I hope to help you communicate to your students both what we know as political scientists and how much fun we had in being part of the process of discovering it and teaching about it.

FEATURES AND CHANGES

The eighth edition retains many of the features from the previous editions.

The Constitution Today

"The Constitution Today" was a new feature in the sixth edition. Again in this new edition each chapter opens with a vignette that highlights the continuing relevance, even centrality, of the Constitution to our most critical modern political debates and controversies. The United States is very unusual in this regard. The Founders invented the idea of a written constitution resting on the foundation of popular sovereignty. Many nations now have written constitutions, but no nation reveres its constitution the way Americans do theirs. Moreover, no nation gives its constitution the central role that Americans do in shaping the outcome of important substantive political debates and battles. In America, it has often been said, every major political dispute eventually will end up before the courts so that the proposed political outcomes can be measured against the Constitution.

The first two chapters in this book deal with the origins of American political principles and how those principles informed and shaped the Declaration of Independence and the Constitution. We open these chapters with explorations of the idea of "American exceptionalism" and of the deep historical resonance of Barack Obama's famous "Speech on Race" delivered during the 2008 presidential campaign. In Chapters 3 through 16, we highlight the relevance of key provisions of the Constitution to our most important contemporary political battles. This feature, "The Constitution Today," spotlights the way that the provisions of the Constitution shape and structure our fights over issues like gay marriage, gun control, campaign contributions and free speech, states rights, congressional redistricting, health care reform, domestic surveillance, war powers, and much more. These vignettes bring to life otherwise obscure provisions of the Constitution by highlighting the critical issues that they decide. They are identified in the text by the following symbol. The Constitution TODAY

Focus Questions

Each chapter opens with a set of focus questions that prepare the student for the major points made in the chapter. The questions later appear in the margin where the text addresses that particular question, allowing students to easily scan the chapter for a quick review after they have completed their reading.

"Pro & Con" and "Let's Compare" Boxes

As in the previous edition, the book includes two different types of boxed features. "Pro & Con" features offer opposing viewpoints to controversial issues currently in the news and "Let's Compare" features place the discussion of U.S. institutions and processes in a global context, giving students a sense of possible alternatives to the American political tradition.

What Do You Think?

New to the eighth edition is a feature called *What Do You Think?* Throughout the book, where an important and interesting question has been discussed, we pose a couple of questions designed to make students stop and think. These are also an invitation to teachers to pause the lecture and engage the class in a discussion of an important issue.

End-of-Chapter Features

Each chapter closes with a summary, a list of central concepts and cases, and suggestions for additional reading. Finally, this new edition directs students to the Internet for more information on topics discussed in the text. At the end of each chapter are URLs that direct students to further information on issues, institutions, groups, and data discussed in the book.

Companion Reader: **Perspectives on American Government**

To supplement the new eighth edition of *American Government: Political Development and Institutional Change*, I joined with David Robertson of the University of Missouri, St. Louis, to develop an American Government reader. The second edition of this reader, which we have called *Perspectives on American Government: Readings in American Political Development and Institutional Change* (Routledge, 2014), facilitates deeper exploration of key themes in the text. The chapter order of the text and the reader has been aligned so that they can be assigned together if instructors wish. Each chapter of the reader is composed of six selections, usually two or three classic readings, from Locke, the Federalist, Jefferson, Tocqueville, and the like, and three or four of the most outstanding American Political Development (APD) essays of recent years from today's top scholars. This reader will deepen and enrich the learning experience of students using this text. A sample of these readings are identified in the Suggested Readings sections at the end of each chapter of this volume by the following symbol ✎.

Online Resources

American Government offers a website for both students and instructors at **www. routledge.com/cw/jillson**. This site contains a wealth of useful resources to help students as they learn about American politics and instructors as they prepare their courses.

For Instructors

Instructor Manual　　Chapter by chapter, the manual provides answers to the text's Focus Questions; chapter outlines; lecture outline suggestions with options for behavioral, APD, institutional, or political theory approaches to the course; projects, exercises, and activities; and additional resources.

Test Bank　　A full test bank for each chapter, with multiple choice, fill-in-the-blank, short answer, and essay questions, available as Word documents, for the Respondus testing software, or in formats compatible with uploading to Blackboard, WebCT, or other Virtual Learning Environments.

PowerPoint Lecture Slides　　Instructors can access sample lecture slides, mirroring the lecture outlines provided in the Instructor Manual and complete with figures and tables from the text.

Course Management Cartridges　　Instructors have access to course cartridges to upload into Blackboard, WebCT, or Moodle, making all the features of both the student site and instructor resources readily accessible in the platform you're already using.

For Students

Chapter Summaries   Summaries help students home in on the main points of each chapter.

Practice Quizzes   Self-tests for each chapter provide students instant feedback on their answers.

Flashcards   Interactive flashcards allow students to test their knowledge of the book's key concepts.

Participation Activities   Activity prompts encourage students to explore further the themes of the book, asking them to apply those themes to their own experiences.

Interactive Timelines   These timelines bring to life key dates and eras illustrated in each chapter of the text through links to relevant articles, videos, and websites, thus enhancing students' understanding of these pivotal milestones in American politics.

Links   Useful websites and resources are provided here to allow for further investigation of the material.

Updates

The eighth edition has been updated and revised in several important ways. Most importantly, a renewed focus on student engagement and classroom discussion has informed this new edition. At multiple points in each chapter, controversial issues, surprising comparisons, unexpected developments, and puzzling facts are highlighted as jumping off points for class discussions, impromptu debates, or brief essay assignments. There are four to eight or nine such prompts in each chapter of this new eighth edition and each is identified by an icon like this— 🔖. Finally, the eighth edition has been thoroughly updated to provide complete coverage of the Obama presidency, including the 2012 presidential election, the 2014 congressional elections, the ongoing rollout of the Obama health program, and much more.

PLAN OF THE BOOK

This eighth edition of *American Government: Political Development and Institutional Change* is divided into sixteen chapters. Each chapter begins with a vignette and several focus questions designed to introduce and display the main themes of the chapter. The subject matter of each chapter is presented in five or six major sections, with each major section divided internally into subsections, in explicit outline form, so that it is easy for students to understand and study.

Chapters 1 through 3 present the political principles and constitutional foundations of American politics. Chapter 1 describes the ideas about government that the colonists carried from the old world to the new and the effects of the openness and bounty of the new continent on those ideas. Chapter 2 describes the social, economic, and political institutions that were in place in the American colonies as the Revolution approached. The historical and practical knowledge of the revolutionary generation provided the menu of institutional possibilities from which they chose as they first designed their state governments, the Articles of Confederation, and later the U.S. Constitution. Chapter 3 describes changes in the broad structure of American federalism as the nation evolved from agriculture, to industrial powerhouse, to global superpower.

Chapters 4 through 8 describe how Americans learn about politics, organize their thinking about politics, and come together in interest groups and political parties to affect the course of politics. Chapter 4 describes how Americans get their political information and what the distribution of partisan and political opinion among Americans looks like. Chapter 5 describes the American mass media and the role that they play in determining which political issues and what political information comes to our collective attention. Chapter 6 describes how Americans come together in interest groups to press their ideas, interests, and demands for change on government. Chapter 7 describes the changing role that political parties, including third parties, play in elections and governance. Chapter 8 describes how citizens, variously informed and organized, use the process of campaigns, elections, and voting to select their political leaders and, much more broadly, the policies that their leaders will implement.

Chapters 9 through 12 describe the major institutions of the national government and how they relate to each other and to the problems and issues that confront them. Chapter 9 describes the structure of the Congress and the legislative process through which it seeks to represent and respond to the ideas, needs, and interests at large in the country. Chapter 10 describes the range of responsibilities and expectations that confront the American president and the American presidency. Chapter 11 describes the bureaucratic structure of the national government and the dilemmas that face the bureaucrats who staff them as they seek to deliver a wide range of services fairly, efficiently, and at a reasonable cost. Chapter 12 presents the structure of the federal judiciary and the ongoing controversy over whether its role should be one of judicial activism or of judicial restraint.

Finally, Chapters 13 through 16 provide a broad overview of the domestic and international policy issues and opportunities facing the United States in the new century. Chapters 13 and 14 link the changing scope and character of our civil liberties and civil rights to the evolving character of our society. Chapter 15 explores the tension between our desire to provide social programs to aid and assist the neediest among us and our desire to keep taxes low so that citizens can enjoy the fruits of their labor and American companies and products can remain competitive in the global economy. Chapter 16 seeks to place America and its future, both the futures of its individual citizens and of the nation collectively, within the broad and rapidly changing context of the world economy and the world political environment.

Acknowledgments

Many debts were incurred in the writing and revision of this book. My greatest debt remains to all the authors who went before and upon whom I had the good fortune to draw. Completion of this new edition of *American Government* leaves me with a renewed sense of pleasure and pride in our collective enterprise—political science.

Much of this sense of pleasure and pride comes from remembering how many fine people contributed to the conception, development, and completion of this book, particularly the Routledge team and the reviewers. Michael Kerns, acquisitions editor, was unwavering in support of this enterprise. The team that he assembled eased my way tremendously. Lillian Rand, editorial assistant, and Lisa Salonen, senior production editor, pulled all of the pieces together in the end and actually made a book of the raw materials that I provided them.

I owe special thanks to David Tatom and Stacey Sims for their early support of this book. I also received wonderful support from the staff of the Political Science Department and the John Tower Center for Political Studies at Southern Methodist University. Several colleagues, including Dennis Ippolito, Dennis Simon, Joe Kobylka, Jim Gerhardt, Brad Carter, Matthew Wilson, and Jim Hollifield came to my aid more frequently than either they or I would like to remember.

Finally, the expertise and patience of friends and colleagues around the country were shamelessly exploited. Among the reviewers, whose invaluable and constructive feedback I've incorporated throughout the book, were Steve Anthony, Georgia State University; Debra August, Florida Atlantic University; Ross K. Baker, Rutgers University; Tom Baldino, Wilkes University; Brian Bearry, University of Texas at Dallas; Paul Beck, Ohio State University; Robert A. Bernstein, Auburn University; Michael Binford, Georgia State University; James Brent, San Jose State University; Susan Burgess, Ohio University; Gregory A. Caldeira, Ohio State University; Cecilia Rodriguez Castillo, Southwest Texas State University; Paul N. Chardoul, Grand Rapids Community College; Roger H. Davidson, University of Maryland; Byron W. Daynes, Brigham Young University; Kevin Deegan-Krause, Wayne State University; Jim Duke, Richland College; Larry Elowitz, Georgia College; Art English, University of Little Rock; Brian Farmer, Amarillo College; Cecilia Ferradino, University at Albany, State University of New York; Terri Susan Fine, University of Central Florida; Charles J. Finocchiaro, University of South Carolina; Paul Goggi, University of Utah; Dennis J. Goldford, Drake University; George J. Gordon, Illinois State University; Paul Goren, Southern Illinois University at Carbondale; James J. Gosling, University of Utah; Craig Grau, University of Minnesota at Duluth; Gerard S. Gryski, Auburn University; Thomas J. Hoffman, University of Illinois, Champaign-Urbana; Judson L. Jeffries, Purdue University; Mark R. Joslyn, University of Kansas; Nina Therese Kasniunas, Goucher College; Thomas Keating, Arizona State University; William E. Kelly, Auburn University; Joseph A. Kunkel, III, Mankato State University; Christopher Lawrence, Texas A & M International University; Christine Ludowise, Georgia Southern University; Donald Lutz, University of Houston; Rolin G. Mainuddin, North Carolina Central University; James Mitchell, California State University, Northridge; Thomas Mortillaro, Nicholls State University; Ayo Ogundele, Kilgore College; Anthony J. Nownes, University of Tennessee, Knoxville; Richard M. Pious, Barnard College; Daniel Ponder, Drury University; Robert Porter, Ventura College; John Pottenger, University of Alabama in Huntsville; Ronald Rapoport, William and Mary; Christopher C. Robinson, Clarkson University; Joseph Romance, Drew University; Winfield H. Rose, Murray State University; Raymond Sandoval, Richland College; Robert Sahr, Oregon State University; Michael Semler, California State University, Sacramento; Raymond Smith, Columbia University; Robert Speel, Penn State Erie; A. Jay Stevens, California State University, Long Beach; Walt Stone, University of Colorado, Boulder; Martin P. Sutton, Bucks County Community College; Alexander Thompson, Schoolcraft College; Sylvia Ann Thompson, University of Miami; William Wallis, California State University, Northridge; Jeffrey S. Walz, Wheaton College; Marcella G. Washington, Florida Community College at Jacksonville; Ronald Weber, University of Wisconsin, Milwaukee; Robert S. Wood, University of North Dakota; Frank Zinni, State University of New York at Buffalo; and Louis C. Zuccarello, Marist College.

Credits for the Chapter opener images are as follows:
Chapter 1: Getty Images AFP/Jewel Samad
Chapter 2: Getty Images/William Thomas Cain
Chapter 3: Getty Images/Seth McConnell
Chapter 4: Getty Images/Alex Wong
Chapter 5: Getty Images AFP/Mladen Antonov
Chapter 6: AP Photo/J. Scott Applewhite
Chapter 7: Luke Sharrett/*New York Times*
Chapter 8: © Susana Raab/Sygma/Corbis
Chapter 9: The Granger Collection, New York
Chapter 10: Getty Images/The White House
Chapter 11: Getty Images/Win McNamee
Chapter 12: Chuck Kennedy/MCT/Landov
Chapter 13: © Brooks Kraft/Corbis
Chapter 14: Jacob Silberberg/Reuters/Landov
Chapter 15: Spencer Platt/Getty Images
Chapter 16: Photo by Bill O'Leary/*Washington Post* via Getty Images

THE AUTHOR

Cal Jillson earned a PhD from the University of Maryland and has taught at Louisiana State University and the University of Colorado, where he chaired the Department of Political Science from 1989 to 1993. He joined the faculty of Southern Methodist University in 1995 as professor and chair of the Department of Political Science (1995–2001). He is a member of the American Political Science Association and several regional political science associations. Professor Jillson has written a number of books dealing with the origins of the American political culture and the health and performance of contemporary American politics and political institutions. His most recent book, *Lone Star Tarnished: A Critical Look at Texas Politics and Public Policy*, appeared in 2012.

Chapter 1

THE ORIGINS OF AMERICAN
POLITICAL PRINCIPLES

*❝ What Athens was in miniature, America will be in magnitude. The one was the
wonder of the ancient world; the other is becoming the admiration of the present. ❞*

THOMAS PAINE,
The Rights of Man, Part 2, 1792

AMERICAN EXCEPTIONALISM?

Every American believes at some level in "American Exceptionalism." You may not know the phrase, but you know the broad assumptions and the underlying feelings of national pride and confidence. American exceptionalism is the conviction, embedded in the American psyche from the first generation of colonists, that America is blessed and that God has destined her to play a uniquely positive role in the world.

Virtually every president and presidential candidate in the past half century, including John Kennedy, Ronald Reagan, Bill Clinton, and George W. Bush, have endorsed American exceptionalism. The reason is simple—any presidential candidate who can communicate unwavering commitment to America's fundamental values while drawing his opponent's commitment to those values into question has gained a great advantage. Not surprisingly, American exceptionalism was again front and center in the 2012 presidential contest.

Even before winning the Republican nomination, Mitt Romney told Wisconsin voters that President Obama "doesn't have the same feelings about American exceptionalism as we do." Moreover, he said, the 2012 presidential election provided the opportunity "to restore to this country the principles that made this nation the greatest nation in the history of the earth." President Obama felt compelled to fight back, declaring "My entire career has been a testimony to American exceptionalism." In 2009, during his first trip abroad as president, he had spoken at length about American exceptionalism, saying "I think we have a core set of values that are enshrined in our Constitution, in our body of laws, in our democratic practices, in our belief in free speech and equality, that, though imperfect, are exceptional."

Many Americans believe that America is God blessed and that it is superior to other countries in the world, but how many others would add with President Obama that little phrase "though imperfect?" When the Pew Research Center asked Americans in 2012 whether they thought their culture was superior to others, the responses varied by age and education. Just 37 percent of 18–29 year olds answered yes, while more than 60 percent of those over 50 did. Fifty-two percent of those without college degrees answered yes, while 43 percent of those with degrees did. Why the variation? How would you answer this question?

Is America exceptional? If America is exceptional, what made it so? Most American leaders have answered the first question in the affirmative. Answers to the second question have varied, with many, including Ronald Reagan and George W. Bush, offering that God made America exceptional. Others have argued that American exceptionalism, while real, flowed from the fortuitous combination of remarkable leaders drawing lessons from the history of Europe and from their own colonial experience to craft new institutions that left Americans free to make a bountiful continent bloom.

The belief in American exceptionalism has worked for good and ill both in our domestic and international politics. Domestically, the belief that America is distinctively the home of freedom, equality, and opportunity has encouraged striving and entrepreneurship, but it has also encouraged us to believe that the results are natural and perhaps even blessed. Internationally, the belief that America is leading the world into a brighter future has encouraged the fight against tyranny but also has led to a sense that America can do no wrong.

In this opening chapter, we show that the roots of American politics are buried deep in the intellectual and political soils of Europe.

WHAT DO YOU THINK?

- Did the growth of old Europe, transplanted to America, bear new fruit?
- Is there any danger in seeing our nation's fundamental values and institutions as shaped by God rather than by more fallible human hands?
- Does the former promote hubris while the latter suggests caution, maybe even humility?
- In a dangerous world, is hubris or humility the better stance?

Focus Questions: from reading to thinking

Q1 What are the broad purposes of government?

Q2 How should government be designed to achieve its purposes?

Q3 What lessons about government did colonial Americans draw from the history of ancient Greece and Rome?

Q4 What circumstances led Europeans to leave their homelands to settle in America?

Q5 What did democracy mean to our colonial ancestors, and did they approve it?

Change is a constant in politics. When your grandparents were born, much of Asia, Africa, and the Middle East were colonies governed from Europe. When your parents were born, Germany, Italy, and Japan were recently defeated tyrannies; and the Soviet Union was the source of a communist ideology that threatened to spread around the globe. Today things look much different; much has changed.

Just in your lifetime, democracy has taken root around the world. In some places, like Russia (the Soviet Union is no more) and central Asia, the roots have not penetrated far, but in others, like South Africa and much of central Europe, they have sunk deep enough to support vibrant new democracies. In the Middle East, long a bastion of authoritarian government, the Arab Spring suggests a desire for democracy, though the odds seem long.

Even as you settle into your study of our democratic government and politics, the United States and its allies have been seeking for more than a decade to plant democratic institutions in Afghanistan and Iraq. Despite their long histories, neither nation has had much more than passing exposure to democracy. Most recently, both countries were abject tyrannies: the religious tyranny of the Taliban in Afghanistan and the secular tyranny of Saddam Hussein's Baath Party in Iraq. Their paths to democracy, assuming they can stay on them at all, will be long and rocky. But their struggles do raise the broader question of how nations, peoples, and their leaders draw upon their own historical experiences and those of others when the opportunity arises to chart a new course into the future. Our nation faced just such an opportunity more than two centuries ago. In fact, the presence of "Tea Party" and the "Gay Rights" movement on the nation's streets suggest that the struggle to define and refine our democracy is ongoing.

Before we begin our study of American politics, let me ask you to think for a moment about the title of this book: *American Government: Political Development and Institutional Change.* The thought behind this title is that American government is best understood historically, as a set of carefully designed political institutions that have evolved and changed over the course of American political history as the nation itself has evolved. To further clarify our purposes, we need to define two terms—American political development and institutions.

American political development (APD) is the study of American politics from an historical perspective. APD assumes that understanding contemporary American political institutions or practices is enriched and deepened by understanding their origins, as well as the changes and reforms they have undergone in arriving at their modern forms. As we shall see time and again throughout this book, history regularly empties ideas and institutions of their original meanings and refills them with different, though never completely different, meanings more relevant to the new day.

Finally, we need to define the word institution and talk a little bit about how institutions change. *The Oxford English Dictionary* defines **institution** as "An established law, custom, usage, practice, organization, or other element in the political and social life of a people." An institution can be an organization, like Congress or the Supreme Court, but it can also be a legally defined custom or practice, like marriage, slavery, or voting. But institutions are always historical, they exist within a context or a specific historical environment. As that environment changes, evolves, and becomes more layered and complex, political institutions from Congress, and voting to slavery and marriage have had to change as well. Congress, marriage, and voting are not the same institutions they were in the nation's early years, but we can trace these contemporary institutions back to their roots and see how they adapted over time. In other cases, slavery is an obvious example, social change has been so profound that the institution no longer exists. But even here, vestiges of the old institution may persist in norms and assumptions, even if no longer in law. So welcome to the story and the study of American government and politics.

American political development (APD) The study of development and change in American political processes, institutions, and policies.

institution A custom, practice, or organization, usually embedded in rules and law, that defines and structures social and political activity.

A TRADITION TO DRAW FROM

Human beings have always wondered about what government should be and do. What benefits should government provide to citizens, and how should it be organized to achieve the best results? History and experience provided lessons upon which the American Founders drew in designing American political institutions. To know why they made the choices they made and how they believed that the institutions they chose would work, we must be familiar with the historical evidence and examples that they took to be persuasive.

Through most of the history that the American Founders knew, no women and few men had been free. A few societies, such as those of Athens and Rome, while free for some, had been based on immigrant and slave labor. From the fall of Rome in the fifth century A.D. through the stirrings of modern Europe in the sixteenth and seventeenth centuries, virtually all people had been subjects of kings and tyrants rather than citizens of free societies. Colonial American societies, while somewhat more free, were by no means free for all. While most white men were citizens, religion, law, and politics held these white men to be superior to women, minorities, and immigrants. How, then, did America become what Seymour Martin Lipset, the prominent mid-twentieth-century political sociologist, called the "first new nation"; the first nation in which free people lived under democratic institutions?[1] The answer, of course, is slowly.

In the first part of this chapter we will describe three general perspectives on how government should be organized and what it should be designed to do that the Founders knew, respected, and thought deeply about. (1) The ancient world, which usually means Athens and Rome, thought that government should foster human excellence. (2) Medieval Christendom thought that government should facilitate the Christian life. (3) Early modern Europe came to believe that government should establish and maintain order and prosperity.[2]

Q1 What are the broad purposes of government?

In the second part of this chapter we will explain the factors that convinced thousands and then tens of thousands of people to abandon their homelands in Europe for what to them seemed the vast, unsettled expanses of America. Few Europeans of comfortable circumstance left for America—ever—but very few left in the beginning. Those who did leave were refugees from religious, economic, and social contests in their homelands. They were, almost always, the losers in these contests. The winners remained at home to enjoy the benefits and opportunities that their victories had secured.

When those individuals and groups who were cast off by Europe fled to America, they brought with them the experiences of their own societies and their knowledge of how societies in history had been organized. They sifted both their own experiences and the experience of history in search of patterns of political, social, and economic organization that they believed would serve their interests and protect their individual rights and liberties. What lessons did colonial Americans draw from the history of earlier societies?

The Ancients: Who Rules and for What Purposes?

Athens and Rome formed the centers of the two greatest European societies of the ancient world. Athens defined the human and political values—justice, openness, and excellence—that Western societies still pursue today. Rome embedded these values in political and legal institutions—equality before the law, federalism, separation of powers, and checks and balances—that are still central to our thinking about politics. Yet, both Athens and Rome were slave societies; they made their vaunted rights and liberties available only to citizens and both fell to social and political instability. What did the Founders see, and what lessons did they learn when they looked back on the history and politics of Athens and Rome?

The Granger Collection, New York

Athens was a direct democracy in which the people gathered to debate and decide the public business. Here, Pericles, leader of Athenian democracy, addresses the citizens of Athens. Crowds can be emotional and precipitous, so think about the criticism that direct democracy too often produces injustice and instability.

The Greeks: Monarchy, Aristocracy, Democracy. Much of the way that Europeans, and after them Americans, have thought about politics and government was set by two Greek political theorists: Plato (428–348 B.C.) and Aristotle (388–322 B.C.). Both lived in Athens, and Aristotle was Plato's student. Their discussions of the nature and purposes of political life and of the fairly limited number of ways in which politics might be organized to achieve these purposes were well known and deeply respected by the American Founders.

The Greeks believed that the task of politics is to organize the **polis,** or political community, to foster human excellence and that the main obstacles to be overcome are political instability and injustice. Plato argued that the ideal political order would be one ruled by a **philosopher-king**, an excellent leader who knows the nature of justice and acts justly in every instance.

Plato knew that the pure intellect of the philosopher-king would rarely be available in the real world, so he concluded that good government would be uncommon and short-lived.[3] Hence, under most circumstances, the philosophically-minded would be well advised to avoid the strife and tumult of politics.

Aristotle was much less interested than Plato in the normative or abstract question of what form of government was best. Rather, he asked the more practical questions of what kinds of government exist in the world and which could be made to work reasonably well under most circumstances.[4] He concluded that governments could take three basic forms and each form could be motivated

polis Greek term for political community on the scale of a city.

philosopher-king A term, closely identified with Plato, denoting ideal political leadership. The philosopher-king would know the true nature of justice and what it required in every instance.

either by the broad public interest or by narrow private and class interests. Good governments could be organized around the best man in the community, a **monarchy**; around a few good men, an **aristocracy**; or around the well-intentioned many, a **democracy.** Yet, like Plato, Aristotle knew that good governments decayed into their bad counterparts with depressing frequency. Monarchy became tyranny, aristocracy became oligarchy, and democracy became mob rule (see Table 1.1).

Aristotle saw class conflict as the great bane of politics. Rulers tend to govern in their own interest until those being oppressed rebel. Aristotle defined "**oligarchy** . . . as the constitution under which the rich, being also few in number, hold the offices of the state; and . . . democracy . . . as the constitution under which the poor, being also many in number are in control."[5] Aristotle's great insight was that while most governments are rendered unstable and oppressive by class conflict, elements of oligarchy and democracy might be merged to form a working approximation of the good government that he called **polity**. Polity promised to reduce class conflict by respecting the needs and interests both of the few wealthy and the many poor.

Unlike Plato, Aristotle had a fundamental respect for the common citizen. The many had a collective judgment that could be very useful to the state. Individually, however, the many poor were unlikely to have had the benefits of sufficient leisure and education to allow them to serve well in positions where individual judgment and decision were required. Therefore, Aristotle advised constitution makers to think carefully about laws governing the right to vote and hold office. Property qualifications for holding office could be set high enough to gratify and reassure the few rich. Qualifications to vote could be set low enough to reassure and gratify the many poor. In this way, the individual judgment of the few and the collective judgment of the many could be put into the service of the community.[6]

Although the Athenian democracy promised liberty and justice, class conflict frequently produced instability and injustice. The few rich and the many poor ruled in their narrow class interest whenever they had the opportunity. Moreover, meeting together in the Assembly (see the picture on page 6), the few rich and the many poor could see too readily how much their interests differed. Our Founding Fathers agreed with Plato and Aristotle that factionalism compromised both oligarchy and democracy. Aristotle's claim that a balanced government, or polity, promised stability seemed right, but the Greek world offered no working

monarchy For the ancients, monarchy meant the rule of one man in the interest of the entire community. More broadly, monarchy denotes kingship or the hereditary claim to rule in a given society.

aristocracy For the ancients, aristocracy meant rule by the few, who were usually also wealthy, in the interest of the entire community. More broadly, aristocracy denotes the class of titled nobility within a society.

democracy Rule by the people. For the ancients, democracy meant popular rule, where the people came together in one place, in the interest of the community. More broadly, democracy denotes political systems in which free elections select public officials and affect the course of public policy.

oligarchy For the ancients, and more generally, oligarchy denotes the rule of the few, usually an economic elite, in their own interest.

polity The general meaning of polity is political community. Aristotle used it to denote a political community in which the institutions of oligarchy and democracy were mixed to produce political stability.

Q2 How should government be designed to achieve its purposes?

TABLE 1.1 Aristotle's Typology of Governments

Number of Rulers	Purposes of Government		
	Broad Public Interests		Narrow Private Interests
One	Monarchy	→	Tyranny
Few	Aristocracy	→	Oligarchy ⎫
Many	Democracy	→	Mob Rule ⎭ → Polity

examples of such a government. More frequently, it seemed that power produced stability at the expense of liberty.

The Romans: Republicanism and Mixed Government.   Rome, like Athens, began as a small city–state. At the height of its glory, Rome was a **republic**, with a limited and mixed government that represented the rights and liberties of both the rich and the poor. However, Rome continued to expand and evolve until it became a world empire that stretched from England to Egypt and from Germany to North Africa. Roman political thinkers had to envision political life on a broader scale.

republic A limited government in which power is widely, though not neccessarily equally, vested in the people either directly or through their elected representatives.

Polybius (204–122 B.C.) and Cicero (106–43 B.C.) were principally responsible for turning the wisdom of Plato and Aristotle to the practical purposes of Roman law and administration. Like Aristotle, Polybius believed that mixed government promotes political stability. However, whereas Aristotle thought that political stability could be achieved by balancing the rich and the poor within the narrow parameters of the city–state, Polybius thought that Rome's strength came from balancing political institutions and offices within the political structure of government. From Polybius came early hints of the importance of separation of powers, checks and balances, and federalism.

Cicero's great contribution to political thought was to summarize the wisdom of the ancient world in regard to personal liberty and the rule of law.[7] Cicero believed that Natural Law is the source of human dignity and that service to one's community is the highest human purpose. For Cicero, political legitimacy and stability flowed from the informed consent of the individual citizen, and consent assumed both liberty and equality. These ideas still remain integral to our thinking about politics.

The lessons that the American Founders took from Polybius and Cicero were that natural rights could be protected by the rule of law and that the mixed constitution generated great power and stability because it engaged the interests of the few rich and the many poor and drew the best from monarchical, aristocratic, and democratic institutions.[8] However, it seemed equally clear that Plato had been correct: even the best-formed state would decay, weaken, and eventually fall. Rome's expansion ultimately led to the fall of the republic and the rise of the Roman Empire under Julius Caesar and his successors. In sum, the Founders thought that the ancients had described the goals of politics beautifully, that they had even identified institutions and mechanisms that might produce peace, justice, and stability for a time, but that they had been unable to figure out how to maintain a just political order through time. The Founders would have to solve this puzzle.

Struggling Toward Democracy

Not surprisingly, political science professors love the fact that Aristotle described politics as the master science, or architectonic science, of the good. He said, "the highest good . . . belongs to the . . . most comprehensive master science, and politics clearly fits this description. . . . Thus it follows that the end of politics is the good for man."

What do you think?
- What positive benefits for society can politics, or political science for that matter, produce?
- Is Aristotle's conception of politics the same as people commonly understand it today?

Q3 What lessons about government did colonial Americans draw from the history of ancient Greece and Rome?

The Middle Ages: The Secular Serves the Sacred

The Christian view of political life, most forcefully stated by St. Augustine (354–430) and St. Thomas Aquinas (1225–1274), differed from that of

Pro & Con

Pursuing Democracy: Ancient Fears, Modern Hopes

Democracy was rarely taken seriously as a form of government in the ancient world. In the ancient Greek, *demos* meant "people," and *kratia* meant "rule" or "authority," so *democracy* literally meant "rule by the people." Thoughtful students of politics well into the eighteenth century doubted that "direct democracy," in which the whole body of citizens met to discuss and decide all public issues, could provide stable government.

Yet, we frequently hear the phrase "Athenian democracy," so let us consider Athens in the fifth century B.C. and ask whether it was a democracy in any sense we would recognize. The demos, or the people, came together in the Assembly to discuss and decide the major issues of the day. All citizens were entitled to participate in the Assembly. Debates were free, open, and wide-ranging, and each citizen had a single vote. Offices were filled by lot from rotating panels of eligible citizens. Government by representatives was thought undemocratic because it seemed to deny the people as a body their full authority. So far, this is almost our ideal image of democracy.

There were, however, several key aspects of the Athenian democracy that we would consider to be decidedly undemocratic. First, a large class of slaves (one-fifth of the total population) provided much of the physical labor that kept Athens going, and resident aliens (another two-fifths), mostly tradesmen, could never become citizens. Second, Athens had little sense of individual rights and liberties. Persons whose opinions were unpopular could be expelled from the city or, as with Socrates when he was accused of "corrupting the youth," put to death by simple majority vote. Finally, public discussion in the Assembly often produced class conflict. The many poor could easily see both that their interests differed from those of the few wealthy and that they were in the majority. Does Athens sound more like a democracy or an oligarchy?

How about modern democracies? Has the passage of 2500 years taught us solutions to the problems Athens experienced with popular government? Not until the eighteenth century did popular election and devices of government structure like federalism, separation of powers, and checks and balances allow the idea of democracy to attach to societies as opposed to small cities. In fact, "representative democracy" has more to do with political equality and the right to vote than it does with citizens participating directly in making governmental decisions.

As a result, scholars still go back to Aristotle to ask about the relationship of democracy to oligarchy. In a recent issue of *Perspectives on Politics*, a journal of the American Political Science Association, Jeffrey Winters and Ben Page, both of Northwestern University, explored "Oligarchy in the United States." Winters and Page concluded that "oligarchy and democracy are not mutually exclusive but rather can coexist comfortably—indeed, can be fused integrally—into governments that Aristotle conceived to be an 'admixture of the two elements.'"

What do you think?
- Does democracy require a thorough-going equality or can structures of privilege, especially economic privilege, coexist with democracy?
- When does democracy become oligarchy?

PRO	CON
All citizens met face-to-face	Most residents were not citizens
Discussion of issues was open to all	Individual rights were not protected
Each citizen had a single vote	Direct debate produced class conflict

the ancients in dramatic and fundamental ways. Most important, medieval Christian thought held that the greatest human aspiration is to achieve salvation, not some temporal, transient, local, even if glorious, good in this world.[9]

For the Middle Ages, the Christian's first and only concern should be to live according to the law of God in order to deserve salvation.[10] To guide man, God imprinted the **Natural Law** on all of creation and most particularly on the heart and mind of man. Natural law directed all of nature, including man, to its best development and fulfillment, but man was free to make other choices and too frequently did. The message of the medieval church to the faithful was that people cannot simultaneously act according to the values of this world and "live rightly" in the eyes of God. Therefore, the temporal world—the world of peoples and nations and human history—is too often a distraction. Those who allowed themselves to become caught up in the endless struggles for preference and power, even if they achieved the glory of a Caesar, would pay a heavy price. They would be damned to burn in hell for all eternity.

The political implications of the medieval Christian vision were clear. The first was that religious concerns were so much more important than **secular** concerns, the politics and economics of daily life, that the secular world

Natural Law God's act of creation entailed a just and proper end or purpose for the natural world, including man. God's purpose for man, the Natural Law, is imprinted on the mind and heart of man.

secular The nonreligious, this-worldly, everyday aspects of life.

Picture Desk / Art Archive

Frankish King Charlemagne, who established the first empire in Western Europe after the fall of Rome, was emperor from A.D. 768 to 815. He is shown here being crowned King of Italy by Pope Adrian I of Milan. Note the symbolism of the emperor kneeling before the pope to receive his crown; politics was to serve religion.

should be organized to protect and facilitate religion. The second was that because the world was awash in sin, the goal of politics should be to maintain order so that religious life could proceed in peace. The third was that hierarchy in politics, economics, religion, and society in general was the best guarantee of peace, order, and stability.[11] For stability and order to prevail, power had to flow down these hierarchies and obedience had to flow up.[12] Resistance to established order was resistance to God and the punishment was damnation.

Community, obedience, and belief were the dominant values of the medieval world. The pope sat at the apex of the universal Catholic Church, and the king, ordained to his position by the pope, sat at the apex of society exercising a dominant role in its political and economic life. The medieval vision held that political authorities maintain order in the world so that the religious authorities can lead the faithful to salvation in the next.

The Puritans of the early Massachusetts Bay colony shared many of the medieval European commitments to community, order, and hierarchy. One hundred and fifty years later, the Founders were still, with a few exceptions, religious men, but they were religious men in a religiously diverse society. Most of them had come to believe that religious diversity made it impossible for politics directly to serve religion. Therefore, the Middle Ages provided them with negative examples and warnings rather than with ways of understanding and conducting politics that they wished to emulate.

Secularism, Individualism, and the Idea of Progress

Secularism is the sense that life in this world is not simply preparation for eternity, but is worthy of attention and respect in its own right. The ideas of individualism, opportunity, and choice—and behind them the even more fundamental idea of progress, of development and improvement in the world—emerged slowly. The rise of **individualism,** first in politics, then in religious thought, and later in economics, was the solvent that weakened and ultimately dissolved hierarchy as the dominant way of thinking about social organization. The idea that freedom has an order and structure of its own found its brightest moment in the era of the American Revolution.[13]

individualism The idea that the people are the legitimate sources of political authority and that they have rights that government must respect.

Secularism as a Focus on Humans in the World.   In Europe, beginning with Niccolo Machiavelli (1469–1527) early in the sixteenth century, attention began to shift from concentration on salvation to concentration on the social, political, economic, and religious experiences of people. In fact, Machiavelli forced this change so abruptly that the word "Machiavellian" became a short-hand for dangerous political thinking. Machiavelli scandalized his own and later generations by asserting that: "how we live is so far removed from how we ought to live, that he who abandons what is done for what ought to be done, will rather learn to bring about his own ruin than his preservation."[14]

Machiavelli's rejection of ethical idealism in favor of political realism was, in his view, demanded by the danger and instability of his times. Italy,

Machiavelli's homeland, was a cauldron of petty tyrants, private armies, and warring city–states. Pervasive political instability resulted in weakness, vulnerability, and poverty for many. Machiavelli concluded that one man, "The Prince," would have to gather absolute political power into his hands to enforce social and political order. Order and safety, once established, would allow men to pursue their individual goals and interests. Perhaps, but Machiavelli's ideas were so radical, so wholly at odds with earlier thinking, that they were suppressed for another century.

Individualism and the Protestant Reformation.   In the meanwhile, the leading theorists of the Protestant Reformation acknowledged the importance of the individual but were unwilling to accept the political implications of individualism. Martin Luther (1483–1546) and John Calvin (1509–1564) rejected the Catholic tradition and liturgy, with its stress on "works" or the visible performance of ritual, in favor of what Luther called "justification by faith alone." Latin mass and an unapproachable religious hierarchy were replaced by hymns, sermons, and religious services in the language of the congregation. Luther and Calvin both argued for an active, participatory, informed congregation that Luther called the "priesthood of all believers." The Bible was translated into the languages of Europe so that individual Christians could approach their religion and their God on a personal basis.

Nonetheless, both Luther and Calvin accepted monarchy as necessary and

Thomas Hobbes thought that only a sovereign, an absolute monarch, could constrain self-interest and secure social peace and order.

desirable. Martin Luther made his peace with rulers by informing subjects that: "An earthly kingdom cannot exist without inequality of persons. Some must be free, some serfs, some rulers, some subjects."[15] Denying hierarchy in the religious realm while retaining a commitment to it in the political, social, and economic realms reflected the traditional value that religious communities placed on peace and order. Once the religious wars of the Reformation and Counter-Reformation ended, some theologians, mostly but not exclusively Protestants, began to question political hierarchy as well.

Science and the Idea of Human Progress.   During the seventeenth century, hierarchy and privilege fought individualism and opportunity for control of people's minds. Although the outcome remained in doubt for most of the century, Francis Bacon (1561–1626), Thomas Hobbes (1588–1679), John Locke (1632–1704), and Charles Secondat, the Baron de Montesquieu (1689–1755), represented the growing commitment to science and progress that would come to dominate thinking in Europe and America. Once the battle was won, this period became known as the Age of Reason.

Bacon believed that science and discovery work to the eternal benefit of human society. The sense that progress might characterize the future was a dramatic departure from both ancient and medieval views. Human history need not always collapse back into tyranny and barbarism. Christians need not merely suffer through life in this world in order to earn salvation in the next. Rather, social, economic, and political progress—perhaps interrupted now and again by backsliding and slippage, but always tending toward discovery and improvement—could be the new future of humanity in the world.

Unfortunately, English politics in the half-century following Bacon's death in 1626 seemed to mock this vision of peace and progress. England's rising middle class and its representatives in Parliament challenged the monarchy and landed aristocracy for the right to guide the nation's future. England's ruling elites fought back and the nation devolved into the misery and violence of civil war.

For many, including Thomas Hobbes, the constant political conflict and frequent violence inspired such fear that absolute monarchy seemed the only way out. Hobbes' classic work, *Leviathan* (1651), argued that individual self-interest, unconstrained by political force, would produce a war of all against all in which life would be, in his memorable phrase, "solitary, poor, nasty, brutish, and short."[16] Only after an all-powerful monarch had established and assured peace was it even reasonable to think about social or economic progress. Like Machiavelli and Luther, Hobbes thought that individualism without hierarchy would result in chaos. Hobbes was wrong. After nearly fifty years of political conflict and civil war, Parliament and England's new commercial middle class finally triumphed in the Glorious Revolution of 1688.

John Locke thought that the Glorious Revolution ushered in an era of peace and progress that would be based on deliberation and free choice. In the second of his famous *Two Treaties of Government* (1689), Locke drew the Natural Law tradition forward into the modern world. He reasoned that "Men being by Nature, all free, equal, and independent, no man can be subjected to the Political Power of another, without his own Consent, by agreeing with other Men to join and unite into a Community, for their comfortable, safe, and peaceable living one amongst another."[17] Clearly, free men, thinking about what kind of government would be most useful to them, would choose a limited, moderate, constitutional regime to protect rather than to threaten them. Locke's **social contract theory**, which held that only the consent of the governed can produce political legitimacy, peace, and prosperity, and Montesquieu's description of separation of powers as a means to limit and control government authority, underlay the political thinking of the American eighteenth century.[18]

The famous frontispiece to Thomas Hobbes' *Leviathan* shows the sovereign towering over the state. On close inspection, one sees that the sovereign's body is made up of hundreds of individual citizen persons.

John Locke thought that the rule of law and limited government could produce peace and order.

social contract theory
Argument identified with Hobbes and Locke that the legitimate origin of government is in the agreement of a free people.

The Granger Collection, New York

Montesquieu thought that groups in society and separation of power in government would check and control political power.

Montesquieu made two points that shaped the thinking of the American Founders. The first was that a nation's institutions and laws must fit its people and their circumstances. Poverty and ignorance might require the strong hand of a monarch, but widespread property and freedom made moderate government, a government of laws and not of men, possible. The second was that political power can best be limited if social groups form a buffer between the people and the government and if it is distributed across executive and legislative offices and institutions—separation of powers.

Within less than a century, Adam Smith (1723–1790) had applied the ideas of free choice and consent to the economic realm, arguing that commerce and markets, when not regulated by the state, have a natural order as well.[19] The implication was that hierarchy and compulsion are not required to assure peace and order in religious, political, and economic life. Peace and order are compatible with—in fact, they might require—freedom and choice as opposed to hierarchy and compulsion.

These ideas had to struggle for recognition in the societies of Europe, with their titled nobilities, state-supported churches, and managed economies. In America, on the other hand, questions about what kinds of political and economic institutions men would create if their society had none—questions that seemed merely academic in Europe—were of immediate and even urgent importance. Over time, as these new ideas influenced law and policy, Americans evolved from subjects to citizens.

THE ROOTS OF AMERICAN POLITICS

Q4 What circumstances led Europeans to leave their homelands to settle in America?

classical liberalism Doctrine identified with Hobbes, Locke, and Smith favoring limited government and individual rights. The dominant American political and social ideology in the nineteenth and twentieth centuries.

The English civil wars and similar disturbances in other European lands drove tens of thousands of settlers to America during the seventeenth century. Throughout the colonial period, individuals and groups fled religious persecution in their own countries to settle in America. Others fled poverty, starvation, and a seemingly permanent lack of economic opportunity. Still others fled from political oppression. Many of these early settlers sought to guarantee their new liberties by oppressing others, but they soon found that vast open spaces, cheap land, and a diverse population made freedom and toleration too difficult to deny. Ideas that were radical in Europe—individualism, freedom, liberty, and equality—seemed invited by the vast openness of America to fulfill themselves, at least for some. Over the course of the seventeenth and eighteenth centuries, what we now refer to as **classical liberalism**, the Lockean idea that the people are the legitimate sources of political authority and that they have the right to place contractual limits on government came to dominate American political thought. Classical liberalism expected government to protect the lives and property of citizens but otherwise to leave them free.

But these Lockean ideas were not unchallenged. An older tradition, that we now refer to as civic humanism or **classical republicanism**, challenged and mixed with classical liberalism. Classical republicanism drew its inspiration from the Roman Republic, Machiavelli's Florence, and the historical patterns of English country life.[20] Citizens are not thought of as motivated principally by self-interest, as in liberal tradition, rather, they look to the good of their community. Classical republicanism encourages citizens to display civic virtue by sacrificing private interests and concerns to the common good. Classical republicanism expected government actively to check bad behavior (gambling, for example) and promote socially positive behavior (militia service, for example).

As we shall see more fully below and in the chapters that follow, both sets of ideas, classical liberalism and classical republicanism, were at large and influential in the revolutionary and founding periods. They clashed, interacted, and mixed to shape the intellectual commitments of the new American nation.

classical republicanism
Doctrine identified with Montesquieu and Hume that highlights concern for the common good over the self-interest of individuals.

Oppression in Europe and the Settlement of America

Seventeenth- and eighteenth-century Europe were still largely dominated by social elites who controlled politics, religion, and economic opportunity. In most cases, a complex mix of religious persecution and denial of social and economic opportunities led Englishmen and other Europeans to abandon their own societies for the unsettled expanses of North America.

Religious Persecution. Over the course of American colonial history, wave after wave of European immigrants were driven to American shores by a desire to worship God in a way denied them by authorities at home. The English Pilgrims and Puritans came first and they were followed by rising tides of English Quakers, French Huguenots, German Pietists, and many others.

English Pilgrims and Puritans came generally from among the middling merchants, artisans, yeomen, and husbandmen, usually free and often successful, but barred on the basis of their religious beliefs from advancing through the social and political hierarchies of the day. Puritan religious and secular leaders worked with Puritan parliamentary leaders to open up English society. Not surprisingly, the king, the established Anglican Church, and economic elites benefiting from royal favor opposed Puritan demands for equality of social and economic opportunity.

From 1629 to 1640 Charles I pushed back against Puritan demands. First, because Puritan influence was strong and rising in Parliament, he ruled England without calling Parliament into session. Second, he supported Archbishop William Laud in purging Puritan members from the Church of England. Twenty-one thousand English Puritans led by John Winthrop and John Cotton departed for New England. They were willing to sever ties to the place of their birth in exchange for the opportunity to build what they intended to be a more godly society in America.

Corbis

The *Mayflower* in Plymouth harbour.

Others facing religious oppression in their homelands made similar decisions. In 1682, the first English Quakers left for Pennsylvania to pursue William Penn's "holy experiment" in peace. Only three years later, Louis XIV's revocation of the Edict of Nantes, the century-old promise of toleration to Protestant French Huguenots, led fifteen thousand of them to flee to America. Several colonies, including Pennsylvania, Delaware, and Maryland, were established as safe havens for the oppressed of one or all of these religious groups.

Denial of Social and Economic Opportunity.   Although religious motivations were strong, defeat in the social and economic struggles that swirled around the religious conflicts in England and the rest of Europe also helped to people America. For example, when Oliver Cromwell and Parliament rose up against Charles I and Archbishop Laud, defeat of the royalists in 1642 and again in 1651 led thousands to flee to the new settlements in Virginia. Even after Charles II was restored to the throne in 1660, the exodus to Virginia of land-hungry second and third sons and cousins of English country lords continued.

Longing for economic betterment that seemed impossible within the constrained social systems of Europe drove many to America. For most men below the propertied classes, feudal restrictions made the prospect of obtaining one's own land almost inconceivable. Visions of immense opportunity, of free or cheap land in a society that had no entrenched and oppressive hereditary aristocracy, energized the poor and even the middle classes to consider removal to America.

Q5 What did democracy mean to our colonial ancestors, and did they approve it?

Political Participation in the Early Colonies.   Although freedom of conscience and equality of opportunity drove many from Europe to America, few came in search of democracy. John Winthrop and John Cotton, the leading political and religious figures of early Massachusetts, openly rejected democracy. Their comments reflect a tradition of thought that stretched back through

Citizens attend a town meeting in New England to discuss the issues before their community. Though most male freeholders were entitled to attend, the hierarchical social and political norms of the day expected the elite to lead.

Hobbes and Aquinas to Plato and Aristotle. Winthrop wrote that "A Democratie is accounted the meanest & worst of all formes of Governmt & Historyes doe recorde, that it hath been allwayes of least continuance & fullest of troubles." Cotton concurred, writing that "Democracy, I do not conceyve that ever God did ordeyne as a fitt government eyther for church or commonwealth. If the people be governors, who shall be governed?"[21]

Nor was the New England town meeting initially a democratic institution. Rather, it was the vehicle through which the Puritan oligarchy of religious and secular leaders informed and led the members of the community. The purpose of the town meeting was not to find the majority will through debate and voting, but rather to create a consensus through a guided discussion designed to persuade and educate the community.[22] If elements of the community declined to be educated, they were as likely to be driven out as allowed to live in peace.

The political institutions of the southern colonies were even more explicitly oligarchical than were those of New England. The leading political and religious institutions of Virginia were the county and the parish. Both the county courts and the parish vestries were dominated by plantation gentry. This Virginia elite based its wealth and social position on slavery. Most of its members had little sense that concepts like freedom, liberty, and equality applied to individuals below their own class, regardless of whether these were landless whites or black slaves.

Struggling Toward Democracy

In colonial America, women had few rights separate from their husbands and were expected to play strictly limited public roles. Anne Hutchinson (pictured on page 18) was charged with sedition for challenging the religious and political elites of early Massachusetts. Though she defended herself brilliantly at trial, she was convicted and banished with her family and followers by a panel of 49 male judges.

What do you think?

- Does our modern culture still place clear limits on women's public roles or not?

Copyright © North Wind / North Wind Picture Archives

Anne Hutchinson (1591–1643), described by Governor John Winthrop as a most "disorderly woman," was tried for heresy, really for having her own religious and political opinions, and expelled from Massachusetts.

Space, Diversity, and Dissent in Colonial America

Few colonists came to America willing to live and let live. Most whites came, as the Puritans did, to establish societies in a particular form and for particular purposes. America, however, was simply too spacious, too open and bountiful, to permit elites to hold common men to purposes and patterns that were not their own. Throughout the colonial period, it was possible to go just down the road or just over the next hill to organize one's political, religious, or economic life just as one wished. Open space and a diverse population corroded hierarchy in colonial America.

"Space" for Dissent. Puritan or Quaker dissent in England was difficult because Anglicanism was the official state religion. Wherever the dissenter went within England, he or she faced orthodoxy (the sanctioned belief of the official state church) and only a few choices—comply, resist, or leave. In America, the options facing the dissenter looked much different. As in England, there was often orthodoxy, but in America there were huge spaces between pockets of orthodoxy in which its influence was barely felt.

As a result, when Roger Williams ran afoul of the orthodoxy of John Winthrop and John Cotton in Massachusetts, they could simply banish him, as they did, and he could simply flee south with his followers into what is now Rhode Island, which he did. Similarly, when Anne Hutchinson and her followers became too troublesome, they too were banished and made their way to Rhode Island.

Similarly, the arrival of the Scotch-Irish in Quaker Philadelphia beginning around 1720 was deeply troubling to the Quakers. The Quakers considered the Scotch-Irish to be dirty, ignorant, quarrelsome, violent, and given to heavy drink. The Quaker response was to hurry them through Philadelphia to the frontier. The Scotch-Irish, drawn forward by the promise of cheap land, filled the inland hills and valleys of Pennsylvania, Virginia, and the Carolinas.

In America, the orthodox seldom felt the need to destroy the unorthodox if they were simply willing to move out of sight. Orthodoxy weakened as it became clear that drawing lines too starkly encouraged resistance and upheaval. Hence, the historian Daniel Boorstin noted that "Puritanism in

LET'S COMPARE

The Settlement of North America: Comparing the British and French Styles

Most Americans, if asked to name the one country in the world that is most like their own, would probably name Canada. That makes perfect sense. America's neighbor to the north is a wealthy, free-market democracy, as is the United States. But the United States and Canada were not always so similar. The United States was cast in a British mold, whereas Canada was cast in a French mold.

Once the Spanish and Portugese empires went into eclipse in the late sixteenth century (Britain defeated the Spanish Armada in 1588), Europe's most dynamic imperial states were Britain and France. Their competition for control of the world's trading routes and resources ranged from India to the Americas. Over the course of this competition, England rejected the absolutist pretensions of the Stuart kings to become a commercial republic with a limited monarchy featuring parliamentary supremacy, a rising middle class, religious toleration, and a strict defense of property rights. France, over the same period, went the other way, becoming increasingly absolutist

under Louis XIV, the "Sun King," and his heirs, with a highly centralized political system, a state church, and feudal traditions of landholding and property rights. Frenchmen remained subjects long after Englishmen became citizens. Not surprisingly, Britain and France shaped their North American colonies differently.

The diversity of the British colonies made them more comfortable and welcoming destinations for immigrants. With the welter of religions, languages, and ethnicities present in British colonies, immigrants could often find residents willing to help them settle in and learn the ways of their new country. Once settled, immigrants could expect to secure their own land in fee simple (untrammeled ownership) upon which to work. French authorities, both at home and in Canada, closely monitored immigrants for loyalty to Church and Crown. Lands in Canada were granted to settlers *en seigneurie*. The grantee swore fealty to the Crown, which retained rights to minerals, a one-fifth equity share at sale, and certain corvee (service) rights. Not surprisingly, French Canada grew slowly while its southern neighbors doubled in population about every twenty years. Once Canada passed to Britain at the conclusion of the French and Indian War in 1763, Canada's growth sped up, but British population did not surpass the French for nearly half a century.

Social and Cultural Comparisons

	British Colonies	French Canada
Religion	Various	Catholic
Language	Various	French
Ethnicity	Various	Gallic (French)
Newspapers	First in 1690, 23 by 1764	None
Land Tenure	Fee simple, individual ownership	Feudal tenure with corvee duties
Immigration	700,000 or 4,500 annually (1607–1760)	27,000 or 200 annually (1608–1760)
Total Population, 1760	1,600,000	56,000

Sources: Edward J. Perkins, *The Economy of Colonial America*, 2nd ed. (New York: Columbia University Press, 1988), 1; John J. McCusker and Russell R. Menard, *The Economy of British America, 1607–1789* (Chapel Hill: University of North Carolina Press, 1985), 54; Bernard Bailyn, *Voyagers to the West* (New York: Knopf, 1986), 24–25; G. Thomas Tanselle, "Some Statistics on American Printing, 1764–1783," in Bernard Bailyn and John B. Hench, *The Press and the American Revolution* (Worcester, MA: American Antiquarian Society, 1980), 347.

New England was not so much defeated as it was eroded by the American climate."[23] Similarly, and more generally, Clinton Rossiter wrote that "under the pressure of the American environment Christianity grew more humanistic and temperate—more tolerant with the struggle of the sects, more liberal with the growth of optimism and rationalism, more experimental with the rise of science, more individualistic with the advent of democracy."[24]

Economic Opportunity and Social Fluidity. The social and economic openness of the British colonies in North America to white men during the eighteenth century was distinctive in the world. The populations of all of the colonies were overwhelmingly rural and agrarian. Even as late as 1765, only five American cities—Boston, New York, Newport, Philadelphia, and Charleston—could claim more than eight thousand inhabitants. These cities contained only 5 percent of the population, and fully eight in ten Americans drew their livings directly from the land. Throughout the colonial period, as William Penn noted, America was "a good poor Man's country." Although "land was easier to acquire, keep, work, sell, and will in the colonies than in any other place in the Atlantic world," it was the special combination of "cheap land, high wages, short supply, and increasing social mobility [that] permitted the worker to shift for himself with some hope of success."[25] Although great wealth was rare, sufficiency was available to the hardworking, and movement into the ranks of the gentry was open to the smart and the fortunate.

Heterogeneity. As the colonies filled up during the seventeenth and eighteenth centuries, the free population of New England, coastal Virginia, Charleston, and a few other areas remained largely English. Other areas rapidly became buzzing hives of sociocultural diversity. William Penn arrived in Pennsylvania in 1682. Within a few years he was reporting to correspondents back in England that his neighbors were "a collection of Divers Nations in Europe: as, French, Dutch, Germans, Swedes, Danes, Finns, Scotch, and English, and of the last equal to all the rest."[26]

Throughout the colonies, of course, citizens of English origin predominated, but they were by no means alone. In 1765, out of a total population of 1,850,000, only about 53 percent were of English origin, 11 percent were Scotch and Scotch-Irish, 6 percent were German, 3 percent were Irish, 2 percent were Dutch, 22 percent were African, and the remaining 3 percent were from a scattering of nations including Sweden, Denmark, France, and elsewhere.[27] When the Declaration of Independence was signed only a little more than a decade later, fully eighteen of the fifty-six signers were of non-English extraction and eight were immigrants.[28]

More striking yet was the religious diversity in America. An accounting by religious denominations of the congregations active in the colonies in 1775 shows the following: "Congregational, 668; Presbyterian, 588; Anglican, 495; Baptist, 494; Quaker, 310; German Reformed, 159; Lutheran, 150; Dutch Reformed, 120; Methodist, 65; Catholic, 56; Moravian, 31; Congregational-Separatist, 27; Dunker, 24; Mennonite, 16; French Protestant, 7; Sandemanian, 6; Jewish, 5; Rogerene, 3," with complex doctrinal disputes common throughout.[29] Few colonial Americans could avoid the sense that their neighbors hailed from a variety of places and believed a variety of things.

Equality and Tolerance.   For a few of America's immigrants, most prominently Quakers and Baptists, equality and tolerance were principles central to their religious and social thinking. Both faiths rejected church hierarchy and liturgy to place individuals in a direct and personal relationship with their God. This radical individualism reflected the Baptist conviction that God did not see nation, race or class when he looked into the believer's heart and the Quaker view that "the light of God," God's personal presence, shone in each believer and justified his or her faith. For most, however, equality and tolerance were not abstract principles to which one might commit intellectually; they were the solid counsel of memory, experience, and necessity. Memory reminded some that they or their ancestors had fled the oppression of an established church somewhere in Europe. Experience reminded others that they had been victims of oppression—Quakers at the hands of Puritans, Catholics at the hands of Anglicans, Jews at the hands of all—by the dominant churches in the separate colonies. Necessity warned that active suppression of such diversity was simply and plainly impossible.

Still, to be entirely true to our early history, we must always keep clearly in mind that these lofty ideals applied only to propertied white men.[30] While we often describe freedom, liberty, and opportunity in colonial and founding America in general terms, they applied to white women through their fathers and husbands, and they applied to Indians and slaves not at all. American history has been and remains a slow and as yet incomplete unfolding of equal rights for all.

Chapter Summary

TABLE 1.2 Stages and Giants in the Western Intellectual Tradition	
Stages	**Giants**
The Ancient World (to A.D. 500)	Plato (428–348)
	Aristotle (388–322)
	Polybius (204–122)
	Cicero (106–43)
	St. Augustine (354–430)
The Middle Ages (500–1350)	St. Thomas Aquinas (1225–1274)
The Renaissance (1350–1600)	Niccolo Machiavelli (1469–1527)
The Reformation (1500–1650)	Martin Luther (1483–1546)
	John Calvin (1509–1564)
The Enlightenment (1600–1800)	Francis Bacon (1561–1626)
	Thomas Hobbes (1588–1679)
	John Locke (1632–1704)
	Montesquieu (1689–1755)
	Adam Smith (1723–1790)

The lessons of history upon which colonial Americans drew were clear, although they were as often warnings and cautions as positive models. Ancient Athens warned that each of the three basic governmental forms—monarchy, aristocracy, and democracy—is subject to distinctive and inevitable flaws. Monarchy inevitably succumbs to tyranny, and both aristocracy and democracy degenerate into class conflict. Aristocracy becomes selfish oligarchy, and democracy becomes mob rule. However, Aristotle understood—and the history of Rome seemed to demonstrate—that stability can be attained, at least for a time, by balancing the interests and influence of the few wealthy and the many poor.

The spectacular rise of Rome seemed to indicate that mixed governments, by harnessing the vision of the aristocracy to the power of an armed populace, could generate great wealth and power. Yet, the equally spectacular destruction of Rome by barbarian armies from the Germanic North seemed to teach that great success breeds complacency, complacency breeds weakness, and weakness inevitably succumbs to strength. Good political institutions might generate strength, but only the character of individual citizens could maintain it over time.

The medieval period was also rich in lessons, almost all of them negative, for colonial Americans. The dominance of hierarchical structures—the papacy, absolute monarchs, hereditary nobility, feudal tenure in land, and mercantile organization of the economy—represented much of what the colonists had sought to escape by abandoning Europe. These social, economic, and political structures represented denial of the opportunity to strive and to achieve outside the narrow boundaries of one's class and position in society.

The lessons that Americans drew from the more recent history of Europe, and especially of England, were a mixture of the promising and the ominous. The promise resided in the Glorious Revolution of 1688, in which the forces of Parliament finally and conclusively overcame the forces of the king to create a limited and constitutional monarchy. The threat resided in the fact that it was these reformed institutions that had sought to oppress the colonies. Although Americans continued to admire the ideas and institutions of English politics, they came increasingly to believe that these ideas and institutions were not directly transferable to the American setting.

Americans were convinced that their distinctively middle-class society, lacking both the aristocracies and the peasantries of Europe, required new political institutions and new distributions of power within them. There would be no monarch and no aristocracy. The people's representatives would be paramount. This much was clear. What remained unclear for nearly a decade after the revolution was how justice and stability would be assured in a system in which class interest did not check and balance class interest. In Chapter 2 we show how this puzzle was addressed by the Founding Fathers.

Key Terms

American political development 4	Natural Law 10
aristocracy 7	oligarchy 7
classical liberalism 14	philosopher-king 6
classical republicanism 15	polis 6
democracy 7	polity 7
individualism 11	republic 8
institution 4	secular 10
monarchy 7	social contract theory 14

Suggested Readings

Readings marked with this icon can be found in the companion reader to this book, *Perspectives on American Government*.

Ferguson, Niall. *Civilization: The West and the Rest.* New York: Penguin, 2011. Ferguson offers six reasons—competition, science, the rule of law, medicine, consumerism, and work ethic—to explain the West's rise to dominance.

Ferris, Timothy. *The Science of Liberty: Democracy, Reason, and the Laws of Nature.* New York: HarperCollins, 2010. Ferris describes the role of science in sparking thought about freedom, innovation, and individual rights in the Age of Reason.

Hulliung, Mark. *The Social Contract in America: From the Revolution to the Present Age.* Lawrence, KS: University Press of Kansas, 2007. This book explores the role and meaning of social contract ideas over the course of American history.

Lilla, Mark. *The Stillborn God: Religion, Politics, and the Modern West.* New York: Alfred A. Knopf, 2007. Lilla asks why the "Great Separation" between Church and State came to the West first and whether it is applicable to other cultures as well.

Morone, James. "The Democratic Wish," 1998. Morone argues that the American Creed of a people capable of governing themselves in the broad public interest is a myth—longstanding and influential—but a myth nonetheless.

Richard, Carl J. *Greeks and Romans Bearing Gifts: How the Ancients Inspired the Founding Fathers.* New York: Rowman and Littlefield, 2008. Richard explores the lessons the Founders took from the ancients about politics.

Smith, Rogers M. "The Multiple Traditions in America," 1993. Smith identified three conflicting streams in American intellectual life—liberal, republican, and ascriptive or racist—and described how their interplay shaped American political history.

Web Resources

For practice quizzes, key term flashcards, videos, links, and other study tools, visit the *American Government* website: www.routledge.com/cw/jillson

1. **www.archives.gov/exhibit_hall/featured_documents/**
   The document issued by King John confirmed that the power of the king was not absolute. This site provided by the National Archives and Records Administration (NARA) reveals the political antecedents of American government.

2. **www.ilt.columbia.edu/academic/digitexts/locke/bio_JL.html**
   Columbia University's John Locke page. This page provides a short biography, list of works, and links to the founder of British empiricism and social contract theory. The site includes links to other philosopher pages such as Thomas Hobbes.

3. **www.lawmoose.com/internetlawlib/8.htm**
   The complete text of Federalist Papers and other founding documents can be found at the Internet Law Library, formerly maintained by the U.S. House of Representatives.

4. **www.tocqueville.org**
   This page is maintained by C-SPAN and provides a plethora of information on Alexis de Tocqueville. Resources include selected writings and essays.

5. **www.ted.com/talks/long/en/michael_sandel_the_lost_art_of_ democratic_debate.html**
   Michael Sandel, a leading Harvard philosopher, links Aristotle's views on justice to modern debates such as those surrounding health care.

Chapter 2

THE REVOLUTION AND
THE CONSTITUTION

Should the states reject this excellent Constitution, the probability is that an opportunity will never again offer to make another in peace—the next will be drawn in blood.

GEORGE WASHINGTON,
Pennsylvania Journal and Weekly Advertiser, November 14, 1787

OBAMA'S SPEECH ON RACE

On March 18, 2008, the Obama presidential campaign was in deep trouble. The Obama family's long-time minister, the Reverend Jeremiah Wright, was on tape railing against America, its fundamental values, and its history. Barack Obama and his inner circle, and everyone else for that matter, knew that America and its white majority would not elect the nation's first black president if that person seemed deeply alienated from America, its history, and its values. Damage control was the order of the day. But Obama accomplished much more than damage control; he offered a tutorial on race in American history that not only moved Jeremiah Wright off center stage but was accepted by most Americans as positive and healthy. Here is the core of what Obama said in his Philadelphia speech on race:

> "'We the people, in order to form a more perfect union.'
>
> Two hundred and twenty one years ago, in a hall that still stands across the street, a group of men gathered and, with these simple words, launched America's improbable experiment in democracy. . . .
>
> The document they produced was eventually signed but ultimately unfinished. It was stained by this nation's original sin of slavery, a question that divided the colonies and brought the convention to a stalemate until the founders chose to allow the slave trade to continue for at least twenty more years, and to leave any final resolution to future generations.
>
> Of course, the answer to the slavery question was already embedded within our Constitution—a Constitution that had at its very core the ideal of equal citizenship under the law; a Constitution that promised its people liberty, and justice, and a union that could be and should be perfected over time.
>
> And yet words on parchment would not be enough to deliver slaves from bondage, or provide men and women of every color and creed their full rights and obligations as citizens of the United States. What would be needed were Americans in successive generations who were willing to do their part—through protests and struggle, on the streets and in the courts, through a civil war and disobedience and always at great risk—to narrow the gap between the promise of our ideals and the reality of their time. . . .
>
> The profound mistake of Reverend Wright's sermons is not that he spoke about racism in our society. It's that he spoke as if our society was static; as if no progress had been made; as if this country—a country that has made it possible for one of his own members to run for the highest office in the land and build a coalition of white and black; Latino and Asian, rich and poor, young and old—is still irrevocably bound to a tragic past. But what we know—what we have seen—is that America can change. That is the true genius of this nation. What we have already achieved gives us hope—the audacity of hope—for what we can and must achieve tomorrow."

Focus Questions: from reading to thinking

Q1 What are the decisive events and arguments that produced the American Revolution?

Q2 What changes in institutional design and allocation of powers were reflected in the first state constitutions?

Q3 How did the Articles of Confederation differ from the U.S. Constitution?

Q4 How did the Virginia and New Jersey Plans differ about the kind of national government that each envisioned?

Q5 What role did the debate over a bill of rights play in the adoption of the U.S. Constitution?

Consider for a moment how differently the traditional vision of "American Exceptionalism" in the vignette introducing Chapter 1, and Barack Obama's view here, understand and use history. Leaders need to make a strong and resonant connection with their people if they are to lead effectively. Every president tries to put his or her own political goals into the broader context of American history; how have we gotten to this point, what problems do we face, and how will my political agenda move us forward or get us back on track? If a president, or a candidate for president can tell a story of American history that seems to call for his or her policies as a logical, even necessary, next step, their political way will be smoothed. Different politicians not only see American history differently, they see the road into the American future as leading off in different directions.

Ronald Reagan saw American values as God-given and only in need of restoration for all to be well. Barack Obama saw American values as compromised at birth and realized only by a long history, generation after generation and continuing today, of struggle. In Chapter 2, we review the American founding period, from the coming of the American Revolution through the adoption of the United States Constitution.

WHAT DO YOU THINK?

• Which view of history and of America's place in history, Reagan's or Obama's, seems more consonant with your understanding of American history?
• Is racial injustice America's original sin or is it a preoccupation we should put behind us?

BACKGROUND TO THE REVOLUTION

Revolutions are inherently tumultuous affairs. Among the great revolutions of modern history—the American (1774–1781), the French (1787–1800), the Russian (1917–1921), and the Chinese (1911–1949)—all but the American Revolution ended in social upheaval and civil war. In the American case, after an initial period of instability, the founding generation recast the revolutionary ideals of the Declaration of Independence on the sturdy foundation of the United States Constitution.[1]

The Declaration and the Constitution are the founding documents of the American nation. As we inquire into the nature and character of these documents, we will discover that Thomas Jefferson, Abraham Lincoln, Franklin Roosevelt, and many others believed that the Declaration set the goals of American politics, while the Constitution outlined the means by which those goals were to be pursued.

This chapter opens with a look at the political circumstances surrounding the fight for American independence. First, we ask how the British governed their

North American colonies and what problems arose to disrupt this 150-year-old imperial relationship. Second, we ask what kinds of state and national political institutions the citizens of the new nation chose in the immediate wake of the revolution and what problems they experienced with these institutions in the first decade of independence. Third, we describe what the U.S. Constitution is, what role it plays in our politics, and we highlight the document's key provisions. Fourth, we ask what role the promise to add a bill of rights to the new Constitution played in the ratification debate. Finally, we ask what reforms or constitutional amendments are most frequently called for today.

The Colonial Political Environment

British rule rested lightly on the colonists in America. For the most part, although the opportunity to direct and control was always there, imperial administrators in London chose not to involve themselves deeply in the political and economic affairs of the colonies.

Political Control in Colonial America.   The basic structures of the colonial governments varied little. Familiar ideas drawn from Locke and Montesquieu, popular sovereignty, separation of powers, checks and balances, representation, and bicameralism were present from the beginning.[2] Each colonial government was headed by a governor. Generally, governors were empowered to call and dismiss legislatures, collect taxes and propose expenditures, enforce imperial and colonial laws, command troops, and appoint officers of the executive branch. Behind each governor stood the power and majesty of the British king and Parliament.

There were, however, important limitations on the powers of the governors, and these limitations became tighter over time. Each governor faced a legislature composed primarily, if not exclusively, of colonials. Most of these colonial legislatures had an upper house selected by the governor and a lower house elected by the people. The upper house, often referred to as the Governor's Council, represented the interests of the governor and the empire to the lower house and to the people of the colony. The lower house, frequently called the House of Representatives, the House of Burgesses, or simply the Assembly, used the "power of the purse" to control and limit the independence of colonial governors. In almost every colony, the people's representatives gained the upper hand over the governor and his council.

The rights and responsibilities of citizenship also varied by colony. In all of the colonies there were limitations on who could vote. Most commonly, the limitations involved race, gender, and property holding. Moreover, most of the colonies had restrictions on office holding. These restrictions often increased with the prestige of the office or required that service in a less prestigious office precede service in a more prestigious office.[3] Nonetheless, the average white man in colonial America wielded an economic and political influence enjoyed by the mass of men in no other place on earth because most had access to property.

Adding Economic Muscle.   In the seventy-five years preceding the American Revolution, the people and economy of the British colonies in North America became self-sustaining. Between the year 1700 and independence, the population of the colonies doubled approximately every twenty years, rising from 250,000 to 2,500,000. As population grew, the domestic economy became more important and the burden of imperial regulations less obviously beneficial.[4]

Removal of the French Threat.   The political implications of the social and economic growth of the colonies were masked for a time by the presence of the French in Canada. This was particularly true while the massed forces of the British and French empires clashed worldwide between the mid-1750s and 1763 in the Seven Years War. In North America, this conflict was known as the French and Indian War. British victory in the Seven Years War made Canada a British colony, thereby removing the threat that hostile French troops had posed. Dangers still lurked all around, Indians on the frontier, the Spanish to the South and West, but the greatest threat of the past century had, it seemed, been removed.

The Assertion of British Imperial Authority.   The Seven Years War left England with a national debt twice what it had been at the war's beginning. In the view of the British government, because an important part of the war had been fought in North America, it seemed reasonable that the colonists would help bear some of the cost. The American colonists took a different view. They regarded imposition of a tax designed to raise revenue in America to fill British coffers in London as a dramatic change of imperial relations.

In the past, British taxes collected in America had been designed to control and direct the flow of trade within the empire: a legitimate, if not entirely welcome, activity in the view of most Americans. Taxes to raise revenue were another matter. Passage in Parliament of the Sugar Act late in 1764 and the Stamp Act early in 1765 brought protests and threats of boycott from individual colonial legislatures and from an intercolonial meeting called the **Stamp Act Congress**. Howls from London merchants that their valuable colonial trade was being harmed (what we would call interest group activity today) led Parliament in February 1766 to rescind the Stamp Act and to modify the Sugar Act.

To cover its retreat on the Stamp Act, Parliament passed the **Declaratory Act,** which restated its right to make laws binding on the American colonies "in all cases whatsoever." Relations remained strained between Parliament and the American colonies, erupting most strikingly in the **Boston Massacre** on March 5, 1770 and the **Boston Tea Party** on December 16, 1773. The Boston Tea Party was an act of civil disobedience in which the Boston Sons of Liberty, disguised as Indians, dumped three ship loads of tea into Boston Harbor rather than pay the taxes levied on it. The imagery of this famous tax protest fuels the imagery if not the substance of the modern Tea Party Movement.

Parliament's reaction to continued colonial resistance was broad, firm, and inflammatory. Collectively, Parliament's actions have come to be known as the **Intolerable Acts**. First, General Thomas Gage, commander of the British

---

Q1 What are the decisive events and arguments that produced the American Revolution?

Stamp Act Congress Delegates from nine colonies met in New York City in October 1765 to coordinate their resistance to Parliament's attempt to tax the colonies directly. They argued that only colonial legislatures could levy taxes in the colonies.

Declaratory Act An act passed in Parliament in March 1766 declaring that the British king and Parliament had the right to pass laws binding on the colonies in America "in all cases whatsoever."

Boston Massacre A clash on March 5, 1770 between British troops and a Boston mob that left five colonists dead and eight wounded.

Boston Tea Party Boston patriots oppose British attempts to tax the colonies by dumping tea into Boston Harbor rather than pay the required taxes.

Intolerable Acts Acts passed in Parliament during the spring of 1774, in response to the Boston Tea Party and similar events, to strengthen British administration of the colonies.

Corbis

Tensions between British troops and colonists erupted in the Boston Massacre on March 5, 1770. Five colonists were killed immediately, and eight others were wounded. Two of the wounded died later.

troops in Boston, was appointed governor of Massachusetts. Second, citizens were required to house his troops in their homes. Third, the port of Boston was closed to commerce. Fourth, town meetings were suspended, and the right to appoint the Governor's Council was removed from the Assembly and transferred to the king. And fifth, colonists were informed that Crown officials accused of committing crimes while pursuing their official duties were to be tried not in Boston but in Nova Scotia or London.

A young Thomas Jefferson spoke for many Americans when he declared that "single acts of tyranny may be ascribed to the accidental opinion of a day, [but] a series of oppressions pursued unalterably plainly prove a deliberate and systematic plan of reducing us to slavery." Jefferson's conclusion seemed equally obvious: "when tyranny is abroad, submission is a crime."[5] Few Americans chose to submit, but fewer still had any idea of how far resistance would take them.

First Steps Toward Independence

After Americans decided to resist, and the authorities in London decided to meet their resistance with force, the impulses that led to Lexington, Concord, Bunker Hill, and independence took over. Misinterpretation of motives, overreaction on both sides, and the difficulties of transatlantic communication led first to heated rhetoric and then to a spiral of threats and violence that neither side knew how to stop.[6]

The First Continental Congress.   The publication of the Intolerable Acts in America in May 1774 brought calls for an intercolonial conference to develop a coordinated response. Every state but Georgia appointed delegates to meet in the First **Continental Congress**. The Congress met in Philadelphia and began its deliberations on September 5, 1774.

    Independence was not on the agenda. Most of the delegates hoped to heal the rift that had developed between the colonies and England. Therefore, the Congress appointed two committees. The first was to compose a petition stating grievances and seeking redress, and the second was to state the rights of trade and manufacture due the colonies and to identify the grounds upon which these rights rested. The petitions that resulted from the work of these committees were adopted by the Congress and forwarded to the king and Parliament in London. The delegates to the First Continental Congress adjourned on October 26, 1774, after agreeing that if necessary they would hold a second Congress in the spring.

Revolutionary Action.   British authorities took the mere fact that a Continental Congress had met in America to be defiance. The American petitions were rejected summarily, and talk in Parliament quickly turned to the use of force. Parliament ordered reinforcements to Boston, extended the trade sanctions then in place against Boston to all of New England, and ordered General Gage to seize arms and military stores that might be used by colonial rebels. Benjamin Franklin, then in London as agent for several of the colonies, sent word to Congress that "three regiments of foot, one of dragoons, seven hundred marines, six sloops of war, and two frigates are now under orders for America."[7]

    Preparation and posturing on both sides erupted into violence early on the morning of April 19, 1775. A column of British troops dispatched from Boston to seize weapons clashed with colonial militia at Lexington and Concord. Finding no military stores in either place, the troops sought to withdraw to Boston. The militia harassed the redcoats from cover all along the line of march, inflicting substantial casualties. When the column finally reached Boston, the militia took up defensive positions on the hills surrounding the city to block further incursions into the countryside.

    Blood had been shed on both sides, but many colonists still hoped for reconciliation. It was not to be. Into this volatile situation stepped a recent Irish immigrant named Thomas Paine. Paine captured the

Continental Congress Met in September 1774 and from May 1775 forward to coordinate protests against British policy and then revolution. The Continental Congress was superseded by the Confederation Congress when the Articles of Confederation went into effect on March 1, 1781.

Struggling Toward Democracy

Support for the American Revolution was by no means universal. The best estimates are that 40 percent of adult white males were patriots, 20 percent were loyalists, and 40 percent were bent mostly on staying out of harm's way.
What do you think?
- What values do you suppose those who opposed the revolution thought they were defending?
- What issues today would likely divide those same types of groups?

emotion of the moment in an incendiary pamphlet called *Common Sense*. Paine denounced King George as the "royal brute," called for immediate independence, and declared that "the cause of America is in a great measure the cause of all mankind." *Common Sense* sold 120,000 copies in the first three months of 1776 and shifted the tone of public discussion toward confrontation.

The Second Continental Congress.   New England delegates returning to Philadelphia for the Second Continental Congress in early May 1775 traveled roads clogged with militia moving to reinforce the patriots encamped on the hills around Boston. Delegates arriving from the southern colonies pledged their firm support. By May 10, 1775, forty-nine delegates, virtually all of them veterans of the first Congress, were present.

The second Congress agreed to organize a Continental Army (really to adopt the troops around Boston). Colonel George Washington, a delegate from Virginia, was selected to take command of this new army. Congress also authorized the raising of foreign loans and contacts with foreign governments, particularly the French. The French could be expected to support anyone willing to give their British enemies a difficult time.

The Declaration of Independence

On May 15, 1776, the Virginia House of Burgesses voted to instruct its delegates in Congress to propose independence. On June 7, 1776, Virginia's Richard Henry Lee introduced the following resolution: "These United Colonies are, and of right ought to be, free and independent States, that they are absolved from all allegiance to the British Crown, and that all political connection between them and the State of Great Britain is, and ought to be totally dissolved." Lee's resolution was set aside in order to give each member time to consider its implications.

On June 10, 1776, Congress elected a committee of five of its leading members—Thomas Jefferson, John Adams, Benjamin Franklin, Roger Sherman, and Robert R. Livingston—to prepare an explanation and justification of Lee's motion. Jefferson's reputation as a literary craftsman led the committee to assign him the task of producing a draft. Jefferson's draft declaration was lightly revised, mostly by Franklin and Adams, and submitted to the full Congress. The work of this committee, debated and amended in Congress in early July and adopted on July 4, is the document that we call the **Declaration of Independence**. In fact, the actual declaration, Lee's resolution, had been passed two days earlier.

Decades later, Jefferson explained that in crafting the Declaration of Independence, he drew upon "the elementary books of public right, as Aristotle, Cicero, Locke, Sidney, etc." as these had become embedded in the common mind.[8] The imprint of John Locke's social contract theory is especially heavy on the Declaration of Independence (the Declaration is Appendix A in the back of this book). Jefferson put human rights, the right of individuals to security, respect, and self-development, at the core of the American promise. The justly famous second paragraph of the Declaration reads, "We hold these truths to be

Declaration of Independence   The document adopted in the Continental Congress on July 4, 1776, to explain and justify the decision of the American colonies to declare their independence from Britain.

self-evident, that all men are created equal, that they are endowed by their Creator with certain unalienable Rights, that among these are Life, Liberty, and the pursuit of Happiness.—That to secure these rights, Governments are instituted among Men, deriving their just powers from the consent of the governed,—That whenever any Form of Government becomes destructive of these ends, it is the Right of the People to alter or to abolish it, and to institute new Government, laying its foundation on such principles and organizing its powers in such form, as to them shall seem most likely to effect their safety and Happiness."

The opening sentence of that paragraph makes two key points. First, it defines as "self-evident," that is, beyond demonstration and dispute, "certain unalienable rights," "among" which are "Life, Liberty, and the pursuit of Happiness." The idea of self-evidence is a striking way of saying, despite all of the evidence of difference and inequality that you see around you, a free society must treat people as fundamentally equal. Moreover, the simple phrase "among these" suggests that there may be, and probably are, self-evident and inalienable rights in addition to life, liberty, and the pursuit of happiness.

Second, John Locke's identification of life, liberty, and property as fundamental rights was significantly softened, broadened, and enriched by Jefferson's substitution of "pursuit of Happiness" for property. Life and liberty remain fundamental for Jefferson, as for Locke, and there is no doubt that Jefferson valued property, but "pursuit of Happiness" is an open promise while property is defensive and exclusionary.

The Declaration argues that free men create governments, through a process of social contract, to create order and security and if government fails to do so, they can redesign or replace it. The king, through repeated arbitrary acts and tyrannous behavior, had violated the contract. The American colonists concluded that they must sever relations with Britain and its king and establish governments of their own design. The Declaration of Independence announced to the world the Congress's decision for independence and the reasons that lay behind it. But it did more than that. Thomas Jefferson's declaration defined the goals of American public life—the promise of Life, Liberty, and the pursuit of Happiness—in positive and expansive language that has thrilled and challenged every subsequent generation of Americans.

Today we think of the Declaration of Independence as a great literary achievement, as a wonderful expression of American political commitments and values. The men who signed it understood it differently. Each man knew that affixing his signature to the document was an admission of treason. Benjamin Franklin reminded them of the importance of unity at such moments, saying "We must hang together, gentlemen . . . else, we shall most assuredly hang separately."

GOVERNANCE DURING THE REVOLUTIONARY PERIOD

In May 1776, the Continental Congress advised states that had not already done so to discard institutions based on ties to Britain and to establish

Q2 What changes in institutional design and allocation of powers were reflected in the first state constitutions?

governments grounded on their own authority. This was a more complicated instruction than might first appear. No nation in the world, including Great Britain, had a written constitution. The colonies had had written charters, but these assumed the superior authority of British laws and institutions. Ten new or revised state constitutions were produced in 1776 alone. Between 1776 and 1787 all thirteen states produced at least one new constitution. The architects of the U.S. Constitution drew on these state constitutions both for examples and for inspiration.

In the American experience, constitutions are written documents that describe and define the structure and powers of government. They usually begin with a preamble describing the goals and purposes of government and contain a bill of rights designed to prohibit government from imposing on the freedom and liberty of citizens. The bulk of the document, usually in a series of numbered articles or sections, describe the structure of the government, how the parts relate to each other, their respective powers, and how one achieves election or appointment to these offices. Constitutions frame and legitimate politics; they are prior to and superior to regular laws and other decisions of government, so they must be approved by popular vote and can only be amended or changed by popular vote.[9] Because constitutions make all citizens aware of the rules for winning office and the rights and limits pertaining to each office, supporters of the losing candidates are more likely to see their loss as legitimate and fair, and wait for the next election to try again. Losers seeing winners as legitimate is critical to orderly democratic politics.

Although the focus of attention in 1776 was on revising state constitutions, Americans were keenly aware that some kind of central authority would also be necessary. The Continental Congress produced the Articles of Confederation in 1777, but their formal adoption was not achieved until 1781. These initial efforts required reconsideration, adjustment, and reform over the course of the decade that followed.

Thomas Jefferson and his colleagues prepare the Declaration of Independence. The declaration was meant to provide the reasons justifying American independence from Great Britain.

Independence Sparks Constitutional Change

The call to armed resistance and ultimately to revolution, based as it was on the rhetoric of liberty, equality, and popular sovereignty, sparked extensive political change. Political institutions were redesigned to remove powers from their more aristocratic elements and add powers to their more democratic elements. Despite the rousing rhetoric of the Revolution, few white men imagined and even fewer argued that rights and liberties should be expanded to groups—women, slaves, Indians—that had not previously enjoyed them.

The State Constitutions.   Most of the new state constitutions retained the basic structure of a legislature with an upper and a lower house and an executive branch headed by a governor, although the distribution of power within and among the institutions shifted dramatically. In all of the constitutions of 1776, most power was lodged in the lower house of the legislature. The upper house and the governor, suggesting the monarchical and aristocratic elements of the old regime, were reduced in influence. Governors frequently lost the veto power, appointment power, and control over the budget. Popular involvement was usually assured through an expanded suffrage and through annual, or at most biannual, elections.

The new state constitutions were careful to expand and make more explicit the protection of individual rights and liberties traditionally enjoyed by white men including trial by jury, free speech, press, and assembly, and protections against unreasonable searches and standing armies in peacetime. These rights and others like them were widely seen as part of the fundamental law that controlled and limited the power of government over society and citizens.

The Articles of Confederation.   The Confederation Congress produced a "league" of states, not a nation of citizens (the Articles are Appendix B in the back of this book). Each state delegation had a single vote, and the presidency of the Congress rotated among the states. There was no executive, no judiciary, no separation of powers, and no checks and balances. The revolution created an increased sense of unity among Americans, but not yet a sense of nationhood.

The **Articles of Confederation** granted the **Confederation Congress** authority over foreign policy, including sending and receiving ambassadors, negotiating treaties and alliances, and making decisions of war and peace. Congress was empowered to regulate its own coinage, fix the standards for weights and measures, establish a postal system, regulate trade with Indians living outside the individual states, and appoint the senior officers of army and navy units serving under the control of the Congress. Congress was authorized to borrow money and to requisition the states for money, men, and materials needed to fight the war and support Congress's other activities.

On the other hand, certain critical powers were denied to Congress altogether. Congress had no power to regulate trade and commerce between the states or to tax the citizens of the individual states. Congress's only domestic source of revenue was requisitions on the states. Finally, amendments to the Articles required the unanimous approval of the thirteen state legislatures. No amendment ever passed because at least one state always opposed, no matter how critical the need seemed to the others. Despite the powers granted to the

Articles of Confederation
Written in the Continental Congress in 1776 and 1777, the Articles outlining America's first national government were finally adopted on March 1, 1781. The Articles were replaced by the U.S. Constitution on March 4, 1789.

Confederation Congress
The Congress served under the Articles of Confederation from its adoption on March 1, 1781, until it was superseded by the new Federal Congress when the U.S. Constitution went into effect on March 4, 1789.

Congress by the Articles, the reality was that the states remained almost completely sovereign, obeying the Congress only when they saw fit.

In a nation not yet born but fighting its way to independence, the flaws and weaknesses of the Articles were frustrating to many and infuriating to some—including General Washington. The root of the problem was that while Congress could requisition from the states the men and supplies needed to fight the war, it was the hard-pressed states that decided whether to comply in full, in part, or not at all. The story of Washington's army suffering through the winter of 1776–77 at Valley Forge is, in major part, a story of inadequate supply and is just one such story. Not surprisingly, large states bristled at the fact that the small states had an equal vote in Congress and most states, large and small, were frustrated that just a single state could block amendments to the Articles. Even after the war ended in victory, Congress's inability to resolve commercial disputes, or even consistently to keep a quorum, deepened pessimism about the new nation's future.

Political Instability during "The Critical Period"

Volatile state legislatures and a weak and impoverished Congress created a sense of instability and drift in the new nation. Many Americans came to believe that the weakening of the executives and the upper houses of the state legislatures and their total elimination at the national level had left American governments unable to ensure social stability and foster economic growth. State governments sought to address this instability through constitutional reform. By 1780 both New York and Massachusetts had adopted new constitutions that reempowered their governors and upper houses.

Other states, especially Rhode Island, but Pennsylvania, North Carolina, and Georgia as well, seemed to drift toward a dangerous populism. The right to vote had been expanded and new men, sometimes poor farmers and debtors, challenged traditional elites for places in town councils and state legislatures. Wartime inflation threatened the value of property and state legislatures frequently sided with poor debtors. Men of property and wealth concluded that a national government capable of restraining the too democratic state governments was necessary to restore order, security, and prosperity. The new men were wary but circumstances played into the hands of the traditional elites.

The Annapolis Convention.   In 1786, Virginia proposed an interstate conference to discuss commercial regulation. Although disputes between Maryland and Virginia concerning trade on the Chesapeake provided the focus, other states were invited in the hope that a general set of commercial recommendations might be crafted. Delegates from five states—New York, New Jersey, Pennsylvania, Delaware, and Virginia—attended. The **Annapolis Convention** met on September 11, agreed that trade issues were parts of a larger set of federal issues that needed to be dealt with together, and adjourned on September 14. Its report, sent to Congress and the states, called for a general convention to meet in Philadelphia in May 1787 "to render the constitution of the Federal

Annapolis Convention Held in Annapolis, Maryland, in September 1786 to discuss problems arising from state restriction on interstate commerce, it was a precursor to the Constitutional Convention.

Government adequate to the exigencies of the Union." Events conspired to suggest that the Philadelphia meeting would be of the utmost importance.

Shays's Rebellion.   Although a modest conflict by any realistic measure, **Shays's Rebellion** was taken by many to be a warning of worse to come. The conservative administration of Massachusetts Governor James Bowdoin had increased taxes on land. This bore heavily on the small farmers of central and western Massachusetts who frequently found their farms seized for back taxes. In August 1786 and throughout the subsequent winter, farmers under the leadership of Daniel Shays, a Revolutionary War veteran and local office-holder, closed courts, opposed foreclosures by force of arms, and clashed with local militia called out to restore order.[10]

By February 1787, troops of the state militia, paid with $20,000 in private money raised mostly among the merchants and tradesmen of Boston, put the rebels to flight in a series of skirmishes. Several aspects of the Shaysite controversy remained profoundly worrisome to conservatives throughout the country even after order had been restored. First, they knew from Aristotle,

Massachusetts farmers led by Daniel Shays rose up against high taxes and oppressive government during the winter of 1786–1787. The movement—a scene from which is shown here—came to be called Shays's Rebellion.

Copyright © North Wind / North Wind Picture Archives

Shays's Rebellion An uprising of Massachusetts farmers during the winter of 1786–1787 that convinced many Americans that political instability in the states required a stronger national government.

Struggling Toward Democracy

In the wake of Shays's Rebellion, 4,000 rebels confessed to taking part and received pardons. Eighteen leaders were tried and sentenced to death, though only two, John Bly and Charles Rose, were actually hanged. The rest were eventually pardoned. Shays escaped, hid out until tensions died down, and eventually was pardoned too. He died poor and obscure in Conesus, New York, in 1815.

What do you think?
- In a democracy, should public protest, even if it slides toward violence, be lightly punished or not?
- Would you be willing to engage in protest over something you felt strongly about, even if it became violent?

Polybius, and Montesquieu that domestic instability, pitting the rich against the poor, had been the classic pattern of failure in popular regimes throughout history. Second, that this should happen in Massachusetts suggested that even the best state constitution, the Massachusetts Constitution of 1780, was unable to produce peace and stability. Federal constitutional reform seemed the only remaining possibility.

THE CONSTITUTIONAL CONVENTION

Q3 How did the Articles of Confederation differ from the U.S. Constitution?

Constitutional Convention
Met in Philadelphia between May 25 and September 17, 1787, and produced the U.S. Constitution. It is sometimes referred to as the Federal Convention or Philadelphia Convention.

Failure of the Annapolis Convention and concern over Shays's Rebellion focused great attention on the **Constitutional Convention** (also called the Federal Convention) held in Philadelphia from May to September 1787. Virginia, the largest and most prominent state, sent a delegation that included George Washington, Governor Edmund Randolph, James Madison, and George Mason. Other states also sent their leading citizens. These men were concerned that the new nation, independent only for a decade, was beginning to show the classic signs of instability that had characterized popular government since ancient times.

History and experience offered the delegates several pieces to the still-unsolved puzzle of democratic constitutionalism— limited government, separation of powers, checks and balances, bicameralism, and federalism—but no persuasive description of how the pieces fit together to produce justice, strength, and stability over time. Most delegates shared a sense that the central government had to be strengthened and that, at minimum, this meant that authority to control commerce and collect taxes had to be lodged with the Congress. This suggested, however, that the central government would need executive agencies to enforce its laws and judicial agencies to resolve disputes. Nonetheless, it was unclear whether the necessary reforms, whatever they turned out to be, would add up to a truly national government or merely to a series of amendments to the existing Articles of Confederation.[11]

The Delegates and Their Backgrounds

Fifty-five delegates from twelve states (Rhode Island refused to send delegates) attended and took some part in the proceedings of the Federal Convention. Thirty-nine delegates remained to the end and signed the final document. The delegates were often relatively young, generally well educated, and usually well placed within their state's social, economic, and political elite.[12]

Most of the delegates had already seen extensive public service. Twenty-four had served in the Continental Congress between 1774 and 1781, and thirty-nine had served in the Confederation Congress between 1781 and 1787. Twenty-one had fought in the Revolutionary War, seven had served as governors of their states, and fully forty-six had served in their state legislature. They knew firsthand the problems that faced the new nation, and they knew how to pursue solutions in a political setting.[13]

A Foundation of Basic Principles

The delegates shared a broad consensus on the most fundamental political and constitutional issues before them. They drew upon a common body of historical knowledge and upon shared experiences with existing state and national political institutions. As a result, the range of political principles and institutional possibilities that were actually on the table was fairly narrow.[14]

The delegates knew that they wanted a limited government, but one more capable than the Articles of Confederation had proven to be. They knew that if they gave more power to government, especially a distant national government, they would have to take great care in distributing that power and hedging it in. Unfortunately, no one knew how to do this.

Limited Government and the Idea of a Written Constitution.   John Locke had grounded the case for limited government on individual rights and popular sovereignty. But the written constitution is an American invention. The Founders believed that a written constitution allows for a precise distribution and limitation of power between and within the institutions and offices of government. Citizens could then watch to ensure that the powers neither expand nor move within the system.[15]

Representative Government.   In a country that numbered almost four million persons and stretched from New Hampshire to Georgia and from the Atlantic to the Mississippi, direct democracy on the model of Athens or the

Historically, most Americans have assumed that the values embedded in the U.S. Constitution are universal. Here "Uncle Sam" learns that that may not be so.

representative government
A form of government in which elected representatives of the people, rather than the people acting directly, conduct the business of government.

New England town meeting was impossible. **Representative government** required those entitled to vote, generally propertied white men, to select from among themselves those who would actually govern. Nonetheless, how to design representative institutions that would reliably produce stable and effective decisions was not entirely clear. Some worried that national institutions, too far removed from the real lives of individual citizens, would be unresponsive, whereas others worried that local institutions were inherently unstable.

federalism A form of government in which some powers are assigned to the national government, some to lower levels of government, and some, such as the power to tax, are exercised concurrently.

Federalism.   As we will see in more detail in the next chapter, **federalism** is a form of government that divides the powers of government between national and subnational levels. One of the main reasons for summoning the Constitutional Convention was to adjust the balance of power between the national and state governments. Nonetheless, attachments to the state governments were strong, and it was clear to most delegates that a plan that leaned too obviously toward a consolidated national government would have difficulty.

separation of powers The idea that distinctive types of governmental power, most obviously the legislative and executive powers, and later the judicial power, should be placed in separate hands.

Separation of Powers.   As we saw in Chapter 1, the basic insight behind **separation of powers** is very old. The Roman republic had been organized to give two social classes—the few rich and the many poor—separate institutions and officers to protect their distinct interests. In the seventeenth and eighteenth centuries, Locke and Montesquieu argued that distinct governmental tasks—most critically the legislative task of making laws and the executive task of enforcing laws—needed to be in separate hands. Only with the American founding did the judicial function come to be seen as a third distinctive governmental task.

The problem with a simple separation of powers, as no less an authority than John Locke had pointed out, was that it made the law-making power supreme. The power to make the law is simply a more fundamental power than the power to enforce the law. If political power is dangerous, and the founding generation thought that it was, then power concentrated in the legislature is a problem.

checks and balances The idea that government powers should be distributed to permit each branch of government to check and balance the other branches.

Checks and Balances.   Although the ideas of **checks and balances** and separation of powers frequently occurred together in the founding period and still do today, they are distinct. In fact, checks and balances provide a solution to the problems associated with a pure separation of powers. Checks and balances blur a pure separation of powers by giving the actors of one branch a role in or leverage over the activities of the other branches. The executive veto of legislative acts, the legislature's participation in treaty making and appointing senior executives, and the right of the judiciary to declare acts of the legislature and the executive unconstitutional all are checks that violate an institutional separation of powers. **Bicameralism**, the idea of dividing the legislative power between two separate houses, is a check that does not violate the principle of separation of powers.

bicameralism A two-house, as opposed to a unicameral or one-house, legislature.

Despite widespread agreement on common principles, delegates were sobered by the recognition that history offered no examples of these principles informing a working national government. State constitutions incorporated many of these principles, but it was the instability of state governments that had convinced many of the delegates that a more powerful national government was necessary. Delegates awaited the opening of the convention nervously, knowing that they had many of the pieces of a new national government before them, but knowing just as well that they did not know how the pieces fit together.

The Convention Debates

Although the delegates making their way toward Philadelphia shared a broad commitment to the ideas of limited and representative government, federalism, separation of powers, bicameralism, and checks and balances, it was not at all clear where these commitments would lead once the discussions began. The northern states had interests that the southern states did not share, and large states hoped that their greater numbers and wealth would be reflected in greater influence over the national councils. Political principles and practical political interests would clash loudly and repeatedly at the convention. Finally, most delegates thought the new nation's fate depended upon creating a more powerful national government. Delegates and delegations willing to threaten the convention's success were likely to be accommodated— if only grudgingly.[16]

Virginia's James Madison had thought long and hard about what benefits might flow from a more powerful national government.[17] He laid out his ideas in letters to Washington, Jefferson, and Virginia Governor Edmund Randolph in March and April of 1787. Madison's boldest ideas were communicated only to Washington, who responded warmly. Confident that Washington's influence in the convention would be great, Madison molded his ideas into a draft constitution to be laid before the upcoming convention.

The Federal Convention began on May 25, 1787. Its first act, to no one's surprise, was to elect Washington to preside. On the first day of the convention, and on every day thereafter, Madison took a position in the front of the room, facing the members, to record the debates and decisions of the body. Most of what we know about how the convention worked and how the Constitution actually took shape during the debates we owe to James Madison. Keenly aware of the delicate task before them, the delegates adopted brief rules of procedure, closed the windows and doors, swore one another to secrecy, and set to work.

The Virginia Plan. The **Virginia Plan** was written by Madison, endorsed by Washington and by most of the delegates from the large states, and introduced on May 29 by Governor Edmund Randolph, leader of the Virginia delegation. The Virginia Plan envisioned a powerful national government. The legislature was to be the dominant branch. It would consist of two houses, the first elected by the people, the second elected by the first from among

James Madison is widely regarded as the father of the U.S. Constitution.

Q4 How did the Virginia and New Jersey Plans differ about the kind of national government that each envisioned?

Virginia Plan Outline of a strong national government, written by Virginia's James Madison and supported by most of the delegates from the large states, that guided early discussion in the Constitutional Convention.

The Granger Collection, New York

George Washington presides over the Federal Convention that met from May 25 through September 17, 1787. Having led the American revolutionary armies to victory, Washington was the most trusted man in America. His calm and serious presence as presiding officer kept the members of the Convention focused on the task at hand.

nominees put forward by the state legislatures. The numbers in each house were to be proportional to state population. The proposed Congress was to have authority to legislate in all cases where it might judge the individual states to be "incompetent" or in which it conceived that their individual legislation would disrupt the "harmony" of the new nation.

Both the executive and the judiciary would derive their appointments from the legislature. The executive would be chosen by the national legislature for

TABLE 2.1 The Virginia and New Jersey Plans	
Virginia Plan	**New Jersey Plan**
Based on popular sovereignty	Based on state sovereignty
Bicameral legislature	Unicameral legislature
Congressional seats allocated according to state population or contributions	Equal votes for states in Congress
Broad powers to legislate where the "harmony" of the U.S. requires it	Authority of the old Congress plus limited powers over taxation and commerce
"A National Executive" chosen and removable by Congress	Multiple executives chosen by Congress and removable upon petition of the states
Federal court system with broad powers	Supreme tribunal with narrow powers
Ratification by the people	Ratification by the states

a single term of seven years. A national judiciary, to consist of one supreme court, would be appointed by the Senate, with lower courts to be created by the national legislature. The new Constitution was to be ratified by popularly elected state conventions rather than by the state legislatures.[18] Most of the major provisions of the Virginia Plan were adopted by the convention during the first two weeks of debate.

The New Jersey Plan.   On June 14, the New Jersey delegation asked that time be given to allow delegates who had been developing a "purely federal" plan to complete their work. The **New Jersey Plan,** presented to the convention on June 15, represented a more limited national government. Absence of powers to tax and regulate commerce were widely seen as the key deficiencies in the confederation government. The New Jersey Plan would add these powers to the existing Congress, but even here, it would hedge them in with state powers and discretion.

New Jersey Plan A plan to add a limited number of new powers to the Articles, supported by most of the delegates from the small states, introduced into the Constitutional Convention as an alternative to the Virginia Plan.

The national executive and judicial powers envisioned by the New Jersey Plan, while new, were limited. The Congress would elect a federal executive who would be ineligible for a second term and removable by Congress upon petition of a majority of the state executives. The national judiciary was even more constrained. Virtually all original jurisdiction over American citizens was to be exercised by the state courts. Following three full days of debate over the merits and deficiencies of the two plans, the convention voted 7–3, with one delegation deadlocked, to approve the Virginia Plan as amended instead of the New Jersey Plan. Though defeated in this first major encounter, the supporters of the New Jersey Plan continued to press their demands. Before moving on, ask yourself how the federal government might look today if the New Jersey Plan, rather than the Virginia Plan, had been selected as the basis for the new constitution.

The Great Compromise on Representation.   After delegates determined that the Virginia Plan still would provide the general outline for the convention's work, it was clear to all that the next major stumbling block was the issue of representation. Large states wanted seats in both the House and the Senate to be distributed according to population (commonly referred to as proportional representation). The small states wanted each state to have one vote in each house. The southern states wanted their slaves to be counted for representation; the northern states opposed unless their property was counted too.

As early as June 11, delegates from Connecticut proposed a compromise in which the states would be represented on the basis of population in the House and each state would be represented equally in the Senate. The convention took five more weeks of intense debate to move grudgingly toward the middle ground that the Connecticut delegation had identified.[19] Finally, on July 12, the northern states agreed to count each slave as three-fifths of a person for purposes of representation if the southern states agreed to apply this proportion to taxes as well. They so agreed. That slaves were to be counted for purposes of representation meant nothing to them, but it did enhance the political clout of their white owners. On July 16, the convention narrowly adopted proportional representation in the House, as the large states wished, and equal votes in the Senate, as the small states demanded.

The Commerce and Slave Trade Compromise.   Once the issue of representation was settled, new regional differences over commerce and slavery rose to threaten the convention. Delegates representing northern commercial interests were little concerned with slavery, although a few did speak stirringly against it, but they were quite determined to control national commercial and trade policy. Delegates representing southern interests sought to limit northern control of southern exports, slavery, and the slave trade. In the face of southern threats to abandon the convention, the delegates agreed to acknowledge northern control of commerce and southern control over slavery, although limits on importation of new slaves after 1808 were permitted. This noxious bargain was renegotiated on the battlefields of the Civil War.

The Compromises on Voting and Presidential Selection.   Like students of politics going back to Plato and Aristotle, the members of the Constitutional Convention were, at best, reluctant democrats. Some of the northern states allowed male citizens over 21 the right to vote, but some southern states had high wealth and property qualifications for voting. Rather than trying to debate and battle their way to a constitutional rule for suffrage, they agreed to allow each state to set the rules for voting and conducting election. Universal suffrage, even universal white manhood suffrage, was not yet a principle for which most American leaders were willing to fight.

Not surprisingly, as the convention approached the completion of its business, the contentious topic of presidential selection remained unresolved. Delegates advocating a powerful national government wanted an independent executive strong enough to check a volatile legislature, whereas those who opposed great power at the national level wanted an executive dependent upon, even selected by, the legislature. But legislative selection of the executive seemed too obvious a violation of separation of powers.

As they had with other difficult issues, the convention voted to turn the issue of executive selection over to a committee composed of one member from each state. This committee, known as the Brearley Committee, crafted a solution that many believed balanced the interests of the large and small states. The Brearley Committee proposed an electoral college in which the number of electors per state was equal to the number of House and Senate seats assigned to each state. However, many delegates were convinced that electors voting in their separate states could not coordinate their votes to elect a president on the first round and that candidates from the larger states would likely receive the most votes. If no candidate received a majority, the Senate, where the small states had equal votes, would select the president from among the top five candidates.

Floor debate on the Brearley Committee proposal raised the troublesome issue of whether the power to select the president from a list of five candidates, in addition to the Senate's other powers, might make the Senate a dangerous aristocracy. Connecticut's Roger Sherman proposed that the final selection be made by the House of Representatives, voting by states. This solution left the advantage over final choice among candidates to the small states, but removed the objection that the Senate was too powerful. With this last major deadlock broken, the Federal Convention moved rapidly to conclude its work.

The Constitution as Finally Adopted

After nearly four months of debate broken only by a brief respite to observe the Fourth of July, thirty-nine delegates signed the Constitution on September 17, 1787 (the Constitution is Appendix C in the back of this book). How did the principles and interests that the delegates brought to the convention show up in the final document?

The Preamble: A Statement of Our Goals.   The Preamble declares the Constitution to be an act of the sovereign people of the United States to secure the public purposes that they held most dear. The Articles of Confederation had been an agreement among the states, whereas the Constitution was an act of the people. The Preamble reads: "We the people of the United States, in Order to form a more perfect Union, establish Justice, insure domestic Tranquility, provide for the common defence, promote the general Welfare, and secure the Blessings of Liberty to ourselves and our Posterity, do ordain and establish this Constitution of the United States of America." These goals—like the self-evident truths enumerated by Thomas Jefferson in the Declaration of Independence, "that all men are created equal, that they are endowed by their Creator with certain unalienable rights, that among these are Life, Liberty, and the pursuit of happiness"—have continued to challenge and inspire each new generation of Americans.

Article I: The Legislative Branch.   It was widely assumed that the legislature would be the core of the new government and that its powers and responsibilities needed to be laid out with care. Article I, section 1, states: "All legislative Powers herein granted shall be vested in a Congress of the United States, which shall consist of a Senate and House of Representatives." This language seems a stark adoption of separation of powers theory, although the bicameral design shows that the idea of checks and balances was not ignored. Sections 2 through 6 are largely given over to legislative housekeeping.

Section 7 lays out the president's role in the legislative process. The president has the right to review all legislation before it becomes law. If he concurs, he signs the legislation; if he strongly opposes the judgment of the legislature, he can veto the legislation subject to an override by two-thirds of each house or he can ignore the legislation, in which case it becomes law after ten days. Both bicameralism and the presidential veto were intended as checks on the legislature's ability to act rashly.

Section 8 of Article I describes the powers of the Congress. What makes Article I, section 8, utterly fascinating is that it begins by listing seventeen

Gathering Momentum: The Growth of Democracy in the World

Upon leaving the Federal Convention at the completion of that body's work, Benjamin Franklin was asked by a group of citizens what kind of government had been settled upon. Franklin replied, "A republic, if you can keep it." What he meant by "a republic" was a limited government adopted by the body of eligible citizens and administered by elected officials sworn to uphold the citizens' rights and liberties. Franklin did not call the new government a "democracy" because, in the founding period, democracy meant direct rule by the citizens themselves. By the time Thomas Jefferson became President, the new nation thought of itself as a democratic republic. And by Andrew Jackson's day, most Americans were comfortable thinking of their nation simply as a democracy.[20]

Although our history books speak boldly of Jacksonian democracy, in fact, the United States took almost a century and a half to grow into its democracy. In Jackson's day, less than 40 percent of American adults, only white men, were eligible to vote. Black men were made eligible to vote with adoption of the Fifteenth Amendment in 1870, women with adoption of the Nineteenth Amendment in 1920, and young people ages 18 to 21 with the adoption of the Twenty-sixth Amendment in 1971. Still, until the late 1960s most blacks were denied the right to vote and today, even in our most important elections, only a little more than half of the electorate casts a ballot.

Yet, the world wears a much more democratic face than it did when the American democracy was born. The number of demo-cratic nations in the world grew slowly throughout the nineteenth century and a good part of the twentieth century. In 1820, as stability returned to Europe in the wake of the Napoleonic Wars, there were twenty-three nation-states and only three of them were democratic. As the twentieth century dawned, there were fifty-five nations and thirteen democracies, but great changes lay ahead.

The two world wars of the twentieth century, World War I from 1914 to 1918 and World War II from 1939 to 1945, destroyed the great colonial empires of previous centuries. The result was a more than three-fold increase in the number of independent nations in the world. The family of nations increased from 55 in 1900, to 80 in 1950, to 195 today. Even more remarkably, the number of democracies increased from 13 in 1900, to 22 in 1950, to 117 today.

Almost exactly half of the world's democracies became democracies after 1990 (61 of 117). Many of the new democracies are poor and have little historic familiarity with democratic habits and practices. Hence, many fall short on respect for human rights, free and fair elections, and open and responsive government. Democracy is not like a light switch, either on or off; rather, it is more like a dimmer switch. Even when it is on, it can get dimmer or brighter. Over time, with the support of the world's mature democracies, most new democracies should get brighter.[21]

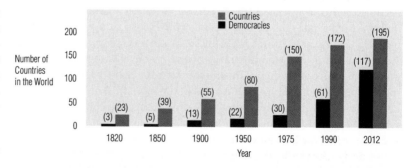

Sources: J. David Singer and Melvin Small, "The Composition and Status Ordering of the International System, 1815–1940," *World Politics* 18, no. 2 (January 1966): 236–270; Francis Fukuyama, *The End of History and the Last Man* (New York: Free Press, 1992), 48–51; and various Freedom House publications including "Democracy's Century" and "Freedom in the World 2013."

specific congressional powers. Foremost among these **enumerated powers** are the powers to levy taxes and to control commerce. The right to tax has been central to the growth of national power, but, as we shall see more fully in Chapter 3, the obscure sounding commerce power has supported increasingly broad national authority as well. Most of the remaining enumerated powers involve financial and monetary policy and regulation and the right to raise and support an army and navy. Section 8 closes with language that has come to be known as the "**necessary and proper" clause**: "To make all Laws which shall be necessary and proper for carrying into Execution the foregoing Powers, and all other Powers vested by this Constitution in the Government of the United States, or in any Department or Officer thereof." To many, the broad sweep of the "necessary and proper" clause seemed to defeat the purpose of a finite list of enumerated powers.

enumerated powers The specifically listed or enumerated powers of Congress found in Article I, section 8, of the Constitution.

"necessary and proper" clause The last paragraph of Article I, section 8, of the Constitution, which states that Congress may make all laws deemed necessary and proper to carry into execution the powers specifically enumerated in Article I, section 8.

Article II: The Executive Branch. Article II, section 1, declares that "The executive Power shall be vested in a President of the United States of America." It also describes the process by which the president will be selected, the qualifications of the office, the succession of the vice president in the case of presidential death or incapacity, and the presidential oath. Section 2 describes one set of powers that is explicitly granted to the president and another set that is granted to the president "with the Advice and Consent of the Senate." The first set of powers is modest indeed. The president serves as commander in chief of the army and navy, may require the opinions in writing of the principal officers of the executive branch, and may grant reprieves and pardons for offenses against the United States. With the **advice and consent** of two-thirds of the senators present, the president can conclude treaties, and with the approval of a simple majority of the Senate he can appoint ambassadors, members of the Supreme Court, and other public ministers and administrative officers of the United States.

advice and consent Article II, section 2, of the Constitution requires the president to seek the advice and consent of the Senate in appointing Supreme Court justices, senior officials of the executive branch, and ambassadors, and in ratifying treaties with foreign nations.

Section 3 provides several opportunities for presidential influence but gives no additional powers. The president is required to give the Congress, from time to time, information on the "State of the Union," and he is entitled to "recommend to their consideration such Measures as he shall judge necessary and expedient." Also in section 3 is a clause that charges the president to "take care that the Laws be faithfully executed." The "**take care**" **clause** has been read by presidents since Abraham Lincoln as a command that they see that the laws of the United States are both faithfully executed by the government and obeyed by the citizenry. Finally, section 4, the impeachment clause, warns against misuse of power by the president and his associates and officers.

"take care" clause Article II, section 3, of the Constitution requires that the president "take care that the laws be faithfully executed."

Article III: The Judicial Branch. Section 1 declares simply that "The judicial Power of the United States shall be vested in one supreme Court, and in such inferior Courts as the Congress may from time to time ordain and establish." Section 2 sketches a very limited jurisdiction for the federal courts. The federal courts are to handle cases arising under the Constitution or federal laws and treaties; involving ambassadors and other public ministers; or involving the

United States, two or more states, citizens of different states, and states with citizens of other states. Only in those unusual cases where the jurisdiction of a single state does not cover the parties involved do the federal courts have jurisdiction. The Supreme Court has original jurisdiction in cases involving ambassadors, other public ministers, and cases in which one or more states are involved. In all other cases, their jurisdiction is appellate.

republican government
Mixed or balanced government that is based on the people but may retain residual elements of monarchical or aristocratic privilege. Americans of the colonial period were particularly impressed with the example of republican Rome.

full faith and credit Article IV, section 1, of the Constitution requires that each state give "full faith and credit" to the legal acts of the other states.

privileges and immunities clause Article IV, section 2, of the Constitution guarantees to the citizens of each state the "privileges and immunities" of the several states.

Articles IV and VI: Federal Relations.   Article IV provides for reciprocity between the states, for the admission of new states into the union, and for guarantees of **republican government** and protections against domestic violence in the states. Article IV, section 1, guarantees that **full faith and credit** will be given by each state to the legal acts of the other states. More generally, the full faith and credit clause, together with the **privileges and immunities clause** of Article IV, section 2, guarantees that normal social and economic transactions would have effect across state lines within the new nation. Article IV, section 3, guarantees that new states can be admitted into the union but that they will not be carved out of existing states or parts of existing states except with the consent of the states involved. Section 4, in direct response to the concern created by Shays's Rebellion, promises that "The United States shall guarantee to every State in this Union a Republican Form of Government, and shall protect each of them against Invasion; and on Application of the Legislature, or of the Executive (when the Legislature cannot be convened) against domestic Violence."

Article VI declares: "This Constitution, and the Laws of the United States which shall be made in Pursuance thereof . . . shall be the supreme Law of the Land." Moreover, all public officials, "both of the United States and of the several States, shall be bound by Oath or Affirmation, to support this Constitution." The "supremacy clause" declared federal authority supreme within its authorized areas of responsibility. Nonetheless, Joseph F. Zimmerman, a leading scholar of American federalism, has noted, "The U.S. Constitution was the first written document in the world to provide for the distribution of significant powers between the national government and territorial governments."[22]

Article V: The Amendment Process.   Article V outlines two methods by which amendments can be proposed and two methods by which they can be approved or rejected. Congress can, by a two-thirds vote of both houses, propose amendments to the Constitution, or, in response to a call from two-thirds of the state legislatures, must summon a convention to consider proposing amendments. Regardless of whether Congress or a convention proposes amendments, they must be ratified by the legislatures of three-fourths of the states or by special conventions called in three-fourths of the states.

Although the Founders quite clearly wanted the Constitution to be subject to amendment, they just as clearly did not want to see it changed easily or often. In fact, the Constitution has been amended only twenty-seven times in more than two hundred years. Congress has always exercised close control over the amendment process. All twenty-seven amendments to the Constitu-

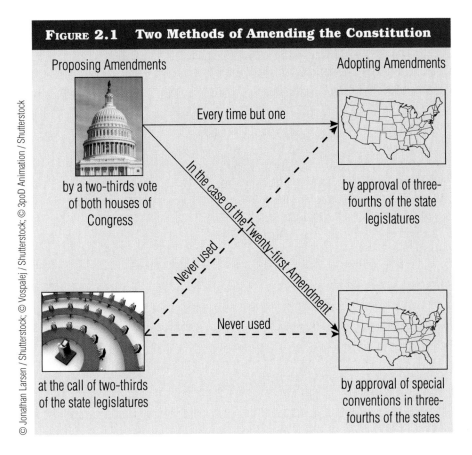

FIGURE 2.1   Two Methods of Amending the Constitution

Proposing Amendments

Adopting Amendments

Every time but one

In the case of the Twenty-first Amendment

Never used

Never used

by a two-thirds vote of both houses of Congress

by approval of three-fourths of the state legislatures

at the call of two-thirds of the state legislatures

by approval of special conventions in three-fourths of the states

tion were proposed by Congress. Congress has only once, in the case of the Twenty-first Amendment, chosen the state convention approach to considering amendments proposed by Congress. In every other case, Congress has specified that consideration of proposed amendments occur in the state legislatures.

Finally, the Constitution is also quite interesting for what it leaves out. This includes any discussion of parties, the internal organization of Congress, the membership and role of the president's cabinet, the structure of the bureaucracy or bureaucratic agencies, and the structure and jurisdiction of the federal courts below the level of the Supreme Court. All of these things and many more were left to the Congress to decide.

THE STRUGGLE OVER RATIFICATION

The members of the Federal Convention made every effort to tilt the ratification process in favor of the proposed Constitution. They knew that if they followed the amendment process laid out in the Articles of Confederation—adoption by

TABLE 2.2	State Ratification of the Proposed Constitution		
State	**Date**	**Approve**	**Reject**
Delaware	Dec. 7, 1787	30	0
Pennsylvania	Dec. 12, 1787	46	23
New Jersey	Dec. 18, 1787	38	0
Georgia	Jan. 2, 1788	26	0
Connecticut	Jan. 9, 1788	128	40
Massachusetts	Feb. 7, 1788	187	168
Maryland	Apr. 28, 1788	63	11
South Carolina	May 23, 1788	149	73
New Hampshire	June 21, 1788	57	47
Virginia	June 25, 1788	89	79
New York	July 26, 1788	30	27
North Carolina	Nov. 21, 1789	194	77
Rhode Island	May 29, 1790	34	32

the Congress and "the legislatures of every State"—the prospects for ratification were literally zero. Therefore, the convention proposed a ratification process that included neither explicit congressional approval nor a role for the state legislatures.[23] The intent of the convention was that the Constitution "be submitted to a Convention of Delegates, chosen in each State by the People thereof, under the Recommendation of its Legislature, for their Assent and Ratification."[24]

Article VII of the proposed Constitution made approval by nine states sufficient to put the new government into effect among the approving states. Some states were overwhelmingly supportive and were ready to move immediately; others had grave reservations and wished to have time to gather their arguments and to watch early developments. Therefore, while the first wave of decisions took only a few weeks and several were unanimously positive, it took nearly seven months to secure the ninth ratification and two more years to secure the thirteenth.

Moreover, the vote in some major states was close; Massachusetts approved by 187 to 168, Virginia by 89 to 79, and New York had to vote twice. In the first vote, on June 17, 1788, the Constitution went down 19 to 46. After the Federalists rallied, agreeing to 31 proposed amendments, a second vote on July 26 narrowly succeeded 30 to 27.

Federalists Supporters of a stronger national government who favored ratification of the U.S. Constitution.

Anti-Federalists Opponents of a stronger national government who generally opposed ratification of the U.S. Constitution.

Federalists versus Anti-Federalists.   Although **Federalists** supported the proposed Constitution and **Anti-Federalists** opposed it, they were not divided by deep and irreconcilable differences. Historian Ralph Ketcham noted that both Federalists and Anti-Federalists "were conditional democrats. They were for or against the ideas of majority rule, representation, broad suffrage, and so on insofar as those processes seemed likely to result in order, freedom, justice, prosperity, and the other broad purposes of the Constitution."[25]

Pro & Con

Do We Need a Bill of Rights?

The Federalists contended that adding a bill of rights to the Constitution was not only unnecessary, but positively dangerous. It was unnecessary for two reasons: first, because the structure of the Constitution was designed to protect the rights of the people through the principles of delegation, representation, separation of powers, bicameralism, checks and balances, and federalism; and second, because the Constitution was composed of delegated powers and powers not given were retained by the people. It was positively dangerous because to list some rights might suggest that rights not listed were not retained or claimed by the people.

James Wilson, a leading member of the Philadelphia convention and an important lawyer in that city, was the chief defender of the proposed Constitution in Pennsylvania. In his famous State House speech of October 6, 1787, Wilson presented an argument that became the standard Federalist case against adding a bill of rights to the Constitution. Wilson's "reserved powers theory" held that the Constitution provides for a government of limited and enumerated powers, so "every thing which is not given" to the national government "is reserved" by the people. Under these circumstances, Wilson contended, no bill of rights would be needed because the government has power to act only where power has been expressly granted. Wilson further reasoned that "If we attempt an enumeration, everything that is not enumerated is presumed to be given. The consequence is that an imperfect enumeration would throw all implied power into the scale of the government; and the rights of the people would be rendered incomplete." Wilson was by no means the only prominent Federalist to oppose a bill of rights.

Anti-Federalists argued that the people demanded explicit protection for traditional rights including freedom of speech, press, religion, search and seizure, speedy trial, and more. If Federalists worried that a short list of rights might leave something off, make a long list. Besides, they argued, clear protection of some critical rights and liberties was better than none.

Eventually, Thomas Jefferson and others convinced James Madison of the importance of a national bill of rights. Madison convinced his colleagues in the first House of Representatives that a bill of rights was necessary to "quiet that anxiety which prevails in the public mind" and to "stifle the voice of complaint, and make friends of many who doubted [the Constitution's] merits." The first ten amendments to the Constitution, known as the Bill of Rights, went into effect on December 15, 1791.

What do you think?
- If the Federalists had prevailed, and no Bill of Rights had been added to the Constitution, how might that have changed the course of our national development?
- Would those changes have been for good or ill?

PRO	CON
The people deserve a bill of rights	The Constitution's structure protects rights
Make a long list	Some rights might be left off any list
Protecting some rights is better than none	Powers not granted cannot be abused

The problem was that the Federalists and Anti-Federalists disagreed about how the national government described in the proposed Constitution would actually work. Many Americans were concerned that the proposed Constitution was simply too powerful to leave their liberties secure. James Madison,

Alexander Hamilton, and John Jay teamed up to write a series of newspaper columns intended to explain and support the new Constitution during the ratification struggle in New York. These columns, which came to be known as the Federalist Papers, turned the debate in New York in favor of the Constitution and were reprinted by supporters up and down the Atlantic coast.

The Federalists believed, as James Madison would explain in numbers 10, 48, and 51 of the Federalist Papers, that a large nation, an "extended republic" in the phrase of the day, makes a powerful and stable national government possible if that government is wisely and carefully crafted. Extensive territory means a broad diversity of groups and interests, no one of which, or no combination of which, would constitute a stable majority capable of oppressing a stable minority. Rather, the diversity of religious, social, economic, and regional interests would check and balance each other (Federalist Numbers 10 and 51 are included in Appendix D in the back of this book).

If diversity means that no oppressive majority is likely to form in society and press its demands on government, then one has only to guard against oppressive tendencies arising within government itself. Madison and his colleagues believed that they had in fact guarded against governmental tyranny by constructing a careful system of limited and enumerated powers, by supplementing a pure separation of powers with appropriate checks and balances, and by leaving important governmental powers to the states and rights and liberties to the people.

The Anti-Federalists were not so sure. They thought that popular governments can exist only in "small republics" where the people can come together, as in county court days in the South or town meetings in New England, to conduct the public business. They did not believe that a nation as diverse as theirs could have a single public interest. Rather, they thought that sectional divisions would divide the national councils and that legislators serving so far from home would forget the interests of their constituents. The Anti-Federalists believed that the blessings of the revolution—local people controlling local governments according to local needs, interests, and customs—would be endangered by a powerful national government.[26] Before moving on, ask yourself how the divisions between Federalists and Anti-Federalists in the founding period relate to the divisions between Republicans and Democrats today. What issues that divided Federalists from Anti-Federalists back then still divide Republicans and Democrats today?

Q5 What role did the debate over a bill of rights play in the adoption of the U.S. Constitution?

A Concession to the Opposition: The Bill of Rights. As the ratification debate progressed, Anti-Federalist opinion settled on the absence of a bill of rights as the fundamental deficiency of the proposed Constitution. The public was responsive to this criticism. The idea of rights and resistance to their violation had been a rallying cry for Americans since the mid-1760s. However, staking their campaign against the Constitution on the absence of a bill of rights eventually led to the Anti-Federalists' downfall. When the Federalists accepted the demand that a bill of rights be added to the Constitution, the Anti-Federalists were stripped of their key reason for opposing its ratification. New Hampshire was the ninth state to ratify the new Constitution in June 1788.

What kind of bill of rights should be added to the new Constitution remained an open question for some time. Madison concluded that a bill of rights designed to secure the traditional rights of citizens could, assuming that its provisions did not weaken the legitimate powers of the government, win over those citizens still worried that the new government was too powerful. On September 28, 1789, largely due to Madison's efforts, Congress approved and sent to the states for ratification twelve amendments to the Constitution. Ten of these were approved and have come to be known as the **Bill of Rights**.

The Bill of Rights, broadly conceived, accomplished two things. First, it defined a preserve of personal autonomy, choice, and expression where government power should not intrude. The First Amendment offered the expansive assurance that "Congress shall make no law respecting an establishment of religion, or prohibiting the free exercise thereof; or abridging the freedom of speech, or of the press; or of the right of the people peaceably to assemble, and to petition the government for a redress of grievances."

Second, the Bill of Rights defined how persons would be subject to the power of government. Isolated individuals, especially common people, cannot stand up to the concentrated power of government unless that government is required to proceed slowly, carefully, and according to well-known rules and procedures. Hence, the Bill of Rights confirmed the rights to a speedy trial before an impartial jury, to confront witnesses, and to have the aid of counsel (Amendment 6). The Bill of Rights protected citizens against "unreasonable searches and seizures" (Amendment 4), double jeopardy and self-incrimination (Amendment 5), and excessive bail or cruel and unusual punishments (Amendment 8). The Ninth Amendment, like the Declaration of Independence, suggested that citizens, as human beings, have more rights than those specifically listed in the Constitution and its amendments. The Ninth Amendment said, "The enumeration in the Constitution, of certain rights, shall not be constructed to deny or disparage others retained by the people." Finally, the Tenth Amendment declared that, "powers not delegated to the United States by the Constitution, nor prohibited to it by the states, are reserved to the states respectively, or to the people." These reassuring commitments encouraged citizens to give the new Constitution a chance. Just as Madison had hoped, support for the Constitution increased to near unanimity within a few years.

Bill of Rights The first ten amendments to the U.S. Constitution, proposed by the first Federal Congress and ratified by the states in 1791, were intended to protect individual rights and liberties from action by the new national government.

CONSIDERING CONSTITUTIONAL REFORM

The U.S. Constitution was written in an undemocratic age. The Founders did not intend to write a democratic constitution. They did not intend to treat minorities and women as equals. They intended to write a constitution that would check, balance, and limit political power while protecting the individual and property rights of white men.[27] While white Americans tend to slide over the narrow sense of equality in the Constitution, others do not. Thurgood Marshall, a top lawyer for the National Association for the Advancement of Colored People (NAACP) and the first black justice of the United States Supreme Court, appointed by President Lyndon Johnson in 1967, was invited on the 200th anniversary of the Constitution to give a speech celebrating the genius of the Founding Fathers and of the document they crafted. Justice Marshall both educated and discomfited his audience by moving quickly past praise for the Founders and the Constitution to take a clear-eyed view of the weaknesses and shortcomings of both.

Marshall said: "I do not believe that the meaning of the Constitution was forever 'fixed' at the Philadelphia Convention. Nor do I find the wisdom, foresight, and sense of justice exhibited by the Framers particularly profound. To the contrary, the government they devised was defective from the start, requiring several amendments, a civil war, and momentous social transformation to attain the system of constitutional government, and its respect for the individual freedoms and human rights, we hold as fundamental today. When contemporary Americans cite 'The Constitution,' they invoke a concept that is vastly different from what the Framers barely began to construct two centuries ago."[28] Modern critics of the U.S. Constitution find many of its key structural elements undemocratic and call for their removal or revision.

Robert A. Dahl, perhaps the most prominent democratic theorist of the second half of the twentieth century, wrote a book in 2002 called *How Democratic Is the Constitution?* Dahl's answer was, "Not very." Dahl leveled particular criticism at the role of the Electoral College in presidential selection, the equal representation of the states in the Senate, and the power that judicial review gives judges to overturn the actions of elected executive and legislative officials.[29]

More recently, University of Texas law and government Professor Sanford Levinson agreed with Dahl that the Electoral College, the Senate, and the federal courts were undemocratic in their origins and operations. In *Our Undemocratic Constitution* (2006), Levinson pointed out that most modern democratic nations are governed by untrammeled, unicameral, parliamentary majorities. Levinson contends that the slow and painful need to reach a consensus in our "tripartite" system of House, Senate, and presidency is an unnecessary and inefficient check on democratic governance. He calls for, though he does not expect, a nationwide petition campaign demanding that Congress and the state legislatures authorize a new constitutional convention.[30]

Many agree with Dahl and Levinson that our politics are broken and the Constitution is the root cause. Others believe that the Electoral College, Senate and Supreme Court are curiously configured and mildly undemocratic, but they do not believe that wholesale constitutional reform is necessary. What do you think?

Chapter Summary

During the eighteenth century, the population of the colonies doubled approximately every twenty years. As the economy grew and matured, domestic markets

TABLE 2.3	**From Revolution to Constitution**
1763	British win Seven Years War, secure Canada
1765	Parliament passes Stamp Act
	Americans hold Stamp Act Congress
1766	Parliament withdraws Stamp Act
	Parliament passes Declaratory Act
1770	Boston Massacre
1773	Boston Tea Party
1774	Parliament passes Intolerable Acts
	First Continental Congress meets
1775	Violence erupts at Lexington and Concord
	Second Continental Congress meets
1776	Congress passes Declaration of Independence
1777	Congress writes Articles of Confederation
1781	Articles of Confederation ratified
	Independence secured with British surrender at Yorktown
1786	Annapolis Convention meets
	Shays's Rebellion
1787	Philadelphia Convention drafts U.S. Constitution
1788	Constitution ratified
1789	Congress proposes Bill of Rights
1791	Bill of Rights ratified

became increasingly important, and the desire for free access to international markets beyond Britain became more compelling. After British victory in the Seven Years War cleared the French threat from Canada, Americans could see less and less benefit from British intrusion into their economic and political lives.

Independence brought its own difficulties. The decade leading up to the revolution was dominated by talk of British tyranny and American freedom. The argument was that American rights and liberties were threatened by the power of a distant government in London. Not surprisingly then, when Americans set about creating their own political institutions they sought to limit political power by keeping it local wherever possible. Where political power had to be exercised at a distance, as with the national government under the Articles of Confederation, it was made as modest as possible.

Yet, history suggested that popular political institutions are volatile and unstable. Shays's Rebellion convinced many that a more powerful national government was needed to stabilize politics in the states and to encourage national economic opportunity and development. The delegates that each state sent to the Constitutional Convention of 1787 understood quite clearly that they were to propose reforms that would secure the social, economic, and political stability of the new nation.

The delegates shared a number of broad principles that were rarely challenged in the convention. They agreed that written constitutions provide the surest guarantee of limited government. They agreed that federalism permits the assignment of power and responsibility to the level of government best suited to fulfill them efficiently and safely. They agreed that at both levels of the federal system—national and state—the principles of bicameralism, separation of powers, and checks and balances provide the best assurance that political power will be exercised in the public interest. The delegates differed relatively little over these issues.

They did, however, differ over the distribution of power within the federal system and how to ensure that their states and regions were well placed to exercise decisive influence in the new system. Men from small states believed that their interests would suffer if men from the large states dominated, and men from the South believed that their interests would suffer if men from the North dominated.

The Federal Constitution of 1787 reflected the particular configuration of ideas and interests present in the convention during the summer of 1787. As that configuration has changed and as ideas have asserted their steady influence, the Constitution has been brought to reflect more fully the values of liberty, equality, and opportunity that were so important to the rhetoric of the revolution and so clearly stated by Thomas Jefferson and his colleagues in the Declaration of Independence.

No greater compliment can be paid to the U.S. Constitution than to say that it has aspired to embody the values of the Declaration of Independence.[31] Perhaps more important, the Constitution has been vastly strengthened by the fact that values only implicit there are luminously explicit in the Declaration of Independence. The Declaration of Independence remains an open invitation to those not enjoying the full fruits of liberty and equality to make their case for a fuller share.

Key Terms

advice and consent   47

Annapolis Convention   36

Anti-Federalists   50

Articles of Confederation   35

bicameralism   40

Bill of Rights   53

Boston Massacre   29

Boston Tea Party   29

checks and balances   40

Confederation Congress   35

Constitutional Convention   38

Continental Congress   31

Declaration of Independence   32

Declaratory Act   29

enumerated powers   47

federalism   40

Federalists   50

full faith and credit   48

Suggested Readings

Amar, Akhil Reed. "America's Constitution," 2005. Amar argues that the Constitution's promise of self-government put the U.S. on a path to expanded democracy, however slowly, that ultimately would include all adult white men, women, and racial minorities.

Beeman, Richard. *Plain, Honest Men: The Making of the American Constitution*. New York: Random House, 2009. Beeman tells the story of the Constitution's drafting by highlighting the compromises that permitted success.

Gibson, Alan. *Understanding the Founding: The Crucial Questions*. Lawrence, KS: University Press of Kansas, 2007. Gibson explores the historical and intellectual influences on the Founders and the Constitution.

Levinson, Sanford. *Our Undemocratic Constitution*. New York: Oxford University Press, 2006. Levinson contends that impotant provisions of the Constitution are insufficiently democratic.

Maier, Pauline. *Ratification: The People Debate the Constitution*. New York: Simon & Schuster, 2010. The first full account of the debate in the thirteen states over whether to approve the Constitution.

Storing, Herbert. "What the Anti-Federalists Were For," 1981. The anti-federalists believed that the Constitution marked a step in the wrong direction, away from small government values and toward a centralized government beyond the people's control.

Wood, Gordon S. *Revolutionary Characters: What Made the Founders Different*. New York: Penguin, 2006. Wood offers eight brief but compelling biographies of leading Founders and two essays on the nature of their times.

Web Resources

For practice quizzes, key term flashcards, videos, links, and other study tools, visit the *American Government* website: www.routledge.com/cw/jillson

1. **www.archives.gov/**
   The national archives provide a treasure trove of information on the Constitution. Click on "America's Historical Documents."

2. **www.mlkcelebration.com/speech_negroconstitution.php**
   This noteworthy page offers the essay titled "The Negro and the Constitution" by Martin Luther King Jr. The essay sheds light on the disparity in rights between Anglo and African Americans despite the Constitution.

3. **www.earlyamerica.com**
   The Archiving Early America page offers links to historical documents and to the *Early America Review,* a journal about eighteenth-century America.

4. **www.constitutioncenter.org**
   A non-partisan center focused on increasing knowledge and understanding of the U.S. Constitution.

5. **www.constitution.org/afp/afp.htm**
   A good selection of anti-federalist writings opposing the Constitution and good directions to secondary literature.

6. **www.youtube.com**
   To get more information on the events and personalities of the revolutionary and constitution convention eras, go to YouTube and type in your interest. Many fascinating clips are available.

Chapter 3

FEDERALISM AND AMERICAN POLITICAL DEVELOPMENT

" *The proposed Constitution, so far from implying an abolition of the state governments, makes them constituent parts of the national sovereignty ... and leaves in their possession certain exclusive and very important portions of sovereign power. This fully corresponds ... with the idea of a federal government.* "

ALEXANDER HAMILTON,
Federalist Number 9

IF MARIJUANA IS ILLEGAL, WHY ARE THEY SELLING IT IN CALIFORNIA?

Article VI: "This Constitution, and the laws of the United States which shall be made in pursuance thereof . . . shall be the supreme law of the land."

Tenth Amendment: "The powers not delegated to the United States by the Constitution, nor prohibited by it to the states, are reserved to the states respectively, or to the people."

In 1970 the Congress passed and the president signed the Controlled Substances Act (CSA). The CSA declared marijuana, first made illegal in federal law in 1937, to be a Schedule I drug with a "high potential for abuse" and no legitimate medical use. The CSA is federal law to this day; yet new claims regarding the medical benefits of marijuana led California to enact a medical marijuana law in 1996. By 2014 medical marijuana was legal in twenty states and D.C. (Alaska, Arizona, California, Colorado, Connecticut, Delaware, Hawaii, Illinois, Maine, Massachusetts, Michigan, Montana, Nevada, New Hampshire, New Jersey, New Mexico, Oregon, Rhode Island, Vermont, and Washington) and the Obama administration had instructed federal law enforcement officials not to enforce the CSA in those states. However, when the number of pot shops in California proliferated beyond apparent medical needs, federal authorities cracked down. In 2012, two states, Colorado and Washington, upped the ante when citizen referenda approved marijuana use by any citizen over 21. Can federal and state laws conflict like this and, when they do, is not federal law supposed to prevail over state law? Yes, well usually, but occasionally federalism, the topic of this chapter, is messier than we would like.

The question of the relative priority of federal versus state law plagued the Founders during the Constitutional Convention, was one of the central issues over which ratification was fought, and has surfaced time and again throughout American history. In the 1860s we fought a bloody Civil War over just this issue—national versus state authority within the federal system.

For most of American history, the claims of state officials that federal officials construed their powers too broadly and thereby infringed on the state powers protected by the Tenth Amendment were taken seriously in the federal courts. All of that changed during the "Great Depression," in 1937 to be exact. President Franklin Roosevelt moved aggressively to deal with the depression, but the Supreme Court resisted, striking down major parts of his agenda.

Focus Questions: from reading to thinking

Q1 How did the meanings of the terms *federal* and *federalism* change over the course of the founding and early national periods?

Q2 What powers and responsibilities did the U.S. Constitution give the national government in relation to the states and to the states in relation to the national government?

Q3 How did the expansion and integration of the American economy shape the balance of governmental power and authority within the federal system?

Q4 What fiscal and political forces led to the change in American federalism called "devolution"?

Q5 Have the complexities of the twenty-first century rendered our government essentially national, or do state and local governments still have important roles to play?

FDR responded by trying to "pack" the Court with new and more compliant members. The Court blinked, almost wholly abandoning its traditional role of limiting government regulation of the economy in favor of a focus on civil rights and liberties. The federal government initiated expansive social programs and an aggressive regulatory agenda. Only in the mid-1980s did the Court begin to challenge federal powers, but only occasionally on the basis of the Tenth Amendment.

How then can states push back against unwelcome actions by the federal government? One option is through nullification, the idea that states can render federal laws null and void within their boundaries if they believe the laws are unconstitutional—meaning touching matters beyond the scope of the Congress's enumerated powers. To understand this claim we must distinguish between formal and informal nullification. Formal nullification would involve a state government declaring an act of Congress void and the federal courts upholding that claim. The federal courts would have to declare that the federal action was an unconstitutional violation of the "reserved rights" of the states under the Tenth Amendment. The Supreme Court has done so only twice in the last half century. In the most notable case, *Printz v. U.S.*, the Court struck down a provision of the Brady Handgun Violence Protection Act for requiring state officials to conduct background checks on persons seeking to buy a handgun.

Informal nullification, as with the case of medical marijuana or the broader marijuana use approved by Colorado and Washington, is more common and is well within the American traditions of political bargaining, popular democracy, and federalism. Informal nullification occurs in a variety of ways, most involving state and public reluctance to comply with a particular federal statute. State legislatures may pass contrary laws or decline to enforce federal mandates and public opinion and action might demonstrate an unwillingness to comply. If state authorities do not challenge federal authority directly, or do so carefully, federal authorities may react to the opposition by withdrawing the act or at least limiting enforcement.

WHAT DO YOU THINK?

- On what other issues, besides medical marijuana use, do state and federal laws come into conflict?
- How about capital punishment, gay marriage, abortion, and environmental regulation?
- Should these be federal issues, state issues, or what?

FEDERALISM AND AMERICAN
POLITICAL DEVELOPMENT

This chapter completes our discussion of the origins of American political cal ideals and institutions and serves as a transition to our treatment of contemporary American politics. In this chapter we explore the origins

TABLE 3.1 Strengths and Weaknesses of Federalism	
Strengths	**Weaknesses**
Limits concentrated national power	Leaves state power vulnerable
Encourages innovation by the states	Complex overlapping responsibilities
Encourages pluralism and citizen involvement	Lack of uniformity
National minorities may be subnational majorities	Encourages race to the bottom

of the American federal system and ask how the federal structure has affected and been affected by political development and change within the broader American society.

A federal system divides political power and responsibility between national and subnational levels of government.[1] We describe how the nature of American federalism and the balance of power within it have evolved over time to address new issues and problems in a rapidly growing, increasingly complex, national and now international environment.

The Founders knew that the structure and character of the American government would affect the path of the nation's development. That is why they were so concerned about what kind of government they were creating: national or federal. Just as the Founders used separation of powers and checks and balances to allocate and limit executive, legislative, and judicial functions within the national government, they used federalism to allocate and limit political power and responsibility between levels of government. Some among the founding and later generations always wanted more power and initiative at the national level, others always wanted less. The struggle between and among national and state actors for the power and resources to define and address the dominant issues of American political life has been and remains the drama of American federalism.

As we shall see, twenty-first-century American federalism involves a complicated array of authorities and actors. The nation now spans a continent and contains more than 320 million citizens. These citizens are served, at most recent count, by 89,527 governments within the federal system. There is, of course, only one national government. There are fifty state governments. Within the states are 3,031 county governments, 19,519 municipalities, 16,360 towns and townships, 12,880 school districts, and 38,266 special districts that deliver all manner of services.[2] As you read this chapter, think about the tremendous growth and change that our nation has undergone over the course of its history. From small colonies scattered along the Atlantic seaboard, the U.S. is now a global economic and military powerhouse. Is the "social contract" that the founding generation struck and wrote into the Constitution still in force today? Has that social contract changed and, if so, when? How did the Constitution adapt to permit and even facilitate the evolution of our federal political structure? How healthy is contemporary American federalism and what are the system's prospects for effective governance in the twenty-first century?

Q1 How did the meanings of the terms *federal* and *federalism* change over the course of the founding and early national periods?

THE ORIGINAL MEANING OF FEDERALISM

Federalism is a very old idea. The word *federalism* and several closely related terms including *federal*, and *confederation* are drawn from the Latin root *foedus*, which means "treaty, compact, or covenant." The idea that people can establish lasting compacts or covenants among themselves by discussion and consent has been central to American political thought and development. Before the first Pilgrim stepped onto Plymouth Rock, the entire *Mayflower* company approved the famous Mayflower Compact to define the kind of society and government that they would have.

The great difficulty involved in thinking about government as resting on the ideas of compact and covenant is the obvious fragility of such an arrangement. Political scientist Samuel Beer remarked that, "Among the consequences of thinking of federal government as based on a contract was the idea of secession, 'the idea of simply breaking a disagreeable contract whenever any pretext of bad faith on the part of any other party arose.'"[3]

Nonetheless, the best thinking of their day told the Founders that governments over large territories had to take one of two forms. One is a consolidated or **unitary government** like the empires of the ancient world and the monarchies of Europe. These centralized states were subject to the will of one man or woman who could wield his or her power both offensively and defensively. The other is a **confederation** of smaller republics. The confederal solution left the individual republics fully sovereign, fully in control of their own domestic affairs, but pledged to coordinate their foreign affairs and to assist each other if attacked. Not surprisingly, confederations, including our own Articles of Confederation, proved to be weak and unstable in times of crisis.[4]

What made the choice between consolidation and confederation seem so stark was the idea of sovereignty—that in any political system, ultimate or final political authority must rest somewhere specific. In English history, disagreement about whether the king or Parliament was sovereign resulted in almost fifty years of civil war between 1640 and 1688. In the American case, it seemed that sovereignty had to be located either in a national government or in individual states that might then confederate together. The Articles of Confederation allocated specific modest powers to the Confederation Congress, but unambiguously left sovereignty with the individual states. Article II read: "Each state retains its sovereignty, Freedom and independence, and every Power, Jurisdiction and right, which is not by this confederation expressly delegated to the United States, in Congress assembled." The powerful idea that several governments might operate in the same space and in relation to the same citizens if each was limited in its authority and jurisdiction was not yet widely understood or accepted.

The Constitutional Convention of 1787 set aside familiar names (confederation) and outdated assumptions (sovereignty) and let the problem that they were trying to solve guide their thinking in new directions.[5] Initially, James Madison and the supporters of the Virginia Plan called for a powerful national

unitary government Centralized government subject to one authority as opposed to a federal system that divides power across national and subnational (state) governments.

confederation Loose governing arrangement in which separate republics or nations join together to coordinate foreign policy and defense but retain full control over their domestic affairs.

Library of Congress

Benjamin Franklin created this image of the separated serpent to convince his fellow colonists to unite, warning them to "Join or Die."

government capable of overriding the states where necessary. Madison's opponents rallied behind the New Jersey Plan's demand that the national government be grounded on the sovereignty of the states. Eventually, the Convention came to understand, if only vaguely, that neither old model applied well in the new nation and that a new understanding of federalism was required.

Q2 What powers and responsibilities did the U.S. Constitution give the national government in relation to the states and to the states in relation to the national government?

FEDERALISM IN THE CONSTITUTION

The Founders' most fundamental insight was that the apparent choice between a consolidated national government and a loose confederation of sovereign states was false. The ideas of constitutionalism and limited government laid open the possibility that within a single territory there might be two sets of governments and two sets of public officials assigned clear and specific responsibilities and powers through written constitutions.[6]

If political power derives from the people, why should the people cede sovereignty either to a consolidated national government or to loosely confederated sovereign states? James Madison gave the classic answer to this question in Federalist Number 51 (see Appendix D). Madison explained: "In the compound republic of America, the power surrendered by the people is first divided between two distinct governments, and then the portion allotted to each is subdivided among distinct and separate departments. Hence, a double security arises to the rights of the people." After this double security is in place, the Federalist concluded, "Every thing beyond this, must be left to the prudence and firmness of the people; who, as they will hold the scales in their own hands, it is to be hoped, will always take care to preserve the constitutional equilibrium between the General and the State Governments."[7]

The Constitution gives certain powers to the national government, bars the states from making policy in certain areas, offers them guarantees and assurances in other areas, and leaves still other areas open to the authority of both national and state governments. Despite Madison's assurances that the constitutional equilibrium between the national and state governments would be maintained by a watchful people, only occasionally has federalism been the target of popular tumult, as with the modern "Tea Party" movement. More commonly, the Congress, the Supreme Court, and ever-watchful state and local officials have shaped American federalism. In fact, the American political system has been involved in one of its periodic reassessments of the balance of power and authority within the federal system since the mid-1990s.[8]

Enumerated, Implied, and Inherent Powers

James Madison arrived at the Constitutional Convention determined to strengthen the national government. The Virginia Plan envisioned a national Congress with both a broad grant of legislative authority and the right to review, amend, or reject acts of the several state legislatures. This strong national federalism, in which the states would play a decidedly secondary role, was rejected in favor of a national Congress wielding specifically listed or enumerated powers. The nationalists' disappointment was assuaged somewhat by the Convention's adoption of the **supremacy clause** in Article VI. Article VI read in part: "This Constitution, and the laws of the United States which shall be made in pursuance thereof; and all treaties made, or which shall be made, under the authority of the United States, shall be the supreme law of the land; and the judges in every state shall be bound thereby; anything in the Constitution or laws of any State to the contrary notwithstanding." Moreover, all state officials were required to take an oath "to support this Constitution."

supremacy clause Article VI of the U.S. Constitution declares that the acts of the national government within its areas of legitimate authority will be supreme over the state constitutions and laws.

The enumerated powers of Congress are laid out in Article I, section 8, of the U.S. Constitution. Article I, section 8, lists seventeen enumerated powers, including the powers to tax, to regulate commerce and coinage, to declare war, and to raise armies and navies. In theory, Congress is limited to making law and policy within its areas of enumerated power. But other language in the Constitution seems to give Congress **implied powers** that go beyond its specifically enumerated powers. The closing paragraph of Article I, section 8, grants Congress the power to "make all laws which shall be necessary and proper for carrying into execution" its enumerated powers. The "necessary and proper" clause, frequently referred to as the "elastic clause," suggests that Congress has a general authority beyond and in addition to its enumerated powers.

implied powers Congressional powers not specifically mentioned among the enumerated powers, but which are reasonable and necessary to accomplish an enumerated end or activity.

If the enumerated powers are fairly specific, and implied powers are somewhat broader but still must be a means to achieve enumerated purposes, the idea of inherent powers is only loosely related to specific constitutional provisions. Both Congress and the Supreme Court have accepted the idea, especially

inherent powers Powers argued to accrue to all sovereign nations, whether or not specified in the Constitution, allowing executives to take all actions required to defend the nation and protect its interests.

relating to the president and foreign affairs, that nationhood entails the right and necessity, without reference to specific language in the Constitution, to deal with other nations from a footing equal to theirs. In fact, these **inherent powers** of nationhood were what the Declaration of Independence referred to when it announced to the world: "That these United Colonies are, and of Right ought to be Free and Independent States; that . . . they have full Power to levy War, conclude Peace, contract Alliances, establish Commerce, and to do all other Acts and Things which Independent States may of right do."

One example of presidential initiative, taken in threatening circumstances, but with no narrow constitutional authorization, will suffice to clarify the nature of inherent powers. Early in 1861 President Lincoln took several steps in the immediate wake of the secession of the southern states, including calling up additional troops and spending substantial sums of money, even though Congress was not in session and had not previously authorized these actions. When critics complained Lincoln simply asked, "Was it possible to lose the nation and yet preserve the Constitution?" Lincoln assumed that the answer was "no" and that his actions required no further justification.

Concurrent Powers

concurrent powers Powers, such as the power to tax, that are available to both levels of the federal system and may be exercised by both in relation to the same body of citizens.

The idea of **concurrent powers** is central to the Founders' conception of a complex republic in which national and state governments exercise dual sovereignty. Dual sovereignty suggests that in some fields, such as the power to tax and borrow, to regulate commerce, to establish courts, and to build roads and highways, the national and state governments have concurrent powers. Both levels of the federal system are authorized to act in these and similar areas of law and policy. Your tax bill is a good example of a concurrent power. In all but seven states citizens must fill out income tax returns for both the national and state levels (and sometimes the local level, too).

Powers Denied to the National Government

Article I, section 9, of the Constitution denied certain powers to the national government. Congress was forbidden to suspend normal legal processes except in cases of rebellion or grave public danger, to favor the commerce or ports of one state over another, to expend money unless lawfully appropriated, and to grant titles of nobility. Other limitations on national power have been added to the Constitution by amendment, but students should notice that this is a brief paragraph.

Powers Reserved to the States

In a course on American government, like this one, students often miss, even in the federalism chapter, how important the states are and have always been. The fundamental logic of American federalism is that the states possess complete power over matters not delegated to the national government and not denied them by the U.S. Constitution or by their own state constitutions. As Madison explained in Federalist Number 39, the jurisdiction of the Congress "extends to certain enumerated objects only, and leaves to the several States a residuary and inviolable sovereignty over all other objects."[9] Nonetheless, widespread concern that the new national government might encroach upon the powers of the states and the rights of their citizens led many to demand that protections be added to the Constitution itself. The first Congress initiated a process that led to adoption of ten amendments to the Constitution—the Bill of Rights—in 1791. The Tenth Amendment reads as follows: "The powers not delegated to the United States by the Constitution, nor prohibited by it to the states, are reserved to the states respectively, or to the people."

Joseph Zimmerman has usefully divided the **reserved powers** of the states into three categories: "the police power, provision of services to citizens, . . . and creation and control of local governments."[10] The "police power" covers regulation of individual and corporate activities in order to protect and enhance public health, welfare, safety, morals, and convenience. States also provide services such as police and fire protection, road construction, and education. Finally, local governments are created and regulated by the states.

reserved powers The Tenth Amendment to the U.S. Constitution declares that powers not explicitly granted to the national government are reserved to the states or to the people.

Powers Denied to State Governments

The Founders wanted to be very sure that the problems experienced under the Articles of Confederation, where individual states had antagonized dangerous foreign powers and tried to create economic advantages for their own citizens

Olivier Douberg, Abaca Press

Demonstrators on both sides of Arizona's strict illegal immigration law debated the provisions outside the U.S. Supreme Court. At issue was whether federal authority over immigration policy preempted state authority.

to the detriment of citizens of other states, were not repeated. Article I, section 10, of the U.S. Constitution forbids the states to enter into treaties or alliances either with each other or with foreign powers, to keep their own armies or navies, or to engage in war unless actually invaded. Foreign and military policy belongs to the national government. States are also forbidden to coin their own money, impair contracts, or tax imports or exports.

Federal Obligations to the States

The U.S. Constitution makes a series of explicit promises to the states. Most of these are found in Article IV, sections 3 and 4, and in Article V. The states are promised that their boundaries and their equal representation in the Senate will not be changed without their consent and that their republican governments will be protected from invasion and, at their request, from domestic violence.

Relations among the States

Article IV, sections 1 and 2, of the U.S. Constitution deal with interstate relations. Provisions require the states to respect each other's civil acts, deal fairly with each other's citizens, and return suspected criminals who flee from one state into another.

Full Faith and Credit.   Article IV, section 1, of the U.S. Constitution requires that "Full faith and credit shall be given in each state to the public acts, records, and judicial proceedings of every other state." Stated most directly, "public acts are the civil statutes enacted by the state legislatures. Records are documents such as deeds, mortgages, and wills. Judicial proceedings are final civil court proceedings."[11] Through this simple provision, the Founders largely succeeded in creating a national legal system requiring the states to recognize and respect each other's legal acts and findings. Nonetheless, over the course of American history, social issues such as religious toleration, slavery, and, most recently, the decision by some states to permit gay marriage, have strained reciprocity and cooperation between the states.

Paul v. Virginia (1869) This decision declared that the privileges and immunities clause of the U.S. Constitution guarantees citizens visiting, working, or conducting business in another state the same freedoms and legal protections that would be afforded to citizens of that state.

Privileges and Immunities.   Article IV, section 2, of the U.S. Constitution declares that "The citizens of each state shall be entitled to all privileges and immunities of citizens in the several states." The classic statement of the reasoning behind the privileges and immunities language was delivered by the Supreme Count in the 1869 case of *Paul v. Virginia*. The Court explained that citizens visiting, working, or conducting business in other states have "the same freedom possessed by the citizens of those States in the acquisition and enjoyment of property and in the pursuit of happiness; and it secures them the equal protection of the laws."

extradition Provision of Article IV, section 2, of the U.S. Constitution providing that persons accused of a crime in one state fleeing into another state shall be returned to the state in which the crime was committed.

Extradition.   Article IV, section 2, provides for a legal process called **extradition**: "A person charged in any state with treason, felony, or other crime, who shall flee from justice, and be found in another state, shall on demand of the executive authority of the state from which he fled, be delivered up, to be removed to the state having jurisdiction of the Crime."

Fundamentally, the Constitution left the states in charge of their own internal police and gave the national government responsibility for military and foreign policy. Yet, the Constitution also sought to lower trade and regulatory barriers among the several state economies to create a national economy, an American free trade zone, that would stretch from Maine to Georgia and from the Atlantic coast to the farthest edge of western settlement. Not surprisingly, the boundary line between the national government's supremacy within its areas of constitutional responsibility and the states' reserve powers has been fuzzy, contested, and shifting over the course of American history. In fact, it is fair to say that the principal point of tension in thinking about American federalism is how to balance federal power, grounded in the elastic clause and the supremacy clause, and the powers reserved to the individual states by the Tenth Amendment. As we shall see, these tensions arose early and remain with us today.[12]

DUAL FEDERALISM AND ITS CHALLENGERS

The view of American federalism that held sway from the founding period through the first third of the twentieth century was dual federalism. **Dual federalism**, often referred to as layer-cake federalism, sees the nation and the several states as sovereign within their areas of constitutional responsibility, but with little policy overlap between them. During the nation's early history and, to a lesser extent, throughout the nation's history, dual federalism had two challengers, one a nation-centered federalism and the other a state-centered federalism.[13] The national vision of federalism was championed by a long series of American statesmen including Alexander Hamilton, Chief Justice John Marshall, Senator Henry Clay, and President Abraham Lincoln. The fundamental idea was that the nation preexisted the states and in fact called the states into existence in June of 1776 when the Continental Congress instructed the colonies to sever ties to England.

A second set of American statesmen took a different view. Thomas Jefferson, John C. Calhoun, the South's great antebellum political theorist, and President Jefferson Davis of the Confederate States of America all believed that the states preexisted the nation and created it by compact among themselves. On this state-centered vision of federalism, the original parties to the compact, that is, the individual states, could secede from the Union if the national government violated the compact by encroaching upon the sovereign prerogatives of the states. Short of secession, states could nullify, or declare unenforceable, federal laws they believed fell outside Congress's Article II, section 8, enumerated powers.

The nation-centered and state-centered visions of federalism fought on even terms through the early decades of the country's history. However, as the

dual federalism Nineteenth-century view of federalism envisioning a federal system in which the two levels were sovereign in fairly distinct areas of responsibility with little overlap or sharing of authority.

Q3 How did the expansion and integration of the American economy shape the balance of governmental power and authority within the federal system?

John Marshall, Chief Justice of the U.S. Supreme Court from 1801 to 1835, established the judiciary as a co-equal branch of the national government.

Marbury v. Madison (1803) Chief Justice John Marshall derived the power of judicial review from the Constitution by reasoning that the document was supreme and therefore the Court should invalidate legislative acts that run counter to it.

McCulloch v. Maryland (1819) The Court announced an expansive reading of the "necessary and proper" clause, holding that Congress's Article I, section 8, enumerated powers imply unspecified but appropriate powers to carry them out.

Gibbons v. Ogden (1824) This decision employed an expansive reading of the commerce clause, the doctrine of the "continuous journey," to allow Congress to regulate commercial activity if any element of it crossed a state boundary.

industrial economy of New England outstripped the agrarian economy of the South during the 1840s and 1850s, state-centered federalism became increasingly isolated and strident. When Abraham Lincoln was elected president in 1860, the South seceded and two visions of American federalism faced off on the battlefields of the Civil War.[14]

Chief Justice John Marshall and National Federalism. As early as 1791, a federal court declared a Rhode Island state law unconstitutional, and in 1803 Chief Justice John Marshall, in the famous case of *Marbury v. Madison*, declared a section of an act of Congress, the Judiciary Act of 1789, to be unconstitutional. The broad result of the *Marbury* decision was to establish the Supreme Court as the final arbiter of what is and is not constitutional, and, hence, of the meaning, shape, and boundaries of American federalism.

The importance of the Supreme Court's role as arbiter of the meaning of the Constitution was highlighted by the Court's 1819 ruling in *McCulloch v. Maryland*. The issue in McCulloch, whether Congress could legitimately charter a bank, permitted the Court to interpret the powers of Congress broadly and to limit state interference with them. No power to establish a bank appeared among the enumerated powers of Congress, so opponents of the bank, arguing from the state-centered or compact vision of federalism, denied that Congress had the power to create a bank at all. Chief Justice Marshall, writing from the nation-centered vision, rested the right of the Congress to establish and administer a bank on the "necessary and proper" clause. Marshall noted that Congress's enumerated powers include the power "to coin money" and "regulate the value thereof." He argued that the bank was an "appropriate," though perhaps not an "indispensable," means to this end. Marshall's classic interpretation of the "necessary and proper" clause makes this point as follows: "Let the end be legitimate, let it be within the scope of the Constitution, and all means which are appropriate which are plainly adapted to the end, which are not prohibited, but consistent with the letter and spirit of the Constitution, are constitutional." This expansive interpretation of national power came at the expense of the Tenth Amendment "reserved powers" of the states.

A third decision completed Chief Justice Marshall's attempt to embed the nation-centered vision of federalism in the Constitution. The 1824 case of *Gibbons v. Ogden* dealt with the regulation of interstate commerce, that is, commerce conducted across state lines. While the court's interpretation of the commerce clause may seem arcane, even boring, it has been absolutely central to the expansion of congressional power from Chief Justice John Marshall's day to our own day. In fact, the broad interpretation of Congress's commerce power, just as much as the necessary and proper clause, has fueled and legitimated the expansion of national power in our federal system.

The issue in *Gibbons* was whether a steamship company operating in a single state was in interstate commerce and subject to the regulatory powers of the Congress. Advocates of the state-centered vision said no. Marshall, writing for the majority, held that the Congress's power to regulate interstate commerce applies to navigation, even in a single state, if any of the passengers or goods being carried on the steamship are engaged in a "continuous journey" that finds or will find them in interstate commerce. Clearly, this is a very expansive ruling because it is almost inconceivable that not a single person or piece of cargo on such a steamship had been or would later be in interstate commerce. These decisions laid the foundation for the triumph of national federalism, though it would be another century before the structure was fully built. In the meantime, Marshall's opponents would have their century-long day in the sun.

Chief Justice Roger Taney and the States.   Upon John Marshall's death in 1835, President Andrew Jackson named Roger B. Taney to be the new chief justice, an office he held until 1863. Chief Justice Taney was a strong advocate of state-centered federalism and of a limited national government. A stronger advocate still was South Carolina Senator John C. Calhoun. Senator Calhoun, convinced that the South was threatened by an overbearing northern majority, proposed "the doctrine of the **concurrent majority**," whereby each major region would have the right to veto national laws that threatened their fundamental interests. If the South was denied such security, Calhoun argued that the sovereign states could nullify illegitimate national laws and, as a last resort, secede from the Union. These ideas are occasionally still heard.

Chief Justice Taney's most infamous opinion was ***Dred Scott v. Sandford*** in 1857. Taney held that Congress had no right to prohibit a slave owner from taking his property, even his human property, into any state in the Union, even a free state, and holding that slave as property. The next year, in the Illinois Senate election of 1858, Senator Stephen A. Douglas argued that the deep American commitment to "popular sovereignty" meant that the citizens of individual states should be able to vote for or against slavery. Douglas's opponent, then a little-known former congressman named Abraham Lincoln, argued for the right of the national government to limit slavery to those states where it currently existed. Lincoln lost.

The strong arguments by Taney and Douglas in favor of an expansive view of states' rights and the state-centered federalism helped set the stage for the Civil War. Northern opinion mobilized against the expansion of slavery and Lincoln rode that mobilization to the

The Granger Collection, New York

Roger Taney, author of the Dred Scott decision, is often seen as the Supreme Court's most infamous Chief Justice.

concurrent majority South Carolina Senator John C. Calhoun's idea for restoring balance between the North and South by giving each region the right to reject national legislation thought harmful to the region.

Dred Scott v. Sandford (1857) The Court declared that African Americans, whether free or slave, were not citizens of the U.S. Moreover, slaves were property and could be carried into any state in the union, even a free state, and held as property.

cooperative federalism Mid-twentieth-century view of federalism in which national, state, and local governments share responsibilities for virtually all functions.

presidency in the election of 1860. The South seceded, the North resisted, and America went to war with itself over the nature of its federal Union.

FROM DUAL FEDERALISM TO COOPERATIVE FEDERALISM

Although the idea of the Constitution as a compact from which states might secede was a casualty of the Civil War, the idea of states' rights—a large and secure place for the states in the federal system—certainly was not. Congress did little to regulate state and local affairs until the Great Depression seemed to demand change in the broad character and basic structure of American federalism. After the 1930s American federalism was better described as cooperative federalism than as dual federalism.

The defining aspects of **cooperative federalism**, or marble-cake federalism as it is often called to highlight the sharing or mixing of national and state responsibility, have been nicely described by political scientist David Walker. Walker made two key points that distinguish cooperative federalism from dual federalism. In cooperative federalism, national, state, and local officials share "responsibilities for virtually all functions," and these "officials are not adversaries. They are colleagues."[15] Over time, however, concern about the national government's dominance of the federal system, usually by attaching mandates to federal funds provided to states and communities, has became a growing concern.

The Industrialization and Urbanization of America

Social change in America between the elections of Abraham Lincoln in 1860 and Franklin Roosevelt in 1932 was massive. During this period, the nation went from one mostly of small towns and isolated farms to one of burgeoning cities and large-scale industry. More important, the nation was bound ever more tightly into a web of commerce and communication that seemed to demand tending above the levels of states and communities. As the web of commerce expanded over the course of the nineteenth century and into the twentieth century, debate raged over the reach of congressional power channeled through the Constitution's commerce clause.

Consider two related developments: the rise of railroads and the telegraph. Prior to the arrival of railroads and the telegraph, businesses were local or at most regional. The size of a business was determined by the distance over which finished products could be distributed efficiently by wagon, barge, or boat. After the telegraph made it possible to order and advertise over long distances and railroads made it possible to deliver products quickly over long distances, businesses expanded rapidly. By the last decades of the nineteenth century, huge monopolies or trusts in basic service and product lines like banking, railroads, communications, steel, oil, and sugar dominated the nation's business landscape.

Pro & Con

The Continuing Relevance of States' Rights

The language of the U.S. Constitution is ambiguous about the relative power of the national and state governments. Although Article VI suggests national supremacy ("This Constitution, and the laws of the United States which shall be made in pursuance thereof . . . shall be the supreme law of the land"), the powers granted to Congress are enumerated rather than general. Moreover, the Tenth Amendment, adopted as part of the Bill of Rights in 1791, reads: "The powers not delegated to the United States by the Constitution, nor prohibited to it by the states, are reserved to the states respectively, or to the people."

Prior to the Civil War most discussions of the rights of the states in the new Union revolved around the ideas of nullification and secession. **Nullification** was the idea that a state could suspend within its borders the operation of an act of the national government with which it disagreed. **Secession** was the idea that a state might actually withdraw from the Union if it disagreed deeply with the general pattern of policy activity of the federal government.

Although the Civil War destroyed both nullification and secession as practical ideas within the American political system, the broader idea of states' rights retained its importance. Some now believe that the fights against the racism and poverty of the 1960s and 1970s, important though they were at the time, left behind programs that no longer work and a federal government too large and intrusive for the needs of the twenty-first century. Therefore, many, mostly conservatives, believe that federal money and authority should be transferred back to the states, closer to the problems that need to be solved and to the people in the best position to know how to solve them.

Some others, mostly liberals, worry that the old states' rights arguments for the virtues of local control will once again be used by powerful local majorities to ignore the needs of weaker local minorities and that, as in the past, the most vulnerable (women, blacks, gays) will be among the first to suffer. The modern opponents of states' rights claim that fairness and justice require that national standards be set and maintained, not just in the obvious area of equal rights for minorities and women, but also in such diverse areas as health, welfare, and education. Absent such standards, they believe, some states will do much less than others to assist their neediest citizens.

On the other hand, it is mostly liberals who cheer the movement of some states to provide the rights of marriage to gay people. Conservatives talk of a constitutional amendment to forbid gay marriage in the states. Although there are principled reasons to stand for states' rights or national uniformity, there is also a long national tradition that the party that dominates Washington is comfortable with uniformity while the opposition party looks for partial victories in friendly states.[16]

What do you think?
- What are the pros and cons of allowing each state to decide how they want to go on critical issues like gay marriage, legalization of marijuana, abortion, guns, prayer in schools, and other hotly debated issues?
- Why might liberals or conservatives have conflicting views of state–federal powers depending on the policy issue?

PRO	CON
State differences are real	Natural standards for justice are critical
Problems should be addressed close to home	Many problems require national coordination
States' rights no longer about secession	Local minorities are still vulnerable

nullification The claim prominent in the first half of the nineteenth
century that states have the right to
nullify or reject national acts that
they believe to be beyond national
constitutional authority.

secession The claim that states
have the right to withdraw from the
Union.

U.S. v. E.C. Knight (1895) The
Court held that Congress's power
to regulate interstate commerce
extended only to transportation
of goods across state lines, not to
manufacturing or production.

How could states, let alone localities, control and regulate a railroad that stretched across half a dozen states, or a steel, sugar, or tobacco trust that did business in every state in the Union? They simply could not. Yet, the Supreme Court declared in ***U.S. v. E.C. Knight*** (1895) that Congress's power to regulate interstate commerce did not reach manufacturing or production, only the transportation of goods across state lines. Hence, as the twentieth century dawned, the nation's largest businesses were beyond the reach of congressional and state regulation and control.

Knowing that changes are needed is not the same thing as knowing what changes are needed, much less knowing how to get political agreement to adopt and implement a particular set of changes. President Theodore Roosevelt threatened "trust busting" to encourage large private sector actors to accept more federal oversight. Future president Woodrow Wilson, still president of Princeton in 1908, urged a broader dynamic view of federalism. His *Constitutional Government in the United States* argued that the principles and institutions of government must adapt to serve an evolving society: "The question of the relation of the States to the federal government is a cardinal question of our constitutional system. . . . It cannot, indeed, be settled by the opinion of any one generation, because it is a question of growth, and every successive stage of our political and economic development gives it a new aspect, makes it a new question."[17] Although the Progressive Era administrations of Theodore Roosevelt and Woodrow Wilson did establish a beachhead for the regulatory authority of government, the Roaring 20s saw a return to *laissez faire*. Not until Franklin Roosevelt rose to confront the Great Depression of the 1930s did the balance of American federalism begin a decisive shift of responsibility and authority to the national level.

In the early years of the twentieth century, state and local governments accounted for about 70 percent of total government spending in the United States, whereas the federal government accounted for about 30 percent (see Figure 3.1). However, in 1913, President Wilson proposed and the Congress passed the federal income tax. This meant that the national government could, for the first time in American history, raise large amounts of money by taxing the annual incomes of citizens and residents. As the national government moved to address each major crisis of the first two-thirds of the twentieth century, its share of spending rose markedly. When each crisis passed, the federal share of total spending fell back toward, but never all the way to, precrisis levels. Since the mid-1960s, the federal government has accounted for about 65 percent of all government expenditures while state and local governments have accounted for the remaining 35 percent. Federal spending in 2009 jumped up to 68 percent in response to stimulus spending to combat the recession and has remained there since.

The Great Depression

Nothing made the fact that the American economy had become an integrated whole more clear than its collapse in late October 1929. "The Crash," in which

FIGURE 3.1 **Percent of Government Expenditures by Level of Government, 1902–2012**

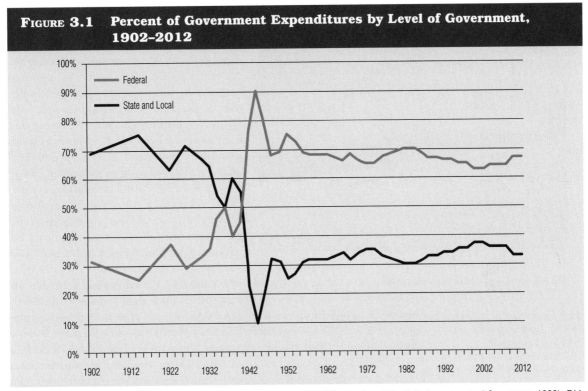

Source: *Historical Statistics of the United States, Colonial Times to 1957* (Washington, D.C.: U.S. Department of Commerce, 1960), 711, Series Y254–257, and 726, Series Y536–546. Post-1960 figures come from *Budget of the United States Government, Fiscal Year 2014*, Historical Tables (Washington, D.C.: Government Printing Office, 2014), Table 15.2, 350–351.

the stock market lost almost a quarter of its value in two days of panic trading, began a decade of deep economic depression and persistent unemployment. Just as the depression eased, World War II erupted.

The 1930s and 1940s were a period of national emergency. By the time Franklin Roosevelt assumed office early in 1933, the country had already been mired in depression for more than three years. The Depression was a national, even worldwide, economic collapse. The economy had declined by 40 percent from its 1929 high, and fully one-third of the workforce was unemployed. State and local governments were overwhelmed by the needs of their citizens. Roosevelt's dramatic response, known as the "New Deal" and initiated during his "first hundred days" in office, included "an extraordinary assumption of federal authority over the nation's economy and a major expansion of its commerce and taxing powers."[18] The Supreme Court, still committed to maintaining as much of the logic and operation of "dual federalism" as possible, declared virtually all of it unconstitutional.

Roosevelt threatened to ask the Congress to expand the size of the Supreme Court so that he could "pack" it with new members more favorably disposed to his vision of an activist role for the federal government. The Supreme Court

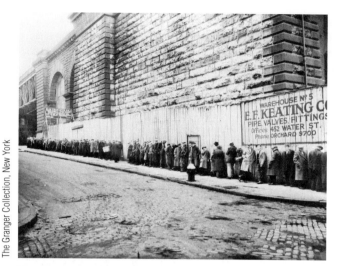

The poor and unemployed wait for a free meal—Christmas dinner—at the Municipal Lodging House in New York in 1931.

Wickard v. Filburn (1942) The Court rejected the narrow reading of the commerce power in *U.S. v. E.C. Knight* to return to the broader reading in *Gibbons v. Ogden* by which Congress could regulate virtually all commercial activity.

blinked. Some members changed their votes, a few retired, and Roosevelt soon had a Supreme Court that would bless a vastly expanded role for the federal government. By June of 1935, the Court had approved several key economic programs including the National Labor Relations Act, the Railway Labor Act, the Farm Mortgage Act, and the Social Security Act. These decisions amounted to the end of "dual federalism" and the beginning of a period in which the national government would have the broad power to set and regulate economic activity in the states. The proportion of total government spending accounted for by the national government rose from 28 percent in 1927 to 50 percent in 1936.

Wickard v. Filburn shows how far the Supreme Court had moved by 1942. Roosevelt's program for rejuvenating agricultural prices, the Agricultural Adjustment Act (AAA), regulated the acreage that farmers could plant. Roscoe Filburn was authorized to plant 11 acres of wheat on his Ohio farm. He planted 23 acres, arguing that the wheat from only 11 acres would be sold and the other 12 would feed livestock. The Supreme Court, for decades a staunch defender of free markets and of a limited role for Congress in economic regulation, held that feeding the excess wheat to his own animals meant that he did not have to buy that wheat in the open market and that tiny effect on "interstate commerce" was enough to bring him under the purview of Congress's legitimate constitutional authority.[19] The balance between national and state authority within American federalism had shifted dramatically to the national level.

World War II drove the federal share of total government spending to 90 percent by 1944. When the war ended in 1945, the United States remained engaged in international politics, aiding in the rebuilding of the European and Japanese economies and constructing a military alliance to confront Soviet expansionism. Although the federal share of total government spending fell below 60 percent in 1950, the Korean War of the early 1950s drove it back up toward 70 percent. It has ranged between 60 and 70 percent for the past half century. Moreover, consolidation of political authority at the national level involved domestic policy as much as it did foreign and national security policy.

THE RISE OF FISCAL FEDERALISM

For most of American history, the limited congressional authority outlined in Article I, section 8, of the Constitution was understood to forbid national control of broad policy areas including education, health care, income and retirement security, and much more. Slowly, beginning with Theodore Roosevelt's "Square Deal" and picking up speed with Franklin Roosevelt's "New Deal," federal authorities highlighted the first clause of Article I, section 8, permitting Congress to "lay and collect taxes . . . to pay the debts and provide for the common defense and general welfare of the United States." Especially during the "Great Depression," need in the nation's states and communities seemed to call for an activist federal government.

The reach of the national government within the structure of American federalism continued to expand during the 1960s and early 1970s. John Kennedy was elected president in 1960 on the promise to "get the country moving again" after the calm of the Eisenhower years. The fuel that would power this new movement was federal money. The favored device for delivering federal funds to states and localities was the **categorical grant**. Each categorical grant program offered state and local governments opportunities to receive federal funds if they would engage in a certain narrow activity and if they would do so in compliance with detailed federal mandates on eligibility, program design, service delivery, and reporting.

categorical grant A program making federal funds available to states and communities for a specific, often narrow, purpose and usually requiring a distinct application, implementation, and reporting procedure.

Only five categorical grant programs were in place in 1900 and only fifteen by 1930. Fifteen more were added during FDR's first two terms as president, but major transfers of funds from the national government to state and local governments did not begin until after World War II. Figure 3.2 shows that federal expenditures for grants to state and local governments rose dramatically and continuously from 1950 through the late 1970s.

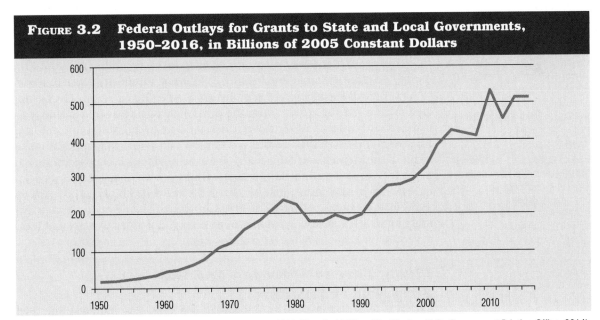

FIGURE 3.2 Federal Outlays for Grants to State and Local Governments, 1950–2016, in Billions of 2005 Constant Dollars

Source: Budget of the United States Government, Fiscal Year 2014, Historical Tables (Washington, D.C.: Government Printing Office, 2014), Table 12.1, 257–258. The numbers for 2013 to 2016 are official estimates from the same table.

Federal expenditures in constant 2005 dollars rose from more then $20 billion in 1950 to $236.1 billion in 1978. President Carter and the Congress reduced spending on grants to state and local governments modestly in 1979 and 1980, before the new Reagan administration slashed them by more than 20 percent in the early 1980s and then held them at that level through the remainder of the decade. Not until the early 1990s did federal grants to state and local governments begin to increase as part of the Clinton administration's aggressively domestic focus. Republican congressional majorities first elected in 1994 supported the devolution of federal authority to the states, but the Clinton administration resisted and then the Bush administration's homeland security initiatives dramatically increased federal transfers to state and local governments between 2002 and 2005 before they leveled off.

But national emergencies—whether they take the form of external threats, like World War II or 9/11, or economic catastrophes, like the Great Depression of the 1930s or the Great Recession of 2008 and 2009—invariably call out for concerted national action. Not surprisingly, then, the Obama economic stimulus program, passed just one month into the new administration, pumped tens of billions of new dollars into the states. Republican gains in the 2010 House elections led to initial cuts, but the struggling economy seemed to call for more stimulus. Obama administration projections, reflected in Figure 3.2, suggest a leveling off of federal transfers to the states, but skepticism is warranted.

LBJ: Creative Federalism and Grants-in-Aid

By the time John Kennedy entered the White House in early 1961, 132 categorical grant programs were in operation. During the five years that Lyndon Johnson was president, he and his overwhelmingly Democratic Congresses passed more than two hundred new categorical grant programs covering the full range of U.S. domestic policy initiatives. **Creative federalism** was the term used to describe the range and breadth of Johnson administration activities.

creative federalism 1960s view of federalism that refers to LBJ's willingness to expand the range of federal programs to support state and local activities and to bring new, even nongovernmental, actors into the process.

coercive federalism A pejorative term to describe the federalism of the 1960s and 1970s, suggesting that the national government was using its financial muscle to coerce states into following national dictates as opposed to serving local needs.

The "Great Society" initiatives of the 1960s were driven, not just by Democratic activism in the White House and the Congress, but also by a federal judiciary determined to end racial discrimination and segregation, protect civil liberties, reform criminal justice procedures, and afford new protections to rights of the accused and convicted.[20] Every new federal grant program passed and every expansive judicial decision handed down increased the federal bureaucracy's range of regulatory control. By the time LBJ left office early in 1969, his opponents had begun to refer to creative federalism as **coercive federalism**. In 1970, nearly one dollar out of every four spent by state and local governments came from the federal treasury.[21]

Nixon: Revenue Sharing and the First New Federalism

Republican President Richard Nixon's "New Federalism" was intended to enhance the discretion of the states in deciding how best to use the financial resources they received from the national government. President Nixon undertook two major federalism initiatives. The first, called **special revenue sharing (SRS)** or **block grants**, bundled related sets of categorical grants into a single SRS or block grant program. States and localities were permitted to decide how to allocate the money across the eligible program activities. The second Nixon initiative, called **general revenue sharing (GRS)**, provided $30.2 billion to the fifty states and approximately thirty-eight thousand local governments over a five-year period. Unlike categorical grants or even block grants, general revenue sharing funds had few strings attached. States could set their own priorities.

Nixon's New Federalism was purchased from the Democratic Congress at a high price. Congress exacted from President Nixon both increased expenditures and expanded regulation of state and local governments in other areas including civil rights, consumer protection, workplace safety, and environmental affairs. As a result, the late 1960s and early 1970s witnessed the greatest expansion of federal regulation of state and local governments in American history. Conservatives in Congress became increasingly concerned about the expense of federal mandates and regulations while many state and local officials complained about the complexity of application, administration, and reporting requirements. By the late 1970s, Democratic President Jimmy Carter began to trim federal transfers to state and local governments.

Not surprisingly, the rapid rise in federal spending and of federal transfers to the states over the past half century and more has sharpened the long-running conflict between nation-centered and state-centered federalism. In the 1960s and 1970s especially, the federal government used its financial resources to encourage state and local governments to follow their lead. In other policy areas, the federal government displaced state and local authorities altogether.

The modern version of the long-running historical battle between national federalism and states rights federalism is the battle between "preemption" and "devolution." **Preemption** is the power of the national government, based on the "supremacy clause" in Article VI, to preempt or push aside state law. Joseph F. Zimmerman, one of the nation's leading federalism experts, has written that Congress passed 678 preemption statutes between 1790 and 2011 in policy areas ranging from banking and commerce to health care and the environment.[22] Fully 70 percent of them were passed after 1970.

Alternatively, **devolution** stems from the idea that the Tenth Amendment to the U.S. Constitution guarantees the states against undue intrusion by the national government. Supporters of devolution call for returning both authority and financial resources to the states so that they can deal with the issues that seem most critical to them.

Reagan Turns Off the Tap: The Second New Federalism

Ronald Reagan came to the presidency early in 1981 with a view of American federalism unlike that of any president since Herbert Hoover. Reagan's first inaugural address declared his "intention to curb the size and influence of the

special revenue sharing The Nixon administration developed block grants that bundled related categorical grants into a single grant to enhance state and local discretion over how the money was spent.

block grants Federal funds made available to states and communities in which they have discretion over how the money is spent within the broad substantive area covered by the block grant.

general revenue sharing Program enacted in 1974, discontinued in 1986, that provided basically unrestricted federal funds to states and localities to support activities that they judged to be of highest priority.

preemption The Article VI declaration that national statutes are "the supreme law of the land" allows Congress to preempt or displace state authority in areas where they choose to legislate.

devolution The return of political authority from the national government to the states beginning in the 1970s and continuing today.

Federal establishment and to demand recognition of the distinction between the powers granted to the Federal Government and those reserved to the States or the people."

The Reagan administration concluded that the national and state governments were doing too much and would do less only if they had less money. The Economic Recovery Tax Act (ERTA) of 1981 reduced the individual income tax rates by 25 percent over three years and reduced corporate income tax rates. The top bracket for individual income taxes was reduced from 70 percent to 50 percent in 1981 and reduced again by the Tax Reform Act of 1986 to 28 percent. Although tax rates were adjusted marginally upward during the late 1980s, federal revenue losses were massive.

Moreover, huge annual budget deficits put very heavy pressure on domestic spending in general and on transfer payments to state and local governments in particular. Strikingly, states were dropped from general revenue sharing in 1980 and the program was allowed to lapse in 1986. "[R]eal outlays to state and local governments fell by 33 percent between 1980 and 1987."[23] State and local governments were left to decide whether to pick up the slack or take the heat for program cuts.

Virtually all state and local governments, unlike the national government, are required, either constitutionally or by law, to balance their budgets each year. Declining federal support to states and communities makes them particularly vulnerable to economic downturns. When an economic downturn takes hold and revenues decline, the federal government can run a budget deficit but the states have to cut spending and, hence, programs and people feel it.

The Process of "Devolution" in Contemporary Federalism

Q4 What fiscal and political forces led to the change in American federalism called "devolution"?

Since 1980, only the first President Bush and Barack Obama were not governors before becoming president. Ronald Reagan, Bill Clinton, and the second President Bush all served as governors and all thought they knew how the national government should relate to the states. Ronald Reagan thought government, national, as well as state and local, was too big, too intrusive, and too expensive. He cut taxes at the national level and cut revenue transfers to the states so that government's role in American life would shrink.

Bill Clinton thought that government had an important role to play in American life, but that many problems were better addressed by people in their states and communities. He sought to redirect both financial resources and programmatic responsibilities to the states. After 1994, President Clinton's desire to produce a balanced budget joined with the Republican Congress's desire to shift primary responsibility for social welfare policy in the United States from the national to the state level to produce a dramatic overhaul of federal relations. In key policy areas like welfare, health care, job training, and transportation, Congress and the president rolled dozens of separate grant programs into a few large block grants. Each block grant gave the states

greater flexibility in deciding how to spend the money allocated to them. However, the block grants often included only about 70 percent of what the federal government spent on the same programs when it administered them.

President George W. Bush accelerated the process of moving financial resources and policy responsibility to the states, especially in the areas of education, health care, homeland security, and electoral reforms. However, like Reagan, Bush also cut taxes, and the resulting budget deficits put new pressure on federal support for the states.[24]

Just as momentously, in a series of narrow 5–4 judicial decisions, beginning with **U.S. v. Lopez** (1995) and extending through **U.S. v. Morrison** (2000), the Supreme Court moved to limit the ability of the president and Congress to use the commerce clause to push states in directions that they did not wish to go. In *Lopez*, the Court decided that the national government's prohibition on guns near schools was too loosely connected to regulating commerce to be justified. Similarly, in *Morrison*, the Court held that the 1994 Violence Against Women Act was unconstitutional because its impact on commerce was too remote to displace the rights of the states to legislate as they see fit in this area. *Lopez* and *Morrison* were the first cases in more than 70 years, since *Wickard v. Filburn* in 1942, in which the Court struck down an attempt by Congress to regulate some realm of public activity under the commerce clause.

However, constitutional interpretation rarely goes in a straight line. In the 2005 case of *Gonzales v. Raich*, the Supreme Court upheld Congress's power under the commerce clause to make marijuana possession illegal. The Court declared that regulating possession and use of marijuana fell "squarely within Congress's commerce power." The Court's conservatives, led by then-Chief Justice Rehnquist, then-Justice O'Connor, and Justice Thomas, were

U.S. v. Lopez (1995) The Court found that Congress's desire to forbid carrying handguns near schools was too loosely related to its power to regulate interstate commerce to stand. The police powers of the states cover such matters.

U.S. v. Morrison (2000) Citing *U.S. v. Lopez*, the Court found that the Violence Against Women Act was too loosely related to Congress's power to regulate interstate commerce to stand.

LET'S COMPARE

The Prevalence of Federal Systems in the World

Although the number of democratic nations in the world has grown dramatically over the past two hundred years, the number of federal systems is small and has grown slowly. Although all the nations that employ federal systems are democratic, it is certainly not the case that all democratic systems are federal. In fact, only about a dozen nations employ federal systems, and they have little in common except the fact

that they are all democratic and most are reasonably well-off by world standards.

The countries that have chosen to employ federal systems vary in geographical size, population, wealth, and ethnic and religious diversity. Most frequently, federal systems are chosen by the political leaders of countries who believe that some of the efficiency of centralization should be sacrificed to local and regional autonomy. In the United States, the claim is often made that federalism leads to bold experimentation and problem solving in the "laboratories of democracy" that are the fifty states.

Nation	Population	Area (Sq Km)	GDP Per Capita	Ethnic Diversity	Religious Diversity
Argentina	42,610,981	2,780,400	18,400	Low	Low
Australia	22,622,501	7,686,850	43,300	Low	Medium
Austria	8,221,646	83,870	43,100	Low	Low
Brazil	201,009,622	8,511,965	12,100	Medium	Low
Canada	34,568,211	9,984,670	43,400	Medium	Medium
Germany	81,147,265	357,021	39,700	Low	Medium
India	1,220,800,359	3,287,590	3,900	Medium	High
Malaysia	29,628,392	329,750	17,200	Medium	High
Mexico	116,220,947	1,972,550	15,600	Low	Low
Russia	142,500,482	17,075,200	18,900	Low	Low
Switzerland	7,996,026	41,290	46,200	Medium	Medium
United States	316,668,567	9,826,630	50,700	Medium	Medium

Source: Central Intelligence Agency, *The World Factbook*, 2014 (Washington, D.C.: U.S. Government Printing Office, 2014).

dismayed. Justice Thomas argued that "if Congress can regulate this under the Commerce Clause, then it can regulate virtually anything, and the federal government is no longer one of limited and enumerated powers."[25]

A far larger battle broke out in 2010. The Obama health care program, passed in early 2010, was quickly challenged by twenty-six mostly Republican Attorneys General as an abuse of the commerce clause and an unconstitutional intrusion into the policy domain of the states.

Most close observers thought that there was at least an even chance that the Supreme Court would strike down all or most of Obamacare. Chief Justice

John Roberts, writing for a divided court, surprised almost everyone, especially conservatives, by upholding most of Obamacare, not on commerce clause grounds, but under the federal government's power to tax. He did, however, acknowledge the role of the states in the federal system by holding that the national government could not pressure the states into expanding Medicaid as part of health care reform.

Another line of cases decided since 1995 has strengthened the sovereign immunity of states against being sued in their own courts or the federal courts by state government employees or citizens.[26] Moreover, the findings limit the ability of Congress and the president to make federal law binding on state governments. So far, federal laws concerning worker rights, patent protection, and age discrimination have been struck down as they apply to state governments. In 2006, the U.S. Supreme Court rejected U.S. Attorney General John Ashcroft's attempt to intervene in opposition to an Oregon assisted-suicide law. The court noted that general regulation of medical practice traditionally had been a state responsibility. Nonetheless, the stark fact is that over the course of the twentieth century, the weight and focus of government in the United States shifted from the state and local levels to the national level.

> **Struggling Toward Democracy**
>
> State governments receive more than one-third of their general revenue directly from the federal government. State officials claim that strings attached to the federal funds limit their ability to confront state and local problems as they think best.
>
> **What do you think?**
> * When the federal government sends money to the states, do they have the right to define how it can be used or not?
> * Should the federal government withdraw its funding if states fail to comply?

THE FUTURE OF AMERICAN FEDERALISM

Federalism has been a part of American constitutionalism since several Puritan communities founded the New England Confederation in 1643. After more than 350 years of experience with federalism, one might think our commitment to it would be secure. It is not. Some still wonder whether American federalism has been compromised, perhaps irreparably, by American political development and, more recently, by the globalization of the world communication, finance, and trade structures. They support the devolution of recent decades and call for more. Others believe that globalization of commerce, the serious threat of global warming, international terrorism, and the pandemic threats of Aids and bird flu require more national authority, not less.

Q5 Have the complexities of the twenty-first century rendered our government essentially national, or do state and local governments still have important roles to play?

Clearly, American political development—the progressive integration of our social, economic, and moral lives—has caused massive political change over the last 130 years or so. Hurricane Katrina highlighted the need to strengthen the abilities of local, state, and national forces to coordinate their efforts in dealing with natural disasters. Man-made disasters may confront us with worse in the future and our federal system must be prepared to respond.[27]

Social networks must be tended. Consider the nation's transportation infrastructure. There is a sense in which initially it builds itself. Footpaths may not need to be managed, but roads are community projects. As a result, from the earliest days, New England villages elected town officers to monitor, improve, and extend roads and trails as growth and new settlements required. Highway systems, to say nothing of air traffic control systems, require management and integration above the level of towns, cities, and even states. Fundamentally, as societies and their economies grow and mature, more and more of their activities occur nationally and internationally.

For example, the North American Free Trade Agreement (NAFTA) signed by Canada, the United States, and Mexico in 1993 both permits free trade throughout North America and limits each nation's ability to manage its own internal trade and national labor markets. Similarly, the General Agreement on Tariffs and Trade (GATT), the worldwide trade agreement approved by virtually every nation in the world in 1994, restricts each nation's ability to protect and nurture its particular national industries. Finally, instantaneous satellite and Internet communications allow twenty-four-hour-a-day trading in every nation's stocks, bonds, and currencies. This makes each nation's financial markets much less subject to national control and management than they once were. These developments pose great challenges to American federalism. Once again, the resilience of the American federal system will be tested.[28]

Chapter Summary

Federalism is a system of government that divides political power and responsibility between national and subnational levels of government. Initially, the distribution of political power described in the Constitution seemed to indicate that the national government would be responsible for dealing with foreign and military affairs and for economic coordination between the states and with foreign powers. The states would retain the power to deal with domestic affairs. The rights and liberties of the people would remain unfettered in broad areas where power had not been granted to either the national or subnational level of government.

However, as the nation grew in size and complexity, many issues that had once seemed appropriate for state or local resolution, such as building and tending a transportation system, seemed to require support and coordination from the national level. As problems seemed to move within the federal system, power within the federal system had to be redistributed or realigned. After the founding there were two historical eras during which power was redistributed dramatically upward within the American federal system: the Civil War era of the 1860s and the Depression era of the 1930s.

Both the 1860s and the 1930s marked distinctive phases in the integration of the American economy and society. In the two decades before the Civil War and the two after, a national structure of communication and transportation was developed. Railroads and telegraph not only permitted goods and information to move nationally, but also permitted the businesses and corporations that produced these goods and information to become national entities. By the final decade of the nineteenth century, it had become clear that

TABLE 3.2	The Evolution of American Federalism
Stages	**Events**
National Federalism	John Marshall appointed Chief Justice (1800) *Marbury v. Madison* establishes judicial review (1803) *McCulloch v. Maryland* defines "necessary and proper" (1819) *Gibbons v. Ogden* defines "interstate commerce" broadly (1824)
State Federalism	Roger B. Taney appointed Chief Justice (1835) *Dred Scott v. Sandford* lets states define property (1857) U.S. Civil War (1861–65)
Dual Federalism	*U.S. v. E.C. Knight* limits federal commerce power (1895) *Plessy v. Ferguson* limits federal citizenship rights (1896) 19th Amendment approves federal income tax (1913)
Cooperative Federalism	FDR's New Deal (1935) *Wickard v. Filburn* expands federal commerce power (1941) LBJ's Great Society (1965) Nixon's Special Revenue Sharing (1972) Nixon's General Revenue Sharing (1974)
Devolution	Reagan's tax reform (1981) Clinton's welfare reform (1997) *U.S. v. Morrison* limits federal commerce power (2000) Obamacare approved; Medicaid expansion made discretionary (2012)

corporations dominating key sectors of an integrated national economy could be effectively regulated only from the national level. By the time FDR assumed the presidency in March of 1933, most Americans had become convinced by their experience with the Depression that federal regulation of the economy needed to be enhanced.

FDR's "New Deal" and LBJ's "Great Society" initiatives involved the federal government in almost every area of policymaking. Many of these areas, including education, job training, health care, and welfare, had traditionally been the exclusive responsibilities of state and local governments. Initially, states and localities were too eager to receive the federal funds to worry much about the rules and regulations that accompanied them. However, the rules and regulations that seemed reasonable when there were thirty categorical grant programs in the 1930s seemed unreasonable as the number of such programs passed four hundred in the 1960s, and by 1970 nearly one dollar in every four spent by state and local governments came as a transfer from the federal government. The complexity of applying for, administering, and reporting on all of these grants worked a hardship on state and local governments.

By the late 1980s and early 1990s the problems of fiscal federalism and of American federalism in general had been redefined. Ronald Reagan thought that government at all levels of the federal system was too big, demanding, and expensive. Reagan sought to scale back governments at all levels by denying them funds. Although Bill Clinton sought to restore federal assistance to states and localities, he and the Republican Congress that he faced through most of his administration agreed that federal responsibilities as well as funds should be devolved to the states where possible.

In the latter half of the 1990s, Congress moved to reconstitute the federal system by repackaging dozens of social programs into block grants, cutting the funds allocated to them by up to 30 percent, and returning primary responsibility for them to the states. This policy reversal, called "devolution," in which President Bush joined enthusiastically, was the largest reallocation of authority within the federal system since LBJ's "Great Society" and perhaps since FDR's "New Deal." Nonetheless, it was reversed, at least temporarily, when the "Great Recession" of 2008–2009 strained state budgets and the Obama Administration offered help as part of its stimulus strategy. Today, the federal government supplies more than one in every three dollars spent by state and local governments.[29] The struggle within the American federal system for authority and resources is unending.

Key Terms

block grants 79	inherent powers 66
categorical grant 77	*Marbury v. Madison* 70
coercive federalism 78	*McCulloch v. Maryland* 70
concurrent majority 72	nullification 74
concurrent powers 66	*Paul v. Virginia* 68
confederation 63	preemption 79
cooperative federalism 72	reserved powers 67
creative federalism 78	secession 74
devolution 79	special revenue sharing 79
Dred Scott v. Sandford 72	supremacy clause 65
dual federalism 69	unitary government 63
extradition 68	*U.S. v. E.C. Knight* 74
general revenue sharing 79	*U.S. v. Lopez* 81
Gibbons v. Ogden 70	*U.S. v. Morrison* 81
implied powers 65	*Wickard v. Filburn* 76

Suggested Readings

Beer, Samuel H. *To Make a Nation: The Rediscovery of American Federalism*. Cambridge, MA: Harvard University Press, 1993. Beer traces thinking about federalism from the ancient world through the American founding period.

Karch, Andrew. *Democratic Laboratories: Policy Diffusion Among the States*. Ann Arbor: University of Michigan Press, 2007. Karch describes the influences on policy innovation and adoption among the states.

LaCroix, Alison L. *The Ideological Origins of American Federalism*. Cambridge, MA: Harvard University Press, 2010. LaCroix traces the roots of American federalism in law, theory, and practice.

Mettler, Suzanne. "Gender and Federalism in New Deal Public Policy," 1998. Mettler shows that the Social Security Act of 1935 was designed around male workers in cities. Relatively few women and minorities were part of the fulltime workforce and so were ineligible for the program.

Robertson, David Brian. *Federalism and the Making of America*. New York: Routledge, 2012. Robertson shows how America's federal structure has shaped the nation's politics, especially in critical areas like economic policy and race.

Weir, Margaret. "States, Race, and the Decline of New Deal Liberalism," 2005. Weir's analysis shows that federalism can explain a great deal about the way politics and political institutions have evolved over the decades and shaped the political landscape today.

Zimmerman, Joseph F. *Contemporary American Federalism: The Growth of National Power*. 2nd ed. Albany, NY: State University of New York Press, 2008. An excellent survey of the broad stages of the development of American federalism and of its contemporary strengths and weaknesses.

Web Resources

For practice quizzes, key terms flashcards, videos, links, and other study tools, visit the *American Government* website: www.routledge.com/cw/jillson

1. **www.theamericanpartnership.com/federalism-links/**
   This site highlights dozens of top websites dealing with federalism.

2. **publius.oxfordjournals.org**
   Home page for *Publius*, a scholarly journal dedicated to the study of federalism. The journal provides the reader with a better understanding of the dynamics of federal/state relations.

3. **www.access.gpo.gov/usbudget/index.htm**
   If an individual has an interest in fiscal federalism, this website is of great assistance. The page provides access to current budget sta-

tistics as well as a useful section entitled "A Citizen's Guide to the Budget."

4. **www.ncsl.org**
   The National Conference of State Legislators' (NCSL) home page offers links to information about state legislators, tax and budget issues, and general news relevant to state policymaking.

5. **www.statelocalgov.net/index.cfm**
   State and Local Government on the Net (SLGN) has links featuring various local governments within each state.

Chapter 4

POLITICAL SOCIALIZATION
AND PUBLIC OPINION

A government retains its sway over a great number of citizens … by that instinctive, and to a certain extent involuntary, agreement which results from similarity of feelings and resemblances of opinion.

ALEXIS DE TOCQUEVILLE,
Democracy in America, 1835

The
Constitution
TODAY

WHAT EXPLAINS THE U.S. COMMITMENT TO THE DEATH PENALTY?

Eighth Amendment: "Excessive bail shall not be required, nor excessive fines imposed, nor cruel and unusual punishments inflicted."

Since late 2003, Bianca Jagger, 1960s bad girl, fashion icon, first wife of ageless rocker Mick Jagger, and human rights activist, has been a Goodwill Ambassador in the Council of Europe's fight against the death penalty. Her main target has been the United States. The Council of Europe, established in the immediate wake of World War II, is now a 47-member regional organization opposed by charter to the death penalty. No member country has employed the death penalty since the late 1990s.

How is it that the U.S. views the death penalty so differently than its closest allies and now stands as one of the practice's last defenders and regular users in the world? Perhaps because Europe in the twentieth century saw government sanctioned death wholesale, not just in war, but in the far more heinous example of the Holocaust. Death in war, while obviously state-sanctioned, can be seen as necessary, even noble. But the Holocaust, state-sanctioned killing of millions of innocents, done by and to Europeans, created a revulsion not as directly felt in the United States. Our state-sanctioned killing, the death penalty, was more democratic, something the public visited on its miscreant members. It remains legal today.

In a February 2010 speech in Geneva, Ambassador Jagger explained Europe's post-World War II commitment to abolition of the death penalty, saying,

> Since it was founded in 1949 the Council of Europe has played a leading role as a guardian of our fundamental rights and freedoms. . . . In 1989, abolition of the death penalty was made a prerequisite of accession for all new member states . . . . The idea now is to spread these values to the rest of the world, starting with the two countries that enjoy observer status to the Council of Europe: the United States and Japan. . . . I am shocked and appalled at the unabated . . . application of the death penalty in the U.S., China, Iran, North Korea, Saudi Arabia, Iraq, Vietnam, Afghanistan, Japan, Yemen, and Somalia among others.

Think about this list for a moment—except for the U.S. and Japan, this is a list of the world's rogue states—precisely Jagger's point, right!

But the U.S. is unblinking in its commitment to the justice and utility of the death penalty. For decades, Gallop has shown a fairly steady two to one support for the death penalty in the U.S, rejecting Jagger's declaration that "The death penalty is the ultimate denial of human rights, a pre-meditated and cold-blooded killing of a human being by the state." Nonetheless, the U.S. has been sensitive to the charge made by Jagger and others that "The death penalty is unfair, arbitrary and capricious often based on jurisprudence fraught with racial discrimination and judicial bias." In fact, the Supreme Court struck down the death penalty on just these grounds in *Furman v. Georgia* (1972). A popular backlash and hastily revised state and federal statutes led the Court to reinstate the death penalty in *Gregg v. Georgia* (1976). Still, in recent years the Court has prohibited execution of the mentally challenged (IQ under 70) and the young (under 18).

Finally, though the United States seems unlikely to abolish the death penalty anytime soon, some parts of the country have already done so for all intents and purposes. The Death Penalty Information Center reports that since 1976 when the death penalty was reinstituted, 1,142 inmates have been executed in the South, while only 4 have been executed in the Northeast. The Midwest and West fall in between, at 173 and 85, respectively, but it is the difference between the Northeast and the South that commands attention.

This chapter will raise important questions about American political culture and how the country's residents form political opinions. But as you read the chapter bear in mind that culture and opinions are not always monolithic across the entire nation; they often diverge along regional or other lines.

Focus Questions: from reading to thinking

Q1 What does it mean to say that America is the only country in the world based on a creed—on principles and ideals?

Q2 Where do individual Americans get their opinions about politics, and what are the forces that shape those opinions?

Q3 How well informed and well organized is public opinion in America today?

Q4 Do Americans support or oppose abortion, or is the distribution of opinion more complicated than that?

Q5 What does it mean to be liberal or conservative, libertarian or populist, in America today?

WHAT DO YOU THINK?

- What accounts for these stark regional differences in attitudes toward the death penalty?
- Do you expect these regional differences to persist or do you think the differences will narrow over time?
- If they narrow over time, do you think the Northeast will move toward the South or the South will move toward the Northeast?

POLITICAL INFORMATION IN AMERICA

Earlier chapters introduced the basic ideas—liberty, equality, opportunity, limited government, the rule of law—and the basic institutions—separation of powers, federalism, Congress, the presidency, the courts—of American politics. We traced the American roots of these ideas and institutions back into British and European history and showed how they shaped the Founders' thinking in the Declaration of Independence and the Constitution. In this chapter, we ask how widely those broad ideas about government and politics are accepted today, how and how well they are transmitted from one generation to the next, and what contemporary Americans think about the major political issues of the day.

Historically, Americans held firmly to the broad political principles of their society, but had access to comparatively little "real-time" information about their government and its policy debates. Consider the situations of the first citizens who moved over the Alleghenies into Kentucky and Tennessee in the 1780s and the settlers spreading out across the Midwest in the 1870s. Most were farmers, the farms were isolated, and interactions with outsiders were limited. Newspapers, when they arrived at all, were often well out of date. In the more settled parts of the country, of course, information was more plentiful.

How did political learning occur under these circumstances? Generally, parents talked about politics in the normal course of the day, and children, having few alternative sources of information, learned from their parents. Today the social and informational contexts facing citizens are very different. Numerous sources send wave after wave of politically relevant information washing over the social landscape. Parents face stiff competition for the attention of their children from peers, social groups and clubs, radio, TV, movies, the Internet, and social media. These competitors are both powerful and unremitting.

How do people today, especially young people, come by their political views? Do different kinds of people, considered in terms of categories like age, sex, race, income, and region, hold similar views, or do they hold moderately, perhaps even completely, different views? How coherent are the opinions that Americans hold on public issues? Where did you get the ideas that you hold about politics and how coherent are your political ideas? These are important questions because democracy assumes political participation by an informed citizenry.

Brief definitions of three important concepts—political culture, political socialization, and public opinion—will help us understand how Americans come by their ideas about politics and public life. The term **political culture** refers to patterns of thought and behavior that are widely held in a society and that define the relationships of citizens to their government and to each other in matters affecting politics and public affairs.[1] Our political culture has long been referred to as the *American Creed.* Both terms refer to the ideas of the American founding: liberty, equality, opportunity, popular sovereignty, limited government, the rule of law, and the like.

Political socialization refers to the process by which the central tenets of the political culture are communicated and absorbed. Political socialization is the process by which the next generation of children and the next wave of immigrants come to understand, accept, and approve the existing political system and the procedures and institutions through which it operates.[2] In the main, political socialization is a conservative process because, it reproduces in new citizens the dominant political ideas of the culture.

Public opinion is the distribution of citizen opinion on particular matters of public concern or interest. Because the American political culture operates at a fairly general level, and political socialization impacts blacks somewhat differently from whites and women somewhat differently from men, public

political culture Patterns of thought and behavior that are widely held in a society and that refer to the relationships of citizens to their government and to each other in matters affecting politics and public affairs.

political socialization The process by which the central tenets of the political culture are transmitted from those immersed in it to those, such as children and immigrants, who are not.

public opinion The distribution of citizen opinion on matters of public concern or interest.

HON. DANIEL WEBSTER ADDRESSING THE CITIZENS OF BOSTON IN FRONT OF THE REVERE HOUSE.

Senator Daniel Webster, one of the premier political orators of the nineteenth century, could reach a few thousand people at a time.

opinion varies on and across the major issues of the day. Now we turn to the origins of the American political culture, then to political socialization, and then to the nature and content of public opinion in America today. We conclude by pondering some possibilities for political reform.

POLITICAL CULTURE: DEFINING THE "AMERICAN CREED"

Louis Hartz, one of the leading American historians of the mid-twentieth century, described colonial America as a "fragment society."[3] Hartz meant that the English men and women who immigrated to America in the seventeenth century did not represent the full range of English, let alone European, political, social, and religious opinion. Royalists had no desire to abandon their comfortable lives and benefits; the very poor were limited in their ability to emigrate; but the "middling class" of farmers, merchants, and craftsmen could see the chance for more—and they had both the desire and the means to move. The fragments of English society and thought that wave after wave of settlers carried to the New World drew heavily but selectively on the Old World.

Q1 What does it mean to say that America is the only country in the world based on a creed—on principles and ideals?

Getty Images for Meet the Press

Obama administration foreign policy official Susan Rice and others go on Sunday morning talk shows to shape both elite and mass opinion on administration policy.

The seventeenth-century Protestantism that the Puritans and Quakers carried to America rejected monarchy and the state religions of Europe in favor of local control of towns and churches. By the early eighteenth century, the Glorious Revolution in England and the beginning of the European Enlightenment brought increased attention to arguments for natural rights, popular sovereignty, limited government, and the rule of law. To this British heritage, immigrants from other parts of Europe added a rich and leavening diversity. We discussed these influences in some detail in Chapter 1, especially as regards the ideas of John Locke and Baron de Montesquieu. Students needing a review may wish to flip back to pages 12–14.

Colonial Americans drew on this cultural and intellectual heritage to create communities that then developed and evolved in interaction with the vast and wealthy continent itself. By the late eighteenth century, America's self-image, its political culture was set. Thomas Jefferson and his colleagues in the Congress of 1776 drew heavily on Locke in grounding the new nation's independence on the declaration that "all Men are created equal, that they are endowed by their Creator with certain unalienable Rights, that among these are Life, Liberty, and the pursuit of Happiness." The Declaration of Independence put liberty, equality, and opportunity at the core of the American Creed.[4] As we shall see below and throughout this book, these creedal values were aspirations, not realities, in the founding generation and our own.

Contemporary analysts still point to the same familiar ideas and concepts as fundamental to the American Creed. One prominent scholar, Samuel

Huntington, concluded his study of the American Creed by declaring that "the same core values appear in virtually all analyses: liberty, equality, individualism, democracy, and the rule of law." Another, Seymour Martin Lipset, concluded that "the American Creed can be described in five terms: liberty, egalitarianism, individualism, populism, and *laissez faire*."[5] These ideas form the basis of the American political culture and are almost universally approved within the American society.

Despite the near universal support for the fundamental principles of the American political culture, there are disagreements about what they mean and what, if anything, should be done to realize them more fully. For example, thoughtful people disagree about the real meaning of liberty and equality. Isaiah Berlin's famous distinction between negative liberty (freedom from outside control) and positive liberty (the real ability to achieve desirable ends) still sparks heated debate. Equality has been variously argued to mean—in the eyes of God, before the law, of opportunity, and of outcomes. Moreover, liberty can conflict with equality, individualism can conflict with democracy, and *laissez faire* competition can conflict with the rule of law. As we shall see in later chapters of this book, much of politics is a battle over the right to define the meanings of terms like liberty and equality.

Finally, although we often think that a deep gulf between liberals and conservatives, Democrats and Republicans, make our politics rough-and-tumble, the ideological spectrum in the U.S. is fairly narrow by European and certainly by global standards. There are virtually no monarchists in America and precious few fascists, socialists, or communists. While our politicians might call each other fascists and socialists, most Americans were socialized to a fairly narrow range of democratic-capitalist ideals.

POLITICAL SOCIALIZATION: WHERE OUR IDEAS ABOUT POLITICS COME FROM

How are the broad ideas of the American political culture taught by one generation of Americans and learned by the next? Political scientist Fred Greenstein described political socialization as the study of "(1) who (2) learns what (3) from whom (4) under what circumstances (5) with what effects."[6] Greenstein's fundamental interest was in how young children acquire their first impressions of politics and political leaders. More recently scholars have asked how easily early political learning is modified as people move through the life cycle. Do people change their political views as they experience school, work, marriage, family, retirement, and old age? Do poor children who get rich in adult life change political assumptions and beliefs?

Political engagement involves a desire and a willingness to be involved in the political world—to follow political news and events, to join in political discussions, perhaps to work to advance one set of political ideas or issues over others, and to vote and maybe even to stand for election. Students of

Q2 Where do individual Americans get their opinions about politics, and what are the forces that shape those opinions?

political engagement study how people feel about politics, how interested they are in politics, how much they actually know about politicians, politics, and public policy, and how and how much they engage in politics. As we shall see, scholars find that political engagement varies by age, education, income, race, region, and much more.[7]

Agents of Socialization

How does it happen that the vast majority of Americans come to believe that market competition is the best way to organize an economy, that elections are the best way to pick political leaders, and that the flag, the White House, the Lincoln memorial, and the Capitol dome represent a political heritage and culture worth passing on, worth defending, even worth dying for? As we shall see, while political socialization is a powerful process, much of it takes place informally, below the radar screen, almost automatically. Neither those who teach nor those who learn are much aware that they are doing it.

Agents of socialization are the persons by whom and the settings in which the process of political socialization is accomplished. Persons include parents, family, friends, teachers, coworkers, and associates of various kinds, as well as those whose views are transmitted through the media. Settings include homes, churches, schools, workplaces, clubs, union halls, and professional associations.

Agents of socialization are also categorized by the timing, scope, and intensity of their influence. Students of political socialization distinguish between primary groups and secondary groups. **Primary groups** are face-to-face groups with whom the individual has regular, often frequent, contact. These include close personal associations like family, friends, and coworkers. Primary groups are usually made up of persons of similar background (income, education, race, religion) engaged in frequent conversation on a wide range of topics including politics.

Secondary groups are broader and more diffuse. Examples include churches, unions, the military, and clubs and professional associations such as the Sierra Club, the National Rifle Association, and the Chamber of Commerce. Their members come from a variety of income, educational, racial, and religious backgrounds. Moreover, secondary groups usually have a substantive focus—that is, they are environmentalists, business owners, or gun owners. Their influence is limited to a distinctive set of issues to which the group is thought relevant.

New technology, like the Internet and social media, and new uses of old technology, like talk radio, allow geographically disparate groups to form around and act on shared interests. Rush Limbaugh's "ditto heads" learn a coherent ideology and arguments supporting their positions by tuning in every day. Meetup.com, YouTube, and Facebook allow like-minded people to find each other and share enthusiasms, ideas, and plans. And where like-minded people do not find each other, pollsters, political strategists, and niche marketers work to identify people with shared values and interests so that they can target them with political information designed to mobilize them to political action.[8]

---

agents of socialization The persons, such as parents and teachers, and settings, such as families and schools, that carry out the political socialization process.

primary groups Face-to-face groups, such as families and friends, with whom an individual has regular, often continuous, contact.

secondary groups Broader and more diffuse than primary groups, secondary groups often serve a particular role or purpose in the life of the member, and often do not meet together as a full membership.

Family, School, and Work. Everyone agrees that the first and most important agent of political socialization is the family. Virtually all American families
teach respect for democracy and capitalism, but they differ on the lessons they
teach regarding participation, partisanship, politics, and public policy. Studies
show that 80 to 90 percent of married couples share the same party affiliation.
In such homes, children receive consistent messages from both parents. In
Democratic households, children hear favorable comments about Democrats
and unfavorable comments about Republicans as parents converse at the
dinner table and as they respond to what they see and hear on the evening
news. Parents rarely sit young children down and tell them that they are
Democrats and not Republicans, or vice versa, but children learn just as
effectively by overhearing their parents, observing their actions and reactions,
and sensing their party affiliation.

Over the past half century, scholars have consistently shown that high
school and college-age young people generally adopt their parents' partisan
identification. If both parents share the same party affiliation, Democrat or
Republican, 60 to 65 percent of young people adopt the family partisanship,
about 30 percent abandon it for an independent stance, while only about
10 percent join the opposition party. Young people from those uncommon
households where Mom is a Democrat and Dad is a Republican or vice versa
scatter with remarkable uniformity across Democrat, Republican, and independent categories. In households where both parents are independents, the children
choose independent status at least two-thirds of the time, while the remaining one-third divide equally between the Democrats and the Republicans.[9]

Schools also play an important role in early political socialization. School
curricula lay down layer after layer of American history, civics, and social

Bob Daemmrich / The Image Works

Schools begin each day with a recital of the Pledge of Allegiance, a traditional induction into the process of political socialization. History, civics, and social studies classes reinforce a positive sense of
American ideas and institutions.

studies. Students learn patriotic songs and rituals (who has not been either a Pilgrim or an Indian in a Thanksgiving day pageant?), they learn about political heroes such as Washington ("I cannot tell a lie") and Lincoln (reading law books by candlelight), and they cast their first presidential straw ballots. Moreover, school, even elementary school, offers a broader horizon than the family. Respect for diversity, equality, fair play, toleration, majority rule, and minority rights is required for the first time in a setting where people actually differ.

Fred Greenstein's seminal work with schoolchildren in New Haven in the late 1950s and early 1960s remains fascinating even today. Greenstein found that children begin to learn about politics in their elementary school years. Second graders can name the president. Over the remainder of the grade school years, children become aware of other branches of government and other levels of government. Initially, children see Congress as the president's "helpers." By eighth grade, they know that Congress can differ with the president and that this is how the system is supposed to work. A half century of subsequent scholarly work, best summarized by Robert Erikson and Kent Tedin in their classic *American Public Opinion*, affirms "the primacy principle" that early learning has staying power. Still early views are not set in stone. Students begin their college careers somewhat more liberal than the adult population and become somewhat more liberal still by their senior year. Scholars attribute this to education challenging stereotypes and prejudices and to the diversity of the college environment. Later life may roll back some of these changes, but, as some parents worry, college tends to be a liberalizing experience.[10] Childhood political socialization can be deepened or partially reshaped during "the impressionable years" of 17 to 29.[11] Socialization continues after early adulthood, but early foundations are deeply set.

Work has both general and specific effects on political socialization. In fact, employment, quite apart from the nature of the job, has a profound effect on a person's political outlook. Having a job is one's ticket to participate in a whole range of social and political processes. Having a good job teaches confidence that carries over into political activity. Unemployment, particularly chronic unemployment, takes away the status, time, opportunity, and confidence that political participation requires. Having a bad job, where you put in long hours at low pay, saps confidence and discourages political activity. Not surprisingly, studies show that higher income people are more aware of politics, issues, and candidates than are lower income people. The wealthy are socialized to a more active political life than are the poor.[12]

The Media.   The media, like the schools, provide pervasive and continuous support to effective political socialization simply by routinely reporting political and economic events. The president's latest statements, the work of the Congress, and the latest Supreme Court decisions are all reported on the evening news and in the morning paper. Trade figures, corporate profits, and the rise and fall of the stock market are reported in ways that assume the fundamental legitimacy of democratic capitalism. Even talk radio and the Internet offer few hints that politics or economics might be organized differently. The role of the media in American politics will be treated more fully in Chapter 5.

The Impacts of Transformative Events and Personalities. Political socialization is the process by which families, schools, and the media transmit the
American political culture to young people and newcomers, but that broad
process of cultural teaching and learning, of memory and renewal, can be
disrupted. Some events including wars, economic upheavals, social turmoil,
and political scandal can transform the way people see and understand their
society. Depending upon how these challenges are handled by political leaders, the nation's faith in its political culture, its confidence in its basic ideals
and institutions, is renewed and strengthened or called into doubt and weakened. Leadership interacts with crisis to convince people that society and government are or are not up to the task of confronting the major issues of the day.

AP Photo

In his famous "fireside chats," President Franklin Roosevelt used radio to educate and reassure
Americans through a dozen years of economic depression and world war. Though modern presidents
still use radio, they depend more heavily on television when they need to address the nation.

Abraham Lincoln held the nation together through a terrible Civil War, and Franklin Delano Roosevelt did the same through a dozen years of economic depression and world war. Both gave the Americans who witnessed their virtuoso political performances the confidence to confront their world forcefully and for the most part successfully. Alternatively, leaders that misperceive or mismanage the major threats of their time, as Herbert Hoover misperceived the threat posed by the Great Depression of the 1930s, may raise doubts about the viability of the nation's most basic political assumptions. Leaders facing crises must respond effectively to challenges and do so in ways that protect and strengthen the nation's basic principles. President Bush believed that his War on Terror would bring the nation and the world through to a safer, more peaceful, and democratic future. Critics contend that his policies failed and the means that he used to pursue them have undercut U.S. rights and liberties and weakened our national security. President Obama retained some Bush initiatives, such as intensive surveillance, and rejected others, like enhanced interrogation and Guantanamo. History will judge both men on how well they protected the nation's ideals, institutions, and citizens.

THE NATURE OF PUBLIC OPINION IN THE UNITED STATES

The agents of socialization discussed above, although they all work within a general American political culture revolving around capitalism and democracy, do not teach the same lessons to all members of society. The poor and the wealthy are socialized to different roles; minorities are socialized differently from whites, and women are socialized differently from men. Hence, public opinion varies across a wide range of social group characteristics.[13] Public opinion, in its most general formulation, is simply the current distribution of citizen opinion on matters of public concern or interest.

Before we can discuss public opinion in detail, we must address a prior question. How do we measure public opinion and how confident should we be in those measurements? Once we understand how public opinion is measured, we can ask how attitudes and opinions vary within the American public by class, race, ethnicity, and gender.

History of Public Opinion Polling

Citizens have always wondered how others see the leading candidates and major issues of the day. Informal preference polls for the leading presidential candidates in the election of 1824 were reported in the press. In fact, the partisan press of the nineteenth century regularly reported on rallies, straw polls, and citizen reports of voter attitudes in their area. (See Table 4.1 for a summary of the ways public opinion has been expressed and assessed through history.) As late as 1916, a prominent national magazine called the *Literary Digest* simply asked its readers to send in whatever information they had from

TABLE **4.1**	Historical Techniques for the Expression and Assessment of Public Opinion
Periods	**Techniques**
5th century B.C.	Oratory/Rhetoric
16th century	Printing
17th century	Crowds
Late-17th century	Petitions
18th century	Coffee houses and taverns
Late-18th century	Revolutionary movements
Early-19th century	Strikes, General elections, Straw polls
Mid-19th century	Modern newspapers, magazines, photography
1920s	Radio
1930s	Sample surveys
1940s	Television
1980s	Cable television
1990s	Internet, Web, E-mail
2000s	YouTube, Twitter, Tumblr

Source: Susan Herbst, *Numbered Voices* (Chicago: University of Chicago Press, 1993), p. 48. Updated and expanded by the author.

their areas about the presidential contest between Democrat Woodrow Wilson and Republican Charles Evans Hughes. Over the next two decades, the *Literary Digest* conducted huge and reasonably accurate surveys in the presidential elections of 1920 through 1932. However, the famous failure of its survey in 1936 helped usher in a new era in the history of polling.

In 1936, the *Literary Digest* mailed 10 million ballots to citizens—whose names were compiled from automobile registration lists, telephone directories, and magazine subscription lists—asking them to choose between the Democrat, Franklin Roosevelt, and the Republican, Alf Landon. The 2 million ballots that were returned suggested a big win for Landon; in fact, Roosevelt won in a landslide, carrying the popular vote 57 percent to 43 percent and the Electoral College 523 to 8. Analysts concluded that the *Literary Digest* poll results were so far off because the magazine's subscribers were mostly wealthy, those who owned cars, had phones, and subscribed to literary magazines. The poll missed less wealthy voters, who did not own cars or subscribe to literary magazines, and who were more likely to vote for Roosevelt.[14]

Scientific Polling. In the same year that *Literary Digest*, with its 2 million responses, was completely wrong about the election outcome, George Gallup, with a much smaller but scientifically selected sample of voter opinion, predicted the outcome correctly. Gallup and his competitors—Louis Harris, Elmo Roper, and others—gauged citizen opinion on public issues and political candidates with "quota samples" of the broader electorate. The new scientific pollsters did well in the 1940 and 1944 elections as well, but then disaster struck again in 1948.

Quota samples were supposed to defend against the skewed sampling that had undermined the *Literary Digest* poll, but more subtle biases became evident in 1948. Pollsters might fill their quotas, securing the right number of men, women, blacks, Catholics, rich, poor, etc., but they might avoid a dangerous or hard to reach neighborhood. As a result, even a quota sample might be skewed. In 1948, all of the supposedly scientific polling firms projected that the Republican Thomas Dewey would defeat the incumbent Democratic President Harry Truman. Truman won and subsequent inquiries concluded that quota samples should be replaced by more dependable "probability samples." They also concluded that pollsters, lulled into overconfidence by Dewey's stable lead, stopped polling too early and missed Truman's late surge.[15]

probability sampling A sampling model in which every person in the target population has an identical chance of being selected for the sample to be polled.

Probability sampling is based on a statistical model in which every person in the target population has an equal or known chance of being selected for the sample to be polled. In a simple probability sample, all members of the population have an equal chance of being selected. In a stratified probability sample, the population is first divided by some theoretically relevant characteristic—like gender, income, or likelihood of voting—and then the population is randomly sampled within each category. Pollsters have understood for more than half a century that a well-constructed national sample of just 1,000 persons produces results that have a sampling error of +/– 3 percent with a confidence interval of 95 percent. What do these ominous phrases, sampling error and confidence interval, actually mean?[16]

Assume we had a well-designed poll of 1,000 adults telling us that 60 percent of them approved a certain policy. Remember, we have not asked all American adults whether they support the policy, just a carefully selected sample of them, so we know that our 60 percent result is unlikely to be precise. The 3 percent sampling error is the pollster's admission, or at least sampling theory's admission, that in a sample of 1,000 the results could be off as much as 3 percent either way—so maybe not precisely 60 percent, but somewhere between 57 and 63 percent support the policy. The 95 percent confidence interval is another admission. It says that if you polled 100 similarly drawn samples, at least 95 of them would produce results in that 57 to 63 percent range; meaning that the remaining 5 might be off by more than 3 percent either way.[17] None of this means that polls are always wrong, just that even well-constructed polls can be off within a certain known range and should be interpreted appropriately.

On the other hand, consumers of polling information should also keep in mind that not all polls are trying to be accurate. Polls released by campaigns are often—surprise—intended to serve political purposes, to suggest momentum or to trigger positive news stories. Polling analyst Nate Silver of FiveThirtyEight.com has found that campaign polls tend to be about six points more favorable to their candidate than independent surveys.[18] As we shall see below, some polls strive for accuracy, some have other purposes. Sophisticated consumers of polls, as you are about to become, know how to tell the difference.

Kinds of Polls.   Different kinds of polls and surveys are designed to produce different kinds of information. Polls play a large role in political campaigns, to gauge who is ahead and why, but they are also conducted between elections to determine what citizens think about the major issues of the day. The main kinds of polls are benchmark polls, preference polls, opinion surveys, focus groups, tracking polls, and exit polls.

A candidate considering a particular election or a group considering a particular issue campaign will often run a **benchmark poll** to see where they stand before undertaking the campaign. A benchmark poll might seek to determine a candidate's name recognition, how he or she is viewed by potential voters, critical issues in the district, and key demographic information on the district's voters. **Preference polls** offer respondents a list of candidates for a particular office such as the presidency and ask which candidate they prefer. Preference polls show whether a candidate enters a race from a position of strength or from way back in a crowded field.

Opinion surveys may be conducted within the context of a campaign, but they are much more broadly used by the media, civic and interest groups, marketers, and others who wish to know how opinion is distributed across particular questions and issues. Focus groups are not really polls, but they are often used in conjunction with polls and provide similar but richer information. A **focus group** is made up of ten to fifteen carefully selected people who are led through an in-depth discussion of their thoughts and reactions to particular policy issues, candidates, or campaign themes and arguments. Focus groups are meant to supplement surveys by uncovering why people think what they think.

A **tracking poll** provides constantly updated information on the rise and fall of support for a candidate or policy. Late in a presidential campaign, for example, tracking polls provide daily updates on the status of the race—is the gap narrowing, or does the leader seem to be widening his or her margin? Tracking polls interview several hundred new people a day and then average the samples for the last two or three days to create a continually updated picture of the race. An **exit poll** is taken after voters have cast their ballots; it is a survey of actual voters rather than of potential or even likely voters. Exit polls interview carefully selected samples of voters as they exit the polls to find out how they voted and why they voted that way. Exit polls are used by the media to "call" elections, sometimes even before the polls close.

Should Citizens Believe Polls?   Many Americans are skeptical about polls and there are some good reasons to be skeptical. Doubts about polls were deepened, particularly among conservatives, when the Romney campaign polls and those of other conservative groups and interests showed a dead-heat if not a Romney advantage in the closing days of the 2012 presidential campaign. When Romney lost most of the Midwestern swing states and the national vote by three to seven points, conservatives argued publicly about how their pollsters could have been so far off.

Polls are not easy to conduct well, and the increasing use of answering machines, caller identification devices, cell phones, and the general unwillingness of citizens to respond to surveys make it more difficult. The Romney campaign "turnout model," meaning the campaign's best estimate as to how

benchmark poll A poll conducted early in a campaign to gauge the name recognition, public image, and electoral prospects of a candidate.

preference poll A poll that offers respondents a list of candidates for a particular office and asks which is preferred.

opinion survey Poll or survey used by political campaigns, the media, civic organizations, and marketers to gauge opinion on particular questions or issues.

focus group A small but carefully selected group of ten to fifteen persons led through an in-depth discussion of a political issue or campaign to delve behind opinions in search of their root causes.

tracking poll Frequent polling using overlapping samples to provide daily updates of the status of a race.

exit poll A poll taken after voters have cast their ballots to get an early sense of who won and why.

many whites, blacks, Hispanics, etc. would turn out on election day, was off. They estimated more whites and fewer minorities than actually showed up on election day—and they lost. Political pros also know that poll results can be shaped and manipulated by the order in which questions are asked and by the way that they are phrased.[19]

push poll A push poll is not a real poll; instead it is designed to influence voters by providing negative, often, false information.

Moreover, every election cycle includes reports of **push polls**. Push polls are pseudo polls, not really intended to gather information about the respondent's opinions, but to use negative and often false information to push the respondent away from a particular candidate. Push polling is among the dark arts of politics. In the guise of a simple question, such as, "Would you be more or less likely to vote for Candidate X if you knew he tortured kittens?" Candidate X may love kittens, he may even contribute to the local Humane Society, but a push poll, employed late in a campaign when no effective response is possible, can do real damage. Concern about push polls deepens public skepticism about all polls.

Still, skepticism should be directed toward some polls more than others. As a general rule, citizens can trust polls from organizations that have reputational incentives to be accurate—major polling organizations like Gallup, major news outlets like ABC and the *New York Times*, and major research organizations like the Pew Charitable Trusts. Citizens might well mistrust polls from groups that pop up in the middle of a campaign or that have a dog in the fight—an advocacy group, candidate, Super PAC, or political party.

Variations in Socialization by Class, Race, and Gender

What then do reputable polls tell us about how citizens differ in regard to politics and public opinion by class, race, ethnicity, and gender? Broadly, the more thoroughly and comfortably integrated a person is into the community and society, the more likely he or she is to be politically active. Wealthy, well educated, professionals tend to be engaged in lots of ways, and not just voting, while those for whom life is more difficult tend to be less active politically.

Class.   Poor children enter school with fewer skills than wealthy children and less is expected of them. Children from lower-class backgrounds have less information about politics than children from upper-class backgrounds. Extensive research, summarized by Chris Garcia and Gabriel Sanchez, reports that schools serving children of the working class and poor "are less involved in preparing future leaders, and instead emphasize the importance of becoming good law-abiding citizens, paying taxes, serving one's country, and similar 'subject' rather than participant . . . styles."[20] Many studies have shown that these early differences in knowledge and confidence can translate into differences in political participation that last a lifetime.

The most recent National Election Study found that poor adults were only about half as likely as the wealthy, 22 percent to 38 percent, to say that they paid attention to public affairs "most of the time." But they were 18 points

"What I drink and what I tell the pollsters I drink are two different things."

more likely, 59 percent to 41 percent, to agree with the statement that "people don't have a say in what government does." The poor believe, rightly in many cases, that society and government do not move to their commands. They also know that they are not expected to lead, perhaps not even to participate, and so many times they do neither.

Race. An important new book, entitled *Black Politics Today*, by political scientist Theodore J. Davis, argues that blacks have not fully embraced the dominant political culture because it has not rejected and moved to dismantle cultural and institutional racism in the country. The cultural gulf has produced deep and systematic divisions between white and black opinion across a wide range of issues. Davis reports that 81 percent of blacks felt that society had not dealt fairly with their racial group (only 15 percent of whites agreed), 76 percent thought government should spend more to improve conditions among blacks (only 27 percent of whites agreed), and 55 percent felt that there still was a fair amount of discrimination against blacks (only 28 percent of whites agreed).[21]

In the 2012 presidential election, a remarkable 93 percent of blacks voted for Obama, as did 71 percent of Hispanics, but just 39 percent of whites. Moreover, blacks and whites have tended to differ on a broad range of policy issues, sometimes quite dramatically. Blacks are more supportive of government spending on health care, education, and job training than whites and less supportive of spending for defense and corporate subsidies. For example, over the last three decades, blacks have been 20 to 30 points more favorable than whites toward busing to achieve desegregation of public schools and 30 to 40 points more favorable than whites to the idea that government should guarantee fair treatment in jobs. Scholars explain the cohesion in black opinion by positing a "linked-fate" hypothesis in which blacks stand uniformly against racial discrimination because each individual knows that if it occurs he or she will be impacted by it.

Finally, in foreign policy, a *New York Times* poll taken in late March 2003 as war with Iraq loomed, found that 82 percent of whites and only 44 percent of blacks supported military action to oust Saddam Hussein. By early 2008, a CNN poll reported that while white support for the war had fallen to 45 percent, black support had fallen all the way to 9 percent.

Ethnicity.   Political scientists Chris Garcia and Gabriel Sanchez, in *Hispanics in the U.S. Political System*, contend that, "most Latinos would grow up in a subcultural environment, that is, a cultural environment that is different from the majority mainstream environment in some ways." They describe the traditional Latino family as more controlled, gender defined, and patriarchal than the dominant cultural model of the family.[22]

Until recently, Hispanic Americans were less likely than blacks to feel that discrimination was a major problem for their community. In a 2002 Pew Hispanic Center poll, 47 percent of Hispanics claimed that discrimination was a major problem. But by 2010, after several years of public debate about immigration and border control, 61 percent believed that it was and another 24 percent believed it was at least a minor problem.[23]

Hispanics favor special efforts to remedy past discrimination and help minorities get ahead by 76 percent to 14 percent and favor a bigger government

From silent personal protests, like this one, to the recent Ferguson, Missouri, mass protest, minorities and women, but especially blacks, see a pervasive injustice in U.S. society.

offering a wider array of services by 75 percent to 16 percent. On the other hand, Hispanics favor tax cuts over deficit reduction by a margin of two to one, 59 percent to 30 percent, and are twice as likely as non-Hispanics, 44 percent compared to 22 percent, to think that abortion should be illegal.[24] Hispanic public opinion is often said to reflect an "in-between" community, with life experiences and attitudes in-between those of blacks and whites.

Asian-Americans, after Hispanics, are the fastest growing racial and ethnic minority in the nation. Asians currently make up about 5 percent of the population. In a recent major survey, 32 percent of Asians claimed a Democratic party affiliation, 12 percent claimed a Republican affiliation, 19 percent were Independent, and 35 percent were non-partisan. Chinese, Filipino, Indians, Japanese, and Koreans tend to lean Democratic, while Vietnamese tend to lean Republican. Like most Americans in 2012, Asian-Americans identified the economy as the most important issue.

An interesting difference among Asian-Americans showed up in regard to Iraq policy. While a majority of Asian-Americans supported withdrawing from Iraq, only 15 percent of Vietnamese-Americans did. Vietnamese-Americans obviously remember the Vietnam War of the 1960s and 1970s where U.S. withdrawal led to the fall of South Vietnam. These figures also remind us that no broad racial or ethnic group is monolithic.[25]

Gender.   Similar differences, although not so large and across a narrower set of issues, exist between men and women. Women have consistently been more supportive than men of gun control, stern punishments for drunk driving, and spending on education and health care, and less supportive of capital punishment at home and the use of force abroad. Women oppose force at home and abroad about 10 percent more than men and favor the "moralistic" position on domestic issues about 3 or 4 percent more consistently than men.[26]

The terrorist attacks of September 11, 2001 and the subsequent conflicts with Al-Queda, Afghanistan, and Iraq put these historical differences between men and women on stark display. In early September 2001, just prior to the attacks, 41 percent of men, but only 24 percent of women, favored additional defense spending. In the immediate wake of the 9/11 attacks, support for increased defense spending among men increased to 53 percent, but among women it nearly doubled to 47 percent, still 6 points below men. Nonetheless, only a year and a half later, as war with Iraq loomed in late February 2003, women were about 10 percent less willing than men to consider the potential costs in troops and treasure acceptable.[27] And in late 2011, as the last troops were being withdrawn from Iraq and the Afghan War ground on, men remained 17 points more supportive of the war than women, 43 percent to 26 percent.[28]

In later chapters we will see how variations in political socialization by class, race, ethnicity, and gender affect partisan identification and voting throughout a lifetime. A quick look ahead to Table 7.5 in the chapter on political parties and Table 8.1 in the chapter on campaigns and elections will suggest clearly the lifelong impact of political socialization on the way individuals view and act in the world.

Properties of Public Opinion

Although public opinion differs across class, race, and gender lines, it also displays a number of general properties or characteristics. Most Americans hold to certain broad ideas about politics, although they have little detailed information about institutions, leaders, or policies.

Public opinion scholars distinguish between elites or "opinion leaders" and the mass public. Opinion leaders are those few, usually thought of as around 10 percent of the adult population, who follow public affairs closely and know a good deal about them. These people possess a lot of well-organized and readily accessible information about politics and public policy; they know the leading actors, the major issues, and the key policy choices.[29]

Members of the mass public, on the other hand, are busy with work and family and do not spend their free time puzzling over political issues. What they learn about politics comes in disconnected bits and pieces that do not add up to a coherent view of the political world.

Q3 How well informed and well organized is public opinion in America today?

How Detailed Is Public Opinion?   The first aspect of public opinion that we must note is its lack of detail for most Americans. In one sense, most Americans "know" very little about politics, public policy, and political leaders. For example, in survey after survey over the past fifty years, most Americans knew who the president was (usually 95 percent plus) and almost as many could identify the vice president. Only about half of adult Americans knew that there were two U.S. senators from their state, could name their representative in Congress, or could identify the majority party in the House and Senate. Fewer than 10 percent could name the chief justice of the Supreme Court or the chairman of the Federal Reserve Board.[30]

Can you name the chief justice of the Supreme Court? Does it matter? How much specific information do citizens need to evaluate government and to decide whether they approve of its performance? Do citizens need to know who the chief justice is to be able to decide whether they like what the Court has done on civil rights, on the rights of persons accused of crimes, or on school prayer? Some suggest that detailed knowledge is not required because citizens quite sensibly make broader judgments about how political and other national institutions, like business, labor, education, and religion, are doing. Others note that, at least for some purposes, partisanship and ideology can stand in for detailed information.

Struggling Toward Democracy

There is debate over how well citizens need to be informed about details of the current political environment to act politically.

What do you think?

- What does it mean for our democracy that at any given time nearly half of adults do not know which party has majority control of the U.S. House of Representatives?
- How much do citizens need to know about government and politics to play a meaningful role in them?

Even if one assumes that the average citizen does not need to know much about particular public officials, one should be a little nervous to learn that in surveys taken before every congressional election (every two years) over the past half century, an average of only 55 percent of respondents correctly identified the majority party in the U.S. House of Representatives. Remember: there are only two major parties, the Democrats and the Republicans, so just a moment's thought tells you that one or the other is the majority party.

LET'S COMPARE

Attitudes on Gender Equality in Nineteen Societies

WorldPublicOpinion.org reported a survey of twenty countries concerning attitudes toward gender equality. The nations included in the survey represent about 60 percent of the world's population and majorities in most countries favored gender equality and favored government doing more to promote it. Steven Kull, director of WorldPublicOpinion.org, noted that "The idea that women should have equal rights is fairly new in the context of world history. It is quite extraordinary that there is now such a global consensus across cultures not only that women should have equal rights but also that it is the responsibility of government to prevent discrimination."

It is certainly true that gender equality has made major advances in the past half century or so, but it is also true that these advances have been uneven. Some cultures still socialize men and women to distinctive social roles and limit women mostly to secondary roles. Public opinion in Egypt, Russia, Iran, and India, for example, neither favors gender equality nor wants government to do much to promote it. On the other hand, public opinion in Mexico, China, France, and Indonesia, both favors gender equality and more effort by government to promote it. The U.S. favors gender equality but is ambivalent about additional government effort to promote it.

Finally, Turkey will be an interesting case to follow in the coming years. Turkey is a Muslim country that had an aggressively secular government for the last century. Hence, the survey showed strong support for gender equality and pretty strong support for more government effort to promote it. But Turkey now has a Muslim government that proposes to give religion a larger public role. What impact will this have on the role of women in Turkish society?

Country	Gender Equality Very Important	Government Should Do More	Country	Gender Equality Very Important	Government Should Do More
Britain	89	52	Jordan	55	29
Mexico	89	83	Thailand	49	72
Turkey	80	60	Ukraine	44	46
U.S.	77	48	Nigeria	44	61
China	76	70	Iran	44	36
France	75	68	South Korea	43	73
Argentina	71	51	India	41	23
Indonesia	71	69	Russia	35	39
Kenya	66	69	Egypt	31	17
Azerbaijan	55	40	**Survey Average**	**59**	**53**

Source: http://www.worldpublicopinion.org/incl/printable_version.php?pnt=453.

Softening this picture just a bit are the findings of two new lines research. One suggests that citizens do better in remembering political and other information if given more time and if given incentives to take surveys seriously, but performance remains pretty poor.[31] Another distinguishes between recall and recognition. Unassisted recall involves simply remembering your member of

Congress's name, which only about half of citizens can do. But many more citizens are able to recognize the name of their member from a list of several names.[32] Unaided recall is hard, but many political activities, like voting, involve the easier task of recognition—so maybe citizens and voters are not in such bad shape after all.

General Principles versus Real Choices.   A second worrisome aspect of public opinion is that there is often a wide gap between the general principles that citizens claim to hold and specific choices they make in their communities. The most famous evidence of this gap comes from a study done by political scientists James M. Prothro and Charles M. Grigg in the late 1950s. Many more recent studies confirm these findings with minor revisions. Prothro and Grigg found 95 to 98 percent support for majority rule, minority rights, and free speech. However, they found that only 44 percent of respondents were prepared to let a communist speak in their community and only 63 percent were prepared to let someone with antireligious views speak. Prothro and Grigg concluded that when one moves from general principles of the American political culture to specific applications of those principles, "consensus breaks down completely."[33]

The puzzling relationship between general principles and specific cases has spawned a great deal of research. Generally, findings confirm broad respect for the nation's general principles, but deep uncertainty about how they should apply in specific cases. Important research by James Gibson suggested that whether respondents initially gave a tolerant or intolerant response to a specific case, their minds could easily be changed by the presentation of counterarguments. Though the relationship between general principles and specific cases seems tentative, on some broad issues of fairness and inclusion, public opinion has clearly changed.[34]

For example, opinion on whether white and black children should attend the same schools has moved from only 30 percent responding yes in 1930 to more than 90 percent responding yes by the early 1980s.[35] Even more striking, the Gallup organization has been asking Americans whether they would be willing to vote for a woman for president since 1937. In 1937 only 33 percent said yes. The number rose to 48 percent in 1949, 57 percent by 1967, 82 percent by 1989, and 95 percent in 2012. A similar path was traced by willingness to vote for a black candidate for president. It began at 38 percent in 1958 and reached 96 percent by 2012.[36]

Hillary Clinton (female), Barack Obama (black), and Mitt Romney (Mormon) put opinions such as these to the test in the 2008 and 2012 presidential nomination and general election contests. Gallup polling in June 2012, just as the 2012 presidential contest got fully underway, reported that the vast majority of respondents said they could vote for a black or female president, but only 80 percent said they could vote for a Mormon and only 54 percent said they could vote for an atheist.[37]

Q4 Do Americans support or oppose abortion, or is the distribution of opinion more complex than that?

The Ambivalence of Public Opinion.   On some issues, such as broad equity issues regarding minorities and women, the last six decades have seen a

Pro & Con

Must Voters Be Knowledgeable?

People differ about how much knowledge a citizen needs to be a constructive and legitimate participant in the politics of the community, state, and nation. The first instinct of many, including most college students, is to assume that society would benefit if its political judgments and choices were made by its best informed citizens and that society ought to take reasonable actions to ensure this outcome. Others believe that a democracy must allow citizens to participate in their own governance and must permit those citizens to decide what kind of information and how much information they need to form their judgments.

It is almost natural to assume that democracy would work best if all participants—officials and voters—knew all of the issues inside out, knew what each party and politician proposed to do on each major issue, and knew where their interests and the broader public interests lay on each issue. Those who believe that knowledge should be the basis for political participation simply contend that good public decisions cannot be made by people who know as little about politics as most surveys show voters know. They believe that the right to vote entails a personal responsibility to prepare oneself adequately for the task.

Others believe that insurmountable moral and political difficulties attach to the idea of sorting legitimate from illegitimate participants in democratic politics based on what they know. They point out that it is aristocratic politics, not democratic politics, that begins from the assumption that only some members of the community have the knowledge and therefore the right to participate in making political decisions for their community. Democratic politics begins from the assumption that all of those impacted by political decisions made in their communities have a right to participate in making those decisions or in selecting those who do make them.

More generally, however, they argue that using ignorance to exclude people from participating in the political life of their community ignores the fact that participation is educational. People who participate in politics learn about the issues that face their communities, the alternative approaches to dealing with these issues that might be available, and the arguments and policy approaches that various political leaders and parties propose.

Moreover, skeptics point out that citizens can get a lot of mileage out of a few relatively general pieces of information. For example, Ronald Reagan's question to voters in 1980, "Are you better off today than you were four years ago" was enough to elicit a "throw the bums out" response from voters who decided the answer was "no." Similarly, the wealthy can reasonably assume that they will usually get a better deal from the Republicans, whereas the poor can usually assume that they will get a better deal from the Democrats. Whether either group needs to study a lot to figure out "how much better" the deal will be is an open question.

What do you think?

- How much do citizens and voters need to know to be legitimate, to be valuable, participants in our democratic society?
- If a particular level of knowledge is required, how would you go about testing for it? Have we been down this road before?

PRO	CON
By definition, good citizens are knowledgeable	Democracy requires broad participation
Making complex choices requires knowledge	At base, many political decisions are simple
If it is required, citizens will become informed	Participation itself is educational

slow, steady, and apparently permanent improvement that represents a fuller realization of the basic principles of our political culture. On the other hand, as was suggested earlier, there are several senses in which public opinion reflects a deep ambivalence on the part of the American people across a wide range of issues. Several examples will suffice to make a number of related points.

Perhaps the classic example of policy ambivalence in American politics has to do with abortion and the circumstances under which it should be available. About 55 percent of Americans believe that human life begins at conception (at the moment that the male sperm fertilizes the female egg), but only about 15 percent of Americans believe that abortion should be illegal in all cases. This suggests that 40 percent of Americans are in the uncomfortable position of believing that ending young human life is sometimes necessary. Extensive polling suggests that about 25 percent of Americans think abortion should always be legal, 50 percent think it should sometimes be legal, and about 20 percent say it should always be illegal.[38] In the end, most Americans want abortions to be available with restrictions. In fact, about 85 percent of Americans want abortion to be available when a woman's life is in danger and more than 75 percent want it available when a woman's health is in danger or a pregnancy results from rape or incest. On the other hand, 88 percent of Americans want doctors to inform women of alternatives to abortion, 78 percent favor a 24-hour waiting period, and 73 percent want parental consent for women under eighteen.

Similarly, political scientists Robert Erikson and Kent Tedin highlighted the results of a survey on attitudes toward pornography. Eighty percent of respondents agreed that "people should have the right to purchase a sexually explicit book, magazine, or movie if they want to." But 65 percent of the same respondents also said that "community authorities should be able to prohibit the selling of magazines or movies they consider to be pornographic." On many issues, including obviously this one, most people have not thought enough about it to have well-formed views. Hence, they can easily give responses that seem to be in conflict with each other to alternative formulations of poll questions.[39]

Moreover, Americans are ambivalent about government in general. Two important pieces of data suggest that public satisfaction with American politics and public life moves up and down in broad waves. The American National Election Studies (ANES) have regularly asked, "How much of the time do you think you can trust the government in Washington to do what is right?" In 1964, 76 percent of those polled answered, "just about always" or "most of the time," whereas only 22 percent answered, "some of the time" or "none of the time." The low point was reached in 1994 when only 21 percent registered trust in the national government and an astounding 77 percent said it could be trusted only some of the time or not at all. From there, trust in government slowly rebounded through the 1990s before soaring 12 points in the wake of 9/11. In 2002, 56 percent responded, "just about always" or "most of the time," while only 44 percent responded, "some of the time" or "none of the time." In 2008, trust was back down to 30 percent and mistrust had risen to 70. A 2011 Gallup poll put trust at 19 percent and mistrust at 81 percent.

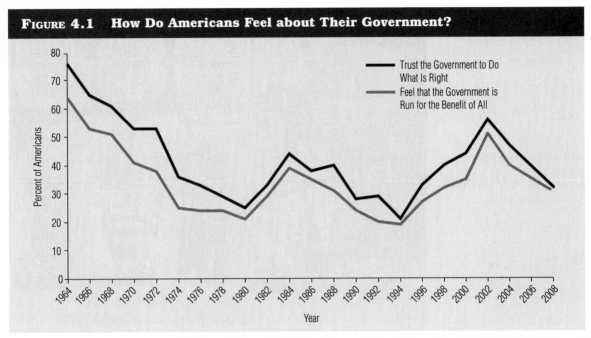

FIGURE 4.1 How Do Americans Feel about Their Government?

Trust the Government to Do What Is Right

Feel that the Government is Run for the Benefit of All

Source: The ANES Guide to Public Opinion and Electoral Behavior at www.electionstudies.org/nesguide/toptable/tab5a_1.htm and electionstudies.org/nesguide/toptable/tab5a_2.htm.

Similarly, in 1964, 64 percent of Americans said that government is run "for the benefit of all," while 29 percent said that government serves "a few big interests." By 1994, only 19 percent responded, "for the benefit of all," whereas fully 76 percent said it served "a few big interests." Other data show that over this same period the public experienced a loss of confidence in business, labor, and other private and public institutions. Again, faith in the fundamental fairness of American national institutions improved through the late 1990s. In the wake of 9/11 and a 16-point bounce, 51 percent of Americans said government worked "for the benefit of all," while 48 percent still said it served "a few big interests." And in 2008, just 29 percent of respondents said "for the benefit of all," while 69 percent said "a few big interests."

Political Ideology and the Coherence of Public Opinion

We have seen that most Americans do not pay close attention to politics. Nonetheless, some Americans know more about politics, some a great deal more than others do, and this small subset of citizens shapes the politics of the country.[40] The people who participate fully in American politics and who make and react to public policy are generally people whose interests, livelihoods, and futures depend upon it in some direct fashion. They are, of course, politicians and senior bureaucrats, but they are also business, media, and education elites for whom understanding the implications of particular political choices is a full-time job. These elites help set the assumptions, terms, and standards by which others understand and interpret the political spectacle. The average citizen, on the other hand, with only a modest education, an hourly wage, and modest savings and investments, is much less likely to be motivated to explore the complexities of interest rates, trade deficits, and whether the dollar is falling against the Euro.

political ideology An organized and coherent set of ideas that forms a perspective on the political world and how it works.

How Many Americans Think in Ideological Terms?   A **political ideology** is an organized and coherent set of ideas that forms a perspective on the political world and how it works. In some nations, the ideological spectrum is quite broad, stretching from traditional monarchists on the right to communists on the left. In the United States, the ideological spectrum is bound by a political culture that highlights democracy and capitalism. Nonetheless, this still leaves room for Americans to differ on how large a role government should play in the nation's social and economic life.

The landmark study of the incidence of ideological thinking in the U.S. entitled "The Nature of Belief Systems in Mass Publics" was conducted by political scientist Philip Converse on data collected during the Eisenhower era, 1956–1960.[41] Converse assumed that ideology in America was best conceived on a left/right, liberal/conservative continuum. He found that only about half of Americans even vaguely understood liberalism and conservatism and only about 10 percent of Americans (remember the "opinion leaders") responded to politics from a consistent liberal or conservative perspective. Fully two-thirds of Americans responded to politics based on how they, their neighbors, and the country seemed to be doing. Almost one-quarter of Americans seemed to ignore politics altogether. Many subsequent studies have left Converse's basic findings intact even though they have refined and elaborated them.[42]

Q5   What does it mean to be liberal or conservative, libertarian or populist, in America today?

Most public discussions of politics among partisans, politicians, and the media still assume that liberalism and conservatism define the political fight in America. When asked, many Americans do place themselves within a liberal/conservative context. In 2008, 32 percent identified as conservative, 22 percent as liberal, but 22 percent of respondents placed themselves in the middle of that spectrum, calling themselves moderates, and another quarter simply refused to locate themselves on the spectrum at all.

This fuzziness in the traditional liberal/conservative ideological spectrum is aggravated by the fact that the widely respected General Social Survey has reported since 1972 that most Americans say they want smaller government and lower taxes *and* they want to spend more, not less, on most government activities. In 2012, although 52 percent of respondents thought their income taxes were too high, most favored increased spending on education (76 percent), the poor (64 percent), alternative energy sources (62 percent), health (61 percent), social security (56 percent), among other programs.[43] This is a classic paradox in American public opinion.

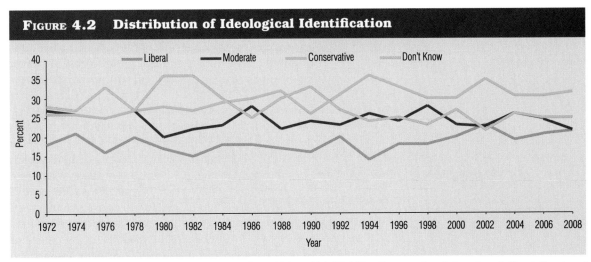

FIGURE 4.2   Distribution of Ideological Identification

Source: ANES website at http://www.electionstudies.org/nesguide/toptable/tab3_1.htm. For ease of analysis, extremely liberal, liberal, and slightly liberal were collapsed to liberal; extremely conservative, conservative, and slightly conservative were collapsed to conservative; don't know and haven't thought about it were collapsed to don't know.

Ideological Types in the United States.   Many scholars now contend that the traditional distinction between liberals and conservatives does not capture the range and variety of political ideology in America. William Maddox and Stuart Lilie were among the first to argue that the ideological spectrum in the United States is best understood along two dimensions rather than one. Americans differ both on the extent of government involvement in the economy and on the extent of government involvement in securing and expanding personal freedoms. Figure 4.2 clearly shows that conservatives have outnumbered liberals for decades.

A recent book by Christopher Ellis and James Stimson, entitled *Ideology In America*, has sought to unwind this paradox by explaining that a majority of Americans are "symbolically" conservative (they self-identify as conservatives) and "operationally" liberal (they support government services and spending). Moreover, they show that while liberals are generally consistent in policy terms, conservatives tend to be less so. Many conservatives are attracted to the conservative label because they read it to mean careful, thoughtful, and responsible. Others read it to reflect a commitment to traditional social and religious values about family and sexuality. Nonetheless, many of these conservatives support an active government working to improve services and solve problems.[44]

In broadest terms, Maddox and Lilie contend that "A person who supports government intervention in the economy and the expansion of personal freedoms is a **liberal**. One who opposes government intervention in the economy but supports government restrictions on personal freedoms is a **conservative**. A person who opposes government intervention both in the economic sector and in the private lives of citizens is a **libertarian**. One who supports

liberal A liberal generally favors government involvement in economic activity and social life to assure equal opportunity and assistance to those in need.

conservative A conservative generally favors small government, low taxes, deregulation, and the use of market incentives where possible.

libertarian A libertarian generally favors minimal government involvement in the social and economic lives of individuals and believes that government should be limited mostly to defense and public safety.

Figure 4.3   A Two-Dimensional View of Political Ideology in America

		Government Intervention in Economic Affairs	
		For	Against
Expansion of Personal Freedoms	For	Liberal	Libertarian
	Against	Populist	Conservative

Source: William S. Maddox and Stuart A. Lilie, *Beyond Liberal and Conservative: Reassessing the Political Spectrum* (Washington, D.C.: Cato Institute, 1984), p. 5.

populist A populist generally favors government involvement in the economy to assure growth and opportunity but opposes government protection of individual liberties that seem to threaten traditional values.

government activity in the economy but opposes the expansion of personal freedoms is a **populist.**"[45]

More broadly, a liberal favors taxes high enough for government to deliver a crucial range of services including education, health care, job training, and other supports to all who need them. Liberals also favor government action to expand and protect individual rights and opportunities including the rights of minorities, women, and gays to enjoy the full range of opportunities and choices offered by American life.

A conservative favors smaller, less expensive, government that protects property, personal security, and social order. Conservatives believe that markets and competition distribute opportunities and rewards to individuals in society far better than government. On the other hand, conservatives believe that government should foster religion, morality, the family, and law as the bases for social order. Hence, conservatives often favor increased spending on the military and police as well as legal regulation of pornography, abortion, affirmative action, and sexual activity.

A libertarian favors the maximum of human freedom and personal choice consonant with social order. Hence, libertarians often agree with conservatives that government should be small and inexpensive, but with liberals that women should be able to choose abortions and gays should be able to choose their marriage partners. Libertarians favor a government limited to national defense, the protection of persons and property, and little more.

A populist favors an activist government, but expects it to defend the traditional social order. Hence, populists tend to agree with liberals on the size of government and the range of its activities and with conservatives on the importance of traditional social and religious mores. Populists usually want government to be active in supporting individual opportunity and advancement, to provide access to education, health care, job training, and unemployment compensation when it is needed. They usually oppose social changes, whether in regard to minorities or women, that run ahead of traditional values and local norms.

Have you thought much about where you fit on the ideological spectrum? Are you a liberal or a conservative, libertarian or populist? There is a relatively brief, 25-item, survey on the website of the Pew Research Center for the People and the Press. The survey is entitled "Beyond Red and Blue" and you can find it at http://typology.people-press.org/typology. Give it a try.

PONDERING REFORM POSSIBILITIES

Given what we know about political socialization, polling, and public opinion, what reforms, if any, would improve the workings of our democracy? Should we, for example, reform our elementary and secondary schools, our colleges and universities for that matter, to better educate students about our political institutions, how they operate, and who runs them and works within them? Or is that dangerously close to indoctrination? What do young people need to know to play a full and productive role in our society and in its politics?

How about immigrants? Immigration, legal and illegal, has been a divisive issue in our recent politics. How easy or difficult should it be to earn citizenship in our nation? What do immigrants need to know about American history, institutions, and politics to fulfill the role of citizen? Does one have to be able to speak English to play an informed and productive role in American life?

Should we be concerned that only about 10 percent of the American public plays an attentive and well-informed role? Should we be grateful, or perhaps at least relieved, that these "opinion leaders" guide their less well-informed citizen brethren, or are they usurping the role that self-governing citizens should play for themselves? In either case, what could we do short of strapping average citizens down in front of CNN for a couple of hours each evening to encourage a better-informed citizenry? These are interesting and important questions, but they remind us that changing what citizens know is a daunting, probably impossible, task.

Chapter Summary

This chapter asked how people come by the political information they have, how much of it they have, and how well it is organized. We found that the process of political socialization is quite effective at transmitting the broad principles of the American political culture—respect for democratic institutions, majority rule, minority rights, diversity, and competition—from one generation to the next. On the other hand, we found that the relationship between broad democratic principles and the opinions that citizens hold on the issues of the day is not at all close. Numerous studies show that most Americans pay so little attention to politics that their opinions are loosely held, often inconsistent, and subject to frequent change.

Political socialization is the process by which the fundamental norms and expectations of the society concerning politics are passed from one generation to the next. Early studies of political socialization were focused on the roles and relative impact of primary groups, secondary groups, and the media on the political information and attitudes acquired by children and adolescents. More recently, studies have focused upon how early socialization responds to an individual's movement through the life cycle and to social, political, and economic change, turmoil, and crisis.

Beyond what Americans think about particular issues, the academic study of public opinion is also interested in how much people know, how well organized that information is, and how it is employed in political life. Most Americans are not very interested in politics and do not follow it closely. As a result, public opinion displays a number of properties that some find worrisome. First, the opinions that many Americans hold on political issues are based on very little information. Second, there is often a gap between the principles that people claim to approve and the choices that they make in their own lives and communities. Third, Americans demonstrate a pervasive ambiguity in their thinking about public issues such as abortion, welfare, and government spending.

Fundamentally, public opinion in the United States is shaped by the top 10 percent of the population who think consistently and systematically about politics and public affairs. These are the political elites, the media and educational elites who watch and study them, and the corporate and social elites whose jobs and incomes are directly affected by politics and public policy. When this elite is united, as it has been in recent decades on equal rights for minorities and women, all of the information and arguments reaching the general population are uniform, and broad public opinion will conform to it. When the elite divides, as it frequently does on issues like affirmative action and size of government, the public will receive mixed signals and will be divided as well.

Key Terms

agents of socialization   96
benchmark poll   103
conservative   115
exit poll   103
focus group   103
liberal   115
libertarian   115
opinion survey   103
political culture   92
political ideology   114

political socialization   92
populist   116
preference poll   103
primary groups   96
probability sampling   102
public opinion   92
push poll   104
secondary groups   96
tracking poll   103

Suggested Readings

Asher, Herbert. *Polling and the Public: What Every Citizen Should Know.* 7th ed. Washington, D.C.: CQ Press, 2007. Asher seeks to make citizens better consumers of polls by describing their design, methodological issues, and interpretation.

Cantril, Albert H. and Susan Davis Cantril. *Reading Mixed Signals: Ambivalence in American Public Opinion about Government.* Baltimore: The Johns Hopkins University Press, 1999. Extensive survey data and analysis suggest that while Americans hold conservative opinions in the abstract, they generally support liberal views in practice.

Dalton, Russell J. *The Good Citizen: How a Younger Generation Is Reshaping American Politics.* Washington, D.C.: CQ Press, 2007. Dalton argues that young Americans are more engaged than they get credit for.

Ellis, Christopher and James A. Stimson. *Ideology in America.* New York: Cambridge University Press, 2012. This book explains why so many Americans call themselves conservatives but still support active government and oppose spending cuts.

Erikson, Robert S. and Kent L. Tedin. *American Public Opinion.* 8th ed. New York: Longman, 2011. The leading general text on American public opinion.

Sunstein, Cass. "Polarization and Cybercascades," from chapter 3 of *Republic 2.0.* Princeton, NJ: Princeton University Press, 2007. Sunstein argues that the Internet has strengths and weaknesses as a forum for sharing political information.

Verba, Sidney. "The Citizen as Respondent: Sample Surveys and American Democracy," *American Political Science Review*, vol. 90, no. 1, March 1995, 1–7. Verba's address as president of the American Political Science Association highlights the importance of good polling to democratic politics.

Web Resources

For practice quizzes, key term flashcards, videos, links, and other study tools, visit the *American Government* website: www.routledge.com/cw/jillson

1. **www.cnn.com/politics/**
   This Time Warner website is operated by CNN and is dedicated to providing news and features concerning politics. It provides up-to-date political information.

2. **www.fair.org**
   Official home page of Fairness and Accuracy in Reporting. This organization is a media watchdog group that reports on the performance of media outlets.

3. **www.electionstudies.org/nesguide/nesguide.htm**
   The major academic survey of voting behavior in U.S. national election is done by the National Election Studies (NES). The site gives online access to tables and graphs that reveal the trends in public opinion.

4. **www.gallup.com**
   The Gallup organization website affords use of an enormous number of polls and analyses, both current and archived.

5. **typology.people-press.org/**
   This is the website for the Pew Research Center for the People and the Press. Take the survey to see where you fit in the political typology.

6. **www.charneyresearch.com/2007July9_CampaignElections_Top10 ways.htm**
   Excellent list, with examples, of ten ways in which polls can be misleading. Reputable pollsters guard against these errors, but the intelligent consumer of polls—you—should be aware of them.

Chapter 5

THE MASS MEDIA AND
THE POLITICAL AGENDA

"There is nothing so fretting and vexatious, nothing so justly TERRIBLE to tyrants, and their tools and abettors, as a FREE PRESS."

SAMUEL ADAMS,
Boston Gazette, March 4, 1768

The Constitution TODAY

EDWARD SNOWDEN AND THE JOURNALISTS WHO HELPED HIM

First Amendment (in part): "Congress shall make no law ... abridging the freedom ... of the press."

A great international drama surrounded Edward Snowden's massive release of National Security Agency (NSA) secrets and his subsequent flight to avoid criminal prosecution in the U.S. While Snowden can look forward to prosecution, conviction, and jail if he returns home, the journalists who helped him make his secrets public are looking forward to honors, fame, and—maybe—Pulitzer prizes for their reporting. In fact, the Pulitzers were duly delivered in April 2014. If releasing national security secrets is criminal, perhaps treasonous, why is publishing these same secrets not only not criminal, but praiseworthy?

Before exploring this question, we need to ask—who is Edward Snowden and what exactly did he do to create such havoc? Edward Snowden was a 29-year-old computer specialist working for a contractor at the NSA. In June 2013, Snowden copied and stored sensitive NSA documents concerning programs that mined data from nine Internet companies, including Microsoft and Google, evesdropped on American citizens without the required warrants, swept up meta-data on millions of foreign communications, listened in on friendly foreign leaders, including Germany's Chancellor Angela Merkel, and released the "black budget" from which sixteen intelligence agencies are funded.

Many argue that U.S. national security has been compromised by Snowden's actions. U.S. opponents and enemies, including Russia, China, Iran, and North Korea, now know more than they did about U.S. surveillance capabilities and how to evade or exploit them. Leaders and publics of allies like Germany, France, and Spain have felt compelled to complain about U.S. data collection and spying, even though their own intelligence agencies often participated in or benefited from the U.S. efforts. The Obama administration has defended its intelligence systems and activities, but has also been forced to undertake a full review to insure that they are legal and likely to produce more benefit than harm. Moreover, two weeks after Snowden fled the U.S., first to Hong Kong and then to Russia, the U.S. Justice Department filed three felony charges, including espionage, against him.

While Snowden faces serious prison time, the journalists who worked with him to make public the NSA data collection and surveillance programs do not. Three journalists were most directly involved: Barton Gellman (of the *Washington Post*) and Glenn Greenwald (of London's *Guardian*), both U.S. citizens, and Sarah Harrison, a British journalist and Wikileaks staffer. Sarah Harrison spent almost four months with Snowden in Russia. When she left Russia, she went to Berlin rather than back home to Great Britain on her lawyers' advice. In a statement posted on the Wikileaks website, Harrison said, "It should be fanciful to suggest that national security journalism . . . should be called terrorism, but that is how the U.K. is choosing to interpret this law."

U.S. journalists, protected by the First Amendment declaration that "Congress shall make no law . . . abridging the freedom of . . . the press," feel less legal jeopardy. In 1973, the U.S. Supreme Court ruled in *New York Times Co. v. United States*, the Pentagon Papers case discussed more fully in Chapter 13, that journalists cannot be prohibited from publishing, even secret materials, unless the likelihood of imminent harm can be proven. Journalists and the government do negotiate over what details might be withheld from a story, or what harm disclosure might cause, but in the end journalists make the decision based on their sense of the "public's right to know."

WHAT DO YOU THINK?

- Which legal system makes most sense—the British system of punishing both leakers and journalists or the U.S. system of punishing leakers and not journalists?
- How does the press's wide freedom on what they report help or harm American democracy?

Focus Questions: from reading to thinking

Q1 How has the role of the media changed over the course of American history?

Q2 Does the increasing concentration of media control in the hands of a few private corporations threaten the accuracy and diversity of information available to citizens?

Q3 How do the media shape the ideas and information that citizens have about their world?

Q4 How do the media affect how elections are conducted and how government works in the United States?

Q5 What role should the media play in a democratic society, and what can we do to get our media to play this role?

THE MASS MEDIA

After the family and maybe schools, the media are among the most powerful shapers of the American political culture and public opinion. But family and schools are personal and local, so one senior scholar of the media and politics has noted that, "for many Americans, the media are their only contact with the world of public affairs."[1] In a sense, this is obvious—we do not all live in Washington D.C., so we cannot have personal knowledge of what Congress and the president are doing. But it also means that everything—everything—we know about what is going on in Washington we learn through the media. Are you comfortable with that thought?

What roles do the modern media play in our democracy? Inevitably, the media play several potentially conflicting roles; they draw attention to some issues and not others, they inform as well as entertain, and they operate as profit-making businesses. Some media analysts worry that entertainment and opinion may squeeze out hard news and that the ideological preferences or profit-making concerns of the major corporations that provide most of our news may taint the coverage. Can we depend upon the media to provide the news and information we need to be responsible democratic citizens?

Many Americans complain that the media do a poor job, either because they are understaffed, too timid, sloppy with the facts, or overtly biased. The media may be guilty on all these counts, but citizens have a lot to answer for as well. Fewer Americans than ever before read newspapers and fewer still read them closely. Circulation for newsmagazines like *Time* and *Newsweek* is down, as is viewership for Sunday newsmaker shows like *Meet the Press* and *Face the Nation*. Young people in particular view these "old media" offerings as staid, boring, and, quite likely, biased.[2]

Many now claim to get their news from the Internet and talk radio. Is this possible? Can a person be well and thoroughly informed based on information gleaned from the Internet and talk radio? Yes and no, but certainly not without careful effort. Talk radio should be viewed as entertainment as much as information, as should cable news, though to a somewhat lesser degree, and the Internet should be scanned broadly and then mined deeply. No one, whether they read newspapers, watch broadcast television or cable news, or surf the net, should be dependent upon one or even a few sources of news and information. Only when you get roughly the same story from a number of sources on a major issue—health care reform, the safety of the banks, or global climate change—can you be confident that you "understand" the issue.

In this chapter we ask how the media, first print and then electronic, developed over the course of American political history. We explore the implications of the fact that the United States is virtually the only advanced industrial country in the world in which the media are both privately owned and lightly regulated. We then ask how the media gather and present news and information to citizens and how citizens receive and use that information to participate in politics and to evaluate policies and politicians. Finally, we ask what responsibility, if any, the media have for the fact that citizen opinion about government and politics is, at best, mixed.

Historical Development of the Media

Q1 How has the role of the media changed over the course of American history?

Through most of human history virtually all news traveled by word of mouth. The merest trickle of news traveled as pages of handwritten text until mass printing came to Europe in the middle of the fifteenth century, when Johannes Gutenberg invented a printing press that featured single, movable, reusable, metal letters. The Gutenberg press increased the speed and flexibility of printing while dramatically reducing its cost.

The first newspaper appeared in Strasbourg in 1609, and London got its first newspaper in 1621 and its first successful daily, the *Daily Courant*, in 1702. Tension between government and the press was almost immediate. English courts early developed the idea of **seditious libel**, which held that public criticism of government officials or policies was illegal, whether the allegations made were true or not, because criticism tended to reduce the prestige and authority of government.

seditious libel English legal principle, influential in America into the twentieth century, that criticism of government officials and policy that reduced the prestige and influence of government was punishable.

America's first newspaper was published in Boston on September 25, 1690. It was, in modern terms, a tabloid. One of the reports in its first edition, that the king of France had "lain with" his son's wife, led the governor and council to close the paper, observing that it contained "doubtful and uncertain Reports." A less entertaining but more important clash between colonial authorities and the press occurred in New York in 1735. High-handed actions by the new royal Governor, William Cosby, spawned resistance among the colonists. Opposition leaders hired a German immigrant, John Peter Zenger, printer of the *New York Weekly Journal*, to carry the public fight against the government. Governor Cosby responded by arresting Zenger for seditious libel. Zenger's lawyer made the argument that truth should be a defense against the charge of seditious libel. While Zenger's jury agreed, public officials from that day to this have looked for ways to limit and control press criticism.

The Partisan Press, 1776–1880

Most eighteenth-century American newspapers were sold by subscription to members of the upper class and were dedicated mostly to foreign and commercial news. American independence and the adoption of a national constitution brought political news to the fore.[3] Even in President Washington's first term, divisions formed between adherents of Alexander Hamilton, who wished to promote commercial development and foreign trade, and Thomas Jefferson, who wished to foster agrarian development of the West. Both Hamilton's Federalists and Jefferson's Republicans awarded government printing contracts to newspapers willing to trumpet the party line and vilify the opposition.

The arrival of Jacksonian democracy and mass parties in the 1820s made partisan newspapers even more common, since candidate positions and party platforms had to be communicated to a far larger audience than before. The **partisan press** made no effort to present the news in an evenhanded way; their role was to inform and energize the party faithful. The **penny press** grew up alongside and eventually mixed with the partisan press. In September 1833, Benjamin Day published the first edition of the *New York Sun*

Culver Pictures

A famous cartoon by Thomas Nast depicts New York City's Tammany Hall Democratic Party leader William "Boss" Tweed. Tweed and his confederates were reputed to have defrauded the city of millions during the 1860s.

partisan press Most papers in the nineteenth century were identified with a political party and served to rally the party faithful rather than to objectively inform the entire public.

penny press Popular newpapers of the early nineteenth century that sold on the street for a penny and oriented their coverage toward the common man.

Newsboys hawking papers in the street were a classic feature of nineteenth-century urban America.

and sold it on the street for a penny. *The Sun*, appealing to a new audience, the common man, supplemented coverage of news with large doses of sensationalism. Crimes, natural disasters, fires, and the unusual—man bites dog, a two-headed goat, a bearded lady—became the staples of the penny press.

Technological developments, including the steam press in the 1830s and the telegraph in the 1840s, changed how the news was gathered, packaged, and distributed. The traditional Gutenberg press produced about 125 newspapers per hour, whereas the steam press by the end of the 1840s produced nearly 20,000 per hour. The telegraph allowed news of distant events to be reported almost as they happened. In 1848, six New York newspapers formed the Associated Press (AP) to coordinate gathering and distribution of the news. Still, until late in the nineteenth century, the media market was highly fragmented, all newspapers were local and there were thousands of them.

Muckraker Journalism, 1880–1920

The late nineteenth century was a time of tremendous social change, and the media, like the rest of society, were forced to respond. First, urbanization brought millions of potential readers within the easy reach of newspapers, allowing owners and editors to derive their income from subscribers and advertisers rather than political parties. Second, industrialization produced national corporations, like John D. Rockefeller's Standard Oil and Andrew Carnegie's Carnegie Steel Company, and raised important new issues about whether government should act to control and regulate them. Third, immigration rose to unprecedented levels, pouring millions of new residents into the nation.

muckraking tradition Progressive journalism of the late nineteenth and early twentieth centuries that dedicated much of its attention to uncovering political and corporate corruption.

The print media responded in three ways. One was to compete for the attention of the working classes by ramping up the sensationalism that had long characterized urban newspapers. Another was the **muckraking tradition** of investigative journalism that fed the middle-class demand for reform of business and politics. Finally, some newspapers tried to educate the new immigrants, to teach them about the opportunities and dangers of life in America.

Two newspapermen, Joseph Pulitzer and William Randolph Hearst, led journalism's response to the evolving society of late nineteenth-century America. Both Pulitzer and Hearst took over struggling papers and built them into national publishing empires by the 1890s. Hearst pursued his causes and interests so noisily that sensationalism threatened to overwhelm reform politics in his newspapers. Joseph Pulitzer eventually lost the head-to-head competition with Hearst, but in retirement he created the famous prizes for excellence in journalism that still bear his name.

The purest strain of muckraking investigative journalism was found in the new monthly magazines of the day. Magazines like *McClure's* and *Collier's* gave free rein to aggressive editors and writers like Lincoln Steffens, Ida Tarbell, and Upton Sinclair, who dedicated whole editions to political and corporate abuses. Stories highlighted how corporate and partisan elites cooperated to benefit themselves at the expense of the public interest. Advances in photography produced pictures that gave these stories new punch.

Although progressive journalism brought political and economic corruption to light, it also had the effect of driving many Americans away from politics in disgust. The understanding of machine politics—the spoils system, cronyism, and electoral fraud—that emerged from the Progressive Era made political activity, even the simple act of voting, seem almost to be a willing participant in corruption.[4]

The Granger Collection, New York

William Randolph Hearst (1863–1951) was one of the nation's leading newspaper publishers from the 1890s through the late 1920s.

THE EVOLUTION OF THE MODERN MEDIA

World War I blunted the muckraking tradition of investigative journalism as it became clear to most Americans that big government and big business would have to work together to win the war in Europe. War and emergency, as we shall see, almost always give government the upper hand over the press, at least for a time.

Moreover, a new appreciation of science, engineering, objectivity, and rationalism pervaded American life in the wake of the war. Adolph S. Ochs, owner and publisher of the *New York Times* from 1896 to 1935, is the figure most identified with the movement toward professionalism and objectivity among newspaper reporters and editors. This new commitment to objectivity highlighted facts as opposed to opinions or interpretations. Professionalism in the news business brought reform and expansion of national news agencies. The Associated Press was reorganized and expanded in 1900, the United Press was founded in 1907, and the International News Service was founded in 1909. The news services offered simple, factual stories so that editors from all over the nation could take them straight off the wire without rewriting them according to a particular political slant.

Increasingly, journalists were expected to consult experts, provide at least two sources for contested or controversial statements, and provide both sides or all relevant sides of every story. The ideal of **objectivity** was best represented by stories organized on an inverted pyramid model. The **inverted pyramid model** placed the most important information at the top of the story and the less important secondary and supportive information thereafter. The "lead"

objectivity The demand for objectivity in journalism required that reports present readers with facts and information rather than opinion and interpretation.

inverted pyramid model The idea that newspaper stories should put the most important facts in the opening paragraph, followed by less important supporting facts and details as the story goes on.

paragraph delivered the story in brief, detailing the "who, what, how, when, and where" of the event.

Critics of objectivity argue that it is not enough and is often misleading. For example, a journalist simply reporting two sides of an issue—Republicans contend X and Democrats contend Y—may mislead readers if the journalist knows that one side or the other has the better argument. The dilemma of modern journalism is how to get beyond simply reporting what disputants say to identify for readers the better argument without triggering criticism for partisan or ideological bias. It is a difficult task and seldom accomplished.

The Rise of the Electronic Media

Radio and television burst onto the media scene in the years between World Wars I and II. On November 2, 1920, the first commercial radio station, KDKA in Pittsburgh, went on the air. By the end of 1922, nearly six hundred radio stations were operating in the United States, and American Telephone & Telegraph (AT&T) had created the first modern network by linking a series of stations along its existing telephone wires. Affiliated stations paid an access fee for the right to broadcast network programs. The first commercial to be carried over the network was a ten-minute "spot" that sold for fifty dollars.

Within a few short years competing radio networks were in place. The National Broadcasting Corporation (NBC) was founded in the early 1920s. Complaints of monopoly were heard as early as 1924, and by 1927, NBC split into two networks: NBC and the American Broadcasting Company (ABC). In 1928, William S. Paley established the Columbia Broadcasting System (CBS), and an increasingly intense competition for domination of the airwaves was underway. By 1935, two-thirds of city dwellers and one-third of rural people had radios in their homes.

Network competition, as well as the presence of independent or unaffiliated stations, made it clear that some regulatory authority was required to keep the signals of competing stations from overriding and interfering with each other. Congress and the industry worked closely together to produce the Radio Act of 1927 and create the Federal Radio Commission (FRC). The FRC was charged to allocate scarce space on the public airwaves in exchange for stations' agreement to act in the "public interest, convenience, or necessity."

The radio networks soon faced a new challenge: television. The radio networks responded by competing to capture and perfect the new technology. By 1941, CBS was broadcasting two fifteen-minute television news shows each day to a small audience in New York City. NBC and ABC also moved into TV. More than one hundred television stations were broadcasting to several million homes by the end of the decade, and the real boom was yet to come.

Television expanded dramatically in the 1950s and became the defining broadcast medium of the twentieth century. By 1952, 62 percent of American homes had TVs and by 1962 fully 90 percent did. Television brought national and world politics as well as entertainment into every American home. In 1952, television covered both the Democratic and Republic National Conventions, and in 1960 all three networks covered the debate between presidential candidates Richard Nixon and John Kennedy. The fact that Kennedy's youth and vigor were so evident in the televised debate is often credited for his narrow victory over Nixon in the November election.

A series of events throughout the 1960s riveted Americans to their television sets. First came the grainy footage of John Kennedy's assassination in Dallas. Then, within days, the alleged assassin, Lee Harvey Oswald, was assassinated on television by Jack Ruby. Moreover, the preeminent social concerns of the 1960s—the civil rights movement and the Vietnam War— were eminently visual, and television made the most of them. No American could ignore what segregation meant to black children trying to enter school between walls of angry whites or the unforgettable image of the little Vietnamese girl, clothes burned completely off by American napalm, fleeing down an open road among other terrified children. Televised images have the power to stop and stun that words alone seldom do.[5]

The Modern Media Explosion

The modern media form an increasingly complex, diffuse, but interactive information production and distribution system. The modern media include more than fourteen hundred daily newspapers, seven thousand weeklies, fifteen thousand journals and magazines, twenty-six hundred book publishers, ten thousand radio stations, and twenty-seven hundred cable and television stations. Many companies like Google, Bing, and iTunes specialize in presenting and managing information on the World Wide Web.

Newspapers and Magazines.   Newspaper and magazine readership has been on the decline for decades. Fewer than 90 million Americans, about 40 percent of the 230 million Americans over the age of 16, read a daily newspaper. Slightly more, about 120 million people, receive a Sunday paper. Twenty percent of these spend less than 30 minutes scanning headlines and checking out the sports scores, market statistics, and weather forecasts before they move on. That leaves only about one quarter of adults who can be said to read a paper in depth each day.

A 2012 study by the Pew Research Center for the People and the Press found that younger Americans spend only half the time older Americans spend following the news. The study also found that those under 30 were disconnected from newspapers and increasingly from television. Just 13 percent of those under 30 said that they read a newspaper yesterday and just 34 percent said they saw any television news. By contrast, two-thirds of adults 50–64 years old and three-quarters of those over 65 watched television news the previous day. Younger Americans, at least those who are consuming news, are as likely to do so on social networking sites (33 percent) as they are on television (34 percent).[6]

Only about half a dozen papers have circulations of more than five hundred thousand, and only three—the *Wall Street Journal* (2.3 million), *USA Today* (1.7 million), and the *New York Times* (1.6 million)—sell more than a million

CJ Gunther for the *New York Times*

Out of Town News, which opened in 1955, closed its famous store in Harvard Yard, victim of a shrinking audience.

copies a day. The *Wall Street Journal*, along with the *New York Times, Los Angeles Times* (606,000), and the *Washington Post* (551,000), are considered authoritative "papers of record" and together dominate the industry.[7]

The leading national news magazine, *Time*, sells 3.4 million copies weekly. *U.S. News & World Report* went digital years ago. In 2010, *Newsweek* joined with *Daily Beast* and in late 2012, the print edition of *Newsweek* was discontinued. In the digital age, people are less willing to wait a week to get the news in a print magazine. The more ideologically edgy opinion magazines of the right and the left have tiny subscription bases. For example, the left-leaning *The Nation* has a circulation of only 165,000, while the right-leaning *National Review* boasts 155,000. Although the number of people reading the nation's top papers and news magazines has declined, they still exercise a disproportionate influence over public opinion because their readers are the opinion elite. Newspapers and news magazines have tried to hold their influence and their readership by dramatically upgrading their presence on the Web.

Broadcast Radio and Television.   Many American listens to radio at some point during the day. All news and politically-oriented talk radio have proliferated in recent years. Conservative domination of talk radio is led by Rush Limbaugh's "ditto-head" audience of 15 million a week. Liberals tend to gravitate toward National Public Radio (NPR), whose "Morning Edition" has an audience of 12 million a week, but Rush enjoys an advantage because NPR's programming is not explicitly ideological.

Fully 98.5 percent of American homes have one or more television sets on for an average of seven hours each day. Americans watch a lot of TV, but they do not watch a lot of news. While 22 million Americans tune in the nightly news on one of the three major networks on an average day, that is less than one-tenth of adult Americans. All three networks focus their attention on the

LET'S COMPARE

Commercial vs. Public Radio and Television

While it is generally true to say that the U.S. drew heavily from the cultures of Europe, the earliest white settlers were mostly middling men—farmers, craftsmen, and shop owners—seeking to escape the religious, political, and economic hierarchies of Europe. From the beginning, American culture has been more focused on individual rights and liberties than the more traditional, hierarchical, and centralized cultures of Europe.

Interestingly, the U.S. preference for small government and a robust private sector is particularly clear in regard to media ownership and regulation. From the initial commercialization of radio in the 1920s and television in the 1930s, the U.S. developed a regime of private ownership subject to modest and declining public regulation. Europe, on the other hand, developed a public radio and television model featuring government ownership and regulation.

Public Media Funding and Market Share in Leading Democracies					
Country	Year of Public Media Founding	Public Funding as % Total Funding	Per Capita Public Funding ($)	Per Capita Total Revenue ($)	Market Share
Australia (ABC)	1932	82.3%	34.01	41.34	19%
Belgium (VRT)	1930	77.8%	74.62	95.92	32%
Canada (CBC)	1936	63.6%	30.42	47.83	9%
Denmark (DR, TV2)	1925	91.0%	130.52	143.42	69%
Finland (YLE)	1926	95.0%	99.00	104.21	41%
France (F2, F3)	1963	74.0%	51.56	69.68	30%
Germany (ARD, ZDF)	1950, 1961	86.2%	131.27	152.23	40%
Ireland (RTE)	1960	45.6%	71.65	157.13	37%
Netherlands (NPO)	1919	68.0%	50.0	73.30	28%
Norway (NRK)	1933	95.0%	133.57	140.62	32%
Sweden (SVT)	1956	93.0%	57.87	62.22	34%
U.K. (BBC)	1922	77.96%	90.70	116.43	38%
U.S. (PBS/NPR)	1970	40.0%	3.75	9.37	1%

Source: Rodney Benson and Matthew Powers, "Public Media and Political Independence," New York: Freepress, February 2011. Revised by the author.

As the table shows, most European nations established their public radio and, a little later, television channels as early as 1919 and all but a few were in place by the 1930s. Germany followed in 1950, Sweden in 1956, Ireland in 1960, and France in 1963. The U.S. established PBS and NPR in 1970. Established late, they have less public funding, at 40 percent of total funding, than any other nation listed in the table. The average share of public funding is over 75 percent. Finally, the U.S. lags dramatically on both per capita public funding and

per capita total funding. U.S. public funding per capita, at $3.75, is just about one-twentieth of the thirteen country average. And, not surprisingly, PBS has by far the smallest market share of any nation in the table.

What do you think?
- Should the U.S. spend more on public radio and television, or should we continue with the private sector model?
- What are the pros and cons of more public involvement in our national media landscape?

TABLE 5.1		The Ratings Race among the Broadcast Networks		
Program Format	**Rank**	**Program**	**Network**	**Viewers**
News Magazines	1	60 Minutes Sunday	CBS	11.1 million
	2	20/20 Friday	ABC	5.2 million
	3	Dateline Sunday	NBC	5.2 million
	4	48 Hours	CBS	5.0 million
	5	Dateline Friday	NBC	4.8 million
Sunday Newsmaker	1	Face the Nation	CBS	3.0 million
	2	Meet the Press	NBC	2.9 million
	3	This Week	ABC	2.6 million
Morning	1	Good Morning America	ABC	5.3 million
	2	Today	NBC	4.6 million
	3	Early Show	CBS	2.8 million
Evening News	1	Nightly News	NBC	8.3 million
	2	World News Tonight	ABC	7.6 million
	3	Evening News	CBS	6.1 million
	1	Late Show	CBS	4.2 million
	2	Nightline	ABC	4.0 million
	3	Tonight Show	NBC	2.6 million

Source: Pew Project for Excellence in Journalism, "The State of the News Media, 2013," see http://www.stateofthemedia.org/2013/index.htm.

major events of the day in Washington, in the nation's major cities, foreign capitals, and the most visible foreign or domestic trouble spot of the moment. TV newsmagazines such as *60 Minutes*, *20/20*, and *Dateline* provide softer and more sensational fare. The Sunday morning interview shows led by *Meet the Press* are rigorously substantive, but their audiences are quite small (see Table 5.1).

These statistics on media exposure highlight the distinction made in the previous chapter between the "attentive public," the 10 percent of Americans that knows a lot about politics, and the "mass public," the 90 percent that pays no more than intermittent attention to newspapers, the evening news, and the Sunday morning talk shows. They also explain why many analysts and commentators are concerned that too many Americans get their news from talk radio or the monologues of Jay Leno, David Letterman, and Conan O'Brien.

The authoritative voice of the mainstream media, represented by Edward R. Murrow during the 1940s and 1950s and by Walter Cronkite during the 1960s and 1970s, has been weakening for decades. Nonetheless, most Americans still get most of their news from these sources and they are the main sources of independent reporting.

Cable, Satellites, and the Web. On June 1, 1980, Ted Turner's Cable News Network (CNN), the first all-news, twenty-four-hour, cable news channel, went on the air. In 1996, Rupert Murdoch's Fox News and MSNBC, a joint venture by the old and new media titans, NBC and Microsoft, moved to challenge CNN with their own twenty-four-hour cable news channels. Almost 85 percent of American homes have cable or satellite TV and many packages offer hundreds of channels. We watch the Moscow evening news on C-SPAN and we regularly see live news reports from London, Beirut, and Kuala Lumpur.

Despite the proliferation of new media channels, the transition from old to new media is not as rapid or complete as one might expect. First, no matter how many channels people have on their cable package, they tend to regularly use only about fifteen. Most viewers have a comfort zone that includes both old media and new. Second, with the partial exception of cable news, the new media do little original reporting. Rather, they offer analysis and commentary on news gathered elsewhere. Nonetheless, some viewers, especially those looking for an overtly political slant on the news, value commentary as a supplement, sometimes a corrective, to the original reporting of the old media.

Cable news audiences grew tremendously in the wake of the terrorist attacks of 9/11 and the subsequent U.S. wars with Afghanistan and Iraq. Fox News' unabashedly supportive stance toward the war in Iraq powered it past the more moderate and journalistically traditional CNN. Fox overtook CNN in January 2002 and is now the most watched cable news channel by far. In 2009, MSNBC, the liberal alternative to Fox, also passed CNN in the prime time news hours. The major networks' response to the rise of cable has been to embrace them. All of the broadcast networks have a growing list of cable holdings and cooperative relationships.

JASON REED / Reuters / Landov

Oprah Winfrey's endorsement of Barack Obama's candidacy for president during the 2008 Democratic Party nomination fight fueled his campaign.

While cable was maturing, so was the Internet and its progeny, the World Wide Web. By the mid-1990s, the Web offered massive amounts of information to tens and then hundreds of millions of people in real time. The Web is the new frontier, the Wild West, of American politics. It is great for organizing, networking, fundraising, and getting a candidate's or party's message out, but its relative anonymity allows for the easy spread of lies, rumors, doctored photos, and the like. The best of them, like the "Obama Girl" ad, and the worst of them, like the charge that Obama was secretly a Muslim, spread virally.[8]

Just around the corner is a far vaster data, audio, and video universe. Communications companies are on the verge of lifting many of the barriers on the amount of information that is available and when and where it can be accessed. HD technology, TiVo, digital video recorders (DVRs), and video on demand (VOD) allow the consumer unprecedented control over content, timing, and location of use. Slightly further down the road, but only slightly further, is the transition from network TV to the Internet, freqently called IPTV, where every website can function as a media channel. Trying not to be left behind, old media have sought to partner-up with new media. In 2012, social media like Facebook, Twitter, and Foursquare were a fully integrated part of national election coverage.

These technological developments raise important questions of quality, inclusion, and privacy.[9] First, with so much information available, it is largely up to the consumer to sort the good from the bad, the trustworthy from the biased or the haphazard. Will most consumers of news be able to tell CNN from the Drudge Report? Second, we must find a balance between broad access and personal privacy. How do we guarantee free speech on the Internet while giving parents the tools they need to protect their children from violent images and pornography? Third, will the market provide access for the poor to systems that may become fundamental to social inclusion, even political participation? Table 5.2 suggests, not very surprisingly, that the answer is probably not, or at least not yet. Fourth, the spread of technology from electronic scanners in supermarket checkout lines, credit cards and banking records, law enforcement files, national security agency meta-data sweeps, and data collecting "cookies" embedded in Internet sites means that increasingly detailed and difficult-to-challenge files on citizens are becoming available. How will they be used and who will use them?

OWNERSHIP AND REGULATION OF THE MEDIA

Through most of human history, individuals learned most of what they knew about their towns or villages directly, through what they saw and heard from others. Today, we still learn a lot of what we know about the world by directly observing or by talking with friends and neighbors, especially when we are

TABLE 5.2 Home Broadband Demographics, 2013	% with Home Broadband
All Americans aged 18+ (n=2,252)	70%
Gender	
Men	71
Women	69
Race/Ethnicity	
White, Non-Hispanic	74
Black, Non-Hispanic	64
Hispanic	53
Age	
18–29	80
30–49	78
50–64	69
65+	43
Education	
No high school diploma	37
High school grad	57
Some college	78
College+	89
Household Income	
Less than $30,000/yr	54
$30,000–$49,999	70
$50,000–$74,999	84
$75,000+	88
Urbanity	
Urban	70
Suburban	73
Rural	62

Source: Pew Research Center's Internet and American Life Project Spring Tracking Survey, April 17–May 19, 2013.

young. But as we age, we learn more and more through the media. This means that our information, our news, is selected and shaped by others before it is presented to us. Who controls the media and what impact does such control have on what we learn about our world?

In most of the world, governments own, finance, and regulate the mass media. Although government control of the media is under review throughout Europe, the United States remains the only advanced industrial country in the world in which the ownership of major media outlets—radio, network and cable TV, satellites, Internet access, and telecommunications systems more generally—is private.

Eighty-eight percent of households making more than $75,000, but only 54 percent of those making less than $30,000, use the Internet.
What do you think?
- What implications does this "digital divide" have for our democracy?
- Should free Internet access be made available by state or local governments, especially in low-income areas?

Q2 Does the increasing concentration of media control in the hands of a few private corporations threaten the accuracy and diversity of information available to citizens?

Communications Act of 1934 Established the Federal Communications Commission (FCC) as the federal agency responsible for regulating the media.

Federal Communications Commission (FCC) Established by the Communications Act of 1934, the FCC is a five-member commission empowered to regulate the media in the public interest.

Media Consolidation and Diffusion

Not only are the major U.S. media outlets privately owned, they are concentrated in the hands of a few large corporations.[10] All three major broadcast TV networks have in recent years been acquired by conglomerates: Comcast bought NBC from General Electric, Capital Cities Communication bought ABC and then was bought by Disney, and Viacom bought CBS. In fact, by 2009, four companies—Viacom, Comcast, Disney, and the News Corporation—dominated access to the broadcast and cable TV audiences. The driving idea behind most media mergers is to link a "carrier" like an Internet, telephone, or cable company with a content provider like a television network, movie studio, video chain, or, more recently, user-generated content provider like YouTube or Pinterest.

At the same time, cable and satellite systems that offer dozens, sometimes hundreds, of TV stations and the Internet that offers literally millions of Web and blog sites, create a radically diverse information environment. Some argue that media consolidation is a pressing danger, while others argue that citizens enjoy access to more information than corporations or governments could ever dream of controlling.[11]

Public Regulation

The desire in a democratic society to regulate the media is eminently understandable. After all, citizens need accurate and plentiful information if they are to play a meaningful public role. However, as the number and type of media outlets have grown in recent years, the rationale for government regulation has shifted and, in the minds of many, at least until recently, almost disappeared.

Congress defined government's role in mediating between the electronic media and the public interest more than seventy years ago. In the **Communications Act of 1934**, Congress created the **Federal Communications Commission (FCC)** and charged it with regulating the communications industry. The need for the FCC's regulatory role was that the airwaves were limited resources that belonged to the public. The mandate to the FCC was to assure that radio and television transmissions were properly assigned by power, frequency, and hours of operation so that they did not interfere with each other. In exchange for the licenses, licensees agreed to act according to the "public interest, convenience, and necessity."

When available technology required that each city have only a few radio and television stations, it also made sense to worry that the major networks might gain monopoly control over information available to the public. Therefore, the FCC limited the number of radio and television stations that an individual or corporation could own and prohibited ownership of more than one TV station in most markets and cross-ownership of newspapers, TV stations, and cable companies in the same city.

Broadcasters challenged these FCC regulations as outmoded and anticompetitive once cable, satellite, and Internet technology led to a vast proliferation of media outlets. The landmark Telecommunications Act of 1996 and subsequent FCC regulatory reforms moved to lift limits on the number of radio and television stations that one company could own and allow the ownership of multiple radio stations in a single city and multiple television stations in the nation's largest cities. Most importantly, they allowed cross-purchases of major media corporations in print, radio and television, telecommunications, and the Internet, spectacularly fueling the process of media consolidation during the past decade. The logic behind loosening these restrictions on media ownership and control was that with so many sources of information and entertainment available, citizens need not worry that someone, or even some small group of individuals or corporations, might control them all.[12]

Nonetheless, Congress continues to worry about media concentration and content. In 2003, Congress reinforced penalties for offensive images and words. As media outlets proliferated, Internet pornography and graphic language and images became more common, initially on cable and the Internet, but increasingly on broadcast radio and television. Many citizens have long wanted a filter on the "public" airwaves to assure that they and their children were not surprised by offensive language and pictures. Howard Stern famously jumped from Clear Channel Communications, the nation's largest broadcast radio group, to Sirius Satellite radio to avoid regulatory constraints.[13] In 2007 Don Imus was fired, at least for a time, for sexually charged racial insults aimed at the national champion Rutgers women's basketball team.

Consider for a moment that commercial television is "free" to the consumer. You do not pay to watch *The Big Bang Theory* or *Criminal Minds*. Rather, network television creates programming that will attract viewers to whom advertisers can attempt to sell their products. In other words, the networks do not sell their TV shows to viewers; they sell viewers to advertisers. Selling viewers to advertisers is big business. Advertisers paid a top price of $4.5 million for a thirty-second spot during the Super Bowl. Moreover, a thirty-second spot on *American Idol*, one of the most popular shows on TV, cost over $360,000 during the 2014 season, over $600,000 for the finale. With that much money on the table, it is unlikely that big media will antagonize the Congress and the FCC into reregulating them.

Old media companies, usually print and broadcast media, are struggling both to hold their shares of readers and viewers and to convince advertisers that they are still the vehicles through which to reach most Americans. New media sources, usually cable, satellite, and Internet sources, are winning larger market shares year by year. Advertisers spent $170 billion in 2013, 40 percent on television (about evenly between network, local, and cable), 25 percent on the Internet, 10 percent on newspapers, 9 percent on radio, and 9 percent on magazines.[14]

If government regulation of the media has been decreasing, the same certainly cannot be said of the media's role in politics and government. The media serve as a principal intermediary and filter between politicians and government and the citizens they must lead.

MEDIA INFLUENCE AND THE POLITICAL AGENDA

Q3 How do the media shape the ideas and information that citizens have about their world?

The traditional media—newspapers, magazines, and television—select from among all the things that happen in our country and the world and present a very thin slice to us as news. The new media—talk radio, wireless communication, and the Web—repackage, interpret, and critique the product of politics and the traditional media. In this section, we see how the media collect the news, what kind of news they find most compelling, and how citizens receive and process the news that is presented to them. We pay particular attention to how the media present elections and government. We find that the media not only present information, but they raise certain issues and not others, and they suggest how the issues that they raise should be understood. As a result, the media play a significant role in shaping public opinion in the United States.[15]

The Media, the Politicians, and Public Opinion

Not only do public officials and journalists need each other, neither can do their jobs without the other. Public officials, and especially politicians, need to communicate with their constituents, and journalists need exciting and up-to-date news and entertainment to attract and hold audiences for their advertisers. The press and politicians are engaged in an exchange relationship: the exchange of information for publicity, from which both benefit. Increasingly, the new media give citizens a chance to say whether they do benefit and to complain and criticize when they do not. Mainstream journalists and politicians are struggling to respond to this rapidly changing environment.

Although politicians and the press need each other, there is a natural tension between them that occasionally bursts into view. Since 1966, the **Freedom of Information Act (FOIA)** has required government to provide citizens including the media with most information in its possession upon written request. Reporters want every scrap of information that is available on the topics of their interest while politicians want to give reporters only those scraps of information that put themselves and their policies in a good light. And some stories, especially those dealing with war, secrecy, scandal, and corruption put politicians and the media at cross purposes. The ongoing political and legal battles swirling around Wikileaks, Snowden, the NSA, and global Internet giants like Google and Microsoft over national security and privacy are an excellent, but just the most recent, example.

Freedom of Information Act (FOIA) Passed in 1966, FOIA requires government agencies to provide citizens including the press with most kinds of information in their possession.

Where Do the Media Get the News?   Our image of where the traditional media get the news comes from a romanticized version of Bob Woodward

Pro & Con

Is the Media Biased?

The American media are frequently condemned both as unduly liberal and as hopelessly conservative. How can this be? Some critics cite surveys of print and electronic journalists that consistently show that journalists identify themselves as liberals in higher proportions than do American citizens in general and that they tend to vote for Democratic candidates for president in much higher proportions than do Americans in general. Others argue that editors, publishers, and owners—those who manage, control, and own the media—tend to be more conservative than Americans in general. Moreover, newspapers have traditionally endorsed candidates for office and have usually favored Republicans.

This ongoing battle over bias in the media has new champions: two books. Tim Grosecolse's *Left Turn: How Liberal Media Bias Distorts the American Mind* (2012) used advanced statistical techniques to demonstrate that most U.S. media outlets lean left and that this affects what voters think and how they act. John Nichols and Robert W. McChesney in *Dollarocracy: How the Money and Media Election Complex Is Destroying America* (2013) argue that aggressive wealth, mostly right leaning and conservative, works through the media to dominate our electoral and democratic processes.

The values of journalists are always present, even when they try to manage and control them, and during elections the power of money is evident. The structure of the news media also plays a substantial role in how they work.

Two major factors help to explain why traditional news organizations gather and disseminate the news in cautious and predictable ways. First, news organizations are or are part of large, bureaucratic, for-profit corporations that make money by selling space or time to advertisers. Network executives know that most viewers and the large corporate advertisers who wish to sell to them do not wish to be disturbed or shocked by what they receive from the media. Network executives who thought they were losing viewers and the advertising dollars that pursue them because of the content of their news programs would make immediate changes.

Second, both the print and electronic media must efficiently organize and assign work to their reporters, editors, and production people. This requires both deadlines and beats. Deadlines are required because a morning paper must be on doorsteps by 6 a.m. and the evening news must go on precisely at its scheduled time. Therefore, reporters must submit their copy and pictures by set times if the whole process of producing the paper or the newscast is to work.

Moreover, reporters are assigned to news beats that usually revolve around institutions like the White House, the State Department, the county court house or police station where news is expected to occur on a regular basis. Having committed these resources, editors and producers have little choice but to report what happened on the main beats each day. As a result, most news reporting shows a strong bias toward formal and prescheduled events occurring on the beaten track.

The new media of talk radio, cable, and Internet with their smaller, but more intense, 24 × 7 audiences are edgier, more personality-driven, and more overtly ideological. But they are "mom and pop" operations when compared with the hundreds, even thousands, of people employed by traditional media such as the *New York Times*, *Time Magazine*, and the *Associated Press*. For example, drudgereport.com, a news aggregation site that drives more traffic than the Huffington Post, Fox News, and CNN, has a total of four paid employees.

PRO	CON
Most reporters admit to voting Democrat	The media are businesses that focus on the bottom line
Credible studies have purported to find bias	No business want to offend customers
Some media outlets clearly proclaim their biases	Journalists have a professional commitment to objectivity

Getty Images

Top leaders like President Obama, Vice President Biden, and Senate Majority Leader Harry Reid (D-NV) are always in the media spotlight. Political leaders need the media to get their message out and the media need access to political leaders if they are to have anything to report.

and Carl Bernstein, the young metro desk reporters at the *Washington Post* who uncovered the Watergate scandal. Sometimes the relationship between politics and the media works this way, but not usually. In general, reporters do not spend their days searching for big news stories, and they do not do extensive background research in preparation for writing their stories. Rather, reporters depend heavily on routine and official channels of information including press conferences, formal briefings, press releases, background and for-the-record interviews, and leaks.

Political scientist Gadi Wolfsfeld's recent book, *Making Sense of Media and Politics*, explains that politicians have the advantage over the media under normal circumstances. Wolfsfeld writes that, "Political power can usually be translated into power over the news media. One of the most enduring lessons in the field of political communication is that those who have political power not only find it much easier to get political coverage, but also are in a much better position to get their messages across."[16] At other times and for various reasons, politicians lose control of the flow of information or the narrative of a story and then the advantage shifts to the media.

The tension between administration officials and the press is particularly evident in time of war. The administration of the first President Bush sought to control information during the first Gulf War by limiting journalists to official briefings. Media complaints led the Pentagon under the second President Bush to improve wartime access during the 2003 Iraq War by "embedding" reporters with military units in the field. While embedded reporters provided unprecedented real-time access during the war, some were concerned that the dependence of reporters on the military created a bond that produced unquestioningly positive coverage during the sprint to Baghdad.

After the end of major combat operations, administration officials thought the media focused too much on continuing resistance and not enough on rebuilt schools, bridges, and electrical grids. At home, President Bush sought to work around the national press corps by giving exclusive interviews to friendlier local TV correspondents. The President explained, saying "I'm mindful of the filter through which some news travels, and sometimes you have to go over the heads of the filter and speak directly to the people."[17]

As tensions over Iraq policy grew during 2005 and 2006, the Bush administration struggled to control the news cycle and the press resisted. In mid-2006, the mainstream press—the *New York Times, Washington Post, Wall Street Journal,* and *Los Angeles Times*—reported on a number of sensitive administration programs including secret CIA prisons, clandestine wiretapping of overseas calls, and tracking of international financial transactions.

As attention shifted from Iraq to Afghanistan during the Obama administration, embarrassing revelations of Koran burnings and abuse of dead Taliban fighters produced new tension between the administration, the U.S. military, and the press. In early 2012, the *Los Angeles Times* received photographs of U.S. troops posing with body parts of dead Afghan insurgents. The Pentagon asked the newspaper not to print the photos because they might incite retaliatory violence and further endanger American troops. The *Times* published two of the photos, arguing their readers' right to know, and the military was outraged. Clearly, in wartime, the government's penchant for secrecy and its understandable interest in not being embarrassed conflict with the press's right to inquire, know, and publish conflict. The press usually wins this conflict.

Where Does the Public Get Its News?   Although both public officials and the media have a profound interest in getting and holding the public's attention, the public tends to ignore them. For most people, politics and public affairs play an occasional and usually secondary role in their lives. Their attention is normally focused on their jobs and families, and during their free time they turn not to politics but to leisure, sports, and entertainment. They may catch snatches of news and pieces of information throughout the day if the news is on while they dress, as they glance over the morning paper, listen to the car radio on the way home from work, or hear parts of the evening news over conversation at dinner. Most Americans get their news from more than one source, but asked by Gallup for their main source of news—55 percent said they look to TV, but 21 percent said the Internet, 9 percent said newspapers, 16 percent the radio, and 2 percent magazines.[18]

Struggling Toward Democracy

Some scholars and media analysts have argued that new media—the Internet, the web—are powerfully democratic, allowing all of us to express our ideas and opinions.

What do you think?

- What does it mean for the democratic potential of "new media" that they originate little news, instead circulating or linking to news created by the "old media" stalwarts of print and broadcast?
- What other value, then, does new media have in a democracy?

As we shall see later in the chapter, an appreciable number of viewers, many of them young, prefer the pseudonews of Jon Stewart to the "real" news of Diane Sawyer. What media do you pay particular attention to and what are you looking for from those particular media sources?

Moreover, the way that the media gather and report the news makes it difficult for citizens to see patterns and relationships. The media are focused on the events of the day: who said what about the latest act of random violence, the most recent unemployment figures, or the latest campaign poll or candidate promise. Citizens, with most of their attention directed elsewhere, may have heard about the latest isolated event or statement, but will not have the time, inclination, or related information to place it within an appropriate and meaningful context. Only citizens who already have high levels of information on a particular topic can readily make sense of the next piece of information that they receive on that topic. To the uninformed citizen, a new piece of information on a complex topic makes no sense and is likely to be ignored.

Because the number of citizens who get most of their news from the Internet is growing steadily, the Internet played a larger role in the 2012 presidential contest than in any previous election. Internet sites like Meetup.com and MoveOn.org changed the way national campaigns identify supporters, recruit volunteers, raise funds, and get their messages out. As candidates prepared for 2012, they sharply increased their use of e-mail, interactive websites, candidate and party blogs, smarter cell phones and other mobile devices, and social media to organize and energize potential supporters.

Did the Internet Democratize Politics and the News?   The promise of the Internet has been and remains its breadth and openness. Like space, the Internet is limitless; there is room for everyone and millions have found there a forum for their views. The early assumption was that the public sphere would be expanded, more voices would be heard, and a wider range of ideas and opinions would thus be presented—this would energize and enrich our democracy. Evidence suggests that this promise has yet to be realized. Much of this was predictable because it springs from our own limitations—limitations of time, attention, and patience. Even more ominously, the web itself seems to spawn information monopolies.

First, most news on the web originates with "old media" sources like the AP, Reuters, Bloomberg, the BBC, the *New York Times, Wall Street Journal, Washington Post*, or the like. These original news reports are then reposted or linked on other sites that might comment on them but do little or no original reporting of their own. Gadi Wolfsfeld writes that only 3.5 percent of news stories originated on the web and then flowed into the traditional media. The other 96.5 percent flowed the other way, from the old media to the web.[19]

Second, web traffic tends to concentrate on a few sites rather than diffuse across the greater number of sites that the web seemingly permits. Top newspapers like the *Wall Street Journal* and the *New York Times* get a share of the web traffic that is two and one-half times greater than their share of print readership. Smaller papers get a smaller share of the web traffic than of print readership.[20] Most people who get news online focus on just a few sites and those tend to be the most prominent. A survey by the Pew Research Center's Project for Excellence in Journalism reported that while only 21 percent of respondents used just one online news source, 57 percent used only two to five sources.[21]

Third, traffic on political blogs is just as concentrated as online news sites. More than one million people have a political blog, but only a small portion of these blogs attract appreciable traffic. Anyone can start a political blog and say whatever they want on it, but if no one beyond family and friends see it, the gain to our democracy is negligible. Only a few dozen blogs, led by Daily Kos, Fire Dog Lake, and Talking Points Memo on the left and RedState, Powerline, and InstaPundit on the right draw readers in the thousands and tens of thousands. Interestingly, however, unlike in talk radio, liberal blogs outdraw conservative blogs by two to one.[22]

Finally, John Nichols and Robert W. McChesney, a Washington journalist and an academic, note that, "In grand irony, the Internet has arguably become the greatest generator of monopoly power in the history of economics. Everywhere enormous firms all ranking among the most valuable in the world—Google, Apple, Amazon, and Microsoft, with eBay and Facebook not far behind—have monopolistic domination of huge digital markets . . ."[23] These companies facilitate some of our most important activities, but we must remember that they are, first and last, business enterprises and they know a very great deal about each one of us.

While the Internet has expanded the consumption of news and the range of news sources, it has not done so nearly as much as its boosters hoped. Most citizens have a limited interest in politics and even more limited time to spend on it. The time they do spend is focused on familiar sites. A relatively few people, however, with more education, income, interest and time, have a plethora of hard news, analysis, and opinion available to their eyeballs.

The Media and the Electoral Process

Elections, like war, put the cooperative tension that exists between public officials and the press under heavy pressure. Candidates want as much favorable publicity as they can get and no unfavorable publicity, whereas the media want to cover the campaign in ways that make it seem dramatic and exciting. Candidates need to bring their cases before the public. The press, on the other hand, decides which aspects of the campaign constitute news and which do not.[24] Almost invariably, they highlight the simple but exciting "horse race" (who's winning and who's losing) "strategy" (why did they say that or go there), and "character" (who's flawed and how) stories to the virtual exclusion of the more complicated and inherently ambiguous issues of policy. Increasingly, new actors with motivations all their own, like Swift Boat Veterans for Truth in 2004, STOPHillary.com in 2008, and the Super PACs of 2012, are having profound impacts.

Q4 How do the media affect how elections are conducted and how government works in the United States?

Money and Media Access.   In politics, as in most other arenas of American life, the price of admission is a certain amount of money. The higher the political office, the higher the price of admission. Much of the cost of modern elections goes to pay media outlets for candidate-controlled access to their audiences, that is, for paid political advertisements directed at potential voters. Campaigns must also pay media professionals and campaign consultants to develop and test themes, strategies, target audiences, and conduct polls, surveys, and focus groups to take a candidate's message to the media for transmission to voters. Approximately 40 percent of the total campaign expenses of presidential campaigns, one-third of U.S. Senate campaigns and one-fourth of the total expenses of U.S. House campaigns goes for radio and television advertising.[25]

Candidates for the U.S. Senate and House and their supporters raised and spent more than $2 billion. Incumbents of both parties were forced to raise and spend unprecedented amounts of money to hold their seats and many faced tidal waves of "outside money," mostly raised by ideological groups and very wealthy individuals. Most "outside money" went to buy television and other media time for hard hitting, usually very negative, commercials. In the most expensive Senate race of the 2014 cycle, North Carolina Democrat Kay Hagan lost to North Carolina House Speaker Thom Tillis by two points. Of the $118 million spent in this race, $80 million came from outside the campaigns themselves. Similarly, in the race for California's 7th U.S. House district, Democrat incumbent Ami Bera and Republican challenger Doug Ose each raised about $5 million, while $13.5 million was spent on the race by

As this cartoon suggests, journalists are often criticized for reporting trivial campaign slogans, conflicts, and horserace polls while avoiding the hard work of analyzing candidate records and issue positions. In the last panel of the cartoon, a voter is shocked to have found a new and useful piece of information.

outside groups. Bera held his seat by 1,400 votes out of 183,000 cast. With so much outside money pouring into so many races, candidates often feel they have lost control of their own races.

Horse-Race Political Coverage. The print and electronic media give more coverage to campaigns as games and less coverage to the political experience and policy positions of candidates than they used to. Game stories deal with winning and losing, campaign strategy and tactics, appearances and hoopla, whereas policy stories deal with issues, a candidate's strengths and weaknesses, past record, and potential for future performance. The favorite game analogy, the campaign as a horse race, highlights the competitive aspects of the campaign such as who raised the most money, who is ahead in polls, and who is likely to win. Moreover, the game stories tend to overwhelm the policy stories when campaign themes and policy statements are interpreted not according to their merits but according to "how they play" with this or that element of the electorate.

An important study by the Pew Research Center's Project for Excellence in Journalism analyzed stories that appeared throughout the campaign in four major newspapers, seven network news programs, two cable news programs, and five blogs. During the first half of 2012, nearly two-thirds of all campaign stories dealt with the "horse race" and the "inside baseball" of campaign strategy and tactics. Twelve percent of stories dealt with the candidates personal lives, and just 11 percent and 6 percent dealt with their policy positions and public records respectively.[26]

The Character Issue. The attraction of the press to framing political campaigns in game terms as opposed to policy terms has contributed to a second major development in campaign coverage. In recent decades, the press has been much more willing, even eager, to deal with the private lives and personal failings of candidates. Certainly through the presidency of John Kennedy, reporters generally tried to draw a line between a candidate's public political performance and his private life, unless personal issues such as unusually heavy drinking seemed directly to threaten performance in office.

More recently, the sex lives of candidates, their abuse of alcohol and drugs, their candor, and many similar issues have been the subjects of what political scientist Larry Sabato has termed the media "feeding frenzy."[27] The barrier between the public and the private has been broken down as part of the more general shift from party-centered to candidate-centered campaigns. Personal appeal and promises bring a personal scrutiny that party politicians rarely faced even thirty years ago. On the Republican side in 2012, Newt Gingrich's multiple marriages, infidelity, and tendency toward bombast was a topic of frequent, if not always serious, conversation.

Below the level of presidential campaigns, personal attacks are both more common and direct. Candidates and their handlers know that a successful attack on an opponent's character—honesty, faithfulness, candor—could cripple, even end, their campaign. Hence, candidates and their handlers know that they have to hit back quick and hard if they are attacked. The common wisdom of modern campaigns is that no charge should go unanswered. Not surprisingly, the cut and thrust of modern campaigns makes it hard for the survivors to reach out to the other side when the campaign is over and it is time to govern.[28]

The Media and Defining Successful Governance

How then do the media, and especially the electronic media, affect how citizens understand, think about, and evaluate their government and its officials? The broad answer to this question was famously delivered by Bernard Cohen in 1963 and has been affirmed many times since: "The press . . . may not be successful much of the time in telling people what to think, but it is stunningly successful in telling its readers what to think about."[29]

The media have at least four broad effects on what and how the public thinks about government, politics, and politicians. The first is an **educational effect** as the public learns from and is informed by what it hears and sees in the media. The second is an **agenda-setting effect** as the public's attention is directed toward issues to which the media give special or disproportionate attention. The third is a **framing effect** as the way that the media present the issue suggests who or what should be held responsible for the current state of affairs and for addressing it if need be. The fourth is a **persuasion effect** whereby the media can occasionally change the substance of what citizens believe or think they know.

The leading contemporary analysts of the effect of television news on what Americans know about politics and of how that knowledge is structured are political scientists Shanto Iyengar and Donald Kinder. Iyengar and Kinder summarized their path-breaking book, *News That Matters: Television and Public Opinion*, first published in 1987 and updated in 2010, by writing, "the power of television news . . . appears to rest not on persuasion but on commanding the public's attention (agenda-setting) and defining criteria underlying the public's judgment (priming)."[30]

Iyengar and Kinder and others have shown that the more attention television news gives to a particular issue, whether that issue is crime, economic performance, or war, the higher that issue rises in the public's ranking of important issues facing the nation. Even more intriguingly, Iyengar and Kinder distinguish two general ways in which television news reports present or frame an issue. Framing can be predominantly episodic or thematic. A television news report on poverty that is framed episodically might involve pictures of or interviews with one or several poor people describing the difficulties of their situation. A report framed thematically might involve an analyst or official explaining the extent of poverty in the country and whether it is increasing or decreasing.

Episodic framing leads to placing responsibility for poverty on the individual poor person, whereas thematic framing leads to placing responsibility on society and government. Iyengar notes that "since television news is heavily episodic, its effect is generally to induce attributions of responsibility to individual victims or perpetrators rather than to broad social forces."[31] Episodic framing discourages the public from seeing the connections between issues

educational effect The public learns from wh at it sees discussed in the media and cannot learn, obviously, about issues that are not taken up by the media.

agenda-setting effect The extent to which the amount of media coverage of an issue affects the public's attention to and interest in that issue.

framing effect The way an issue is framed or presented in the media, either episodically or thematically, suggests to the public where the praise or blame should be laid.

persuasion effect The way an issue is presented by the media can sometimes change the substance of what people think about the issue.

and from attributing responsibility for the patterns to elected officials and political institutions.

Political operatives, of course, know all of this and so struggle mightily to shape the media narrative to the benefit of their clients. Politicians have long had media advisers on their campaign staffs, but over the past several decades media advisers have become central to the daily political struggle. Frank Luntz, a Republican media specialist, has been at this longer and more effectively than anyone else. In 1994, Luntz helped Republicans, led by Newt Gingrich, develop their Contract With America and learn to talk about issues in new ways. The inheritance tax became the death tax, tax cuts became tax relief, and drilling for oil became exploring for energy. Luntz's 2006 book, *Words That Work: It's Not What You Say, It's What People Hear*, is well worth a read. Democrats have their own message gurus, led by George Lakoff, author of *Moral Politics: How Liberals and Conservatives Think*, but the Republicans got there first and have generally been more effective in framing the national political debate—socialized medicine anyone? How about death panels?

The President: Passing His Program. Television has added immensely to the prominence of the president and to his apparent centrality to consideration and resolution of most major issues. Television requires pictures to accompany the words in which a story is told, and those pictures must be of something. Among the many institutions and actors who might be involved in resolving a major issue, the president is likely to be among the most important. His position and role as the leading figure in the government are well understood and, because he is a single individual, he is easily pictured.

Watch the evening news broadcast on any of the major networks. Note how thoroughly the presentation is nation-centered and president-centered. On almost any evening, there will be several stories about national issues and the government policies and programs in place or under consideration to address them. Most of these stories will describe the president's position in relation to the issues and show film of him doing something relative to the issues— perhaps visiting an area damaged by storms or flooding, proposing a new program, or signing a bill into law in the White House Rose Garden.

The visibility and centrality of the president in contemporary American politics create a double-edged sword that can as easily wound the president as it can his opponents. A president riding a crest of popularity is likely both to be able to sweep his opponents before him and to keep media attention focused on his political agenda. But in American politics, momentum inevitably slows, opponents stall and block, and the losses pile up. When this occurs, popularity declines, opponents are emboldened, and press attention shifts to issues on which the president is not well positioned and on which he cannot help but appear awkward and indecisive. These no-win issues include war, abortion, immigration, deficits, and many others.

Moreover, Iyengar and Kinder have demonstrated that the more television coverage interprets situations or events as resulting from the president's actions, the more important those situations or events will become in the viewers' evaluation of the president. When television coverage minimizes the president's connection to an issue, citizens tend not to use the issue in developing their sense of how the president is doing.

Presidents, of course, know this and they know that they do not control it. At the depth of the economic recession of the early 1980s, President Reagan complained that, "you can't turn on the evening news without seeing that they're going to interview someone else who has lost his job. Is it news that some fellow out in South Succotash someplace has just been laid off and that he should be interviewed nationwide."[32]

Recent scholarship contends that the relationship between the president and the press has become increasingly distant and hostile. Negative campaign ads and campaign coverage have increased from 20 to 25 percent in the 1960s and 1970s to about 60 percent in 2008. The Pew Research Center's Project for Excellence in Journalism reported that in 2008, while Barack Obama's coverage was slightly more positive than negative, John McCain's coverage was four times more negative than positive.[33] In 2012, both Obama and Romney had more negative than positive stories, though Obama's coverage was slightly less negative than Romney's.

Congress: Gridlock and Localism.   Coverage of Congress is as diffused as that of the president is focused. Congress is an institution built around public resolution of partisan disagreement. The partisan disagreement can go on for months or years, while the resolution is usually grudging and is always brief because the institution moves on to the next subject of partisan disagreement. And all of this is done on live TV. C-SPAN, a satellite cable TV company, dedicates round-the-clock coverage to the debates of Congress, committee hearings, interviews with members, outside experts, and other individuals and groups interested in business before Congress.

Congress is made up of 535 members, each elected largely on the basis of his or her own efforts to represent constituents and districts with radically differing interests. Congress is a difficult institution to lead, not because it has no leaders, but because it has so many. Congress has party leaders, committee and subcommittee leaders, and the leaders of special caucuses, regional groups, liberal and conservative study groups, and many more. Additionally, Congress is hard to lead because nearly half the members, those of the minority party, feel a special obligation to oppose the leaders and disrupt the activities, programs, and projects of the majority party. As a result, Congress moves slowly, by fits and starts, and always seems to be somewhat out of control.

How do the media cover Congress, and what effect does this pattern of coverage have on how the public thinks and feels about Congress? As with elections and politics more generally, coverage of Congress is most often done in a game frame—who's winning and who's losing—rather than in a policy frame where the questions would be what is the issue and what do people propose to do about it? The public generally assumes that the nation's problems go unresolved while the Congress bickers. Hence, the average Gallup poll approval rating of Congress over the past four decades has been a mediocre 34 percent. In recent years, it has bumped along at about 20 percent and in early 2012 reached and settled in at an all-time low of about 9 percent.[34]

The Federal Courts: Ideological Imbalance.   The media have a difficult time covering the courts because the judicial branch is much less open than the executive and legislative branches and they do their work in a technical, legal language with which most reporters and citizens are unfamiliar. Most reporters respond by placing the courts' activities into their standard horse race and conflict frames. Coverage of the federal courts, particularly of the Supreme Court, falls along two dimensions. The first asks how the next important decision—whether that decision deals with abortion, affirmative action, gun control, or some similarly divisive issue—will be received by relevant interest groups and their sponsors in Congress and the administration. The second asks how the racial, ethnic, gender, religious, and/or ideological composition of the federal courts, and of the Supreme Court in particular, is changing. One frequently sees reports on how the pattern of appointments to the federal courts by the incumbent president compares with that of his predecessors. Is the incumbent president appointing more minorities or women than his predecessor? Do the courts include more or fewer liberals or conservatives? And when an opening occurs on the Supreme Court, the inevitable question is: will the appointment tip the balance in regard to abortion rights, gun control, or some other hot-button issue?

MEDIA RESPONSIBILITY IN AMERICAN POLITICS

In a mass society such as ours it is difficult for political leaders and citizens to communicate directly with each other. Ideally, the media and public officials would cooperate to ensure accurate reporting on the issues demanding political decisions, on the options available, and the actual effects, good and bad, of existing policies.[35] Realistically, politicians struggle mightily to ensure that only good news is reported and that the blame for any bad news does not attach to them. The media, on the other hand, gravitate strongly toward stories about conflict, scandal, corruption, and gaffe. Clearly, both public officials and the media bear responsibility for the kinds of news and information reported and upon which citizens must base their judgments.

Q5 What role should the media play in a democratic society, and what can we do to get our media to play this role?

Entertainment versus Information

Many observers worry that "hard" news is being displaced by a softer, breezier, more personalized combination of news and entertainment that they refer to as "infotainment." Even newspapers now devote more space than they once did to special features and sections such as Arts and Entertainment, Home

Sales and Improvement, Health and Beauty, and Personal Investment. In fact, several major newspapers have launched brief, breezy, tabloid style papers "with big, bright photographs and snappy articles that focused heavily on subjects like entertainment, all wrapped in a package so thin it could be scanned in the time it took to ride an elevator."[36]

Even more radical changes have affected the television news business in the past decade or so. Broadcast deregulation; the purchases of the major networks by conglomerates; the rise of competition from cable, satellites, and the Internet; and the constant struggles for audience share have led to an orientation that is less serious and more entertaining. The success of the Fox News Channel has led some analysts to bemoan the "Fox Effect" and the moves of competitors like MSNBC to copy the fast-paced, blunt, and opinionated Fox style. Others worry that too many Americans get some, if not all, of their news from Leno, Letterman, Comedy Central's Jon Stewart and Stephen Colbert, and the animators at JibJab.

WHAT DO YOU THINK?

- Do the media have a responsibility in a democracy to provide more substantive coverage of our political institutions?
- Or do you think there is plenty of good political information out there for those willing to look for it?

President Obama and Jimmy Fallon slow jam the news that the president is urging Congress to act so that the interest rate of Stafford student loans do not rise. Presidents try every way they can think of to get their message out.

Why Americans Distrust Politics

Americans distrust politics because so much of what they see of it seems more show than substance. First, issues that need to be resolved politically are complex, but politicians and the press often treat them simplistically. For example, the question of whether poverty springs from individual deficiencies of character and effort or from social pathologies such as racism and selfishness is in some sense irresolvable. The answer is certainly both. Yet, politics treats the origin of poverty as either individual or social pathology, with each side forcing the other to an extreme position because seeing this and similar problems as individual means lower taxes and less government, whereas seeing social responsibility means higher taxes and bigger government. Citizens know that both the problem and its causes are complex, even though politicians talk about them in simple partisan terms.

Second, the media aggravate public skepticism by presenting politicians in unrealistically negative terms. An extensive study by political scientist Thomas Patterson of news coverage of politicians showed that in the 1960s, only about one-third of the media's stories about political leaders were negative. In the 1980s, and 1990s, fully 60 percent were negative.[37] Patterson is concerned that the unremitting negativity of the media toward politics and politicians threatens to damage the media's credibility as well as the credibility of the politicians upon whom they report.

Finally, citizens and voters are often concerned that their candidate is being treated unfairly by the press. Partisans, of course, see criticism of their candidate as unfair and criticisms of the opposition as not just fair, but as late in coming and less than deserved. Late in the 2008 campaign, the respected Project for Excellence in Journalism released a study showing that 60 percent of McCain's coverage had been negative but just 30 percent of Obama's had been.[38] Was Obama the better candidate? Was McCain weighed down by Bush fatigue? Or were the media playing favorites? In 2012, Republicans scoffed at media reports that showed Obama leading in most swing states until, and even after, election night results bore them out. Distrust of the media is now baked into conservative politics.

MEDIA REFORM OR PERSONAL RESPONSIBILITY

When citizens are not as well informed as we think they should be, or the media do not perform the educational role that we think they should, it is natural to wonder whether thoughtful reforms might improve things. In the previous chapter, we found that concerns over inadequate political socialization and lack of political knowledge quickly ran into issues of the personal freedom to know and not know what one chooses and the dangers of political indoctrination and propaganda.

Similarly, in this chapter, we find that concerns about the role of the media in our culture and politics quickly run into concerns about freedom of speech and press. Radio and television have been subject to regulation because they use the public airwaves. Print, cable, satellite, and the Internet are subject to much less regulation, though Congress has attempted to address issues of indecent language and images, especially where children might be exposed to them.

The trade-off, of course, is between freedom of thought and expression and the right of people, including parents and their children, to be free from unwanted and unpleasant content. Our courts have generally held that the Constitution privileges free expression and that parents must take care, though V-chips and other means of blocking undesirable content, to protect their children.

WHAT DO YOU THINK?

- Should the government do more to limit indecency in the public square, or is it up to individual citizens to change the channel if they hear or see something they do not like?
- If the government should do more, can you think of reforms that would help and that could also pass constitutional muster?

Chapter Summary

There are two general models of the relationship between the media and politics. One sees the media playing a "hegemonic" role. In this model, the mainstream media's control over information is said to be used to support the existing institutions and power relationships in society. The media are seen as the mouthpieces for the dominant corporate, class, and political institutions of the society and their individualist, free-market, competitive ideologies. The other model might be referred to as the "demonic" model. In this model, the increasingly negative coverage of politics and society by the new media undercuts and reduces support among citizens for the fundamental efficiency and fairness of American political institutions and the corporate, economic, and social institutions that connect to them.

Yet, there is a real sense, especially from the politician's perspective, in which the "demonic" model has always seemed too prevalent. Both the partisan press of the nineteenth century and the muckrakers of the late nineteenth and early twentieth centuries gave no quarter to politicians with whom they differed. The same is true of today's media in general and of certain elements of the media, like the tabloids, talk radio, and the blogosphere, in particular. Three things, however, have changed markedly. First is the scale upon which the political dialogue now occurs and the speed at which it occurs. It is truly national and instantaneous. Second is the number of players involved and the literally dozens of ways that they have to communicate their views and opinions to us. Third is that political parties, the institutions that formerly mediated between citizens and political information, sorting and interpreting information for the party faithful, have broken down.

Finally, we have seen several troublesome developments in how the information that the media report is received and used by citizens and how it affects their views of society and politics. For example, we have seen that the media's penchant for horse race coverage of elections and conflict framing of presidential, congressional, and judicial activity sours citizens' evaluations of their elected representatives. Moreover, episodic, as opposed to thematic, framing of issues like poverty leads to harsher evaluations of some groups of people than others. Specifically, depicting individual cases of black poverty leads to higher levels of assumed individual responsibility than does depicting identical cases of white poverty.[39]

Horse race coverage, the conflict focus, and episodic framing all encourage negative evaluations of politics and politicians. Evidence indicates that policy coverage, a process focus, and thematic framing leave citizens with a more positive sense of what politics is about and what politicians are trying to do. But there is no evidence that the media are about to change how they report on politics. Therefore, we are left with only the hope that knowing how the media work and what their effects are will be some defense against the negative influences involved.

Key Terms

agenda-setting effect   146

Communications Act of 1934   136

educational effect   146

Federal Communications Commission (FCC)   136

framing effect   146

Freedom of Information Act (FOIA)   138

inverted pyramid model   127

muckraking tradition   126

objectivity   127

partisan press   125

penny press   125

persuasion effect   146

seditious libel   124

Suggested Readings

Bollinger, Lee C. *Uninhibited, Robust, and Wide-Open: A Free Press for a New Century.* New York: Oxford University Press, 2010. Bollinger describes the history of freedom of the press in America and warns of the government's proclivity to erect barriers.

Iyengar, Shanto. *Media Politics: A Citizen's Guide,* 2nd ed. New York: W.W. Norton, 2011. A good Media Politics textbook by one of the leading researchers in the field.

Kernell, Samuel. "The Early Nationalization of Political News in America," 1986. Kernell demonstrates that nineteenth-century communities were never cut off from national news, though the proportion of local, state, and national news varied over time.

Ladd, Jonathan M. *Why Americans Hate the Media and Why It Matters.* Princeton, NJ: Princeton University Press, 2011. Ladd argues that the public's distrust of the traditional media has led many to turn to alternative partisan media outlets.

Patterson, Thomas E. *Informing the News: The Need for Knowledge-Based Journalism.* New York: Vintage Books, 2013. Calls for a journalism that does not hide behind false objectivity but gives the public the facts they need to make the democracy work.

Wolfsfeld, Gadi. *Making Sense of Media and Politics.* New York: Routledge, 2011. Wolfsfeld highlights five principles that summarize the key findings of the modern political communications literature.

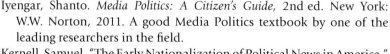

Web Resources

For practice quizzes, key terms flashcards, videos, links, and other study tools, visit the *American Government* website: www.routledge.com/cw/jillson

1. **www.ropercenter.uconn.edu**

   This site provides access to one of the most comprehensive public opinion research facilities. It is a nonprofit organization located at the University of Connecticut. Visitors may have online access to public opinion data collected over the past fifty years.

2. **http://www.aim.org**

   A website dedicated to exposing what it believes to be liberal bias in the news.

3. **www.fair.org**

   A website dedicated to exposing what it believes to be conservative bias in the news.

4. **www.csmonitor.com**

   A prestigious newspaper with national stature. It is an excellent source for domestic and international coverage.

5. **www.aapor.org**

   This site functions as the official homepage of the American Association for Public Opinion Research (AAPOR). This organization publishes the *Public Opinion Quarterly,* a scholarly journal dedicated to research in the field of public opinion studies.

6. **appcpenn.org**

The Annenberg Public Policy Center of the University of Pennsylvania offers students a site for media research. It features various research projects and reports covering topics such as campaign advertising, children's television, and health communication.

Chapter 6

INTEREST GROUPS
The Politics of Influence

❝ *Public … measures are too often decided, not according to the rules of justice and the rights of the minor party, but by the superior force of an interested and overbearing majority.* ❞

JAMES MADISON,
Federalist Number 10

THE FIRST AMENDMENT RIGHTS
TO ASSEMBLE AND PETITION
AND THEIR LIMITS

The Constitution TODAY

First Amendment (in part): "Congress shall make no law . . . abridging the right of the people peaceably to assemble, and to petition the government for a redress of grievances."

Citizen protest, usually peaceful, sometimes not, is a constant running through American history from the Boston Massacre, through the civil rights marches of the 1960s, to the Tea Party and Occupy Wall Street (OWS) movements of recent years. Authorities almost always push back against protesters; usually it is the protesters that give in, but sometimes it is the authorities who are forced to give ground.

On September 17, 2011, several hundred protesters, calling themselves the Occupy Wall Street (OWS) movement, occupied Zuccotti Park in the financial district of lower Manhattan. OWS was a grassroots movement; it had no leadership structure, made decisions by direct democracy, and articulated a diffuse list of complaints including social injustice, economic inequality, and corporate dominance of government. Nonetheless, their signature slogan, "We are the 99 percent," protesting the greed of the 1 percent, captured the nation's attention.

Within a month, the OWS movement had spread to all of America's large cities and to hundreds of smaller cities and towns. Soon, police forces around the U.S. were moving in on OWS encampments, sometimes gently, sometimes forcefully, usually citing violations of city laws and codes, to break up the camps. OWS resisted government attempts to end their occupations by citing the First Amendment "right of the people peaceably to assemble, and to petition the government for a redress of grievances." Protesters always believe that the right to assemble and petition should be viewed broadly, but city governments and police are the established order, so no one should be too surprised that their patience with protest is limited. The rights of citizens to assemble and protest has been contested throughout our history. Look back to the depiction of the Boston Massacre on page 30 to remind yourself why the right of citizens to assemble and protest might have been front of mind for the Founders.

"The right of the people peaceably to assemble" means that citizens may gather in public to share their views, hear from each other, and organize for further action. The right "to petition the government for a redress of grievances" means that, individually or in groups, citizens have the right to address complaints, criticisms, and demands for change to public officials. These First Amendment rights are the foundation for modern interest group organization (assembly) and lobbying (petition), but they have much broader application as well.

Until well into the twentieth century, First Amendment limits applied only against the national government (recall that the First Amendment begins, "Congress shall make no law") unless individual state constitutions provided similar protections. In the late 1930s the Supreme Court began using the "due process clause" of the Fourteenth Amendment (more about this in the Civil Liberties chapter) to limit the action of state and local governments as well. The modern meaning of the right to peaceably assemble was established in *Dejonge v. Oregon* (1937). Oregon had made it a crime for radicals, in this case Communists, to meet. The Supreme Court held that "peaceable assembly for lawful discussion cannot be made a crime." Justice Oliver Wendell Holmes made the even more challenging point that the Constitution was needed to protect "free thought—not free thought for those who agree with us but freedom for the thought that we hate."

Freedom for the thought that we hate is hard. *National Socialist Party v. Skokie* (1977) was decided by the U.S. Court of Appeals for the Seventh Circuit. The U.S. Supreme Court agreed with the findings of the Seventh Circuit and so declined to hear an appeal. The facts of this remarkable case are that public officials in Skokie, Illinois, had passed ordinances trying to prohibit a march by American Nazis, swastikas and all, through the small city of Skokie, near Chicago. The Nazis wanted to parade in Skokie because it was home to many Jews, some of whom were Holocaust survivors. Drawing on Justice Holmes' "freedom for the thought that we hate" argument, Judge Bernard Decker held that "It is better to allow those who preach racial hate to expend their venom in rhetoric rather than to be panicked into . . . permitting the government to decide what its citizens must say and hear." Does that sound right to you? Some would argue that excluding Nazi hate speech, or speech directed against blacks, gays, or Muslims from the public square is no great loss.

Still, as with most rights, there are limits on the rights to assemble and express one's views publicly. Courts have upheld the rights of cities to require permits and control the size, location or route, and timing of gatherings, parades, demonstrations, and similar events. In the case of the OWS movement, Zuccotti Park was a private park to which the public usually had access, which makes it a little murky, but many of the Occupy sites around the country clearly were public property.

WHAT DO YOU THINK?

- Should governments confronting protests lean toward protecting the rights of the protesters to be heard or the rights of other citizens to the general peace and order of their city?

Focus Questions: from reading to thinking

Q1 Have the Founders' concerns about factions been borne out in current American national politics?

Q2 What types of interest groups are most influential in American politics?

Q3 How do interest groups try to influence public policy?

Q4 What role do lobbyists play in the political process?

Q5 What role did interest groups play in the battle over health care reform?

INTEREST GROUPS

In previous chapters we saw that most Americans share a broad commitment to ideas like individualism, liberty, equality, democracy, constitutionalism, and the rule of law. These commitments are said to be embodied in a political system built around openness, fairness, due process, freedom of speech and assembly, and the rights of citizens to petition their government for redress of grievances. But beneath this broad agreement on basic principles are politics and the struggle for political advantage.

In this chapter and the next, we ask how individuals who see politics similarly come together to press their opinions on society and government. As we shall see, the answer is that citizens who share interests relevant to politics come together in interest groups and political parties. In this chapter we look at interest groups. If there are villains in American politics, and there are, in the minds of many they are the ever present interest groups and their lobbyists. They are generally blamed for the behind closed doors, influence peddling, pork barrel character of our politics. But this view is too simple; interest groups come in many forms and they have many goals, some of them clearly laudable—who could argue with job creation or a clean environment? So let's reserve judgment on the role of interest groups in American politics until we know more about what they do and why they do it.

We begin from the simple observation that no society, not even a democratic society such as ours, listens to each of its citizens with equal interest.

Getty Images

Thomas Donohue in his office. Donohue has been head of the U.S. Chamber of Commerce, the nation's top business lobby group, since 1997.

Every society has insiders and outsiders. The insiders are the voters and the members of interest groups whose mostly mainstream views are represented in and reflected by the political system. The outsiders are the citizens who may or may not vote, may or may not belong to interest groups, but whose views are seen as unorthodox or radical and are regularly ignored and sometimes suppressed by the political system and the broader society.

Generally, the insiders dominate. Interest groups and their lobbyists engage elected and appointed officials every day. They offer advice, information, and support to assure that their views are heard and their interests addressed. Some interest groups, though not most, are closely identified with one party or the other—the Chamber of Commerce with the Republicans and the AFL-CIO with the Democrats—so they join in the electoral fray with all they have. Most hang back during elections in order to preserve the option of working closely with whoever comes out on top. Once the ballots are counted and the winners take office, politics as usual continues largely as before. Democratic insiders may replace Republican insiders, as they did when the Obama administration arrived in Washington in 2009, or Republican insiders may return, as they did with the triumphant House Republicans in 2011, but many Americans see little real difference.

Occasionally the outsiders rise up and demand that the political system be changed to better represent them and reflect their views, interests, and needs. Frustration builds in groups with unmet needs. Some groups eventually win enough public support that the political system is forced to respond with significant reforms. The "Tea Party" movement has exercised significant influence inside the House Republican caucus since 2010. More commonly, the outsiders are co-opted with minor concessions and promises or ignored and ridiculed until they weaken and collapse. This was the fate of the "Occupy Wall Street" movement and now they are largely gone.

In this chapter we describe the history of the interest group system in America, the types of groups that form, the resources they bring to the political fight, and the tactics they employ to get their way. We close the chapter with a case study, the passage and early implementation of health care reform, to show the many ways that interest groups seek to exercise influence in American politics.

INTEREST GROUPS IN AMERICAN POLITICS

The American Founders were keenly aware that, at least since the ancient Greeks and Romans, students of politics had warned that social divisions of class, party, and group threaten political stability. James Madison called all of these social divisions "factions" and was particularly wary of them. Madison declared a faction to be "a number of citizens . . . who are united by . . . some common impulse of passion, or of interest, adverse to . . . the permanent and aggregate interests of the community."[1] The most prominent contemporary definition of **interest groups** comes from David B. Truman's classic

interest groups Organizations based on shared interests that attempt to influence society and government to act in ways consonant with the organization's interests.

study of the governmental process. In terms similar to Madison's, Truman defines an interest group as "any group that, on the basis of one or more shared attitudes, makes certain claims upon other groups in the society."[2] Others highlight the interplay of interest groups and government. Graham Wilson notes that "interest groups are generally defined as organizations, separate from government though often in close partnership with government, which attempt to influence public policy."[3]

The obvious presence and influence of interest groups have led politicians and scholars to ask whether interest groups strengthen or weaken democracy. Historically, two answers, two perspectives on the role of interest groups in the American democracy, have been offered. One perspective, **pluralism**, suggests that interest groups represent the interests of citizens to government and that the struggle between groups produces a reasonable policy balance. The other, **elitism**, contends that effective, well-funded interest groups are much more likely to form, win access, and exercise influence on behalf of the interests of the wealthy and the prominent than of the poor and the humble.

Let us keep the insights of pluralism and elitism in mind as we explore four key aspects of the development, structure, and operation of interest groups in America. First, we look at the growth and development of interest groups from the founding period to contemporary times. Second, we describe the variety of interest groups now active in American politics. Third, we ask what resources lead to influence for groups. And fourth, we ask what strategies interest groups use to affect the policymaking process.

pluralism The belief that the interest group structure of American politics produces a reasonable policy balance.

elitism The belief that the interest group structure of American politics is skewed toward the interest of the wealthy.

The Rise of Interest Groups

Social change and economic development alter the environments in which people live, work, and govern. Geographic expansion, industrialization, urbanization, immigration, and related changes redistribute resources, raise new issues, and mobilize new groups. Initially, it was assumed by David Truman and many others that as change adversely affects people's interests they naturally and automatically form groups to protect themselves.

In recent decades, scholars like Mancur Olson, Jack Walker, Robert Salisbury, Frank Baumgartner and Dan Tichenor showed that some kinds of groups form more easily than others and that the group system is more complicated and diverse than previously thought.[4] Business, corporate, and professional interests are well represented. On the other hand, it takes the support of wealthy patrons, foundations, and even government agencies to encourage groups to form around and fight for interests—the poor, the disabled, children, and the mentally challenged—that otherwise might not form so readily or fight so effectively.

A couple of quick examples will help make the point that some potential interest groups form more easily and fully than others. First, the pharmaceutical industry is fairly concentrated, with just a few dozen major drug companies leading the way, and a large sum of money at stake. They care a great deal about the length and expense of the government's drug testing and approval process. They are highly organized and very effective. Civil rights groups, consumer safety groups, and environmental groups, on the other hand, though they have huge potential membership—after all, we all want clean air—often attract only a small fraction of their potential members into the group as dues paying members.

Why wouldn't environmental groups form and be powerful if we all want clean air? Because, scholars have explained, the good—clean air—is non-excludable. If only some join the environmental group, pay their dues, and some policy success leads to cleaner air, the non-joiners cannot be excluded from breathing the cleaner air. They are called "free-riders" in the interest group literature and we are all free-riders in the sense that we benefit from the efforts of many groups—clean government groups, consumer safety groups, or education reform groups—that we do not join and actively support. Do you see why a business group like the drug companies might form a group, contribute funds to it, hire lobbyists, and win their policy battles more readily than environmental groups or consumer safety groups?

Analysts see five major periods of interest group formation in American history. The first occurred in the decades immediately preceding the Civil War as technological developments—steam power, the telegraph, and railroads—allowed the growth of national businesses intent on seeing that regulation did not inhibit their opportunities. The second occurred in the 1880s and early 1890s as industry boomed, cities grew rapidly throughout the North, and white-collar professionals organized to stabilize and secure their places in the rapidly changing society and economy. The third occurred during the Progressive and New Deal eras of the early twentieth century as skilled and then unskilled labor demanded government recognition of their economic and social interests. The fourth occurred in the 1960s and 1970s as the civil rights, consumer, women's, and environmental movements flowered.

Finally, a fifth burst of group formation is under way today. New electronic technologies allow those with shared interests, no matter how broadly they are spread across the country or even the world, to communicate, plan, organize, and act almost instantaneously and at next to no cost. While low-cost long-distance calling, the FAX, and computer mail merges began this process, smart phones, instant messaging, the Internet, and social media have personalized, democratized, and dramatically accelerated organized political behavior.

Q1 Have the Founders' concerns about factions been borne out in current American national politics?

Madisonian Assumptions.   James Madison and many in the founding generation assumed that human nature is self-interested and that people who share interests would join together to protect and enhance them. In Federalist Number 10 (see Appendix D) Madison wrote that "the causes of faction are sewn in the nature of man," leading inevitably to a multiplicity of interests. He argued that "a landed interest, a manufacturing interest, a mercantile interest, a moneyed interest with many lesser interests grow up of necessity in civilized nations and divide themselves into different classes actuated by different sentiments and views." Because factions or interests could not be eradicated, they needed to be accommodated and controlled. Fortunately, Madison thought, there were two lines of defense against an undue influence of factional interests on the new national government.

Madison assumed that the size of the new nation and the primitive means of communication then available would make it hard for people who shared an interest to identify each other and coordinate their activities. He thought that the interests that did form would be so numerous that no one of them or combination of them would be powerful enough to dominate the national government. He also thought that the structure of the new government, with its separation of powers, checks and balances, and bicameral legislature, would make it difficult for interests to control the whole policymaking process.[5] Hence, Madison concluded that with factions held at bay by the size of the country and the complex structure of the national government, government officials would debate, bargain, and compromise with each other in a search for the common good.

During the new government's first decade, when it was located in New York City, commercial and financial leaders were close at hand and mixed socially with congressmen and senior officials of the executive branch. But once the government moved to the new capital at Washington in 1800, it was thoroughly isolated. The most prominent historian of the nation's early governing establishment wrote that, "no national associations made the government's headquarters their headquarters, and few came on errands to Washington. Resident lobbyists, in the modern definition of the term, there were none."[6] With the government very much in isolation in the new capital, Madison's assumptions held reasonably well through the first quarter of the nineteenth century. But then change came on in a rush.[7]

National Groups Emerge.   In the decades immediately before and after the Civil War, the telegraph and railroad created a national market for goods and services. After the war, the pace of industrialization and urbanization in the northern economy quickened. Businesses that had been local became regional conglomerates, and some became national trusts or monopolies. These powerful new business interests bought or at least rented compliant state legislatures to assure friendly treatment and to control the appointments of U.S. Senators. The business-friendly Senate of the late nineteenth century was known as the "Millionaires' Club."[8]

The first business associations and labor unions had their origins in the final decades of the nineteenth century. Farmers groups and unions were a powerful force in the late nineteenth century as the nation was still predominantly rural and most labor was engaged in agriculture. But the most powerful interest group of the period was the Grand Army of the Republic (GAR). The GAR, a national organization of Union Army veterans lobbied intensively for better pensions and expanded eligibility for pensions. The Dependent Pension Act of 1890 severed the link between war injuries and pension eligibility and by 1906 simple old age was disability enough for a Union military service pension.[9]

Urbanization and economic development soon spawned a new class of professionals in accounting, engineering, finance, law, medicine, education, science, and many other skills and occupations. Trade and professional societies formed to protect their members from corporate and employer power above and economic competition below. Trade groups and professional societies set educational and training standards, controlled entry to the trade or profession, shared information, and worked to advance the social and economic interests of members.[10]

Modern Group System.   The modern group system was formed in two key phases—the Progressive and New Deal eras of the early twentieth century and the Great Society years of the 1960s and early 1970s. By the end of the Progressive Era, mass circulation newspapers, magazines, radio, and telephones were in place. By the end of the Great Society, television was a dominant force, and computers, fax machines, and satellites were looming on the technological horizon. Today, the Internet and mobile cellular technology makes communication—for advertising, recruitment, fundraising, and more—instantaneous.

In addition to technological developments, the increasing size and scope of government contributed to expansion of the interest group system. Not only did the number of business groups increase as government expanded its regulatory reach, but a thick network of public interest groups grew up to press their views as government expanded into civil rights, welfare, health care, education, parks and recreation, and agriculture. So dense is the modern group system that nine out of ten Americans belong to at least one voluntary association or membership group like a professional association, a church, a social club, or a civil rights organization. The average American adult belongs to four groups.[11]

Moreover, Robert Salisbury has pointed out that the interest group system extends beyond membership groups to include a "diverse array of . . . individual corporations, state and local governments, universities, think tanks, and most other *institutions* of the private sector. Likewise unnoticed are the multitudes of Washington representatives, freestanding and for hire, including lawyers, public relations firms, and diverse other counsellors."[12] Scholars place the number of registered lobbyists at about 12,000 but loose rules allow as many as 100,000 people to spend up to 20 percent of their time lobbying before they have to register. The broader influence industry is hundreds of thousands more.[13]

Not surprisingly, many now wonder whether James Madison was not simply wrong to think that the dangers of factionalism could be managed by the size of the nation and the institutional defenses of federalism, separation of powers, checks and balances, and staggered terms of office. The Internet allows people with shared interests and concerns, even if they are spread thinly across the country, to find each other, organize, and press their concerns on government. And as we shall see in more detail in the chapter on campaigns and elections, some see the entry of Super PACs, permitted to raise unlimited funds from sometimes unidentified donors, as a new kind of threat within the nation's interest group system. Do you share these concerns or do you think everyone, wealthy as well as poor, should be able to use their resources as they see fit to effect political outcomes?

Types of Interest Groups

The most comprehensive study of interest groups in America comes from the work of Frank Baumgartner and Beth Leech. In 1959, the *Encyclopedia of Associations* listed fewer than 6,000 groups. Today the same source lists over 25,000. These groups now spend about $3.5 billion each year lobbying Congress and the executive branch. Baumgartner and Leech summarize an extensive literature showing that fully three-quarters of the group system reflects occupational interests. Almost 40 percent of interest groups are private sector occupational groups, including corporate, business, and labor interests, and about 35 percent of public sector, not-for-profit, occupational groups, drawing members from educational, health, religious, science, and public affairs occupations. The remaining 25 percent of the interest group system is comprised of public interest and citizen membership groups. These draw members based on substantive interests, such as consumer, environmental, or international affairs, and member attributes such as ideology, partisanship, race, ethnicity, and gender.

In recent decades the nonprofit and citizen group sectors have grown faster than the traditional business, professional, and labor sectors. Although corporate interests still dominate because of their superior command of money, prestige, and expertise, the balance of interests in American politics is fuller and fairer than it was only a few decades ago (see Figure 6.1).

Q2 What types of interest groups are most influential in American politics?

As we shall see more fully below, private sector business associations and groups include such well-known names as the Chamber of Commerce, the United Auto Workers (UAW), the American Bar Association (ABA), and the Pharmaceutical Research and Manufacturers of America (PhRMA). The nonprofit and citizens' groups are similarly familiar, including such names as the National Association for the Advancement of Colored People (NAACP), the League of Women Voters, the Wilderness Society, the National Rifle Association (NRA), and the Christian Coalition.

Not surprisingly, given the wide array of interest groups in our society, organizations and individuals have an equally wide array of reasons for joining interest groups. Scholars have sorted these reasons into three broad categories; material benefits, purposive benefits, and solidary benefits. Material benefits are the real and tangible benefits, like lower taxes, lighter regulation, higher wages, and group insurance rates that often come with or are at least hoped to result from group membership. Purposive benefits refer to the substantive, partisan, and ideological goals, like helping Haiti, fighting hunger, supporting Republicans, or battling socialists that might lead a person to join a group. And solidary benefits are the simple joys and social rewards of meeting, getting to know, and working with like-minded people. Organizations and persons often join groups for a mix of reasons, but anticipation of material, purposive, and solidary or social benefits is almost always among them.

Private and Public Sector Occupational Groups. Groups representing the economic interests of their members are the oldest as well as the most

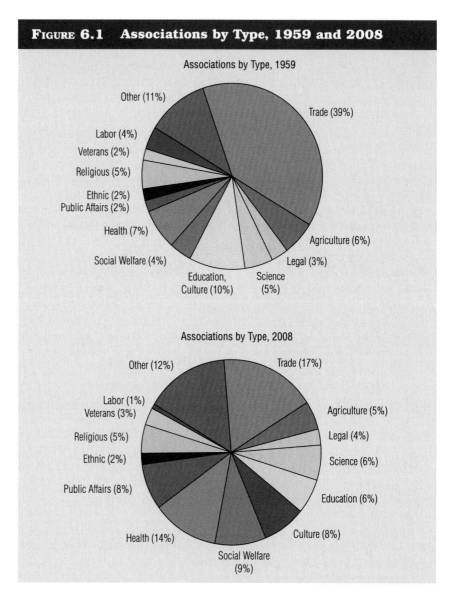

FIGURE 6.1   Associations by Type, 1959 and 2008

Associations by Type, 1959

Other (11%)
Trade (39%)
Labor (4%)
Veterans (2%)
Religious (5%)
Ethnic (2%)
Public Affairs (2%)
Health (7%)
Agriculture (6%)
Social Welfare (4%)
Legal (3%)
Education, Culture (10%)
Science (5%)

Associations by Type, 2008

Other (12%)
Trade (17%)
Labor (1%)
Veterans (3%)
Agriculture (5%)
Religious (5%)
Legal (4%)
Ethnic (2%)
Science (6%)
Public Affairs (8%)
Education (6%)
Health (14%)
Culture (8%)
Social Welfare (9%)

Source: Frank L. Baumgartner and Beth Leech, *Basic Interests: The Importance of Groups in Politics and Political Science* (Princeton, NJ: Princeton University Press, 1998), 109.[14] Updated by the author from *Encyclopedia of Associations*, 45th edition.

numerous members of the interest group system. Such groups form early and in large numbers because members share clearly defined interests that can be helped or hurt in significant ways by the actions of other groups, the government, or the market in general.

The business community has always been the most thoroughly organized part of the interest group system because it has natural advantages of money, organization, and expertise. Throughout American history, government and business have worked closely together to foster economic growth and increase profits. In fact, the political-economist Charles E. Lindblom has famously used the phrase "the privileged position of business" to describe the place of businesses and corporations in capitalist or market economies. Not only do businessmen serve in prominent roles in government, government policy is carefully designed to stimulate business and employment. Elected officials know that their tenure in office depends on a healthy economy and they listen closely when leading business figures talk about what policies will most likely produce the desired results.[15]

Peak Associations represent the interests of business in general. The National Association of Manufacturers (NAM) traces its roots to a meeting held in Cincinnati in January 1895. The NAM is the nation's largest industrial trade association, with 14,000 members. The national Chamber of Commerce, the principal voice of small business in the United States, was founded in 1912. The national organization now includes nearly 3,000 affiliated state and local chambers and an underlying membership of more than 3 million businesses. The newest major group representing American business is the Business Roundtable formed in 1972. The Roundtable is open only to America's largest companies—160 of the Fortune 500 largest corporations were founding members—and is a forum for discussion of their shared concerns and interests.

peak associations Peak associations, like the U.S. Chamber of Commerce, represent the general interests of business.

Of the peak business associations, the Chamber of Commerce is the most politically dynamic and aggressive. The Chamber has been headed since 1997 by 76-year-old Thomas Donahue. Donahue manages an annual budget of $250 million and a staff of 500, including scores of lobbyists, economists, researchers and analysts, and communications experts. The Chamber spent $136 million on lobbying in 2012, three times the $41 million spent by the number two National Association of Realtors. Donahue was paid just under $5 million in 2011. From the perspective of American business, government programs and regulations threaten many interests, so it makes a lot of sense to spend the money needed to influence those programs and regulations.[16]

In addition to the peak associations are almost 6,000 **trade associations**. Trade associations bring together companies in a single business, commercial, and industrial sector. These trade associations go by such familiar names as the Aerospace Industries Association, the American Electronics Association, the American Petroleum Institute, and the Automobile Manufacturers Association. Moreover, many individual corporations are large, wealthy, and diverse enough to constitute formidable concentrations of interest by themselves. Names such as American Airlines, AT&T, Bank of America, General Motors, IBM, General Electric, Microsoft, and Google come immediately to mind.

trade associations Associations formed by businesses and related interests involved in the same commercial, trade, or industrial sector.

Although local associations of workers existed from the nation's earliest days, the modern labor movement began with the formation of the American Federation of Labor (AFL) in 1886. The AFL was a federation of skilled trade or craft unions including the Brick Layers, Carpenters, Cigar Makers, Glass Workers, Pipe Fitters, and Tool and Die Makers. Samuel Gompers of the

Just 11 percent of American workers belong to labor unions, down from 24 percent in 1970 and 35 percent in 1955.

What do you think?

- What are the implications, positive and negative, for the American society and economy of the decline of labor unions?
- Why do you think labor unions have seen such precipitous declines?

AFL-CIO Formed in 1955 when the American Federation of Labor joined with the Congress of Industrial Organizations, the 9 million member AFL-CIO is the largest labor organization in the United States.

Cigar Makers was the AFL's first president. The AFL avoided politics to concentrate on protecting and insulating the crafts and their members by controlling entrance requirements, work rules, and wage and benefit levels.

It was not until the mid-1930s that Franklin Roosevelt and the Democratic Congress, seeking to jump-start the economy in the depths of the Depression, passed and FDR signed the National Labor Relations Act, also known as the Wagner Act, to clear the way for unions to organize, bargain, and strike as necessary. Organization of unskilled workers in industrial sectors like mining, steel, and autos was a top priority of the Roosevelt administration. The Congress of Industrial Organizations (CIO), first headed by John L. Lewis of the United Mine Workers, was formed in 1935. George Meany of the Carpenters, head of the AFL from the mid-1940s, helped engineer a merger of the AFL and CIO in 1955 and became the first president of the new **AFL-CIO.**

The AFL-CIO reached its high point in 1979 with almost 20 million members and fell to as few as 15 million in 1995. John Sweeney's election as AFL-CIO president in 1995 promised a new focus on recruitment; instead, membership continued to decline. When Sweeney refused to step down at the end of his second term in 2005, seven unions with 5.4 million members, including the Teamsters, United Farm Workers, and service employees, withdrew to form the Change to Win coalition. Renewed competition to organize new workers pushed union membership to 16.1 million in 2008.[17] In 2009, the AFL-CIO elected Richard Trumka as its president. Trumka, Secretary-Treasurer of the AFL-CIO and former president of the United Mineworkers, promised once again to focus intently on union organization and expansion. In 2009 and 2010, two of the unions that defected in 2005, Unite Here and the Laborers' International Union, returned to the AFL-CIO. Despite the restored unity, the Great Recession of 2009 hit unions hard, driving membership down to 14.4 million in 2012. The Let's Compare box on the next page shows that American labor is far less organized than is labor in most other advanced industrial countries in the world.

In recent decades, while private sector unions have slipped, public sector unions have expanded. While only 11 percent of all U.S. workers belong to unions, nearly 36 percent of public sector workers belong to unions. About 35 percent of teachers are union members, with the 3 million member National Education Association (NEA) and the 1.5 million member American Federation of Teachers (AFT), an AFL-CIO affiliate, being the largest and most active. The Great Recession of 2009 provided an opening for several Republican governors, led by Scott Walker of Wisconsin and John Kasich of Ohio, successfully to push legislation limiting public sector unions.

Major professional associations, like those that serve lawyers, doctors, social workers, academics, and others formed in the late nineteenth and early twentieth centuries. These professional associations formed to set standards and design admission requirements, share information of general interest,

LET'S COMPARE

U.S. Unions in Global Perspective

The labor movement has never been as central to American life as labor movements in many other advanced industrial countries have been to the lives of their citizens. Nonetheless, labor movements in most parts of the industrialized world have been weakening for most of the past two decades under the onslaught of globalization. The chart below shows the percentages of the nonagricultural workforce belonging to labor unions in select advanced industrial nations. Several points are evident.

First, a small cluster of northern European nations have abiding commitments to unions. Most workers in these nations are represented by unions and these unions deal with business and government from a position of equality. Second, many advanced-

industrial nations have seen the levels of unionization of their workforces decline from about half to less than one-third, sometimes much less. Finally, trade unions in the United States were weak to begin with and declined steadily after 1970. Twenty-four percent of the U.S. workforce was unionized in 1970, but by 2012 only 11 percent of U.S. workers belonged to labor unions.

The forces of global trade, commerce, and investment have borne hard on labor unions since the mid-1970s. Governments and businesses feel the pressures of global economic competition, and unions are often faced with the prospect of reducing wages and benefits or losing jobs to nonunion workers at home and abroad. Moreover, unions have had their strongest hold in the traditional manufacturing industries like steel and autos. The newer service and information industries—such as banking, computers, and communications—have been much more difficult for unions to organize.

Country	1970	1980	1990	2012 or Most Recent	% Change 1970–2012
Sweden	68	78	81	68	+0
Finland	51	69	73	69	+18
Denmark	60	79	75	69	+9
Belgium	42	54	54	50	+8
Norway	57	58	59	55	−2
Canada	32	35	33	27	−5
Germany	32	35	31	18	−14
Netherlands	37	35	24	18	−19
Austria	63	57	47	28	−35
United Kingdom	45	51	39	26	−19
Australia	50	50	41	18	−32
Japan	35	31	25	18	−17
Switzerland	29	31	24	17	−12
United States	24	20	16	11	−13
France	22	18	10	8	−14

Source: Organization for European Cooperation and Development (OECD). http://stats.oecd.org/Index.aspx?DataSetCode=UN_DEN.

and protect member interests against competitors and government regulators at the local, state, and national levels. The American Bar Association (ABA) was established in 1876; many of the nation's academic and scholarly associations were organized in the two decades that followed; and the American Medical Association (AMA) was founded in 1901. These professional associations derive influence from the respect that society awards to their members and from the expertise or specialized knowledge that they possess.

There are also professional associations in the public sector. Among the most prominent would be the National Governors Association (1908), the Conference of Mayors (1933), and the National Conference of State Legislators (1975). But state local budget officers, human service professionals, transportation officials and many others have their own professional groups. Their principal service is to share information, relevant trends, and best practices, but they also lobby state and national agencies for better funding of their activities.

Public Interest and Citizen Groups.   Most private sector and some public sector occupation groups have economic or professional assets, money, expertise, and sometimes numbers to trade for government attention and assistance. The public interest movement, comprised of a diffuse set of membership groups, law firms, think tanks, lobbying groups, and community organizations, depends more on information and publicity to make both business executives and government bureaucrats look beyond narrow self-interests to the broader public interest. Political scientist Ronald Hrebenar defines public interest groups as groups pursuing goods that cannot be made available to some without generally being made available to all.[18] Such goods include honest government, safer toys, highways and workplaces, and cleaner air and water.

Two of the most famous public interest groups are Common Cause and Ralph Nader's collection of Public Citizen groups. Common Cause was established as a "people's lobby" in 1970 by John Gardner, a former Johnson administration official. It focuses on "structure and process" issues such as ethics laws, open government laws, and campaign finance reform.[19] Nader's Public Citizen (1971) groups, of which Congress Watch is the most well known, lobby Congress and the executive branch on a wide range of consumer issues. Other public interest groups include the Wilderness Society, the League of Women Voters, the Young Americans for Freedom, and the Free Congress Foundation. Although it is hard to argue against the importance of pristine wilderness, clean air, and frugal and efficient government, the public interest movement is frequently criticized for limiting itself to an upper middle-class agenda.

Major elements of American society are not well represented either by economic groups or by consumer and public interest groups. Minorities and women, for example, have often felt that they must organize to demand access to America's economic mainstream before occupational and consumer groups can be of much assistance to them. Nonetheless, civil rights organizations, such as the NAACP, the Urban League, the Southern Christian Leadership Conference (SCLC), the League of United Latin American Citizens (LULAC), and the Native American Rights Fund (NARF) work to assure opportunity and fair treatment for the groups from which their members are drawn. Similarly, the National Organization for Women (NOW) has sought to assure women's rights in society, before the law, in the workplace, and in regard to procreation and reproduction.

Interest Group Resources

Different interest groups bring different resources to bear in pursuit of their goals. Some groups have millions of members. Others, like the American Bar Association (ABA), have fewer members, but the members they have are wealthy and have professional expertise upon which the government must draw. Still others like Common Cause and Congress Watch draw their strength from strong leadership, a membership intensely committed to the goals of the organization, and tight networks of strategic alliances with other groups pursuing related interests. In this section we will explore the mix of resources available to American interest groups.

Q3 How do interest groups try to influence public policy?

Size of Membership.   Large groups such as the 40 million member American Association of Retired Persons (AARP) or the 8.4 million member AFL-CIO demand attention simply because of their size. Ultimately, however, both unity and coverage must accompany size if it is to have its full effect.

American unions provide good examples of how the influence that might flow from size can be compromised by a lack of unity within a group and a lack of coverage. If the membership of a group is divided over policy or over candidates in an election, that group will carry less weight than it otherwise might. Coverage is just as important as cohesion. Although 70 percent of Scandinavian workers belong to labor unions, only about 11 percent of American workers do. It should not be surprising then that Scandinavian unions carry more weight with their governments than American unions do with theirs. Unions are not alone. The ABA claims fewer than half of lawyers and the AMA claims only about one-quarter of doctors as members. Public interest and consumer groups include only tiny fractions of potential members if one assumes that all citizens or all consumers are potential members.

Intensity of Membership.   Large majorities of Americans favor some form of gun control and some access to abortion services. However, well-organized and intensely interested minorities can often overcome unorganized majorities. The 5 million member National Rifle Association (NRA), whose clout represents both its size and its intensity, strongly opposes most limitations on the rights of gun owners. Similarly, much of the Right to Life movement favors outright prohibitions of abortion services. Both groups are sufficiently well organized, funded, and motivated that their influence over government decision making in areas of interest to their members far outweighs their numbers.

The National Rifle Association (NRA) had 500 exhibits and nearly 74,000 attendees at its 2012 national convention. A committed membership is a key source of interest group influence.

Financial Resources of Members.   Money, like numbers and intensity, is critical to interest group success. Scholars point out that "quality leadership, access to political decision makers, a favorable public image, and a hardworking and knowledgeable staff are just some of the resources that can be purchased with the careful expenditure of adequate amounts of money."[20] Money helps groups both organize internally and exercise influence externally.

Businesses, interest groups, and labor unions spend $275 million a month on lobbying the federal government. The Open Secrets website tracks lobbying in great detail. In 2010, interest groups spent a record $3.55 billion on lobbying. Three business sectors, pharmaceuticals and health products ($527 million), finance, insurance, and real estate ($480 million), and energy and natural resources ($454 million) led the pack. In 2013, when overall spending had dropped to $2.9 billion the same three sectors again ranked in the top five.[21]

Prestige and Expertise of Members.   Some groups—business, labor, and professional groups, for example—are in better positions than other groups—consumer, wilderness, and civil rights groups, for example—to claim decisive or exclusive expertise. Most members of Congress and most citizens feel that they have enough personal insight and experience to have opinions on

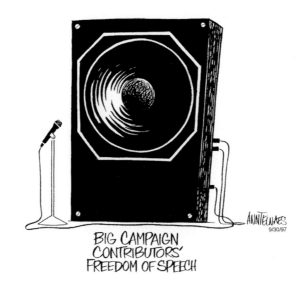

YOUR FREEDOM OF SPEECH

BIG CAMPAIGN CONTRIBUTORS' FREEDOM OF SPEECH

whether we need more national forests or stronger affirmative action laws. Most members of Congress and most citizens do not feel competent to set waste disposal policy without input from the chemical industry or drug approval guidelines without input from the pharmaceutical industry.

Organization and Leadership.   Interest groups are organized either as unitary organizations or as federations. Common Cause, the NRA, NAACP, and NOW are unitary. Members belong directly to the organization, and there is a single level of administrative structure, usually a national office or headquarters. Although the organization may have local chapters, they are all directed from the national headquarters. Federations are made up of member organizations that have a substantial degree of independence. The AMA, for example, is a federation of 180 medical societies, some of which opposed Obama's health care reform agenda, some of which supported it. In general, unitary organizations are more energetic and coherent than federations.

Different kinds of organizations also require different kinds of leaders. Charismatic leaders, of whom Martin Luther King Jr. is the most frequently cited example, lead by force of personality and will. Entrepreneurial leaders, of whom Ralph Nader is a good example, lead by energy, creativity, and strategic sense. Charismatic and entrepreneurial leaders are particularly common in unitary membership organizations, where their energy and ideas can fuel the entire organization. Managers are more common in federated organizations, where consensus must be negotiated among the leaders and members of the constituent organizations.

Some interest groups also have extensive staffs who provide analysis, policy, and legal support to their leaders. The pharmaceutical and health products lobby has more than 1,500 registered lobbyists in Washington and they

Protest marches were held across the country on May 1, 2008. These May Day marches called for access to the American Dream. Opponents called for enforcement of current U.S. Law.

spent $359 million on lobbying in 2011, more than any other industry. The American Petroleum Institute has a Washington staff of 400 and the National Rifle Association (NRA) has a Washington staff of over 460 persons.

Strategic Alliances.   Finally, some groups are able to leverage their own resources by forming strategic alliances.[22] For example, consumer groups often supplement their usually modest resources by coordinating their activities with civil rights groups, environmentalists, and organized labor. Similarly, the Christian Coalition might seek alliances with Right to Life groups, anti-tax groups, and conservative think tanks such as the Cato Institute and the Heritage Foundation.

One example of rival coalitions of interest groups forming to do battle over a major issue involves immigration reform. In 2007, President George W. Bush, most Democrats, the Catholic Church, the United States Chamber of Commerce, the National Association of Manufacturers, the National Council of La Raza, the National Restaurant Association, and many others lined up in favor of comprehensive immigration reform—including increased border security, a guest worker program, and a path to citizenship for undocumented workers already in the country. On the other side were most Republicans, conservative groups like the Eagle Forum, the Heritage Foundation, and anti-immigrant groups led by Numbers USA. After a pitched battle, the opponents blocked comprehensive immigration reform. Congress was able to pass a border security bill, but both sides stored ammunition for future battles.[23]

Many Republican leaders were shocked when Hispanics gave Obama 71 percent of their votes in 2012. Republican National Committee chair Rince Priebus called for immigration reform, as did Florida Senator Marco Rubio, both arguing that the party looked anti-Hispanic. Still, even after the Senate passed a comprehensive immigration reform bill, the anti-immigration interest group alliance held firm and were able to kill the bill in the House. A large and motivated coalition of interest groups is hard to defeat.

Interest Group Goals and Strategies

Most interest groups seek to gather, shape, and disseminate information in the hope of beneficially influencing the opinions and behavior of policymakers and, often, the public. Interest groups employ a fairly standard set of tools in their work. They gather information; consult with government officials; testify before committees, boards, and commissions; participate in campaigns and elections; organize and deploy their members; conduct public education; and build coalitions. Most interest groups do not engage in all of these activities with the same frequency and confidence.

Depending on the type of group and the nature of its resources, some groups employ an "inside" strategy and some an "outside" strategy. Both aim to influence public officials, but in different ways. An inside strategy is aimed at influencing public officials directly, while an outside strategy is aimed at changing public opinion and, thereby, indirectly influencing public officials. Classic elements of an inside strategy might include meeting with a legislator, testifying before a committee, or providing a campaign contribution. Classic elements of an outside strategy might involve running media ads, organizing letter-writing and email campaigns, or perhaps even busing in demonstrators for a rally at the capitol.

The Role of Lobbyists.   An inside strategy often depends heavily on professional lobbyists. **Lobbyists** attempt to influence government decision making in ways that benefit or at least avoid harm to those they represent. Traditionally, the chief instrument of influence for most lobbyists is information that is useful to policymakers in deciding how to proceed on the issues before them. Lobbyists provide information that supports their positions and withhold or suppress information that seems to argue against their positions. Decision makers such as members of Congress must hope that the contest for influence between and among lobbyists will produce enough diverse information to present a reasonably full and accurate picture.

Lobbyists have more than information at their disposal and some have a great deal more. "Super-lobbyist" Jack Abramoff gave $1.4 million to 300 lawmakers between 1999 and 2005. Lobbyists seek to buy access with their campaign contributions, which is not illegal. What is illegal is engaging in a *quid pro quo*—exchanging campaign contributions or gifts for official favors. In the biggest influence-peddling scandal of modern times, Abramoff and several of his colleagues were indicted, convicted, and sent to jail. Several lawmakers

lobbyists Hired agents who seek to influence government decision making in ways that benefit or limit harm to their clients.

Q4 What role do lobbyists play in the political process?

were either jailed, indicted, or defeated for reelection. Lobbyists, at least temporarily, scurried for their ethics manuals and Congress enacted tough new ethics reforms.[24]

The very top lobbyists often move back and forth, through what is referred to as the "revolving door," between important roles in government and lucrative lobbying jobs. Former congressman Billy Tauzin was a Democrat from Louisiana's third congressional district from 1980 to 1995 before switching to the Republican Party and serving until 2005. During his quarter century in the House, he served in the leadership of both parties, a rare feat, and he served as Republican chair of the House Energy and Commerce Committee between 2001 and 2004. Tauzin declined to run for reelection in 2004 and instead became President and CEO of PhRMA, the trade and lobby association for the pharmaceutical industry, from 2005 to 2010. With his broad contacts in Congress and the clout of the pharmaceutical industry behind him, he played a central role in assuring that the Obamacare program that emerged from Congress in 2009 and early 2010 was acceptable to the drug companies. For his services, PhRMA paid Tauzin $11.6 million in 2010. Known as the "Tauzin line," this remains the top lobbyist salary on record.[25] It will be broken.

Many former high-ranking elected officials, military officers, and bureaucrats act as lobbyists after they retire or leave office. The price of a top lobbyist is on particularly stark display when party control in Washington changes hands. During the Bush administration, Mark Racicot, former governor of Montana and Republican Party national chairman, commanded a salary of $1.8 million as head of the American Insurance Association. In the week following Obama's victory, no longer useful to the insurance association, Racicot retired. In the wake of the election, lobbying firms across Washington were bulking up on Democratic influence peddlers and shedding Republicans. The value to the private sector of former government officials like Daschle or Racicot is their access to and perhaps influence over former colleagues and friends still serving in the government.[26] Nearly half of the senators and House members who left Congress between 1998 and 2012 stayed in Washington to lobby.[27]

Family ties are also common between public officials and lobbyists. Literally dozens of legislators and their senior staffers are married to lobbyists. Increasingly, as legislators serve in Congress into their seventies, eighties, and beyond, their grown children join the lobby. Separating family life from business is difficult when you eat together, relax together, and even sleep together.[28] At a slightly less elevated level, but perhaps of more direct interest to political science majors, is the case of Peter Roberson. Roberson earned $124,000 as a staffer on the House Financial Services Committee in 2009 before going to work as a lobbyist for Intercontinental Exchange, Inc., a financial services firm for three to five times that amount.[29]

Struggling Toward Democracy

Nearly half of U.S. congressmen and senators who leave office remain in Washington as lobbyists.
What do you think?
- Is this their right as citizens or is it a threat to our democracy?
- Should there be limits on the public role of former elected officials?

inside strategy Lobbying strategies usually involving direct contact with elected and appointed officials or their staff to shape their view of issues.

Inside Lobbying.   The goal of an **inside strategy** is to convince the elected and appointed officials, usually by means of close and quiet consultation, to develop or modify a policy or to take some action in the interpretation or implementation of a policy that would serve the interests of a group and its members. Since most of Congress's work is done in committee, lobbyists focus there as well. Committees debate pending legislation, adding, modifying, or dropping provisions as they go and along and work hard to have a role in this process. Lobbyists also attend and may testify or present evidence at administrative hearings where laws or regulations affecting their clients may be under discussion and review. Lobbyists need to know what is happening in relation to their clients' concerns at all times and affect the process where they can.

Interest groups pursuing an inside strategy explicitly attempt to establish an exchange relationship, a relationship of mutual assistance and advantage, with government officials. Fundamentally, the exchange is information and financial contributions for access and influence. Interest groups and their lobbyist representatives provide government decision makers with useful information about how a proposed change might actually work and about how it would be received in relevant policy communities and publics. Public officials offer lobbyists access to and some influence, sometimes a great deal of influence, over the policymaking process. At a cruder level, campaign contributions are exchanged for "earmarks," targeted legislative benefits, about which we will hear more in our discussion of Congress.

Outside Lobbying. An **outside strategy** may involve media advertising designed to educate the public, or letter-writing, phone, and fax campaigns by

outside strategy Lobbying strategies intended to inform and shape public opinion as an indirect way of influencing policymakers.

AFP / Getty Images

Supporters of the "Tea Party" demonstrate against the Obama health care program outside the Capitol. People in the streets will often get lawmakers' attention when a quiet meeting in their office will not.

interest group members and others designed to impress public officials with the breadth and depth of concern in the public over a particular issue. The range of outsider strategies may go beyond education campaigns and electioneering to protest and civil disobedience. Protests, demonstrations, and sometimes even violence are weapons of last resort, usually employed only by the poor and the weak. The classic example of the effectiveness of protests and demonstrations is the civil rights movement of the 1950s and early 1960s. The pictures of demonstrators under assault by water cannon, mounted police, and dogs confronted Americans with the tremendous gap between promises of liberty and opportunity and the reality of black lives.

If inside lobbying does not work, as it often does not for unions and citizen groups, then outside lobbying is a way to step up the pressure on public officials by showing that concern in the public is widespread. Elected officials are particularly sensitive to the opinions of persons who care enough to write a personal letter, make a phone call, or show up with signs outside a congressman's office. When demonstrations attract the media, demonstrators get to express their concerns to the broader public and elected officials have to answer uncomfortable questions, often on the record. Lobbying often works, but there are other tools in the interest group toolbox.[30]

Litigation.   Interest groups that fail to influence public officials directly or indirectly by influencing public opinion may turn to the courts. Litigation, which is another name for bringing a case in court, is time-consuming and expensive. Few interest groups have experienced litigators on staff, though some, like the Chamber of Commerce, NAACP, and the Sierra Club, certainly do. Others must either hire a public affairs law firm or join a coalition of like-minded groups that includes such a firm.

litigation Bringing a case in court for the purpose of demanding a beneficial policy change or avoiding an adverse change.

Litigation is rarely a first move. Usually it comes after a failed inside strategy and, perhaps, after or in place of an equally expensive and unlikely outside strategy. The purpose of most interest group **litigation** is to demand a beneficial policy change or forestall an adverse change. Famously, from the 1930s through the 1960s, the NAACP, unable to move the political branches of the government toward equal rights, initiated a series of court cases that eventually brought down segregation and other forms of overt discrimination. The National Organization for Women (NOW), the Mexican-American Legal Defense and Education Fund (MALDEF), and, more recently, the gay rights Lambda Legal Defense and Education Fund, all followed similar strategies.

Litigation is a strategy that interest groups are especially likely to follow in fighting damaging decisions by Congress, the executive branch, or even other groups. For example, as we have already seen, when Congress passed and President Bush reluctantly signed the McCain-Feingold campaign finance bill limiting the right of interest groups to advertise for and against a candidate within 30 days of a primary election and 60 days of a general election, Wisconsin Right to Life, Inc., sued. In 2007, the Supreme Court, in *Federal Election Commission v. Wisconsin Right to Life, Inc.*, overturned the McCain-Feingold provisions barring spending near elections. Similarly, when the Food and Drug Administration (FDA) overrode a medical advisory panel and blocked access to the morning-after-pill in 2004, a feminist group, the Center for Reproductive Rights, sued. The Center's lawyers argued that the FDA's decision had been made on political rather than medical grounds and demanded that access to the pills be granted. In 2006, the FDA reversed itself and authorized over-the-counter sale of Plan-B to women 18 years of age and older.

THE FIGHT OVER HEALTH CARE REFORM: A LOBBYIST'S DONNYBROOK

The on-going fight over health care reform is one of the great political battles —great interest group battles—of recent memory. Such battles almost never break out unexpectedly. What makes them great battles is that the armies are fully arrayed, the terrain over which the battle will be fought has been cleared, and the opponents' offensive and defensive capabilities are well known—it is main force on main force and both sides have a big stake in the outcome.

The Origins of Health Care Reform

While national health insurance was rarely mentioned in the nineteenth century, it became a major issue in twentieth century U.S. domestic politics. The Democratic Party has been the most consistent advocate of national health insurance. The Republican Party has recognized the importance of the issue, sometimes offering their own programs, but more often opposing more government involvement in health care. Though national health care systems were established across the developed world during the twentieth century, the U.S. remained wary of what was often described as "socialized medicine."

The first initiative in the direction of national health care was taken, not by the Democratic Party, but by former Republican President Theodore Roosevelt (TR) in his unsuccessful third party, "Bull Moose," campaign for the presidency in 1912. TR's distant cousin Franklin Delano Roosevelt (FDR) was elected president in 1932 and included national health insurance in the early versions of the Social Security Act of 1935. Ultimately, he was forced to drop the health provisions in order to pass the rest of the bill. FDR's successor, President Harry Truman, again proposed national health care in 1948, but it was defeated by a coalition of conservative southern Democrats and Republicans. Charges of "creeping socialism" filled the air.

In 1965, Democratic President Lyndon Baines Johnson (LBJ) passed Medicare, health insurance for the retired elderly as an add-on to Social Security, and Medicaid, health insurance for the non-working poor, as part of his "Great Society program." Medicare and Medicaid, along with Veterans' Health Care and a few smaller federal health programs, now account for half of U.S. spending on health care. Finally, in 2003, Republican President George W. Bush passed a bill adding prescription drug coverage to Medicare. At the time, this $400 billion program was the largest expansion of federal involvement in health care delivery since the original adoption of Medicare in 1965. Republicans hoped that their passage of the prescription drug bill would help break the commitment of elderly voters to the Democrats in memory of their passage of Social Security and Medicare.

Between the passage of Medicare and the prescription drug bill a major health care initiative by Democratic President Bill Clinton failed. Clinton won the 1992 presidential election comfortably and enjoyed big Democratic majorities in the House and Senate. With health care as his principal domestic policy initiative, Clinton assigned his wife, Hillary Clinton, to head a task force on health care reform. The task force produced a comprehensive bill, mostly in secret, and forwarded it to the Congress for adoption. Strong opposition from Republicans, employers, and the health care industry sunk the bill. The Democratic majorities in Congress caved and the bill was never brought to the floor for a decisive vote in either the House or the Senate. The public viewed the Democrats as ineffectual and elected Republican majorities in both the House and Senate in 1994.

Not surprisingly, the Obama administration studied the failure of Clinton's health care reform effort closely. Many Clinton administration veterans, including Obama Chief of Staff Rahm Immanuel, played key roles in Obama's effort. They were determined not to repeat Clinton's mistakes—especially offering Congress a complete bill on a near take-it-or-leave-it basis—so they provided only broad guidance and asked Congress to produce a bill. As it turned out, this process nearly collapsed as well.

Interest Groups in the Health Care Debate

Q5 What role did interest groups play in the battle over health care reform?

The health care sector in 2009 comprised fully 17 percent, $2.4 trillion, of the U.S. economy. The stakes of health care reform were huge. Unlike during the Clinton health care debate, when the health care industry generally lined up with the rest of the business community in opposition, the Obama administration worked hard to line up health care industry support before the public debate began. They were generally successful with doctors and hospitals, though they lost the health insurance industry as the congressional and public debates played out. As they had historically been, business and employer groups, led by the U.S. Chamber of Commerce, were opposed.

Because the stakes were so high, the lobbying coalitions on each side were broad and complex. Fundamentally, Democrats and their traditional interest group supporters promoted the reform effort while Republicans and their core supporters opposed. The interest group coalition supporting reform included the AARP, AMA, AFL-CIO, civil rights groups, advocates for the poor and disabled, MoveOn.org, and a coalition of drug companies, doctors, and for-profit hospitals called Americans for Stable Quality Care. Another coalition of supporting groups was called Health Care for America Now. Opponents put together a broad coalition of coalitions as well. The conservative Heritage

Foundation led a coalition called the Health Policy Consensus Group, while another coalition was called Conservatives for Patients' Rights. The opposition was led by the always formidable U.S. Chamber of Commerce and a group called America's Health Care Providers representing the insurance industry. Freedom Works, led by former Republican House Majority Leader Dick Armey, and the "Tea Party" movement were also vocal in their opposition.

Drug companies struck a deal with the White House to guarantee their profits well into the future. They spent almost $270 million on lobbying in 2009, mostly in favor of the bill, though they did hedge their bets when it looked like their deal might not hold. Drug company spending in 2009 was more than any industry had ever spent on lobbying in a single year. Just to put their $270 million into perspective, it is $100 million more than the next largest industry, oil and gas, spent on lobbying in 2009. In addition to their lobbying expenditures, the drug companies spent $120 to 130 million on television advertising and grassroots organizing. Hospitals, who also struck a deal with the White House to support the bill, spent almost $110 million on lobbying.

The insurance companies spent $162 million lobbying against health care reform and the Chamber spent about $144 million on lobbying and another $50 million on television advertising. The insurance companies were always wary and in the end turned fiercely against reform. Initially, the insurance companies were promised that if they agreed to insure all Americans, without reference to pre-existing conditions and annual and lifetime expense caps, the bill would require all Americans to buy health insurance and provide subsidies to assist the poor in doing so. As the debate played out, the insurance

Stephen Crowley / *New York Times*

As the U.S. House prepared to vote on the health care bill on March 21, 2010, demonstrators for and against the bill faced off outside the Capitol.

companies concluded that the requirement to buy insurance and the subsidies to assist the poor would be too weak, and so they bolted.[31] The Chamber of Commerce opposed the effort from the start because it contained employer mandates requiring all employers with over 25 employees to offer health insurance. If companies did not offer health insurance they would have to pay the federal government $750 per fulltime worker per year.

Key Provisions in the Health Care Bill

In an unusual Sunday evening session, on March 21, 2010, House Democrats, with no Republican support, passed the health care overhaul bill by a vote of 219 to 212 and sent it on to the president for his signature. The process of crafting and passing the bill had been long and messy, in fact, a second companion bill had to be passed to seal the deal. The key elements of health care reform were an expansion of coverage, regulation of health insurance industry practices, and taxes and fees to finance the reforms.

First, health care reform sought to expand health insurance coverage to 32 million previously uninsured Americans by 2019 when fully implemented. This would have increased coverage from 83 percent to 95 percent of all Americans. About half of the newly insured were expected to be added to the Medicaid rolls. These would be poor persons, including formerly ineligible childless adults and parents of eligible children, up to 133 percent ($29,327) of the federal poverty line. The other half would select private insurance policies offered within federal and state-run insurance exchanges. A sliding scale of federal subsidies for persons making between 133 percent and 400 percent ($88,200) of the federal poverty line would be available to help make health insurance polities offered in the exchanges affordable. Finally, gaps in federal support of prescription drug coverage for the elderly would be filled by 2020.

Second, health care reform limited certain health insurance industry practices. Since 2010, dependent children up to the age of 26 have been allowed to stay on their parents' health insurance policy and health insurance companies have been prohibited from setting annual or lifetime caps on insurance payouts. And since 2014, insurance companies have been forbidden to deny insurance coverage based on preexisting conditions, such as cancer, diabetes, or congenital defects and abnormalities. Other important regulations required private companies with more than 50 employees to provide health insurance coverage to their employees or pay a penalty and required individuals, mostly self-employed or working for small companies, to purchase health insurance in the state exchanges or pay a penalty.

Third, covering tens of millions of people is not cheap, so new taxes, fees, and penalties were levied to pay the additional costs. The existing Medicare payroll tax was increased by 3.8 percent for individuals making more than $200,000 annually and families making more than $250,000. New taxes and fees were levied on health insurers and medical device makers. Companies selling brand name drugs and high cost "Cadillac" insurance plans were taxed. In both cases, the goal was to save money in health care by moving consumers to generic drugs and to make them more sensitive to medical costs in general by discouraging expensive insurance that covers everything and leaves consumers with no reason to consider the cost of medical care.

Finally, the claim, based on Congressional Budget Office (CBO) analysis, was that these taxes, fees, and savings would more than pay for the cost of health care reform. CBO says health care reform would cost $940 billion over the first ten years, but that revenues would total $1.083 trillion, thereby reducing projected deficits by $143 billion over ten years. While these estimates

Pro & Con

Obamacare: Revise or Repeal

The Affordable Care Act (ACA), better known as Obamacare, was the most important new domestic policy initiative in decades. Democrats put everything they had behind its passage and Republicans did everything they could to block its passage and to delay and disrupt its implementation. Now that most major elements of Obamacare have been implemented, with 7.5 million Americans signing up on the healthcare exchanges and another 3 to 4 million signing up for Medicaid, supporters and opponents have refined, though not changed, their arguments.

Supporters of Obamacare, mostly Democrats, argue that millions of people are benefiting from the program and that Republicans, with nothing comparable to put in its place, would not dare to repeal it. They further claim that the longer the program is in place and people come to see its benefits more clearly, the more popular it will become. Opponents, mostly Republicans, argue that the program will likely collapse as costs escalate, people lose their existing health insurance and doctors, and tens of millions remain without health insurance. They argue that

Obamacare should be repealed, but that their alternative program would retain many of its popular elements, including prohibitions on denial of insurance for preexisting conditions, on annual and lifetime caps, and exclusion of young people from their parents' insurance before the age of 26. Further, they argue, their alternative program would include provisions like the opportunity to buy insurance across state lines, join high risk insurance pools, and participate in health savings accounts (HSAs), to drive down costs.

Public opinion on Obamacare has always varied by partisanship and ideology. On approval or disapproval of Obamacare, opinion is often split almost evenly. Most Democrats support the law, while independents remain ambivalent and most Republicans continue to oppose it. Nonetheless, two-to-one majorities support revision of Obamacare over repeal.

What do you think?

- Is access to health insurance and health care a human right or is it something for which individuals and families should be responsible?
- Is Obamacare a major domestic policy achievement or yet one more entitlement program burdening a national budget already deeply in the red?

PRO	CON
Health care is a right	For most, it is a private responsibility
Millions previously uninsured are now covered	It is a burden on federal and state budgets
Now in place, it cannot be repealed	It must be replaced with a sustainable program

were viewed skeptically by many, they were instrumental in reassuring Democrats that they could support health care reform without busting the budget.[32]

The Fight Goes On—Inside and Outside Lobbying after Adoption

Even after the main battle—win or lose—interest groups have powerful incentives to keep fighting. Once health care reform passed, proponents and opponents shifted their focus from Congress to the executive branch where the implementing regulations would be written. Some opponents took the additional step of preparing to challenge the bill in the courts. Republican elected officials and their supporters continued to work the public with the theme of "repeal and revise."

Inside lobbying focused on the bureaucracy while outside lobbying focused on the courts and the public. Inside lobbyists, whether they supported or opposed the bill, know that federal requirements governing insurance coverage, access to the insurance exchanges, and employer mandates remain to be written. They can be written tight or they can be written loose. Nancy LeaMond of AARP, said "Our role as an advocate does not stop once a piece of legislation is signed. We know that the devil's in the details, and so much of what is actually delivered to our members in this bill is determined at the regulatory level, both at the federal level and in the states."[33] Opponents like the U.S. Chamber of Commerce promised to lobby for more

Eric Thayer / *New York Times* / Redux

Even after an important bill like health care reform passes Congress and is signed into law by the president, the fight often continues in Congress, the bureaucracy, and the courts.

business-friendly regulatory language. But clearly, proponents have the advantage in inside lobbying.

Hence, opponents moved quickly to outside lobbying techniques, such as television commercials, town meetings, and contributions to friendly candidates. The goal of negative public lobbying is to aggravate doubts about health care reform and to defeat Democratic supporters of the bill and replace them with Republicans who will work to revise the legislation if they cannot repeal it. Opponents poured hundreds of millions of dollars into the 2010 midterm elections and helped the Republican Party take back the House. In 2012, Republican presidential candidates promised that, if elected, they would repeal Obamacare "on day one." Proponents promised an equally vigorous educational and electoral campaign. Their hope is that, as with Medicare and the prescription drug bill, early reservations among the public and in the opinion polls will improve as people find out more about the program and experience its benefits.

Opponents also moved immediately to the courts. Within five minutes of Obama's signing the bill, Virginia's Republican Attorney General, Ken Cuccinelli, filed suit contesting its constitutionality. Within weeks, 26 state Attorneys General (mostly Republican), led by Florida's Bill McCollum, filed suit to stop implementation nationally. The Attorneys General argue that the bill dramatically overreached on Congress's Article I, section 8 power to regulate interstate commerce by ordering that every person must have health insurance. They also argue that this vast new federal program would change the relationship between the federal and state governments in violation of Tenth Amendment guarantees of the states' reserved powers.

Beginning in late 2010, several federal district and appellate courts held the law constitutional while several others found part, usually the individual mandate, or all of the law unconstitutional. As the number of conflicting opinions among the lower courts grew, the U.S. Justice Department in September 2011 asked the U.S. Supreme Court to resolve the dispute. The Supreme Court heard an unprecedented five hours of oral argument across three days in March 2012 and ruled in June, just as the 2012 general election campaign for president shifted into high gear.

Stunningly, Chief Justice John Roberts, writing for a narrow 5–4 majority, held that even though the commerce clause could not sustain the health care law, it was constitutional based on the taxing power. While the court generally upheld Obamacare in mid-2012, it also poked a significant hole in it. The court held narrowly that the health care law was constitutional, based on the tax provisions rather than the commerce provisions of the Constitution, though it declared that states could not be forced to expand their Medicaid programs to cover the poorest. About half the states, including large states with lots of uninsured poor like Texas and Florida, initially refused to expand Medicaid, claiming the burden on state budgets was too great.

The Supreme Court's declaration that Obamacare was constitutional ended the enactment phase of the fight, though it did not end the fight itself. Opponents inside and outside of government continued the fight on two key fronts.

The Republican-controlled U.S. House of Representatives voted nearly thirty times in 2012 and 2013 to revise, delay, or defund Obamacare. Outside government, opponents like the Chamber of Commerce and the Catholic Church funded media campaigns and court cases designed to undercut support for the health care law or limit its coverage, especially for contraception and abortion services. Opponents slowed but did not stop Obamacare.

The Obama administration's principal responsibility, in addition to fighting off the law's opponents, was to write the thousands of pages of rules and regulations required to bring the health care law to life and build the federal website that would allow people to sign up for the new insurance. These were always going to be huge and complicated tasks. Unfortunately, at least initially, the administration failed at them. The law required action by many public and private entities and organizations that had to be electronically connected and coordinated. Rules were late, mandates were delayed, and the debut of the federal website on October 1, 2013 was very rocky. Poor website design, construction, and testing meant endless frustration for citizens trying to sign up and data sent from the website to insurance companies were badly flawed. Opponents sprang forward to declare that the fault was not simply in a poorly designed website but in the law itself—irremediably flawed they said.

After weeks of feverish repair work on the website, citizen frustration ebbed and the registration process became smoother. By the end of the official enrollment period, March 31, 2014, nearly 15 million citizens had signed up for health insurance or had been added to the state Medicaid roles. As the numbers grew, Republican opposition began slowly to shift and even to moderate. Some Republican governors, like Rick Scott of Florida and John Kasich of Ohio, approved Medicaid expansion and congressional leaders worried that taking coverage from those that had it was more politically dangerous than opposing a program not yet implemented. Republicans again threatened to repeal the law as soon as they were able. The fight goes on.[34]

Chapter Summary

The Founders were concerned that factions, because they reflect divisions within the community, would make the public interest and the common good more difficult to define and pursue. Madison hoped that the sheer size of the United States would limit the possibility that people with shared interests could come together to press their case on government. In the intervening two centuries, however, technological developments have rendered Madison's hope illusory.

All of the institutions that we have described in this chapter—business and labor groups, professional and volunteer associations, citizens' groups—serve to link groups of citizens to their government and to the political realm. Interest groups, which are often narrow and highly focused, try to influence the development and implementation of policies that affect their members. Interest groups draw upon resources including group size, money, intensity, and leadership to press their case on government. They usually prefer an insider strategy of quiet lobbying but are sometimes forced into an outside strategy of grassroots campaigning and protest.

The debate over Obamacare was one of the great, no-holds-barred, interest group fights of recent memory. Broad and diverse interest groups coalitions formed on both sides of the issue and both sides put hundreds of millions of dollars into the fight. These funds paid for the full range of inside and outside lobbying techniques. Even after the fight seemingly was over and health care had passed, lobbyists were redeployed to influence the work of the regulators and the thinking of the public on health care reform. Moreover, big programs are under almost constant revision and long after public attention has faded the lobbyists will still be at work to see that those revisions work for their clients.

Early in the chapter, students were introduced to two theories about how interest groups organize and operate in the United States. Elite theory holds that interest groups organize and operate readily around corporate interests and the interests of the socio-economic elite more generally. Pluralist theory recognizes the advantages enjoyed by elites but argues that groups will form, perhaps not as readily or thickly, around public and community interests, including those of minorities, the poor, and the unpopular.

WHAT DO YOU THINK?

- Now that you have been through the chapter and better understand how interest groups organize and operate, what assets various groups wield, and how they interact with government and the broader public, does elitism or pluralism seem the better description?
- If elitism is often the better description, what does this mean for our democracy?

Key Terms

AFL-CIO 168

elitism 161

inside strategy 176

interest groups 160

litigation 178

lobbyists 175

outside strategy 177

peak associations 167

pluralism 161

trade associations 167

Suggested Readings

Baumgartner, Frank R., Jeffrey M. Berry, Marie Hojnacki, David C. Kimball and Beth L. Leech. *Basic Interests: The Importance of Groups in Political and Political Science*. Chicago: University of Chicago Press, 2009. In a study of 98 issues, this book found that despite spending millions, lobbyists fail more often than they succeed in changing policy.

Cigler, Allan J. and Burdett A. Loomis. *Interest Group Politics*, 8th ed. Washington, D.C.: CQ Press, 2011. A leading general introduction to the study of interest groups.

Clemens, Elisabeth. "Politics Without Party: The Organizational Accomplishments of Disenfranchised Women," 1997. Prior to women's suffrage, because women had no access to party organizations, they cooperated directly with government agencies to initiate services for vulnerable women and children.

Gibson, Joseph. *Persuading Congress: A Practical Guide to Parlaying an Understanding of Congressional Folkways and Dynamics into Successful Advocacy on Capitol Hill.* TheCapitol.net, 2010. Former top staffer on the House Judiciary Committee describes the nuts and bolts of effective lobbying.

Gray, Virginia, David Lowrey, and Jennifer Benz, *Interest Groups and Health Care Reform Across the United States.* Washington, D.C.: Georgetown University Press, 2013. Review of the Affordable Care Act and how it was dealt with in the states.

Harris, Richard and Daniel Tichenor. "Organized Interests and American Political Development," 2002–2003. Harris and Tichenor found that there was a surge of interest group formation and activity in the Progressive Era, well before the better known expansions of the New Deal and the 1960s.

Lowery, David and Holly Brasher. *Organized Interests and American Government.* Prospect Heights, IL: Waveland Press, 2011. Explores how organized interests try to exercise influence and asks whether these activities are as negative as they as they are often portrayed.

Web Resources

For practice quizzes, key term flashcards, videos, links, and other study tools, visit the *American Government* website: www.routledge.com/cw/jillson

1. **www.naacp.org**
   Official website of the National Association for the Advancement of Colored People (NAACP). This page provides a wealth of information about the organization that spearheaded much of the civil rights movement of the 1950s and 1960s.

2. **www.mojones.com**
   Mother Jones magazine has an online compendium of resources regarding money and political interest. It also contains a database of the 400 largest individual contributors in the U.S.

3. **www.opensecrets.com**
   This is the leading website tracking campaign contributions by candidate, industry, party and much more.

4. **www.aflcio.org/index.cfm**

   This site offers press releases and speeches, as well as links to union affiliates, AFL-CIO state federations, and central labor councils. In addition, it gives information on various grassroots activities, including its project on working women.

5. **www.citizen.org**

   Public Citizen, founded by Ralph Nader in 1971, is a site that informs the activist and consumer about safety issues that are discussed in Congress such as drugs, medical devices, cleaner energy sources, automotive safety, and fair trade. The organization has the goal of maintaining a more open and democratic government by serving the public as a "Congress Watch."

Chapter 7

POLITICAL PARTIES
Winning the Right to Govern

❝ Political parties created democracy ... and modern democracy is unthinkable save in terms of parties. ❞

E.E. SCHATTSCHNEIDER,
Party Government, 1942

SHOULD THE STATES MAKE ELECTION RULES?

Article I, section 4 (in part): "The times, places and manner of holding elections for Senators and Representatives, shall be prescribed in each state by the legislature thereof; but the Congress may at any time by law make or alter such regulations."

The constitutional provision above reflects the Founders understanding that states, under the general supervision of Congress, should set their own election rules. The Founders anticipated, correctly, that states would organize their elections somewhat differently from each other—and in fact universal white manhood suffrage came to some states before others, so did women's suffrage, and some states charged poll taxes on those wishing to vote while others did not. But Congress was empowered to evaluate these differences and to make illegal those they concluded were not just unfair, but unconstitutionally unfair. Universal white manhood suffrage came by state legislative action before the Civil War, but black and female suffrage came by constitutional amendment, the Fifteenth in 1870 and the Nineteenth in 1920, and the poll tax was outlawed by the Twenty-fourth Amendment in 1964.

Today, everyone seems to agree that elections should be open, fair, and honest. Voters should be legally entitled to cast a ballot and officials should count all the ballots legally cast. Reasonable steps should be taken to insure the integrity of the electoral process, but sometimes it is not so easy to tell reasonable from unreasonable steps. For example, there is a heated debate over whether voter ID laws passed by two-thirds of the states in recent years are reasonable or not?

The widely respected National Conference of State Legislatures (NCSL) has tried to help by distinguishing between strict and non-strict voter ID laws and between photo and non-photo laws. Strict voter ID states require voters who show up at the polls without acceptable ID to cast a provisional ballot and to return within a few days with the right ID before the provisional ballot will be counted. Non-strict states may require a voter without acceptable ID to sign an affidavit of identity but do not require them to return with more ID. The strictest states require specific forms of photo identification. For example, Texas requires voters to present one of seven forms of photo ID—a driver's license, election identification certificate, Department of Public Safety personal ID card, military ID, a citizenship certificate, U.S. passport, or a concealed handgun permit. Other states require ID, but allow a much wider range of identification, including a utility bill or a paystub.

Proponents of voter ID laws, mostly Republicans, argue that elections are sacrosanct and it is just common sense to require potential voters to prove they are who they claim to be. They also argue that positive identification, usually a photo ID, is required to board an airplane or check out a library book, and so are not an undue burden on voting—everyone has them.

Opponents, mostly Democrats, argue that voter ID laws are a solution in search of a problem. Reports of voter impersonation, where a photo ID might stop an illegal vote from being cast, are extremely rare. Instead, they argue, strict voter ID laws are intended to exclude those least likely to have the required ID—the poor, the elderly, and ethnic and racial minorities.

In 2013, the first election after the strict Texas voter ID law came into effect, both candidates for governor, the Republican Greg Abbott and the Democrat Wendy Davis, were required to cast provisional ballots because their names on their driver's licenses and on the voter rolls were slightly different. Moreover, 90-year-old Jim Wright, a former Democratic congressman and former Speaker of the U.S. House of Representatives, initially was denied a Texas voter identification card because his driver's license had expired—he's 90.

Focus Questions: from reading to thinking

Q1 How has the role of political parties in American politics changed over the course of the nation's history?

Q2 How did the progressive reforms of the late nineteenth and early twentieth centuries affect political parties in the United States?

Q3 Are American political parties in decline, and, if so, should we be worried about it?

Q4 What roles have minor parties, often called third parties, played in American history?

Q5 Are interest groups or political parties the best vehicle for representing citizen opinion to government?

WHAT DO YOU THINK?

- Are voter ID laws reasonable or unreasonable?
- Are there any groups of citizens you think would have a difficult time getting the required identification?

POLITICAL PARTIES IN THE UNITED STATES

The founding generation was deeply skeptical of what James Madison called "factions" and what today we call interest groups and political parties. The Founders believed that there was a public interest and a common good and that statesmen might discover and act upon them. Factions, groups, and parties reflected divisions and disagreements within the governing class and perhaps the public about the nature, even the existence, of the common good. Not until the 1830s did Americans begin to consider that the clash of political parties might actually be healthy, even necessary, for democracy.

Over the course of the nineteenth century, Americans came to believe that parties could organize, structure, and facilitate democratic politics in ways that made it easier for citizens to participate. Absent parties, voters must study every issue and every candidate independently. But parties have histories, they have reputations as standing for corporate interests or for the common man, and citizens can choose the party that usually represents them best. Choosing a party is easier than studying every issue and every candidate in every election.[1]

Getty Images

Conservative pundit, television personality and former vice presidential candidate Sarah Palin takes the stage to speak during the 41st annual Conservative Political Action Conference (CPAC). The conference, a project of the American Conservative Union, brings together conservatives, politicians, pundits, and voters for three days of speeches and workshops, exemplifying the "party as social networks."

The distinguishing characteristic of a **political party** is that its candidates compete in elections in the hope of winning executive branch offices and majority control of legislatures. Parties recruit and screen candidates, offer platforms, contest elections, and, if they win, attempt to implement their campaign promises. The losing party acts as a watchdog, criticizes the governing party, exposes corruption and abuse of power, and prepares for the next election. Contemporary students of political parties have generally agreed with E.E. Schattschneider that modern democratic politics are unthinkable except in terms of parties. Table 7.1 highlights the several key roles played by parties in our democracy.

While the basic goals of American political parties—winning office, controlling public policy, keeping an eye on the opposition—seem clear, scholars disagree about the origins and driving dynamics of parties. Just as pluralists see a welter of interest groups in society, some scholars see political parties as loose coalitions of like-minded social groups and interests. In this view, parties are "big tents," with the Democratic tent sheltering mostly liberal to moderate people and interests and the Republican tent sheltering mostly moderate to conservative people and interests. Both tents have their flaps up so that new members and new groups can enter. Hence, each party works to attract some of the people and groups that lean toward the other party. The Democratic Party works to attract some small businesspeople, and the Republican Party works to attract some blacks.[2]

political party An organization designed to elect government officeholders under a given label.

TABLE 7.1   Political Parties in Democratic Politics

1. Parties provide channels through which ordinary citizens can affect the course of government.
2. Parties give political leaders reliable bases on which to build support for their programs in the legislature and among the general electorate.
3. Parties offer a means for organizing dissent against the policies of an incumbent administration.
4. Parties, to protect their own rights of free expression, are natural guardians of civil liberties.
5. Parties "keep each other honest," since each party has a political interest in exposing corruption, deception, and abuses of authority by its opposition.
6. Parties perform many of the chores of democracy, such as getting voters registered and to the polls, disseminating information, and organizing public meetings for expression of opinion.
7. Parties recruit and screen candidates for public office, from local election officials to president of the United States.
8. Parties spur the development of new ideas.

Source: A. James Reichley, *The Life of the Parties: A History of American Political Parties* (New York: Rowman and Littlefield, 2000), 340.

An alternative to the big tent view of parties is the "responsible party model." Advocates of responsible parties argue that parties should be clear about what they stand for so voters can know what they will get if they give a party their votes. Responsible parties campaign on coherent and detailed platforms, seek to implement them if elected, and stand to be judged on them when they seek reelection.[3]

Finally, some scholars reject both the big tent and responsible party models. They argue that parties are best seen as "social networks" of party officials, candidates, officeholders, and voters, but also supportive interest groups, social movements, campaign consultants, donors, and partisan elements of the media. Parties as social networks evolve over time, but do not change completely, as new leaders, movements, and issues arise—think of the effect that the "Tea Party" has had on the Republican Party since 2009.[4] As we shall see below, each of these perspectives on American parties provides insights as we look at parties and partisanship in campaigns, elections, and governance.

We now turn to the place of parties in the American political system. First, we describe the broad party eras of American political history in terms of the leading figures, principal issues, and relative successes of the major parties during each period. Second, we assess the state of modern political parties in the electorate, as organizations, and in the government. Third, we assess the special role that minor parties play in American politics and how they, together with the interest groups discussed in the previous chapter, relate to and affect the performance of the major parties. Fourth, we ask what changes the future is likely to hold for American political parties and how we can expect parties to respond to those changes. Finally, we ask whether specifics reforms might improve the performance of parties.

Party Eras in American Politics

Citizens today expect the same things from politics and government that they expected from them two hundred years ago.[5] Citizens expect security, opportunity, and progress; they expect that they and their families will be safe and secure, that they will have opportunities to compete fairly for the good things that society has to offer, and that they and their children will be better off over time if they work hard. Political parties compete by offering alternative visions of how government should assist citizens in achieving a better future.[6]

As we shall see, a party must do more than win a single election to have the opportunity to implement its vision. A party must win the presidency, both houses of the national Congress, most of the governorships, and majorities in most of the state legislatures, and hold them long enough and by margins large enough to overcome opponents entrenched in the bureaucracies and courts of the land. Only then can a party program be enacted into law and allowed sufficient time to see whether it works as promised.

Historically, the American political system has undergone major changes in partisan balance about every thirty-five years (see Table 7.2). In each case, about fifteen years of one-party dominance was followed by fifteen to twenty years of competitive politics in which the major parties alternated in power, third parties rose to contest new issues, and divided government was common. This pattern was particularly clear between the 1830s and the 1960s and was preceded and followed by periods of looser and more fluid partisan activity. Partisanship began making a comeback in the mid-1980s and remains strong today.

There is an extensive literature in political science, called realignment theory or critical realignment theory, describing and explaining this pattern in American political party competition. In 1955, the prominent political scientist V.O. Key published *A Theory of Critical Elections* in which he argued that certain elections, usually fought over critical issues like democracy, slavery, war, and economic turmoil, realign or restructure the political system and the distribution of partisan power within it. For example, Lincoln's election in 1860 and the Civil War that followed left the Republican Party in power for a generation. Similarly, Franklin Roosevelt's election in 1932 and his response to the Great Depression and World War II produced Democratic dominance for a generation. But as these great partisan battles fade, voters loosen their commitment to the established party system in a process called dealignment, new issues arise, and party competition becomes less predictable.

One hears talk of realignment around many presidential elections, as when George W. Bush won reelection and expanded congressional majorities in 2004 or when Barack Obama and the Democrats swept to power in 2008.

Q1 How has the role of political parties in American politics changed over the course of the nation's history?

Some critics of realignment theory, most prominently Yale political scientist David Mayhew, argue that change occurs in all elections and identifying some elections, beyond the obvious candidates like 1860 and 1932, as critical is arbitrary.[7] Others argue that even if critical realignments did happen historically, they cannot any more because the rise of independents limits the number of persons likely to make long-term commitments to either major party. They contend that the electoral volatility of the last two decades is the new normal. Whichever proves to be true, Table 7.2 highlights an intriguing electoral pattern and, hence, is a good teaching and learning tool. One does

TABLE 7.2   Party Control of the Presidency (P) and Congress [House (H) and Senate (S)], 1828–2016

Election Year	P	S	H	Election Year	P	S	H	Election Year	P	S	H	Election Year	P	S	H
1828	D	D	D	1876	R	R	D	1924	R	R	R	1972	R	D	D
1830		D	D	1878		D	D	1926		R	R	1974		D	D
1832	D	D	D	1880	R	R	R	1928	R	R	R	1976	D	D	D
1834		D	D	1882		R	D	1930		R	D	1978		D	D
1836	D	D	D	1884	D	R	D	1932	D	D	D	1980	R	R	D
1838		D	D	1886		R	D	1934		D	D	1982		R	D
1840	W	W	W	1888	R	R	R	1936	D	D	D	1984	R	R	D
1842		W	D	1890		R	D	1938		D	D	1986		D	D
1844	D	D	D	1892	D	D	D	1940	D	D	D	1988	R	D	D
1846		D	W	1894		R	R	1942		D	D	1990		D	D
1848	W	D	D	1896	R	R	R	1944	D	D	D	1992	D	D	D
1850		D	D	1898		R	R	1946		R	R	1994		R	R
1852	D	D	D	1900	R	R	R	1948	D	D	D	1996	D	R	R
1854		D	R	1902		R	R	1950		D	D	1998		R	R
1856	D	D	D	1904	R	R	R	1952	R	R	R	2000	R	R	R
1858		D	R	1906		R	R	1954		R	D	2002		R	R
1860	R	R	R	1908	R	R	R	1956	R	D	D	2004	R	R	R
1862		R	R	1910		R	D	1958		D	D	2006		D	D
1864	R	R	R	1912	D	D	D	1960	D	D	D	2008	D	D	D
1866		R	R	1914		D	D	1962		D	D	2010		D	R
1868	R	R	R	1916	D	D	D	1964	D	D	D	2012	D	D	R
1870		R	R	1918		R	R	1966		D	D	2014	D	R	R
1872	R	R	R	1920	R	R	R	1968	R	D	D				
1874		R	D	1922		R	R	1970		D	D				

D = Democrat. R = Republican. W = Whig.

Source: Jerome M. Clubb, William H. Flanigan, and Nancy H. Zingale, *Partisan Realignment: Voters, Parties, and Government in American History* (Beverly Hills, CA: Sage, 1980), 164. Updated by author.

not have to believe that the next realignment is overdue or just around the corner to see realignment as good shorthand for the argument that the elections of 1800, 1828, 1860, 1896, and 1932 were important turning points in the nation's party history.

The Preparty Period. The founding generation believed that politics can be organized to place the best men in the community in an institutional setting where reasoned debate and inquiry might discover the public interest. Political parties, or factions more generally, they believed, both reflect and aggravate unhealthy divisions within the public and make discovery of the public interest more difficult.

The men who wrote the federal Constitution intended to produce a conservative and stable national government managed by the leading citizens of the new nation. However, what actually happened, even as early as the latter part of President Washington's first term, was that factions formed in the cabinet and the Congress around Alexander Hamilton on the one hand and James Madison and Thomas Jefferson on the other. These competing factional leaders were the unwitting fathers of the American party system.[8]

Alexander Hamilton, secretary of the treasury and President Washington's closest adviser, proposed an economic program that envisioned a powerful national government oriented toward northern commercial and manufacturing interests. Although virtually all of the northern congressmen and even many southern congressmen close to the administration supported Hamilton's programs, a loose opposition made up mostly of representatives of southern agrarian interests began to form around James Madison. Secretary of State Thomas Jefferson opposed Hamilton in the cabinet until it became clear that Washington preferred Hamilton's counsel. Jefferson resigned and returned to Virginia.

The period of Federalist ascendancy barely outlasted President Washington's second term. Although Vice President John Adams, Washington's chosen successor, did win the election of 1796, Thomas Jefferson ran second and, given the rules of that time, became vice president.

1800–1824: Federalists versus Jeffersonian Republicans. Although the divisions in Congress deepened and stabilized during the first half of the 1790s, they did not extend into the electorate until the late 1790s.[9] Both the Federalists and the Jeffersonian Republicans (later called Democrats) assumed that the political conversation was rightly held within the elite. The Federalists, unfortunately, held this view much more publicly than did the Democrats. They were not bashful about explaining to the common man, particularly if he were without property, that he lacked the necessary experience, stability, and judgment to play a full role in the political life of his community.

The Federalists drew their strength from the northern, urban, and commercial interests of the country. The Democrats drew their strength from

---

Struggling Toward Democracy

We think of the U.S. as a democracy, but listen to Alexander Hamilton in the Constitutional Convention— "The voice of the people has been said to be the voice of God; and however generally this maxim has been quoted and believed, it is not true in fact. The people are turbulent and changing, they seldom judge or determine right."

What do you think?

- Do many Americans today share Hamilton's view?
- Should government policy follow the "voice of the people" at all times and on all matters?

the agrarian interests of the South and West. Clearly, in a nation composed more than 90 percent of small farmers, the Democrats had an overwhelming strategic advantage. Jefferson, Madison, and Monroe won two presidential elections apiece between 1800 and 1824. The Federalists were uncompetitive outside New England after 1812. Yet, even in this moment of one-party dominance, the Democrats remained skeptical of parties. They believed that their party had been necessary to oppose the Federalist agenda. Now that the Federalists had been defeated, party itself could be done away with and the Jeffersonians could govern in the interest of the whole community. It was not to be.

1828–1856: Jacksonian Democrats versus Whigs. Political parties as we know them came into being during the 1830s.[10] An expanded electorate and popular election of state executives and presidential electors created organizational, management, and communication problems that had simply not existed earlier. Moreover, Monroe's retirement from the presidency in 1824 produced an intense political scramble. Although Andrew Jackson received the most votes for president, he did not have a majority. By constitutional requirement, the decision was thrown into the House of Representatives, where House Speaker Henry Clay maneuvered to deliver the victory to John Quincy Adams (son of former President John Adams). Adams then quickly named Clay to the coveted office of secretary of state, and charges of a "corrupt bargain" filled the air.

Supporters of Andrew Jackson, led by Martin Van Buren of New York, began to organize for the election of 1828. Van Buren and those around him in the Jackson movement were the first American politicians to make the positive case for parties. They argued that the political party was a vehicle by which common citizens, if well organized, might take control of government and enact the political views of the majority into law. If, as part of the process, the spoils of politics, in the form of offices, contracts, and various other opportunities, fell to the party faithful, so much the better.[11] Andrew Jackson stood for an expanded and democratized Jeffersonian vision of limited government in which average men in their local communities could enjoy the fruits of their labor without fear of arbitrary power. Small government, low taxes, and individual freedom were the watchwords. Democratic candidates for the presidency won three elections in a row, and six out of eight, between 1828 and 1856.

Others, however, thought in broader terms and sought opportunities on a grander, national and even international, scale. Over the course of the 1830s, Henry Clay championed the "American system," a renewed Federalist agenda of high tariffs and internal improvements to protect and foster industrial development. Daniel Webster of Connecticut and Massachusetts, Thurlow Weed and William Seward of New York, and Thaddeus Stevens of Pennsylvania were arguing for similar policies. During the latter half of the 1830s, these various centers of opposition to Jackson, Van Buren, and their programs came together to form the Whig Party.[12]

The Whigs found that they had no choice but to match the Democrats' party organization and electoral techniques if they were to compete with

The Granger Collection, NYC

Whigs hold an election rally during the 1840 presidential campaign. The Whig candidate, William Henry Harrison, defeated the incumbent Democratic president, Martin Van Buren. Note the Whig Party headquarters sign—Democratic Whig—as an attempt to fish in the other party's pond.

them in the electorate. By 1840, the Whigs had won twenty governorships, and they won the presidency in 1840 and 1848. The Democrats and the Whigs were evenly balanced national parties from 1840 to the eve of the Civil War.

1860–1892: The Civil War System. The contest over slavery and its role in America's future reduced the Democrats to a predominantly southern party, destroyed the Whigs, and led to the rise of the Republican Party in the North. The Republican Party of the late 1850s stood for free soil, meaning cheap family farms in the Midwest, and against the expansion of slavery. By 1860, when Abraham Lincoln was elected the first Republican president, his party also enjoyed majority control of both houses of the national Congress, the governorship of every northern state, and both houses of most of the northern state legislatures. Voter turnout in the presidential contest of 1860 was the second highest in all of American history, 82 percent of the eligible electorate.

The Republicans held the presidency and both houses of Congress from 1860 to 1874, when the Democrats broke through in the House. Between 1876 and 1896, Democrats and Republicans again competed evenly, with Democrats behind Grover Cleveland winning two of five presidential elections and enjoying control of the House for sixteen of the twenty-two years between 1874 and 1896. The Republicans held the Senate for eighteen of these years.

Once Reconstruction ended in 1876 and Union troops withdrew from the South, the Republicans developed a broader version of the traditional Federalist and then Whig programs of aggressive economic development. The Republicans combined subsidies to support economic development, high tariffs for commerce and industry, and free homesteads for those who wished to establish family farms in the Midwest, with open immigration to ensure an adequate supply of labor for the factory and the farm. However, when Republican tariff and currency policies bore more and more heavily on the nation's farmers, the party stood resolutely with the interests of corporate capital. The South was left to languish in social dislocation, racial strife, and economic ruin.[13]

Elections in the last quarter of the nineteenth century featured massive torchlight parades, picnics, and rallies to which people would flock by the thousands to hear candidates engage in day-long debates or in speeches that might go on for hours. In cities and counties across the country, the parties controlled hundreds, sometimes thousands, of patronage jobs, contracts, and related opportunities. At the national level, the parties in Congress were as cohesive and militant as they have ever been. Voter turnout was consistently over 80 percent, higher than at any other time in American history.

1896–1928: The System of 1896. Competitive party dynamics during the period from 1896 to 1928 were remarkably similar to those of earlier party systems: a fourteen-year period of majority party dominance, followed by a period of conservatism and drift, leading up to the next realignment. The dramatically different programs offered by the major parties in 1896 made it a decisive election. The Republicans offered William McKinley and the promise of business-led prosperity. The Democrats offered William Jennings Bryan and a program designed to protect farmers and other small interests, mostly in the South and West, from the unrestrained power of commerce and industry.

More than 82 percent of eligible voters turned out to cast their ballots. McKinley and the Republicans took the presidency and both houses of

Congress in 1896, holding all three until the congressional elections of 1910, when the Democrats took control of the House. The Democrats then won the presidential elections of 1912 and 1916, although their inroads into the House and Senate were limited to the first six years of the Wilson presidency. Following World War I, the Republicans held sway until the Democrats again broke through in the House elections of 1930.

Progressive revolts within both major parties between 1900 and 1920 changed the American party system dramatically. Progressives cut away the patronage base of the spoils system by enacting civil service reform to organize and regulate federal government employment. In the years that followed, voter registration requirements, the Australian (secret) ballot, and opportunities for split-ticket voting were widely adopted. These reforms were designed to reduce the control of the political parties over the choices that voters made. Other party-weakening reforms followed. In 1903, Wisconsin adopted a **party primary** system of nomination for office, wherein all of the voters affiliated with the party, not just party bosses and insiders, voted in an election to pick the party's nominee. Fifteen states adopted the primary system by 1912, and twenty-six states were using it by 1916.

The role of the individual citizen and voter was further enhanced by the widespread adoption of **initiative**, **referendum**, and **recall** provisions during this period. In general, initiative allows voters to put questions on the ballot, referendum allows state and local governments to put questions on the ballot, and recall allows voters to remove offensive officeholders before the normal ends of their terms. The party-weakening reforms of the Progressive Era took effect steadily over the first half of the twentieth century.[14]

1932–1964: The New Deal System. Following the stock market crash of October 1929, the onset of the Depression, and President Hoover's ineffective response to it, Franklin Roosevelt and the Democrats swept to power in 1932. The problems faced by the nation during this period were huge. The early years of the Depression saw the gross national product (GNP) fall by one-third, from $104 billion in 1929 to $74 billion in 1933, and unemployment grow from 5 percent to more than 25 percent.

Roosevelt attacked the Depression with federal activity on many fronts. To combat unemployment, he made the federal government the employer of last resort. Both the Civilian Conservation Corps and the Works Progress Administration employed hundreds of thousands of young people. To combat poverty among displaced workers and the elderly, he implemented the Social Security and unemployment compensation systems in 1935. Roosevelt also created or expanded a number of agencies charged with regulating the economy. The Federal Reserve (1913) was supplemented by the Securities and Exchange Commission (1935), the Federal Deposit Insurance Corporation (1935), and the Banking Act of 1935.[15]

Following the successful end of World War II, President Harry Truman built upon Roosevelt's New Deal agenda by promising every American a Fair Deal that moved the federal government into "a broad array of services like

Q2 How did the progressive reforms of the late nineteenth and early twentieth centuries affect political parties in the United States?

party primary An election in which voters identified with a political party select the candidates who will stand for election under the party label in a subsequent general election.

initiative Legal or constitutional process common in the states that allows citizens to place questions on the ballot to be decided directly by the voters.

referendum A legal or constitutional device that allows state and local governments to put questions directly to the voters for determination.

recall A legal or constitutional device that allows voters to remove an offensive officeholder before the normal end of his or her term.

medical care, . . . economic renewal of decaying cities, education, and housing."[16] The period of Democratic ascendancy, interrupted by the Eisenhower years, 1952–1960, culminated in President Lyndon Johnson's Great Society initiatives. The Johnson administration oversaw a massive expansion of federal government responsibility for poverty programs, education, housing, health care, and civil rights.

1968–2016: The Era of Divided Government.   Some argue that the traditional pattern of American party politics has passed from the scene. As with the preparty period that preceded the Jacksonian era, American political parties in the post-Vietnam and post-Watergate period seemed too weak and diffuse to implement coherent programs. The 1980s and 1990s saw a resurgence of the parties that continues through this day.

The period from 1968 to 1992 seemed to be one in which voters wanted Republicans in the White House and Democrats in the Congress. This period saw Republicans winning five of seven presidential elections, whereas Democrats held the Congress except for a brief period, 1980–1986, when the Republicans captured the Senate. The 1990s turned that pattern upside down. Bill Clinton narrowly won the presidency in 1992, only to watch the Republicans take control of both houses of Congress in 1994 for the first time since 1952. Clinton was reelected in 1996, but Republicans retained majorities in Congress. Voters seemed unwilling to permit party government and willing to try almost any variation on divided government.

Doug Mills / *New York Times*

Less than one week after the November 4, 2008 elections, President-elect Barack Obama and Michelle Obama met President George W. Bush and Laura Bush at the White House. Given the nation's history, encapsulated in the previous six pages of this book, this is a remarkable photograph.

The divided government of the late twentieth century was reflected in a deeply divided electorate as the century turned.[17] Although Democrat Al Gore won the popular vote by a margin of more than 500,000 votes over Republican George W. Bush, Bush narrowly prevailed in the Electoral College, 271 to 266, after a month-long court fight over Florida's 25 electoral votes. Just as important, the United States Senate divided perfectly, fifty Democrats and fifty Republicans, and the House Republican majority shrank to a mere handful.

In 2004, George W. Bush won the popular vote by 3.5 million votes, 59.5 million to Kerry's 56 million, and he prevailed in the Electoral College by a margin of 286 to 252. Moreover, Republicans picked up seats in both the House and the Senate to establish margins of 233 to 201 in the House and 55 to 44 in the Senate. Both the House and the Senate had one independent member who normally sided with the Democrats. Republicans emerged from the 2004 elections believing, or at least hoping, that they had established long-term majority control of the national government.

In fact, the Republican majority's hold on power was slipping even as President Bush's second term began. Bush's popularity, below 50 percent when he was reelected slipped through the 40s and into the mid-30s as the 2006 mid-term election approached. Support for the war in Iraq fell below 30 percent with twice as many Americans opposing as supporting the Republican president and Congress's handling of the war. Although the economy was expanding, most middle and working class Americans felt little of the benefit. Democrats took control of both the House and Senate, picking up 30 seats in the House and 6 in the Senate. When the 110th Congress convened in 2007, Democrats enjoyed a 233 to 202 advantage in the House and a narrower 51 to 49 margin in the Senate. Presaging another good year in 2008, Democrats won three special House elections in 2007 and early 2008, all in traditional Republican districts, to move the House margin to 236 to 199.

The Democratic Party advance carried strongly through the 2008 election cycle. Democrat Barack Obama, the first black nominee of a major party, won the presidency over John McCain by 53 percent to 46 percent. Obama carried every state the Democrats won in 2004 plus nine states that the Republicans had won that year. Obama's win was the biggest for a Democrat since LBJ's landslide victory over Barry Goldwater in 1964. Moreover, Democrats won 21 new House seats and eight new Senate seats to control the House 257 to 178 and the Senate 59 to 41. Yet while unified government and large congressional majorities offer the opportunity to govern, they do not guarantee success.

President Barack Obama entered office facing ongoing wars in Afghanistan and Iraq and a U.S. economy teetering on the edge of collapse. Democrats immediately passed a nearly $800 billion stimulus bill to spur economic recovery. Projecting that the stimulus would keep unemployment below 8 percent, Democrats turned to health care reform. Over the course of nearly a year, over staunch Republican opposition, Democrats hashed out a health care bill. In the meanwhile, unemployment continued to rise, breaking 10 percent in 2010. When Democrats faced the voters in the 2010 midterm election, they took, in Obama's words, a "shellacking." Democrats lost 6 seats in the Senate,

though they retained a 53 to 47 majority, and a jaw-dropping 63 seats in the House, where the Republicans took a 242 to 193 majority. Polls showed that voters trusted neither party and were willing to punish whoever was in charge and not getting results.

In 2012, with President Obama standing for reelection, a slow recovery unfolding, but unemployment still near 8 percent, voters seemed unsure who to blame. Nonetheless, President Obama squeaked through to reelection, 51 percent to Romney's 48.5 percent, and Democrats made narrow gains in Congress, picking up two seats in the Senate and seven in the House. Few voters seemed to believe that these status quo election results would produce the kinds of change they wanted and the nation needed. Presidents fortunate enough to win a second term, like President Bush in 2004 and President Obama in 2012, have been in front of the American people for a long time, they have tried most of their good ideas, and voters, especially voter of the other party, have tired of them. As a result, a reelected president's midterm election, Bush's 2006 midterm and Obama's 2014 midterm, tend to be rough. In 2014, with the wars in Iraq and Afghanistan winding down, but the broader Middle East in turmoil, the U.S. economy recovering, but wages stagnant and inequality between rich, especially the super-rich, and the poor increasing, Democrats lost nine Senate seats and control of that body and thirteen House seats. As the electoral dust cleared, President Obama faced a Republican Senate, 54 seats to 46, and a Republican House, 247 to 188. The Republican House majority was the largest in nearly a century. Both parties girded for what they saw as a tossup presidential election in 2016.

Q3 Are American political parties in decline, and, if so, should we be worried about it?

THE STATE OF POLITICAL PARTIES
IN THE UNITED STATES

What is the state of the major political parties in the United States today? We will look at them in each of three classic roles: **party in the electorate**, **party organization**, and **party in government**.[18] In looking at party in the electorate, we ask how steady the commitment of voters to the parties has been in recent decades and how broad and firm it is today. In looking at party organization, we ask how the parties are structured and what kinds of services they deliver to the voters and officeholders associated with them. In looking at party in government, we ask how committed officeholders are to the party labels and programs under which they were elected. Do Republicans and Democrats in the Congress, for example, mostly vote together and against each other? We shall see that the parties are strengthening among the voters, stronger in government, and still stronger as national and, increasingly, as state and local organizations.

party in the electorate The voters who identify more or less directly and consistently with a political party.

party organization The permanent structure of party offices and officials who administer the party apparatus on a day-to-day basis.

party in government The officeholders, both elected and partisan-appointed officials, who ran under or have been associated with the party label.

Party in the Electorate

Harvard political scientist and historian Arthur M. Schlesinger, Jr. observed some years ago that American elections had evolved from labor-intensive enterprises to capital-intensive enterprises.[19] Others have noted that elections that once were party-centered had become candidate-centered. Both formulations make the same point. Elections used to turn on which party could put its troops on the street during the campaign, putting up posters and yard signs, handing out leaflets, signing up new voters, and then getting its voters to the polls on election day. While these party activities are still important, particularly in local elections, in state and national contests, parties and candidates have had to learn a new set of skills. Elections now turn on which candidates can raise the money required to run a state-of-the-art media campaign and get-out-the-vote effort.[20] As we shall see more fully below, as campaigns evolved from labor-intensive to capital-intensive and from party-centered to candidate-centered and media-driven, the voters initially loosened their ties to the parties. More recently, increasing partisanship in government and more ideological media have driven voters back to parties. If voter commitment to party waxes and wanes, weakens and strengthens over time, what kind of commitment is it?

There are two main descriptions of how citizens adopt partisan preferences and update them over time. One has its roots in the 1960 classic, *The American Voter*, which presented party identification as a deep-seated psychological commitment, established early and remaining quite stable over time. Partisans might defect in a given election or move from the partisan ranks into the independent ranks, but few jump from one party to the other and stay. An alternative view, offered by Morris Fiorina, sees partisanship as more a rational calculation than a stable psychological commitment. Fiorina explains partisanship as a "running tally" of positive and negative evaluations of party candidates and policies. A voter whose running tally points consistently toward one party may look like they have made a "standing decision" for that party, but if evidence shifts eventually so may the tally and ultimately the voter's partisan identification. Both views offer insights and should be kept in mind as we think about how voters interact with political parties.[21]

Party Identification: The Ties Loosen. The political science literature refers to the commitment of individual voters to their political party as **party identification**. For over sixty years, the Survey Research Center (SRC) at the University of Michigan has asked voters the following questions: Generally speaking, do you usually think of yourself as a Republican, a Democrat, an independent, or what? (If Republican or Democrat) Would you call yourself a strong (Republican or Democrat) or a not very strong (Republican or Democrat)? (If Independent) Do you think of yourself as closer to the Republican party or to the Democratic party? Answers to these questions distinguish voters who consider themselves stronger and weaker identifiers with one or the other of the major parties, independents who lean toward one of the major parties, and pure independents. Findings are reported in a seven-point scale and a simpler three-point scale.

First, we look at the seven-point scale (see Table 7.3). Only a few fairly straightforward points need to be made about variations in the distribution of party identification over the past sixty years. First, note the continuing breadth and depth of the Democrats' "Roosevelt coalition" through the mid-1960s. Combining strong and weak partisans, we see that Democrats claimed 45 to 50 percent of the electorate, whereas the Republicans, even while Eisenhower was winning two easy elections in 1952 and 1956, claimed less than 30 percent, and independents remained around 23 percent.

Second, the late 1960s and 1970s saw both major parties give up chunks of their partisan base to the independent category. Lyndon Johnson's broad

party identification The emotional and intellectual commitment of a voter to his or her preferred party.

TABLE 7.3 Party Identification in the Electorate, 1952–2012

	'52	'54	'56	'58	'60	'62	'64	'66	'68	'70	'72	'74	'76	'78	'80	'82	'84	'86	'88	'90	'92	'94	'96	'98	'00	'02	'04	'08	'12
SD	23	23	22	28	21	24	27	18	20	20	15	18	15	15	18	20	17	18	18	20	18	15	18	19	19	17	17	19	20
WD	26	26	24	23	26	24	25	28	26	24	25	21	25	24	23	24	20	22	18	19	17	18	19	18	15	17	16	15	15
ID	10	9	7	7	6	8	9	9	10	10	11	13	12	14	11	11	11	10	12	12	14	13	14	14	15	16	17	17	12
I	5	8	9	8	10	8	8	12	11	13	15	18	16	16	15	13	13	14	12	12	13	11	10	12	13	7	10	11	14
IR	8	6	9	5	7	6	6	7	9	8	10	9	10	10	8	12	11	13	12	12	12	12	11	13	13	12	12	12	12
WR	14	15	15	17	14	17	14	15	15	15	13	14	14	13	14	14	15	15	14	15	14	15	15	16	12	16	12	13	12
SR	14	13	16	12	16	13	11	10	10	9	10	8	9	8	9	10	12	11	14	10	11	15	12	10	12	15	16	13	15

SD = Strong Democrat; WD = Weak Democrat; ID = Independent Democrat; I = Independent; IR = Independent Republican; WR = Weak Republican; SR = Strong Republican

Source: American National Election Studies. http://electionstudies.org/nesguide/toptable/tab2a_1.htm.

victory over Barry Goldwater in 1964 and the Watergate scandal and forced resignation of President Richard Nixon in 1973 pushed Republican Party identification under 25 percent, where it remained into the 1980s. Simultaneously, the cumulative effect of the turmoil of the late 1960s and early 1970s including the Vietnam War, social unrest, and economic stagnation shaved a full 10 percent off the Democratic base.

Third, the proportion of voters identifying themselves as independents rose from a steady 23 percent as late as 1964, to 30 percent in 1968, and to 37 percent in 1976, where it has remained relatively stable ever since. Recent figures show that 40 percent of voters identify themselves as independents, whereas only 34 percent identify themselves as Democrats and 25 percent as Republicans. These developments are often presented as evidence that the electorate has become less partisan, more willing to look at candidates from both major parties, and hence that American elections are decided by a large, floating, independent vote.

The fact that more Americans came to call themselves independents over the past four decades than call themselves either Democrats or Republicans is striking. But as we move beyond partisan self-identification to consider partisan behavior, a somewhat different story emerges.

Partisan Identification: The Scales Rebalance. First, an extensive literature suggests that the broad category of "Independent" is more structured, more connected to party, than commonly understood.[22] Not surprisingly, strong partisans tend to turn out at high rates and to vote overwhelmingly for the nominees of their party. Weak partisans turn out at somewhat lower rates than strong partisans and are somewhat less loyal to the candidates of their party. Interestingly, however, independent leaners tend to behave very much like the weak identifiers of the party toward which they lean. They turn out at the same rates and are just as loyal. Only pure independents tend to split their votes between the major parties, and they turn out at lower rates than partisans and leaners.[23]

Table 7.4 presents a picture that better reflects partisan behavior. Independent leaners are allocated to the parties toward which they lean, leaving only the pure independents in the Independent category. Now we see that the number of pure independents more than doubled, rising from 6 percent to 15 percent

TABLE 7.4 Party Identification in the Electorate, 1952–2012																															
	'52	'54	'56	'58	'60	'62	'64	'66	'68	'70	'72	'74	'76	'78	'80	'82	'84	'86	'88	'90	'92	'94	'96	'98	'00	'02	'04	'08	'12
D + L	59	58	52	58	53	56	62	55	56	54	51	52	51	54	52	55	48	50	47	52	50	47	52	51	50	49	50	51	46
I		5	8	9	8	10	8	8	12	11	13	15	18	16	16	15	13	13	14	12	12	13	11	10	12	13	7	10	11	14
R + L	36	34	39	34	37	36	31	32	33	33	34	31	33	30	33	32	40	36	41	36	37	41	38	37	37	43	41	37	39

D + L = Democrats + Leaners; I = Independents; R + L = Republicans + Leaners
Source: American National Election Studies. http://www.electionstudies.org/nesguide/toptable/tab2a_2.htm.

between 1952 and 1976, before receding to 11–13 percent from 1980 onward. Democratic numbers, counting leaners, have fallen 5 or 10 points since the mid-1960s. Despite Democratic losses, the Republicans made little headway until the early 1980s. Ronald Reagan's reelection victory in 1984 expanded the Republican Party to about 40 percent of the electorate, though it has declined a bit in recent years.[24] The Democrats enjoyed a significant advantage in party registration during the 2008 election cycle, and a smaller but still significant advantage in 2012, but the Republicans had their own advantages.

Traditionally, the Democrats have needed a lead just to stay even. Partisan balance would mean Republican advantage. At every level of partisan identification, strong, weak, and leaners, Republicans are five or six percentage points more likely to turn out and until 1996 they were five to ten points more likely to stick with the candidates of their party. With the transition of conservative white southerners from the Democratic Party to the Republican Party now complete, Democrats are more uniformly liberal and Republicans uniformly conservative. Now, both Democrats and Republicans vote consistently for the nominee of their party.[25]

Struggling Toward Democracy

Some whites find it surprising, even disturbing, that blacks voted for Barack Obama over Mitt Romney in 2012 by a little more than 13 to 1.

What do you think?
- Do you find this surprising or disturbing?
- What explains this lopsided support?
- Do you think there was anything Romney could have done to win over more blacks?

The Breakdown of the 2012 Vote. The surest way to win an election is to get the most votes (though as we saw in 2000 this does not always work). The surest way to get the most votes in an election is to do well among large blocs of voters. How did Obama and Romney do among voters when we divide them up by gender, race, education, income, age, ideology, and religiosity? Where did each candidate get most of his votes?

Table 7.5 shows that Obama did best among women, minorities, the poor, the young, liberals, and the lightly churched. Romney did best among men, whites, the comfortable, older voters, conservatives, and regular churchgoers. Obama prevailed because traditional Democratic groups are expanding while traditional Republican groups are not. Winning elections is not easy, but it is not rocket science.

Women accounted for 53 percent of total votes cast and Obama won among women by 55 percent to 44 percent. Men cast 47 percent of the total vote and Republicans usually carry men, as Romney did 52 percent to 45 percent. Whites cast 72 percent of the total vote and Romney won among whites by 59 percent to 39 percent. But Obama carried blacks 93 percent to 6 percent and carried Hispanics and Asians by almost 3 to 1. America is becoming increasingly diverse and while future Democrats may not perform as well as Obama among minorities; Republicans will have to do better among minorities than Romney if they are to remain competitive.[26]

In regard both to education and income, Obama did better with those with less than with those with more, while Romney did better among the middle and upper classes. Romney won among voters over 40, among conservatives, and among those who attend church at least weekly. Obama won among the young, liberals, and moderates, and the more secular.

One group, really many groups, that the parties, but especially the Republicans, have had trouble addressing is immigrants. Two-thirds of Latinos and

TABLE 7.5 Who Voted for Obama and Romney in 2012?	% of Votes Cast	% Obama	% Romney
TOTAL	**100**	**51**	**47**
Gender			
Male	47	45	52
Female	53	55	44
Race			
White	72	39	59
Black	13	93	6
Hispanic	10	71	27
Asian	3	73	26
Education			
< High School	3	64	35
High School	21	51	48
Some College	29	49	48
College Grad.	29	47	51
Post-Grad.	18	55	42
Income			
Under $50,000	41	60	38
$50,000–100,000	31	46	52
$100,000 and up	28	44	54
Age			
18–29	19	60	37
30–39	17	55	42
40–49	20	48	50
50–64	28	47	52
65 and up	16	44	56
Ideology			
Liberal	25	86	11
Moderate	41	56	41
Conservative	35	17	82
Religious Services			
Weekly	42	39	59
Occasionally	40	55	43
Never	17	62	34

Source: Compiled by the author from exit polls and post-election analyses.

87 percent of Asians in the U.S. are immigrants or first-generation Americans. Most immigrants arrive in this country with little sense of U.S. politics, parties, issues, or practices. Even American-born children of immigrants might not see the relevance of the Democratic and Republican parties to the problems confronting them.[27] For most of American history, parties appealed directly to immigrants, sometimes meeting the immigrant ships and offering help and guidance. Today, our capital-intensive, candidate-centered, parties are as likely to ignore as to court immigrants and new Americans.

Pro & Con

Black Commitment to the Democratic Party

For half a century, blacks have given about 90 percent of their votes to Democratic candidates for president and Congress. No other racial or ethnic group has been as deeply committed to one of the major parties over the other as blacks have been to the Democratic Party.

We must first note that this close connection between blacks and the Democratic Party is very curious historically. Consider, after all, that the Democratic Party was the party of the South and slavery during the Civil War and the party most identified with southern racial segregation into the 1960s. Consider also that the Republican Party came into existence in the 1850s as an antislavery party and that it was the Republican Party, the party of Abraham Lincoln and the Emancipation Proclamation, that fought a great civil war to end slavery.

Nonetheless, in the 1930s and then more decisively in the 1960s, black voters left the Republican Party for the Democratic Party. The connection made between the Kennedy brothers and Martin Luther King Jr. during the 1960 campaign and the social activism of the brief Kennedy administration were especially heartening to black citizens. Then the Civil Rights Acts of 1964 and 1965, the Voting Rights Act of 1965, and the whole package of Great Society initiatives—in education, housing, welfare, health care, and job training—firmly attached blacks to what they took to be a new Democratic Party committed to equal rights.

What are the pluses and minuses of the nearly exclusive commitment of blacks to the Democratic Party? Among the pluses are at least the following. First, the Democratic Party's philosophy and programs have been responsive to the needs and interests of blacks. The Democratic Party created and defended the American welfare state and affirmative action. Second, the Democratic Party has been receptive to blacks with political aspirations. All but three of the 46 black members of Congress are Democrats. In 2012, the Democrats reelected Barack Obama President of the United States.

Among the minuses are at least the following. First, Democrats—including Barack Obama—are sometimes reluctant to have their campaigns too closely identified with the black community for fear of scaring away white voters. Second, the fact that both major parties know that most blacks will vote Democrat means that there is no bidding for their votes. Third, the wholesale commitment of blacks to the Democratic Party means that they are almost completely without access when Republicans win.

What do you think?
- How do you read the balance of the pluses and minuses?
- Does the near exclusive commitment of blacks to the Democratic Party enhance or detract from their political clout?

PRO	CON
Democrats have been more responsive	Democrats often take blacks for granted
Democrats support public services and affirmative action	Blacks are isolated when Democrats lose
Most black elected officials are Democrats	Republicans have no incentive to bid for black votes

Party Organizations

What do parties look like in the twenty-first century? The traditional party organization was conceived as a pyramid rising from a broad base of local precincts through a series of intermediate layers—ward, city, county, congressional district, and state central committee—to the national committees and conventions of both parties. With almost 200,000 precincts in the United States and multiple levels of party structure above the precinct level, fully staffed party organizations for only the two major parties would involve over half a million party officials and volunteers.

Well into the 1960s, the locus of activity and influence within the party organizations was much nearer the base than the tip of the pyramid. As campaigns evolved, so did the parties organized to contest them. The focus is now on developing and managing partisan social networks that will identify, train, and support candidates in winning office and taking policy control of government. In other words, party organizations joined the movement to capital-intensive, candidate-centered campaigning. In doing so, they reinvented themselves for the twenty-first century by abandoning much of what they had been in the nineteenth and twentieth centuries.

Local Party Organizations.   The heyday of local party organization was in the two decades on either side of the beginning of the twentieth century. Some local party organizations, often called "machines" by their detractors, controlled hundreds and even thousands of patronage jobs and lucrative city and county contracts. Because the organizations controlled the voters, they could slate candidates, discipline officeholders who did not toe the line, and reward the party faithful with offices and opportunities.

The most famous city machine was the Chicago Democratic organization founded by Mayor Anton J. Cermak in 1931 and run by the formidable Richard J. Daley from 1955 until his death in 1976.[28] In 1989, Daley's son, Richard M. Daley, was elected mayor. Daley won his sixth term as mayor in 2007 but declined to stand for a seventh term in 2011. Both father and son served 21 years as mayor.[29] The machine still controls about 37,000 patronage jobs in Chicago and Cook County, though it has lost some of its clout in statewide and congressional elections.

Over the course of the twentieth century, and especially in its last three decades, several powerful trends served to hollow out most local party organizations. The first was bringing government jobs under civil service regulation. Civil service regulation of government jobs spread throughout the federal workforce by the 1930s and through most state and local governments by the 1970s and 1980s. The second was the movement toward nonpartisan local elections. The idea was that citizens suffer when local politics is a partisan scramble for patronage and that a more efficient and business-like approach to local problems is possible if candidates remove their party labels and run on issues and expertise. Nearly three-quarters of local elections in the United States today are nonpartisan.

Getty Images

The mayor and his city: probably the most powerful of America's big-city bosses and the mayor who presided over the building of many large public-works projects in the city, Richard J. Daley left an indelible stamp on Chicago.

The third trend was technology. By 1960, presidential candidates were using television to take political messages directly to voters in their homes. By 1980, all candidates for statewide offices and many at the local level were employing television as the central component of their campaigns. While "local organizations are still essential for managing some aspects of campaigns, such as carrying on registration drives, arranging rallies, setting up phone banks, facilitating use of absentee ballots, and turning out the vote on election day," more and more campaigning is conducted over the head of the local party structure.[30]

These late twentieth- and early twenty-first-century trends changed political parties in many ways, but one key change was to elevate "purists" over "pragmatists" in party business. In the old days, meaning at least through the 1960s, party officials and officeholders found it pragmatic to share the spoils, bargain with elements of their coalition, assuage dissidents, and, most importantly, select candidates that could win. Purists, on the other hand, care as much and maybe more about issues and ideology than about party and the compromises often required to win elections. Think for a moment about the difficulty that U.S. House Speaker John Boehner, a pragmatist, has had in dealing with the purist "Tea Party" element of his House Republican caucus.

Fifty State Organizations.   At the top of the party structure in each of the fifty states are a Democratic Central Committee and a Republican Central Committee. Although these state central committees still perform a number of traditional tasks, they have evolved remarkably in the last three decades. The traditional responsibilities of the state committees included organizing the state party caucuses and convention, drafting the state party platform, allocating campaign funds, and selecting the state party's national convention and national committee delegates.

On the other hand, few state parties still run large patronage operations or organize and support slates of candidates for statewide office. State party organizations have moved from a focus on electoral mobilization to a focus on campaign management. State party organizations all over the country now offer technical advice to candidates, campaign managers, and workers. The state parties train activists to manage voter lists, run phone banks, do mass mailings, organize election-day turnout, and raise, manage, and account for funds as required by state and federal law.

The National Party Organizations.   The Republican and Democratic National Committees, as well as the House and Senate Republican and Democratic campaign committees, are stronger and more active than at any previous point in their histories. The campaign committees raise funds and provide campaign services to their incumbent members of the House and Senate. Although the McCain-Feingold campaign finance reforms slowed "soft money" contributions to the national parties and campaign committees, they are still far more vibrant and capable than in past decades.

The modern national committees, although they certainly expand and contract their operations with the election cycle, engage in continuous party support and development activity. They recruit and train candidates and their staffs and pay for polling and issues research, media production, fund-raising, consulting, and the ongoing administrative expenses of the operation. Candidates have become dependent on the services provided by the national committees.

Party in Government

Party in government is composed of the officeholders—both elected and partisan-appointed officials—who ran under or have been associated with the party label. Parties present alternative programs to the public during election campaigns and try to enact them once they gain office. Usually, this means the president's program, but it can, as with the Democratic majorities that took control of Congress in 2006, mean the program of the majority party in Congress.

Promoting the President's Program.   The idea that the president should present a program to the Congress each year is relatively new. Prior to the New Deal, the majority party's program was as likely to come from the Congress as it was from the White House. Now, however, **presidential support** hinges

presidential support   Each year *Congressional Quarterly* reports the proportion of votes in Congress on which the president took a clear position and Congress supported him.

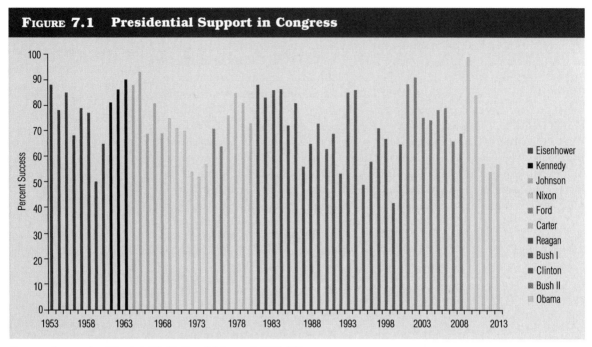

FIGURE **7.1**   **Presidential Support in Congress**

Source: Congressional Quarterly Weekly Report, February 3, 2014, 175.

on the president getting his program through the Congress and consistently convincing his partisans in Congress to support that program (see Figure 7.1).

Congressional voting records show that when presidents enjoy majorities in both houses of the Congress, as Democratic presidents Kennedy, Johnson, Carter, Clinton, and Obama and Republican President George W. Bush did during all or part of their terms, they are successful more than 80 percent of the time. Presidents whose partisans control at least one house of the Congress, as Republican presidents Eisenhower and Reagan did, do nearly as well, at almost 75 percent. Presidents who find both houses of the Congress controlled by the other party, as Republican presidents Nixon, Ford, George H.W. Bush, and George W. Bush did in his final two years, face tough sledding, achieving success only about 60 percent of the time.

President George W. Bush's success rate during 2001 and 2002, his first two years in office, although Congress was evenly divided and control of the Senate shifted from Republican to Democrat and back again, averaged 88 percent, the highest since LBJ in 1964 and 1965. His success scores remained near 80 percent from 2003 to 2006. In November 2006, Republicans lost control of both houses of Congress and Bush's personal popularity touched all-time lows. His 2007 success score plunged to 38 percent, tied with Bill Clinton's post-Lewinsky 1999 low for the worst presidential success scores of the past half century. It recovered modestly, to 48 percent, in 2008.

Barack Obama's first year presidential success rate was an astounding 97 percent. That is the highest on record; higher than LBJ's in 1964 and 1965,

Luke Sharrett / *New York Times*

Senators Lindsey Graham (R-SC), John McCain (R-AZ), and Ted Cruz (R-TX) listen as President Barack Obama delivers the State of the Union address to a joint session of Congress in the House Chamber at the U.S. Capitol. Looking at these men, would you assume bipartisan cooperation is about to break out or not?

higher than Clinton's in 1993 and 1994, and higher even than George W. Bush's in 2001 and 2002. Presidents almost always do best in their first couple of years and then the political gravity of difficult problems, partial solutions, and familiarity, pull them down. Obama's success rate slipped to a still very respectable 86 percent in 2010, but since Republicans took control of the House in 2011 it has languished in the mid-50s.

The Loyal Opposition. The role of loyal opposition falls to the leaders of the party in Congress that does not control the presidency. If this party is also a minority in Congress, as Republicans were during the first years of the Obama presidency, its leaders are mostly restricted to organizing dissent and raising questions about the president's program. Though if the opposition holds together and is adamant, they can, as Republicans did in 2009 and 2010, reshape important parts of the president's program. If this party holds a majority in one house of the Congress, as Republicans did after 2011, it can more effectively bargain with the president on his program. If the party holds majorities in both houses of the Congress, it may well be in a position to offer a program of its own.

In general, **party unity** in Congress—defined as the proportion of votes on which the majority of one party lines up against a majority of the other party—was high during the 1950s and early 1960s, fell throughout the 1960s,

party unity Each year *Congressional Quarterly* reports the proportion of votes in the House and Senate on which a majority of one party lines up against a majority of the other party.

LET'S COMPARE

Electoral Rules and Party Systems in Fifteen Nations

One of the most prominent theoretical and empirical insights in political science is **Duverger's law**. Maurice Duverger noted a direct connection between electoral systems, party systems, and national politics. Specifically, Duverger argued that one set of electoral rules produced two-party politics and another produced multiparty politics.[32]

Among the advanced industrial nations of Western Europe and their cultural offspring, the English-speaking nations have generally adopted electoral systems featuring single-member districts and plurality or majority identification of winners. A single-member district is a geographical district that elects a single member to public office. Plurality winners are those that get the most votes, whether or not those votes total to a majority. A majority winner must obviously win a majority of the votes and that sometimes requires a runoff. Both plurality and majority systems are frequently called—using the imagery of a horse race—first-past-the-post systems.

Most of Europe favors another electoral system featuring multimember electoral districts or list systems and proportional representation (pr). Whether a constituency is national or subnational, parties draw up lists of candidates depending on the number of seats to be filled. Voters then cast their ballots for par-

ties rather than candidates, and the proportion of the total vote won by each party determines the number of seats that each party gets and hence how many candidates on the list get to fill the seats. Some countries, as the adjacent table shows, employ mixed systems designed to get the best of proportional and majoritarian systems. In mixed systems, some legislatures are chosen from a party list and some are chosen in single-member districts.[33]

The key difference between first-past-the-post systems and pr systems is the relative openness and diversity of the party and political system that each fosters. First-past-the-post systems encourage two major parties by awarding seats to the top vote-getters in each district. Consider a hypothetical two-party contest for all 435 seats in the U.S. House of Representatives in which one party got 51 percent in every district and the other party got 49 percent in every district. In a first-past-the-post system, the party with 51 percent would win every seat and the party with 49 percent would win none. Not so in a pr system; each party would win legislative seats in proportion to its share of the total vote. Electoral rules matter. The data in the following table suggest that pr systems encourage a larger number of major parties and make room for minor parties and new social groups.

Finally, proportional representation systems, as opposed to winner-takes-all systems, promote turnout. As we shall see again in the next chapter, electoral rules affect voter behavior. Consider the different incentives to a minority party voter in a pr system where her party will win seats even if they don't run first and a similar voter in a winner-takes-

and began to rise slowly in the early 1970s and then more rapidly during the 1980s (see Figure 7.2). During 1993, the first year of the first Clinton term, the proportion of partisan votes was an all-time high of 65 percent in the House and 67 percent in the Senate. Although this divisiveness moderated a bit in 1994, it shot to record highs in 1995 following the Republican capture of both houses of Congress: 73 percent of House votes and 69 percent of Senate votes were partisan.[31]

all system that will elect no candidates unless they run first. In a winner-takes-all system the incentive for minor party voters simply to stay home is great. In addition, research suggests that supporters of losing parties are happier with the political system in pr countries.[34]

What do you think?
- Would the U.S. be better served by a multi-party system than by our current two-party system?
- Would a multi-party system with proportional representation increase competition and raise turnout?
- Would it lead to more minorities and women being elected?

Nation	Electoral System	Number of Major Parties	% Seats to Minor Parties	% Seats to Women (2013)
United States	Plurality	2.0	.2	17.9
United Kingdom	Plurality	2.3	7.6	22.0
Australia	Majority	2.4	1.9	26.0
Canada	Plurality	3.0	32.3	24.7
France	Mixed	2.4	3.6	26.9
Ireland	pr	3.2	6.2	15.1
Germany	Mixed	3.4	8.6	36.5
Austria	pr	3.5	8.7	33.3
New Zealand	Mixed	3.2	12.6	32.2
Sweden	pr	4.2	16.4	44.7
Norway	pr	4.7	17.4	39.6
Denmark	pr	4.9	17.7	39.1
Finland	pr	5.0	9.3	42.5
Netherlands	pr	5.4	13.0	38.7
Belgium	pr	7.5	15.0	38.0

pr = proportional representation
Source: David M. Farrell, *Electoral Systems: A Comparative Introduction* (New York: Palgrave, 2011), 234–237; Russell J. Dalton and Martin P. Wattenberg, *Parties without Partisans* (New York: Oxford University Press, 2000), 205; Women in National Parliaments, http://www.ipu.org/wmn-e/classif.htm. % of seats to women (2013) is the lower or single house of the Parliament or Congress.

Partisanship declined markedly between 1996 and 1998, before the Clinton impeachment saga of late 1998 and early 1999 soaked the Congress in partisan rancor. President George W. Bush's determination to "change the tone in Washington" by "reaching across party lines" seemed to work initially. Partisan voting declined to 40 percent in the House and 55 percent in the Senate in 2001 and then to 43 percent in the House and 45 percent in the Senate in 2002. It did not last. Once the post-9/11 unity faded, partisanship surged in 2003 to

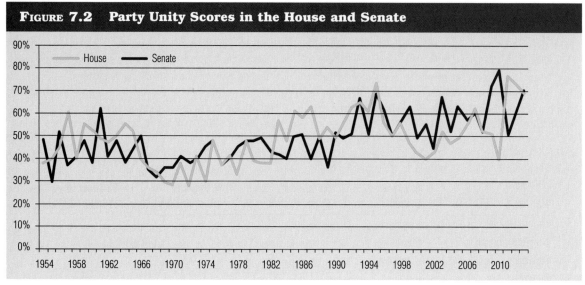

FIGURE 7.2   Party Unity Scores in the House and Senate

Source: *Congressional Quarterly Weekly Report*, February 3, 2014, 190.

52 percent in the House and 67 percent in the Senate. From 2004 through 2008, party unity averaged about 53 percent in the House and 57 percent in the Senate.

Party unity in the House remained in its traditional range in 2009 and 2010, at 51 percent and 40 percent, while Senate party unity shot to all-time highs at 72 percent and 79 percent. Both Democrats and Republicans in the Senate were highly unified because the Democrats had just 60 votes, exactly the number needed to break a filibuster, and the Republicans needed all 40 of their votes and just one Democrat to sustain a filibuster and block the Democrats. In January 2010, when Republican Scott Brown won Democratic Senator Ted Kennedy's old Senate seat, the parties still had huge incentives to stick together.

In November 2010, Republicans swept to control of the House and narrowed the margin of Democratic control in the Senate. In 2011, House Republicans moved to block the Democratic agenda and to offer their own alternatives, driving House party unity scores to an all-time high of 76 percent. The more closely balanced Senate, 53 Democrats and 47 Republicans, was forced into occasional compromise, so party unity slipped back to 51 percent. 2012, a presidential election year, assured continued partisan conflict.

Duverger's law Political scientist Maurice Duverger was the first to note that electoral rules influence party systems. Majoritarian systems usually produce two-party systems, and proportional representation systems usually produce multiparty systems.

Q4 What roles have minor parties, often called third parties, played in American history?

THE IMPACT OF MINOR PARTIES ON AMERICAN POLITICS

The United States is frequently described as a two-party system. In many ways it is: the Democratic and Republican parties have stood against each other since before the Civil War. They get most of the attention and win virtually all of the elections. But the United States as a two-party democracy is only part of the story. In this section, we define minor parties, describe their traditional role in American politics, describe the barriers that the major parties throw up against them, and assess the recent history and future prospects of minor parties in American politics.

Major parties are the Democrats and Republicans, the parties that have the best chances of winning elections, organizing the government, and making public policy. **Minor parties** also seek support, stake out issue positions, and run candidates for election, but they generally have little chance of winning and everyone knows it. But sometimes, when the political stars line up just right, a third party can garner enough attention and votes to change the course of an election. In fact, many believe that the improved opportunities to communicate and organize offered by the Web and other new media suggest that the growth of minor parties is likely to accelerate in the early decades of the twenty-first century.

Perhaps! But in 2012 media attention focused on "Americans Elect," an online movement to select a unity ticket and get it on the ballot in all 50 states. It fizzled without even being able to nominate candidates.

minor party A party that raises issues and offers candidates but has little chance of winning and organizing the government.

The Historical Role of Minor Parties

Minor parties are common if not particularly visible parts of American political life. In the 2012 presidential election, 25 candidates, in addition to the Democrats' Barack Obama and the Republicans' Mitt Romney, appeared on at least one state's ballot for president. Most of the parties represented by these candidates were irrelevant to the conduct or outcome of the election, but in 2000, the Green Party's Ralph Nader was an important factor in the election and did affect the outcome. In fact, he quite likely changed the outcome from a probable Al Gore win to a George W. Bush win.

What role do third parties normally play in American politics and under what circumstances do they have the best chance of affecting the course of an election? Generally, their principal goal is to raise issues that the major parties fear or simply ignore. These are often issues that have no majority potential but can ignite intense followings, like those of the Free Soilers and Know Nothings of the mid-nineteenth century, the Prohibitionists and Populists of the late nineteenth century, the Socialists and Bull Moosers of the early twentieth century, and the Reform Party of recent electoral cycles. (see Table 7.6) These parties raise new, often divisive issues, draw attention to them, build followings if they can, and try to incite change.[35]

Usually, they fail and languish in obscurity, but sometimes they catch fire and force a reaction from the broader political system. Almost always three factors occurring together explain the rise of a third party. First, the third party must be well positioned on a critical issue that the major parties would prefer to ignore. Usually this is an economic issue, but it can be a governance, moral, or cultural issue. Second, it must have an intriguing leader like a

TABLE 7.6 Development of the Party System			
		Major Parties	**Minor Parties**
1789	Federalists	Anti-Federalists	
1796	Federalists	Jeffersonian Democrats	
1820		Jeffersonian Democrats	
1832	Whigs	Jecksonian Democrats	Anti-Masonic Party
1840	Whigs	Democratic Party	Liberty Party
1848	Whigs	Democratic Party	Free Soil Party
1856	Republican Party	Democratic Party	Know Nothing Party
1860	Republican Party	Democratic Party	Union Party
1880	Republican Party	Democratic Party	Prohibition Party, Greenback Party
1888	Republican Party	Democratic Party	Populist Party, Union Labor Party
1900	Republican Party	Democratic Party	Socialist party
1912	Republican Party	Democratic Party	Bull Moose Party
1924	Republican Party	Democratic Party	Progressive Party
1948	Republican Party	Democratic Party	States' Rights Party
1968	Republican Party	Democratic Party	American Party
1972	Republican Party	Democratic Party	Libertarian Party
1980	Republican Party	Democratic Party	National Party
1988	Republican Party	Democratic Party	Green Party
1992	Republican Party	Democratic Party	United We Stand (Reform Party)
1996	Republican Party	Democratic Party	Reform Party
2000	Republican Party	Democratic Party	Libertarian Party, Green Party
2012	Republican Party	Democratic Party	Libertarian Party, Green Party

Ross Perot or a Ralph Nader. And third, it must play its opportunity perfectly because the deck is stacked against it.

Only Abraham Lincoln in 1860 rode a third party to the White House. Others have come close. Theodore Roosevelt ran second in 1912, and Ross Perot, after temporarily leading the presidential contest in June 1992, faltered, withdrew, reentered the race, and eventually finished third, with a still impressive 19 percent of the vote. In American politics, and particularly in a presidential race, third parties that stumble get trampled.

The Obstacles to Minor Party Success

The rules and laws governing elections in the United States were written by Democrats and Republicans. Democrats and Republicans, in state legislatures and governors' offices, in Congress and the White House, wrote the rules governing who gets to run and what it takes to win. Not surprisingly then, these Democratic and Republican elected officials have designed the American electoral system to favor them and to make life difficult for those who would challenge them.

The major parties have three main levels of defense against third party challenges. First, virtually all American elections are conducted in individual districts (often referred to as single-member districts) where the person getting the most votes (the plurality, though not necessarily a majority) wins. This is hard on minor parties.[36]

Second, most election rules are state rules. The states have made access to the ballot automatic for the major parties and difficult for minor parties. Frequently the number of valid voter signatures required to get a minor party candidate on the ballot is very high. At the end of the process of obtaining signatures, partisan election officials often disqualify many signatures for technical reasons. Even when third party candidates make it onto the ballot, the privileged top-of-the-ballot positions are usually reserved for the two major parties. Moreover, the petition process usually has to be redone for each new election cycle.

Even higher hurdles exist for a third party candidate for the presidency. To get on the ballots in all fifty states, a candidate must determine each state's rules and comply with them in detail. The ability of most third party candidates to raise money is miniscule compared to the two major party candidates. Third party candidates are barred from participating in presidential debates unless their support in the national polls is 15 percent (a rule

Struggling Toward Democracy

In 2012 "minor parties" got just 1.6 percent of the presidential vote.
What do you think?
- Is there a role for minor parties in U.S. politics and, if so, are they being allowed to play it?
- Is a protest vote for a third party candidate a "wasted" vote?

Getty Images

Senator Rand Paul (R-KY) speaks to supporters during a Tea Party rally in front of the U.S. Capitol in Washington, D.C. The Tea Party is not a major party like the Republicans. Is it a minor party, interest group, or something else?

Table 7.7 Major and Minor Party Votes in 2012			
Candidate*	**Party**	**Popular Vote**	**Electoral Vote**
Barack Obama	Democratic	61,176,680	332
Mitt Romney	Republican	58,173,364	206
Gary Johnson	Libertarian	1,178,551	0
Jill Stein	Green	414,643	0
Virgil Goode	Constitution	116,399	0

* Twenty others not listed here received at least a scattering of votes for president.
Source: http://www.cbsnews.com/election-results-2012/president.shtml

made by the major party-sponsored Presidential Debate Commission). In a general election, the major party candidates raise hundreds of millions of dollars or receive tens of millions of dollars in public funds to run their campaigns, but third party candidates get nothing unless their parties achieved at least 5 percent of the vote in the last election (a rule made by the major party-dominated Federal Election Commission).

The major parties usually disdain even to notice the demands and machinations of the minor parties. Yet, if a minor party does begin to build momentum, the major parties react. Initially, they take half measures to try to drain off the emotion fueling the growing third party. If that fails, one or both of the major parties will adopt one or more of the key issue positions of the third party. These third party actions and major party reactions were on stark display during recent presidential election cycles as Ralph Nader and others took their shots at challenging the primacy of the two major parties in American politics.

How did the minor parties fare in the 2012 elections (see Table 7.7)? More minor party candidates were on the ballot in 2012 than at any time since the economic tumult of the Great Depression of the 1930s. The Libertarian Party's Gary Johnson was on the ballots in 48 states and the District of Columbia, the Green Party's Jill Stein was on the ballots in 37 states, and the Constitution Party's Virgil Goode was on 26 state ballots.

As anyone who watched the 2012 election saw clearly, life for the third parties is not easy. Gary Johnson, a former-governor of New Mexico, ran briefly for the Republican nomination in 2012 before accepting the Libertarian nomination. Republicans worried that Johnson might siphon votes from Romney, and he did garner almost 1.2 million votes, more than double any other minor party candidate, but neither he nor all of the minor party candidates together polled enough votes to affect the outcome. Third parties barely made their presence felt in 2012. Is there good reason to believe that their presence and clout could grow in the future?

What Is the Future of Minor Parties?

The odds against minor parties are always long. The electoral system is stacked against them and there is little reason to believe that the major parties and their elected officeholders and officials will allow that to change any time soon. Nonetheless, social, political, and technological developments are afoot that should open the door to continued growth for third parties. Citizens and voters are better educated, wealthier, and more secure than ever. Moreover, with the two major parties closely balanced, the defection of only a few voters to minor parties can have important consequences. Democrats continue to be vulnerable to defections to the Green Party and Republicans to the Libertarian and Constitution parties. And communications technology, especially the Internet, makes it easier for like-minded people to find each other, coordinate their activities, and make the political system respond to them.[37]

Do we look for many third parties to develop or for a minor party to rise to challenge and perhaps displace one of the major parties? It's hard to say; but one should probably look to that fertile ground between a too-liberal Democratic Party and a too-conservative Republican Party, where Ross Perot, Jesse Ventura, and Ralph Nader found enough economic conservatives and social liberals to roil the political system in recent elections.

PARTY REFORM IN THE WAKE OF 2012

Recent presidential contests have raised a number of questions about party reform. For example, should the national Democratic and Republican parties be able to organize the primary and caucus process or should each state be able to decide when and how to organize its role in the process? And should the major parties be able to make life difficult for third parties and independent candidates or should their participation be facilitated and even welcomed?

In 2008, more states crowded to the front of the presidential nomination process, close to the traditional first events in Iowa and New Hampshire, to assure that their voters got to weigh in before the nominations were locked up. The Democratic and Republican national committees (DNC and RNC) tried to establish rules about which states would go first and about the earliest dates that others could go. On the Democratic side, Florida and Michigan defied the rules and scheduled their primaries earlier than permitted. The DNC responded by advising candidates not to participate and declaring that the states' delegates would not be seated at the national convention. The RNC had similar problems in 2012. Rogue states, again led by Florida, jumped the line to insure that their voters got to weigh in before the nomination was locked up. Should the national parties be able to design a national presidential nomination process or should states be able to participate in the process as they see fit?

Concern also arose in 2008 over how the national and state parties awarded delegates to their national convention. Democrats tended to award delegates proportional to the state vote; for example, if Obama won a state with 60 percent of the vote to Clinton's 40 percent, the state's delegates to the Democratic National Convention would be divided similarly, 60/40. Republicans tended to award delegates on a winner-take-all basis. In another attempt to stem the front-loading in 2012, Republicans changed their rules to say that caucuses and primaries held before April 1 had to distribute delegates proportionally, while events after April 1 could retain the winner-take-all system. Does proportional or winner-take-all distribution of delegates seem most reasonable?

And finally, should Democrats and Republicans be able to write election rules that make it difficult for third party and independent candidates to compete? Rules govern how third party and independent candidates get on the ballot, whether they remain ballot eligible from one election to the next, and where they appear on the ballot. Common sense says we do need such rules. We do not want hundreds of candidates running for president as a lark. But who should write the electoral rules? The Constitution allows Congress and the states to write the rules, but this means elected Democrats and Republicans. Should the rules perhaps be written by non-partisan commissions to allow fair access to third party and independent candidates, as well as the major party candidates, so voters can choose from a full menu? Could either Congress or the Supreme Court require such a change? Should they?

WHAT DO YOU THINK?

- How should authority over electoral rules be divided between the national party organizations and the states?
- Should delegates to the parties' national conventions be awarded proportionally or should the winner take all?
- Should the rules be more favorable toward third parties? Who should write them?
- Should the rules perhaps be written by non-partisan commissions to allow fair access to third party and independent candidates, as well as the major party candidates, so voters can choose from a full menu?
- Could either Congress or the Supreme Court require such a change? Should they?

THE RELATIONSHIP OF INTEREST GROUPS TO POLITICAL PARTIES IN THE UNITED STATES

Q5 Are interest groups or political parties the best vehicle for representing citizen opinion to government?

In Chapter 6 we discussed interest groups and in this chapter we discussed major and minor political parties. All three are institutional mechanisms for bringing together and promoting interests, ideas, and goals shared by groups of citizens. In a society like ours, based on freedoms of speech, press, and association, with the technical ability to communicate improving every day, interest groups and minor parties are likely to proliferate and the major parties are likely to remain strong. Americans will have more and more ways to join with like-minded fellow citizens to make their views known and to press them on government.

As our political world grows more complicated, we must distinguish between interest groups and political parties and remember what each can and cannot do. As we saw in Chapter 6, interest groups generally press their members' views on government, whichever political party happens to control government at the time. Minor parties rarely win office and almost never win the top offices in government, but they do challenge the major parties and raise issues that might not otherwise get a hearing. Interest groups and minor parties may seem similar, but interest groups focus their attention on influencing government while minor parties often scorn traditional politics and policymaking and spend their energy on educating and organizing the public. Major parties offer candidates for all or most offices from the local to the national level in the hope of winning executive offices and legislative majorities so that they can run the government and make policy.

Finally, though interest groups and political parties compete for a limited supply of political talent, energy, and money, they also complement each other in critical ways. Political parties play the dominant role during elections and when government is being organized. Interest groups are at their most influential, perhaps even dominant, during the normal course of government business—during legislative hearings, program design, and bureaucratic rule-making and policy implementation. Political parties construct the broad public agenda; interest groups shape its details in ways acceptable and often beneficial to interest group goals.

Chapter Summary

Interest groups may be large or small, they may focus on inside or outside lobbying, but they generally focus on a fairly limited range of issues. Political parties serve to link groups of citizens to their government and to the political realm more generally. Minor parties may resemble interest groups, but their goal is to rise to major party status and to contest for control of the nation's political institutions. Major parties compete in elections in the hope of winning majority control of government so that they can affect the full range of policymaking and implementation.

The founding generation was extremely wary of interest groups and political parties because they saw them as representing self-interested differences over the nature of the public interest or the common good. Nonetheless, by the 1830s the two-party system was a well-established part of the American political system, although minor parties were usually present as well. Although political reforms during the twentieth century loosened the holds of parties over voters, most voters still orient themselves toward politics through their partisanship.

In this chapter, we analyzed the major parties in the electorate, as political organizations, and in government. The identification of voters with parties, strong in the nineteenth century, weakened over most of the twentieth century. Rising wealth and education produced voters capable of analyzing complex issues on their own rather than receiving their political information through partisan filters. However, a close partisan balance in Washington, an evenly divided electorate, and more explicitly ideological and partisan media have brought many back to parties. Two-thirds of voters claim partisan labels, more than 90 percent of voters vote for major party candidates, and the emotional attachment of voters to the major parties is stronger than it has been in decades.

Parties have responded to the move to capital-intensive, candidate-centered campaigns by focusing party organizations at the state and national levels on providing high-tech campaign-related services to candidates and their staffs. The national parties have become exceptionally efficient at fundraising, campaign management, and advertising. As a result of closer connections between candidates and party organizations, parties have also become more cohesive and consistent forces in government.

The standard democratic politics of groups and parties serves the interests of most citizens most of the time. Minor parties and protest movements arise when increasing numbers of people conclude that the political system is simply unwilling or incapable of dealing with a set of critical issues about which they feel deeply. Minor parties raise new issues or demand new solutions to old issues. They organize, argue the issues, and run candidates, but have little chance of winning. However, sometimes, as with Ross Perot in 1992 or Ralph Nader in 2000, they gain enough attention to change the course of an election and to demand that the major parties respond.

Key Terms

Duverger's law   218

initiative   201

minor party   219

party identification   206

party in government   205

party in the electorate   205

party organization   205

party primary   201

party unity   215

political party   193

presidential support   213

recall   201

referendum   201

Suggested Readings

Aldrich, John H. "Why Parties Form," 2011. Parties arose because ambitious politicians realized that a stable, coherent party apparatus would help them win elections and policy battles more consistently than they could otherwise.

Flanigan, William H. and Nancy H. Zingale. *Political Behavior of the American Electorate.* 12th ed. Washington, D.C.: CQ Press, 2010. Classic overview of the partisanship and political behavior of the U.S. electorate.

Hanjal, Zoltan L. and Taeku Lee. *Why Americans Don't Join the Party: Race, Immigration, and the Failure (of Political Parties) to Engage the Electorate.* Princeton, NJ: Princeton University Press, 2011. Explores the reasons immigrants and minorities do not readily connect to the major parties and how they might better be addressed.

Hershey, Marjorie R. *Party Politics in America.* 14th ed. New York: Pearson Longman, 2011. This leading textbook on American political parties describes parties as they operate in the electorate, as organizations, and in government.

Sager, Ryan. *The Elephant in the Room: Evangelicals, Libertarians and the Battle for Control of the Republican Party.* New York: John Wiley, 2006. Sager analyzes the division within the Republican Party between small government libertarians and evangelicals who want government involved in issues like abortion, school prayer, and gay marriage.

Schraufnagel, Scot. *Third Party Blues: The Truth and Consequences of Two-Party Dominance.* New York: Routledge, 2011. Analyzes both the means that the dominant parties use to block third parties and the potential benefits that third parties offer to parties and the policy process.

Skocpol, Theda and Vanessa Williamson. *The Tea Party and the Remaking of Republican Conservatism.* New York: Oxford University Press, 2012. Interviews and survey research show that the Tea Party has pushed the Republican Party further right.

Web Resources

For practice quizzes, key term flashcards, videos, links, and other study tools, visit the *American Government* website: www.routledge.com/cw/jillson

1. **www.democrats.org/index.html**
   This serves as the official website of the Democratic National Committee. It includes party news and information on how to become involved in the party. It also provides discussion topics concerning legislative and issue positions.

2. **www.gp.org/index.php**
   Official Web page of the Association of State Green Parties. This international democratic grassroots party is dedicated to environmental and social issues. The page contains profiles on party candidates and officials. It also gives information on how to become an involved member.

3. **www.lp.org**
   Official website of the Libertarian Party which has survived and proliferated longer than any other third party. The site provides insight into Libertarian principles and state-by-state information on its activities.

4. **www.gop.org**
   Official website of the Republican National Committee. It includes information on how to become involved with the GOP. It also contains information on organizations and profiles of elected officials.

5. **www.reformparty.org**
   website for the Reform Party.

Chapter 8

VOTING, CAMPAIGNS, AND ELECTIONS

❝ *(Supporter) Governor, you have the vote of every thinking person. (Stevenson) That's not enough, madam, we need a majority.* ❞

ADLAI STEVENSON, DEMOCRATIC CANDIDATE FOR PRESIDENT, 1956

The Constitution TODAY

DO CORPORATIONS HAVE ALL THE RIGHTS OF PEOPLE?

First Amendment (in part): "Congress shall make no law . . . abridging the freedom of speech"

Fourteenth Amendment (in part): "No state shall . . . deprive any person . . . within its jurisdiction the equal protection of the laws."

Have you, your parents, or someone else you know donated money to a candidate running for office? Along with other forms of engagement in the electoral process, making a campaign contribution has become a popular way to show support for the person you want to win an election, and to back the values and issues that candidate supports.

In early 2010, the United States Supreme Court, in a case entitled *Citizens United v. Federal Election Commission*, held that corporations could spend as much money as they wished to support or oppose candidates, parties, and issues in U.S. elections. The Court cited the First Amendment free speech protections and Fourteenth Amendment equal protection provisions. Students of free speech and of campaign finance reform were stunned and both political parties scrambled to figure out how to benefit from the ruling. Corporations were also puzzled about how, and even if, to deploy their new found freedom to participate openly in elections. A lot of history was upended in the decision.

From the nation's early days, "corporations" have been considered artificial or legal "persons" for a limited range of mostly commercial purposes—buying and selling goods and property, making contracts, and suing and being sued. Chief Justice John Marshall famously defined corporations in the Dartmouth College case (1819) as follows: "A corporation is an artificial being, invisible, intangible, and existing only in the contemplation of law. Being the mere creature of law, it possesses only those properties which the [state] charter of creation confers upon it, either expressly, or as incidental to its very existence."

Some saw corporations, with their great wealth, as a danger from the beginning. In 1816 Thomas Jefferson wrote, "I hope we shall crush in its birth the aristocracy of our monied corporations which dare already to challenge our government to a trial of strength and bid defiance the laws of our country." Abraham Lincoln issued a similar dire warning near the close of the Civil War, saying "as a result of the war, corporations have become enthroned, and an era of corruption in high places will follow."

The Fourteenth Amendment, quoted in part above, was ratified in 1868 to insure that the freed slaves were treated by the states as "persons" entitled to all the rights and privileges enjoyed by whites. Within a few short years, the personhood of blacks had slipped from the Court's view and the personhood of corporations became their focus. The Supreme Court held in *Santa Clara County v. Southern Pacific Railroad* (1886) that corporations are persons within the meaning of the Fourteenth Amendment and therefore enjoy all of the rights and protections of natural persons.

Soon the potential impact of corporations on elections became starkly clear. In 1896, Mark Hanna funded Republican William McKinley's presidential campaign against Democrat William Jennings Bryan with an assessment on the nation's largest corporations, allowing McKinley to outspend Bryan by 10, some say 20, to 1 and easily win the presidency. McKinley was re-elected in 1900 before being assassinated and succeeded in office by his Vice President Theodore Roosevelt. Roosevelt, a reformer, signed the Tillman Act (1907) barring corporate campaign contributions. The Federal Corrupt Practices Act (1925) and the Taft-Hartley Act (1947) strengthened the ban on corporate campaign spending and extended it to labor unions. The Federal Election Campaign Act (1971) and its McCain-Feingold revisions (2002) continued the bans on corporate and union expenditures.

Bans on direct participation in elections by corporations have been motivated by the fact that corporations have access to vast financial resources. Just one stunning example makes the point; in 2013 Exxon made corporate profits of $32.6 billion, just 1 percent of which, $326 million, would allow it to become a major player in every American election in which it took an interest. Justice Stevens, dissenting in the *Citizens United* decision, called "the Court's opinion . . . a rejection of the common sense of the American people, who have recognized a need to prevent corporations from undermining self-government since the founding, and who have fought against the distinctive corrupting potential of corporate electioneering since the days of Theodore Roosevelt."

Focus Questions: from reading to thinking

Q1 Why do so many Americans fail to vote even in important elections like those for Congress, governor, or president?

Q2 How do those who do vote decide which of the parties and candidates to vote for?

Q3 Who chooses to run for political office, and how do they organize their campaigns?

Q4 How does the campaign for the presidency differ from campaigns for other offices that are less visible, powerful, and prestigious?

Q5 Does money dominate presidential elections?

WHAT DO YOU THINK?

- Are limits on corporate electioneering advisable?
- Should corporate persons and human persons have the same means for voicing and defending their interests?

VOTING, CAMPAIGNS, AND ELECTIONS

Voting, campaigns, and elections are among the central structures and acts of democratic political life.[1] Election campaigns put alternative policies, programs, and politicians before voters for consideration and choice. However, fewer Americans take advantage of their rights to vote than do citizens in other advanced, industrial democracies.

We begin by exploring the history of the right to vote in the United States. During the colonial period, the electorate was restricted to white male property holders over the age of twenty-one. The slow addition of poor white males, then black males, then women, and finally young people between the ages of 18 and 21 now make virtually all adult American citizens eligible to vote. But more than a third of eligible voters stay home even in presidential elections. We ask who votes, who does not, and why.

We then ask what motivates some Americans to stand for political office. We ask how congressional campaigns are organized and what accounts for the tremendous advantages that incumbents enjoy over their challengers. Finally, we ask how campaigns for the presidency—the top prize in American politics—are planned and executed from early organization and fund raising, through the long season of competition in state primaries and caucuses, to the national nominating conventions, to the general election where the voters make their final choice.

VOTING AND NONVOTING IN AMERICAN HISTORY

01 Why do so many Americans fail to vote even in important elections like those for Congress, governor, or president?

One of the great puzzles of American political life is that so many of us choose to ignore political rights for which citizens in other countries—China, Kenya, and Iran, just to name a few—still struggle and die. In this section, we discuss when and how Americans achieved the right to vote and what accounts for the fact that some consistently employ this right, whereas others consistently ignore it. Though voter participation has been up in the past couple of electoral cycles, it is still well below levels achieved in earlier periods of our history and in most modern democracies.

Struggling Toward Democracy

In the nineteenth century, less than half of adults were entitled to vote, but about 80 percent of those entitled to vote did. Today, virtually all adults are entitled to vote, but only about half do.

What do you think?
- Which set of facts seems to describe the healthier democracy?
- We think of democracy as the right to vote; is it just as much the right not to vote?

Expanding the Franchise, 1789–2012

No question is more fundamental to a free society than who gets to vote. Recall that the Founders were wary of direct democracy and, frankly, of the participation of the poor and the poorly educated in politics and governance. They knew and were comforted by the fact that republics since ancient Greece and Rome had employed limitations on **suffrage,** which is another term for the right to vote, as a way of balancing the interests of the few wealthy and the many poor. In thinking about the effectiveness of voting, one wants to know two things: what portion of the adult population is eligible to vote and what portion of the eligible electorate actually turns up to vote on election day.

Information about voter eligibility and turnout in early American history is spotty and inconsistent. But even for the early nineteenth century, we have a pretty good sense of the size of the adult population. Then we ask

suffrage Another term for the legal right to vote.

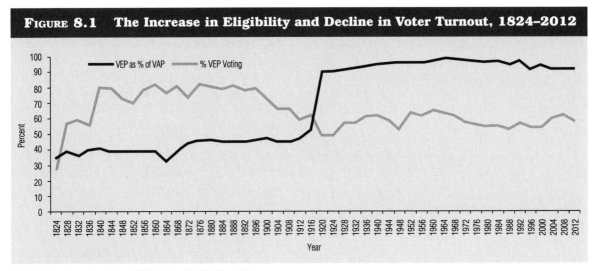

FIGURE 8.1   The Increase in Eligibility and Decline in Voter Turnout, 1824–2012

VAP = Voting-Age Population VEP= Voting Eligible Population
Sources: Data were drawn from the following sources: Department of Commerce, Bureau of the Census, *Historical Statistics of the United States, Colonial Times to 1957* (Washington, D.C.: U.S. Government Printing Office, 1960), Series A 1–22, Series Y 80–128; *Statistical Abstract of the United States, 2012*, 131st ed. (Washington, D.C.: U.S. Government Printing Office, 2011), 246. See also Francis Fox Piven and Richard A. Cloward, *Why Americans Don't Vote* (New York: Pantheon Books, 1989), 30, 54, 125, 161; and Stephen J. Wayne, *The Road to the White House*, 2012, 9th ed. (New York: Wadsworth, 2012), 73–76.

what percentage of these people were eligible to vote under the laws in force at the time and what percentage of those eligible to vote actually turned out on election day. **Voter turnout** is the percentage of the voting eligible population (VEP) that actually turns out to vote on election day. In Figure 8.1, the blue line is the percent of the VAP eligible to vote under the laws of the day while the orange line is the percent of eligibles that actually turned out to vote.

voter turnout That portion of the voting-age population that actually turns up to vote on election day.

The first American electorate was made up of white men whose ownership of land, usually something like fifty acres or the equivalent, suggested that they had a permanent stake in the community that they would help to govern. However, between 1810 and 1850, the rise of mass-based parties, and especially the commitment of the Jacksonian Democrats to universal suffrage for white men, produced expansion both of the eligible electorate and turnout. Turnout among eligible voters in presidential elections jumped from under 30 percent in 1824 to just under 60 percent in 1828. By the 1840s, the eligible electorate was fully mobilized, and turnout held in the 70- to 80-percent range for the next fifty years.[2]

The second important expansion of the electorate occurred in the wake of the Civil War with the enfranchisement of black men. The Congress required southern state governments to ratify the Fifteenth Amendment (1870), which provided a national guarantee of male suffrage regardless of race, as part of the price for ending military occupation. The addition of black men to the electorate spurred white turnout to even higher levels as the South's traditional elites struggled to regain control of southern state governments. Eighty percent of those eligible to vote, black and white men, actually did so into the last decade of the nineteenth century.

Managing the Electorate, 1880–2012

The second half of the nineteenth century was an extraordinarily tumultuous time in American history. Regional conflict culminating in civil war, the end of slavery, and the military occupation of the South from 1865 to 1876 produced a superheated political environment. Voter turnout held around 80 percent as the fate of the defeated South and of the nation to which it would have to be reconciled hung in the balance. Not surprisingly, the two highest-turnout elections in American history were the election of 1860 (second highest), when Lincoln was elected and the nation split, and 1876 (highest), when a tied election (much like the 2000 tie between George W. Bush and Al Gore) produced a compromise that allowed the Republican, Rutherford B. Hayes, to assume the presidency in exchange for ending the military occupation of the South.

Over the course of the next two decades, southern elites regained control of their state politics and steadily moved blacks out of the electorate and to the fringes of social and economic life. In the North, steeply rising levels of immigration and a shift from traditional northern European sources of immigration to new southern and eastern European sources convinced many that limitations on citizenship and suffrage were necessary. Traditional northern and southern elites moved systematically to reduce the electorate to a more dependable, predictable, and manageable size.

The election of 1896, in which William McKinley (R) defeated William Jennings Bryan (D), concluded a series of intensely partisan, volatile, and closely fought national elections. This contest left the conservative business wing of the Republican Party dominant in the North and the conservative planter wing of the white Democratic Party dominant in the South and the national balance favoring the Republicans. Figure 8.1 shows that severe declines in turnout began in the 1880s and continued through the 1920s.

White conservatives in both the North and South employed a number of rules and laws to shrink the electorate in ways that would enhance their control. In the South, the planter class used the Democratic Party to enact poll taxes, literacy tests, grandfather clauses, white primaries, and restrictive voter registration procedures that forced most black and poor white voters off the voter rolls. Voter turnout in the South dropped from 75 percent in 1876, to 57 percent in the election of 1896, to 43 percent in 1900, to 29 percent in 1904. Blacks in the South virtually disappeared from the voter rolls during these years.

Conservatives in the North enacted voter registration and election rules that were intended to hold down the rapidly rising immigrant vote. These reforms, which included civil service exams, city manager and commission forms of government, at-large elections, and personal registration of voters were proposed as good-government measures. In many ways they were, but they also severely weakened political parties and limited voter participation.

Turnout in the North dropped from 86 percent in the election of 1896 to 57 percent in 1924.[3]

The third major expansion of the eligible electorate occurred with the adoption of the Nineteenth Amendment in 1920. The Nineteenth Amendment guaranteed the right of women to vote.[4] Overnight the size of the eligible electorate doubled. As with other new voters, women took a while to become familiar with the electoral process and to gain the confidence necessary to participate in it. Initially, women's suffrage contributed to declining turnout in the early twentieth century.

The percentage of eligible voters casting ballots rose back above 60 percent by the mid-1930s and stayed there until the mid-1960s. A new downward trend began in the mid-1960s and continued through the election of 2000, despite a nice uptick in 1992. This latest period of declining turnout was aggravated by the passage of the Twenty-Sixth Amendment in 1971, which lowered the voting age to eighteen in all American elections. Like women half a century earlier, young people tended to vote in relatively modest numbers. Turnout in 1996 and 2000 averaged slightly over 50 percent of eligible voters, but in 2004 rose to 61 percent and in 2008 to nearly 62 percent. Better, but still below earlier levels. In 2012, turnout dropped to just below 60 percent.

Today, virtually all citizens over the age of eighteen, except the formally institutionalized and about three million former felons, are eligible to vote.[5] Several states recently relaxed legal prohibitions on former felons. In 2007, Florida relaxed its lifetime prohibition, restoring suffrage to 115,000 former felons, though nearly a quarter million remain ineligible. As we shall see, many Americans fail to put their legal eligibility to vote into effect.

What Might We Do to Increase Turnout?

Most analysts argue that the way the United States organizes and administers its voter registration system and conducts its elections explains its low voter turnout rate. First, as shown in the Let's Compare box (see pages 222–223), U.S. voter turnout is substantially lower than in virtually every other advanced industrial nation in the world. Second, recent declines, unlike those in the early twentieth century that were caused by legal and illegal efforts to force blacks and poor whites from the voter rolls, have occurred despite removal of these old obstacles and despite improvements in education, income, and other factors that traditionally have increased turnout and other forms of participation. Recall that in the previous chapter, we discussed the likelihood that the U.S. electoral system, characterized by single-member districts and plurality voting schemes, suppressed turnout. Here we ask which specific rules and procedures suppress turnout and whether specific reforms might encourage turnout.

Analysts have long contended that simplifying **voter registration** and voting was the key to increasing turnout. President Clinton and the Democratic Congress responded by passing the National Voter Registration Act in 1993. The act, also called **Motor Voter**, allows Americans to register to vote at the same time they are doing other things, like getting their driver's license (hence the

voter registration The process by which members of the voting-age population sign up, or register, to establish their right to cast a ballot on election day.

Motor Voter Popular name for the National Voter Registration Act of 1993. The act permits people to register to vote while they are doing other common tasks like getting or renewing their driver's licenses.

LET'S COMPARE

Voter Turnout and the Effects of Alternative Voter Registration Systems

Country	1983, Turnout Percent VAP	Latest Turnout Percent VAP	Compulsory Voting	Automatic Registration
Belgium	94%	93%	Yes	Yes
Italy	92%	68%	No	Yes
Sweden	89%	83%	No	Yes
New Zealand	87%	70%	No	No
Austria	87%	69%	No	Yes
Denmark	86%	82%	No	Yes
Norway	83%	78%	No	Yes
Spain	83%	63%	No	Yes
Finland	81%	70%	No	Yes
Australia	81%	80%	Yes	No
Germany	81%	66%	No	Yes
Netherlands	80%	71%	Yes	Yes
Israel	80%	73%	No	Yes
Ireland	76%	64%	No	Yes
United Kingdom	72%	61%	No	Yes
Japan	68%	60%	No	Yes
Canada	68%	54%	No	No
France	64%	46%	No	No
United States	**53%**	**58%**	**No**	**No**
Switzerland	41%	40%	No	Yes

These data make several things clear. One is that voter turnout has been dropping in most countries of the advanced industrial world during the past three decades. Declines of 10 percent are not uncommon. Another is that most advanced industrial nations have turnouts consistently around 70 percent, and a few are consistently over 80 percent. Still another is that the United States has among the lowest voter turnout rates of any advanced nation. How do the nations that consistently experience voter turnout levels much higher than ours do it? First, three of the countries with turnout over 70 percent have compulsory voting laws. Second, and much more important, virtually all of the countries listed have automatic voter registration. Automatic voter registration means that the government is responsible for seeing that all eligible voters are on the voter registration rolls and entitled to vote on election day.

Only the United States, Canada, Australia, and New Zealand fail to employ either mandatory voting or automatic registration, leaving citizens on their own to decide whether and how to register and vote. In the United States, 80 percent of eligible adults are registered to vote. The following table shows how important registration is to turnout. Only 68 percent of Americans who are registered actually turn out on election day. Still, in the not-too-distant past the percentage was much higher. In 1964, 94 percent of registered voters turned out, and in 1976, 88 percent turned out. The following table compares turnout among registered voters in the United States and other advanced Western democracies.

These figures make it very difficult to argue that our country puts a high value on political participation by all adult citizens. Although we were the first nation to adopt universal manhood suffrage (the states actually did the adopting), it is equally clear that these same states adopted reforms in the late nineteenth century that excluded large numbers of blacks and poor whites from the electorate. To this day, more than a century after the watershed election of 1896, American political parties and institutions remain largely, even curiously, disinterested in voter registration and higher turnout.

Percentage Turnout among Registered Voters			
	Country	**2000**	**Latest**
1	Belgium	96%	89%
2	Australia	95%	93%
3	Denmark	87%	88%
4	Italy	81%	75%
5	Austria	80%	75%
6	Sweden	80%	85%
7	France	80%	55%
8	Netherlands	80%	75%
9	Germany	79%	72%
10	New Zealand	77%	74%
11	Norway	75%	78%
12	Spain	69%	69%
13	Israel	68%	68%
14	United States	67%	68%
15	Finland	65%	67%
16	Ireland	63%	70%
17	Canada	61%	61%
18	Japan	61%	59%
19	United Kingdom	59%	66%
20	Switzerland	45%	49%

Source: Website of the International Institute for Democracy and Electoral Assistance at http://www.idea.int/vt

name *Motor Voter*), signing up for social services, or checking on their property taxes. Most states allow on-line registration. Voter registration is up since 1993, but just a bit.[6]

Other proposals for increasing turnout include reducing the number of elections in which voters are asked to participate by clustering national, state, and local elections on the same day. Elections might also be moved from the traditional Tuesday, a workday for most people, to a Saturday or a few days including a Saturday. Early voting, either in person or by mail ballot, is used in many jurisdictions, and same-day voter registration in a few; both serve to increase turnout moderately. Some advocate voter registration for high school seniors and a few call for mandatory voting.[7]

Not everyone agrees that ease of voter registration and voting is obviously desirable. Republican state legislators in Indiana and three dozen others states passed laws requiring a government-issued photo ID, such as a passport or drivers' license, to vote. Republicans argue that illegal voting is a serious problem, so it is likely that more states will follow Indiana's lead. Democrats argue that existing laws, which allow a wider range of documentation to prove residence, like an electric bill with a name and address on it, are sufficient and that requiring photo IDs will work a particular hardship on the poor, the elderly, and minorities. In early 2008, the Supreme Court upheld the Indiana photo ID law. The court held that, while Republicans had failed to prove that illegal voting was a major problem and Democrats had failed to prove that legal voters were being excluded, the requirement was a constitutionally permissible precaution against illegal voting. However, the court left the door to reconsideration open a crack if Democrats could show real evidence of legal voters being excluded for lack of a photo ID. A number of state courts struck down voter ID laws as unconstitutional and the U.S. Justice Department struck down a Texas law as a violation of the Voting Rights Act. The Supreme Court then struck down key provisions of the Voting Rights Act and Texas implemented its photo ID law. This fight is not over.

Finally, the vote counting debacle in Florida in the 2000 presidential election highlighted the question of whether votes were being accurately recorded and counted. To resolve these questions, Congress passed the Help America Vote Act (HAVA) in 2002. HAVA provided more than $4 billion dollars to replace outdated voting equipment, create statewide voter registration databases, and train election workers. No sooner was the new equipment installed than questions were raised about handicapped accessibility and the dependability of electronic voting equipment, especially when there was no paper trail to assure that votes were cast and counted as voters intended. These issues remain unresolved today.[8]

Two Decisions: Whether to Vote and for Whom to Vote

Q2 How do those who do vote decide which of the parties and candidates to vote for?

Registered voters still have two important decisions to make: whether to vote in a given election and, if they decide to vote, for whom to vote.[9] The first decision depends heavily on the kind of election it is. Voters are more likely to turn out if the offices at stake are important and visible; if the candidates are well known, popular, and attractive; if the main election is competitive; and if other key issues, such as hotly contested initiatives or referenda, are on the ballot. Not surprisingly, local elections among less-known candidates for minor offices draw fewer voters.

How voters decide for whom to vote is an interesting and complicated process. Historically, the less visible the office, the more likely voters were to be guided by their partisan identification. In major elections, when information about the candidates came to hand more readily, candidate attributes and issue positions could move voters away from their traditional party attachments. However, in recent elections, the number of "persuadable" voters has been declining. In 2004, 2008, and 2012 fewer than a fifth of Democrats and Republicans said there was even a chance they would vote for the candidate of the other party. In 2012, although Independents leaned toward the Democrats, nine in ten Republicans continued to support the candidates of their party.

TABLE 8.1   Voting Turnout by Population Characteristics, 1972–2012

	1972	1976	1980	1984	1988	1992	1996	2000	2004	2008	2012
Education											
8 Years or Less	47.4%	44.1%	42.6%	42.9%	36.7%	35.1%	28.1%	26.8%	23.6%	23.4%	21.6%
Some High School	52.0%	47.2%	45.6%	44.4%	41.3%	41.2%	38.8%	33.6%	34.6%	33.7%	32.2%
High School Grad	—	59.4%	58.9%	58.7%	54.7%	57.5%	49.1%	49.4%	52.4%	50.9%	48.7%
Some College	65.4%	68.1%	67.2%	67.5%	64.5%	68.7%	60.5%	60.3%	66.1%	65.0%	61.5%
College Grad or More	78.8%	79.8%	79.9%	79.1%	77.6%	81.0%	73.0%	72.0%	74.2%	73.3%	71.7%
Age											
18–20	48.3%	38.0%	35.7%	36.7%	33.2%	38.5%	31.2%	28.4%	41.0%	41.0%	35.1%
21–24	50.7%	45.6%	43.1%	43.5%	38.3%	45.7%	33.4%	35.4%	42.5%	46.6%	40.0%
25–34	59.7%	55.4%	54.6%	54.5%	48.0%	53.2%	43.1%	43.7%	46.9%	48.5%	46.1%
35–44	66.3%	63.3%	64.4%	63.5%	61.3%	63.6%	54.9%	55.0%	56.9%	55.2%	52.9%
45–64	70.8%	68.7%	69.3%	69.8%	67.9%	70.0%	64.4%	64.1%	66.6%	65.0%	63.4%
65 and Over	63.5%	62.2%	65.1%	67.7%	68.8%	70.1%	67.0%	67.6%	68.9%	68.1%	69.7%
Sex											
Male	64.1%	59.6%	59.1%	59.0%	56.4%	60.2%	52.8%	53.1%	56.3%	55.7%	54.4%
Female	62.0%	58.8%	59.4%	60.8%	58.3%	62.3%	55.5%	56.2%	60.1%	60.4%	58.5%
Race											
White	64.5%	60.9%	60.9%	61.4%	59.1%	63.6%	56.0%	56.4%	60.3%	59.6%	57.6%
Black	52.1%	48.7%	50.5%	55.8%	51.5%	54.0%	50.6%	53.5%	56.3%	60.8%	62.0%
Hispanic	37.4%	31.8%	29.9%	32.6%	28.8%	28.9%	26.7%	27.5%	28.0%	31.6%	31.8%

Source: Department of Commerce, Bureau of the Census, *Statistical Abstract of the United States, 2014* (Washington, D.C.: U.S. Government Printing Office, 2013), Table 418.

Who Votes, Who Stays Home?   Citizens of higher socioeconomic status (SES—a composite measure of education, income, and occupational status) vote, contribute time and money to campaigns, contact public officials, talk about politics with their friends and acquaintances, and engage in other political activities in greater numbers and more frequently than do citizens of lower socioeconomic status.[10]

Education is the most important component of socioeconomic status for influencing turnout. In fact, the data in Table 8.1 show that education is becoming an increasingly powerful determinant of turnout. Note that in the 1972 presidential election, 47.4 percent of people with less than eight years of schooling voted, whereas 78.8 percent of those with four or more years of college voted. This difference of more than 31 points is impressive. But then note that although turnout among the best educated dropped just over seven points between 1972 and 2012, it plummeted almost twenty-six points, from 47.4 to 21.6, for the least educated. The well educated now vote at a rate more than three times greater than the least educated.

Analysts point to three effects of education that facilitate political activity. First, education reduces the sense of complexity and mystery that surrounds politics and policymaking for many. Second, education makes citizens more able to anticipate the probable results for them of government actions on matters such as taxes, trade policy, and interest rates. Third, highly educated citizens are confident that they have the knowledge and skills to influence government and that government listens to people like them.

Age, like education, is an important factor in discriminating between voters and nonvoters. Note in Table 8.1 that by 2000 voters under 35 voted about 10 to

President Obama, with the ladies of "The View," courts the women's vote during the 2012 campaign. Just because it is obvious what you are doing does not mean it will not work.

15 points less than they did in 1972, whereas people 45 and over had dropped 5 to 10 points, and older people voted 5 points more than they had in 1972. Although 2004 and 2008 recorded big increases in the youth vote over 2000, up 12 percent for voters 18–24 and up 5 percent for voters 25–34, they remained almost 20 points behind voters over 45. In 2012, the youth vote dropped back about 5 points, giving up about half the gains since 2000.

The relationship between gender and turnout has developed in interesting ways. Through the 1970s men voted in higher proportions than women, but women began to outvote men in 1980 and have incrementally increased the margin in most elections since. Women cast 53 percent of all votes in 2012. Race and ethnicity provide a final set of interesting comparisons.[11] Although white turnout dipped 7 percent between 1972 and 2012, turnout among blacks rose about 10 percent, putting black turnout 4.4 percent ahead of whites for just the second time (in 2008 it was 1 point ahead) in American history—the Obama effect. Turnout among Hispanic voters in 2012 was just under 32 percent, whereas for blacks it was about 62 percent, and for whites it was almost 58 percent.[12]

Table 8.2 mirrors Table 8.1, but looks just at young people, aged 18 to 29. As a result, Table 8.2 gives us a glimpse into the future, allowing us to think about whether whites will continue to outvote blacks, women will continue to outvote men, and whether Hispanic turnout will increase. First, among young voters, women have a larger turnout advantage over men than they do among all voters, so the gender gap is likely to continue to grow. Second, young black voters have a larger turnout advantage over young white voters than exists among older voters, so the recent trend of blacks outvoting whites may

TABLE 8.2	**Young People's (18–29) Turnout by Population Characteristics, 1972–2012**										
	1972	**1976**	**1980**	**1984**	**1988**	**1992**	**1996**	**2000**	**2004**	**2008**	**2012**
Education											
Less than HS	27.9	22.5	20.2	22.7	19.5	23.1	19.2		18.2	26.3	
High School	51.2	40.7	41.6	41.8	34.5	41.6	29.0	30.3	30.4	39.6	
Some College	72.7	58.6	57.9	59.0	52.7	61.8	46.9	46.3	45.8	57.1	
College Grad or More	82.5	77.2	77.4	75.7	70.1	79.6	63.2	64.4	64.7	71.9	
Sex											
Male	58.4	47.7	47.1	46.9	41.8	49.6	35.4	37.7	45.5	47.2	41.5
Female	55.9	49.8	49.3	51.1	45.7	54.3	42.6	42.8	52.4	54.9	48.6
Race											
White	57.1	51.7	50.9	50.3	45.6	54.9	41.4	42.0	52.3	52.1	46.1
Black	42.7	35.5	38.6	48.3	39.4	45.2	39.0	42.0	49.5	58.2	53.7
Hispanic		32.0	30.2	35.5	33.4	38.9	28.4	29.4	35.5	40.7	36.9
Asian						36.9	34.3	31.8	32.4	42.2	36.2

Source: CIRCLE, www.civicyouth.org
http://www.civicyouth.org/PopUps/WorkingPapers/WP35CIRCLE.pdf

continue even after Barack Obama is out of office. Finally, low turnout among young Hispanic voters suggests that overall Hispanic turnout will continue to lag for the foreseeable future.

How Do Voters Make Up Their Minds?   How do those who vote decide for whom to vote? Among the key factors that voters take into account are party identification if they have one, party images and issue positions, and candidate attributes.

In the end, however, research suggests that voters make their decisions as much and perhaps more from gut reactions as from strictly rational calculations. Fear and anxiety are powerful emotions, particularly in time of war and economic turmoil. Hope and optimism are powerful emotions as well, but they are subject to being undercut by fear and anxiety. In the 2012 campaign, a fight over whether Iran is a great threat or we can talk to them was waged over this terrain. Finally, voters respond positively to candidates they think are like themselves—in terms of social class, race, ethnicity, gender, even region—and, they hope, likely to see and understand the world as they do.[13]

Party Identification.   Partisanship is the strongest and steadiest influence on the political behavior of individuals. Partisanship is a predisposition, often established during childhood and maintained throughout adulthood, to favor one party over the other. Although this commitment can be shaken by the events and personalities of a particular election, all other things being equal, it will be the dominant influence on the voters' decision.

Strong partisans tend to support the candidates of their party more consistently than do weak partisans, and they tend to make their decisions earlier in the electoral cycle. Party regulars tend to listen almost exclusively to their own side in election campaigns, and hence they rarely change their minds during campaigns.[14] Strong partisans are also likely to be more interested in politics, to follow it more closely between elections, and to be better informed than weak partisans and independents. Thirty-four percent of votes were cast early in 2012 and most of those early voters were commited partisans.

Although independents now make up over one-third of the electorate, two-thirds of independents admit that they "lean" toward the Democrats or the Republicans. These leaners behave more like partisans than like "pure" independents. Pure independents tend to have very little information about politics and to vote infrequently.[15] Hence, both major parties have been torn between working to hold their base and reaching out to the fairly small number of independent or swing voters.

Party and Candidate Positions.   Extensive polling data show that some issue information is fixed in the historical images of the two major parties. The Democrats are widely perceived to be more sensitive to the poor and minorities, social welfare issues, and income and employment issues. The Republicans are widely perceived to be better on issues of national security, crime, inflation, and business and regulatory policy. These party images stick in voters' minds and are hard to change.[16] As a result, elections that highlight race, crime, and national security (such as the Nixon elections of 1968 and 1972, the Reagan elections of 1980 and 1984, and the Bush election of 2004) tend to give Republicans the advantage, whereas elections that highlight the economic interests of the common person (such as the Johnson election of 1964, the Carter election of 1976, and the Clinton elections of 1992 and 1996) tend to give Democrats the advantage.[17] However, if the party in power proves ineffectual, especially on their natural issues, voters may well decide to make a change.

The particular dynamics of individual elections encourage candidates to raise some issues and to try to keep others from coming to voters' attention. Candidates seek to raise issues that work to their advantage and to the disadvantage of their opponents and to bury issues that work to the advantage of their opponents and are a disadvantage to them. In general, however, candidates are constrained by positions that they have taken in the past and by the core positions of their party.

In 2012, Mitt Romney was convinced that a focus on slow job growth and instability in the Middle East would work to his and the Republican Party's advantage. Obama believed that a focus on the economic vulnerability of the middle and working classes would work to his and the Democratic Party's advantage. Exit polls showed that 63 percent of Americans ranked the economy as the most important issue facing the country while only 19 percent cited either terrorism or the war in Iraq. Advantage Obama. In 2012, with a maddeningly slow economic recovery in place, Obama focused on solidifying and turning out his base among young people, women, especially single women, and minorities.

Candidate Attributes.   Although partisanship and issue information remain important, attention to candidates and their personal traits and qualities has increased. Voters want to know what kind of person a candidate is—is he or she a strong leader, of good moral character, experienced, and personable?—in order to gain some insight into how he or she will think and react in office.[18]

For some candidates, such as Dwight Eisenhower and Ronald Reagan, qualities such as strength, honesty, and consistency were the foundation of their success. For others, such as Barry Goldwater, George McGovern, and Howard Dean, concerns about personal stability, judgment, and character were hurdles that they could not clear. Yet character is multifaceted, and questions about some aspects of a candidate's character can be overcome if other facets of that character seem to be attractive.

In 1992 and 1996, questions about Bill Clinton's character—in regard to business dealings such as Whitewater, sexual conduct with Gennifer Flowers, Paula Jones, and others, and his early history regarding marijuana and the draft—were widely discussed. Many voters looked past these questions about character to place greater weight on his seemingly deeper empathy for people and on policy proposals for addressing their problems.

In 2008, McCain was seen as heroic and experienced, though often emotional and sometimes impetuous. Obama was seen as articulate, cool, and cerebral, though many voters wondered whether they knew him well enough to truly understand him. When the U.S. and world stock markets turned sharply down in the weeks just before the elections, Obama responded calmly while McCain seemed less steady. In the next two weeks, McCain went from up two or three to down five or six. Candidates reap a big advantage when their personal character and attributes seem to match well the nation's major challenges.

The Result: Volatile Turnout and Polarization.   Two major results have followed from the nature of modern campaigns and elections. First, as voter turnout has declined among some socio-demographic groups—the poor, and the poorly educated—it has held up among older, economically secure, and well-educated people. Well-educated people have become more partisan, more ideological, and more polarized over the last two decades.

Second, candidate-centered campaigns, as opposed to the older party-centered campaigns, increase both the effectiveness and the likelihood of "going negative." Shifting attention from differences on issues to criticisms of character or competence offers the opportunity to call an opponent's fundamental viability as a candidate into question and thereby to destroy the candidacy.[19]

But former senators Jeff Bingaman (D-NM) and Olympia Snowe (R-Maine), both of whom chose not to seek reelection in 2012, argue that harsh, win-at-all-costs campaigns make the kind of bipartisan cooperation necessary to governance just too difficult. Moreover, negative campaigns reduce turnout and compromise the faith of voters in the political system in general.

POLITICAL CAMPAIGNS: AMBITION AND ORGANIZATION

Q3 Who chooses to run for political office, and how do they organize their campaigns?

Where do our political leaders, the people who sit on our city councils, in our state legislatures, in Congress, and even in the Oval Office, come from? What leads them to run for office? Most are driven to run for office and then to run for higher office by their own ambitions. Today politicians at the national level and increasingly those in the larger, more complex states and cities are careerists supported by teams of professional campaign managers and consultants. In this section, we focus on those who run for Congress. We ask what advantages incumbents enjoy, what difficulties challengers face, and how both organize and conduct their campaigns.

The Incumbency Advantage

We should not be terribly surprised to find that incumbent members of Congress usually win reelection. This incumbency advantage derives from the fact that incumbents are likely to be better known, more experienced, and have more established fund-raising prospects than do their challengers.

On the other hand, we might reasonably be concerned to find that over the past six decades, House incumbents standing for reelection won more than 92 percent of the time and incumbent senators won over 78 percent of the time. Our concern might deepen to learn that more than 98 percent of House incumbents seeking reelection won in 1986, 1988, 1998, 2000, and 2004. More than 90 percent of senators seeking reelection won in 1990, 1994, 1996, 1998, and 2004. Even in 2006, when both the House and Senate switched from Republican to Democratic control, and in 2008 when Democrats built on their majorities, 94 percent of House members and 83 percent of senators who chose to stand for reelection won. In 2010 the Republicans took back much of what they had lost in 2006 and 2008, but 84 percent of House members and Senators who stood for reelection still won. In both the House and the Senate, incumbents who chose to stand for reelection in 2012 won 91 percent of the time. In 2014, Republicans retook the Senate, picking up nine new seats, and extended their House majority by winning thirteen new seats. Again, despite a big partisan win, this time for the Republicans, 96 percent of House incumbents and 82 percent of Senate incumbents were able to hold their seat. Even in a difficult year, incumbents have important advantages.

Name Recognition and Advertising.   Voters like to vote for candidates they know, or at least know of, but they do not like to spend time getting to know candidates. As a result, more than half of eligible voters even at the height of a congressional campaign were unable to name either candidate running in their district, and only 22 percent of voters could name both candidates.[20] Voters who could name only one candidate almost always named the incumbent, and almost no one could name only the challenger.

Incumbent members of Congress control a variety of resources that come with the office, including a paid staff distributed between Washington and a number of home district offices, free postage from Washington (called the franking privilege), a travel allowance permitting approximately one trip a week home to the district, and a communication allowance. Members routinely mail newsletters and other information and advertisements throughout their district, and they maintain their district offices principally to handle constituent complaints and problems. These activities keep the names of Congress members before their constituents in a favorable light.

Fundraising Opportunities.   Incumbent members of Congress raise campaign money both within their districts and from national interest group and party sources. Potential contributors know that incumbents almost always win, and no one likes to throw money away on an unknown challenger. As a result, campaign contributions flow much more readily to incumbents than to challengers.

National party sources want to protect their incumbents as a first priority, and interest groups want to make contributions to those most likely to be in a position to help them later. A study conducted by The Center for Responsive Politics reported just prior to the 2014 House elections that House incumbents seeking reelection had, on average, a six-to-one advantage over their challengers in total campaign resources.[21]

Challengers and Their Challenges

Most challengers lack the visibility, organization, and resources to make a credible stand against an entrenched incumbent. Current officeholders seeking to move up to a higher office and former public officials make the best challengers because they are most likely to have the experience, fund-raising ability, and contacts to assemble the organization and resources needed to make a strong showing, perhaps even to win. An experienced candidate—one who has held elective public office before—is four times more likely than an inexperienced candidate to beat an incumbent member of Congress.[22]

Inexperienced challengers tend to think only in terms of the local district and whether they can win the nomination. Experienced challengers know that winning the nomination is an empty prize unless the organizational and financial resources required to run a strong general election campaign against an entrenched incumbent will be forthcoming. Candidates who have held political office before are most likely both to know the local district and to have access to the national party and interest group resources in Washington.

National Influences.   National influences on the prospects of congressional challengers come in two main forms. One is the national political and economic climate. The other is the national system of party committees, interest groups, campaign consultants, and Super PACs. Because few challengers win, the most experienced tend to wait for favorable circumstances before stepping forward. Experienced challengers run when the general prospects of their party look bright and step aside for the sacrificial lambs when the party's prospects look dim.[23] In 2006, President Bush was down in the polls, the Iraq War was going badly, and a majority of voters told pollsters that they were ready for a change. Democrats picked up 30 seats in the House and six in the Senate to take majority control of both for the first time since 1994. In 2008, voters sent Obama to the White House and added 21 seats to the Democratic House majority and eight more to the Senate majority. By 2010, it was President Obama who was down in the polls, the economy was limping and unemployment was stuck at 9.5 percent. Several former Republican congressmen, smelling blood, stepped forward to reclaim their seats and they were joined by high quality challengers to Democratic incumbents. Republicans picked up 63 seats in the House, more than they had lost in 2006 and 2008 combined, and 6 in the Senate. Smart politicians set sail for higher office when the political winds are at their back. Republicans were confident as 2014 approached; Obama was unpopular and the slow economic recovery had left many Americans nervous or scared. Republicans picked up nine Senate seats, to retake control after eight years, and thirteen House seats to extend their majority to 247 seats to the Democrats' 188.

Resources from the national level are critical to most congressional campaigns. National parties and interest groups rarely spend money just to make a statement of support. They give to candidates who have demonstrated that they can raise money in their own districts and who have connections to Washington through previous experience in Congress, the executive branch, the interest group structure, or congressional staff. Sponsorship by political figures already well known in Washington also helps to establish legitimacy.

Local Considerations.   Candidates for whom the political climate is supportive and the necessary resources are available still need campaign skills, appropriate political experience, and local organization and support. Campaign skills are developed in prior electoral contests; appropriate political experience might mean service in the state legislature or city council; and local organization and support means familiarity with and influence within the local party, community, and interest group structure.[24]

Challengers must know the district within which they will run. They must know the voters, divisions or groups that exist among them, and how a majority might be created from them. They must also know the distribution of influence, prestige, and wealth in their district. These are the human and financial resources upon which a campaign must draw.

This cartoon suggests that the voter is at risk of permanent brain damage from overexposure to political advertising.

Running the Race

The American political process is more open than any other in the world. Nonetheless, the higher up the electoral system one goes, the more indirect the contact with voters becomes. At the local level, candidates and their supporters walk the neighborhoods; but in the cities and at the congressional, state, and national levels television and the Internet dominate and campaigns are run by teams of highly paid professional operatives and consultants.

Campaign Organization.   Members of the U.S. Congress are at the juncture of local and national politics. At the local level, congressional campaigns still depend heavily on candidates and volunteers who take the message directly to the voters by going door-to-door and by walking the neighborhoods and shopping malls. Volunteers also organize the district, distributing leaflets and bumper stickers, placing yard signs, sitting at telephone banks, and carpooling voters to the polls on election day. Most congressional campaigns rise or fall on the ability of local experts to identify, contact, and mobilize a candidate's likely supporters.

In addition, most congressional campaigns, especially those for urban districts and Senate seats, seek the assistance of professional political consultants.[25] A high-profile political consultant usually heads a seasoned organization that provides the candidate with information from polling and focus groups, provides debate preparation and opposition research, and handles scheduling, fund-raising, and media. Respected campaign consultants also provide immediate credibility in Washington with the system of interest groups, party committees, and Super PACs.

Crafting the Themes.   A campaign needs to know what likely voters think both of its candidate and of the major issues of the day so that the two can be related to maximum advantage. Baseline polling and focus groups are the sources of this kind of information. The key is to build on candidate strengths, protect against exploitation of weaknesses by the opposition, and try to highlight themes upon which the candidate and his or her party have a natural advantage.

Later in the campaign, sophisticated tracking polls, media technology, and political consultants allow candidates to stay in touch with and respond to the public mood day-to-day. **Micro targeting** is a process borrowed from corporate marketing in which political consultants sort voters into smaller and more precise target groups, using "public items like party affiliation, ZIP-code . . . and fairly detailed consumer preferences such as which car you drive, where you vacation and which entertainment you prefer. That information is augmented by surveys that link those traits and behaviors to attitudes on political and social issues." Campaigns seek to identify the mix of characteristics, preferences, and attitudes held by their supporters and then reach out in a highly targeted way to others that share that political DNA.[26]

Raising Money.   Successful candidates must combine local fundraising with the involvement of the national party and well-disposed independent groups.

micro targeting Campaign consultants analyze dozens of pieces of demographic, political, and consumer data to determine what issues, themes, and arguments are likely to move a voter or group of similar voters toward a candidate.

Local fundraising involves familiar techniques: breakfasts and lunches, picnics and cocktail parties, and visits by party leaders or other prominent figures on the candidate's or party's behalf. National fundraising moves beyond local or even statewide sources of revenue to tap the big money concentrations in Los Angeles, Dallas, Washington, and New York. As the cost of elections has continued to escalate, national sources have increasingly displaced local sources of funds. Successful Senate races in 2014 cost an average of $10.2 million, and successful House races averaged $1.6 million. Outside money, of course, added to these totals; sometimes it added a great deal.

Fully 60 percent of campaign costs go for fundraising, that is, money spent to raise more money, and media and candidate marketing. The need to raise increasing amounts of money has produced "the 'permanent campaign,' with full-time staff, fund-raising activities, and polling that helps candidates calculate their actions in office against the reactions of potential voters in future elections."[27]

Over the past decade, congressional, statewide, and presidential campaigns have come to focus on "Big Data" in ways previously unimaginable. Campaign data analysts now have the expertise and computing power to merge state voter files, census data, various consumer databases, and information provided directly by individuals to coordinate and focus campaign strategy and tactics. These huge databases, if properly constructed and analyzed, can generate probability estimates of who is most likely to volunteer, contribute, or turn out to vote for the campaign and its candidate. While campaigns can get state voter files and census data free, they often have to pay for computer databases, but the most valuable data they get comes from voters themselves.[28]

RUNNING FOR THE PRESIDENCY

The presidency is the focal point of the American political system and, therefore, the ultimate goal of every American politician. The goal is implausible for most state and local politicians, but for sitting and former governors, senators, and leading members of the House, the question is almost never whether they want it, but how it might be accomplished. In the nineteenth century, the road to the White House ran through state and national party conventions, where party bosses held decisive influence. In the twentieth century, the process has shifted to state caucuses and primaries, and influence has shifted from party bosses to candidates, their handlers, and voters.[29]

In this section, we ask how serious candidates for the presidency organize and run their campaigns. Presidential campaigns begin years before the actual election with a series of critical organizational steps that are largely invisible to the public. This organizational phase of the campaign is meant to prepare and position candidates for the usually brief and intense nomination phase, which begins in Iowa and New Hampshire in January, often is over

Q4 How does the campaign for the presidency differ from campaigns for other offices that are less visible, powerful, and prestigious?

by February, early March at the latest, and formally culminates in the mid-summer party nominating conventions. In 2008, the Republican nomination campaign followed this script, but the Democrats had an epic battle between Hillary Clinton and Barack Obama that stretched into June. In 2012, Democrats rested while the Republicans had an extended nomination battle between Mitt Romney, Rick Santorum, Newt Gingrich, and Ron Paul. The fall general election campaign is a national contest between the Democratic and Republican nominees, and occasionally, as with Ross Perot in 1992 and Ralph Nader in 2000, a third party candidate who attracts enough attention to change the character, and perhaps the result, of the race.

Early Organization and Fundraising

For most major political figures, the decision to run for the presidency is momentous. They know that years of preparation, often extending over several election cycles, are required to build the organizational, financial, and partisan support to mount an effective campaign. John McCain, the Republican nominee in 2008, was the normal case. First elected to the U.S. House of Representatives in 1982, to the Senate in 1986, he ran a strong race for the Republican presidential nomination in 2000 before being defeated by George W. Bush. He campaigned extensively for Bush in 2004 and declared early for the 2008 race. He had been around this track a time or two before.

Most politicians, even those of unquestioned national stature, who look at the possibility of running for president ultimately back away. In 2012, close observers watched prominent 2008 candidates Sarah Palin and Mike Huckabee, as well as popular current and former Republican governors Chris Christie (New Jersey), Mitch Daniels (Indiana), and Jeb Bush (Florida) for signs that they would make the race. Each declined as did a number of prominent senators and congressmen.

Nonetheless, ten candidates did step forward to contest for the 2012 Republican presidential nomination. The acknowledged frontrunner was Mitt Romney, a prominent businessman, former governor of Massachusetts, and an experienced candidate, having run well but unsuccessfully in 2008. Former Minnesota governor Tim Pawlenty seemed a well-qualified candidate and likely to be Romney's principal challenger. Texas Congressman Ron Paul, running for the third time, had an intense libertarian following, but his support was widely thought to be capped at 10 or 12 percent. Former House Speaker Newt Gingrich was well known but was widely seen as too bombastic to go the distance. Former New Mexico governor Gary Johnson and former Pennsylvania senator Rick Santorum seemed unlikely national candidates, as did Minnesota congresswoman Michelle Bachmann, businessman Herman Cain, and businessman/entertainer Donald Trump. Many Republicans were hopeful when Texas governor Rick Perry made a late entry into the race.

The Democratic incumbent, President Barack Obama, was unchallenged for the nomination of his party. This gave him time to monitor his rivals, raise money, build a campaign organization, and prepare for the general election campaign. With the Afghan war in disarray, gas prices rising, and unemployment still above 8 percent, Republicans felt confident. However, with ten candidates fighting for the nomination, a divisive contest lay ahead.

Early money and an experienced campaign organization enhance a candidate's chances of being taken seriously by the media and allow time for systematic planning.[30] Howard Wolfson, Hillary Clinton's communications director in 2008, observed that "creating an organization, divising a strategy, and raising the amount of money necessary to conduct a national campaign all takes time."[31]

By early 2011 all of the major candidates had Internet campaigns in place. Each candidate had a website that offered candidate bios, campaign schedules, policy statements and speeches, chat rooms and message boards, and the always urgent appeal for campaign contributions. Candidates competed to sign up friends on Facebook and to keep their supporters entertained and informed with campaign videos on YouTube. Candidates were well aware that twice as many people, 25 percent to 13 percent, claimed to get political news from the Internet than had in 2004.

The Nomination Campaign

The modern presidential nomination campaign is a state-by-state series of primaries and caucuses, beginning with Iowa and New Hampshire in early January, concluding in the spring. A **primary** is a statewide election in which

primary A preliminary election in which voters select candidates to stand under their party label in a later and definitive general election

BILL GREENBLATT / UPI / Landov

Residents of Des Moines, Iowa, caucus at the city's Carpenters' Hall. They are assessing their candidate's strength as supporters of other candidates gather elsewhere in the building.

caucus Face-to-face meeting in which rank-and-file party members discuss and vote on candidates to stand for election to offices under the party label at a later general election.

the voters select among the available candidates for their party's nomination. A closed primary is one in which only registered members of the party are allowed to participate, while an open primary is open to other voters as well. A **caucus** is organized as a set of small gatherings, face-to-face meetings, in which voters debate the merits of the candidates before selecting among them. The separate caucus votes are totaled to county, congressional district, or state totals, and the state's national convention delegate seats are divided accordingly.

Following the 2008 nomination process, many Republican leaders concluded that the long primary battle between Barack Obama and Hillary Clinton had energized the Democratic Party while Senator McCain's relatively early and easy victory had not hardened him for the campaign to come. So the summer 2010 meeting of the Republican National Committee adopted new nomination rules to make the Republican process more like the Democratic process. Most importantly, they switched from a winner-take-all process, where the candidate winning a state primary or caucus got all that state's delegates to the Republican nominating convention, to a proportional process where each candidate gets a share of the delegates equivalent to his/her share of the vote. The goals were to extend the nomination process, let more states have a say before the nominee was decided, energize the Republican base, and toughen up the eventual nominee. It worked too well.

frontloading The crowding of presidential primaries and caucuses into the early weeks of the nomination period.

Republican rule changes also sought, less successfully, to avoid the **frontloading**—more and more states crowding to the front of the electoral

Getty Images

Mitt and Ann Romney, surrounded by children and grandchildren, bask in their party's support at the Republican National Convention.

calendar—that had plagued the 2008 nomination contest when 36 states voted before the end of February. In 2012, the rules allowed Iowa, New Hampshire, South Carolina, and Nevada to vote in February, while all others were to wait until March and incentives were offered to encourage some states to wait until April, May, and even June. A half dozen eager states, led by Florida, Michigan, and Arizona, refused to comply, forcing Iowa, New Hampshire, and South Carolina back in January and disrupting the formal schedule. So much for well-laid plans.

Caucuses and Primaries. In 2012, thirty-four states and the District of Columbia used primary elections to choose their convention delegates. Fifteen states used caucuses. Louisiana employed a mixed caucus and primary system. By tradition, the first event is the Iowa caucuses (January 3, 2012), followed closely by the New Hampshire primary (January 10, 2012). These two states, even though they are small, rural, and homogeneous, play influential roles in the presidential selection process. To enhance the regional, racial, and ethnic diversity of the states earliest in the nomination process, a Nevada caucus and a South Carolina primary occur later in January. Florida held a high profile primary on January 31 and then seven more states, including Colorado and Minnesota, followed on February 7, with Arizona and Michigan on February 28.

The states that had followed Republican National Committee rules began voting after March 1, but the early movers had left holes in the schedule. In 2008, "Super Tuesday" occurred in early February and included 24 states. In 2012, it occurred a month later, on March 6, and included just ten states. Nine more states and D.C. voted by April 3 and then there was a three week hiatus before the final twenty states voted between late April and the end of June.

The Republican field shrunk by half pretty quickly, but then the real battle began. Initially it appeared that Mitt Romney had eked out a narrow win over Santorum in Iowa, but a detailed count two weeks later showed a Santorum win. Meanwhile, Romney did win New Hampshire, before Newt Gingrich took South Carolina. With three different winners in the first three states, the Republican race began to look increasingly unstable. As weaker candidates—Pawlenty, Bachmann, Cain, Johnson, and Perry—dropped from the field, the dynamic of the race became clearer. Though Romney had big advantages in money, organization, and endorsements, he could not connect with Republican primary voters and, hence, could not put the race away. Although Romney won the Florida primary on January 31, Santorum took Minnesota and Colorado on February 7, Romney took Michigan and Arizona on February 28, and then on March 6, Super Tuesday, Romney won six states to Santorum's three and Gingrich's one. Though Gingrich and Paul trailed, they did not leave the race and Romney and Santorum traded blows into early April. Though Santorum trailed in the delegate count, he claimed that he would win Pennsylvania, his home state, on April 24 and Texas on May 29. With party elders urging him to reconsider so the party could come together around Romney, Santorum suddenly, and somewhat unexpectedly, suspended his campaign on

April 10 and Gingrich followed suit two weeks later, assuring Romney of the nomination.

The Declining Importance of the Conventions.   National party conventions were once scenes of high drama. National party leaders, regional leaders, and state "favorite sons" led their followers into the national convention and there struggled publicly, sometimes through dozens of ballots over several days, for the presidential nomination of their party. More recently, the national party conventions have ratified decisions made by the voters in their primaries and caucuses. The Democratic convention of 1952 was the last to take more than a single ballot to select its nominee, though the 2012 Republican convention had more drama than most.

national party convention
The Democratic and Republican Parties meet in national convention every four years, in the summer just prior to the presidential election, to choose a presidential candidate and adopt a party platform.

In recent decades, **national party conventions** have become increasingly controlled and stylized events where the parties seek to present their best face to the voters. With the whole nation watching, the parties try to portray themselves as unified behind a leader and a program. They seek to highlight their key issues and themes, rouse their partisans to action, attract the attention of independent voters, and set the tone for the coming general election campaign. Convention coverage, which used to be almost gavel-to-gavel, was cut back to only three hours in prime time on the major networks. Since 2000, gavel-to-gavel prime time coverage has moved from the networks to cable channels like CNN, FOX, C-SPAN, and MSNBC.

The General Election Campaign

general election A final or definitive election in which candidates representing their respective parties contend for election to office.

The **general election** campaign is a national battle in that all of the states are equally in play at the same time and throughout the process. On the other hand, the logic and rules of the contest force the battle back to the states in certain fundamental ways. Most strikingly, as we saw so clearly in 2000, the winner is not simply the candidate for whom the most people vote; rather, the winner is the candidate who gets the most votes in the Electoral College. What is the Electoral College, where did it come from, and how does it work?

The Electoral College, a creation of the Founding Fathers, confuses and worries many Americans. The Founders were concerned that voters would not have enough information or judgment to select the nation's chief executive. They sought to leaven the voters' judgments with those of the political elite—the electors—in each state. Each state was assigned the number of electors equal to the number of seats

Getty Images

Republican presidential nominee Mitt Romney and his vice presidential selection, Wisconsin Congressman Paul Ryan, campaign together.

in their congressional delegation. Since each state has two senators, no matter their population, this served to increase the influence of the smaller, less populous, states. Each state awards all of its electoral votes to the candidate who gets the most votes for president in that state.

In modern times, electors no longer exercise independent judgment. They are simply party leaders who cast their votes to reflect the popular vote outcome in their state, but all of the state's electoral votes (except in the cases of Nebraska and Maine, which employ a slightly different process) still go to the winner of the popular vote, no matter how narrow that win is. This imperfect relationship between the popular vote and the Electoral College vote opens up the possibility, the reality in 2000, that the winner of the popular vote and the Electoral College vote will differ—in which case the winner of the Electoral College vote is president. It happens only every century or so (the last time prior to 2000 was 1888), but every time it does, Americans scratch their collective heads and wonder what we are still doing with such a system. Still, because the less populous states benefit from the Electoral College system, it is unlikely to be changed any time soon.

Hence, the logic of the general election is not to pile up as many popular votes as possible. Rather, it is to win more votes than your opponent(s) in as many states as possible. Therefore, sound strategy dictates that candidates

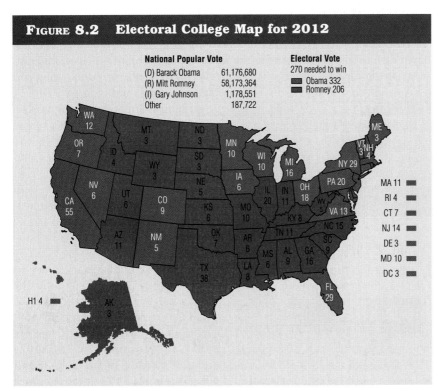

FIGURE 8.2 Electoral College Map for 2012

Source: Federal Election Commission.

shift resources out of states where they are comfortably ahead (because they are going to get all of those states' electoral votes whether they win with 51 percent or 91 percent) to states that are still competitive and whose electoral votes they still might pick up with a little extra time, effort, or advertising money. In recent elections the "battleground" states have tended to be those with large blocs of electoral votes where both parties have been successful in recent elections. In the East, this would be states like Pennsylvania and Virginia, in the Midwest, states like Illinois, Michigan, and Ohio; and the big prize in the South is Florida. In the West, Colorado, Nevada, and New Mexico draw the attention of both parties.

Therefore, general election campaigns are organized both to fight broad battles at the national level and to move resources between and among the states as the flow of the campaign and the changing strategic situation in each of the states seem to suggest. Each campaign has an inner circle of advisers close to the candidate who set strategy and a broader organization that executes the campaign plan.

The Campaign Organization.   Presidential campaigns vary somewhat in their organization, but in general the campaign chairperson organizes the broad operation and acts as liaison between and among the candidate, the party, the presidential campaign, and the congressional campaign committees. The campaign manager assists in setting general strategy, coordinates the state operations, and tries to keep the campaign on message. The finance chairperson runs the crucial fund-raising operation. Recent campaigns, including those in 2012, have taken to using fancier titles, like senior political advisor or chief strategist, for their top officials, but they still play the traditional strategic planning and organizational roles.

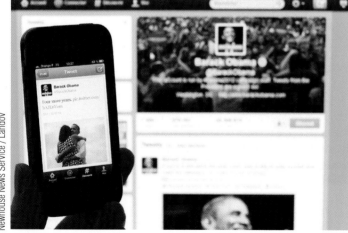

Newhouse News Service / Landov

A person poses with a cell phone in front of a computer screen to check Barack Obama's tweet on November 7, 2012 after his re-election as U.S. president. Barack Obama's sophisticated social media campaign culminated with him proclaiming victory on Twitter and Facebook just as TV networks were breaking the news.

A political director oversees the day-to-day operations, manages the ready response team (discussed below), and sees that resources are allocated and reallocated to achieve the best overall results. Every campaign also has a lead pollster, media consultants, data analysts, communications strategists and technicians, speechwriters, fundraisers, and schedulers.

The candidate's itinerary is set by the campaign scheduling team. The scheduling team's job is to get the candidate to those places and those events that will do him or her the most good or where it will make the most difference. For example, it will do a candidate little good late in a campaign to appear before a large group of committed supporters in a state where he or she is already going to win. The candidate's time would be much better spent appearing before a group of swing voters in a state where he or she is two points ahead, or maybe even better, two points behind.

After the site of a presidential candidate's visit has been determined, an advance team begins work to see that the candidate, an enthusiastic crowd, the media, and anything else required for a substantively and visually satisfying event are in place. The advance team's job is to ensure that the event generates the right message and feeling for both those attending and for the people who will read about it in the paper or see it on the television news. The visuals must be compelling, and the media must be prepped on the theme of the day.[32]

Finally, each national campaign has a ready response team. A **ready response team** is a group assigned to respond immediately and forcefully to any charge or comment from the opposition that, if left unattended, might harm the candidate. The 1992 Clinton campaign organized a "war room" led by strategist James Carville to respond quickly and forcefully to any charges, inaccuracies, or slips by the George H.W. Bush reelection campaign. During the 1990s, candidates' war room operations were focused on managing the traditional print and electronic press.

ready response team A group within a campaign staff that is assigned to respond immediately to any charge or negative comment made by the opposition or the media.

Candidates now have a vastly more complex media landscape to manage. 2004 was the first presidential campaign in which all of the candidates had a presence on the Internet. In 2008, and even more intensely in 2012, candidates sought to craft a hybrid media strategy by balancing "the decentralizing advantages of the Internet with traditional top-down campaign approaches, utilizing new media and online campaign techniques to secure their base while reaching less committed voters through television, direct mail, canvassing, and other traditional means."[33] All of the candidates had profile and friends pages on YouTube and Facebook, and they communicated constantly via Twitter and Tumblr.

The national campaign staff struggles to oversee a structure of campaign operatives that reaches to the state and local levels. The critical responsibility of these state and local operations is to identify and organize volunteers and voters, put up yard signs, and canvass door-to-door. After decades of concentrating on the "air wars" of the media campaign, the Republican Party in 2004 and both parties in 2008 and 2012 put new assets into their "ground game" or GOTV—get out the vote—efforts. Each party worked to create an army of volunteers, armed with palmtop computers loaded with block-by-block voter identification information, to have front-porch contacts with as many potential voters as possible before the election.

Money and the Road to the White House

For most of American political history, presidential campaigns were paid for with funds that the parties and candidates solicited from a limited number of wealthy supporters. Mark Hanna, the famous late nineteenth-century political operative, famously declared that "There are two things that are important

Q5 Does money dominate presidential elections?

Getty Images

President Barack Obama, accompanied by daughter Malia, First Lady Michelle, and daughter Sasha, waves to supporters as he arrives on stage on election night 2012 in Chicago, Illinois. The spouses of presidential candidates have long played an important role in campaigning for their husbands. Why do you think a candidate's spouse is such a key advocate?

in politics. The first thing is money, and I can't remember what the second one is." Even as late as 1972, "Richard Nixon and George McGovern raised an estimated $27 million from fewer than two hundred individual contributors."[34] Nixon and McGovern raised and spent more than $91 million on the general election campaign, almost triple what had been spent only four years earlier. This spending spree set off a flurry of reforms.

Campaign Finance Rules.   The legal basis for regulating the money that flows through presidential campaigns was laid in the early 1970s. The **Federal Election Campaign Act (FECA)** of 1971 and a series of strengthening amendments passed in 1974 set limits on the amount a presidential or vice presidential candidate could spend on his or her own campaign, limited individual contributions to federal campaigns including presidential campaigns to $1,000, and created a presidential election fund to support public financing of presidential elections. Presidential candidates accepting public financing had to abide by state-by-state spending limits during the nomination process. Each major party nominee then received a significant but limited amount for the general election contest. These rules have been revised several times since they initially were passed.

In the latter half of the 1970s, two fairly large holes were poked in the FECA campaign finance system, one by the courts and the other by Congress. In 1976, the Supreme Court, in a case known as *Buckley v. Valeo,* declared provisions

Federal Election Campaign Act (FECA) Campaign reform legislation passed in 1971, with major amendments in 1974 and later, that required disclosure and set limits on campaign contributions and provided public funding of presidential elections.

Buckley v. Valeo (1976) This decision declared provisions of the 1974 Federal Election Campaign Act (FECA) limiting the amount that a candidate could contribute to his or her campaign to be an unconstitutional limitation on free speech.

of the 1974 FECA amendments limiting the amounts that candidates could contribute to their own campaigns to be unconstitutional limitations on free speech. The Court also held that political action committees (PACs) and other groups, as long as they did not coordinate their activities with a candidate's campaign, could spend as much as they wanted on campaign activities. In 1979, Congress passed amendments to FECA permitting political parties to raise unlimited amounts of money for party building, voter registration, and voter turnout activities. These unrestricted funds were referred to as **soft money**.

During the 1990s, these and other holes in the campaign finance system allowed a flood of barely regulated money into presidential elections and spawned a movement for additional reform. In 1992 and 1996, Ross Perot drew on his extensive personal fortune to finance presidential campaigns, and in 1996 Steve Forbes did the same. Meanwhile, the presence of unregulated soft money in presidential campaigns burgeoned from $86 million in 1992, to $262 million in 1996, to $495 million in 2000. To many, the FECA system seemed broken.

Senator John McCain's (R-AZ) focus on campaign finance during his 2000 presidential campaign and the subsequent corporate scandals of 2001 and 2002 broke open an ongoing debate over campaign finance reform. In March 2002, after a seven-year stalemate, Congress passed and President Bush reluctantly signed the **Bipartisan Campaign Reform Act (BCRA)**. BCRA, popularly known as McCain-Feingold after its chief Senate sponsors, John McCain (R-AZ) and Russ Feingold (D-WI), increased the allowable

soft money Amendments to the FECA passed in 1979 allowed unlimited contribution to political parties for party building, voter registration, and voter turnout.

Bipartisan Campaign Reform Act (BCRA) Commonly known as McCain-Feingold, the 2002 BCRA was the first major revision of campaign finance laws since the early 1970s.

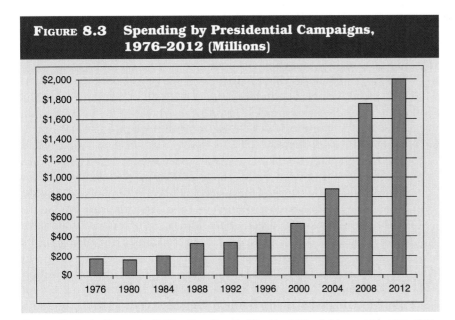

Figure 8.3   Spending by Presidential Campaigns, 1976–2012 (Millions)

Source: Center for Responsive Politics, Open Secrets, "Presidential Fundraising and Spending, 1976–2008," http://www.opensecrets.org/pres08/totals.php?cycle=, Updated by the author.

individual contribution from $1,000 to $2,000 and provided for future increases based on inflation. The maximum allowable contribution for 2012 was $2,500. The BCRA also banned soft money contributed to the national political parties and prohibited issue ads, less flatteringly referred to as "attack ads," within thirty days of a primary election and sixty days of a general election. Many expected the Supreme Court to strike down some or all of these limitations, just as it had in *Buckley* nearly thirty years earlier. Initially, the Court upheld the BCRA, but in 2007 and even more decisively in 2010, after two changes in the composition of the Court, it struck down key elements of BCRA. (See the Pro and Con box on pp. 256–257.)

McConnell v. F.E.C. The Supreme Court upheld all major elements of the Bipartisan Campaign Reform Act (BCRA) of 2002, including those permitting regulation of soft money and issue ads.

Although passage of campaign finance reform was a significant achievement, like all reforms it was incomplete and loopholes remain. PACs are free to accept as much soft money as corporations, unions, and wealthy individuals are willing to give them. Moreover, BCRA placed no limits on the independent, highly partisan "527" groups, such as the conservative Club for Growth and the liberal Emily's List. Finally, the *Citizens United* decision spawned the creation of hundreds of "Super PACs" that can raise unlimited amounts from corporations, unions, and wealthy individuals explicitly for political advocacy. They can expressly advocate for and against individual candidates, though they must register with the FEC and must, eventually, report their donors.

Where Does the Money Come From?   Until 2008 the bulk of the money financing presidential campaigns flowed through the FECA system (now the BCRA system) either as private contributions subject to federal limits and matching or as general election grants to each of the major party candidates. FECA provisions limited candidates operating within the federal campaign funding system to contributions of no more than $1,000, of which only $250 was subject to federal matching. To establish eligibility for federal matching funds, a candidate for the nomination of his or her party had to raise $100,000; $5,000 in twenty different states in amounts of no more than $250. Most of the candidates for president in 2008 stayed within the BCRA system, but Hillary Clinton, Barack Obama, and John McCain all opted out for the nomination phase.

Struggling Toward Democracy

Super PACs associated with Barack Obama and Mitt Romney spent $181 million in the 2012 election cycle. $125 million was spent in support of Romney and $56 million was spent in support of Obama.

What do you think?

- Is this healthy for our democracy or not?
- What do you think this money is meant to buy?

Though Barack Obama and John McCain tentatively agreed in 2008 that if they were the nominees of their parties, they would give back contributions raised for the general election and take the public financing. Obama's extraordinary success at fundraising during the 2008 nomination fight convinced him to forgo public funding for the general election campaign as well. McCain's fundraising lagged badly, so he did take federal funds.

Fundraising is still regulated by, but by no means controlled by, FEC rules. In 2010, congressional campaigns set fundraising records by collecting more than $2 billion. Democrats outraised Republicans, especially in the most competitive races, but outside groups raised and spent another $400 million. Outside groups, many spending large anonymous donations, more than made up the difference by leaning heavily Republican.[35] Republicans won big victories, taking control of the U.S. House, coming close in the Senate, and whetting their partisan appetite for the 2016 presidential election.

Barack Obama raised $745 million for the 2008 campaign and set an even higher target for 2012. Early in 2011, 450 of Obama's top "bundlers," fund-raisers who not only make their own contributions but solicit them from others and bundle all of the contributions together, met to plan for 2012. Each was given a target of $350,000 in contributions for the 2012 cycle. All of the Republican candidates scrambled to sign up the top bundlers from the successful Bush campaigns and from the 2008 McCain campaign. During 2011, President Obama raised $140 million in contributions, almost as much as all of the Republican candidates combined. Mitt Romney, the leading Republican candidate and eventual nominee, raised $57 million in 2011.

President Obama initially discouraged Super PAC fundraising, but Republican Super PAC fundraising success, led by Karl Rove's American Crossroads and Crossroads GPS with $51 million and the Restore Our Future Super PAC supporting Romney with $32 million, forced a change of mind. In February 2012 Obama endorsed Priorities USA Action, a Super PAC organized to support his and other Democratic campaigns. His change of mind, at least in part, was spurred by watching the Republican candidates benefit from Super PAC support. Restore Our Future pounded Gingrich mercilessly in Iowa and Florida and Gingrich only survived because Sheldon Adelson, a Las Vegas casino mogul, and his family gave $16 million to Winning Our Future, a Super PAC supporting Gingrich.[36]

By the time Romney locked up the Republican nomination in early April, he had just $10 million in cash-on-hand compared to Obama's $104 million, but both sides were building expanded fundraising operations for the general election. The Romney campaign quickly announced a goal of $800 million for the general election and the Obama campaign denied the widely circulating rumor that its goal was $1 billion. Republican Super PACs declared that they would spend hundreds of millions more, mostly on advertising, while unions and Democratic Super PACs focused on voter registration and a sophisticated get-out-the-vote operation. Less than a week after Romney's last major opponent withdrew, the Obama campaign launched a $25 million media campaign targeting middle class voters in nine swing states and the general election campaign was, at least unofficially, on.

The 2012 general election campaign was close throughout. Obama generally led narrowly and, after the two party conventions in late August and early September, his lead nationally opened to four or five points. But when Romney decisively won the first debate in early October, Obama's lead evaporated and by late October Romney had built a narrow lead of a point or point and a half. With a week to go before election day on November 6, Obama eased back to even nationally but lead, even if only narrowly, in key swing states, most crucially Ohio. A close general election contest always revs-up fund raisers and donors and certainly did in 2012.

Pro & Con

Is the Supreme Court Right to See Money as Speech?

In a landmark decision known as *Buckley v. Valeo* (1976), the Supreme Court upheld Congress's right to set limits on the amount an individual can contribute to federal campaigns, but struck down limits on overall spending in campaigns, spending by candidates from their own personal wealth, and independent spending by individuals and groups on behalf of a candidate. The only spending limits left in place by the Court were limits attached to voluntary acceptance of public funding. The limits generally held through the 1990s.

The Supreme Court reasoned in *Buckley* that campaign spending is speech intended to communicate ideas and as such is protected from government regulation by the First Amendment. The Court held that "A restriction on the amount of money a person or group can spend on political communication during a campaign necessarily reduces the quantity of expression," even though the clear intent of the First Amendment is to protect political speech. The Court further held that the only ground upon which campaign spending can explicitly be limited is to combat corruption defined as a "financial quid pro quo: dollars for political favors."

The 2002 McCain-Feingold legislation seemed to raise many of the same issues that the Court had dealt with in *Buckley*—restrictions on political spending by groups and individuals through soft money contributions and issue ads in the period immediately before elections. Hence, McCain-Feingold was immediately challenged by a legal team assembled by Senator Mitch McConnell (R-KY), the bill's principal opponent in the Senate.

McConnell v. F.E.C. came before the Supreme Court on September 8, 2003. McConnell's legal team contended that the prohibition of soft money contributions by wealthy donors and interests, as well as the limitations on issue ads thirty days before primaries and sixty days before general elections, were unconstitutional limitations on free speech. Supporters of the McCain-Feingold legislation claimed that the law was the last chance to limit the role of big money in politics and return control to small donors and individual citizens.[37]

Not surprisingly, it was a divided Court, 5–4, that announced its decision on December 10, 2003. The majority opinion, written by Justices John Paul Stevens and Sandra Day O'Connor, rejected the First Amendment free speech claims of the opponents and upheld all of the major provisions of McCain-Feingold. Campaign spending as free speech seemed to have taken a blow.

In 2007, following two new Bush appointments to the Supreme Court, Chief Justice John Roberts in place of Chief Justice William Rehnquist, and, more importantly, Justice Samuel Alito in place of Justice Sandra Day O'Connor, the court reconsidered elements of McCain-Feingold in a case called *Federal Election Commission v. Wisconsin Right to Life, Inc. (551 U.S. 449)*. For a court once again divided 5–4,

President Obama and the Democratic National Committee and Mitt Romney and the Republican National Committee each raised and spent more than $1 billion for the 2012 campaign. The Democrats outraised the Republicans, but the $1 billion raised and spent by outside groups, the so-called SuperPACS and the even murkier non-profit "social welfare groups," leaned heavily to the Republicans. An additional $1.8 billion was spent by congressional campaigns,

Chief Justice Roberts wrote, "Discussion of issues cannot be suppressed simply because the issues may also be pertinent in an election. Where the First Amendment is implicated, the tie goes to the speaker, not the censor." Writing for the dissenters, Justice David Souter said, "After today, . . . the possibilities for regulating corporate and union campaign money are unclear." Senator McCain declared the decision "regrettable."[38]

In 2009, the Supreme Court went out of its way to turn the case of *Citizens United v. Federal Election Commission* into a direct challenge to limits on corporations and unions spending directly from their treasuries on elections. The ban on direct corporate involvement in elections had been in place since 1907, more than a century. Citizens United produced an unrelentingly negative film, *Hillary: The Movie*, for release during Clinton's 2008 presidential nomination campaign. A trial judge found that the movie was a campaign commercial that could be prohibited within 30 days of a primary election under McCain-Feingold.

During oral arguments before the Supreme Court, Chief Justice Roberts asked, if the movie fell under the campaign finance law, how about a campaign book that urged readers to vote for or against a candidate? The government's lawyer, Deputy Solicitor General Malcolm Stewart, responded that such a book could be prohibited. Several justices worried that the government's reading of the McCain-Feingold statute was too broad and instructed the parties to brief the fundamental question of whether banning corporate spending on elections was an unconstitutional denial of corporate and union free speech rights. In 2010, after reargument, the Supreme Court struck down most of the McCain-Feingold limits on corporate and unions campaign contributions.

Justice Kennedy, writing for the majority, declared: "If the First Amendment has any force, it prohibits Congress from fining or jailing citizens, or associations of citizens, for simply engaging in political speech." Many observers were stunned. One particularly interested observer, President Barack Obama, called the decision "a green light to a new stampede of special interest money . . . . It is a major victory for big oil, Wall Street banks, health insurance companies and other powerful interests . . . to drown out the voices of everyday Americans."[39]

What do you think?
- Is money speech?
- Should wealthy individuals, corporations, and unions be able to spend all that they want in election campaigns?
- If so, should they be able to say bluntly, vote for candidate X, or vote against candidate Y?
- If not, how do you justify telling a wealthy person, or a wealthy corporation or union for that matter, that they surpassed their limit of free speech?

PRO	CON
People have a right to express themselves	Our politics are awash in interested money
Spending to communicate is free speech	Big money can erode one-man-one-vote
Limiting speech is unconstitutional	Limits protect everyone's right to be heard

$430 million was spent by outside groups to effect congressional campaigns, and hundreds of millions in shadow money was spent off the books and never likely to be accounted for fully. The Center for Responsive Politics estimated that a total of $6 billion, a record, was spent on the 2012 elections. In 2014, campaigns spent $1.6 billion while outside groups spent an additional $554 million.[40]

CAMPAIGN AND ELECTION REFORM

Even a casual observer of recent American elections, from the Florida debacle in 2000 through the endless presidential campaign of 2012, will have wondered about reform. Is our election system secure and fair? Can we encourage more and better informed voting? How should we fund our political campaigns, especially our presidential campaigns? How should our presidential primary campaigns be organized? And is the Electoral College still an integral part of our presidential election process, or a distracting vestige of the past?

First, how big a problem is electoral fraud in the U.S.? Thirty-four states have passed laws, some upheld by the Supreme Court, requiring voters to present government issued photo IDs to election officials before voting. Clearly, we do not want people voting illegally. But just as clearly, we do not want to throw obstacles in the way of legal voters, especially if we are truly worried about low turnout.

Second, the U.S. is a democratic society with a free market economy, so we expect differentials in wealth and we know that people will spend their money to advance their preferences and interests. But Congress tried to limit the impact of big money by adopting public financing of presidential elections in the early 1970s. That system is now near collapse. While most major candidates abandoned public financing during the nomination phase of the 2008 campaign, Barack Obama was the first major party candidate since 1972 to depend on private fundraising for the general election. In 2012, both major candidates did so.

Third, reform of the state-by-state primary and caucus presidential nomination system is quite likely before 2016. In the 2008 cycle, as states crowded to the front of the process, both parties were forced to punish states that broke the rules and voted too early. In 2012, Republicans again had trouble with states trying to jump ahead on the calendar and they will want to evaluate their experiment with proportional delegate distribution as opposed to winner-take-all by state. One proposal calls for regional contests—east, midwest, south, and west, perhaps—with the regions rotating the order in which they voted from one election to the next. Another, called the Delaware plan, calls for the 12 least populous states to vote in March, the next 13 in April, the next 13 in May, and the 12 most populous states in June. That way, most voters would get to watch the candidates in earlier, smaller, contests before voting. More than half of citizens live in the twelve largest states and so would not vote until June. What do you think would be the pluses and minuses of these plans?

Finally, should we discard the Electoral College in favor of direct, popular, election of the president? Since the Electoral College is mandated in the Constitution and a constitutional amendment would be very difficult to pass, a shortcut has been proposed. States could simply pass a law agreeing to award their electoral votes, not to the winner of the statewide popular vote, as is now done, but to the winner of the national popular vote. If enough states, even just the dozen largest, made this change we would effectively select the president by popular vote without amending the Constitution. Interesting idea? Maybe, but it is still a long shot, though another disputed election like 2000 might make it less so.

WHAT DO YOU THINK?

- What is the appropriate balance between combatting electoral fraud and encouraging turnout?
- Should Congress work to reform the campaign finance system or simply retain the contribution limit and let the marketplace determine the total amount raised and spent on presidential campaigns?

Chapter Summary

Campaigns and elections are the collective processes by which democracies choose the path that they will take into the future. Voting is the one opportunity made equally available to all members of the democracy to affect that critical decision. Yet, almost half of the voting-age population fails to participate even in presidential elections.

In this chapter we have seen that there are some fairly straightforward explanations for the generally low turnout in American elections. We leave citizens alone to figure out how to register to vote, whereas virtually every other wealthy democracy makes that a government responsibility, and a few even mandate voting. Motor Voter has made it easier to register to vote, but we still have more than 50 million Americans of voting age who are not registered to vote.

Those who do vote make their decisions between parties and candidates in light of a number of influences. Party identification is still the most important influence for active partisans and leaners, particularly in low-information elections. In more visible campaigns, where more information is readily available, issue positions and candidate attributes can lead voters to abandon their standing party commitments at least for the current election.

Low turnout raises questions of democratic legitimacy. Stunningly high reelection rates raise questions of responsiveness and accountability. Incumbents benefit from advantages in personal visibility, political organization, and money. Challengers tend to do poorly unless they are experienced politicians able to raise money locally and attract the attention of the national party and PACs or unless they have great personal wealth. Still, some electoral climates, like 2006 for the Democrats and 2010 for the Republicans, are friendlier to challengers as the national currents run strongly against one party or the other.

The race for the presidency is the classic American election. It begins, mostly out of sight, with potential candidates building their own and assessing each other's organizational and financial prospects. Early money and an experienced organization are required to survive an increasingly front-loaded presidential nomination process. Each major party nominee is then presented to the American people in a highly stylized and thoroughly choreographed nominating convention in midsummer. The general election campaign then occurs between late summer and the first Tuesday in November. It is a national contest designed to produce both popular and Electoral College majorities.

Key Terms

Bipartisan Campaign Reform Act (BCRA) 259	Motor Voter 235
Buckley v. Valeo 258	national party convention 254
caucus 252	primary 251
Federal Election Campaign Act (FECA) 258	ready response team 257
frontloading 252	soft money 259
general election 254	suffrage 232
McConnell v. F.E.C. 260	voter registration 235
micro targeting 248	voter turnout 233

Suggested Readings

Fiorina, Morris P., Samuel J. Abrams, and Jeremy C. Pope. *Culture Wars: The Myth of a Polarized America*, 3rd ed. New York: Longman, 2010. Contends that a polarized political class no longer well represents the American public who are more moderate.

King, Anthony. "Running Scared," 1997. King argues that American politics are always running scared because elections are too open and too frequent.

Leighley, Jan E. and Jonathan Nagler, *Who Votes Now? Demographics, Issues, Inequality, and Turnout in the United States.* Princeton, NJ: Princeton University Press, 2014. An important update to Wolfinger and Rosenstone's 1980 classic *Who Votes?* Leighley and Nagler show how important demographics are for understanding voter registration, turnout, and vote choice.

Medvic, Stephen K., ed. *New Directions in Campaigns and Elections.* New York: Routledge, 2011. Leading scholars of U.S. campaigns and elections explore recent changes in how campaigns are organized, funded, and conducted as well as how elections are administered.

Polsby, Nelson W., Aaron Wildavsky, Steven Scheir, and David Hopkins. *Presidential Elections*, 13th ed. New York: Wadsworth, 2012. The standard work on the structure, process, and results of presidential elections historically and in the contemporary period.

Popkin, Samuel L. "The Reasoning Voter," 1991. Popkin argues that voters decide based not on "full information," but on "low information" and "gut reasoning" that draws on past experience and easily gathered information.

Wayne, Stephen J. *The Road to the White House 2012.* New York: Wadsworth, 2012. Like Polsby and Wildavsky, this book describes the process of running for election to the presidency.

Web Resources

For practice quizzes, key term flashcards, videos, links, and other study tools, visit the *American Government* website: www.routledge.com/cw/jillson

1. **www.fec.gov**
   The official website of the Federal Election Commission provides information on campaign contribution laws, how to register to vote, and election results for federal elections. It also gives national and state figures on registration and voter turnouts.

2. **www.fairvote.org**
   Official website of the Center for Voting and Democracy. This organization is dedicated to educating the public about various international voting systems and how they affect voter turnout. It examines the idea of proportional representation in addition to the U.S. federal system of single-member districts.

3. **www.realclearpolitics.com**
   A frequently updated gathering of the most important news stories, commentaries, blogs, videos, and polls.

4. **www.campaignline.com**
   Campaigns and Elections magazine is a premier elections site. It offers in-depth coverage on federal elections and the election system.

5. **www.campaignfinance.org**
   The Campaign Finance Information Center (CFIC) is a project of Investigative Reporters and Editors, a Colombia, Missouri, nonprofit journalism group. CFIC maintains the site with links to databases on state campaign finances.

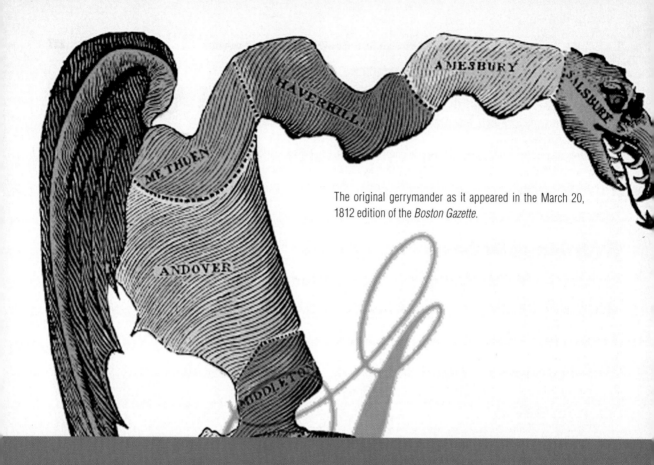

The original gerrymander as it appeared in the March 20, 1812 edition of the *Boston Gazette*.

Chapter 9

CONGRESS

Local Representation and National Lawmaking

❝ *A congressman has two constituencies—he has his constituents at home, and his colleagues here in the House. To serve his constituents at home, he must also serve his colleagues here in the House.* ❞

SAM RAYBURN (D-TX)

THE CENSUS, REAPPORTIONMENT, AND GERRYMANDERING

The Constitution TODAY

Article I, section 2 (in part): "Representatives . . . shall be apportioned among the several states . . . according to their respective numbers. . . . The actual enumeration shall be made within three years after the first meeting of the Congress of the United States, and within every subsequent term of ten years, in such manner as they shall by law direct."

Census results tell us how many people live in the United States and where they live. The population of each state determines how many seats in the U.S. House of Representatives that state gets. State legislatures then must redraw congressional and state legislative district boundaries so that each contains an equal number of residents. Controlling the redistricting process allows lines to be drawn that advantage the dominant party and its candidates and disadvantage their opponents. The struggle over power is and has always been catnip to politicians.

Elbridge Gerry was one of the first to see how redistricting could be used to partisan advantage. Gerry was a great man in his day. A graduate of Harvard College, he signed both the Declaration of Independence and the Articles of Confederation. He attended and took an active part in the Constitutional Convention but refused to sign the final document because it lacked a bill of rights. He died in 1814 while serving as Vice President in the administration of President James Madison. Despite all of these achievements, Gerry is best remembered today as the father of the Gerrymander. As Governor of Massachusetts, Gerry oversaw the redrawing of congressional district boundaries following the 1810 census. One of the oddly-shaped districts, designed to maximize the electoral prospects of his Jeffersonian Democratic Party over the Federalists, reminded a local newspaper editor of a salamander—no, a Gerrymander! And the name stuck.

Article I, section 2, of the Constitution says that the number of seats each state gets in the U.S. House of Representatives shall be based on population as determined by an enumeration—what we call the census—conducted every ten years. Each state is guaranteed at least one seat in the House and then additional seats are awarded based on population. Through the 1910 census, as population grew the size of the House was simply increased so that some states gained but few states ever lost seats. Following the 1910 census, which took place in the middle of a huge immigration surge, the size of the House was increased to 435 seats and fixed there by law. But fixing the size of the House at 435 made reapportionment a much more contentious process. Now, if some states got additional seats because of population growth, other states had to lose seats.

Reapportionment, of course, is not the end of the process. Redistricting, that is redrawing congressional and other electoral district boundaries, must still be done and it is a complex and conflictual political process. From Elbridge Gerry's day to our own, clever politicians have sought to draw lines that advantage them and their parties while disadvantaging their opponents. Incumbents follow this process like hawks because if their district is to be changed, they want it to be made safer, not more competitive. The majority party, though, may have a view somewhat different than its individual incumbents. The party obviously wants to protect its incumbents and disadvantage incumbents of the other party, but they may wish to take excess votes away from their incumbents to try to gain advantage in another district. Finally, the majority party tries to limit the clout of the minority party, either spreading them thinly across a number of districts or packing them into just a few districts.

The Supreme Court has laid out several legal requirements over the years for redistricting. First, each district must have equal numbers of residents. Second, districts should be as compact and contiguous as they reasonably can be. And third, districts may not reduce minority representation. But within these limits, modern computer technology allows levels of partisan manipulation and creativity that Elbridge Gerry could not have imagined. Mapping census data onto precinct voting results from past elections allows redistricting experts to create districts whose partisan tendencies are known down to the city block and even the individual household. How these lines are drawn go a long way toward determining partisan political advantage for the subsequent decade.

Finally, illegal immigration plays a particularly controversial, but delicate, role in the census, reapportionment, and redistricting. It is controversial because the census counts residents, not citizens, and the census numbers then drive reapportionment and redistricting. Counting residents, instead of citizens, adds congressional seats to states like Texas, Florida, and Arizona and subtracts them from states like Illinois, Ohio, and Michigan.

Focus Questions: from reading to thinking

Q1 What purposes were the Founders trying to serve by constructing and empowering the Congress as they did?

Q2 How does the committee system in Congress work to promote specialized knowledge and expertise among members?

Q3 What are the stages of consideration through which most legislation must pass to become a law?

Q4 What pressures operate on a member of Congress as he or she prepares to make an important legislative decision?

Q5 How serious has Congress been in its recent reform efforts?

WHAT DO YOU THINK?

- Should the census just count citizens?
- If so, what would you do with the information found on residents here illegally?

THE UNITED STATES CONGRESS

Americans have always been ambivalent about government. From the revolutionary generation to today Americans have felt that, although government is necessary to foster peace and prosperity, it is frequently given to wasteful spending and intrusive regulation. Furthermore, Americans have always been suspicious of politicians, assuming that society's truly hard-working and creative members are in the private sector, whereas trimmers and schemers tend to gravitate to politics.

Mark Twain, perhaps America's greatest humorist, was merciless in making fun of politicians in general and members of the U.S. Congress in particular. Twain described members of Congress as the "only native American criminal class" and regaled his audiences with jokes like this: "Suppose you were an idiot. Suppose you were a member of Congress. But I repeat myself." Similar attitudes toward Congress have been widely held throughout American history and can be heard any night in the monologues of Jay Leno, David Letterman, Jon Stewart, Stephen Colbert, and many others.[1]

What do we expect from Congress, and why does Congress have such a tough time meeting our expectations? Unfortunately, we expect several at least potentially incompatible things from Congress. First, we think of Congress as a representative institution. Each member of Congress is expected to articulate the views and protect the interests of his or her constituents. Second, we expect Congress to stop talking at some point and enact a policy or program that works for the nation as a whole. As we shall see, Congress has a difficult time moving gracefully from discussion to decision and individual members of Congress have a difficult time lifting their gaze from local constituent interests to national interests.[2]

In this chapter, we ask and answer several important questions. First, what role did the Founders see for the Congress within the broader American political system? Second, how has Congress changed from the early days of the republic to the present? Third, how has Congress organized to do its work? Fourth, what are the key forces or influences that affect congressional deliberation and decision? And fifth, what reforms has Congress undergone in recent decades, and what reforms are now under discussion that might prove helpful?

ORIGINS AND POWERS OF THE CONGRESS

The Founders drew their understanding of legislatures from English theory and practice and from watching and serving in their own colonial legislatures. The English Parliament developed in the twelfth century as an assembly called by the king to approve taxes and fees. Over the centuries, the Parliament's role in approving revenues allowed it to press grievances on the king and finally to engage in open discussion of national issues and of potential solutions to them. By the late seventeenth century, the English political theorist John Locke used the ideas of "popular sovereignty" and "legislative supremacy" to justify the dominance of the Parliament and particularly of its lower house, the House of Commons.

Popular sovereignty is the idea that all legitimate governmental authority comes as a free grant from the people and that the people can reclaim that authority if government becomes neglectful or abusive of it. **Legislative**

Q1 What purposes were the Founders trying to serve by constructing and empowering the Congress as they did?

popular sovereignty The idea that all legitimate governmental authority comes from the people and can be reclaimed by them if government becomes neglectful or abusive.

legislative supremacy The idea that the lawmaking authority in government should be supreme over the executive and judicial powers.

The Granger Collection, NYC

Senator Henry Clay of Kentucky was one of the great orators of the first half of the nineteenth century. Here, late in his career, he offers the "Compromise of 1850" in an attempt to break the worsening deadlock over slavery.

supremacy is the idea that the lawmaking power is supreme, or in Locke's words, that "what can give Law to another, must needs be superiour [sic] to him."[3] If the legislature makes law, and the executive and judiciary merely enforce and adjudicate its meaning, then the lawmaking or legislative power clearly is supreme. Americans began their own thinking about politics from these Lockean ideas of popular sovereignty and legislative supremacy.

Moreover, experience in the colonial American legislatures was consistently that of the people's representatives standing up to seemingly tyrannous royal governors. As tensions grew in the years immediately preceding the revolution, Americans came to see all political power as dangerous and power held by any but the people's most direct representatives as especially dangerous. Hence, when they first had the opportunity to build their own governments, they gave limited power to government, kept whatever power they gave as close to home as possible, and placed it for short terms in the hands of their most directly elected representatives.

The Continental Congress

The first American Congress, the Continental Congress, convened on September 5, 1774. Each colony had one vote, and decisions were made following open

Parliaments and Congresses

The fundamental difference between parliamentary and separation of powers systems is the relationship between executive and legislative authority and officials. In the parliamentary system, members of the majority party or, in some cases, majority coalition in the legislature select the prime minister and cabinet officers from among themselves. In other words, the leaders of the executive branch are and remain leaders of the majority in the legislature. These executive officers maintain their executive positions only as long as they keep the confidence and support of their colleagues in Parliament.

In a parliamentary system, the stability of the whole government hinges on the strength and cohesion of the majority party or coalition. Hence, parties in parliamentary systems tend to exercise close control over their members. The party selects the members who will stand for election in particular districts, organizes and funds their campaigns, and demands their support on party votes in the Parliament. Members who do not adhere consistently to the party's positions are simply not returned to Parliament.

Proponents of parliamentary government argue that this greater centralization of power is more efficient and makes for greater political accountability. It is more efficient because the executive officials, that is, the prime minister and his or her ministerial colleagues, are simultaneously the leaders of the majority in Parliament. They have a natural and

automatic majority in Parliament for their principal policy initiatives. Moreover, there is no confusion in the public about who is in charge or which party is responsible for the good or bad things that happen on their watch.

Separation of powers systems like that in the United States work very differently. First, members of the U.S. Congress are constitutionally prohibited from holding offices in the executive branch. The officials of the executive branch are selected independently of the legislature, for fixed terms of office, and are removable by the legislature only through impeachment. This means that presidents do not need to win every major vote in Congress, that their government will not fall and their term of office end if they lose a big vote, and that legislators, even those of the president's party, can vote their own judgment.

Second, parties are weaker in the United States because less hinges on sustaining continuous majorities in the legislature. Members make their own decisions about whether to run for Congress, raise most of their own campaign money, run their own campaigns, and feel free to use their own judgment, even to the point of differing with a president of their own party.

Third, because separation of powers systems are designed to uncouple the fate of executives and legislators, divided government, in which the executive and legislative branches, in part or whole, are controlled by different political parties, is not just possible—it is common. Divided government, in the minds of many Americans, is not a bad thing. Rather, it is just another way to separate, check, and balance political power.

debate among members on the floor. Congress could recommend actions to the several colonies, but the colonies were free to decide whether to comply in part, in full, or not at all. Once war broke out, Congress and the states felt the need for a clearer distribution of political power and authority.

The Articles of Confederation, drafted in Congress in 1777, although not adopted by all of the states until 1781, were meant to set out the national powers and distinguish them from the powers of the states. Article II clearly said that the states were sovereign and retained all powers not specifically awarded to the Congress. The Articles provided for no national executive or judiciary. They gave Congress broad powers over war and foreign affairs but little direct power over domestic affairs and none over taxation and commercial regulation. Even where Congress had apparent authority, it had no independent revenue with which to pursue its goals.[4]

Congress and the Constitution

The federal Constitution that went into effect in 1789 described a national government in which Congress was to play the central role. Article I comprises fully half of the Constitution and begins with the decisive statement that "All legislative Powers herein granted shall be vested in a Congress of the United States, which shall consist of a Senate and House of Representatives." Article I, section 8, enumerates the powers of Congress in seventeen specific clauses.

The first eight clauses provide the powers over taxation and commerce that had been lacking in the Articles of Confederation. Congress was given power to lay and collect taxes, borrow money on the credit of the United States, establish a national currency, regulate commerce, and establish post offices and post roads. A clause then permitted Congress to establish federal courts below the level of the Supreme Court. Seven clauses set Congress's power over foreign and military affairs. Congress was given the power to punish violations of international law and illegal activity at sea, to declare war, and to raise, train, and equip armies, navies, and the state militias when in the national service. Congress was also given the power to exercise exclusive jurisdiction over a district, not to exceed ten miles square, in which to locate a national capital. Finally, the last clause of Article I, section 8, gives Congress the power "To make all Laws which shall be necessary and proper for carrying into Execution" the previously enumerated powers.[5]

Although the House and Senate have equal roles in the legislative process, each has a few specific powers and responsibilities. Article I, section 7, following both parliamentary and colonial precedents, declares that "All Bills for raising Revenue shall originate in the House of Representatives." The Senate is given the power and responsibility to try impeachments and to advise and consent on treaties, senior executive appointments, and nominations to the Supreme Court.

MEMBERSHIP AND SERVICE IN THE CONGRESS

The constitutional qualifications for service in the U.S. Congress are few and simple. They are age, citizenship, and residency. A member of the House of Representatives must be twenty-five years of age, have been a citizen of the United States for at least seven years, and be a resident of the state from which he or she is elected. A member of the Senate must be thirty years old, have

Alex Wong / Getty Images

Flanked by other Democratic women of the Congress, Nancy Pelosi, the nation's first female Speaker, said all women can rest assured that they "have friends in the Capitol." Pelosi became Minority Leader once the Republicans took control of the House in the 2010 elections.

been a citizen of the United States for nine years, and be a resident of the state from which he or she is elected. Moreover, neither the states nor Congress can add qualifications or limitations without amending the Constitution.

The constitutional qualifications of members have not changed at all since the first Congress, but the kinds of people who serve in Congress and the nature of the congressional experience have changed a great deal. In the nineteenth century, members of Congress were almost all white men. They spent most of the year at home, often worked at regular jobs, and lived in Washington only when Congress was in session. Beginning with the twentieth century, and particularly the latter half of the twentieth century, minorities and women became a growing presence in Congress. Modern air travel allows members of Congress spend almost every weekend and every recess back home.[6] Congress has averaged about 140 days in session each year since 2000, though it dropped to 126 days in 2013 and just 113 days in the election year of 2014.

Member Characteristics

The membership of Congress has always been drawn from the nation's economic, social, and educational elite. Members come disproportionately from the worlds of law and business, although lifetime public service has become increasingly common. Nearly all members have college degrees, and 75 percent have graduate degrees, with most of the graduate degrees being in law (J.D.) and business (M.B.A.). The presence of large numbers of lawyers in Congress is not surprising. Lawyers work in the law, and Congress makes laws. Moreover, lawyers can leave their practices with some ease, and the visibility of having served in Congress usually helps if they return to private practice.

Business careers work differently, and this has an effect on the kind of business person one finds in Congress. Generally, members of Congress come from smaller, often private or family-owned, businesses. When a small business owner is elected to Congress, a spouse, brother, cousin, or partner can maintain the store, insurance agency, or pest control franchise. It is more difficult to get on and off the corporate ladder without losing ground to your colleagues and competitors. Therefore, one rarely finds members who have left senior positions in the corporate or financial world (unless they have retired or have no plans to return) to run for and serve in Congress.

Women now make up about 19 percent of the Congress, blacks make up about 8.6 percent and Hispanics about 6 percent. All are substantially underrepresented in relation to their presence in the population, especially women (see Figure 9.1). In the 114th Congress (2015–2017), eighty-four women served in the House and twenty in the Senate, a modest increase from the last session. The 114th Congress also saw forty-six African American, thirty-two Latino, fourteen Asian/Pacific Island, and two Native American members of the House. The Senate had one black member, three Hispanic members, and one Asian American member. About 29 percent of the members of Congress are Catholic, 8 percent are Jewish, 3 percent Mormon, and most of the remainder adhere to one or another of the Protestant denominations.

Struggling Toward Democracy

Women vote in higher proportions than men and cast more votes than men.

What do you think?
- Why do women hold only 19 percent of seats in Congress?
- What does that say about our democracy?

Finally, members commonly bring considerable political experience with them to Congress. Most members of the House of Representatives prepared for their runs for national office by serving first in local and state offices. Moreover, it is quite common for members of the House to "move up" to the Senate. As a result, half of U.S. House members had prior service in their state legislature and half of current senators served previously in the U.S. House. Another common path to the Senate is from statewide elective offices like governor. As a result, the average age of members of Congress is late-fifties, with senators averaging about five years older than members of the House.

While some members might make more money in the private sector, their congressional salaries and benefits make them among the most comfortable Americans. Members of the 114th Congress receive salaries of $174,000 and generous benefits. Members who serve in Congress for only five years receive modest pensions adjusted each year for inflation and lifetime health benefits. Longer service brings bigger pensions. In 2014, just over 600 former members drew pensions averaging around $60,000.

Texas Congressman Ralph Hall lost his last race and retired at 92, with 34 years in Congress, and an annual pension of $139,000. More than half of members of Congress—268 in all—have a net personal wealth of $1 million or more.[7]

Tenure, Incumbency, and Reelection

Through most of the nation's history, commitment to politics as a career was uncommon. Those who did take time from their real careers to serve in political office mostly chose state and even local office over service at the national level. Washington was a long way off and hard to get to. Hence, average congressional turnover was high, and average length of tenure was low.

During the nineteenth century, member turnover—that is, the proportion of new members from one Congress to the next—consistently ran at 40 to 50 percent. Turnover began to decline near the beginning of the twentieth century, and in the period after World War II the average tenure in office increased. Some members served for extraordinarily long times. Carl Hayden (D-AZ) served for fifteen years in the House and then for forty-two more in the Senate. John Dingell (D-MI), the longest serving member in the history of Congress, entered the House in 1955 and retired after 60 years in 2015. In early 2003, Strom Thurmond

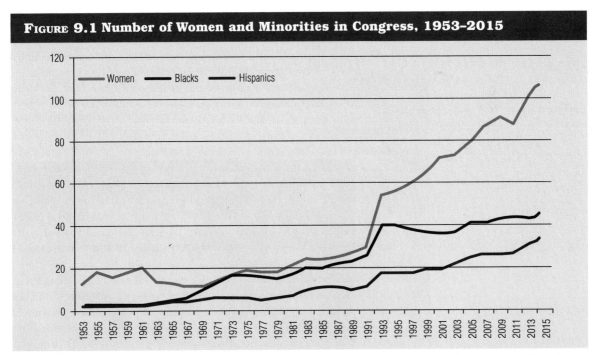

FIGURE 9.1 Number of Women and Minorities in Congress, 1953–2015

Sources: Ornstein, Mann, and Malbin, *Vital Statistics on Congress, 2008*, Tables 1-16, 1-17, and 1-18, pp. 43–45, and Harold W. Stanley and Richard G. Niemi, *Vital Statistics on American Politics, 2007–2008*, Table 5-2, p. 207. Updated by the author.

Pro & Con

Should a Representative Represent Their Conscience or Their Constituents?

For nearly 2,500 years, since Plato and Aristotle lived in ancient Athens, democracy has been understood to mean rule by the people. In the Athenian democracy, all male citizens could gather in public to discuss and resolve the major issues of the day. But modern nation-states are too large and the body of citizens is too numerous for every person to represent him- or herself. Hence, we speak of representative government whereby citizens elect some from among their number to represent them in government deliberation and policymaking.

Serious thinking about the nature of representation is often traced to a famous speech by Edmund Burke (1729–1797), candidate for election to Parliament from Bristol, in November 1774. Democratic ideals were at large, but not yet widely accepted in Britain and her increasingly rebellious colonies in North America. The issue of "instructions," that is, whether voters could bind or instruct elected officials in the performance of their duties was much on people's minds. Burke's opponent had endorsed the idea of instructions and had promised to be bound by the wishes and views of his constituents if elected.

Hence, Burke felt constrained to speak to the issue of instructions and to the responsibility of a representative to his constituents. He did so in these memorable terms: "Certainly, gentlemen, it ought to be the happiness and glory of a representative to live in the strictest union, the closest correspondence, and the most unreserved communication with his constituents. Their wishes ought to have great weight with him; their opinion, high respect; their business, unremitted attention. . . . But his unbiassed [sic] opinion, his mature judgment, his enlightened conscience, he ought not to sacrifice to . . . any set of men living . . . your representative owes you, not his industry only, but his judgment; and he betrays, instead of serving you, if he sacrifices it to your opinion."

Still, stirring as Burke's rhetoric was and is, it essentially says that a representative should listen to his constituents but ultimately use his own judgment. Although many Americans of the founding

Senator Barbara Mikulski, a Democrat from Maryland and chairwoman of the Senate Appropriations Committee, arrives to a Senate Appropriations Committee markup meeting. Mikulski's hand up is holding off the supplicants. Everyone wants something from the powerful chair of the Appropriations Committee.

generation, particularly the Federalist elite that gathered around Hamilton, accepted Burke's view, those who gathered around Jefferson held that legislatures should mirror the broader community and representatives should reflect the views and interests of their constituents.

Today we discuss these issues somewhat, but only somewhat, differently. Scholars use three terms— trustees, delegates, and politicos—to describe who or what modern representatives represent. Trustees, following Burke, believe that although they are responsible for listening to their constituents, they are sent to Congress to use their own knowledge and judgment in the broad public or national interest. Frequently, constituency and national interests will overlap, but where they do not, especially on critical issues, the **trustee** should—must—represent the national or public interest.

A **delegate** takes the mirror view of representation, seeing his or her role as reflecting the views and protecting the interests of constituents. A **politico** tends to move between trustee and delegate stances as issues, circumstances, and pressures vary. On issues about which their constituents are engaged and informed, politicos will often act like delegates. On issues that do not draw constituent attention, or on which constituent opinion is soft or split, politicos will have the latitude to act more like trustees and use their own judgment. In fact, every representative takes the national view on some issues and in regard to some aspects of his or her job, and the local or constituency view on others; but each representative also adopts a general approach and style that marks him or her as a trustee, a delegate, or a **politico.**

What do you think?
- Who or what should a representative represent?
- Are you comfortable with politicians using their own judgment even if they know that their constituents disagree?

PRO	CON
Representatives are accomplished people	Voters know what they think and want
Representatives study and debate the issues	Few issues come up unexpectedly
At least sometimes, representatives must take the broad view	Local views deserve a strong voice

(R-SC) retired from the Senate at age 100 after more than forty-seven years of service. Robert Byrd (D-WV), served six years in the House before being elected to the Senate in 1959. Byrd, the longest serving Senator in U.S. history, died in office on June 28, 2010 at age 92 (see Figure 9.2).[8] Senator Barbara Mikulski (D-MD) is the longest serving woman in the history of Congress. She served 10 years in the House before being elected to the Senate in 1986.

More generally, between 1946 and 2012, 93 percent of House incumbents and 80 percent of Senate incumbents who stood for reelection were returned to office.[9] Only twice since 1980, 1994 and 2010, have more members of Congress been defeated for reelection than retired voluntarily. Even in 2006, when the Democrats picked up thirty seats in the House and six in the Senate to take control of both houses for the first time since 1994, 94 percent of House incumbents standing for reelection and 79 percent of Senate incumbents won. 2010 was bloodier. Only 85 percent of senators and representatives who sought reelection were successful. While 37 senators and representatives

trustee A view of representation that says representatives should listen to their constituents but use their own expertise and judgment to make decisions about public issues.

delegate A view of representation that sees the representative's principal role as reflecting the views and protecting the interests of his or her own constituents.

politico A view of representation that sees representatives following constituent opinion when that is clear and his or her own judgment or political interest when constituency opinion is amorphous or divided.

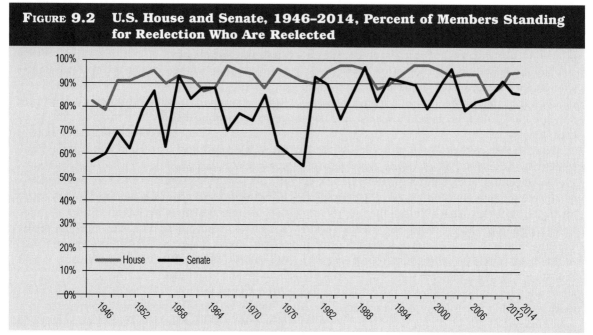

FIGURE 9.2   **U.S. House and Senate, 1946–2014, Percent of Members Standing for Reelection Who Are Reelected**

Source: Ornstein, Mann, and Malbin, *Vital Statistics on Congress, 2008*, Tables 2-7 and 2-8, pp. 57–58 and Stanley and Niemi, *Vital Statistics on American Politics, 2007–2008*, Table 1-17, p. 52. Updated by the author.

retired voluntarily prior to the 2010 elections, 54 were defeated at the polls. In 2012, reelection rates rebounded to 91 percent in both the House and Senate. The year 2014 was very much a normal one: 96 percent of House members and 82 percent of Senators who chose to stand for reelection won.

What explains these extraordinary reelection rates? Two classic works, David Mayhew's *Congress: The Electoral Connection* (1974) and Richard Fenno's *Congressmen in Committees* (1973), have long provided the foundation for our understanding of congressional motivation. Mayhew made a strong case that the dominant motivation of congressmen is reelection—without reelection nothing else in a congressional career is possible. Fenno made the equally compelling case that once reelection is secure, congressmen turn their attention either to policy influence or to broader power within the institution or to some combination of the two. Whatever choice they make, long-term success hinges on a series of successful reelection contests. Members rarely lose focus on their reelection prospects, hence, reelection to the House rarely dips below 90 percent and reelection to the Senate rarely dips below 80 percent.

But as Congress has evolved, so has scholarly thinking about congressional motivation. In Mayhew, party leaders were servants of member interests, working to create party unity without endangering member reelection prospects. In the Senate, this is still largely accurate, but not so in the House. As the ideological distance between the parties in the House has grown, leaders have been re-empowered. Political scientists John Aldrich and David Rohde have led a revision of Mayhew and Fenno called "conditional party government." The "condition" in conditional party government is that if party leaders are ideologically near the middle of their party caucus, members will be willing to empower them and follow their lead. As Mayhew and Fenno explained nearly 40 years ago, members will break with party leaders if their reelection prospects—their careers—depend upon it. But as Aldrich and Rohde explained more recently, as the parties diverged in Congress, leaders were re-empowered, and members increasingly found that following their leaders was in their political and electoral interest.

Finally, 2010 was a census year, so late 2010 and 2011 saw the redrawing of all 435 House districts to assure that each congressperson is representing the same number of constituents. The reelection motivation is on vivid display during redistricting. House members are extremely sensitive about **redistricting** because they won in the old district and they want to be sure that any changes improve, rather than reduce, their chances of winning in the future.

> **redistricting** The redrawing of congressional district boundaries after each census.

State political parties generally drive the redistricting process and their motives are twofold; first, to protect as many of their incumbents as possible, and second, to maximize the overall prospects of the party. Sometimes, to accomplish party purposes, unusual congressional or legislative district boundaries must be drawn. The term **"gerrymander,"** first applied to a strangely shaped district drawn by Massachusetts Governor Elbridge Gerry following the 1810 census, is frequently decried but is a time-tested political tool that is not likely to go away any time soon. Now we turn to how Congress does its work and keeping congressional motivation in mind—reelection, policy influence, and leadership within the chamber—will aid understanding.

> **gerrymander** Refers to the strange shape of some congressional districts that result when parties draw districts intended to maximize their political advantage.

HOW CONGRESS HAS ORGANIZED TO DO ITS WORK

The Congress that came together for its first session in 1789 was composed of sixty-five members in the House and twenty-six in the Senate. Both the House and Senate made most of their important decisions after open discussion among the members on the floor, appointed committees only for specific tasks when that seemed advisable, and empowered leaders only to guide and monitor debate. However, as the number of members in both bodies expanded and their workloads grew, each was forced to develop systems and processes for organizing the members and managing the workload.

Because the size of the House grew much more rapidly than the Senate, the House came earlier and more completely to depend on strong leadership, internal organization, and adherence to explicit rules of procedure. The Senate has remained more informal and individualistic. Fundamentally, the House operates by close enforcement of its rules, whereas the Senate operates by consensus (see Table 9.1).[10]

TABLE 9.1 **Differences between the House and the Senate**		
	House	Senate
Term	Two years	Six years
Size	435	100
Special Role	Taxing and Spending Impeachment Charges	Treaties and Appointments Impeachment Trials
Rules	Rigid	Loose

The leading organizational features of the Congress are parties, committees, and legislative rules and procedures. Parties select the leaders and organize the members of Congress. Committees create a substantive division of labor within the Congress that permits it to discuss issues and make policy, oversee the executive bureaucracy, and serve the needs and interests of constituents. Finally, legislative rules and procedures define the order of events, who is entitled to participate at each stage, and which outcomes are permissible.

The Role of Political Parties

Political parties span the separation of powers and integrate the disparate institutions and actors of the American political system. The Democratic and Republican parties field candidates and compete in elections at every level of the American political system. They offer programs and platforms designed to attract the attention and support of voters, and they are expected to implement these programs once elected.

It falls to the leaders of the majority party in Congress to organize their members, form committees, and control the floor so that as much of their program as possible will pass. Leaders of the minority party organize their members to influence and revise the programs being prepared by the majority and to obstruct their passage where influence is not possible. As we shall see below, the increasing partisanship of the past decade have rendered these traditional majority–minority relationships more deeply and consistently conflictual. The impact on the Senate has been particularly profound.

Party Leaders: Responsibilities and Powers. Party leaders in Congress have responsibilities both inside the institution and in coordinating its activities with other actors and institutions like the president and the executive branch, interest groups, the media, and the public. Moreover, congressional leaders have both institutional and partisan roles and responsibilities.[11] Leaders must organize the chamber, collect and distribute information to members, schedule floor business, and consult and coordinate with the other chamber and the president. At the same time, leaders must organize their parties, promote party unity, ensure that party members are present on the floor for important votes, and provide campaign assistance to the party and its members.

The powers that leaders draw upon in fulfilling their responsibilities are both formal and informal.[12] The formal powers of leaders derive from the rules of each house. Leaders influence the appointment of committee chairs and of committee members, they control recognition of members on the floor and access of their bills to the floor, and they control the staff, space, and financial resources of the institution. The informal powers of leaders derive from their centrality to all that is happening. Leaders know what compromises are likely to be offered and accepted, what the leaders of the other house and the president think, and much more. Leaders also exercise considerable control over the stature and visibility of other members. Members with whom leaders consult and to whom they give important information gain in prestige and influence with their colleagues.

House of Representatives. The presiding officer of the House of Representatives is the speaker of the House (see Figure 9.3). The office of speaker is named but not described in Article I, section 2, of the Constitution, which simply reads: "The House of Representatives shall chuse [sic] their Speaker and other Officers." The speaker is elected at the opening of each Congress by a vote of all the members, although in reality the majority party selects the speaker on a straight party-line vote. Each party also selects a leader and an assistant leader, or whip.

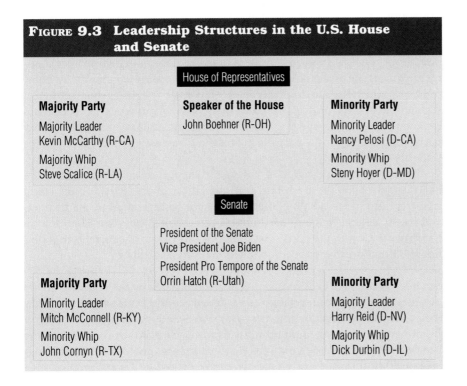

FIGURE 9.3 Leadership Structures in the U.S. House and Senate

House of Representatives

Majority Party	Speaker of the House	Minority Party
Majority Leader Kevin McCarthy (R-CA)	John Boehner (R-OH)	Minority Leader Nancy Pelosi (D-CA)
Majority Whip Steve Scalice (R-LA)		Minority Whip Steny Hoyer (D-MD)

Senate

President of the Senate
Vice President Joe Biden

President Pro Tempore of the Senate
Orrin Hatch (R-Utah)

Majority Party	Minority Party
Minority Leader Mitch McConnell (R-KY)	Majority Leader Harry Reid (D-NV)
Minority Whip John Cornyn (R-TX)	Majority Whip Dick Durbin (D-IL)

For most of the nineteenth century, with the exception of Henry Clay's speakership early in the century, the office was influential but not dominant. It became dominant for about two decades between 1890 and 1910 as Speakers Thomas Reed (R-ME) and Joseph Cannon (R-IL) systematically expanded their powers. The revolt against "Uncle Joe" Cannon in 1910 limited the powers of the speaker and produced a Congress in which committee chairs became increasingly influential.[13] A series of reforms undertaken in 1975 weakened committee chairs and strengthened the speaker as the representative of increasingly coherent House majorities.

The modern speaker of the House enjoys formal and informal powers unprecedented since the era of Reed and Cannon. Nancy Pelosi (D-CA) was the first female Speaker of the House. Her immediate predecessor, Dennis Hastert (R-IL), was the longest-serving (1998–2006) Republican Speaker in history. John Boehner (R-OH) assumed the Speaker's gavel in 2011.

The speaker presides over the House and sets its agenda. He chairs the party committee that assigns members to committees; decides whether to refer legislation to one committee or to several; controls the Rules Committee, which determines whether and how a bill will reach the floor for debate; presides over debate on the floor of the House; and represents his party's positions to the president, the media, and the public.

The speaker's principal deputy is the majority leader. Although formally elected every two years by a secret ballot of the party caucus, the majority leader is usually a close ally of the speaker. In the 112th Congress, Virginia's Eric Cantor was elected majority leader. The majority leader is responsible, working with the speaker, for setting the legislative agenda, maintaining communication with the committees and their leaders, informing members about the flow of major business onto the floor, judging member sentiment concerning issues and legislation, and encouraging support for party positions and bills. The minority leader has little role in agenda setting or scheduling and is principally concerned with organizing her colleagues in committee and on the floor to win moderating adjustments in majority party bills. The closer the partisan balance in Congress, the more leverage the minority enjoys.

The majority whip's job is to encourage support among members of the majority party for the positions and legislation of the party, count votes, advise the senior leadership of the prospects for success or failure on the floor, and try, in general, to mobilize and turn out the majority party coalition on the issues critical to the party. The minority whip's job, of course, is to mobilize and hold together opposition to the majority's agenda.[14]

unanimous consent Legislative device by which the Senate sets aside its standard rules for a negotiated agreement on the order and conduct of business on the floor. Plays roughly the same role as rules or special orders in the House.

Senate.   The Senate is as loosely organized and open as the House is highly organized and rulebound. From its earliest days, the Senate has been informal, collegial, and egalitarian. Moreover, the Senate normally operates by a running consensus called **unanimous consent**. Unanimous consent that the Senate proceed to a particular piece of business or proceed by a particular means, as the term so clearly suggests, can be denied by a single senator.

The Democratic leader, Nancy Pelosi, served as Speaker of the House from 2006 to 2010. She was displaced by Republican leader John Boehner when the Republicans won the majority in 2010.

The Constitution declares that the vice president shall preside over the Senate, although without vote except in cases of a tie. Hence, vice presidents have rarely appeared in the Senate except when it seems that a tie vote on an important issue might provide an opportunity to resolve it in the administration's favor. The Constitution further provides that the Senate appoint a *president pro tempore* to preside in the absence of the vice president. This position has become entirely honorary and usually goes to the most senior member of the majority party. The Senate is actually presided over on any given day by a series of junior members of the majority party who exercise no personal influence over events on the floor.

The majority leader of the Senate is elected by the membership of the majority party, and the minority leader is elected by the membership of the minority party. The majority leader, always in close consultation with the minority leader because of the collaborative nature of the Senate, sets the agenda for the Senate, oversees and manages debate on the floor, and brokers the many agreements, compromises, and deals by which the Senate disposes of its business.

Leading the Senate is an arduous and frustrating process even under the best of circumstances. The Senate's most famous and in many ways most accomplished majority leader was Lyndon Johnson (D-TX). In 1960, Johnson noted that "the only real power available to the leader is the power of persuasion. There is no patronage, no power to discipline, no authority to fire Senators like the president can fire his members of Cabinet."[15]

The Development of the Committee System

Members of the early House and Senate were wary of committees. They preferred to set policy in open debate on the floor before selecting a committee to work out the details and frame a resolution or bill.[16] However, as the workload of the Congress grew, members came to realize that discussion of every issue on the floor was inefficient and time-consuming. By about 1820, both the Senate and the House had developed systems of permanent or standing committees. Standing committees fundamentally changed the way Congress works. By the end of the 1880s, Woodrow Wilson described congressional politics as committee government in which the chairs of standing committees were the dominant figures.

Despite the strong speakerships of Reed and Cannon (1890–1910), Wilson's description of Congress held mostly true into the 1970s. Congressional reforms during the 1970s reduced the power of committee chairs in favor of subcommittee chairs and, more important, the House and Senate leaders. During the 1980s and 1990s the parties became more cohesive, and leaders slowly gained the power to force committee majorities and chairs to support party positions even when they disagreed.[17]

The Division of Labor.   The committee system in Congress during most of the twentieth century represented a division of labor in which legislative work was distributed among stable groups of subject matter experts. Legislative work involves both enacting legislation and oversight and investigation of executive

Q2 How does the committee system in Congress work to promote specialized knowledge and expertise among members?

Roll Call / Getty Images

Senator Chuck Schumer (D-New York) wades through a throng of reporters following his news conference on a critical Senate vote to raise the debt limit ceiling.

branch activities. An integrated set of norms and expectations promised members that if they concentrated on their committee work and developed deep expertise in these subject matter areas, they would be rewarded with influence. These understandings have broken down somewhat during the past several decades. More and more members, first in the Senate and then in the House, forsook their committee specialties to seek more general influence on the floor and in the media. Nonetheless, the division of legislative labor represented by the committee system is still a defining characteristic of the Congress.

Fixed Jurisdictions.   The basis of the division of labor in the modern Congress is the system of permanent standing committees with fixed committee jurisdictions. House rules have required since 1880 that legislation introduced into the House be considered in the committee or committees of appropriate jurisdiction before it is considered on the floor of the House. Senate procedures are similar but based more on precedent than formal rules. While committee jurisdictions are still generally respected, since the mid-1980s House leaders have created special task forces to manage critical bills. Committee chairs and members are often involved, but they have less control than they would in the normal committee process.

Specialization.   Traditionally, members of the House and, to a lesser extent, the Senate were expected to specialize (the **specialization norm**) in the work of their committees and to develop a subject matter expertise upon which the remainder of the body could depend. Members who complied with the specialization norm could expect to have their expertise honored if they were willing to reciprocate (the **reciprocity norm**) by deferring to the expertise of others. Hence, most subject matter areas in Congress are dominated by a few members who understand the process, know the issues inside and out, and know what can and cannot be done.

specialization norm The norm that encourages Congress members to specialize and develop expertise in the subject matter covered by their committee assignments.

reciprocity norm Congressional norm promising that if members respect the views and expertise of members of other committees, their committee expertise will be respected as well.

Seniority and Influence.   The **seniority norm** traditionally provided that the majority party member with the longest continuous service on the committee be given the opportunity to chair the committee. It also provided that members, once assigned to a committee, could stay on the committee as long as they wished. The strength of the seniority system was that it reduced conflict within the Congress. All members knew that their committee seats were secure and that they would move into positions of increasing influence as their seniority accumulated. The weakness of the system was that members advanced to key positions of committee leadership regardless of their talents or the compatibility of their views with the views of the leadership, their colleagues, or the country.

seniority norm The norm that holds that the member of a congressional committee with the longest continuous service on the committee shall be its chair.

In the modern Congress, party leaders depend somewhat less on seniority and somewhat more on ideology, effectiveness, and fundraising prowess in selecting committee chairs. Though respect for seniority is much less automatic than it once was, senior members are still the most active and effective legislators.[18]

standing committees
Permanent committees of the Congress enjoying fixed jurisdiction and continuing automatically from one Congress to the next.

authorizing committees
House and Senate committees that develop or authorize particular policies or programs through legislation.

appropriations committees
House and Senate committees that appropriate or allocate specific funding levels to each government program or activity.

select committees Temporary committees of the Congress that go out of business once they complete their work or at the end of each Congress unless specifically renewed.

joint committees Congressional committees made up of members of both the House and the Senate and assigned to study a particular topic.

conference committees
Committees composed of members of the House and Senate charged to resolve differences between the House and Senate versions of a bill.

Types of Committees.   Committees are the principal vehicles through which the House and Senate do most of their legislative work. There are several different kinds of committees. The most important are the **standing committees** with fixed jurisdictions that automatically continue from one Congress to the next. The broadest distinction that can be made among standing committees is between authorizing committees and appropriating committees.

Authorizing committees produce legislation, policies, and programs. Some of these committees, such as Agriculture, Energy and Commerce, and Transportation, provide members with opportunities to bring specialized benefits back to their districts. Other committees, such as Foreign Affairs and Education and Labor, allow members to be centrally involved in making visible and important public policy.

The power committees of the Congress are those that set taxing and spending levels and determine when and if substantive measures come to the floor. The House Ways and Means Committee and the Senate Finance Committee set the tax rates and policies that determine the revenue available to government. **Appropriations committees** determine how much money will actually be spent on each government activity and program. The House Rules Committee determines which committee bills will come to the floor for final passage and under what circumstances. House rules define Appropriations, Ways and Means, and Rules as "exclusive" committees whose members cannot sit on other committees. The House and Senate Budget Committees are also important and powerful.

Select committees are temporary committees that go out of business unless specifically renewed at the beginning of each Congress. Select committees are usually charged to study and report on a particular topic but lack the legislative authority to receive or offer bills.

Joint committees are made up of members from the House and Senate assigned to do continuing analysis and oversight in a particular substantive area like aging. Joint committees do have authority to initiate legislation and are frequently continued from one Congress to the next. **Conference committees** are composed of members from both houses charged to resolve the differences between bills on the same topic passed in the separate chambers (see Table 9.2).

Committee assignments are critical to both members and leaders in Congress.[19] For members, committee assignments greatly affect whether they will be able to address issues of importance to their constituents. A member from rural Kansas might benefit greatly by an appointment to the Agriculture Committee, whereas an appointment to a committee dealing with urban affairs would require that lots of time be spent on issues of only remote interest to rural constituents. For congressional leaders, making committee assignments provides opportunities both to win gratitude from members and to build committees likely to be receptive to the leadership's agenda.[20]

Because the Senate has about the same number of committees as the House with less than a quarter of the members, each senator must, of necessity, serve on more committees and subcommittees than a member of the House.

TABLE 9.2	Major Committees in the Contemporary Congress	

House	Senate
Power Committees	**Power Committees**
Appropriations	Appropriations
Budget	Budget
Ways and Means	Finance
Rules	
Authorizing Committees	**Authorizing Committees**
Agriculture	Agriculture, Nutrition, and Forestry
Armed Services	Armed Services
Financial Services	Banking, Housing, and Urban Affairs
Energy and Commerce	Commerce, Science, and Transportation
Education and Labor	Health, Education, Labor, and Pensions
Homeland Security	Homeland Security and Governmental Affairs
Oversight and Government Reform	
House Administration	
Foreign Affairs	Foreign Relations
Judiciary	Judiciary
Natural Resources	Energy and Natural Resources
Science and Technology	Environment and Public Works
Small Business	Rules and Administration
Transportation and Infrastructure	Small Business and Entrepreneurship
Veterans' Affairs	Veterans' Affairs
Select, Special, or Other Committees	**Select, Special, or Other Committees**
Select Intelligence	Select Intelligence
Standards of Official Conduct	Select Ethics
	Special Aging
	Indian Affairs

In the 114th Congress, 2015–2016, Senators served on an average of twelve committees and subcommittees, House members served or an average of six. Senators actually seek a wide range of committee assignments because this legitimates their access to the full range of issues likely to affect their states. Hence, Senators tend to be more generalists than specialists.[21]

Committee and Subcommittee Chairs. After the majority party leaders, committee chairs—and below them the chairs of important subcommittees—are the most influential members of Congress. Their influence flows from their long experience and deep knowledge of the subjects with which their committees deal, but also from their control over the resources of their committees and the subjects to which committee attention and resources are directed. Nonetheless, over the past fifty years there has been an interesting ebb and flow of influence from full committee chairs to subcommittee chairs, back to full committee chairs.

Between the 1940s and 1960s, committee chairs were frequently described as "barons," ruling their committees with authority that was not easily challenged by House and Senate leaders or committee members. Committee chairs set the agenda for their committees, appointed subcommittee chairs, called committee meetings, hired staff, and controlled all committee resources.

Power within committees began to shift with passage of the Legislative Reorganization Act of 1970 and the 1973 Subcommittee Bill of Rights, which required that each committee, except the Budget Committee, with more than twenty members have at least four subcommittees with defined areas of jurisdiction, adequate budgets, and the right to hire their own staffs. Nonetheless, committee chairs retained substantial influence at the full committee level.

When the Republicans took control of the House in 1995, they repealed many elements of the Subcommittee Bill of Rights and formally reempowered their committee chairs. Committee chairs appointed subcommittee chairs and members, hired all majority party staff and exercised approval over majority party subcommittee staff, and controlled the committee budget, including the portions formerly under the control of the separate subcommittees. On the other hand, the Republicans moved to constrain their committee chairs by establishing term limits of six years and by enhancing the speaker's power to appoint and remove them and to designate certain issues as leadership issues upon which committee chairs were required to take the party view.[22]

The Staff Structure.   Each member of Congress stands at the center of a small business dedicated to assisting him or her in getting work done. Each member receives a member's representational allowance (MRA) each year to pay for the staffing and operation of his or her office. House members all receive essentially the same allowance, whereas senators receive allowances based on the populations of their states. House members receive about $1.25 million from which he or she hires a staff (which averages about twenty persons) and pays for such things as travel, computers, telecommunications, office equipment, supplies, and mail charges.

Senators receive varying amounts, depending on whether they represent sparsely settled states like Utah or populous states like California. Senate staff average about thirty-five and range from fifteen to seventy. Personnel accounts provide senators with $3 million to $4.7 million for personnel, depending on the sizes of the states they serve. Office expenses, again depending on the size of the senator's state, range from $121,000 to $454,000, while the mail allotment ranges from $32,000 to $300,000.[23]

Member staffs serve the individual members in their offices, whereas committee staffs are hired by the committees and assist the members with their committee work. The numbers of both member staffs and committee staffs grew substantially during the latter half of the twentieth century, though they have remained steady in the Senate and fallen modestly in the House since the mid-1980s.

Staff members play a central role in the Congress. They perform the obvious tasks—handling office correspondence, gathering data and preparing information for committees, arranging meetings and hearings—but they also influence the work and substance of their offices and committees. Staff members develop expertise and policy preferences that they use to try to influence and persuade their members of Congress to adopt certain positions and push certain policies. Senior staff also draft legislation, conduct investigations, and negotiate with other senior staff on behalf of their members of Congress.

Congress also maintains three nonpartisan agencies that provide research and analysis. The Congressional Research Service (CRS) was created in 1914 to provide research support to the committees and members of Congress. The General Accounting Office (GAO), renamed the Government Accountability Office in 2004, was created in 1921 to give the Congress analytic and investigatory capabilities. And in 1974, the Congress created the Congressional Budget Office to provide it with independent information and analysis on budget options and choices. In all three cases, Congress was interested in assuring that it had analytical talent equal to that in the agencies of the executive branch and the offices of interest groups.

THE LEGISLATIVE PROCESS

House committees and their chairs are less powerful now than they were in the 1950s and 1960s, whereas the chamber leaders are more powerful. Although committee leaders are still influential in their committees, the chamber leaders control the floor. Increasingly, House leaders have been willing to bypass normal House procedures if that seems necessary to accomplish the majority party's goals. The legislative process in the Senate, on the other hand, is even more complex and cumbersome than it was in the 1950s and 1960s. Senators have always had the right of unlimited debate and the right to offer any amendment to any bill, but in recent years they have exercised these rights with greater frequency and on less obviously consequential matters. Hence, as political scientist Barbara Sinclair has noted, Senate leadership has "become an exercise in accommodating all interested parties."[24] The traditional legislative process (see Figure 9.4, shown here in a highly simplified version), requires levels of patience and restraint that recent legislative majorities have been incapable of showing.[25]

Q3 What are the stages of consideration through which most legislation must pass to become a law?

Introduction and Assignment

Only a member of the House or Senate can introduce a bill, and then that member is the bill's sponsor. When a bill is introduced into the House or Sen-

FIGURE 9.4   The Traditional Legislative Process: How a Bill Becomes a Law

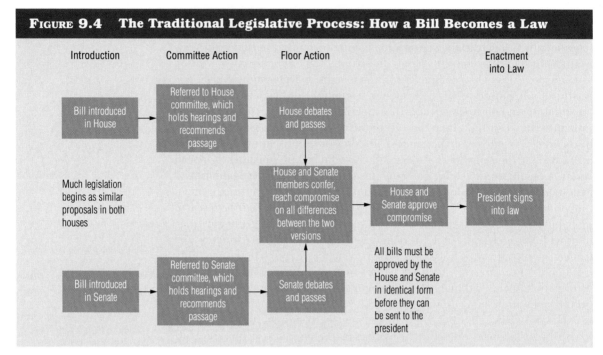

Source: Roger H. Davidson, Walter J. Oleszek, Francis E. Lee, and Eric Schickler, *Congress and Its Members*, 14th ed. (Washington, D.C.: Congressional Quarterly Press, 2014), 207. See also Walter J. Oleszek, *Congressional Procedures and the Policy Process*, 9th ed. (Washington, D.C.: CQ Press, 2014), 14–15 for a good description of the differences between conventional and unconventional law making.

ate, it is given a bill number (HR 1, for example, would be House Resolution 1, whereas S 1 would be Senate Bill 1) and assigned to the committee of appropriate jurisdiction for initial consideration. Whereas Senate traditions still largely require that bills be assigned to one committee, House rules permit simple referral and two kinds of multiple or complex referral: sequential referral and split referral.

referral The process by which a bill is referred or assigned to a standing committee for initial consideration.

Simple **referral** is the traditional practice of referring a bill to the single committee within whose jurisdiction it most nearly fits. The two forms of complex referral used in the House are intended to recognize and account for the fact that many bills contain subject matter of interest to more than one committee. Sequential referral occurs when a bill is sent first to one committee and then to another. Split referral is when a bill is actually split, and relevant sections are sent to different committees. When employing complex referral, the speaker designates one of the committees as primary. When the primary committee reports, the speaker sets deadlines for the other committees to complete their work.

Increasingly, key bills, often the most important bills of the session, and usually the top priorities of the majority party, are removed from some or all of the committee process. These bills are assigned to special working groups or task forces appointed by the majority party leadership. The task force may be drawn at least partially from the membership of the relevant standing committees, but they are led by leadership loyalists and consult with the leadership throughout.[26]

Committee and Subcommittee Deliberation

Most bills are still assigned to one or more standing committees for review. Bills assigned to a committee can be treated at the level of the full committee or assigned to a subcommittee for initial consideration. At either level, the stages of consideration are essentially three: public hearings, markup, and report. However, if a bill receives its initial consideration in subcommittee, full committee consideration will often go right to markup and forgo a second set of public hearings.

Public hearings reflect the open, participatory, democratic character of the legislative process. They create a public record of a broad spectrum of opinion on the issues involved and give interested parties a chance to weigh in before final decisions are made. Until just a decade ago, public hearings almost always took place in the capital itself, open to members, staff, and a small public audience. Since 1979, C-SPAN has been broadcasting select public hearings to a modest audience, but more recently committees have used interactive technology to interview potential witnesses or take testimony from experts anywhere in the country or the world. Teleconferencing can allow committee members to be away from the capital but still participate in hearings.

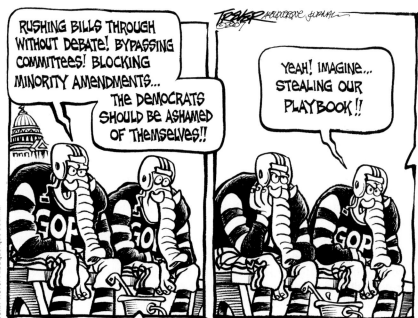

John Trever Albuquerque Journal

The minority party in Congress, Democrat or Republican, always feel that they are being either ignored or mistreated, or both at the same time.

After the hearings have been held, committee members move to the markup or bill-rewriting stage of the process. Here committee members go through the bill paragraph by paragraph, line by line, and word by word, and rewrite the text until it satisfies a majority of them that it is the best treatment of the issues in the bill that is then possible.

Finally, after the bill has proceeded through subcommittee and committee markup and has been approved by a majority vote of the full committee, the committee staff prepares a report that describes the intent of the bill, its major provisions, and the cost of implementation. This report, once approved by committee, is attached to the bill as it is sent to the floor for debate and final passage. The report is important because it is often the only thing that other members read before deciding whether or not to support the bill.

In the modern Congress, with its increasingly fluid and leadership-driven legislative process, bills frequently are changed, usually after a discussion between committee and chamber leaders, to improve the bill's prospects on the floor. Post-committee changes to bills are particularly common on key majority party bills where the pressure to assure passage is great.[27]

Agenda Setting and the Legislative Calendar

Key leadership bills are scheduled for floor consideration at the most advantageous time, while bills reported from the regular standing committees are listed in chronological order on one of several calendars. Calendars are lists of bills awaiting action. The Senate process is simple: All bills go on the Calendar of General Orders, and all treaties and nominations go on the Executive Calendar. In the House it is more complicated. Bills that raise or spend money go on the Union Calendar, other major public bills go on the House Calendar, private bills go on the Private Calendar, and bills that are minor and noncontroversial go on the Corrections Calendar.

Although bills in both the House and Senate go onto the appropriate calendars in the order in which they come from the committees, they do not go to the floor in that order. In the Senate, the majority and minority leaders determine through discussion and negotiation which bills will come up in which order and how they will be discussed. The leaders produce a unanimous consent agreement that describes the way a particular bill will be handled on the floor. Because any senator can block a unanimous consent agreement merely by objecting to it, most divisive issues are bargained out before floor debate even begins.

The House process, again, is more formal, detailed, and rigid. The House Rules Committee shuffles the calendars to put the most important bills up for consideration on the floor in the order and under circumstances most likely to lead to majority party success. The **Rules Committee** sets the conditions for debate and amendment of bills on the floor through a formal rule or special order. The rule lays out when the bill will come up for floor consideration, how long debate on the bill will run, and what kinds of amendments, if any, will be permitted.

Rules Committee Committee that writes rules or special orders that set the conditions for debate and amendment of legislation on the floor of the House.

In general, the Rules Committee produces three kinds of rules or special orders: open rules, closed rules, and modified closed rules. Modified closed rules are also called structured rules. An open rule permits amendments to be offered to any part of the bill. A closed rule forbids amendments to the bill, thereby requiring an up or down vote on the bill as it stands. A modified closed rule prohibits amendments to some sections of the bill and allows them to others. In the contemporary Congress, open rules are rare. About two-thirds of bills are brought up under modified closed or structured rules and one-third under closed rules.

A happy Democratic Party Whip, representative James Clyburn (D-SC), shows how close the vote was on the health care bill.

Special devices exist for bringing minor bills to the floor quickly. Noncontroversial matters can be brought to the floor from the Corrections Calendar on the second and fourth Tuesdays of each month. The suspension of the rules procedure is in order every Monday and Tuesday. Suspension of the rules permits forty minutes of debate, no amendments, and requires a two-thirds vote to pass. In recent years, nearly three-quarters of all bills came to the floor under suspension of the rules.

Floor Debate and Amendment

Floor debate in the House proceeds through a highly structured series of steps to a vote on final passage. House rules empower the Speaker and allow the majority party to work its will with relative ease. In the House, the process of floor debate begins with adoption of the rule describing the way the bill will be handled on the floor. After the appropriate rule has been adopted, the House dissolves itself into a parliamentary form known as the Committee of the Whole House on the State of the Union.

The **Committee of the Whole** is simply the House and all of its members operating under a set of rules that is less restrictive than the formal rules of the House. The key rules that apply in Committee of the Whole are that the quorum required to do business is 100, as opposed to 218 under the regular House rules, debate can be limited, and amendments, if allowed, are considered under a "five minute" rule rather than the hour required under regular House rules.

Committee of the Whole
House convened under a set of rules that allows limitations on debate and amendment and lowers the quorum required to do business from 218 to 100 to facilitate speedier action.

The main stages of floor consideration are general debate, amending, and a vote on final passage by the House. The time allotted for general debate is defined in the relevant rule and is evenly divided between those who favor and those who oppose the bill. Floor managers, usually the bill's sponsor or a senior member from the committee that handled the bill, manage the time available to both sides and parcel it out to members who want to speak to the general merits or demerits of the bill. Floor debate serves to educate uninformed members about the nature and contents of the bill and to surface the strongest arguments in its favor and the most telling points that its opponents have to make.

After general debate, and assuming that the rule under which the bill is being considered allows amendments, the bill is read for amendment. After a particular section is read, any member can offer an amendment (a proposal to change the language of the section) and have five minutes to explain it and argue in its favor. A member opposing the amendment then gets five minutes to explain the basis for his or her opposition. After voting on amendments, the Committee of the Whole "rises" and reports the amended bill back to the full House for a vote on final passage.

The process of floor debate in the Senate is much more fluid than in the House. Each senator enjoys the right of unlimited debate, or **filibuster,** and can block a bill from coming to the floor merely by placing an informal "hold" on it until her or his reservations about the bill are addressed. Because each senator has numerous ways to stop action—filibuster, hold, and denial of unanimous consent being only the most obvious—the Senate moves slowly and by negotiation, rather than in accord with formal rules and procedures as the House does.

Many observers now consider the Senate to be very nearly dysfunctional. While filibusters were once employed only on critical issues—like southern senators standing against civil rights bills in the 1960s—now they are employed with regularity. To stop a filibuster, 60 votes in favor of **cloture** are required. Cloture stops debate and moves, eventually, to a vote on final passage. Gerald Seib, the *Wall Street Journal*'s congressional correspondent, recently argued that filibusters and cloture votes were symptoms of the wider disease of excessive partisanship. Robert Dole, a former senator from Kansas and Republican leader, said "The bottom line is today it's become a 60-vote not a 50-vote Senate."[28]

In 2013, the Senate's majority leader, Democrat Harry Reid of Nevada, moved several times to limit without destroying the filibuster. Early in the year, in a rare moment of bipartisanship, Democrats and Republicans agreed to reduce the number and time allowed for minority party filibusters in exchange for a guarantee to allow at least two minority amendments per bill. In spite

filibuster Senators enjoy the right of unlimited debate. Use of unlimited debate by a Senator to stall or block passage of legislation is called a filibuster.

cloture A cloture vote, requiring a 60-vote majority, is the only way to halt a filibuster in the Senate.

TABLE **9.3** **Senate Action on Cloture Motions, 1950–Present**			
Years	**Motions Filed**	**Votes on Cloture**	**Cloture Invoked**
1951–1960	2	2	0
1961–1970	28	26	4
1971–1980	159	111	44
1981–1990	202	139	54
1991–2000	361	254	82
2001–2010	477	367	204
2011–2014	368	291	228

Source: http://www.senate.gov/pagelayout/reference/cloture_motions/clotureCounts.htm.

of this modest agreement, tensions built throughout the year as Republicans blocked Obama's executive and judicial nominees.

In late 2013, Majority Leader Reid finally resorted to what both sides called the "nuclear option," a simple majority vote approving the most important Senate rules change in decades. By a 52–48 vote, Democrats declared that filibusters would be out of order on executive and judicial nominees, though not on Supreme Court nominees and not on legislation. Democrats then moved a series of previously stalled nominations while Republicans warned of retaliation when they regained control of the Senate and the White House.[29] Republicans did regain control of the Senate in 2015 but did not change the rule.

House/Senate Conference Committees

Bills cannot be sent from the Congress to the president for approval until they have been passed in identical form by both the House and the Senate. However, given the committee and floor consideration processes described earlier, it should not be surprising that many bills pass the House and Senate in somewhat different versions. These differences have to be resolved to the satisfaction of both houses so that both can agree to identical versions of the bill that can be forwarded to the president.

About 10 percent of bills, including many of the most important bills each year, go to conference committees. Conferees are named from the House by the speaker and from the Senate by the majority leader. Conferees are usually leading members of the committee or committees of jurisdiction and include each chamber's most knowledgeable members. Traditionally, conference committees resolve the differences before them by horse-trading over the sections most important to each chamber and by splitting the difference where that is possible. Over the past two decades, as partisanship in Congress escalated, conference committees have been bypassed to simplify and speed up the process. In some instances, rather than bargain out differences, one house just adopts the version of the bill passed by the other house. In other instances, differences are resolved in informal negotiations between leaders of the majority party in the House and Senate.[30]

CONGRESSIONAL DECISION MAKING

Members of Congress are expected to be aware of and open to outside influence as they make the many decisions and choices confronting them. Members must pay attention to the views of their constituents, their staffs, partisan colleagues and leaders, interest groups and their lobbyists, and the president and his representatives in the executive branch. Moreover, members are expected to use their own judgment because they have knowledge and access to information that is available to few others. They also have their own ideological

Q4 What pressures operate on a member of Congress as he or she prepares to make an important legislative decision?

perspectives, political views, and policy interests, or else they would not have run for political office in the first place.[31]

Constituents

A member's constituents, the voters in his or her district, are the only people who can decide whether that member keeps her or his job. Interest groups, party leaders, even the president, can favor or oppose a particular member's reelection, but only the voters in the district can vote them in or out. Naturally, members of Congress pay close attention to opinion in their district. Yet, members have a difficult time deciphering district opinion on many issues. Most states, and even most districts, are diverse, containing voters and groups of voters who hold a wide range of opinions and views.[32] These diverse groups are likely to see issues from several different perspectives.

casework Casework refers to the direct assistance that members of Congress or their staff provide to constituents who need something from a federal agency or department.

Members working to secure reelection have two traditional tools to use in earning the appreciation of their constituents and a new set of online tools with which many members are experimenting. The surest route to constituent approval is through what we call casework. **Casework** is active and direct problem-solving on behalf of constituents. Traditionally, the service that a member of Congress has been most likely to perform for a constituent has been to intervene on her or his behalf with some recalcitrant or unresponsive federal agency. Members can often move an agency to respond, or perhaps even to modify or reverse an objectionable decision. The member's leverage with the bureaucracy comes from Congress's control over the funding, personnel, and programs of the agencies of the executive branch. The member's reward for his or her good services comes in the form of constituent gratitude and votes on election day.[33]

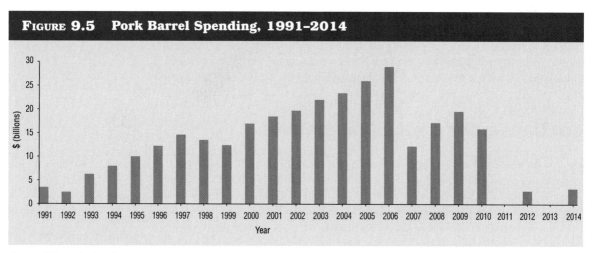

FIGURE 9.5   Pork Barrel Spending, 1991–2014

Source: Citizens Against Government Waste: Pork Barrel Project.

Like casework, bringing federal money back to the district, often called "bringing home the bacon," traditionally produced constituent approval and voter support. While bringing home the bacon is generally expected of members, **pork barrel politics**, which is the same thing, has a less savory reputation. While both citizens and members decry pork barrel politics and often see it as wasteful in other states and congressional districts, some now see projects in their own state or district that way. While Figure 9.5 shows that pork barrel spending increased steadily from 1991 through 2006, intense scrutiny in the 2008 presidential campaign and the 2010 congressional campaign led Republicans to disavow earmarks. There were no pork barrel projects in 2011 or 2013, while the numbers were modest in 2012 and 2014, just $3.3 and $2.7 billion respectively.[34]

As pork barrel spending has faded, many in Congress have looked to new online communication tools to stay in touch with their constituents. Members use "teledemocracy" tools, such as televised town hall meetings, satellite press conferences, cable news appearances posted to YouTube, and blogs to stay in touch with constituents. Other more personal tools, including Facebook, Twitter, Instagram, Tumblr, and Pinterest, allow Members of Congress to show a more personal and casual side to constituents and voters. Critically, though, these new tools are something of a double-edged sword; they allow members to stay in touch, but a thoughtless post can be very difficult to walk back.[35]

pork barrel politics Pork barrel politics usually refers to spending for specially targeted local projects, acquired by a congressman or senator outside the regular appropriations process.

Struggling Toward Democracy

The Constitution gives Congress the power of the purse and congressmen are supposed to represent the interests of their constituents.

What do you think?

- Is there anything wrong with "earmarks" and "pork barrel spending"?
- What, if anything, distinguishes pork from funding useful projects?

Getty/Tom Williams, CQ Roll Call

Members of Congress such as John Shimkus, R-IL, use Facebook, Twitter, and other social media to keep in touch with staff, constituents, donors, and others.

Staff, Colleagues, and Party Leaders

Members of Congress not driven to a particular decision by well-formed constituency opinion often look to their staffs, colleagues, and party leaders for clues on how to vote. Members are too busy to study every issue closely, so they look for guidance to staff members who have been assigned to monitor the relevant issue area. They also look to relevant committee leaders, acknowledged substantive experts, and individual members with whom they most frequently agree. On a few issues, party leaders will demand that members support the party position and members will be under great pressure to do so.[36]

Interest Groups and Lobbyists

When members look past their staffs and colleagues in search of cues about how to vote on a particular issue, they run quickly into interest groups and their lobbyist representatives. Members value interest groups and lobbyists (many of whom are former members of Congress) for the knowledge and information that they can bring to the process. This knowledge and information is particularly valuable at the committee hearing and markup stages while the provisions of a bill are being discussed and shaped. By the time a bill reaches the floor and members are required to make a final decision on it, they are not looking for detailed information so much as for a clear signal on whether to support or oppose it. Members without strong feelings on a bill may trade their support or opposition for future consideration, such as during the next election campaign, from the lobbyist.[37]

The President and the Bureaucracy

The Constitution requires that the president participate in the legislative process. Article I, section 3, requires that the president "give to the Congress Information of the State of the Union and recommend to their Consideration such Measures as he shall judge necessary and expedient." The president follows his State of the Union message each year with a set of administration bills for the consideration of Congress. Moreover, during the past half-century Congress has required the president to report and recommend initiatives in such specific substantive areas as the economy and the environment, and, of course, the president submits an annual budget that structures a great deal of what the Congress does each year.

The president is empowered to consider each law passed by Congress and decide whether to approve or veto it. Knowing that the president possesses this power leads Congress to take his views into account and even to actively bargain with him while bills are being crafted. Individual members of the president's party will support him when they can, which tends to be most of the time, but they will usually choose their constituents over the president when both are watching closely.

PUBLIC DISAFFECTION AND CONGRESSIONAL REFORM

Congress never stands very high in the public mind; hence, waves of reform regularly roil the congressional waters. Congress underwent four major reform waves in the twentieth century. Each was driven by a combination of public and member concern about the representativeness, efficiency, and morality of the institution and its members. The first major reform of the twentieth century occurred in the House in 1910–1911, when members rebelled against autocratic powers that had been gathered by Speakers Reed and Cannon. These reforms weakened the power of the speaker and strengthened committees and their chairman.

Q5 How serious has Congress been in its recent reform efforts?

The second great period of congressional reform came in the immediate post-World War II years. It appeared to most observers that the war had greatly increased the powers of the president in relation to the Congress. The Legislative Reorganization Act of 1946 sought to redress the imbalance by reducing the number of standing committees in the House and Senate, providing them with permanent professional and clerical support, and reasserting Congress's role in the budgetary process.

The third great reform era produced the Legislative Reform Act of 1970. The key reforms enacted during this era were designed to open Congress to greater public scrutiny, enhance its decision-making capabilities in key areas such as legislative management and budgeting, and empower the majority party in Congress. But empowered majorities tend to limit the rights of minorities and to tighten those limits over time as they seek to enact their agenda. This is particularly true of the House where the rules allow for majority party dominance.

House scandals of the early 1990s, including those surrounding the House bank and post office, led to a fourth wave of congressional reform. In the wake of their stunning victories in 1994, House Republicans promised a more open, fair, and accountable Congress. They swore they would not run roughshod over the Democratic minority as it, they claimed, had run roughshod over them. But power is difficult not to wield and opposition soon comes to seem like obstruction. The Republican leadership used closed rules, extended votes, arm twisting, and a proliferation of pork barrel spending to move their agenda through the Congress. After 2003, a series of scandals, many tying back to Majority Leader Tom DeLay (R-TX), and the war in Iraq turned public opinion against the Republican majority.

Democrats claimed that Republicans had fostered a "culture of corruption" in Washington that needed to be replaced. They promised to end gridlock by limiting partisanship and restoring comity in Congress. They also promised

to restore the regular order, allow the minority more opportunity to participate in debate and offer amendments, and open conferences to the public.
Democrats soon backed off these procedural promises, deciding it was more
important to pass bills than to worry unduly about whether the Republicans
were on board.

Democrats were more successful in passing new ethics and lobbying
rules. Members were required to identify and justify earmarks and special tax
provisions that they inserted into legislation. New rules for lobbyists require
them to file quarterly reports certifying that they had not provided gifts to
members and staff in violation of House and Senate Rules. Penalties for failing
to comply with lobbying laws were increased and lobbyists were required to
file semi-annual reports on contributions to members, leadership PACs, and
political parties.

Institutional reform is a continuous process in Congress, as it is in most
major social institutions. The public expects responsiveness (these are the
representatives of the people, after all), efficiency (the ability to identify and
effectively address important issues and problems), and morality (basic honesty) from the Congress. These expectations are rarely fulfilled. Despite their
reform efforts, public approval of Congress sank to all time lows, touching just
9 percent approval in late 2013.

Chapter Summary

Americans of the founding period knew both that government is necessary
and that the powers awarded to government can be misused. First they sought
to limit the danger that political power would be misused by keeping
government weak. The Congress under the Articles of Confederation lacked
the power to tax and to control commerce between the states and with
foreign nations. The instability that resulted from the weakness of the
Confederation Congress led many to conclude that reform was necessary.
The U.S. Constitution envisioned a powerful national government with a
bicameral legislature at its center.

Initially, the new Congress conducted most of its important business in
open discussion on the floors of the House and Senate. Leaders were kept
weak, and committees were used only to draft bills to reflect agreements
reached earlier in floor debate. Only as the membership and workload of
Congress grew early in the nineteenth century did leadership powers expand
and standing committees become central to the legislative business of both
the House and the Senate. The standing committee system in Congress was
built around fixed committee jurisdictions that promoted member expertise.
The seniority norm, which held that the member of the majority party with
longest service on the committee should be the committee chair, further promoted the development of expertise.

The most important committees in the Congress are the standing
committees. They have fixed jurisdictions and continue from one Congress

to the next. When a bill is introduced into the House or the Senate, it is assigned to the appropriate standing committee. The committee consideration process typically involves public hearings, markup, and drafting a report that describes the major provisions of the bill. Floor consideration of bills reported out of committee typically involves general debate, amendment, and a vote on final passage. If the House version and Senate version of a bill differ, a conference committee of members drawn from both chambers is appointed to resolve the difference between the House version and Senate version of the bill. The bill can then be sent on for the president's consideration.

Although the legislative process seems clear enough, the Congress at work always looks slightly out of control. Majorities seem unable to develop and adopt credible programs; minorities seem negative and shrill, accusing the majority of wanting to do hurtful things in ways that will be fraught with waste, fraud, and corruption. Members seem to be pulled to and fro by constituents, party leaders, lobbyists, and representatives of the administration. Naturally, citizens come to think ill of those who seem incapable of solving the nation's problems or even of discussing them sensibly and civilly.

Key Terms

appropriations committees 288

authorizing committees 288

casework 298

cloture 296

Committee of the Whole 295

conference committees 288

delegate 279

filibuster 296

gerrymander 281

joint committees 288

legislative supremacy 271

politico 279

popular sovereignty 271

pork barrel politics 299

reciprocity norm 287

redistricting 281

referral 292

Rules Committee 294

select committees 288

seniority norm 287

specialization norm 287

standing committees 288

trustee 279

unanimous consent 284

Suggested Readings

Davidson, Roger H., Walter J. Oleszek, Francis E. Lee, and Eric Schickler. *Congress and Its Members*, 14th ed. Washington, D.C.: Congressional Quarterly Press, 2014. This textbook highlights the effect on the institution of the fact that members must perform effectively both in Washington and back in their districts.

Deering, Christopher J., and Steven S. Smith. *Committees in Congress*, 3rd ed. Washington, D.C.: Congressional Quarterly Press, 1997. Classic textbook on the changing place and role of committees in the Congress.

Mann, Thomas, and Norman Ornstein. *The Broken Branch: How Congress Is Failing America and How to Get It Back on Track*. New York: Oxford University Press, 2006. The authors trace the origins and effects of partisan deadlock in the modern Congress and how it might be cured.

Mayhew, David. "The Electoral Incentive," 1974. Mayhew explained that members' reelection success depends on their efforts to advertise themselves to their constituents, to claim credit for beneficial public policy, and to take shrewd policy stands.

Polsby, Nelson W. *How Congress Evolves: Social Bases of Institutional Change*. New York: Oxford University Press, 2004. Describes the effects of social and technological changes on the partisan and institutional structures of the House.

Schickler, Eric. "Institutional Development of Congress," 2004. Schickler argues that the reelection and policymaking goals of members have driven the congressional reforms that have produced the modern House and Senate.

Sinclair, Barbara. *Unorthodox Lawmaking: New Legislative Processes in the U.S. Congress*, 4th ed. Washington, D.C.: Congressional Quarterly Press, 2012. This book describes the contemporary legislative process with a particular focus on recent changes in it.

Web Resources

For practice quizzes, key term flashcards, videos, links, and other study tools, visit the *American Government* website: www.routledge.com/cw/jillson

1. **www.statenet.com**

   State Net monitors pending bills and regulations. State Net also publishes a variety of online and print publications such as the nationally popular *State Net Capitol Journal.*

2. **thomas.loc.gov**

   The Thomas home page provides links to the *Congressional Record*, the texts of bills and reports on their status, committee information, and documents on the legislative process and on congressional history.

3. **www.house.gov**

   Official website of the United States House of Representatives. This site includes up-to-date information of legislative activity, votes of members, member biographies, and contact information.

4. **www.senate.gov**

   Official website of the United States Senate. Resources of interest include a virtual tour, legislative news, committee assignments, biographies of members, and an archive searchable by keyword.

5. **www.rollcall.com**

   An online periodical that specializes in covering daily events on Capitol Hill.

Chapter **10**

THE PRESIDENT
Governing in Uncertain Times

"As our case is new, so we must think anew, and act anew. We must disentrall ourselves, and then we shall save our country. Fellow-citizens, we cannot escape history."

ABRAHAM LINCOLN 1862

THE UNITARY EXECUTIVE THEORY OF PRESIDENTIAL AUTHORITY

The Constitution TODAY

Article II, section 1: "The executive power shall be vested in a President of the United States of America."

While the constitutional origins of presidential authority are clear, centering on the clause above, the scope and limits of that authority are hotly contested. Scholars have long noted that while the powers explicitly enumerated in the Constitution's Article II are few—commander-in-chief, pardon power, and, with the advice and consent of the Senate, broad appointment powers—the president has additional unenumerated powers.

Students of executive power all the way back to John Locke (1632–1704) have argued that kings and presidents may have to act outside the law or even in contravention of the law when great dangers threaten. The "inherent powers" of the executive, they argue, may require bold action, even action that would be illegal under normal circumstances, to confront dire threats. Recently, officials of the George W. Bush administration have argued for an even broader "unitary executive" theory of presidential authority. The unitary executive theory holds that the president is the sole authority in the executive branch and any attempt to limit that authority is unconstitutional.

While the Bush administration's view of untrammeled executive authority is distinctive, it is not unprecedented. Presidents, congressmen, Supreme Court justices, and scholars have been wrestling with these issues since the founding period. The key issue is whether presidential authority claims are to be seen within a separation of powers context or a unitary executive authority context.

The classic attempt by the Supreme Court to assess the relative weight of executive branch authority claims came in Justice Robert Jackson's famous concurring opinion in *Youngstown Sheet and Tube v. Sawyer.* Jackson described presidents as being at the height of their power when acting under full statutory authority. In a second category of cases, presidents acting in the absence of, but not in contravention of, explicit statutory authority were acting under inherent executive power. The third class of cases, where presidents act despite an express congressional prohibition, claiming that the prohibition is an unconstitutional intrusion on executive authority, is a claim of unitary executive authority and is where the president is on the thinnest ice.

The Bush administration's "War on Terror" in the wake of the 9/11 attacks raised these issues anew. Though Congress authorized the administration to "use all necessary and appropriate force against those nations, organizations, or persons he determines planned, authorized, committed, or aided the terrorist attacks," administration lawyers led by John Yoo claimed the authorization was unnecessary. Yoo wrote that "the power to initiate military hostilities, particularly in response to the threat of an armed attack, rests exclusively with the president." Moreover, Bush administration lawyers claimed that the president's commander-in-chief powers gave him exclusive control over decisions about how to wage the war against terror.

The Bush administration's unitary executive theory came under Supreme Court review in *Hamdan v. Rumsfeld* (2006). The Bush administration claimed the right to employ military tribunals to try Guantanamo detainees. Writing for the majority, Justice John Paul Stevens declared, "Whether or not the president has independent power, absent congressional authorization, to convene military commissions, he may not disregard limitations that Congress has, in proper exercise of its own war powers, placed on his powers."

Initially, a public in deep shock after 9/11 and Republican majorities in both houses of Congress did not resist expansive presidential authority claims. But as the emergency receded in the public mind, the Afghan and Iraq wars soured, and more information about administration policies emerged, opposition built in public opinion, the courts, and finally in the Congress. The Founders, architects of our system of limited government, separation of powers, and checks and balances would have recognized the process.

Focus Questions: from reading to thinking

Q1 What historical examples of executive power did the Founders consider as they shaped the American presidency?

Q2 How did the Founders limit the powers that they placed with the president?

Q3 What forces account for the growth of executive power over the course of American political history?

Q4 Why does the president have an easier time in shaping and implementing foreign policy than he does domestic policy?

Q5 Should we be concerned that White House staff members have replaced members of the cabinet as the president's closest advisers?

WHAT DO YOU THINK?

- Do you think there are circumstances under which presidents might reasonably "break the law?"
- Do Congress and the courts have ways to push back against claims to presidential authority or are such claims authoritative?

THE PRESIDENT OF THE UNITED STATES

Upon leaving the presidency early in 1857, Franklin Pierce asked, "After the White House what is there to do but drink?" Almost a century later, Vice President Harry S. Truman, upon hearing of the death of President Franklin Roosevelt on April 12, 1945, said to a small collection of reporters, "Boys, if you ever pray, pray for me now." Both men were reflecting on the awesome responsibilities that attach to the office of president of the United States.

President Pierce, drained by his struggle against the deepening divisions between North and South, thought that the peace of the saloon might provide comfort. President Truman would soon learn that the United States possessed an atomic bomb of immense destructive capability and that he would have to decide whether to drop it on Japan. Most presidents, finding that the powers of their office fall far short of the scope and range of their responsibilities, let alone of the scope and range of public expectations of the good that they should do, resort to some mix of drink and prayer.

Fundamentally, the problem is that the office of president of the United States and the expectations that we have of it are inconsistent. Popular expectations surrounding the presidency spring from a civics book image of the president as being in charge of the national government. The reality is somewhat different. Constitutional authority and political resources are shared by the president, Congress, and the courts.[1]

The resulting dilemma is nicely stated by Stephen Skowronek. In describing the mismatch between popular understanding of the president in the American political system and the office's constitutional authority, Skowronek writes, "Formally, there is no central authority. Governing responsibilities are shared, and assertions of power are contentious. Practically, however, it is the presidency that stands out as the chief point of reference . . . it is the executive office that focuses the eyes and draws out the attachments of the people."[2]

Article II of the Constitution outlines the powers of the presidency and its relationships to the other branches only in broad terms. Edward S. Corwin, the leading mid-twentieth-century student of the presidency, warned that the Constitution's broad language concerning the war powers (Congress declares war, the president is commander in chief) was "an invitation to struggle."[3] The Constitution, law, and precedent provide broad parameters to presidential power. Ultimately, within these parameters, each president defines a way of being president and acting in the office that works for him and that others, in government and out, recognize and accept.

George Bush and Dick Cheney, convinced that presidents weakened by Vietnam and Watergate had allowed Congress and the courts to encroach upon the executive's rightful prerogatives, were determined to restore them. During Bush's first term, and especially after 9/11, the administration advocated the unitary executive theory of presidential power. The **unitary executive theory**, discussed above, holds that executive branch authority resides in the president and that, especially in wartime, the president, in his role as commander in chief, is the sole judge of what is required to protect the American people.

Barack Obama entered the presidency facing unprecedented problems; two wars with which the public had grown impatient and national and global economies in deep distress. Big problems require big powers, but not necessarily powers exercised unilaterally. Where Bush demanded compliance from Republican congressional majorities, Obama sought to move quickly and across a broad front but in conjunction with Democratic congressional majorities. Not surprisingly, within a year, critics were complaining that he was not leading the Congress aggressively enough.

In this chapter, we describe the historical examples of executive authority that the Founders had before them as they thought about this new office of president. We then describe and explain the choices that they made concerning the nature of the office of president, the powers that were given to it, and those that were withheld. We follow the growth and development of

unitary executive theory
Strong presidency theory holding that the president embodies executive authority and is the sole judge, particularly in wartime, of what is required to protect the nation and its people.

AFP / Getty Images

President Barack Obama with the four living former presidents. President Obama is flanked by George H.W. Bush and George W. Bush, along with Bill Clinton and Jimmy Carter.

presidential power through the nineteenth and twentieth centuries and into the twenty-first century. We then analyze the range of domestic and foreign policy responsibilities of the modern president. We ask how the presidential establishment—the White House staff, the Executive Office of the President, the cabinet, and the office of the vice president—is organized to assist the president in stretching his powers to meet his responsibilities in an uncertain and dangerous world. We conclude with a discussion of concerns about the presidency and reforms that might be undertaken to address them.

HISTORICAL ORIGINS OF EXECUTIVE POWER

Q1 What historical examples of executive power did the Founders consider as they shaped the American presidency?

The national executives with whom the Founders were familiar were monarchs who possessed broad powers that included the right to conduct foreign policy and make war as they saw fit. Even John Locke, the premier theorist of parliamentary supremacy in England, held that the executive should have a free hand in foreign policy, including war making, and should have the right to ignore or even violate the law in conditions of national emergency.[4] Closer to home, the king's colonial governors wielded legislative and judicial powers in addition to their broad executive powers. The state governors of the revolutionary period were too weak to defend themselves, let alone to check and balance the dominant legislatures of the day. Finding no good models of a republican executive in history or experience, the Founders were forced to invent their own.

Historical Precedents: Crown Governors

In most of the colonies, the governor represented either the king or the proprietor. In the royal colonies, the governor embodied the king's authority, wielding broad powers as commander in chief and as the appointing authority for most colonial offices. In addition, the royal governor could call and disband the legislature at will and veto its acts and requests. His appointed council, usually sitting as the upper house of the legislature, also served as the colony's domestic court of last resort. Proprietary governors were in nearly as strong a position. They were appointed by and served the corporate owners of their colonies.

As the colonies grew in population and wealth over the course of the eighteenth century, local legislatures competed with these powerful executives for control of colonial politics and policy. Colonists saw their legislatures as defending their liberty and property and ultimately their lives against arbitrary and potentially tyrannous executive power. Not surprisingly, when independence brought opportunities for colonists to create their own state governments, they limited executive power.

Historical Precedents: State Governors

The early state constitutions reflected a broad-based consensus on the dangers that concentrated power posed to liberty. Hence, governors were made subservient to state legislatures and many traditional executive powers were removed. Generally, governors were elected by the state legislature, rather than by the people, for short terms, usually one year, and more than half were not eligible for reelection. They were denied the right to veto legislation and were permitted to make appointments only in conjunction with an advisory council. Only the New York constitution of 1777 and the Massachusetts constitution of 1780 gave somewhat more independence and authority to their executives.

Executive Power in the Articles

The Articles of Confederation simply denied the need for independent executive authority. The Articles did not mention an executive branch and gave all power, even over foreign affairs and war making, to the Congress. Although the Congress elected a president each year, that officer's role was to preside in Congress. He had no authority to oversee the work of the committees, affect action on the floor, or even answer correspondence without the express permission of the Congress. His term was one year, and the office circulated among the states.

By the middle of the 1780s, a consensus developed among the nation's conservative elite, in which Washington, Madison, and Hamilton were leading figures, that the Articles were inadequate. Reform proposals focused on the shape and powers appropriate to a national executive strong enough to provide stability and direction but not strong enough to become tyrannous.

THE CONSTITUTIONAL BASES
OF PRESIDENTIAL AUTHORITY

Q2 How did the Founders limit the powers that they placed with the president?

Most of the delegates arriving in Philadelphia in the summer of 1787 for the Constitutional Convention were convinced that executive power had to be both enhanced and restrained simultaneously. No one quite knew how to do that, much less how to describe the result to a skeptical public.

Alternative Conceptions of the Presidency

The Founders had little difficulty establishing the eligibility criteria for the new office. The president would have to be at least thirty-five years of age, fourteen years a resident, and a natural-born citizen of the United States (see the Let's Compare box). Other questions were more difficult: who would choose the president and by what means, how long would he serve, and would he be eligible to serve two or more terms successively? The convention struggled over these questions until within days of final adjournment.[5]

A Messenger for the Congress.   Initially, most members agreed with Connecticut's Roger Sherman that "the Executive magistracy was nothing more than an institution for carrying the will of the legislature into effect." Therefore, selection of the executive by the legislature seemed appropriate to most of the delegates. Yet, some delegates continued to be bothered by the obvious violation of the doctrine of separation of powers, whereas others, particularly those from the smaller states, were concerned that legislative selection advantaged the larger states with the bigger congressional delegations.

A Powerful and Independent Executive.   James Wilson and Gouverneur Morris, eventually seconded by James Madison, argued that popular selection of the chief executive would guarantee his independence and permit him to be given enough power to act as a check on the legislature. Both the president and Congress would draw their authority from and be accountable to the sovereign people; hence, such a president might have a relatively short term of three or four years and be eligible for reelection. But few delegates could imagine that common people, busy with work and family, isolated on frontier farms, with limited knowledge of the leading politicians and issues of the day, could select the nation's chief magistrate. Democracy was still thought dangerously unstable. Another way to select the president was needed.

The Electoral College and Presidential Selection.   The convention struggled with these plans and their flaws for more than three months. Finally, a special committee on "postponed and unresolved parts" reported a compromise solution that satisfied most members. The committee proposed a new institution, the **Electoral College** (each state would have the same number of

Electoral College An institution created by the Federal Convention of 1787 to select the president.

LET'S COMPARE

Qualifying for Leadership around the World

The qualifications listed in the Constitution for service as president seem so sparse that we tend not to think much about them. The qualifications laid out in Article II, section 1, read: "No person except a natural born citizen . . . shall be eligible to the office of president; neither shall any person be eligible to that office who shall not have attained the age of thirty-five years, and been fourteen years a resident within the United States." The age and residency requirements have never drawn much notice, but the elections of Jennifer Granholm (born in Canada) and Arnold Schwarzenegger (born in Austria) as governors of Michigan and California, respectively, raised questions about the nativity requirement. The election of Ted Cruz (born in Canada) as senator from Texas raised these issues again.

More troublingly, the election of Barack Obama set off a "birther movement" that questioned his status as a "natural-born citizen." Obama's father was Kenyan and his mother was an American born in Kansas and ample evidence shows that Obama was born in Hawaii. Yet, some, wishing to draw his very eligibility to be president into question, refused to believe the evidence.

Why do we have these requirements, and how do they compare with the requirements that constitutions of other nations place on their heads of state and government? The age requirement is straightforward. States generally set the age for suffrage at twenty-one (since reduced to eighteen), so the Founders set eligibility for election to the House at twenty-five, the Senate at thirty, and the presidency at thirty-five. Many nations have age requirements for their top leaders (thirty-five to forty is common, with forty the most common).

The residency and nativity requirements are more interesting. The United States at its founding was a land of European immigrants (and African slaves). Europe was governed by monarchs who continued to have designs on America. The Founders wanted to ensure that those elected to office in the United States had lived here long enough to have shed their monarchical principles and adopted her republican principles. Hence, the Constitution requires that candidates for the House have been citizens of the United States for seven years, nine years for the Senate, and for the presidency from birth. Most other nations have citizenship requirements, but surprisingly few have nativity requirements.

A few do: Algeria, Brazil, Bulgaria, the Congo, Egypt, Finland, Indonesia, and the Philippines require native birth. A couple even carry the issue of nativity back to parents and grandparents. Greece requires that candidates for president have been citizens for at least five years and "be of Greek descent from the father's or the mother's line." To run for president of Tunisia, one's "father, mother, and paternal and maternal grandfather [must] have been of Tunisian nationality without interruption." And in 2012, Sheik Hazem Salah Abu Ismail, at the time a frontrunner for the presidency of Egypt, was declared ineligible because his mother had, late in life, become a U.S. citizen.

Even if one believes that the reasons for the Founders' concerns have passed, the Constitution is very difficult to amend, and this is not the kind of issue that is likely to attract broad and sustained political support among politicians or the public.

What do you think?
- How much sense do nativity requirements make in the modern world?
- Do we still need to guard against the tool of a foreign power being insinuated into the presidency?
- If Arnold Schwarzenegger can be governor of California, why shouldn't he be eligible to be president of the United States?

votes as in its combined House and Senate delegations), to choose the president. Because Congress was not involved in the choice, it was thought that the term could be relatively short, four years, and that sitting presidents could be eligible for reelection.

This much made sense to most delegates, but another aspect of the plan added interesting complexity. How would the president be selected if no candidate emerged with a majority in the Electoral College? Again, some form of legislative selection seemed obvious but the Senate was too closely tied to the president in treaty making and appointments to be given a role in executive selection. Selection by the House would advantage the large states, so the small states resisted that possibility. Finally, Roger Sherman and Hugh Williamson suggested selection by the House voting by states.[6] Almost all of the reservations that had been voiced during the convention about the various plans had been solved in this artful design of an electoral college. Students may wish to refer back to Chapter 8 for a fuller discussion of the Electoral College in modern presidential politics.

Struggling Toward Democracy

The Electoral College gets a fair amount of criticism, but the Founders designed it with a purpose.
What do you think?
- Is the Electoral College still a useful element of our system for presidential selection?
- Or is it simply an embarrassing vestige of the Founders' fear of democracy?

Executive Authority in the Constitution

Article II of the Constitution begins boldly, stating: "The executive Power shall be vested in a President of the United States of America." But what did the Founders intend to be included in executive power? In the monarchies of Europe, the executive power was broad indeed, extending to the right to conduct foreign affairs (including war), grant reprieves and pardons, create administrative offices and appoint persons to them, direct the bureaucracy, veto legislation, and call and disband legislatures.

The Founders had a narrower view of executive power. As we shall see, only the pardon power of the traditional executive powers was given exclusively to the president. Most of the president's executive powers, both in domestic legislative and administrative affairs and in foreign and military affairs, were hedged about with legislative and judicial checks. Moreover, the Founders were intent on focusing future presidents on the Constitution as the source of their authority and of limits on that authority. The final paragraph of Article I, section 1, of the Constitution is an oath of office, the only one in the Constitution, which reads, "I do solemnly swear (or affirm) that I will faithfully execute the office of President of the United States, and will to the best of my ability, preserve, protect and defend the Constitution of the United States."

Nonetheless, the Founders knew that they could see the future only dimly, so they constructed the executive power loosely. As the nation has grown, expanded, and matured, the formal or constitutional powers of the presidency have been supplemented by informal powers that have grown up around them.

The Pardon Power.   Article II, section 2, gives the president the right "to grant reprieves and pardons for offenses against the United States except in cases of impeachment." A **reprieve** is a temporary postponement of the effect of a judicial decision to give the executive time to consider a request for a **pardon**. A pardon, whether awarded before or after a formal judicial finding, wipes the slate clean and makes the recipient of the pardon a "new person" in the eyes of the law.

The importance of the pardon power for the Founders was that it permitted the president to set aside inappropriate or unjust applications of the law. It also gave him a means to forestall or negotiate an early end to rebellions and other popular tumults and to heal wounds left in their wake. Over the course of American political history, pardons have been given to petty criminals and former presidents. Recently, pardons have become increasingly controversial, and presidents, not wishing to appear soft on crime, have granted fewer of them.[7]

The Power to Propose and the Power to Veto.   Article II, section 3, gives the president the right to propose legislation to the Congress for its consideration. It states: "He shall from time to time give to the Congress Information of the State of the Union, and recommend to their Consideration such Measures as he shall judge necessary and expedient." This provision of the Constitution legitimates the president's participation in the early or agenda-setting stage of legislative activity in the Congress.

George Washington (seated) meets with members of his cabinet: From left, Secretary of State Thomas Jefferson, Secretary of the Treasury Alexander Hamilton, Secretary of War Henry Knox, and Attorney General Edmund Randolph (background).

The president's **veto power** (veto is Latin for "I forbid") appears in Article I, section 7, of the Constitution. This provision requires that every bill passed by Congress be presented to the president for his evaluation. If he approves, he signs it, and it becomes law. If he disapproves, he sends the bill back to Congress with his objections. After considering the president's objections, Congress can either repass the original bill by a two-thirds vote in each house, in which case it becomes a law over the president's objections, or it can revise the bill to try to win the president's approval.

reprieve A temporary postponement of the effect of a judicial decision to give the executive time to consider a request for a pardon.

pardon A pardon makes the recipient a new person in the eyes of the law as if no offense had ever been committed.

veto power The president has the right to veto acts of Congress. The act can still become law if both houses pass the bill again by a two-thirds vote.

Overriding a president's veto is difficult. Therefore, the veto is as important as a threat as it is in actual use. Members of Congress who know that the president is opposed to certain provisions of a bill are likely to think about revising those provisions in order to avoid a veto. The veto threat allows the president and his representatives to be involved throughout the legislative process rather than simply at the very beginning and the very end.

The "Take Care" Clause.   Article II, section 3, states that "the president shall take Care that the Laws be faithfully executed." Under normal circumstances, the "take care" clause simply requires that the president efficiently administer the laws that Congress has passed. However, under extraordinary circumstances, such as those that faced President Lincoln as the Civil War approached, presidents have argued that extraordinary actions, even actions outside the law, may be required to save the nation. Not surprisingly, presidents sometimes see extraordinary circumstances where others do not.

The Appointment Power.   Presidents argue that if they are responsible to "take care" that the laws be faithfully executed, they must have the power to appoint and remove officials acting on their behalf. The Founders agreed in part. Article II, section 2, split the **appointment power** as follows: "he shall nominate, and by and with the Advice and Consent of the Senate, shall appoint Ambassadors, other public Ministers and Consuls, Judges of the Supreme Court, and all other Officers of the United States, whose Appointments are not herein otherwise provided for, and which shall be established by Law." The president shares the power of appointing senior officials with the Senate and can appoint officers only to positions previously created by the Congress.

Congress's right to create new positions includes the right to define and limit those positions as it sees fit. Moreover, Article II, section 2, states that "the Congress may by Law vest the Appointment of such inferior Officers, as they think proper, in the President alone, in the Courts of Law, or in the Heads of Departments." The Constitution gives the Congress a prominent role in the appointment power from beginning to end.

Treaty Making and Foreign Affairs.   The Founders sought to involve both the Congress and the president in foreign affairs. Article II, section 2, says the president "shall receive Ambassadors and other public Ministers." This right to receive the envoys of foreign nations has evolved into the important right to recognize and initiate formal relations with the nations of the world.

Article II, section 2, also provides that the president "shall have power, by and with the advice and consent of the Senate, to make treaties, provided two-thirds of the Senators present concur." Presidents have liberally supplemented their **treaty-making power** with **executive agreements**. Executive agreements are negotiated between the president and foreign nations and have the same legal status as treaties but do not require Senate confirmation. On the other hand, they remain in force only during that president's term, unless confirmed or renewed by his or her successor.

appointment power Article II, section 2, of the Constitution empowers the president, often with the advice and consent of the Senate, to appoint many senior government officials.

treaty-making power Article II, section 2, of the Constitution gives the president, with the advice and consent of the Senate, the power to make treaties with foreign nations.

executive agreements Agreements negotiated between the president and foreign governments. Executive agreements have the same legal force as treaties but do not require confirmation by the Senate.

Commander in Chief.   Finally, Article II, section 2, provides that "The President shall be commander in chief of the Army and Navy of the United States, and the Militia of the several States, when called into the actual Service of the United States." The Congress was given the responsibility and power to "raise and support" armies and navies and to "declare war." The Founders were quite clear that the choice of peace and war that had rested with the monarchs of Europe would not be given to the president. The president would be in charge after the armed forces were committed to battle, but the decision of whether or not to commit them would rest with the Congress.[8]

Presidents throughout the nineteenth century, with the significant exceptions of Polk and Lincoln, were scrupulous in their adherence to the maxim that the application of force requires prior approval by the Congress except in response to attack. As we shall see below, twentieth-century presidents have taken a different view.

Constitutional Limitations

Presidents at least since Jefferson have pointed to the separation of powers theory to maintain and justify their autonomy and independent authority. In fact, Jefferson argued that presidents have just as much right and authority to interpret the Constitution, especially in regard to presidential powers, as the courts do. Chief Justice John Marshall disagreed and said so authoritatively in the landmark case of *Marbury v. Madison* (1803). Nonetheless, presidents continue to argue that their powers should be construed broadly.

Beginning with Eisenhower, but more formally with Nixon, presidents have claimed and the Supreme Court has recognized a sphere of **executive privilege**—the rights of presidents and their advisers to maintain the confidentiality of their conversations and communications. But the Founders blurred separation of powers to assure adequate checks and balances by giving each branch a role in the other branch's activities. Hence, when Congress calls for information from the executive in pursuit of its oversight responsibilities and the president responds by citing executive privilege, the stage is set for protracted negotiations or legal arguments, often both.

executive privilege The right of presidents, recognized by the Supreme Court, to keep conversations and communications with their advisers confidential.

Congress and the Courts.   The departments and agencies of the executive branch are subject to the simultaneous oversight of Congress, the courts, and the president. Every element of the executive branch, every bureau, agency, and department, was founded and its authority and jurisdiction created by an act of Congress signed by the president. Each year their programmatic responsibilities and authorized personnel levels are reduced, confirmed, or expanded by Congress. Moreover, Congress maintains oversight of the bureaucracy, inquiring into whether programs are being implemented as intended.

The courts play a major but less well-recognized role in overseeing the executive branch. First, courts regularly interpret the meanings of the constitution, laws, executive orders, and bureaucratic regulations. Second, when a presidential instruction or executive order conflicts with a law passed by the Congress, officials are bound to enforce the law, and courts will force them to do so if they are reluctant.

Most citizens assume that the president is "in charge" of the executive branch in some direct and unambiguous sense. In fact, the president and the Congress struggle to control the bureaucracy while the courts act as arbiters to ensure that the struggle takes place on the basis of the legal authorities of both branches. This process was on particularly stark display in regard to the Bush administration's Iraq and terrorism policies and the Obama administration's foreign and domestic surveillance programs. In emergencies, presidents have the initiative, but as the emergency fades Congress holds inquiries and hearings into the actions taken, the courts pronounce upon their ultimate legality and constitutionality, and the public forms its judgments.[9]

The Impeachment Process.   If the president struggles too hard to sustain his own autonomy and influence, or if he steps outside the law, Congress has a final card to play—**impeachment**. Impeachment is the process by which Congress can remove officers of the national government, including the president. Article I, section 2, places "the sole Power of Impeachment," that is, formulating the statement of charges of wrongdoing, in the House of Representatives. Article I, section 3, declares that "The Senate shall have the sole Power to try all impeachments" and that "When the President of the United States is tried, the Chief Justice shall preside."

> **impeachment** The process of removing national government officials from office. The House votes a statement of particulars or charges, and a trial is conducted in the Senate.

Impeachment begins when the House votes a set of charges and proceeds to a trial on the charges conducted in the Senate. A two-thirds vote among senators present is required to convict, and punishment extends only to removal from office and a prohibition against further national government service. Offenders are, however, subject to additional action in the state and federal courts. Only nineteen officers of the national government, including Presidents Andrew Johnson and Bill Clinton, one senator, one cabinet officer, and fifteen federal judges, have been impeached by the House, and only eight federal judges have actually been convicted in the Senate.

THE GROWTH OF PRESIDENTIAL POWER

> **Q3** What forces account for the growth of executive power over the course of American political history?

The Founders were both determined that the president provide energy, focus, and direction to the government and concerned that he work with the Congress and the courts within a framework of law. Therefore, they required the president to share most of his powers and authority with the Congress. Nonetheless, many of the Founders feared that executive power would expand and grow over time and would in the end become overbearing. (See Appendix E in the back of this book for a chronological list of the presidents from Washington to Obama.)

In fact, presidential power remained largely within its constitutional bounds during the nineteenth century.[10] However, the twentieth century

AP images / Ken Lambert

Every president hopes to be remembered among the greats. Only a few are, but the image-makers never stop trying. Here President Bush was carefully positioned at Mount Rushmore to suggest how well he would fit there. History had other ideas.

brought domestic and international crises that demanded bold and concerted actions for which the executive seemed best fitted. Modern presidents in wartime including Franklin Roosevelt, Harry Truman, Lyndon Johnson, Richard Nixon, and George W. Bush have been accused of harboring imperial aspirations. A quick look at Figure 10.1 suggests that greatness requires a great challenge—revolution, civil war, depression and world war—for a president to meet and overcome. Presidential failure comes from facing great challenges ineffectually.

The Early Pattern: Presidential–Congressional Relations

The Constitution provided little guidance for how presidents and their representatives should deal with the Congress. President Washington was very careful and correct in his dealings with the Congress because he knew that traditions were being set and precedents established by his every action. Congress was similarly careful. Both knew that the questions of whether the president would lead or follow the Congress and just what the balance of initiative, consultation and influence between them would be were unclear.

Washington's initial view of the presidency was as a point of non-partisan unity around which the nation might rally. He expected to seek the

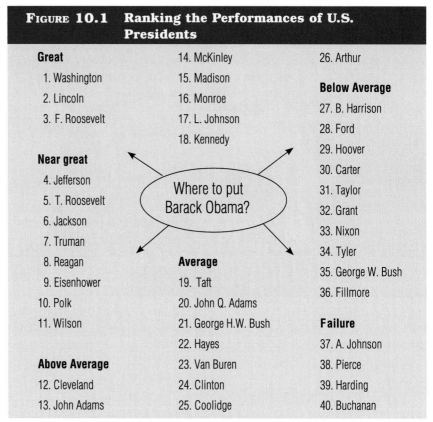

FIGURE 10.1 Ranking the Performances of U.S. Presidents

Great

1. Washington
2. Lincoln
3. F. Roosevelt

Near great

4. Jefferson
5. T. Roosevelt
6. Jackson
7. Truman
8. Reagan
9. Eisenhower
10. Polk
11. Wilson

Above Average

12. Cleveland
13. John Adams

14. McKinley
15. Madison
16. Monroe
17. L. Johnson
18. Kennedy

Where to put Barack Obama?

Average

19. Taft
20. John Q. Adams
21. George H.W. Bush
22. Hayes
23. Van Buren
24. Clinton
25. Coolidge

26. Arthur

Below Average

27. B. Harrison
28. Ford
29. Hoover
30. Carter
31. Taylor
32. Grant
33. Nixon
34. Tyler
35. George W. Bush
36. Fillmore

Failure

37. A. Johnson
38. Pierce
39. Harding
40. Buchanan

Notes: A survey polled 78 scholars—representing a balance of liberals and conservatives—to rank the U.S. presidents from best to worst. William Harrison and James Garfield served for less than a year and are not ranked.

Source: Harold W. Stanley and Richard G. Niemi, *Vital Statistics on American Politics, 2013–2014* (Washington, D.C.: CQ Press, 2013), Table 6.2, 242–243.

advice of his cabinet and arbitrate any debates that might arise on the way to establishing an administration position to submit to the Congress's consideration. Washington expected squabbling in Congress, the legislators were state and local representatives after all, but he did not expect factions to form within his own cabinet.

President Washington's expectations did not survive his first term in office. When Washington sought early in his administration to consult with the Senate about certain aspects of a treaty then being negotiated with the southern Indian tribes, he simply arranged to attend the Senate so that he could pose his questions directly and hear senators' advice. The senators declined to engage the president in direct conversation, wishing instead to receive written questions that they could ponder and discuss among themselves outside of the imposing presence of the president.[11] Washington took offense and never again sought the "advice and consent" of the Senate in person.

On the other hand, the first Congress was guided in its domestic policy-making by a series of detailed reports and legislative proposals prepared by Secretary of the Treasury Alexander Hamilton. Hamilton prepared reports on the domestic economy, tariffs, and the debt, developed bills to address these critical issues, and then coordinated the administration's allies in Congress as they secured passage of the bills. At the height of his influence in the early 1790s, Hamilton seemed to serve as Washington's "prime minister," the leading member of the cabinet and leader of the administration's majority in Congress.

The Jeffersonian Legacy: Congressional Dominance, 1800–1900

As the scope of Hamilton's economic program became clear, Thomas Jefferson, then serving as Washington's secretary of state, and James Madison, one of the leading members in the House, began to organize a systematic opposition. When Washington left the presidency after two terms, Jefferson stood against Vice President John Adams for election as president. Although Adams won, Jefferson finished second and, under the rules of the day, became vice president. Jefferson stood against Adams again in 1800 and defeated him.

Jefferson and his party colleagues were more wary of executive authority than Hamilton and the Federalists had been. In fact, Jeffersonian theory held that the lawmaking authority resided in Congress and was not to be unduly subject to executive influence.[12] During the nineteenth century, Congress, not the president, dealt with the dominant issues of the day: commerce and tariffs, currency and taxation, slavery, sectionalism, and expansion. Presidents rarely gave partisan speeches, campaigned actively for office, or offered legislative programs if elected. The twentieth century would make new demands on the American presidency.

The Modern Presidency, 1901–Present

By the beginning of the twentieth century, the United States was becoming an industrial power with international political and economic interests, but it was not yet a significant military power. The first third of the twentieth century brought threats, both at home and abroad, that demanded immediate and decisive action. Presidents like Theodore Roosevelt, Woodrow Wilson, and Franklin Roosevelt drew power to themselves when Congress was slow to respond.

Theodore Roosevelt is generally credited with expanding presidential power both by how he acted in office, "speak softly [which he did not do] but carry a big stick [which he did do]," as well as how he understood the office. TR articulated what has come to be known as the "stewardship theory" of the presidency. In this view, the president is the nation's elected leader and steward of its security and its future prospects and promise. Following Lincoln, TR argued that "the executive power was limited only by specific restrictions

AP Photo

President Franklin Delano Roosevelt, an early master of radio, was famous for his "fireside chats" with the American people during the darkest days of the Great Depression.

appearing in the Constitution or imposed by Congress under its constitutional powers."

TR's hand-picked successor, William Howard Taft, took a more traditional view, arguing that presidents had "no residuum of power which he can exercise because it seems to him to be in the public interest." Taft's successor, the Democrat Woodrow Wilson, agreed with TR, declaring that the president "is at liberty, both in law and conscience, to be as big a man as he can. His capacity will set the limit." Taft was looking backward to the limited presidency of the nineteenth century; TR and Wilson were heralding the new plebiscitary presidency of the twentieth century.

The greater visibility and broader responsibilities of the president seemed to call for institutional reform. Presidents found that they needed help to lead. During the 1930s a reform commission under the leadership of Louis Brownlow reported that the "canons of efficient government require the responsible and effective chief executive as the center of energy, direction, and administrative management."[13] The commission delivered its report to President Roosevelt in January 1937, and just over two years later Congress approved the Reorganization Act of 1939 that established the Executive Office of the President (EOP) and provided additional staff assistance to the president.

The dominant role of the presidency in American politics at mid-century was a reflection of FDR's dramatic responses to the Depression and World

War II. In domestic politics, Roosevelt bullied the Congress and courts into approving his legislation, but they did, in fact, approve it. In foreign affairs, Roosevelt took a number of actions between 1939 and American entry into the war late in 1941 that were constitutionally dubious. His shoot-on-sight order to American naval forces convoying supplies to England moved the United States to the brink of war. Even more starkly, President Truman's order in 1950 to American air and naval forces to assist the South Koreans against the invading North Koreans was taken unilaterally.[14] Both Roosevelt and Truman informed congressional leaders of what they intended to do, but neither sought congressional advice and counsel before acting.

Where Was the Expanded Authority Found?

Where have the vast new executive powers that have arisen since World War II been found? Generally they have been found outside the Constitution, in **inherent powers** associated with sovereignty and nationhood, in congressional acts and judicial interpretations, and in enlarged public expectations.

inherent powers Powers accruing to all sovereign nations, whether or not specified in the Constitution, allowing executives to take actions required to defend the nation and protect its interests.

Presidents, most prominently Lincoln, FDR, and George W. Bush, have argued that sovereign nations under great threat or operating in the international system have broad rights of self-defense. Inherent powers allow the president to take actions required to protect and defend the nation, whether those actions are explicitly sanctioned by existing law or not. The logic is that it makes no sense to scrupulously adhere to law and procedure if the nation is gravely harmed or destroyed in the process.

Since 1937, the Supreme Court has been willing to sanction extensive government regulation of the economy and of social life. In response to the Court's newly permissive view, Congress transferred vast areas of authority to the president. For example, the Employment Act of 1946 charged the president to "foster and promote free competitive enterprise, to avoid economic fluctuations or to diminish the effects thereof, and to maintain employment, production, and purchasing power."

In foreign and military affairs, Congress's broad authorization of presidential initiative in the Gulf of Tonkin Resolution to carry out the Vietnam War seemed to expand executive authority still further. By the 1970s scholars, politicians, and citizens were warning of an "imperial presidency."[15] Congress's joint resolution of September 14, 2001, broadly authorizing President Bush to "use all necessary and appropriate force" against threats posed by international terrorism raised these questions anew.[16]

THE RANGE OF PRESIDENTIAL RESPONSIBILITIES

Q4 Why does the president have an easier time in shaping and implementing foreign policy than he does domestic policy?

The range of presidential responsibility today is very broad. In domestic affairs, the president acts as chief executive, chief legislator, party leader, and leader of the nation. In foreign affairs, the president acts as commander in chief, chief diplomat, and chief trade negotiator. In a few of these areas, the president has formal constitutional and legal powers that give him a strong position from which to act. However, in most cases, he has only informal powers that give him the right, sometimes merely the opportunity, to be involved and the leverage to affect outcomes but leave him far short of being able to dictate or control events.

Richard Neustadt's classic study, *Presidential Power*, first published in 1960, described "the power to persuade" as the core of presidential leadership.[17] Neustadt pointed out that presidents can rarely command; usually, they have to bargain, compromise, cajole, and inspire to get their way. Presidents must have the political skill to recognize and seize upon opportunities to lead. Presidents must also have a vision that they are capable of communicating and they must be seen as honest, determined, and resilient, as persons who will hold to a course, bounce back from inevitable adversity, and keep moving forward. If they lose the confidence of the people, they lose the ability to lead.

Nonetheless, Aaron Wildavsky's famous essay entitled "The Two Presidencies" pointed out that even highly skilled presidents find it more difficult to lead in domestic policy than in foreign policy.[18] Public opinion, to say nothing of congressional opinion, is commonly split in regard to domestic policy issues. Most things that a president might propose to do with taxes, social security, health care, or environmental policy will generate support from some and opposition from others. Moreover, many interest groups and both major parties have established positions on most of the domestic policy issues of moment, so a fight is virtually guaranteed.

In foreign policy, the president is usually thought to have more current and often more relevant information than either the Congress or the public. The interest group structure involved in foreign affairs is much thinner than that involved in domestic affairs, and most foreign policy conflicts are interpreted as us-against-them events to which citizens respond with a rally-round-the-flag reaction of automatic support for the U.S. position. The relatively free hand that President George W. Bush had in preparing for and conducting the early stages of the wars in Afghanistan and Iraq are excellent examples of this phenomenon. Whereas presidential initiatives in domestic policy tend to be judged immediately, foreign policy initiatives tend to be judged as they play out—well or badly.

The Domestic Policy Presidency

Winning the presidential election opens a window of opportunity to act as national leader, to claim a popular mandate and to govern. The popular mandate of national leader may be extended to early legislative leadership if the new president hits the ground running and is in position to move his program quickly into and through the Congress. In 2001, for example, newly elected President George W. Bush won an extensive package of tax cuts and his No Child Left Behind education bill. President Obama's first priority was economic stabilization, followed by major initiatives on economic stimulus and

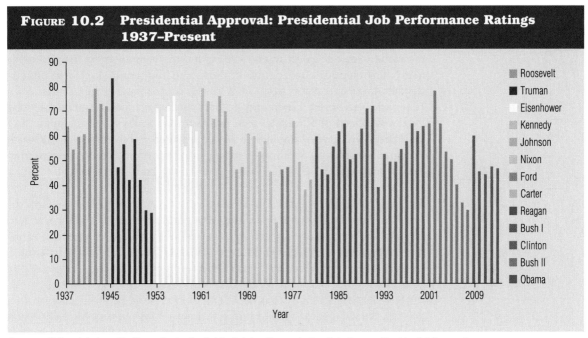

FIGURE 10.2   Presidential Approval: Presidential Job Performance Ratings 1937–Present

Source: Gallup data from the Roper Center for Public Opinion Research. See Data Access, Presidential Approval.

health care. As with most new administrations, some urged a broad assault on all of the major campaign priorities, while others urged winning on one or two major issues before tackling the others.

Each new president knows that he must strike quickly because his clout is likely to decline over time. He knows that nearly half, sometimes more than half, of the members of Congress stand in determined partisan opposition to his program and that many members of his own party have reservations about his ideas and have their own interests to protect and pursue. And finally, the president knows that most of the 2.7 million civilian employees of the federal government are going to do pretty much the same thing the day after he takes office as they did the day before he took office.

A president winning election to a second term faces more limited opportunities. While President George W. Bush claimed that he had "earned political capital" in his 2004 reelection that he intended to spend, his top legislative initiative of 2005, social security reform, immediately ran into a brick wall of public and partisan opposition. In 2012, President Obama won a second term relatively easily, but immigration reform, his top priority, died in the House. Second-term presidents, even assuming they have not used all of their good ideas in the first term, are known quantities: the public has already made judgments about them, their opponents have taken some licks and are looking for revenge and before long, everyone is looking past them as the next presidential election heats up.

Nonetheless, modern presidents have tools for keeping in touch with the public that earlier presidents simply did not have. Franklin Roosevelt made excellent use of the new radio technology in the 1930s and John Kennedy did the same with television in the 1960s. Today's technology gives presidents many new channels for communication with the public. President Obama has held town hall events from the White House via the Internet, Twitter, You-Tube, and Facebook.[19] There are, of course, dangers for presidents in these lightly mediated public exchanges. For example, in President Obama's 2011 YouTube Q&A, 198 of the 200 most highly rated questions had to do with marijuana regulation and drug policy.[20] Who says young people are not interested in politics?

National Leader.   A president's most important relationship is with the American people. Their votes put him into office, their votes can return him to office, and their approval gives him the momentum and confidence to govern. A president who is riding high in the polls is more likely to hold news conferences, make major speeches around the country and to the Congress, and generally try to set the tone for national politics.[21]

However, the strength that presidents derive from opinion polls is often fleeting. Barack Obama's job approval ratings fell from a very healthy 68 percent as he entered the presidency to 50 percent at the end of his first year. Most presidents enter office with job approval ratings at or above 60 percent, but in the last 70 years only four presidents, Franklin Roosevelt, Dwight Eisenhower, Ronald Reagan, and Bill Clinton, left office with approval ratings over 50 percent. Only Bill Clinton left office with higher ratings than he had in his first year. While it is better to be popular than not, high public approval ratings change the presidential–congressional dynamic only marginally. A member of Congress weighing a popular president's desire for support on an issue that most of his or her constituents oppose is unlikely to be swayed much by the president's general popularity.[22]

Chief Executive.   The civics book view of the president is that he supervises the work of the departments and agencies of the executive branch of the national government. His supervision of the executive branch is grounded in the right to appoint, with the advice and consent of the Senate, the leaders of the departments and agencies, propose policies and programs, and oversee their implementation after they are passed into law. The Bush administration challenged this traditional view with its unitary executive theory, but by 2006 Congress and the courts had reasserted the traditional separation of powers view.

Senator and candidate Obama was critical of the Bush administration, but as president he has found that an expansive view of presidential power does have its charms. As a former constitutional law professor and a new president, Obama said he would use signing statements with "restraint" and only in cases where he had "well-founded constitutional objections." In fact, President Obama has employed signing statements only about one-fifth as often as President Bush did.[23]

Doug Mills / *New York Times* / Redux

Presidents have to campaign forcefully to win office and then they have to campaign just as forcefully to rally the American people, or at least their party's faithful, behind their agenda and program.

The executive branch of the national government employs civilian workers in offices scattered all over the country. These civilian employees of the national government work for fifteen major departments and 140 separate agencies. The departments range in size from 765,000 in the Department of Defense to 4,300 in the Department of Education. The departments cover such diverse fields as homeland security, foreign policy, health care, and management of the nation's public lands.

The president's control of this massive and far-flung bureaucracy hinges on his right to control the appointments and subsequent conduct in office of 3,400 senior policymakers. These political appointees serve at the pleasure of the president and are subject to removal at his discretion. The president also has the right to move within or between agencies about 8,500 members (grades 16 through 18) of the Senior Executive Service. Below the political appointees and the Senior Executive Service are nearly 2.7 million career civil servants who work in and are protected by the merit-based civil service system.

Chief Legislator.   The idea that the president should be the nation's chief legislator is a new one. Until 1921, the executive departments and agencies submitted their own budgetary requests and legislative

Struggling Toward Democracy

Congress has not declared war since 1941 in the wake of the Japanese attack on Pearl Harbor. Yet we have engaged in a lot of conflict and several major wars—Korea, Vietnam, Iraq, Afghanistan—since 1941.
What do you think?
- Is the American way of going to war broken?
- If so, is there a democratic way of going to war in the modern world?

proposals to the Congress. Creation of the Bureau of the Budget in 1921 gave the president the institutional tools to exercise better control over budgeting and policy development.

The modern president's legislative leadership hinges on the fact that each year he prepares a budget and a legislative program and submits them to Congress for consideration. The president and his representatives lobby for his program and against proposals that conflict with it, trading favors to get what they want and threatening vetoes when it looks like they might lose.

In general, presidents have more legislative success early in their terms than they do later. Political scientist Paul Light found that new presidents since 1960 have enjoyed 72 percent success rates on bills sent to Congress between January and March of their first years, 39 percent on bills sent between April and June, and 25 percent on bills sent between July and December.[24] Light also showed that a new president's prospects are enhanced not only by acting quickly but also by having a clear substantive focus and message.

Presidents depend on their legislative liaison staffs to keep them in touch with Congress and to structure the trades, bargains, and compromises necessary to nudge their bills through the process. Still, presidents frequently are reduced to bargaining behind the threat or actual use of their veto power. Some presidents have depended on the veto much more heavily than others, but for all presidents it represents significant leverage in their dealings with Congress (see Table 10.1).

TABLE 10.1   Presidential Vetoes and Overrides, 1933–2014

President	Number of Bills Vetoed	Number of Vetoes Overridden	Percent of Vetoes Overridden
Roosevelt	635	9	1.4
Truman	250	12	4.8
Eisenhower	181	2	1.1
Kennedy	21	0	0
Johnson	30	0	0
Nixon	43	7	16.3
Ford	66	12	18.2
Carter	31	2	.5
Reagan	78	9	11.5
Bush	46	1	2.2
Clinton	37	2	6.0
Bush	12	4	33
Obama	4	0	0

Source: Harold W. Stanley and Richard W. Niemi, *Vital Statistics on American Politics, 2013–2014* (Washington, D.C.: Congressional Quarterly, 2013), Table 6.9, 255–256. See also http://www.presidency.ucsb.edu/data/vetoes.php

President Bush took a different tack. He cast his first veto on a bill designed to broaden access for federal funds for stem cell research on July 19, 2006, nearly six years into his presidency. By the time he cast his first veto, he had bargained behind the threat of a veto at least 135 times. More importantly, he issued signing statements challenging 1,200 sections of bills passed by Congress, more than all previous administrations combined.[25] Previous presidents used signing statements to claim credit for the passage of a law or to provide their sense of the law's meaning and import. The Bush administration used signing statements to declare that provisions that it believed intrude on executive authority are not binding on the president. Michelle Broadman of the Justice Department's Office of Legal Counsel said, "The president must execute the laws faithfully, but the Constitution is the highest law of the land. If the Constitution and the law conflict, the president must choose."[26]

Critics contend that signing statements intrude on Congress's lawmaking power and on the federal courts' right to declare what is and is not constitutional. In July 2006, an American Bar Association panel declared signing statements to be "contrary to the rule of law and our constitutional system of separation of powers. . . . The President's constitutional duty is to enforce laws he has signed into being unless and until they are held unconstitutional by the Supreme Court. . . . The Constitution is not what the President says it is."[27] As we saw earlier, this is an old debate, running back to Thomas Jefferson and John Marshall, but very much alive today. President Obama issued eight signing statements in his first year in office.

Party Leader. The president is the titular leader of his party and does have some influence over its activities. He gets to select the party's national leaders including the national party chairman and he can affect though often he cannot absolutely determine the positions taken by the national party in its platform and other statements. However, the president does not control his party members in Congress; they select their own leaders, take positions determined in their own caucuses, and control their own campaign resources. The president exercises even less control over his party at the state and local levels; they recruit their own candidates and design and run their own campaigns. The president makes no attempt to control his party below the level of the national apparatus.

The Foreign Policy Presidency

During most of the nineteenth century, presidents took the initiative in foreign policy generally but left decisions concerning the use of force to Congress. Since the early twentieth century, presidents have increasingly held sway over all of foreign policy including the use of force. Presidents argued and Congress generally agreed that the heightened global dangers of the modern world, the president's ability to act quickly, and his superior sources of information and access to expertise make him the dominant force in U.S. foreign policy. Every president since Truman has deployed U.S. forces around the world and even moved them toward and into conflict situations on his own authority.[28]

Commander in Chief.   The president commands U.S. armed forces during war and peace. He commissions the officer corps and nominates its members for promotion; deploys troops, ships, and other military assets as seems most reasonable; and participates in setting overall military and defense strategy. However, the Constitution gives to Congress the right "to declare war" and the power to regulate all of the president's activities through the power of the purse. Hence, the president and Congress have struggled over the meaning and boundaries of the president's role as commander in chief.

Two key aspects of the post-World War II period led to broad changes in the constitutional positions of Congress and the president in regard to war making. First, in the wake of World War II, presidents negotiated and Congresses approved and provided funds for a worldwide network of defense treaties including NATO, SEATO, CENTO, ANZUS, and the Rio Pact that obligated the United States to come to the aid of member nations if they were attacked.

Second, the U.S. policy of "containment" directed against the Soviet Union, China, and communism in general was central to our Cold War strategy. Opinion leaders in and out of government as well as the general public were convinced that the United States was engaged in a worldwide struggle against communism (today you could substitute radical Islam for communism). Presidents were thought only to be acting responsibly as they moved American military assets around the world to have them always in position where they might be most needed. Increasingly, presidents came to argue that their powers as commanders in chief gave them the constitutional right to initiate hostilities and to determine their scope and duration. Congress's reaction to the implications of presidential war making in Vietnam was to pass the **War Powers Resolution** in 1973. Nonetheless, a workable balance between legislative and executive influence over war making has been elusive (see Pro and Con box).

President George W. Bush went to Congress and the United Nations prior to the 2003 Iraq war. A compliant Congress, with most Democrats joining all of the Republicans in both the House and Senate, gave the president authority to use force if he deemed it necessary to control the dangers posed by Saddam Hussein. Failing to receive the full support of the United Nations Security Council, Bush declared Iraq to be a gathering danger and launched the war in March 2003.

Although the Republican Congress initially was reluctant to set limits on President Bush's claims to broad powers as commander in chief in wartime, the Supreme Court rejected some of his claims. Throughout the Afghan and Iraq wars, the Bush administration claimed that the president as commander in chief could hold "enemy combatants" including American citizens for the duration of the conflict, with no access to lawyers or courts, and try them in military tribunals as he thought best. In a series of cases in

War Powers Resolution
Passed in Congress in 1973 requiring the president to consult with Congress on the use of force and to withdraw U.S. forces from conflict should congressional approval not be forthcoming.

Pro & Con

Must Presidents Have the Initiative in War Making?

Article I, section 8, declares that "the Congress shall have Power . . . to declare War," whereas Article II, section 2, says that "the President shall be Commander in Chief of the Army and Navy." The president is, of course, empowered to respond to attacks on the United States because an attack would initiate a state of war and render Congress's "declaration" unnecessary.

That logic seemed to work through the middle of the twentieth century. But every president of the past sixty years has argued that U.S. involvement in international collective security organizations like the UN and NATO, along with the stationing of U.S. military forces on bases and at sea around the world, means that U.S. interests, territory, and sovereignty are exposed and in essence constantly engaged. Presidents also contend that they have the right to move American troops, planes, ships, and equipment around the world to where they are most likely to be needed. Finally, they contend that an attack on an American treaty ally or on American forces, citizens, or interests anywhere in the world is an attack on the United States and permits action by the president as commander in chief.

What room is left for Congress in decisions about going to war? Congress tried to answer that question in 1973 by passing, over President Nixon's veto, the **War Powers Resolution** designed to reassert Congress's role in authorizing the use of U.S. military force in the world. Effectively, Congress offered to give up its right to prior approval to gain some leverage over how long presidential uses of force could be sustained without congressional approval.

The War Powers Resolution contains three key provisions:

1. Section 3 requires that "The President in every possible instance shall consult with Congress before introducing United States Armed Forces into hostilities or into situations where imminent involvement in hostilities is clearly indicated."
2. Section 4 requires that when U.S. forces are engaged, "the President shall submit within 48 hours" to the Congress information concerning "the circumstances necessitating the introduction; . . . the constitutional and legislative authority under which such introduction took place; . . . the estimated scope and duration of the hostilities or involvement."
3. Section 5 requires that "within 60 calendar days" of the submission of the report mentioned in point 2, "the President shall terminate any use of United States Armed Forces . . . unless the Congress" agrees.

No president has ever acknowledged the constitutionality of the War Powers Resolution. Each has argued that his powers as commander in chief are sufficient to deploy U.S. armed forces around the world and that participation in congressionally approved collective security regimes like the United Nations permits presidents to use force in defense of U.S. interests and those of our allies.

What do you think?
- What should the respective roles of Congress and the president be in determining the use of U.S. military force in the world?
- Is Congress too addled, divided, and slow to play a credible role in decisions on such critical matters?
- After the performances of Presidents Johnson and Nixon in regard to Vietnam and Bush in regard to Iraq, how can we be confident that presidents will use good judgment?

PRO	CON
Modern conflicts happen too fast for debate	The constitution says congress shall declare war
U.S. Interests are engaged globally	Conflict rarely breaks out without warning
International agreements contain security commitments	Consultation with congress is still required

2004, the Supreme Court reminded the Bush administration that "a state of war is not a blank check for the president when it comes to the rights of the nation's citizens."[29]

In 2006, the Supreme Court struck down the Bush administration's plan to try Guantanamo detainees before military commissions. The Court found that the proposed commissions were not authorized by Congress and rejected the administration's contention that the federal courts had no jurisdiction to hear the case. Justice John Paul Stevens, writing for the Court's majority, declared, "The executive is bound to comply with the rule of law that prevails in this jurisdiction."[30] In 2008 the Court affirmed the right of detainees to have access to U.S. courts, but Congress has blocked the Obama administration from bringing detainees to trial in U.S. federal courts.

Chief Diplomat.   The president and Congress share control of our relations with other nations. The president has the initiative in nominating U.S. ambassadors to other nations as well as the leading members of the policymaking teams at the Departments of State and Defense and the National Security Council and in negotiating treaties and multilateral agreements with other nations. The Senate must confirm or reject the president's nominations and actions, and the House and Senate both must agree to provide necessary funds.

Congress can also make policy on a whole range of matters including foreign aid, trade, immigration, and intellectual property that affect our relations with the rest of the world. Alternatively, the president can use executive agreements instead of treaties to bypass Congress on issues when he thinks they are important but anticipates trouble with Congress. Not surprisingly, presidents prefer executive agreements to formal treaties (see Table 10.2).

Chief Trade Negotiator.   As markets and trade have become global, the president's role as chief trade negotiator has become more important. Most economists agree that global free trade benefits consumers by providing them access to high-quality goods at competitive prices. However, imports challenge domestic goods and the businesses and workers that produce them. Decline in the U.S. share of the world market in sectors like steel, autos, and electronics in recent decades highlighted some of the negative impacts of free trade. Public opinion generally favors protection of U.S. markets and interests, and Congress gave the president new powers to punish unfair international trade practices.

The United States has pursued a two-track international trade strategy. One track has been to pursue bilateral negotiations with nations such as Taiwan, Japan, and China with which the United States has a significant trade deficit to ensure that their markets are as open to U.S. goods as our markets are to their goods. A second track has been to pursue multilateral trade agreements that lower trade barriers either regionally or globally. Both strategies were successful during the second half of the twentieth century, although global trade negotiations have lagged since 2001. However, protectionist sentiment remains prominent, particularly among businesses and workers who believe that they are

TABLE 10.2	Treaties and Executive Agreements, 1789–2014	
Period	Number of Treaties	Number of Executive Agreements
1789–1839	60	27
1839–1889	215	238
1889–1932	431	804
1933–1944 (F. Roosevelt)	131	369
1945–1952 (Truman)	132	1,324
1953–1960 (Eisenhower)	89	1,834
1961–1963 (Kennedy)	36	813
1964–1968 (Johnson)	67	1,083
1969–1974 (Nixon)	93	1,317
1975–1976 (Ford)	26	666
1977–1980 (Carter)	79	1,476
1981–1988 (Reagan)	125	2,840
1989–1992 (Bush 41)	67	1,350
1993–2000 (Clinton)	209	2,048
2001–2008 (Bush 43)	147	1,990
2009–2014 (Obama)	20	1182

Sources: Harold W. Stanley and Richard G. Niemi, *Vital Statistics on American Politics, 2013–2014* (Washington, D.C.: Congressional Quarterly Press, 2014), Table 9.1, 345; Office of the Assistant Legal Adviser for Treaty Affairs, U.S. Department of State, Washington, D.C.

suffering from foreign competition. In the 2012 campaign, Republicans generally held to a free trade agenda while Democrats promised "fair trade" that would offer greater protection to American jobs.

Presidents must juggle all of these responsibilities, domestic and foreign, in periods of calm and crisis, while maintaining their relationships with and support among the American people. Obviously, presidents need help. How do presidents organize their offices and staff support to ensure that they get the advice and information they need to make all of the choices and decisions that come before them?

Q5 Should we be concerned that White House staff members have replaced members of the cabinet as the president's closest advisers?

THE PRESIDENTIAL ESTABLISHMENT

Most presidents come into office promising "cabinet government," that is, that they will look to members of their **cabinet** as their most prominent sources of advice. However, it does not take long for presidents to realize that they do not know or trust their cabinet secretaries nearly as much as they do their senior White House aides. Senior White House aides are totally dedicated to the president, whereas cabinet secretaries must represent a broader

cabinet The secretaries of the fifteen executive departments and other officials designated by the president. The cabinet is available to consult with the president.

range of interests. Therefore, most presidents leave office having abandoned any pretense of cabinet government in favor of a tight circle of senior advisers from the White House staff. President Obama made no early pretense of cabinet government, depending instead on a strong White House staff from the beginning.[31]

The Executive Office of the President

Executive Office of the President (EOP) Established in 1939, the EOP houses the professional support personnel working for the president.

The **Executive Office of the President (EOP)** was established in 1939 as part of an attempt to ensure that the president had adequate staff support. The EOP was to consist of six administrative assistants and three advisory boards. Today the EOP consists of nearly 1,700 professionals who assist the president in his relations with the bureaucracy, the Congress, interest groups, the media, and the public. Figure 10.3 illustrates the EOP.

Organizationally, the White House staff falls within the EOP and is its nerve center. Other key offices in the EOP are the Office of Management and Budget and the National Security Council.

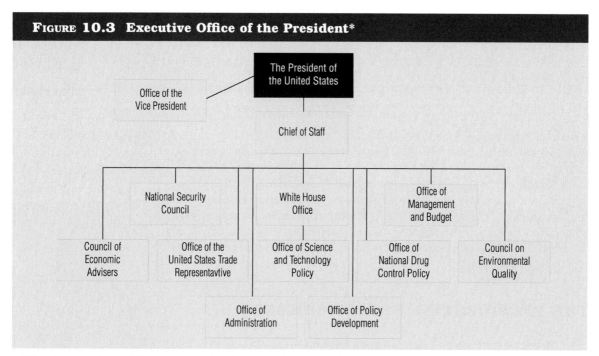

FIGURE 10.3 Executive Office of the President*

* There is no formal or legal hierarchy among the offices within the Executive Office of the President, but there are patterns of greater and lesser influence. The top tier of offices is generally more influential than the lower tiers. Nonetheless, even among the top officials including the Vice President, Chief of Staff, National Security Adviser, and Office of Management and Budget Director, much depends upon the ease and frequency of access to the President.

Source: U.S. Government Manual, 2013 (Washington, D.C.: U.S. Government Printing Office, 2013), 21.

The White House Staff. Although each president organizes his staff as he thinks appropriate, there have been two broad approaches to staff organization at least since Franklin Roosevelt. Roosevelt organized his staff on the model of a wheel on which each spoke, each key staffer, led directly to the president. Roosevelt even assigned overlapping responsibilities to his aides so that he would never be dependent on information and advice from a single source. Truman, Kennedy, Johnson, Carter, and Clinton followed similar designs.

Eisenhower used a hierarchical staff design, familiar from his military experience, in which lines of authority and reporting were clear, with a dominant Chief of Staff who served as gatekeeper to the president. Nixon followed an even more rigidly hierarchical system, whereas Reagan initially employed the "troika" of James Baker, Edwin Meese, and Michael Deaver in place of a single Chief of Staff.

Like Eisenhower, President George W. Bush named a seasoned and influential cabinet including Colin Powell at State and Donald Rumsfeld at Defense, and sought to lean on them for advice and counsel. Bush's White House staff revolved around the efficient and discrete Chief of Staff, Andrew Card, and Karl Rove, the president's long-time political adviser and strategist. What made the Bush first term distinctive was the outsized role, often behind the scenes, but still unmistakable, of Vice President Dick Cheney.

Former New York Governor Mario Cuomo once said that politicians campaign in poetry and govern in prose. In this cartoon, President Obama finds out just how difficult governing is.

The Obama cabinet looked a lot like George W. Bush's first term cabinet. Similarities to the Bush cabinet included powerful figures like Hillary Clinton at State, and the Republican holdover Robert Gates at Defense. In 2011, Gates retired and was replaced by an equally experienced Washington hand in the person of Leon Panetta. On the White House staff were longtime counselor and policy aide Valerie Jarrett, and David Axelrod, the political strategist from the 2008 campaign. President Obama's first Chief of Staff was the gruff, demanding, and sometimes profane Rahm Emanuel, a former Clinton White House staffer, and top House leader. Emanuel resigned in late 2010 to return to Chicago and run, successfully, for mayor. His successors, all lower key inside players, were Pete Rouse, Bill Daley, and Jack Lew.[32] Vice President Joe Biden, former five term senator from Delaware and a foreign and domestic policy expert, played the role of senior adviser and counselor, rather than the independent power center and policy shop that Dick Cheney had made of his office.

Obama's second term team highlighted political allies and trusted staff aides that he had worked with for a long time. Massachusetts Senator John Kerry, an early endorser on Obama's first presidential campaign, replaced Hillary Clinton at the State Department. Jack Lew, a former OMB director and White House Chief of Staff, replaced Timothy Geithner at Treasury. In something of a departure from pattern, Obama named former Nebraska Senator Chuck Hagel, a Republican, as Defense Secretary. Inside the White House, long-time aides were promoted to new positions. Denis McDonough became Chief of Staff, Susan Rice replaced McDonough as National Security Advisor, and Rob Nabors, formerly Obama's congressional liaison, became Deputy Chief of Staff. Finally, when the flawed rollout of Obamacare disrupted the first year of the second term, Phil Schiliro, Obama's first congressional liaison, returned to manage the administration's critical health care initiatives.

No matter how the White House staff is organized, its job is to get the right people and information to the president in a timely fashion and in the right amounts to permit him to make his decisions. The president must know the issues that he is being asked to decide, the options that are available to him, the opinions of his senior staff and cabinet advisers especially if they differ, and how the decision is likely to be received by key interests and the public. Finally, the staff must assist in transmitting the president's decisions and the reasons for them to the departments and agencies, Congress, the media, opinion leaders, and the public.

Office of Management and Budget (OMB) Part of the Executive Office of the President that provides budgetary expertise, central legislative clearance, and management assistance to the president.

Office of Management and Budget (OMB).   The history of OMB dates back to 1921 when the Bureau of the Budget was created within the Department of the Treasury. The Bureau of the Budget was moved from Treasury into the Executive Office of the President in 1939, and in 1970 it was renamed the **Office of Management and Budget** to highlight its management tasks as well as its more obvious budgetary responsibilities.

The main responsibilities of the OMB include assisting the president in preparing the annual budget, performing the central legislative clearance function to ensure that the legislative priorities of the departments and agencies of the executive branch comport with the president's program, and monitoring the implementation of programs to ensure that they are both effective and cost-efficient. Fundamentally, the OMB is responsible for ensuring that the rest of the federal government reflects both the programmatic and budgetary goals of the administration.

National Security Council (NSC).   Although the importance of the **National Security Council**, established in 1947, has varied from administration to administration, it is the EOP entity responsible for coordinating advice and policy for the president on national security. The statutory members of the NSC include the president, vice president, and the secretaries of state and defense. Statutory advisers to the NSC include the chairman of the Joint Chiefs of Staff and the directors of the Central Intelligence Agency and the Arms Control and Disarmament Agency.

The inevitable temptation that the NSC holds out to presidents is to extend its responsibility beyond policy coordination and advice to policy implementation. The high point of NSC policy dominance occurred during the Nixon administration when Henry Kissinger, assistant to the president for national security affairs, so eclipsed Secretary of State William Rogers that Kissinger was eventually named to replace Rogers while retaining the NSC position. The low point of the NSC came during the Iran–Contra debacle of the second Reagan administration. Nonetheless, when conflicts between State and Defense over control and implementation of postwar Iraq policy became too intense, President Bush named Condoleezza Rice as his National Security Adviser and head of the NSC to manage Iraq policy. She failed. But once Rice became Secretary of State in 2005 and Gates replaced Rumsfeld as Secretary of Defense in late 2006, they cooperated closely on Iraq policy and much else. The NSC receded to its appropriate policy coordination role, where it generally has remained during the Obama administration.

National Security Council (NSC) Part of the Executive Office of the President, established in 1947, that coordinates advice and policy for the president on national security issues.

The Cabinet

The Constitution permits the president to request in writing the opinions of the principal officers of the executive departments on issues related to the business of their departments. The Constitution does not require that these officers meet together as a cabinet to consult with the president and give advice. Nonetheless, every president from Washington forward has brought the secretaries of the executive branch departments together as a cabinet. Some presidents have made much more substantive and consistent use of their cabinet than have others.

Most nineteenth-century presidents provided for cabinet discussion of most of the major issues of the day. Cabinet officials were often politicians of independent importance and so could not be easily ignored. Moreover, alternative sources of advice were less readily available than they are to modern presidents, the White House and support staffs were small to nonexistent, parties were mostly state and local operations, and the interest group structure was much thinner than it is today. Presidents since FDR have had alternative sources of information and advice. Increasingly, the White House staff and the professionals in the EOP have displaced the cabinet and even its individual members as principal sources of programmatic and political advice to the president.

The Apparent Possibility of Cabinet Government.   Initially, the cabinet seems an obvious and natural place for the president to turn for advice. The cabinet is composed of the heads of the departments of the executive branch. Presidents have usually added the vice president to the cabinet, and recent presidents have also added the U.S. ambassador to the United Nations and senior trade and national security officials. Why not tap this impressive collection of expertise for advice on the critical issues facing the administration? A key reason is captured in President Kennedy's query, "Why should the postmaster sit there and listen to a discussion of the problems of Laos?"

Several presidents, most notably Nixon, Reagan, and George W. Bush formed cabinet councils of groups of related cabinet departments to provide coordinated staff and policy work below the level of the whole cabinet but above the levels of single departments. Often a senior White House aide is assigned a directing role and the cabinet council meetings are held in the White House to highlight for the cabinet secretaries the president's stake in the policy formulation and coordination process. Still, cabinet councils have tended to pull apart because the cabinet secretaries have constituencies besides the president to whom they must be sensitive.

Divided Loyalties, Mixed Motives.   Cabinet members well know that they have been appointed to their positions by the president and can be removed by him if he becomes dissatisfied with their work. Cabinet members know just as well that they have been confirmed in their positions by the Senate and are dependent on Congress for approval of their programs and budgets and that they remain subject to congressional scrutiny and investigation.

Cabinet secretaries also find that the career bureaucrats in their departments have their own ideas and interests, some of which conflict with the president's. Moreover, each department has ties to organized interests that care deeply about the programs administered by the department and work closely with the career bureaucrats in the department to protect and enhance them.

Effective department secretaries must find a way to work with all of the constituencies in and around their departments. On occasion, this will mean that they will have to stand up to the president on behalf of their departments, their programs, and the interests they serve. Presidents understand this, but they do not like it, preferring to work most closely with staff aides who have no interest but the president's (and perhaps their own) to consider. Presidents worry that cabinet officers will be "captured" by the ethos and interests of their departments. Hence, cabinet secretaries usually come to be seen as friendly emissaries to their departments and the interests they serve rather than as fully integrated and completely trustworthy members of the president's inner policy circle.

The Vice President

John Adams, the nation's first vice president, declared it "the most insignificant office that ever the invention of man contrived or his imagination conceived." Franklin Roosevelt's first vice president, former House Speaker John Nance Garner of Texas, declared the office not "worth a bucket of war spit." For most of American political history such characterizations of the vice presidency seemed entirely accurate. The Constitution says simply, "The Vice President of the United States shall be President of the Senate, but shall have no Vote, unless they be equally divided." The vice president has no other duty but to preside in the Senate unless specifically assigned other duties by the president. Typically, vice presidents have languished, restricted largely to representing the president to groups of secondary importance and, with the advent of jet travel, attending funerals of foreign dignitaries.

But the stature of the office has risen in recent decades. President Jimmy Carter, with no Washington experience before the presidency, leaned heavily on Vice President Walter Mondale, a Washington insider and long-time senator from Minnesota. Mondale gave candid advice, always confidentially and often in private, and Carter included him in all major discussions and decisions. George Bush, vice president during the Reagan years, was involved in many important decisions but never fully trusted by the Reagan insiders. Bill Clinton made Al Gore an integral part of his policy team. Gore set his daily and weekly schedule after the president set his so that he could select which of the president's meetings he wished to attend.

Dick Cheney was clearly the most influential vice president in American history. Like Carter, Reagan, and Clinton, President George W. Bush came to office with no previous Washington experience. Cheney had previously served in the House leadership, as Chief of Staff in Gerald Ford's administration, and as Secretary of Defense in the first president George Bush's administration. Vice President Cheney became the senior day-to-day manager in the Bush administration. However, Cheney became so closely identified with major administration policies in foreign policy, especially the war in Iraq, interrogation techniques, and domestic wiretapping, that he drew widespread criticism. The indictment and conviction in early 2007 of his chief aide, Lewis "Scooter" Libby, robbed Cheney of a shrewd policy strategist and effective bureaucratic infighter. President Bush's refusal to pardon Libby drove a wedge between him and his vice president.

President Obama undoubtedly wanted Vice President Biden to help him shoulder the burdens of office, but both saw the Cheney model as a step too far. The vice president's role is always somewhat awkward, but Biden has consistently been a senior advisor to President Obama and a problem-solver when critical issues arise domestically or internationally.

The president's job is intensely demanding, and every holder of it recognizes the value of having a second seasoned and successful politician of independent national stature with whom to discuss the central issues of the day. This makes the choice of vice president more important than it has ever been. The vice president not only steps in if the president should die or otherwise be incapacitated but, if the choice is well made, serves as a valuable resource and partner day-to-day.[33]

PRESIDENTIAL REFORM TODAY

Demands on the modern presidency are many, shortcomings are evident, and talk of reform is effectively continuous. Americans watch hopefully as each new president struggles to turn campaign promises into political and policy accomplishments. What lessons might presidents learn from their predecessors and what reforms to the presidency seem most pressing?

First, American presidents must recognize and acknowledge that they are one participant, though a leading participant, in a system of shared powers and legal limits. The view held by President Bush and Proved to be Vice President Cheney, that the presidency in wartime is an office essentially without limits in domestic and international law, is historically implausible and proved to be politically untenable. Emergencies recede, opponents find their voice, and, just as James Madison anticipated in Federalist Number 10, ambition moves to check ambition. Better to sacrifice sole control and early speed for broader support in Congress, the courts, and the public. Broad support is more likely to last even after initial momentum and early success fade.

Second, but related, presidents should adhere to the traditional understandings of political process and law in regard to signing statements. Through most of American history, signing statements were usually innocuous, remarking on the importance of the new law or calling for related legislation. The Bush administration not only wrote more signing statements than all previous administrations combined, they used them for new and troubling purposes. Signing statements were used to identify elements of laws that the administration believed intruded on presidential powers and prerogatives and to declare that the president would not be bound by these provisions. Traditionally, acts of Congress that the administration thought unconstitutional, or merely ill-advised, were vetoed and Congress was left to revise the law or try to override the veto. Using signing statements in lieu of vetoes short circuits the political process established in the Constitution.

Third, many worry that how the nation goes to war is dangerously murky. The Founders believed that no question was more critical to a free society. War empowers government, so the Constitution requires that the people's representatives in Congress declare war before the president is authorized to conduct it. But Congress has not declared war since the Japanese attacked Pearl Harbor in December 1941. Rather, in Korea in the 1950s, Vietnam in the 1960s, and Afghanistan and Iraq in the wake of 9/11, often in conditions of fear, confusion, and apparent danger, Congress has hurried to give the president a bipartisan blank check. Discussion might center on reform of the War Powers Act, but it might well require that the U.S. Supreme Court affirm the War Powers Act and define what counts as a declaration of war in the twenty-first century.

Finally, thinking clearly about the roles of the vice president, cabinet, and White House staff is critical. Presidents have massive responsibilities and need a lot of help in fulfilling them. But if the helpers are out of position they do the president—who let them get and stay out of position—harm. An outsized vice president undercuts the president by raising doubts about who is in charge. Presidents need vice presidential partners, but vice presidents should act as senior advisers, not as gate-keepers or alternative points of decision.

Despite the almost universal sense that the complexities confronting the modern president require a well organized, generally hierarchical White House staff, with a clearly designated and empowered Chief of Staff, complaints about the White House staff abound. Critics call for staffers to act as honest brokers, facilitators, and process managers, rather than as policy advocates and program managers. And finally, critics point out that the president's interest and the public's interest are not the same and that the White House staff too frequently mistakes the former for the latter.

Chapter Summary

Early discussions in the Constitutional Convention revolved around whether the executive should be a messenger for the legislature, simply implementing the laws that it passed, or an independent center of power capable of standing up to and checking the legislature. In the end, the convention invented the Electoral College to select the president, thereby securing his independence and allowing great powers in both domestic and foreign affairs to be allocated to him.

Yet, most of the powers awarded to the executive in the Constitution were to be shared with the legislature. The president alone wields pardon power, but his appointment power, treaty-making power, and war-making power all require advice and consent of the Senate or prior action by the whole Congress. On the other hand, the president is expressly invited into the legislative process by his proposal and veto powers. The Founders produced a system of shared powers in which the president simply cannot succeed without the ongoing cooperation—sometimes grudging, to be sure—of both Congress and the courts.

Most nineteenth-century presidents followed the Congress in domestic policy and in decisions about the use of force but led in foreign affairs. Presidents were not expected to produce legislative programs and rarely even campaigned openly for election. The development of a mature industrial economy at the turn of the twentieth century and the movement of the United States into world politics in the first half of that century placed new demands on the national government to which Congress seemed ill-equipped to respond. Presidents from Theodore Roosevelt, through Woodrow Wilson, to Franklin Roosevelt moved to fill the void.

The presidency reached its full stature in the middle of the twentieth century just as the United States emerged as a dominant world power. The presidency that we know today was created by Franklin Roosevelt, reached the height of its power under Truman and Kennedy, and began to come apart under Johnson and Nixon. Presidents from Jimmy Carter, through Ronald Reagan and George H. W. Bush, to Bill Clinton sought to maintain the U.S. position in the world while recognizing that U.S. resources are limited. George W. Bush reached further, fell, and future presidents will be sobered by his example. What lessons Barack Obama has learned from his predecessors remain to be seen.

Key Terms

appointment power   316

cabinet   333

Electoral College   312

executive agreements   316

Executive Office of the President (EOP)   334

executive privilege   317

impeachment   318

inherent powers   323

National Security Council (NSC)   337

Office of Management and Budget (OMB)   336

pardon   315

reprieve   315

treaty-making power   316

unitary executive theory   309

veto power   315

War Powers Resolution   330

Suggested Readings

Baker, Peter. *Days of Fire: Bush and Cheney in the White House.* New York: Doubleday, 2013. Baker, a White House reporter, explores the relationship between Bush and Cheney and how it affected the operation of the White House and the Bush administration.

Cohen, Jeffrey E. *The President's Legislative Policy Agenda, 1789–2002.* New York: Cambridge University Press, 2012. Cohen marshals an impressive array of data to show the president's influence with Congress has changed over the course of the nation's history.

Fisher, Louis. *Presidential War Power,* 3rd ed. revised. Lawrence: University Press of Kansas, 2013. Fisher's thesis is that although the decision to use force was given by the Founders to Congress, presidents have usurped it in the twentieth century.

Goldsmith, Jack. *The Terror Presidency: Law and Judgment Inside the Bush Administration.* New York: W.W. Norton, 2007. Describes how the Bush administration sought to exclude Congress and the Courts from war powers and terrorism policy.

Han, Lori Cox, ed. *New Directions in the American Presidency.* New York: Routledge, 2011. Leading scholars of the U.S. presidency and the executive branch explore how the office of the President and related institutions have evolved and changed in recent decades and over the course of the nation's history.

Jones, Charles O. *The Presidency in a Separated System,* 2nd ed. Washington, D.C.: The Brookings Institution, 2005. Jones stresses that ours is not a presidential system but rather a separated system in which presidents share power with Congress and the courts.

Skowronek, Stephen. "The Conservative Insurgency and Presidential Power: A Developmental Perspective on the Unitary Executive. "*Harvard Law Review,* 2009, vol. 122, 2070–2103. Skowronek traces arguments about the origins and scope of presidential power to the recent conservative argument for a "unitary executive."

Web Resources

For practice quizzes, key term flashcards, videos, links, and other study tools, visit the *American Government* website: www.routledge.com/cw/jillson

1. **www.ipl.org/div/potus/**
   The Internet Public Library includes a POTUS (Presidents of the United States) site that provides excellent information and links for each president.

2. **www.whitehouse.gov**
   Official site of the president; includes a White House history, virtual tour, press releases, documents, and photographs.

3. **loc.gov**
   The Library of Congress site provides links to all federal websites. You can find access points to any agency within the executive branch and learn about the president's relationships with these groups.

4. **douglassarchives.org**

   Northwestern University maintains Douglass Archives of American Public Address, archiving hundreds of historic speeches by presidents.

5. **www.firstladies.org**

   Virtual library of books, manuscripts, journals, news articles, and other resources on first ladies.

Chapter 11

BUREAUCRACY
Redesigning Government for the Twenty-First Century

❝ I think I underestimated the inertia and the momentum of the Federal bureaucracy …
it is difficult to change. ❞

JIMMY CARTER, OCTOBER 23, 1977

The Constitution TODAY

IS THE FEDERAL RESERVE (THE FED) DANGEROUS?

Article I, section 8 (in part): "The Congress shall have the power to lay and collect taxes, . . . to pay the debts . . . of the United States; . . . To borrow money on the credit of the United States; . . . To coin money, regulate the value thereof, and, . . . To make all laws which shall be necessary and proper for carrying into execution . . . powers vested by the Constitution in the government of the United States."

Former Congressman Ron Paul (R-TX), father of Kentucky Senator Rand Paul, is one of the more interesting characters in modern American politics. Trained as a medical doctor, Paul was first elected to Congress in 1976. He was defeated in a run for the Senate in 1984 and as the Libertarian nominee for president in 1988. Paul was again elected to the U.S. House in 1996 and in 2008 and 2012 he ran for the Republican nomination for president. While he was never a serious threat to win the Republican nomination, he was extremely popular with young people, especially in the 2012 race. Ron Paul is credited by many with inspiring the grassroots "Tea Party" movement. He did not run for his House seat in 2012.

Throughout his career, monetary policy and the role of the Federal Reserve system (the Fed) was his dominant concern. So focused was Congressman Paul on the Fed and the dangers that he believed it posed to American prosperity and freedom that he was considered by many to be something of a crank. While this reputation was not completely undeserved, his concern with the Fed came to be much more widely held in the wake of the recent financial turmoil. Congressman Paul filed a bill, HR 1207, "the Federal Reserve Transparency Act," calling for a complete audit of the Fed. The bill quickly gained 300 co-sponsors in the House before being folded into a broader financial reform bill. Bernie Sanders, the Independent-Socialist senator from Vermont, introduced a companion bill in the Senate. When a man of the Libertarian right joins with the only declared Socialist member of Congress to call for a closer look at a powerful Washington institution like the Fed, it is worth asking why.

The Federal Reserve system was established in 1913 and strengthened in the 1930s to manage the nation's money and credit systems, to forestall bank panics, and facilitate steady economic growth. The Fed is the central bank of the United States. Most nations have a central bank, but ours is more insulated, some would say secretive, and independent than most. The top Fed officials, currently led by Chairman Janet Yellen, are nominated by the president and confirmed by the Senate, but they do not have to clear their policy decisions with anyone. The fact that the Fed did not see the recent crisis coming and was forced to take extraordinary action to stem the subsequent financial turmoil has brought intense, really unprecedented, scrutiny on them.

Ron Paul long charged the Fed with being misguided, secretive, and unaccountable. In an open letter to members of Congress urging support for his bill, HR 1207, Paul wrote; "Whereas, Congress, the Federal Reserve, and the

U.S. Treasury have put the American taxpayer on the hook for over $12 trillion in bailouts and loans, and Whereas, allowing the Fed to operate the nation's monetary system in almost complete secrecy leads to abuse, . . . It's time to hold the Fed accountable." The Fed naturally fought back and, while additional transparency was required, it was awarded important new powers as part of the 2010 Dodd-Frank financial regulatory reform legislation.

Finally, Congressman Paul has a weekly constituent newsletter, called "Texas Straight Talk," in which he explained that in the absence of the Fed the free market could set the money supply and interest rates—"no one knows what the market needs more than the market itself."

WHAT DO YOU THINK?

- Should setting monetary policy, including the money supply and interest rates, be in the hands of the Fed or the markets?
- What arguments, pro and con, can you think of in regard to Congress setting monetary policy?

Focus Questions: from reading to thinking

Q1 What is bureaucracy, and what role does it play in government?

Q2 How have the size and role of the federal bureaucracy changed over the course of American political history?

Q3 What should the government do to foster economic growth in the United States?

Q4 Why is the federal bureaucracy less flexible, dynamic, and innovative than most large corporate bureaucracies?

Q5 How do the president, Congress, and courts exercise control over the bureaucracy?

BUREAUCRACY

When we think of the federal government, we usually think of Congress and the president. Their elections, their policy battles, their triumphs and scandals are the stuff of our evening news. But there is another federal government, the permanent government of departments and agencies with their 2.7 million civilian employees that we think about less frequently. Although the permanent government, often referred to simply as "the bureaucracy," does critical work, from national defense to medical research, it has been regarded through most of American history as big, expensive, and at least potentially oppressive.

In fact, one of the key complaints that Thomas Jefferson noted in the Declaration of Independence was that the king had "erected a multitude of new offices, and sent hither swarms of new officers to harass our people and eat out their substance." After independence, the Founders sought to defend against tyranny, both petty and grand. They defended against the petty tyranny potential in mettlesome bureaucrats by giving elected officials multiple points of control over the permanent government. They defended against the grand tyranny potential in kings, presidents, congressional majorities by careful use of separation of powers, checks and balances, bicameralism, and federalism.

As a result, the president, Congress, and the courts all have important constitutional and legal roles in organizing and monitoring the bureaucracy; yet, none has the exclusive right to control and direct it. This creates ambiguity and invites a continuous struggle for influence over what the bureaucracy does and how it does it. Scholars have expressed this insight in a number of interesting ways. Herbert Simon and his colleagues note that "the separation of powers . . . somewhat beclouds the right of the chief executive to control administration." Richard E. Neustadt describes the design and structure of the U.S. political system as "separated institutions *sharing* power."[1]

The key distinction here is between policymaking, which is what Congress and the president do, and policy-implementation, which is what the bureaucracy does. Every agency of the national government is established by law and its budgets and personnel levels are set by Congress and the president annually. For example, the National Highway Traffic Safety Administration (NHTSA) was established in 1970 to administer programs on auto and traffic safety. As a federal bureaucracy, in normal times NHTSA is charged with being inefficient, overbearing, and expensive. Then along comes a global recall of millions of cars for sticking accelerators and bad brakes and the finger pointing begins. Elected officials, those who grudgingly authorized programs, personnel levels, and budgets demand to know why NHTSA did not catch the defects earlier. Hearings are held in which preening congressmen rake crestfallen bureaucrats over the coals. In a nation that begrudges taxes and mistrusts bureaucrats, this is a familiar scene. The bureaucracy does important work—is your car safe?— but this is often hard to see before the crisis is upon us.

This chapter explains how bureaucracy works and why Americans feel about it the way they do. First, we define bureaucracy and describe how the meaning

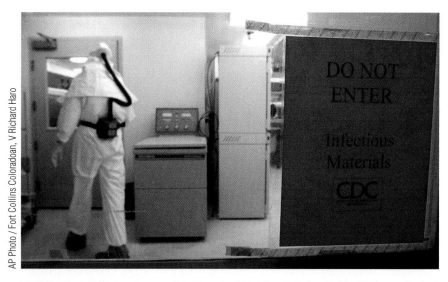

The federal bureaucracy covers everything from the Forest Service to the Centers for Disease Control, commonly known as the CDC.

of the term has changed over time. Second, we describe the origins, growth, and structure of the federal bureaucracy in the United States. Third, we describe the role of the bureaucracy in making and implementing public policy. Fourth, we describe how and how effectively the political branches guide, check, and control the bureaucracy. Finally, we describe the difficulties encountered in creating a new Department of Homeland Security after the 9/11 attacks.

WHAT IS A BUREAUCRACY?

Although governments throughout time have had their officials and functionaries, the term **bureaucracy** suggests modern systems of organization, communication, and control. It refers to a hierarchical organization in which offices have specific missions and employees are assigned specific responsibilities based on merit, knowledge, and experience.

During the first century of American history, federal government employees were directly accountable to elected politicians because they held their positions as **patronage** appointments. When a new president came into office or one party replaced the other in the majority, it replaced large numbers of government workers with its own partisans. As government grew and the tasks that it confronted became more complex, more order and structure seemed necessary. Great Britain, with her more advanced economy and far-flung empire, adopted a government personnel or civil service system in 1854 that was based on merit as opposed to party politics and patronage.

One of the key events that led to the creation of the U.S. civil service system was the assassination of President James Garfield on July 2, 1881 by a disgruntled supporter whose expectation of a government job was disappointed. The **Pendleton Act** of 1883 replaced the spoils system with a system in which hiring, pay, and promotion were based on demonstrated and measurable merit and performance. The main goals of the **civil service system** were to hire on merit, manage employees efficiently, and treat them fairly.[2]

The principles of merit and tenure were supplemented with passage of the Classification Act in 1923. Legislators and agency administrators were systematically to define the tasks for which each agency would be responsible. Personnel experts were then to define the qualifications required to perform each task in the agency and link employee skills with pay scales.

In 1949, Congress extended job classification to all civilian federal employees except those specifically excluded. As a result, more than 90 percent of civilian federal employees were placed into one of eighteen government service rankings (GS-1 through GS-18). Each GS ranking is divided into internal steps, with related pay grades through which employees proceed.

The civil service system has always had its critics. Modern critics contend that the civil service system has come to be "characterized by extreme procedural formalism and even rigidity in hiring, firing, promotion, career movement."[3] The Clinton–Gore "reinventing government" initiatives and the Bush administration's "management agenda" sought to provide options to the

Q1 What is bureaucracy, and what role does it play in government?

bureaucracy A hierarchical organization in which offices have specified missions and employees are assigned responsibilities based on merit, knowledge, and experience.

patronage The awarding of political jobs or contracts based on partisan ties instead of merit or expertise.

Pendleton Act The Pendleton Act of 1883 was the original legislation establishing the civil service system.

civil service system Rules governing the hiring, advancement, pay, and discipline of civilian federal employees.

Modern life seems to demand the order and structure of bureaucracies such as this IRS processing center.

formal civil service system and to remove sensitive classes of employees such as those working in homeland security and defense from its constraints and protections. Today only about half of federal employees are covered by the civil service system.

Modern analysts have seen bureaucracy as posing both promises and threats. The promises are of public services delivered with efficiency, order, and fairness. The threats are that bureaucracy will be too powerful for its political superiors to control and too willful to listen to its clients. The early nineteenth-century French novelist Honore de Balzac described bureaucracy as "that giant power wielded by pygmies."[4] The great German sociologist Max Weber, more respectful than Balzac and, hence, known as the father of modern bureaucracy, warned early in the twentieth century that "the power position of a fully developed bureaucracy is always overtowering. The political master finds himself in the position of the dilettante who stands opposite the expert, facing the trained official who stands within the management of administration."[5] From Weber forward, one of the key questions about the place of the bureaucracy in democratic society has been how to balance efficiency and fairness with political responsiveness and accountability.

Q2 How have the size and role of the federal bureaucracy changed over the course of American political history?

THE GROWTH OF THE AMERICAN BUREAUCRACY

The civilian workforce of the federal government grew slowly through most of the nineteenth century (see Table 11.1, Expansion of the Federal Bureaucracy).

TABLE 11.1	**Expansion of the Federal Bureaucracy**	
	Department, Commission, or Agency	**Total Bureaucracy**
1790	State, Treasury, War, Justice, Post Office	2,000
1825	Department of the Interior	10,000
1883	Pendleton Act authorized U.S. Civil Service	100,000
1887	Interstate Commerce Commission (ICC) is founded	
1889	Department of Agriculture	
1903	Department of Commerce; Department of Labor	250,000
1913	Federal Reserve (Fed) System	
1914	Federal Trade Commission (FTC)	
1933	Federal Deposit Insurance Corporation (FDIC)	
1934	Federal Communications Commission (FCC)	
1935	Social Security Administration	1,000,000
1949	Department of War renamed Department of Defense	
1953	Department of Health, Education, and Welfare (HEW)	
1965	Department of Housing and Urban Development (HUD)	
1966	Department of Transportation (DOT)	
1970	Environmental Protection Agency (EPA)	3,000,000
1977	Department of Energy	
1979	HEW renamed Department of Health and Human Services (HHS) Department of Education	
1989	Department of Veterans Affairs (VA)	
2003	Department of Homeland Security (DHS)	2,700,000

It did not break 10,000 employees until about 1830, 100,000 until 1880, and 1 million until 1940. By the late 1960s it had reached 3 million where it remained into the early 1990s. During the 1990s, despite the creation of more than 20 million jobs in the private economy, the federal workforce actually shrank to 2.7 million. Despite a slight uptick following 9/11, the federal civilian workforce remains at 2.7 million.[6]

Nonetheless, these remarkable numbers must be taken with something of a grain of salt. Though full-time federal government employment remains below where it was a half century ago, the federal government's use of contract workers has increased dramatically, especially since 2000. Federal contracts totaled $207 billion in 2000 and $537 billion in 2011. Paul C. Light of New York University calls the uncounted secret army of contractors a "slight of hand," allowing "successive administrations to brag about cutting the federal workforce." Astoundingly, Light estimates that 10.5 million employees work for the federal government "off the books" on federal contracts and grants.[7]

The Initial Establishment

The first Congress created only three departments of the federal government—the Departments of State, Treasury, and War, each headed by a secretary.

The attorney general was the nation's top legal officer and a member of the president's cabinet. The three departments, the attorney general, and the post office provided the basic services of government at the national level: foreign relations, currency and finance, defense, justice, and delivery of the mails. In 1790, the first year of President Washington's first term, the federal bureaucracy employed about 2,000, most of them in the postal service.

The federal bureaucracy remained small, even as the country began its westward expansion. Most of its tasks were routine—collecting revenue at ports, recording land deeds and citizenship records, and delivering mail. In fact, the two most prominent presidents of the first half of the nineteenth century, Thomas Jefferson and Andrew Jackson, were explicitly antibureaucratic.[8]

President Jefferson reduced the size of government and President Jackson made government jobs part of the "spoils" of party victory. Jackson said, "The duties of all public officers are, or at least admit of being made, so plain and simple that men of intelligence would readily qualify themselves for their performance." Jackson made the bureaucracy a direct extension of the nation's rough-and-tumble party politics.

Government as Promoter of Economic Activity

The federal bureaucracy numbered just over 36,000 when Abraham Lincoln assumed the presidency in 1861. Lincoln believed that national government policy and power should be employed to help the economy produce growth and opportunity. Lincoln's Republican Party stood for generous land grants to railroads willing to push rapidly west, tariffs and subsidies to spur industrial development, cheap land to speed settlement of the Midwest, and land grant colleges to improve agricultural science and education. Even as the Civil War raged, Congress created the Department of Agriculture in 1862. President Lincoln called it "the people's department."[9]

The idea behind the mid-nineteenth-century Republican Party's domestic policies was to spur economic development. Hence, although the bureaucracy grew, reaching more than 250,000 by the end of the century, its tasks remained largely those of parceling out the country, especially the unsettled lands in the West, to farmers, railroaders, and industrialists. However, as commerce and industry boomed through the final decades of the nineteenth century, national corporations, trusts, and monopolies emerged for the first time in American history. How government should respond, or whether it should respond at all, was the fundamental political issue of the era.[10]

Government as Regulator of Economic Activity

The demand for government regulation grew as the problems of industrialization became more evident and pressing. National trusts and monopolies in banking, railroads, steel, and oil—also in daily staples such as sugar, flour, and cooking oil—frightened consumers who felt powerless to fight back. The wealth and power of these new corporate giants seemed to demand that government develop new means to deal with them. Government needed a more skilled workforce, one with more expertise and technical competence, as it moved to take on new responsibilities. Hence, as noted earlier, the Pendleton Act of 1883 established the civil service.

Moreover, late in the nineteenth century, Congress turned to a new type of bureaucratic entity. The **Interstate Commerce Commission (ICC)**, chartered in 1887 to regulate the railroads, was given a broad mandate to develop, implement, and adjudicate "fair" and "reasonable" freight rates. In creating the ICC, Congress set aside the idea of separation of powers. Instead, Congress reasoned that the scope of the businesses involved and the complexity of their operations required that experts make policy, enforce it, and punish violations.

The independent regulatory commission became a fixture of the American government during the twentieth century. For example, Congress created the Federal Reserve Board charged with regulating the money supply and overseeing the nation's banks, and the Consumer Product Safety Commission charged with monitoring the quality and safety of the products offered to consumers. In a dozen separate policy areas, it was thought that the nation would be best served by the application of nonpartisan expertise to complex problems.

Q3 What should the government do to foster economic growth in the United States?

Interstate Commerce Commission (ICC) First independent regulatory commission established in 1887 to develop, implement, and adjudicate fair and reasonable freight rates.

Government as Distributor of Wealth and Opportunity

Americans continued to believe through the first third of the twentieth century that although government might be needed to restrain large concentrations of

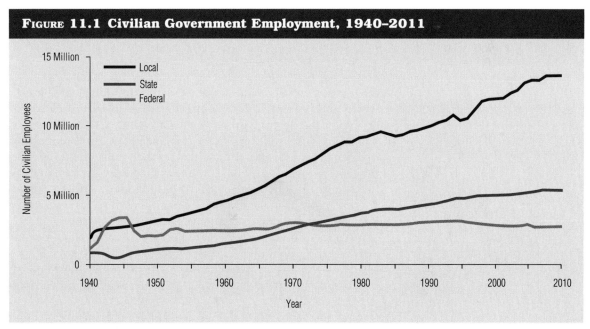

FIGURE 11.1 Civilian Government Employment, 1940–2011

Source: Annual issues of the *Statistical Abstract of the United States*, U.S. Department of Commerce, Bureau of the Census. 2014 edition, Table 481, Government Employment and Payrolls, 1982 to 2011.

LET'S COMPARE

General Government Employment as a Percentage of Total Employment among Fifteen OECD (Wealthy) Nations

Americans spend a lot of time worrying about the size and expense of government. The data below show that government in the United States is smaller than in most other wealthy nations and that it has not been growing—in fact, it has been shrinking a bit—in recent decades. A close look at these data reveal several interesting points. Broadly speaking, there are Scandinavian, European, and Anglo-American approaches to size of government.

When we look at change, we see that, for most countries, most growth in public employment took place before 1985 and has stabilized—in some cases,

fallen—since then. Public employment in Norway, Finland, Portugal and Spain continued to grow after 1985. In the case of Portugal and Spain, entrance into the European Union and rapid economic growth brought them into line with their neighbors. A few European nations including France and Italy stabilized after 1985. Denmark, the United States, Canada, and Japan changed little between 1980 and 2005. Several European nations, including Germany and the United Kingdom, grew until 1985 and then reined in government growth dramatically, ending well below 1980 levels.

Two explanations for these patterns are most prominent. The first is political leadership. A phalanx of conservative leaders—Margaret Thatcher (Britain, 1979–1990), Ronald Reagan (U.S., 1981–1989), and Helmut Kohl (Germany, 1982–1998)—came to power and stressed smaller government and more competitive economies. The second factor is globalization, which renders businesses in every country open to competition from businesses in every other country. The high taxes required to support large public bureaucracies represent costs to business and entrepreneurship that may render them uncompetitive with businesses elsewhere.

Struggling Toward Democracy

By European standards the U.S. has a small public sector, though many Americans remain convinced that it is too large.

What do you think?
- Does the idea of democracy necessarily suggest a large public sector or a small public sector?
- Does a large public sector increase or decrease freedom and opportunity?

economic power, competition should define the individual's place in society. The Depression of the 1930s changed many minds in this regard. In the depths of the Depression—1932, 1933, and 1934—one-third of the adult workforce was unemployed or dramatically underemployed. Banks failed by the thousands, businesses by the tens of thousands, homes were foreclosed by the hundreds of thousands, and jobs disappeared by the millions.

Men and women who worked hard all their lives lost everything in a national economic catastrophe over which they had no control. Many turned to government as the only power capable of dealing with the scope of the disaster. The key change that the Depression era brought to American government was the rapid growth of bureaucratic rules and services (see Figure 11.1). The Social Security Administration requiring workers to save for retirement and the Federal Deposit Insurance Corporation placing federal guarantees behind bank deposits are examples of new bureaucracies created in response

	1980	1985	1990	1995	2000	2005	Latest
Sweden	35%	37%	36%	36%	33%	33%	33%
Norway	28%	30%	33%	35%	34%	34%	34%
Denmark	32%	33%	32%	33%	33%	32%	32%
Finland	23%	26%	27%	31%	29%	29%	29%
France	23%	26%	25%	26%	24%	25%	25%
Canada	23%	25%	25%	26%	24%	25%	25%
Belgium	23%	25%	24%	23%	22%	22%	22%
United Kindom	30%	29%	25%	23%	21%	22%	22%
Ireland	21%	22%	20%	19%	16%	17%	17%
Itlay	20%	22%	22%	23%	21%	21%	20%
Portugal	15%	18%	19%	24%	24%	25%	24%
Spain	12%	16%	16%	18%	17%	17%	18%
United States	18%	17%	17%	16%	16%	16%	16%
Germany	16%	17%	16%	14%	13%	12%	12%
Japan	12%	12%	11%	10%	10%	10%	10%

Source: Center for Economic Studies (CESifo), Ludwig Maximillian University and University of Munich. Derived from OECD: Employment, Public Sector Pay and Employment Data.

to the Depression. World War II further expanded the national government, particularly in its military and national security apparatus.

A second great surge in bureaucratic growth came with Lyndon Johnson's Great Society initiatives of the 1960s. President Johnson's social programs were designed to break the cycle of poverty and decay in the nation's central cities and among its most disadvantaged citizens. Programs such as Medicare and Medicaid were established, the Department of Health, Education, and Welfare grew rapidly, and two new departments—the Department of Housing and Urban Development and the Department of Transportation—were created. The federal bureaucracy reached its greatest size during these years, but as Figure 11.1 highlights, federal grants to state and local governments spurred even more bureaucratic growth there.

Ronald Reagan's election as president in 1980 signaled a turn in the fortunes of the federal bureaucracy. President Reagan believed that the bureaucracy had grown too large and intruded into too many areas of economic and social life. Reagan argued that the federal bureaucracy was fraught with "waste, fraud, and abuse" and needed to be reduced in size and cost. The Democratic Congress disagreed and generally blocked his plans, but the growth of the bureaucracy was slowed.

President Bill Clinton had a more positive view of bureaucracy, but he also thought it should be smaller and more efficient. Clinton was successful both in reforming and trimming the federal bureaucracy, cutting more than

377,000 federal jobs and streamlining systems and procedures from purchasing to personnel. Until 9/11, the Bush administration directed its attention to upgrading the management and information systems of the bureaucracy. Thereafter, it undertook the creation of a domestic security bureaucracy—the Department of Homeland Security—the largest reorganization since the end of World War II.

Who Are the Bureaucrats?

The bureaucrats are the permanent employees of the government. Unlike officials elected or appointed to fixed terms of office, bureaucrats often make careers of public employment. College students facing the job market soon learn that nearly one in six employed adults works for government. The federal government employs about 2.7 million civilian and 1.4 million military personnel for a total federal workforce of 4.1 million. State governments employ another 5.3 million workers, and local governments employ 14.5 million more. These government employees do every kind of work imaginable, from mopping floors to tending to the national forests to doing cancer research. Hence, the bureaucracy, particularly at the federal level, is an increasingly accurate reflection of the society it serves. The proportions of the federal bureaucracy made up of blacks, Hispanics, and women have all nearly doubled during the post-World War II period (see Table 11.2).

THE STRUCTURE OF THE NATIONAL BUREAUCRACY

The modern federal bureaucracy is large and complex. Its most important components are the fifteen cabinet departments, each headed by a secretary

TABLE 11.2	Demographic Characteristics of the Federal Bureaucracy		
	Percent Blacks	**Percent Hispanics**	**Percent Women**
1950	9.3		24.0
1960	11.7		25.0
1970	15.0	3.3	27.0
1980	15.5	4.1	35.1
1990	16.6	5.3	42.7
2000	17.9	6.6	45.0
2010	17.9	7.8	43.0
2013	18.2	9.3	42.7

Source: Office of Personnel Management, *The Fact Book, 2008* (Washington, D.C.: U.S. Government Printing Office, 2010), 10–11. OPM, Common Characteristics of the Government (CCOG), April 2014. Tables 9, 11.

nominated by the president and approved by the Senate (see Table 11.3). The bureau or service is the basic unit of the departmental bureaucracy from which programs are administered. In addition to the departments are dozens of regulatory commissions and agencies and literally hundreds of government corporations, institutes, and advisory panels and boards.

Cabinet Departments

The departments of the federal government are of three broad types and have appeared in three broad waves. As noted earlier, the initial federal establishment consisted of the attorney general and three departments assigned the basic tasks of government. A second wave of departments, most charged with serving the needs of specific clientele groups, was added between the mid-nineteenth and the early twentieth centuries. A third wave of general social service departments was added after World War II, mostly in the 1960s and 1970s. The Department of Homeland Security was established in 2003.

The departments of the federal government employ most of the federal workforce and administer most of the federal government's programs. They manage our foreign affairs, see to our defense, administer the federal parks and forests, and run our welfare, urban renewal, and transportation programs.

TABLE 11.3 Cabinet Departments of the U.S. Government

Departments	Founded	Employees
Original Departments		
Department of State	1789	33,200
Department of the Treasury	1789	112,700
Department of War (renamed Defense in 1947)	1789	765,000
Attorney General (Department of Justice established in 1870)	1789	117,700
Clientele Departments		
Department of Interior	1849	69,800
Department of Agriculture	1862	90,700
Department of Commerce	1903	43,000
Department of Labor	1903	17,500
Department of Veterans Affairs	1989	319,300
Service Departments		
Department of Health, Education, and Welfare (renamed Department of Health and Human Services in 1979)	1953	76,200
Department of Housing and Urban Development	1965	9,200
Department of Transportation	1966	57,600
Department of Energy	1977	15,900
Department of Education	1979	4,300
Department of Homeland Security	2003	191,000

Source: *Budget of the United States Government: Analytical Perspectives, Fiscal Year 2014* (Washington, D.C.: U.S. Government Printing Office, 2013), Table 10-2, 112. All numbers are 2012 estimates.

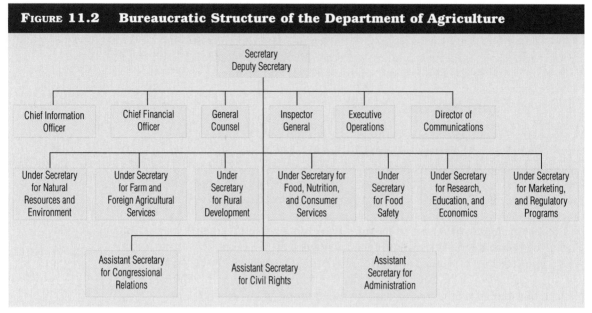

FIGURE 11.2   **Bureaucratic Structure of the Department of Agriculture**

Source: United States Department of Agriculture. http://www.usda.gov/img/content/org_chart_enlarged.jpg

In general, these are large organizations structured in the classic bureaucratic fashion. They are multilayered, hierarchical organizations in which lines of authority run from the secretary to the bureau chief and his or her operational subordinates (see Figure 11.2).

The Department of Agriculture, for example, is headed by a secretary, currently Tom Vilsack, who is appointed by the president and confirmed by the Senate. Cabinet officers like Secretary Vilsack made $201,700 in 2014. The Deputy Secretary is usually the day-to-day manager of the department ($181,500). Six staff offices provide financial, legal, communications, and other services to the secretary. Each line office, under which the major substantive programs of the department fall, is headed by an undersecretary ($167,000). Each undersecretary administers related programs that deliver benefits and services to the department's clients. The bureau or service is the basic organizational unit of the federal government.

Regulatory Commissions and Agencies

regulatory commissions
Commissions headed by bipartisan boards charged with developing, implementing, and adjudicating policy in their area of responsibility.

Today there are twelve independent regulatory commissions (see Table 11.4). Several of the more prominent are the Securities and Exchange Commission (SEC), the Federal Reserve (Fed), the Consumer Product Safety Commission (CPSC), the Federal Trade Commission (FTC), and the Federal Communications Commission (FCC). **Regulatory commissions** are headed by boards

Agency	Number of Members	Term in Years	Partisan Balance
Consumer Product Safety Commission	5	7	No more than three from one party
Federal Communications Commission	5	5	No more than three from one party
Federal Election Commission	6	6	No more than three from one party
Federal Energy Regulatory Commission	5	4	No more than three from one party
Federal Maritime Commission	5	5	No more than three from one party
Federal Reserve Board	7	14	No partisan limits
Federal Trade Commission	5	7	No more than three from one party
National Labor Relations Board	5	5	No partisan limits
National Mediation Board	3	3	No more than two from one party
National Transportation Safety Board	5	5	No more than three from one party
Nuclear Regulatory Commission	5	5	No more than three from one party
Securities and Exchange Commission	5	5	No more than three from one party

TABLE 11.4 Membership, Terms, and Partisan Balance of Federal Regulatory Agencies

Source: Robert E. DiClerico, *The American President*, 4th ed. (Englewood Cliffs, NJ: Prentice-Hall, 1995), 168. Revised and updated by the author.

rather than single executives. The boards must be bipartisan, with relatively long and overlapping terms. Commissioners can be dismissed only for "inefficiency, neglect of duty, or malfeasance."

The regulatory commissions direct and monitor critical parts of our national life. For example, the Federal Reserve monitors the banking system and adjusts money and credit markets to produce steady economic growth. The Federal Communications Commission regulates the nation's airwaves, and the Consumer Product Safety Commission tests and licenses many of the products that we use every day.

The 2013–2014 *United States Government Manual* listed four dozen more major agencies, boards, and institutes. These include such familiar names as the Environmental Protection Agency (EPA), the National Transportation Safety Board (NTSB), and the National Institutes of Health (NIH). You hear about the EPA whenever an environmental hazard like an oil spill occurs, about the NTSB following a plane crash, and about NIH during a health crisis. These entities are of various designs and, because they are more technical than political, they generally lack the explicit partisan balance of independent regulatory commissions.

Government Corporations, Boards, and Commissions

The Congress has also created institutions to pursue specialized tasks and to seek advice from particular constituencies. Some government corporations

Getty Images

John Koskinen, commissioner of the Internal Revenue Service (IRS), waits to begin a House Oversight and Government Reform Subcommittee hearing in Washington, D.C. The IRS has been under congressional scrutiny for more than a year since it said it had given extra attention to small-government groups seeking tax-exempt status.

have organized and administered major undertakings, for example, the U.S. Postal Service, the Tennessee Valley Authority, and AMTRAK. On the other hand, there are approximately 1,000 minor advisory boards, committees, and commissions with as many as 60,000 members that give particular groups access to government. Even though many of these boards and commissions rarely meet and exercise no real authority, they are points of access and are tenaciously defended.

Q4 Why is the federal bureaucracy less flexible, dynamic, and innovative than most large corporate bureaucracies?

spoils system Patronage system prominent between 1830 and 1880 in which strong political parties struggled for control of Congress and the presidency with the winner taking the bureaucracy and its jobs as a prize.

POLICY IMPLEMENTATION AND ITS PITFALLS

The nineteenth-century **spoils system** involved strong political parties fighting for control of Congress and the presidency with the winner taking the bureaucracy as a prize. Control of the bureaucracy allowed jobs and contracts to be awarded to supporters and denied to opponents. During the Populist and Progressive eras of the late 1880s through about 1915, reformers sought to replace the patronage system with a nonpartisan, merit-driven, civil service.

Policymaking, the reformers argued, is the struggle among elected officials to set law and policy through a process characterized by conflict, bargaining, and compromise. Policy implementation, on the other hand, should be the nonpartisan, professional, almost scientific selection and application of means to achieve the goals that politicians set. Progressives believed that politicians should set policy and nonpartisan civil servants should implement it with fairness and efficiency.

However, as clear as the distinction between politics and administration seemed, it was extraordinarily difficult to maintain in practice.[11] Politicians forced to compromise during the policymaking process often struggle to shape implementation in ways that secure as many of their original goals and interests as possible. Hence, bureaucrats work almost perpetually within a highly charged partisan environment in which the push and pull of politics clouds administration.

The Process of Policy Implementation

Congress and the president not only make law and policy but also define the broad process by which bureaucrats implement them. The **Administrative Procedures Act (APA)** of 1946 is the single most important attempt by Congress to define the nature and process of bureaucratic decision making. The APA mandated the processes and standards for rationality and fairness in bureaucratic rule making and administrative adjudication. The APA defines the procedures by which bureaucratic decisions are to be made and offers bureaucrats some protection against political pressure so long as they abide by the procedures.

Administrative Procedures Act (APA) Passed in 1946, the APA remains the single most important attempt by Congress to define the nature and process of bureaucratic decision making.

Rule Making. Congress passes laws that authorize government programs; the bureaucracy then writes specific rules that define how the program will be administered (see Figure 11.3).[12] The process of **rule making** establishes eligibility criteria for services and benefits. For example, Congress has legislated that all citizens below a certain level of income are eligible for food stamps. Rules must be written to declare what shall count as income, what shall be exempt, and why. Well-made rules produce uniform and predictable outcomes for which agencies can be held accountable. The bureaucrat needs merely to apply the rule or regulation rather than reach a personal judgment.

rule making Process of defining rules or standards that apply uniformly to classes of individuals, events, or activities.

The process of rule making encourages administrators to think clearly about the needs to be served, consider all of the groups and interests that might be affected, and then produce a rule that will both be fair and achieve the best result under the conditions most likely to prevail. Nonetheless, some bureaucratic decisions do not lend themselves to the simple application of a rule. Therefore, the Supreme Court ruled in *S.E.C. v. Chenery* (1947), only a year after the APA went into effect, that "the choice between proceeding by general rule or by individual, ad hoc litigation lies primarily in the informed discretion of the administrative agency."

Administrative Adjudication. **Administrative adjudication** is case-by-case resolution of disputes between parties before an agency or between

administrative adjudication Procedures designed to allow resolution of complex issues based on specific facts rather than general rules.

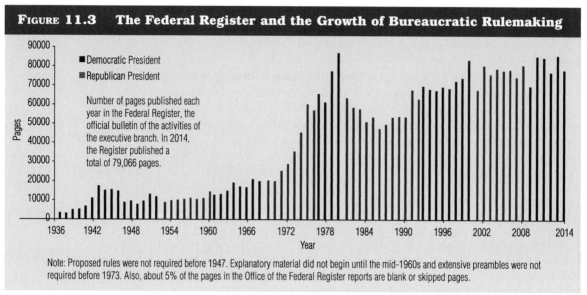

FIGURE 11.3   **The Federal Register and the Growth of Bureaucratic Rulemaking**

Note: Proposed rules were not required before 1947. Explanatory material did not begin until the mid-1960s and extensive preambles were not required before 1973. Also, about 5% of the pages in the Office of the Federal Register reports are blank or skipped pages.

Source: Office of the Federal Register.

individuals and an agency. The APA established administrative adjudication as a quasi-judicial process. Administrative law judges hold hearings in which they administer oaths, take testimony, receive or exclude evidence and information, and make binding judgments in regard to agency rules and regulations. These rigorous procedures are intended to ensure that those subject to bureaucratic decisions receive fair and impartial hearings.

Administrative adjudication is far more common than one might imagine. Between 2000 and 2005, administrative law judges heard 283,000 disputes concerning Medicare services alone. In each case, a claimant protested the denial of services and the judge was required to decide whether, under the Medicare law and rules, the denial of services was legitimate. Social Security disability claims were even more numerous, averaging 560,000 annually. Both Medicare and Social Security disability claimants won 60 precent of these disputes.[13]

Policy Design and the Limits on Implementation

implementation The process of making a program or policy actually work day-to-day in the real world.

Implementation is the process of making a program actually work in the real world. The way most programs are designed makes efficient implementation difficult. First, federal departments, agencies, and bureaus are given multiple and sometimes contradictory goals. Second, responsibility for some tasks like national defense or child welfare is spread so widely through the bureaucracy that it is impossible to decide who is responsible for whatever results occur. Third, measures of success are frequently in dispute. Finally, much of the actual

Pro & Con

Should the Market Set Student Loan Rates?

Bureaucratic rule making is one of those eye-glazing topics that students dread. But hear this: your college costs recently went up because Congress and the Department of Education have changed the formula for determining eligibility for federal aid. Congress writes the law governing student financial aid, but then the Department of Education writes the detailed rules for implementing the program. What families see is a mix of law and regulation.

Nearly $115 billion in financial aid is awarded by educational institutions and governments each year. Eligibility for aid is determined by a single complicated formula called the federal need analysis. A family's personal financial information including savings, equity, income, and expenses is run through this formula to determine how much discretionary income is available to meet college expenses. Unmet need triggers eligibility for financial aid.

The last big fight over how financial aid is awarded occurred about a decade ago. The law then required the Department of Education to recalibrate the federal needs formula on a regular schedule using updated data on average income, expenses, and college costs. When it did so in 2003, the result—largely because of an economic recession—was that millions of students faced reduced eligibility for financial aid.[14] Depending on family income, these changes cost students anywhere from a few hundred to several thousand dollars (the average for 2005 was $1,749). When the formula revision was introduced, Joe Paul

Case, head of financial aid at Amherst College, said in the press, "The seemingly insignificant publishing of an obscure table in the *Federal Register* has serious consequences on the individual."

When Democrats took control of Congress in 2006, they moved to lower interest rates on most government sponsored loans from the pending 6.8 percent to half that, 3.4 percent, where it was held through 2013. In 2013, budgetary pressure allowed the Republican House majority to secure the agreement of President Obama and the Democrat led Senate to move from fixed interest rates to market rates. The base Stafford loan interest rate for 2013–14 loans was 3.86 percent, but it likely will rise with broader interest rates in future years.

But bureaucratic decisions, legally binding while in effect, are not the last words. Congress, through its committees, engages in legislative oversight in which top bureaucrats are called on to answer questions. If the oversight hearings raise serious questions about the way current law is being administered, Congress can amend or revise the law. Because rules follow or implement current law, the implementing rules must change if the law changes. The lesson, then, is don't just watch the flashy players—the presidents and legislators. Watch the bureaucrats, too; what they do is important and can have a direct effect on you.

What do you think?
- Should Congress set student loan rates low enough to promote access to college, making up the difference from federal funds?
- Or should we let the market set rates on student loans as it does on most other loans?

PRO	CON
Paying interest is the cost of borrowing money	Controlling costs facilitates broad student access
Student loans should track the cost of other loans	Student loan rates should be held down to promote access
Markets allow continuous adjustment of rates	Congress should set loan rates to insure broad access

implementation of programs overseen from the federal level occurs at the state and local levels and hence is difficult to monitor closely.

Politics and Program Requirements.   Public policymakers, more frequently than their counterparts in business and industry, are required to address several goals or to serve several values at once. The main goal of a program might be to promote the national defense, assist preschoolers preparing to read, or assure the upkeep of the national highways. In each case, however, a number of secondary or contextual requirements are involved. For example, a requirement may specify that contracts go to the lowest bidder and that a fair share go to minorities and women. Sometimes these requirements conflict.[15]

Political scientist James Q. Wilson argues that the prevalence of secondary goals and political constraints in public policymaking encourages managers to focus more on equity and process than on efficiency and outcomes.[16] Hence, public sector managers tend to hide behind rules and procedures and to be more risk-averse than innovative.

Imprecise and Contradictory Goals.   Some agencies are charged with tasks that seem inconsistent or perhaps even contradictory.[17] The Food and Drug Administration (FDA) is responsible for insuring that drugs are safe before being brought to market and that life-saving drugs are made available as quickly as possible.[18] Schools are expected to feed hungry children, report suspected child abuse, provide day care before and after school, and teach reading and arithmetic if there is time. A police officer is expected to be a friend to the neighborhood children and a match for the most violent criminal. Border patrol agents are expected to stop illegals and drug traffickers without disrupting the flow of people or commerce.

Fragmentation and Faulty Coordination.   Responsibility for creating, monitoring, and implementing federal government programs is diffuse. Both in Congress and in the bureaucracy, no one with an interest in a program wishes to be without influence over it. For example, eighty-four committees and subcommittees of the House and Senate are involved in oversight of various defense programs, and eighty-eight committees and subcommittees have some oversight of the Department of Homeland Security.[19]

Imprecise Measures of Success.   Much of what government does is hard to assess under the best of circumstances. For example, did the collapse of the Soviet Union come from its own internal decay or from pressure applied by the Reagan arms buildup? What are the precise benefits that the nation derives from foreign aid, Head Start, midnight basketball, or faith-based delivery of social services?

Proxy Administration.   Finally, the federal government frequently establishes rules and provides resources rather than actually administering programs

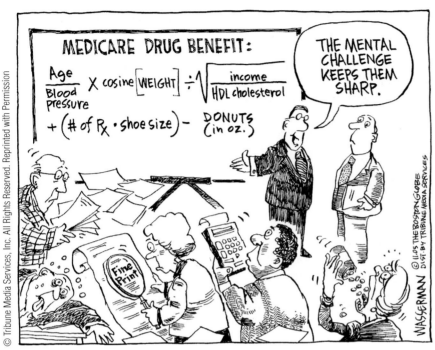

This cartoon pokes fun at the maze of confusing choices confronting seniors in the Medicare prescription drug program.

and serving individual citizens. Many federal programs are administered by contractors or by service providers at the state and local levels. Scholars have described this as "proxy administration." Proxy administration often creates serious problems of coherence and coordination as local administrators in Birmingham, Alabama, and Bellingham, Washington, decide to approach the same task from very different directions.[20]

BUREAUCRATIC AUTONOMY AND ACCOUNTABILITY

Over the course of the twentieth century, Congress, quite sensibly from some perspectives, responded to the increasing number and complexity of the issues that came before it by creating new bureaucracies with impressive new expertise and delegating to them the responsibility for defining and addressing the major issues in their area. Congress also sought to shield the bureaucracy from undue political manipulation—that is, from the undue influence of politicians, mainly its own members and the president and his advisers.

From another perspective though, the bureaucracy must remain subordinate to the people and their elected representatives. Congress, the president,

Q5 How do the president, Congress, and courts exercise control over the bureaucracy?

AFP / Getty Images

Keeping the massive federal bureaucracy on track is no easy task. Here Attorney General Eric Holder (center right, leaning forward) chairs an Interagency Task Force to Monitor and Combat Trafficking in Persons.

and the courts limit the bureaucracy by placing detailed controls on personnel administration, accounting and financial management, government contracting and procurement, property management, and access to information. Political scientist Martha Derthick argues that "the divided and pluralist nature of American government creates an inherently burdensome institutional setting for bureaucracy, making it a pawn in the ongoing institutional struggle between the branches of government."[21] What should be the balance between bureaucratic autonomy and accountability today?

Sources of Bureaucratic Autonomy

The sources of bureaucratic autonomy are several. They can be thought of as internal and external. Internal sources of influence derive from the nature of bureaucracy, whereas external sources of influence involve ties into the broader political community and society.

The first and most important internal source of bureaucratic influence is expertise. The president has several dozen reasonably close personal advisers. Congress has several thousand staff to advise members and committees. The civilian bureaucracy consists of 2.7 million men and women, many of them highly educated technical experts, who run programs that draw directly on their education and experience.

The expertise available in the bureaucracy is deepened by the way bureaucracy is organized. First, experience brings knowledge of history, people, personalities, and options. The Department of State was established in 1789, the Department of Agriculture in 1862, and the Departments of Labor and Commerce in 1903. These institutions have been working their issues for a long time. Within each department, division of labor and specialization mean that workers and managers focus on one program or one task. Hence, they come to know more about their program or task—about how it works, what it does well, and how it could be improved—than anyone else in or out of government. If information is power, as is commonly said, then bureaucracies are storehouses of power.[22]

Constituency ties are another of the bureaucracy's stoutest lines of external defense against serious challenges to its power, independence, and privileges. The phrase "iron triangles" has long been used to describe strong ties among the bureaucrats who administer programs, the legislators who authorize and fund them, and the constituents who benefit from them. Similar, although looser and more occasional, constituency relationships are variously described as issue networks, policy communities, and advocacy coalitions.

Controlling the Bureaucracy

In our constitutional system of separation of powers and checks and balances, the bureaucracy takes direction from many sources.[23] The president exercises influence over the bureaucracy through his power of appointment, his power to propose new programs and budgets, and his power to restructure and reorganize. The legislature grants or refuses new programs and funding, confirms nominees, and engages in oversight and investigation. The judiciary intervenes to resolve disputes over interpretation of statutes and to monitor due process and fairness. These constitute powerful limits on bureaucratic discretion and make the bureaucracy more responsive to its several masters than is commonly realized.[24]

Executive Control. The president has three main sources of control over the bureaucracy. These sources of control have the potential to enhance coordination and accountability in government. First, the president can use his power of appointment and removal to place loyal and competent executives in the top layers of the bureaucracy. Second, the president can alter administrative procedures and reorganize agencies and departments to better achieve his purposes. Third, the president can centralize decision-making authority over personnel, programs, and budgets in the Office of Personnel Management (OPM), the Office of Management and Budget (OMB), and his various policy councils.[25]

Presidents select, often subject to Senate confirmation, the officials who serve at the top levels of the bureaucracy. These officials serve as the president's representatives in and to their departments and agencies. Presidents try in numerous ways—through the heavy hand of the OMB, through participation in policy councils and other decision-making groups, and through personal meetings and communication with senior White House officials—to keep their appointees committed to their programs.

Some presidents, often Republican presidents, use their leverage over the bureaucracy to limit its intrusion into the private sector. Conservatives tend to think that compliance with bureaucratic rules and regulations constrains competitiveness and drives unnecessary costs into business. Some presidents, often Democratic presidents and certainly Barack Obama, empower the bureaucracy to insure that federal laws and regulations are closely followed. For example, the Obama administration blamed lax regulation of the financial industry for permitting the great recession of 2009 and 2010. They proposed a council of regulators to monitor systemic risk and a new consumer financial protection agency to insure that consumers understood the financial products they used. Many Republicans argued that increased bureaucracy would stifle financial innovation and limit consumer choice. Is increased financial regulation a good idea or not?

Every president reorganizes his White House staff, and nearly every president seeks—some at the margins, some more thoroughly—to reorganize the bureaucracy. Political reform often is simply an attempt to upgrade communications, personnel, and financial systems—to bring the "best practices" of the private sector into the public sector. Eleven major reform efforts were undertaken during the twentieth century (see Table 11.5).

Sometimes broader attempts are made to reorganize the bureaus, agencies, and departments of the federal government. Since World War II, several new cabinet-level departments have been added to the federal bureaucracy. President Truman reorganized the national security bureaucracy. President Johnson divided the Department of Health, Education, and Welfare into the Department of Health and Human Services and the Department of Education. President Carter added the Department of Energy, President Reagan added the Department of Veterans Affairs, and President Bush added the Department of Homeland Security.

The president's fiscal powers also provide the means for centralizing control over the bureaucracy. Presidents use their power to propose budgets to set the priorities of their administrations. Departments and agencies are required to submit legislative proposals and new rules and regulations to the Office of Management and Budget in the Executive Office of the President for approval before submitting them to Congress or putting them into effect. This gives the White House an opportunity to assure that all new proposals coming from the executive branch comport with the president's program.

Finally, the Bush administration won new flexibility in the wake of 9/11 in organizing the federal workforce. Congress revised civil service rules covering civilian workers in the Department of Defense and the Department of Homeland Security to provide greater flexibility in hiring, promoting, and assigning personnel.

Congressional Control.   Although the president is chief executive and has day-to-day responsibility for managing the bureaucracy, federal agencies are

TABLE 11.5	Major Attempts to Reform the Federal Bureaucracy

1. Keep Commission, 1905–1909: Personnel management, government contracting, and informaton management.

2. President's Commission on Economy and Efficiency, 1910–1913: The case for a national executive budget.

3. Joint Committee on Reorganization, 1921–1924: Methods of redistributing executive functions among the departments.

4. President's Committee on Administrative Management, 1936–1937: Recommended creation of the Executive Office of the President.

5. First Hoover Commission, 1947–1949: Comprehensive review of the organization and function of the executive branch; including creation of the Department of Defense, Central Intelligence Agency, and National Security Council.

6. Second Hoover Commission, 1953–1955: Follow-up to the first Hoover Commission; focused more on policy problems than on organizational structure.

7. Study Commissions on Executive Reorganization, 1953–1968: Series of low-key reforms that produced quiet but important changes.

8. Ash Council, 1969–1971: Proposal for a fundamental restructuring of the executive branch, including creation of four new super departments to encompass existing departments.

9. Carter Reorganization Effort, 1977–1979: Bottom-up, process-based effort to reorganize a government that mostly ended in failure.

10. Grace Commission, 1982–1984: Large-scale effort to determine how government could be operated for less money.

11. National Performance Review, 1993–2000: Attempt to reinvent government to improve its performance.

12. President's Management Agenda, 2001–2009: Attempt to introduce the "best practices" of business into government.

Source: Ronald C. Moe, *Reorganizing the Executive Branch in the Twentieth Century: Landmark Commissions, Report 92–293 GOV* (Congressional Research Service, March 1992), revised and updated.

profoundly dependent on the Congress. Congress creates the agencies, establishes their programs, and allocates funding to them annually. Congress defines their organizational structures, sets personnel ceilings, and enacts such management systems as procurement and accounting standards. Finally, congressional committees closely monitor departments and agencies within their jurisdiction.

Formal committee oversight is often referred to as the "police patrol" approach to congressional review of agency activities. Committees patrol their bureaucratic territories just as the police patrol the neighborhoods assigned to them. Congress also employs the "fire alarm" approach to administrative oversight. Fire alarms include notice and consent provisions that require agencies to submit proposed policies or regulations to committees of Congress before they can go into effect, statutory provisions that mandate the participation of outside groups in agency decision making, and freedom of information and open meeting requirements. These devices constitute an early warning system to which Congress can respond before problems get really serious.

Finally, Congress and its committees draw on several specialized agencies to help with their oversight responsibilities including the Congressional Budget Office (CBO), the General Accounting Office (GAO), and the Congressional Research Service (CRS). Hence, bureaucrats try to assure that administrative actions are consistent with congressional preferences in order to anticipate and avoid adverse reactions.

Judicial Control.   The courts play a central role in enforcing the constraints that they and the Congress have imposed. They do this through the weight of established precedents (past decisions) and the potential for judicial review of current and future bureaucratic actions. The judiciary acts directly through issuing court orders, assessing awards and damages, and setting new standards in landmark rulings.

On the other hand, judicializing administrative decisions is costly in terms of both time and money. The courts require not only that agency decisions be fair and consistent but also that they be based on substantive evidence laid out in a written record. Knowledge that agency decisions are likely to be reviewed by courts makes administrators unduly conservative and encourages parties with disagreements before agencies to be stubborn.

Citizen Participation and Oversight.   Finally, citizens keep a close eye on government, and some feel compelled to speak out. The Administrative

Syracuse Newspapers / Steve Ruark / The Image Works

A citizen voices concerns at a school board meeting held to discuss school closings. The national government usually has to be approached indirectly, by mail, phone, fax, or through groups with a Washington presence.

Procedures Act of 1946 required that citizens have opportunities to participate in and comment on rule making. Rules must be published for public notice and comment at least thirty days before they go into effect. Political scientists Richard Harris and Sidney Milkis highlight the importance of citizen participation. Increased petitioning opportunities, publicly funded intervenor and monitoring programs, advisory committees, sunshine provisions, and freedom of information laws are among the devices that assure citizens participation in the government and bureaucratic processes.[26]

Opportunities to follow government activity have exploded just over the last decade. Walter Oleszek of the Congressional Research Service reports that "the federal government has an estimated 24,000 Internet sites, with many departments and agencies hosting 'blogs, Facebook pages, YouTube channels, Twitter feeds,'" and similar means of outreach.[27] This bureaucratic openness is both to fulfill sunshine requirements and to keep supporters of agencies and their programs informed and connected.

Internet access, increased petitioning opportunities, and advisory committees are meant to give interested members of the public the opportunity to comment during rule making. Publicly funded intervenor programs encourage community organizations to monitor program implementation. For example, public monies have been made available to fund citizens' groups to monitor federal implementation of welfare, clean air and water, and endangered species programs.

Sunshine laws are intended to open—to let the sun shine on—all government deliberations. These laws apply to both legislative and executive officials and are designed to ensure that policy discussions and decisions occur in full public view and not in closed-door sessions. Public meetings must be announced beforehand. Freedom of information laws give the public access to most government records. In general, the assumption is that records are subject to disclosure under the Freedom of Information Act unless they involve personnel records, court records, national security issues, or business and trade secrets.

Chapter Summary

The United States was born in a war against arbitrary and bureaucratic government. Not surprisingly then, when the Founders created their own government, they were careful to limit and check the power that they placed there. Not only did they give the president, Congress, and courts the power to check each other, but they also gave all three, but no one or two alone, prominent roles in directing and controlling the federal bureaucracy.

Although governments have always had their functionaries and officials, true bureaucracy is a modern phenomenon. The term *bureaucracy* refers to a large, complex, hierarchical organization, whether public or private, in which offices have specific missions and employees have specific responsibilities based on merit. Bureaucracy promises uniformity, order, and fairness in the implementation of public policies and programs. On the other hand, there is always the fear that bureaucracy will become rigid, arrogant, inefficient, and expensive.

The federal bureaucracy grew slowly through the nineteenth century. For three-quarters of the nineteenth century, the federal workforce delivered the mail, collected customs duties in the ports, recorded land deeds and marriage certificates, and did little more. During the last quarter of the nineteenth and first quarter of the twentieth centuries, the federal government took on an increasing range of regulatory responsibilities. From the 1930s through the 1970s, the federal government developed and implemented a wide range of programs that provided a social and economic "safety net" below the nation's most vulnerable citizens. In recent years, the size of the federal workforce has begun to increase again.

The federal bureaucracy is divided into fifteen major cabinet departments, twelve independent regulatory commissions, fifty-four major agencies, boards, and services, and literally hundreds of advisory committees and panels. The cabinet departments are organized hierarchically. Below the cabinet secretary are several layers of undersecretaries and assistant secretaries before one gets to the level of the bureau or service where the actual administration of programs and delivery of services take place. Program implementation is made difficult by the presence of imprecise and contradictory goals, fragmentation and faulty coordination, and imprecise measures of success.

The president, Congress, and courts all have prominent roles in guiding and directing the work of the bureaucracy. Congress creates bureaucratic entities, sets and limits their responsibilities, and allocates funding and personnel levels to them annually. The president appoints their leaders, proposes new programs and annual funding levels, and oversees their daily operations. The courts review bureaucratic decisions and actions, act directly through court orders, and assess awards and damages. The bureaucracy often appears to be unable to move in any direction without offending one or more of its masters.

Bureaucratic reorganization and reform are nearly continuous processes. The creation of the Department of Homeland Security during 2002 and 2003 was the largest reform in more than half a century. It will be many years, perhaps decades, before fair and informed judgments can be made about the success or failure of the reforms that created DHS.

Key Terms

administrative adjudication 361	patronage 349
Administrative Procedures Act (APA) 361	Pendleton Act 349
bureaucracy 349	regulatory commissions 358
civil service system 349	rule making 361
implementation 362	spoils system 360
Interstate Commerce Commission (ICC) 353	

Suggested Readings

Aberbach, Joel D. *Keeping a Watchful Eye: The Politics of Congressional Oversight.* Washington, D.C.: Brookings Institution, 1990. Study showing that congressional oversight of the bureaucracy is a multifaceted and ongoing set of activities that has become increasingly important since the early 1970s.

Carpenter, Daniel. "The Evolution of the National Bureaucracy," 2005. Carpenter highlights the professionalization of the federal bureaucracy as it has evolved away from basic services toward professional and managerial services.

Carpenter, Daniel. *Reputation and Power: Organizational Image and Pharmaceutical Regulation at the FDA.* Princeton, NJ: Princeton University Press, 2010. Carpenter shows how important the FDA's culture of competence has been in encouraging pharmaceutical companies to respect and obey FDA guidelines and commands.

Eggers, William and John O'Leary. *If We Can Put a Man On the Moon: Getting Big Things Done in Government.* Cambridge, MA: Harvard Business School Press, 2009. The process by which important legislation is passed in Congress makes the resulting programs difficult for the bureaucracy to administer.

Goodsell, Charles T. *The Case for Bureaucracy: A Public Administration Polemic*, 4th ed. Chatham, NJ: Chatham House, 2004. The bureaucracy is subject to a great deal of criticism. Goodsell draws on a wide range of argument and information to make a strongly positive case for the bureaucracy.

Kettl, Donald F. *System under Stress: Homeland Security and American Politics.* Washington, D.C.: CQ Press, 2004. Kettl critiques the design and early implementation of the Department of Homeland Security.

Lynn, Laurence E., Jr. "Theodore Roosevelt Redux: Barack Obama Confronts American Bureaucracy." *International Journal of Public Administration*, 2009, 32, 773–780. Lynn describes the difficulties bureaucrats had in spending wisely the stimulus funding during the early Obama administration.

Web Resources

For practice quizzes, key term flashcards, videos, links, and other study tools, visit the *American Government* website: www.routledge.com/cw/jillson

1. **www.whitehouse.gov/government/independent-agencies.html**
   The White House's comprehensive page links to all federal government websites. These sites will give you an insight into bureaucracy.

2. **www.usajobs.opm.gov**
   The Federal government's official site for those interested in jobs. The site is run by the Office of Personnel Management.

3. **www.faculty.rsu.edu/~felwell/Theorists/Weber/Whome.htm**
   This site offers access to several of Max Weber's writings on bureaucracy and government in general.

4. **www.gpoaccess.gov/index.html**
   The Government Printing Office website opens onto many sources covering the bureaucracy as well as the legislative and judicial branches. Don't miss "Ben's [Ben Franklin's] Guide to U.S. Government."

5. **www.lcweb.loc.gov/global/executive/fed.html**
   A Library of Congress page dedicated to listing links to all federal government websites.

Chapter 12

THE FEDERAL COURTS
Activism versus Restraint

The Judicial Department comes home in its effects to every man's fireside: it passes on his property, his reputation, his life, his all.

CHIEF JUSTICE JOHN MARSHALL
Debates of the Virginia Convention, 1829

The Constitution TODAY

DOES THE CONSTITUTION ENVISION JUDICIAL REVIEW?

Article III, sections 1 and 2 (in part): "The judicial power of the United States shall be vested in one Supreme Court, and in such inferior courts as the Congress may from time to time ordain and establish .... The judicial power shall extend to all cases, ... arising under this Constitution, the laws of the United States, and treaties made, ... under their authority."

Each January the president delivers a "State of the Union" address to a joint session of Congress. While these speeches are broadcast live in prime time and closely watched, few of them are memorable. President Obama's 2010 State of the Union address was memorable because he criticized the Supreme Court, seated directly in front of him, for a recent decision. The court overturned a century of law and judicial precedent barring corporate spending on elections, declaring these limits to be unconstitutional violations of corporate free speech rights. Obama thought those laws and precedents not just constitutional, but critical defenses of the integrity of American elections. Could Obama have simply said "I disagree," and ordered the Justice Department and Federal Election Commission to continue implementing the legal prohibitions on corporate campaign spending? No, but this is not the first time the question had come up.

One of the most consequential fights in American political history occurred in Thomas Jefferson's first term as president. The federal government was still relatively new and the relationships between the executive, legislative, and judicial branches were not yet set. The judiciary was an independent branch of government, but as Alexander Hamilton famously wrote in Federalist Number 78, it was considered the "least dangerous branch." The president commanded the power of the sword; the Congress commanded the power of the purse; but what power resources did the courts command?

Judicial review, the power to declare federal and state laws null and void, became the foundation of judicial power. The basic storyline behind the Supreme Court's first use of judicial review in *Marbury v. Madison* (1803) is well known. Thomas Jefferson and his Jeffersonian Republicans won the election of 1800, displacing Federalist President John Adams and the Federalist majorities in Congress. Before the new administration took power, President Adams and the Federalists in Congress sought to maintain control of the judiciary by creating new courts and filling them with dependable Federalist judges. Jefferson dismantled the new courts and refused to seat most of their judges. The issue was carried into the courts, setting up a confrontation between Chief Justice John Marshall and President Thomas Jefferson.

Marshall knew that he was playing the weaker political hand. He could order Jefferson to deliver Marbury's judicial appointment papers. But Jefferson could simply ignore the order, thus highlighting and perhaps permanently establishing the weakness of the court. Instead, Marshall deftly masked the court's current weakness to lay the foundation for its future strength.

Marshall declared that while Marbury deserved his judicial appointment, the court could not order its delivery because the law by which the previous Federalist Congress and president had created the new courts was unconstitutional. Marshall both avoided issuing an order that Jefferson might ignore and employed a power, judicial review, that the Supreme Court had not previously exercised. Marshall made two critical points; one, that laws which contravene the Constitution are void, and, two, that it is the court's particular duty to declare them so. Marshall wrote that the very logic of written constitutions and limited government "must be, that an act of the legislature repugnant to the constitution is void." He then added that, "it is emphatically the province and duty of the judicial department to say what the law is."

Jefferson and most observers agreed with Marshall's first point, a law that contravenes the Constitution is void, but many, including Jefferson, disagreed with his second point, that it is distinctively the court's role to say which acts of government are constitutional and which are not. Jefferson believed that each department of government, the executive, legislative, and judicial was entitled to interpret the Constitution in regard to its own powers and responsibilities. Jefferson laid out his "departmental" view of constitutional interpretation in a letter to Abigail Adams, former President Adams' wife, concerning pardons that he had issued to journalists convicted under the Alien and Sedition Acts. He wrote that the executive and judicial branches "are equally independent in the sphere of action assigned to them. The judges, believing the law constitutional, had a right to pass a sentence of fine and imprisonment, because that power was placed in their hands by the constitution. But the executive, believing the law to be unconstitutional, was bound to remit the execution of it; because that power has been confided to him by the constitution." Jefferson held to his "departmental" view of constitutional interpretation throughout his life.

WHAT DO YOU THINK?

- Do you think Obama agrees with Marshall or Jefferson?
- With which do you agree?
- What dangers might the "departmental" view of constitutional interpretation hold?
- What is the alternative—judicial supremacy?

Focus Questions: from reading to thinking

Q1 What are the main differences between the civil code tradition and the common law tradition?

Q2 How did the theory and practice of judicial review arise in the United States?

Q3 What is the place of the Supreme Court in the judicial system of the United States?

Q4 How have the climate and tone surrounding the process of nomination and confirmation to judicial posts changed since the mid-1950s?

Q5 Is judicial activism necessary because some issues are just too difficult for the political branches of the government to confront?

THE FEDERAL COURTS

L aw and the courts play a larger and more powerful role in the United States than in any other country in the world. In most countries, the courts simply apply current law. In the United States, courts judge current law and policy in light of the more fundamental law of the U.S. Constitution. The temperature around our judges and courts has risen in recent decades because they decide so many critical issues.

Political scientist Herbert Jacob defines **law** very simply as "authoritative rules made by government."[1] Another student of the American judicial system, Henry Abraham, offers a similar but somewhat more descriptive definition. Abraham says that "law, broadly speaking, represents the rules of conduct that pertain to a given political order of society, rules that are backed by the organized force of the community."[2] Although all law is backed by the legitimate authority of the community, there is a hierarchy in U.S. law based on the source from which it flows. The Constitution is the most fundamental source of law; legislation is next; and executive orders and agency rules and regulations are the lowest. To be legally binding, agency rules must implement valid statutes, and statutes to be valid must fall within the range of legislative authority granted in the Constitution. Disagreements about what law requires, permits, or prohibits are taken before courts for resolution.

In this chapter we describe the origins, development, structure, and role of the U.S. federal courts. First, we describe the English common law background

law Authoritative rules made by government and backed by the organized force of the community.

KEVIN LAMARQUE / Reuters / Landov

Chief Justice John G. Roberts Jr. was sworn in on September 29, 2005, by Justice John Paul Stevens as President Bush and Jane Sullivan Roberts watched.

of American law and the formal origins of U.S. courts in Article III of the Constitution. Second, we describe the evolving substantive focus of the federal courts from economic issues to individual rights and liberties. Third, we describe the three-tier structure of the federal courts, rising from the district courts, through a layer of appellate courts, to the United States Supreme Court.

We conclude the chapter by dealing with two volatile issues—judicial selection and judicial philosophy. Judicial selection involves the process and politics of selecting persons to serve in the federal courts. After more than eleven years in which the U.S. Supreme Court did not change at all, it acquired four new members, Chief Justice John Roberts in 2005, Associate Justice Samuel Alito in 2006, Associate Justice Sonia Sotomayor in 2009, and Associate Justice Elena Kagan in 2010. Judicial philosophy involves the disputed role of judges in our democracy. Should judges merely apply the law or should they interpret and expand the law to fit new cases and address pressing social issues?

THE COMMON LAW ORIGINS OF THE AMERICAN LEGAL SYSTEM

Two legal traditions are dominant in the West. One is the civil code tradition that has its roots in ancient Rome, the medieval Catholic Church, and more recently in France. The other is the common law tradition that has its origins in England and in which the United States shares. The civil code tradition is older and more widely used.

The **civil code** tradition envisions a comprehensive legal system that is promulgated or announced complete at a particular point in time. The civil code tradition has its origins in the fourth century Roman Empire, when the Emperor Justinian created a complete and detailed statement of Roman law that came to be known as Justinian's Code. This tradition was carried forward through the Middle Ages in the ecclesiastical law of the Roman Catholic Church and into the modern period by Napoleon late in the eighteenth century. The Napoleonic Code was designed to be a complete and comprehensive legal system based on simple principles that could be readily understood by citizens and applied by judges and magistrates.

The legal traditions of the United States derive from those of England and were deeply embedded in the American mind well before national independence. The English **common law** tradition involved the slow and incremental accumulation of judicial decisions over time. The phrase *common law* refers to the law as announced by the king's judges and therefore common to the whole realm as opposed to the customs and traditions of one local community or region. Over the centuries this judge-made common law expanded into a "broad jurisprudence of right and remedy" that colonial Americans identified as a principal defense of their liberties.[3] The common law limited the power of government and constrained the ways in which power might assert itself against individual citizens.

Q1 What are the main differences between the civil code tradition and the common law tradition?

civil code Legal tradition that envisions a complete and fully articulated legal system based on clear statutes that lay out legal principles and commands in plain language that citizens can understand and obey.

common law Judge-made law, as opposed to a fully integrated legal code, developed over time as judges consider particular legal disputes and then future judges cite earlier decisions in resolving similar issues.

Two statements by England's most famous jurist, Sir Edward Coke, chief justice of the King's Bench during the early seventeenth century, describe the role of the common law and the courts in limiting political power. On November 13, 1608, in response to the king's assertion that he could decide legal disputes on his own royal authority, Chief Justice Coke responded that "the King in his own person cannot adjudge any case . . . but that this ought to be determined and adjudged in some Court of Justice, according to the law and custom of England."

Bonham's Case (1610) British case in which Sir Edward Coke, chief justice of the King's Bench, laid the foundation for judicial review.

Two years later, in ***Bonham's Case*** (1610), Coke noted that "It appears in our books, that . . . when an Act of Parliament is against common right and reason . . . the common law will controul it, and adjudge such Act to be void."[4] During the colonial and early national periods American jurists developed the idea that political power is constrained by law and that some acts of the political authorities are null, void, and unenforceable because they conflict with the fundamental traditions of the community as articulated initially in its common law, and later in its written constitution.

Two judicial principles, precedent and *stare decisis*, help explain the nature and development of the common law. The common law is a body of legal traditions and principles developed over time as judges consider and solve particular legal problems and disputes. Judges cite these earlier decisions as **precedents** or controlling examples in resolving later cases that involve similar issues. The judicial principle of ***stare decisis***, which is Latin, meaning "let the decision stand," is the injunction to depend on earlier cases or precedents to decide later cases of a similar nature.

precedent A judicial decision that serves as a rule or guide for deciding later cases of a similar nature.

stare decisis The judicial principle of relying on past decisions or precedents to devise rulings in later cases.

British colonists brought the common law with them when they emigrated, but in the intervening four centuries American legislatures have refined and specified common law principles in state and federal statutes. While the principles of the common law—the key role of judges, case law, and precedents—are still clearly visible in American law, specific rights and responsibilities are ensconced in statutes.

THE CRIMINAL LAW AND THE CIVIL LAW

Within both the common law and the civil code traditions there is a distinction between two general types of statutory law. **Criminal law** prohibits certain actions and prescribes penalties for those who engage in the prohibited actions. Murder, rape, and burglary are violations of the criminal law. Criminal charges are brought by government against an individual or individuals, and convictions can result in jail time or even in the death penalty in jurisdictions that permit it. The **civil law** deals primarily with relations between private persons or organizations as in marriage and family law, contracts, and the buying and selling of property. Civil charges are brought by one individual against another, and violations result more in judgments and fines than in incarceration or physical punishment.

criminal law Criminal law prohibits certain actions and prescribes penalties for those who engage in the prohibited conduct.

civil law Civil law deals primarily with relations between individuals and organizations, as in marriage and family law, contracts, and property. Violations result more in judgments and fines than punishment as such.

Surely the most famous example of the difference between criminal law and civil law and the penalties related to both types involves the prosecutions between 1995 and 1997 of O. J. Simpson for the deaths of Nicole Brown Simpson and Ronald Goldman. Simpson was a former USC and NFL running back, a national celebrity, so the cases drew extraordinary attention. In the criminal trial, the charge was murder and penalties ranged up to imprisonment for life. Simpson was acquitted because the evidence was not conclusive "beyond a reasonable doubt." He was later convicted on the charge of wrongful death in the civil trial in which the standard was "a preponderance of the evidence" and the jury awarded the Brown and Goldman families large monetary awards for damages. In a remarkably similar pair of criminal and civil cases during 2004 and 2005, the actor Robert Blake was acquitted of murdering his wife, Bonnie Lee Bakley, only to be found guilty of "intentionally causing her death" in a subsequent civil case.

CASES AND THE LAW

The American legal system is set in motion only when a case or controversy brings parties, one of which may be a governmental entity, who are directly involved in a dispute before an appropriate court. Henry Abraham notes that "the presence of the following four conditions: (1) an adversary process, (2) a justiciable issue, (3) ripeness for judicial determination, and (4) an actual disposition" are required in disputes that come before the American judiciary for resolution.[5]

American courts deal in real cases and controversies; they do not give advisory opinions or respond to hypothetical or "what if?" queries from individuals or from public officials. The adversary process involves a complainant who alleges a specific wrong act and a respondent who denies that the act was wrong or denies that he or she committed the act if it was wrong. Courts judge whether an individual has standing or eligibility to come before the court by whether he or she is suffering or threatened with real harm from the act complained of.

Second, a court must determine whether the controversy brought before it is justiciable. **Justiciability** simply means subject to judicial resolution. Some issues are thought to require political rather than judicial resolution, and the courts have traditionally declined to enter what has been referred to as the "political thicket." For example, in the late 1970s, President Jimmy Carter on his own authority cancelled the Common Defense Treaty with Taiwan in order to establish diplomatic relations with China. Senator Barry Goldwater (R-AZ) asked the Supreme Court to declare that the president could not abrogate treaties without the consent of the Senate. The Court declared this to be a political dispute and declined to intervene.

justiciability Legal term indicating that an issue or dispute is appropriate for or subject to judicial resolution.

Third, courts consider whether an issue is ripe for judicial resolution. Ripeness involves the questions of timeliness and necessity. For example, a legislative action like the passage of term limits that threaten harm somewhere down the road but have not yet produced harm by displacing a public

LET'S COMPARE

Worldwide Usage of the Common Law and Civil Code Traditions

In a world in which distances have shrunk dramatically and people and capital move rapidly about, how the various societies of the world are organized makes a big difference. American corporations seeking to do business in the successor states of the former Soviet Union, eastern Europe, Asia, and Latin America must understand the legal systems of these countries. Each nation's legal system defines how property is established and transferred, the kinds of business endeavors and practices that are permitted, and the kinds of taxes and other charges to which businesses and their employees are subject.

Just as religious scholars identify several major religious traditions—Christianity, Judaism, Islam, Buddhism, Shintoism—so legal scholars identify several major legal traditions. The common law and civil code traditions are the most widely practiced, although the particular legal traditions of many nations are mixes of the common law or civil code tradition and the religious rules and traditional mores of their societies.

Finally, the collapse of communism in the former Soviet Union and eastern Europe led these nations to reassess their positions in the world economy and to adjust their legal systems accordingly. Hence, most communist legal systems were recast in the early 1990s to reflect the assumptions of private property and capitalist enterprise. Most of the nations that abandoned communist legal systems have put civil code systems in their place.

Attention now focuses on the struggle of the Islamic or Muslim legal tradition, particularly its conservative Shari'ah strain, to find its place in the modern world. The 2007 "Girl of Qatif" case, in which Saudi courts sentenced a 19-year-old who had been gang raped to prison and 200 lashes, drew worldwide attention. The court ruled that the woman had erred by being alone in a car with a man who was not a relative. International outrage eventually led the Saudi King to commute the sentence. In 2009 a Saudi child bride, eight years old, was granted a divorce from her 50-year-old husband.

Civil Code Tradition[a]	Common Law Tradition[b]	Religious and Traditional Law[c]
France, Italy, Spain, Portugal, Germany, Austria, Switzerland, Denmark, Sweden, Holland, Norway, Finland, Greece, Chile, Brazil, Argentina, Japan, Taiwan, Thailand, South Korea, Indonesia	United Kingdom, United States, Ireland, Jordan, Australia, New Zealand, South Africa, Canada	*Muslim Law* Pakistan, Morocco, Tunisia, Syria, Iran, Indonesia, Mauritania, Algeria, Saudi Arabia, Yemen, Kuwait *Hindu Law* India *Jewish Law* Israel

[a] Most of Europe, all of Latin America, much of Africa, some of Asia.
[b] Mostly Great Britain and her former colonies.
[c] In most cases, religious law exists alongside the secular law of the state. Areas like family law, marriage, and succession are most likely to be shaped by religious law. In extreme cases, secular law is a thin veneer behind which the customary or religious law holds sway.

official would be avoided. The courts would assume that the legislature that passed the bill might retract it before anyone was actually injured. Courts do not act until someone has been harmed or harm is clearly imminent. Finally, courts treat only cases in which their findings will, at least potentially, resolve or dispose of the issue. U.S. courts, for example, will dismiss cases in which there is insufficient evidence to convict or in which evidence has been illegally obtained.

THE BIRTH OF THE AMERICAN LEGAL SYSTEM

The English colonies in North America were born into the common law tradition. After independence, they sought to purge that tradition of its monarchal and aristocratic elements but retain its fundamental procedures and its focus on individual and property rights. Each state thought itself sovereign and developed an independent judiciary. Although the states were loosely bound together by the Articles of Confederation, the confederation provided no national judiciary.

Adoption of the federal Constitution changed that, providing for a national government with separated, defined, and limited powers. Article III, section 1, of the Constitution declared: "The judicial power of the United States, shall be vested in one Supreme Court, and in such inferior courts as the Congress may from time to time ordain and establish." Other key provisions in the Constitution provided the foundation for the independence and stature of the American judiciary and of the Supreme Court in particular. Although the foundation of judicial power was laid in the Constitution, the structure of judicial authority remained to be built. That construction occurred during the new nation's early history.

As President Washington and the first Congress took office, it remained unclear what role the judiciary would play in American political life, how much power it would have, and how it would defend itself and check its competitors in Congress and the executive branch. The checks and balances that were to hold the executive and legislative powers in place seemed clear; but how the judiciary would defend itself was much less clear. Alexander Hamilton famously noted in Federalist Number 78 that the federal judiciary was "the least dangerous branch" of the new government. Congress wielded the power of the purse, and the executive wielded the sword. Moreover, the other branches would have to set the judiciary in motion. The president would have to nominate the judges who would be subject to Senate approval, and Congress would have to give structure and authority to the lower federal courts with, of course, the president's approval.

Yet ideas and practices were at large that suggested an important role for American courts. In a series of decisions between 1780 and 1787, state courts had held state statutes void because they violated provisions of state constitutions. Moreover, elsewhere in Federalist 78, Hamilton explained that "the courts were designed to be an intermediate body between the people and the legislature, in order among other things, to keep the latter within the limits assigned to their authority." Hamilton reasoned that if the limits on government embedded in the Constitution were to be meaningful, "the courts of justice . . . must . . . declare all acts contrary to the manifest tenor of the Constitution void. Without this, all the reservations of particular rights or privileges would amount to nothing." Hamilton was right. Nonetheless, the judiciary had to fight to establish its place and power in the new government.

The Judiciary Act of 1789 and the Early Courts

Q2 How did the theory and practice of judicial review arise in the United States?

Judiciary Act of 1789 Originating act for the federal judiciary passed by the first Congress.

The first Congress under the new Constitution turned immediately to organizing the federal judiciary. The **Judiciary Act of 1789** constituted the Supreme Court with six justices and created a two-tiered system of lower federal courts. Moreover, section 25 charged the federal courts to review acts and decisions of the state governments for compatibility with the Constitution and with federal statutes. The Judiciary Act of 1789 is still the basic law governing the federal courts though, of course, it has been amended many times.

The Judiciary Act of 1789 defined the structure and basic procedures of the federal court system. Each state had a district court to exercise trial jurisdiction, and there were three circuit or appellate courts—the eastern, the middle, and the southern districts. The circuit courts were composed of two Supreme Court justices (one after 1793) and the local district judges "riding circuit" throughout their territory. During the first 120 years of the Supreme Court's history, the requirement that justices ride circuit for much of the year, and at least part of the year until 1912 made the job arduous and unappealing.

The Marshall Court, 1801–1835

Virginia's John Marshall served as chief justice of the U.S. Supreme Court for thirty-four years, from 1801 to 1835. During that time, Marshall took a Court whose power and position in the new government were unclear and established it as an equal and coordinate branch of the national government (see Table 12.1). In addition to establishing its own place and power in the national government, the Marshall Court also gave content and weight to the supremacy clause.

In the famous case of *Marbury v. Madison* (1803), Marshall declared judicial review to be the prerogative of the courts. He wrote, on behalf of a unanimous Supreme Court, that "it is, emphatically, the province and duty of the judicial department, to say what the law is. . . . So, if a law be in opposition to the constitution; the court must . . . decide that case . . . conformable to the constitution, disregarding the law."

Marshall's goal of securing the position and importance of the judiciary in the new national government did not go unopposed. Years later, President

TABLE 12.1 The Court in American Political History	
Substantive Regime	**Justices and Cases**
Founding	Judiciary Act of 1789 is passed (1789)
National Consolidation	John Marshall is appointed Chief Justice (1801)
	Marbury v. Madison (1803)
	McCulloch v. Maryland (1819)
States' Rights	Roger B. Taney is appointed Chief Justice (1836)
	Charles River Bridge v. Warren Bridge (1837)
	Dred Scott v. Sandford (1857)
Civil War	Thirteenth Amendment ratified (1865)
	Fourteenth Amendment ratified (1868)
	Fifteenth Amendment ratified (1870)
Laissez-Faire	*Santa Clara v. Southern Pacific Railroad* (1886)
	Plessy v. Ferguson (1896)
	"Court packing" plan submitted to Congress (1937)
Judicial Activism	Earl Warren appointed Chief Justice (1953)
	Brown v. Board of Education (1954)
	Thurgood Marshall is first black Supreme Court justice (1967)
	Justice William Rehnquist appointed (1971)
	Sandra Day O'Connor is first woman Supreme Court justice (1981)
Conservative Reaction	William Rehnquist appointed Chief Justice (1986)
	*Antonin Scalia appointed to the court (1986)
	*Anthony Kennedy appointed to the court (1987)
	*Clarence Thomas appointed to the court (1991)
	*Ruth Bader Ginsburg appointed to the court (1993)
	*Stephen Breyer appointed to the court (1994)
	*Chief Justice John Roberts appointed to the court (2005)
	*Samuel Alito appointed to the court (2006)
	*Sonia Sotomayor first Hispanic on the court (2009)
	*Elena Kagan appointed to the court (2010)
	Citizens United v. FEC (2010)

*Current members of the United States Supreme Court

Jefferson was still arguing that Marshall's expansive reading of the judiciary's role violated separation of powers. Jefferson argued to Virginia Judge Spencer Roane in a letter of September 6, 1819 that each of the three branches of government "has an equal right to decide for itself the meaning of the Constitution in the cases submitted to its action ... and that the Court is neither more learned nor more objective than the political branches of the government." Nor was Jefferson alone in his resistance to the dominant role that John Marshall claimed for the federal courts in constitutional interpretation. In 1832 President Andrew Jackson claimed that "the Supreme Court . . . ought not to control the coordinate authorities of the Government. The Congress, the Executive, and the Court must each for itself be guided by its own opinion of the Constitution."[6] Nonetheless, Marshall's view, firmly pressed over his three and one-half decades as chief justice, prevailed.

Judicial Review

judicial review Power of any federal court to hold any law or official act based on law to be unenforceable because it is in conflict with the Constitution.

Judicial review is the power of the federal courts to hold any law or any official act based on law to be null, void, and unenforceable because it is in conflict with the Constitution.[7] Although the federal courts have used the power of judicial review sparingly, particularly in regard to federal statutes, the fact that judicial review exists has acted as a constraint on the president and Congress.

Judicial Review of Congressional Legislation.   Although the exercise of judicial review is usually thought of as striking down acts of the president and Congress, this has in fact been fairly uncommon (see Table 12.2). On only

TABLE 12.2	Number of Federal Statutes Held Unconstitutional by the Supreme Court, 1790–2014		
Period	**Number**	**Period**	**Number**
1790–1799	0	1900–1909	9
1800–1809	1	1910–1919	6
1810–1819	0	1920–1929	15
1820–1829	0	1930–1939	13
1830–1839	0	1940–1949	2
1840–1849	0	1950–1959	4
1850–1859	1	1960–1969	18
1860–1869	4	1970–1979	19
1870–1879	7	1980–1989	16
1880–1889	4	1990–1999	24
1890–1899	5	2000–2009	16
		2010–2014	13
		Total	177

Source: Lawrence Baum, *The Supreme Court,* 11th ed. (Washington, D.C.: Congressional Quarterly Press, 2013), 168; see also Harold W. Stanley and Richard G. Niemi, *Vital Statisticson American Politics, 2015–2016* (Washington, D.C.: Congressional Quarterly Press, 2015), 289.

two occasions before the Civil War, the landmark cases of *Marbury v. Madison* (1803) and *Dred Scott v. Sandford* (1857), did the Supreme Court strike down acts of Congress. Judicial review became more frequent after the Civil War and more frequent still after 1960. Its rate of use increased again in the mid-1990s. Still, only 168 acts of Congress have been declared unconstitutional over the entire history of the country.

Judicial Review of State Legislation. One of the main reasons for replacing the Articles of Confederation with the stronger federal Constitution was so some national government entity could oversee, monitor, and coordinate the activities of the several state governments. Many people, including Madison, argued for a mandatory national review of all state laws before they went into effect. Although this requirement, referred to in the Constitutional Convention as the "universal negative," was not included in the Constitution, the supremacy clause did allow review of state actions that appeared to conflict with the national Constitution. Not surprisingly, the federal courts have employed judicial review more frequently against the states than against Congress and the president (see Table 12.3).

About 1,300 state laws and provisions of state constitutions have been declared unconstitutional since 1790. Judicial review of the acts of the states was used with increasing frequency until the late 1980s. Since then, the high

Table 12.3	Number of State Laws and Local Ordinances Held Unconstitutional by the Supreme Court, 1790–2014		
Period	Number	Period	Number
1790–1799	0	1900–1909	40
1800–1809	1	1910–1919	119
1810–1819	7	1920–1929	139
1820–1829	8	1930–1939	92
1830–1839	3	1940–1949	61
1840–1849	10	1950–1959	66
1850–1859	7	1960–1969	151
1860–1869	24	1970–1979	195
1870–1879	36	1980–1989	164
1880–1889	46	1990–1999	62
1890–1899	36	2000–2009	38
		2010–2014	16
		Total	1,321

Source: Lawrence Baum, *The Supreme Court,* 11th ed. (Washington, D.C.: Congressional Quarterly Press, 2013), 163; see also Harold W. Stanley and Richard G. Niemi, *Vital Statistics on American Politics, 2015–2016* (Washington, D.C.: Congressional Quarterly Press, 2015), 289.

court's increasing respect for the rights and autonomy of the states led to a precipitous drop in those numbers.

Judicial Review of Lower Court Action.   The Supreme Court exercises a particularly intensive form of judicial review over the lower courts of the federal system. As the vast majority of cases that the Supreme Court hears come as part of its discretionary jurisdiction, as opposed to the mandatory cases that it must hear, only cases that are important and might have been wrongly decided by the lower courts are chosen for hearing and decision. Hence, fully two-thirds of the cases reviewed by the Supreme Court result in reversal of the lower court in whole or in part.[8]

THE SUPREME COURT AND THE EVOLUTION OF INDIVIDUAL RIGHTS

John Marshall's death in 1835 allowed President Andrew Jackson to appoint Roger B. Taney in his place. Jackson, Taney, and the Democratic Party sought to make the rights to property and contract that had been the focus of the Marshall Court more compatible with the broader rights of the community. Orestes A. Brownson, a prominent Jacksonian editor, expressed the Democratic Party's philosophy in the following terms: "We believe property should be held subordinate to man, and not man to property."[9]

During the post-Civil War period, when the Republican Party was ascendent, the rights of property, and particularly its corporate form, reasserted themselves dramatically. The Court largely rejected the government's right to regulate property because the majority believed that the rights to hold property and to contract are sacred and inviolate. The Great Depression of the 1930s brought the Democrats back to power and convinced many Americans that the economy did require government management and intervention. President Franklin Roosevelt forced the Supreme Court to permit increased government regulation of the economy. The Warren and Burger Courts of the mid-1950s through the 1970s increasingly shifted their focus to individual rights and liberties. The Rehnquist and Roberts Courts have sought, with increasing success, to swing the pendulum from a focus on individual rights back in the direction of property rights.

The Taney Court and States' Rights

Charles River Bridge v. Warren Bridge (1837) The Court limited the more expansive property rights precedents of the Marshall Court and concluded that any ambiguity within a contract should be interpreted to benefit the public interest, asserting the rights of the community without fundamentally damaging property rights.

The chief contribution of the Taney Court was to assert the rights of the community without fundamentally damaging the rights of property. The critical ruling in this regard came in the case of ***Charles River Bridge v. Warren Bridge*** (1837). The Massachusetts state legislature awarded a charter for a toll bridge across the Charles River near Boston. When a second bridge was proposed, one that would charge a toll only until costs were recouped and would be free thereafter, the owners of the Charles River Bridge sued on the claim that the charter was exclusive and should be read as prohibiting competitors.

The Taney Court held that to read the Charles River Bridge company's charter as exclusive was to permit a private company to dictate the future growth and progress of the community. The community had the right to enjoy and benefit from economic development and scientific advance unless charters expressly awarded monopoly rights. This and similar decisions, although less categorical in defense of property than the Marshall Court might have rendered, both facilitated rapid economic development and gave government some means to guide and direct it.

The darker side of the Taney Court's legacy came in its defense of states' rights and, more explicitly, of property in human beings. In fact, the Taney Court overstepped disastrously in attempting to secure the southern position on states' rights and the place of slavery in the Union in its infamous *Dred Scott v. Sandford* (1857) ruling. In essence, the Court ruled that blacks could not be citizens and that slaves carried into free states and territories remained property. This decision did much to bring on the Civil War by suggesting that free states and territories could not exclude slavery even if they wished.

Laissez-Faire and Property Rights

The results of the Civil War, while resolving the issue of national power over the states, reasserted the rights of corporate property. Industrial capitalism was given an enormous boost by the demands of the Civil War. Even as the northern economy expanded dramatically, the Supreme Court developed constitutional interpretations that severely limited the power of government to regulate private enterprise. It interpreted the Fourteenth Amendment, passed initially to protect the rights of newly freed slaves, as providing near-absolute protection for private property against government regulation.

In the case of **Santa Clara County v. Southern Pacific Railroad** (1886), the Court held that the word "persons" in the Fourteenth Amendment applied equally to corporations and to individuals and that hence corporations would enjoy the same benefits of due process and equal protection as did individual persons.[10] The Court sought to protect the free operation of the market by declaring most attempts at government regulation to be violations of **substantive due process,** in other words, by declaring that the mere attempt to regulate was a violation of the due process rights of property holders.

As the focus on property rights increased, attention to the civil rights accorded to former slaves decreased. The Thirteenth, Fourteenth, and Fifteenth Amendments, all passed in the immediate wake of the Civil War, seemed to promise federal protection of civil and political rights for blacks. However, within a decade of their passage, the federal government including

Santa Clara County v. Southern Pacific Railroad (1886) The Court interpreted the word "persons" in the Fourteenth Amendment to apply equally to corporations. The substantive right to enter into contracts was also founded in this decision and used subsequently as a justification for striking down government regulation of business.

substantive due process Late nineteenth-century Supreme Court doctrine holding that most attempts to regulate property were violations of due process.

Getty Images

A Southern Pacific locomotive at the head of a passenger train, circa 1887. A year earlier the U.S. Supreme Court declared that both the passengers on the train and the corporation that owned the train were "persons" for certain legal purposes.

the courts had abandoned their implementation. The period from 1880 to 1930 saw property rights ascendant and civil rights, particularly for blacks, in steep descent.

Nine Old Men and the Switch in Time

When Franklin D. Roosevelt assumed the presidency early in 1933, 78 percent of the federal judiciary and six of nine Supreme Court justices were Republicans, and most were deeply committed to stout judicial defense of private property in a laissez-faire economy. Nonetheless, the grim reality of the Depression steadily drew into question the logic of laissez faire and government nonintervention.

In the 1935–36 Supreme Court term, the justices struck down thirteen administration bills, including two of the mainstays of President Roosevelt's response to the Depression: the National Industrial Recovery Act and the Agricultural Assistance Act.[11] The president's reaction was swift and fierce. President Roosevelt declared: "We have . . . reached the point as a nation where we must take action to save the Constitution from the Court."[12] Roosevelt's attempt to "pack" the Court with more compliant justices failed, but it did shock some of the offending justices into retirement and others became more compliant. Between 1937 and 1943, FDR was able to nominate and have easily confirmed eight new justices.

The new Court followed a tradition of judicial restraint championed by Justices Oliver Wendell Holmes and Louis Brandeis. Both contended, and the Roosevelt administration certainly agreed, that the Court should not obstruct the work of the people's elected representatives in Congress and the White House. The new Court accepted a wide range of new federal government programs designed to stabilize and manage the economy. After 1937 the Court rarely intervened in issues of federal economic regulation.[13]

The Expansion of Individual Rights and Liberties

The appointment of Earl Warren as chief justice of the Supreme Court in 1953 marked a new era. Warren was an accomplished political leader and former governor of California rather than a judicial scholar or sitting judge. He moved the Court from the New Deal posture of judicial restraint and deference to the political branches of the government to the posture of an assertive, even demanding, advocate of individual rights and liberties.[14]

The Warren Court made a long series of dramatic rulings expanding individual rights in such diverse areas as freedom of speech, press, and religion, the rights of minorities to equal political rights and economic opportunities, the rights of accused to counsel and to fair and speedy trials, and the rights of citizens to due process before legislative and administration committees and boards. Many citizens came to feel that the Warren Court was moving too far too fast in areas such as civil rights and the rights of the accused.

Earl Warren's 1969 resignation gave President Richard Nixon the opportunity to nominate his replacement. Republicans and southern conservatives, hoping that the new chief justice would lead the Court in rolling back some of the Warren Court's more liberal initiatives, were heartened by the nomination and Senate approval of Warren Burger. Burger was a conservative jurist with thirteen years of experience on the District of Columbia Circuit Court of Appeals.

Yet, those who expected the Burger Court to be aggressively conservative were disappointed. No major decision of the Warren Court was overturned by the Burger Court, and in fact the Burger Court did more to consolidate than to challenge the legacy of the Warren Court. It upheld affirmative action programs, recognized a woman's right to seek abortion services, and expanded the rights to counsel and against self-incrimination for persons accused of crimes.

Modern Judicial Conservatism Ascendent

William Rehnquist served on the high court for 33 years, the last 18 as chief justice. He was named an associate justice by President Nixon in 1972 and elevated to chief justice by President Reagan in 1986. He died in 2005. Rehnquist's legacy is to have limited the scope of the federal government while strengthening the role of the judiciary against both Congress and the executive. He encouraged the court to strengthen the role of the police, limit the appellate rights of convicts, allow indirect government funding of religious schools and enhance the role of the states in American federalism.[15]

The Rehnquist Court sought to limit, where it could not overturn, the ban on school prayer, affirmative action, gay rights, and the rights of women seeking abortion services.[16] For example, *Roe v. Wade* (1973), decided in Justice Rehnquist's first year on the court, established a woman's right to choose abortion, especially early in her pregnancy. As the court became more conservative and soon after Rehnquist was elevated to chief justice, **Webster v. Reproductive Health Services** (1989) provided an opportunity to limit access to abortion services. While not overturning *Roe,* the decision in *Webster* upheld the rights of states to regulate abortion clinics and to prevent public money and facilities from being used to perform abortions.

Civil rights provides another good example of the Rehnquist Court trimming but not completely overturning major liberal precedents. In 1973, in *Regents of the University of California v. Bakke,* the court approved the use of race as one criterion although not as the sole criterion in college admissions. In 1995, the Supreme Court ruled that preferences based on race in government decisions and programs such as hiring and awarding contracts and grants were suspect and usually unconstitutional. But Rehnquist never marshaled a majority that would overturn affirmative action. In 2003, the Supreme Court held that the University of Michigan could employ race as one of a number of criteria for admission and expressed the hope that twenty-five years hence it might no longer be necessary.

While William Rehnquist undoubtedly moved the high court to the right, he was "unable to assemble a majority of justices willing to take the court—and the nation—as far to the right as he wanted to go." Nonetheless, as Richard Gannett of the Notre Dame Law School noted, "Chief Justice Rehnquist changed the conversation. He brought back to the table certain ideas about limited government, federalism, and textualism."[17]

The high court's conservative momentum picked up speed once John Roberts became Chief Justice.[18] Roberts graduated from Harvard Law School, clerked for Justice Rehnquist in 1980, and then worked in the Justice Department and the White House Counsel's Office in the Reagan administration. He was in private practice in Washington when President George W. Bush nominated him to the D.C. Circuit Court of Appeals in 2003. Roberts was initially nominated to the Supreme Court to replace Associate Justice Sandra Day O'Connor when she resigned in 2005. Just prior to the start of Roberts's confirmation hearings, Chief Justice Rehnquist died of cancer. Roberts's nomination was switched from Associate Justice to Chief Justice and Sandra Day O'Connor agreed to remain on the court until a second nomination could be made and confirmed.

Roe v. Wade (1973) With this landmark decision, the Court struck down a Texas law regulating access to abortion as a violation of a woman's fundamental right to privacy.

Webster v. Reproductive Health Services (1989) The Court upheld all abortion regulations in question and concluded that such regulations did not prohibit a woman from having an abortion, but reasonably furthered the state's interest in encouraging childbirth. The trimester analysis was rejected; *Roe,* however, was not overturned.

Roberts performed masterfully in his Senate confirmation hearings, arguing that the courts should decide issues narrowly, speak modestly, and act unanimously where possible. Despite objections from a wide range of liberal interest groups and some Democrats, he was confirmed by a Senate vote of 78 to 22 in September 2005. President Bush then nominated Samuel Alito to succeed O'Connor. Alito had spent fifteen years on the Third U.S. Circuit Court of Appeals, so he was very knowledgeable but less smooth and personable than Roberts. Despite a more determined opposition in the Senate and among liberal interest groups, Samuel Alito was confirmed 58 to 42 in February 2006.

The Roberts Court started slowly but quickly gained momentum. In the 2005–2006 session, most of the early decisions were unanimous, though as the session went along, issues of executive power arose that created divisions, intense argument, and sharp language in the written opinions. The 2006–2007 session dealt with even more divisive issues, including whether to permit or overturn voluntary integration plans in public schools. Chief Justice Roberts, writing for a deeply divided, 5–4, court, declared that school districts could not use race in an attempt to maintain school integration. Roberts reasoned that discrimination, even in an arguably good cause, was no more legal than discrimination in a bad cause. He wrote that, "The way to stop discrimination on the basis of race is to stop discrimination on the basis of race."[19] The 2007–2008 session was highlighted by a case dealing with the right to bear arms. A 5–4 conservative majority led by Justice Antonin Scalia declared for the first time that the Second Amendment right to bear arms is an individual right rather than a collective right tied to militia service.[20]

In the 2008–2009 session, Chief Justice Roberts continued to guide the court to the right even as the nation elected a Democratic president and expanded the Democratic margins in Congress. The court moved to the right in a range of cases dealing with voting rights, employment, and criminal procedure. Even more ominously, at least from the perspective of the liberal minority, Chief Justice Roberts led the court in rescheduling *Citizens United v. Federal Election Commission* for reargument in a special late-summer session. Citizens United was a case involving a group that produced an anti-Hillary Clinton movie during the 2008 presidential primaries. A lower court barred the group from showing the movie within 30-days of a primary as a violation of the McCain-Feingold campaign finance law. In rescheduling the case, the court instructed the parties to focus on the broad question of whether limits on corporate speech in campaigns were constitutional or not.

In the first big decision of the 2009–2010 session was the *Citizens United* case. The court overturned decades of campaign finance law by finding that corporations and unions have the same free speech rights as individuals in campaigns. Republicans cheered, Democrats howled, and analysts of both the courts and campaign finance debated the meaning and implications of the court's action. Writing for the court in another 5–4 decision, Justice Kennedy wrote that, "If the First Amendment has any force, it prohibits

Congress from fining or jailing citizens, or associations of citizens, for simply engaging in political speech." Writing for the minority, Justice Stevens declared that "The rule announced today—that Congress must treat corporations exactly like human speakers in the political realm—represents a radical change in the law. The court's decision is at war with the views of generations of Americans."[21]

The Roberts court's fifth term, 2010–2011, was notable for a cluster of First Amendment, free speech, decisions, but also for the teeing-up of a number of blockbuster cases for future terms. In 2010–2011, the court found even for distasteful plaintiffs, funeral protesters, violent video game makers, and wealthy political donors in free speech cases. The court also continued to support business interests, including WalMart, the nation's largest employer, and AT&T Mobility against class action suits by employees and consumers. Scholars argue that the Roberts court is the most business friendly court in decades.[22]

In the two most recent court terms, Chief Justice Roberts has continued to nudge the court in conservative directions, though usually no further than Justice Kennedy is willing to go. With four conservative and four moderate to liberal justices, Kennedy is the classic swing vote. Kennedy, a moderate conservative, votes with the four staunch conservatives about two-thirds of the time on divided votes, but about one-third of the time he swings to the four liberals, often making them a majority. Kennedy has voted with the majority 83 percent of the time in recent terms, more than any other justice. This sometimes requires Chief Justice Roberts to maneuver awkwardly to maintain control of the court.

Justice Anthony Kennedy

Associate Justice Anthony Kennedy is often the swing vote on the nine person United States Supreme Court.

Justice Kennedy is consistently conservative on business issues, careful to balance federal and state power on federalism issues, moderate on affirmative action issues, and consistently liberal on issues of sexual preference. Since his vote often makes a 5–4 majority one way or the other, he can make the court seem somewhat erratic—or at least hard to summarize simply. For example, in the 2011–2012 term, the court struck down most of the Arizona illegal immigration law, but affirmed most of President Obama's health care law. In the Arizona case, decided 5–3, Kennedy and Roberts joined three liberals in declaring that Arizona could not intrude on federal power to regulate immigration policy, but they let stand a controversial position allowing police to check a person's immigration status while enforcing other laws if "reasonable suspicion" exists that the person is in the country illegally.

Justice Kennedy again dominated the 2012–2013 term. Two critical civil rights cases, one affecting blacks most directly and one affecting gays, were decided. Both were decided 5–4 and Kennedy was the only justice to be in the majority in both cases. ***Shelby County v. Holder*** struck down critical elements of the Voting Rights Act of 1965 subjecting states with a history of voter discrimination to federal oversight. Civil rights groups and the Obama administration took this decision to be a major defeat and vowed to fight back. In the other case, ***United States v. Windsor***, the court struck down the part of the Defense of Marriage Act denying federal benefits to gay couples, even when married in states allowing gay marriage. Gay rights groups and the Obama administration took this decision to be a major victory.

THE STRUCTURE OF THE FEDERAL JUDICIAL SYSTEM

Article III, section 1, of the Constitution outlines the structure and powers of the federal judiciary. It provides that "The judicial Power of the United States, shall be vested in one supreme Court, and in such inferior Courts as the Congress may from time to time ordain and establish." This provision clearly assumed that Congress would specify the makeup of the Supreme Court and would establish a system of inferior courts as the needs of the nation developed over time. The federal court system now consists of three layers with the U.S. district courts at the base, the U.S. courts of appeals in the middle, and the U.S. Supreme Court at the top.

Article III, section 2, provides that the judicial power of the federal courts "shall extend to all Cases, in law and equity, arising under this Constitution, the Laws of the United States, and Treaties made, or which shall be made, under their Authority." Most cases that arise in the federal courts fall into three categories. Political scientist Lawrence Baum describes these categories as follows: "First are the criminal and civil cases that arise under federal laws, including the Constitution. . . . Second are cases to which the U.S. government is a party. . . . Third are civil cases involving citizens of different states if the amount in question is at least $75,000."[23]

The Lower Federal Courts

The lower courts of the federal system are composed of the U.S. district courts and a number of special courts of limited jurisdiction. The **district courts** are the primary trial courts of the federal system. The special courts hear cases within defined subject matter jurisdictions like taxation, bankruptcy, or military law.

District Courts. The district courts have authority to try most cases within the federal court system. Twenty-six states have a single district court, whereas some of the larger and more populous states have as many as four district

Shelby County v. Holder (2013) The Court struck down elements of the 1965 Civil Rights Act including the critical "preclearance" provisions. The Court argued that the data used to decide which states were covered by the preclearance provisions were outdated.

United States v. Windsor (2013) The Court declared that the Defense of Marriage Act, defining marriage as between one man and one woman, was an unconstitutional denial of gay persons' Fifth Amendment protection of equal liberty.

03 What is the place of the Supreme Court in the judicial system of the United States?

district courts The ninety-four general trial courts of the federal judicial system.

courts. There are ninety-four U.S. district courts in the fifty states, the District of Columbia, and the U.S. territories. In the 2013 term, the district courts processed about 295,310 civil cases and 81,226 criminal cases.[24] Bankruptcy court filings fell dramatically following Congress's 2005 passage of bankruptcy reform, from 1.2 million cases in 2005 as people sought to beat the deadline, to 600,000 in 2006. After a modest increase in 2007, the 2008–09 recession produced 1 to 1.5 million bankruptcies annually through 2012. As the economic recovery took hold, bankruptcies fell to 963,739 in 2013.

Most cases in the district courts are tried before a single judge. Each district has at least two judges, and some have up to twenty-eight. There are 677 federal district court judges in the ninety-four districts. An additional 300 retired or senior judges continue to work part time. A very few cases, usually cases that are important and require expedited treatment, are tried before special three-judge panels composed of two district court judges and one court of appeals judge. District court judges, like members of Congress, make $174,000.

Special Courts.   Congress is empowered in Article I, section 8, of the Constitution to "constitute tribunals inferior to the Supreme Court." These legislative courts include the U.S. Tax Court, the U.S. Court of Military Appeals, territorial courts, and the U.S. Court of Veterans Appeals. In addition, each district court employs special legislative judges, called bankruptcy judges and magistrate judges. Bankruptcy judges handle the specialized workload in their area. Magistrate judges are appointed by district judges to assist with pretrial motions, rule on routine matters, and try and decide minor civil and criminal cases.

Courts of Appeals

courts of appeals Thirteen courts that form the intermediate level of the federal judicial system and hear appeals of cases tried in the federal district courts.

During the first hundred years of federal court history, appeals of district court findings were heard by three-judge panels made up of a Supreme Court justice and two district court judges. Not until 1891 was a formal U.S. court of appeals structure inserted between the district courts and the Supreme Court. Today there are thirteen U.S. **courts of appeals**. Twelve have jurisdiction over certain regions of the country. The thirteenth is the U.S. Court of Appeals for the Federal Circuit that has jurisdiction over tax, patent, and international trade cases (see Figure 12.1). Each court of appeals has six to twenty-eight judges, depending on the workload, with a total of 179 appeals court judgeships authorized in 2013. Usually judges sit in groups of three, with two constituting a quorum, to decide cases. Occasionally, in critical cases, all of the judges assigned to the appeals court will sit as a single panel. Appeals court judges make $184,500.

The purpose of the courts of appeals is to provide a forum for review of decisions made by the district courts. Appeals usually deal with questions of procedure and of the application of rules of law rather than of facts or interpretation of facts, although questions of law and fact are sometimes difficult to disentangle. The courts of appeals also hear appeals of decisions of the Tax Court, Court of Federal Claims, Court of Veterans Appeals, and certain federal agencies. The courts of appeals handled 54,988 cases in 2013.

FIGURE 12.1 Courts of Appeals Circuit Boundaries

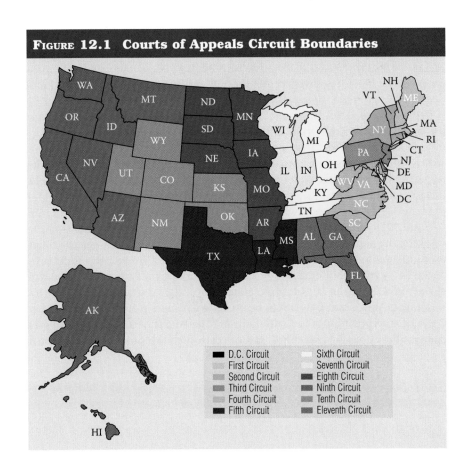

■ D.C. Circuit	Sixth Circuit
First Circuit	Seventh Circuit
Second Circuit	■ Eighth Circuit
■ Third Circuit	■ Ninth Circuit
Fourth Circuit	■ Tenth Circuit
■ Fifth Circuit	■ Eleventh Circuit

The U.S. Supreme Court

The U.S. **Supreme Court** is the most powerful judicial tribunal in the world. Over the course of its history it has addressed, sometimes successfully, sometimes not, the most important and often the most contentious issues facing our society. In the past half century, the Supreme Court has determined policy in regard to civil rights, voting rights, flag burning, abortion, and a host of equally contentious issues. In the hotly disputed 2000 presidential election, the Supreme Court ultimately stepped in to decide the contest, some would say directly, others indirectly, in favor of George W. Bush.

Although the Supreme Court is not explicitly political—its decisions are not reached through the same sort of vote trading and deal making so characteristic of legislative politics—the combatants in most major conflicts in our society seek the judgment of the Supreme Court at some point. In the 2013 term, litigants brought about 7,376 cases and applications to the Supreme Court. Of these, the Court heard arguments and wrote full opinions in only seventy-three. Associate Justices of the Supreme Court make $213,900 and the Chief Justice makes $223,500.

Supreme Court The high court or court of last resort in the American judicial system.

Federal judges can supplement their income modestly through teaching, speaking, and book royalties. Supreme Court justices are allowed about $25,000 a year for teaching, usually a summer law school class, and honoraria for speeches. Book royalties are not limited and some federal judges and justices make significant income from them.

The Supreme Court has both original and appellate jurisdiction. However, the Court exercises the **original jurisdiction** outlined in Article III, section 2, of the Constitution less than once a year on average, or just under 200 times since 1789. The **appellate jurisdiction** of the Supreme Court derives from its responsibility to oversee and review the decisions of the U.S. courts of appeals, the U.S. district courts, the special legislative courts, the territorial courts, and the state courts of last resort when a federal question is at issue (see Figure 12.2).

Since 1988, the Supreme Court has had almost complete discretion over the cases that it chooses to hear and resolve. Observers complain that the court has used this discretion to dramatically cut its workload. In 1985 the court produced 146 signed opinions. By 2000 the number of signed opinions was down to the mid-70s. In the 2013 term it fell to just 67 signed opinions.

The Supreme Court chooses to hear particular cases primarily when differences of interpretation have arisen among the courts of appeals. Most cases come to the Supreme Court by a **writ of certiorari**—an order to a lower court

original jurisdiction Mandatory jurisdiction of the Supreme Court as laid out in Article III of the Constitution.

appellate jurisdiction Substantive area in which a higher court may hear cases appealed from a lower court.

writ of certiorari Judicial instrument that makes a formal request that a case be reviewed by a higher court.

FIGURE 12.2   How a Case Gets to the Supreme Court

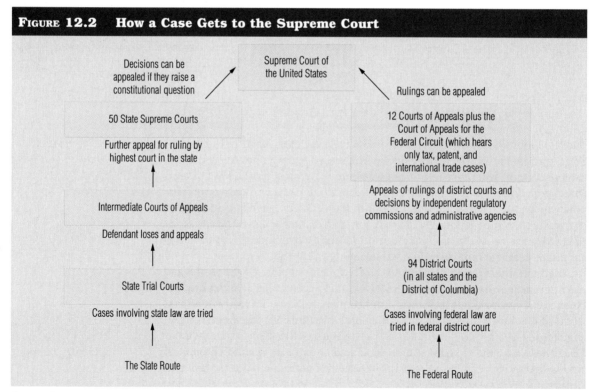

Source: Derived from David M. O'Brien, *Storm Center: The Supreme Court in American Politics*, 8th ed. (New York: Norton, 2008), 168.

to produce a case for review. The justices' law clerks review the thousands of "cert" requests that come to the Court each term and advise the justices on which cases raise interesting and important federal and constitutional issues. The **rule of four** requires that four justices agree before a writ of certiorari will be granted and a case heard before the Supreme Court.

The U.S. Supreme Court holds one term each year beginning on the first Monday in October. The term is divided into a series of sittings of about two weeks, during which the Court sits to hear oral arguments and decide cases, and recesses of two weeks or more during which the justices do their legal research and writing. The justices meet in conference during their sittings and less frequently during recesses to discuss the cases before them. After mid-May, the Court hears no more new cases and holds formal sessions only to announce decisions.

During sittings, arguments are usually heard Monday through Wednesday from 10 a.m. to 3 p.m. with an hour off for lunch. Each case usually receives one hour, with the time equally divided between the two sides. Prior to **oral argument** the justices read the **briefs** or written arguments of the disputants and any **amicus curiae briefs** written by interested persons or groups who are not formal parties to the case. The justices then question the lawyers about the legal arguments and logic offered in their written and oral presentations.

Each week the justices meet in a conference or closed session from about 3 p.m. to 6 p.m. on Wednesdays and from 10 a.m. to 6 p.m. on Fridays to discuss the cases heard that week. The chief justice leads these discussions and can, by the way he frames the questions at issue, try to shape the results of the discussions. Following the conference discussion and a preliminary vote by the justices, the chief justice, if he is in the majority, assigns the drafting of the Court's decision to himself or to one of his colleagues. If the chief justice is not with the majority, the assignment is made by the senior justice in the majority. Distribution of the Court's workload among the justices is usually very balanced although the chief justice and some of the senior members close to him get a disproportionate number of the most important cases.

The Supreme Court's decision is called an **opinion.** Each justice writes six to ten opinions each term. The justice assigned to write the Court's opinion produces a draft that is circulated to the other justices for their comments, suggestions, and advice. Several drafts may be written and circulated before enough justices are willing to adopt the opinion as the final statement of the Court in the case at hand. A decision of the Court may receive various levels and kinds of support or opposition from the nine justices.

Each justice assigned to draft an opinion for the Court hopes to produce a unanimous opinion—that is, an opinion that each justice will approve and sign. However, this is not always possible. A majority opinion is an opinion that a majority of the Court, although not every member, has approved and signed. A minority opinion is one that several members, but not enough to constitute a majority, produce as preferable to the majority opinion. Finally, individual justices may produce opinions that vary in some large or small way from the view that any other justice is willing to adopt. A concurring opinion is produced by a justice who concurs with or accepts the basic thrust of the

rule of four Four justices must approve a writ of certiorari before a case will be heard on appeal before the Supreme Court.

oral argument The opportunity in a case before the Supreme Court for the opposing lawyers to present their legal arguments orally.

briefs Written arguments prepared by lawyers in a case outlining their view of the relevant law and the decision that should be rendered based on the law.

amicus curiae brief An argument filed with the court by a party interested in a case but not directly involved in it as a contending party. *Amicus curiae* is Latin for "friend of the court."

opinion Written finding or decision of a court.

Getty Images

Justices of the Supreme Court of the United States. Standing from left to right are Justice Sonia Sotomayor, Justice Stephen Breyer, Justice Samuel Alito, and Justice Elena Kagan. Seated from left to right are Justice Clarence Thomas, Justice Antonin Scalia, Chief Justice John Roberts, Justice Anthony Kennedy, and Justice Ruth Bader Ginsburg.

affirm Action of a higher court supporting the decision of a lower court.

reverse Action by a higher court to overturn the decision of a lower court.

remand To send a case back to a lower court for further consideration.

Court's majority opinion but wishes to provide a somewhat different rationale for the result. A dissenting opinion is produced by a justice who disagrees with the Court's finding as stated in the majority opinion and wishes to explain why.

The result of the Supreme Court's deliberations is usually to affirm the lower court, reverse the lower court, or remand the case back to the lower court for further consideration. If the Supreme Court agrees with the ruling made by the lower court, it is said to **affirm** the lower court. If the justices **reverse** the lower court, this means that they disagree in whole or in part with the result at that level and they say what the result should have been. Finally, they may **remand** the case back to the lower court to consider certain issues or to focus on certain specific questions.

JUDICIAL NOMINATION AND APPOINTMENT

Q4 How have the climate and tone surrounding the process of nomination and confirmation to judicial posts changed since the mid-1950s?

The formal process for selecting federal judges is very straightforward. Each of the approximately 1,000 active federal judges was nominated by the president and confirmed by a majority of U.S. senators present and voting on the nomination. Once confirmed, federal judges hold their positions "during good behavior," which essentially means for life, because they can be removed from office only by the difficult and cumbersome process of impeachment by the House of Representatives and conviction by the Senate.[25]

Many observers feel that the judicial nomination process has become so politicized that even good candidates are rejected. The cartoon suggests that even Jesus could not get confirmed—perhaps a bit of an overstatement, but not by much.

Backgrounds of Members of the Federal Judiciary

Historically, more than 90 percent of the nominees to the federal bench have shared partisan affiliation with the presidents who nominated them and two-thirds have been prominent political activists.[26] Half have had experience as judges, and nearly half were sitting judges on lower benches when nominated to the federal bench. Almost 90 percent have been male, and almost 90 percent have been white, although both of those number are slowly coming down.

Most presidential nominations to the judiciary are approved by the Senate. About forty-five to fifty judges a year are nominated and confirmed to the federal bench. A president has an opportunity to shape a significant part of the federal judiciary by the nature of his nominations. Political scientists Deborah Barrow, Gary Zuk, and Gerald Gryski have shown that "modern presidents . . . change anywhere from 35 to 60 percent of the membership on the lower federal courts during their stay in office."[27] Moreover, partisan change in the White House can lead to substantial change in the ideological coloration of the judiciary in a relatively few years.

When Franklin Roosevelt assumed the presidency early in 1933, after many years of Republican rule, only 22 percent of federal judges were Democrats. FDR achieved a Democratic majority among federal judges by 1940, and the Democratic ascendancy peaked during the presidency of Lyndon Johnson, when 70.5 percent of federal judges were Democrats. Ronald Reagan reversed these numbers in the 1980s. During eight years as president, Reagan appointed 48.9 percent of all federal judges, and at the end of the first President Bush's

TABLE 12.4   Demographic Characteristics of Federal Judicial Appointments from Presidents Johnson through Obama

President	Party	% White	% Black	% Hispanic	% Asian	% Female
Johnson	Dem.	93.4	4.1	2.5	.0	1.6
Nixon	Rep.	96.0	2.7	.9	.4	.4
Ford	Rep.	90.6	4.7	1.9	3.8	1.9
Carter	Dem.	78.3	14.3	6.2	1.2	15.5
Reagan	Rep.	93.5	1.9	4.1	.5	7.6
Bush I	Rep.	89.2	6.5	4.3	.0	15.7
Clinton	Dem.	74.9	16.7	6.8	1.4	29.2
Bush II	Rep.	81.9	7.5	9.4	1.3	21.6
Obama	Dem.	64.3	17.9	11.3	6.5	40.5

Source: Harold W. Stanley and Richard G. Niemi, *Vital Statistics on American Politics, 2013–2014*, Washington, D.C.: CQ Press, 2013, 278–280.

term in 1992 over 70 percent of all federal judges were Republican. President Clinton appointed 46.6 percent of the federal judiciary and at the end of his eight years in office (1993–2001), 53.4 percent of federal judges were Democrats. President George W. Bush appointed 37 percent of sitting federal judges by the end of 2008. About 60 percent of sitting federal judges and six of nine Supreme Court justices were appointed by Republican presidents.[28]

By late 2014, 307 of President Obama's judicial appointments had been approved by the Senate. Obama's appointments constitute about 30 percent of the federal judiciary and have brought the balance between judges appointed by Democrats and Republicans back to 50/50. Moreover, following the Sotomayor and Kagan appointments, four of nine justices have been named by Democratic presidents, the most since the Nixon years.

The Nomination Process

Presidents follow different nomination processes in regard to the lower federal courts than they do in regard to the Supreme Court. A nomination to a U.S. district court is cleared with the U.S. senators, a process called **senatorial courtesy,** and other political figures of the president's party from the state in which the nominee will serve. Senators and state political figures play a smaller role in nominations to the U.S. circuit courts of appeals because the circuits include several states. Moreover, judges are usually elevated from the district court bench, so the Senate has already passed on them once and their judicial records and performance are more clearly established.

Since the Eisenhower administration (1953–1961), the Standing Committee on the Federal Judiciary of the American Bar Association (ABA) has been given early notice of judicial nominations. The ABA's committee studies the nominees' legal and judicial record and declares the candidate either "well qualified," "not opposed," or "not qualified." The Bush administration (2001–2009)

senatorial courtesy Expectation that the president will clear federal district court judgeship appointments with senators of his party from the state in which the judge will serve.

suspended the ABA's traditional role, arguing that the committee had a liberal bias, but the Obama administration brought them back into the process as soon as it took office.

Nominations to the Supreme Court are so important that presidents and their close advisers hold these nominations for themselves even though they are inundated with advice from others.[29] As soon as a nomination is made, the White House appoints a team of experienced confirmation managers, former senators or White House operatives, to help the nominee navigate the process successfully. Nominees are ushered through a series of meetings with senators, beginning with members of the leadership and the Judiciary Committee. The managers also organize a series of twelve to fifteen "murder boards" to prepare the nominees for the questions they might expect from members of the Judiciary Committee.[30]

Coalitions of interest groups favoring and opposing the nomination seek to make their case to the public and to the senators who will vote on the nomination. Tens of millions of dollars are spent by both sides. As the spending and the rhetoric ratchet steadily higher, senators, dependent on these same interest groups for political and campaign support, are caught in the middle. In 2005, the judicial nomination and confirmation process in the Senate nearly exploded as Senate Democrats threatened to filibuster conservative nominees including Roberts and Alito and Republicans threatened the "nuclear option" of declaring judicial filibusters unconstitutional. Only when a group of fourteen moderates, seven Democrats and seven Republicans, led by Senate veterans Robert Byrd (D-WV), and John Warner (R-VA), negotiated a compromise was the crisis defused.[31]

The Confirmation Process

The Senate takes very seriously its responsibility to advise and consent on presidential nominations to the Supreme Court. Of the 160 Supreme Court nominations forwarded to the Senate by presidents during the country's history, 124 were approved. Seven of the men confirmed to the Supreme Court, mostly early in the nation's history, declined to serve—so 117 men and women have sat on the high court. The Senate took no action on ten nominees, postponed three, rejected twelve, and eleven were withdrawn.[32]

Nonetheless, the climate of confirmation politics began to change after the *Brown v. Board of Education* desegregation decision in 1954 and certainly after the Great Society initiatives of the mid-1960s raised the temperature of our social life. Eight of the twenty-one nominees since 1968 have received twenty-five or more negative votes in the Senate and five have been rejected or withdrawn. Mark Silverstein points out that "powerful groups from all points along the ideological spectrum now consider a sympathetic judiciary essential to the development and achievement of important policy goals."[33]

The most intensely public forum in which the scrutiny of a judicial nominee occurs is the **confirmation hearing** held by the Senate Judiciary Committee.

Struggling Toward Democracy

Over the course of American history, Supreme Court Justices have served an average of 15.65 years each.

What do you think?

- Does the fact that federal judges have lifetime appointments make them better servants of our democracy or somehow undemocratic?

Brown v. Board of Education (1954) This landmark case overturned Plessy and declared that separate was inherently unequal. Consequently, the segregation of public schools was unconstitutional.

confirmation hearing Setting in which nominees for federal judicial posts appear before the Senate Judiciary Committee to respond to questions from the members.

Judge Sonia Sotomayor at the first day of her confirmation hearings in Washington. Judge Sotomayor spoke of her background, the people and principles that had the greatest influence on her, and the need for independent-minded jurists. July 14, 2009.

Committee staff members gather extensive information about the nominee and investigate questions and issues that arise. After the preparation and inquiry are complete, public hearings are scheduled in which the nominee is questioned at length, often over the course of several days, and others, both those favoring and those opposing the nomination, provide their views to the committee.

Senators ask questions that they hope will suggest how a nominee might think about, if not how he or she might vote, on the key social and political issues that come before the court. Nominees invariably decline to respond in ways that would suggest that they have prejudged important and controversial issues that might later come before them. The confirmation hearing is a frustrating exercise for all concerned.

Following the public hearing, the members of the Judiciary Committee vote on whether to report the nomination to the full Senate with a positive, negative, or split recommendation. The full Senate then debates the nomination and a confirmation vote is taken. Most senators agree that judicial nominees should be judged on qualifications, experience, character, and temperament. More recently, senators have begun to argue that it is appropriate to take ideology into account as well.[34] Until Elena Kagan joined the Supreme Court in 2010, every member had been elevated from one of the U.S. circuit courts of appeals.

Q5 Is judicial activism necessary because some issues are just too difficult for the political branches of the government to confront?

THE DISPUTED ROLE OF THE FEDERAL JUDICIARY

How do we explain the fact that American courts play a far more formative role in politically sensitive policy areas such as race, the availability of abortion services, the role of religion in political life, and the rights of the accused than do courts in any other nation? The idea that the courts rather than legislative majorities can and do decide fundamental political issues seems on its face to be blatantly undemocratic.

Some argue, as noted earlier, that one of the main roles of American courts is to limit the political branches of the government to their constitutionally mandated responsibilities. Hence, the federal courts must strike down initiatives, even popular initiatives that command legislative majorities and presidential support, if the courts believe that the Constitution forbids them. Since the mid-1990s, the courts have challenged Congress on the scope of its power to regulate interstate commerce, and since 2005 they have challenged the president on the scope of his commander-in-chief powers.[35] This is what they are supposed to do, but it does worry some people when appointed judges overrule elected officials.

Others note that the courts never stay for long outside the mainstream of American political life. Judges, like other members of the nation's social and political elite, share in the broad flow of popular opinion concerning the major issues of the day. Moreover, judges know that the few times when the courts have strayed too far from the mainstream—as with Federalist judges in the Jeffersonian era on issues of free speech and press, or conservative judges in the New Deal era on the expansion of federal authority—popular and political pressures have asserted themselves, and the courts have been forced to back down. Courts and judges know that they must maintain the confidence and respect of the public if their rulings are to be obeyed. They generally know not to overplay their hand.[36]

Limits on Judicial Activism

The courts constitute an equal branch of the national government, but as Alexander Hamilton noted in Federalist Number 78, they are the "least dangerous branch," lacking access to both the purse of the legislative branch and the sword of the executive branch. Neither of the other branches can directly command the courts, and judges are constitutionally protected against reduction of salary and removal from office except by impeachment. However, the courts are by no means autonomous.

Political scientist Henry Abraham argues that the courts are subject to multiple pressures from other elements of the political system: "First, the Supreme Court's rulings may be effectively reversed by other participants in the processes of government; second, they are almost inevitably responsive to overall policy formulations, sooner or later; third, for enforcement they must look to the executive branch of the government; and fourth; . . . compliance with them is not necessarily automatic."[37]

Presidential Influence.   One of the most obvious constraints on the independence of the courts is that their membership is defined by the political branches of the government. Presidents nominate judges who must gain majority support in the Senate before they can ascend to the bench. Although

judicial activism Active policymaking by courts, especially in sensitive cases such as desegregation and abortion.

judicial restraint The idea that courts should avoid policymaking and limit themselves to implementing legislative and executive intent.

Pro & Con

Does the U.S. Political System Need Judicial Activism to Work?

Courts cannot avoid making policy. Every time a court applies an existing law to a new situation or interprets an existing statute in a novel way, it is reshaping and to some extent elaborating the law. Nonetheless, at some stages in American political history the courts have seemed more eager to lead the national policy conversation than at others. These courts—the Marshall Court of the early national period, the laissez faire courts of Fuller, White, and Taft in the late nineteenth and early twentieth centuries, and the Warren Court of the mid-twentieth century are the three most obvious cases—are said to be engaging in **judicial activism,** and their leading members are called activist judges. Activist judges and courts believe that social, economic, and political problems should be addressed and that the courts are one vehicle for doing so. **Judicial restraint** is the less glamorous view that judges are to follow the lead of the political branches of the government and to avoid policymaking of their own.

Judicial activism and restraint have no natural or logical identity with liberalism or conservatism, big government or small government, active government or passive government. The Marshall Court of the early nineteenth century had a big government, pro-business cast. During the late nineteenth century and the first third of the twentieth century—that is, during the era of laissez faire—judicial activism had a decidedly free market, even antigovernment, cast. Judicial restraint during both of these periods was the stance of those who wanted the courts to step aside so that state and national legislatures and executives could legislate to control large and powerful economic entities like corporations, banks, and railroads. In fact, the same court can be activist in regard to some

issues, say commercial regulation, and restrained in regard to others, say presidential war powers.

Beginning in the mid-1950s, many would even say with the appointment of Earl Warren as chief justice, judicial activism came more commonly to be understood as aggressive pursuit of equal rights in areas as diverse as civil rights, gender equity, the rights of the accused, and, many feared, social and economic outcomes. Judicial restraint was generally understood as the courts following the political branches of the government rather than trying to induce political change on their own.

Many contemporary observers including former President Clinton see judicial activism as a device that is sometimes necessary to assist society in addressing a particularly difficult issue. In presenting a Presidential Medal of Freedom in 1997 to Judge John Minor Wisdom of the U.S. Fifth Circuit Court of Appeals, President Clinton said that activist judges "did the whole nation and especially the South a signal service by the courage with which they carried out the civil rights revolution from the 1950s through the 1970s, when so many of the elected officials from the region were dragging their feet."[38]

Many others including former President George W. Bush argue that democracy requires that the judiciary follow the political branches of the government—the Congress, the president, and the executive branch. In this view, it is the responsibility of the elected representatives of the people to make policy by passing statutes that will be binding on all citizens. It is the role of the courts to evaluate charges that the statutes have been breached and to assess penalties if the courts conclude that the charges are true. Judicial restraint involves an explicit commitment by judges to keep their courts out of policymaking and to limit them to implementing legislative and executive intent.

What do you think?
- Which makes most sense to you—judicial activism or judicial restraint?
- Are charges of judicial activism just a way of saying one doesn't agree with the judge's decision?

PRO	CON
Some problems are too hard for politicians to solve	The Constitution gives Congress the lawmaking power
Justice demands an advocate	Politicians can solve hard issues if given time
Constitutional rights cannot be ignored	Courts must not "find" new rights

less commonly noted, it is also true that presidents affect the activities of the courts by the substance of their litigation policy and by the nature of their appointments in the Justice Department.

Presidents also affect the role and status of the federal courts by the kind of support or lack of support they show to Congress and the public for the decisions of the courts. A famous example of the limits on judicial authority derives from an 1832 conflict between Chief Justice John Marshall and President Andrew Jackson. Marshall ruled in the case of *Worcester v. Georgia* that Indian tribes had to be treated as sovereign and autonomous by both the national and state governments. Upon hearing of Marshall's decision, President Jackson is reported to have declared, "John Marshall has made his decision, now let him enforce it." President Eisenhower's cool reception of the Supreme Court's controversial desegregation 1954 ruling in *Brown v. Board of Education* signaled members of Congress and southern politicians that they would not face presidential ire if they resisted the Court.

Much more recently, President Obama used the very high profile occasion of his 2010 State of the Union address, delivered before a joint session of Congress, with six of the nine justices arrayed in front of him and 48 million Americans watching on television, to call the Supreme Court out for its *Citizens United* campaign finance ruling of the previous week. This rare public presidential rebuke of the court was made particularly memorable by Justice Samuel Alito's equally public reaction—shaking his head no and mouthing the words "not true." President Obama called on congressional Democrats to find a constitutional way to stem the potential tide of corporate money in elections. Do you think the political branches or the Supreme Court will win this fight?

Legislative Reaction and Court Curbing. Congress exercises several forms of fairly direct control over the courts. First, every federal judge must pass Senate confirmation. In 2005, Senator Arlen Specter (R-PA), chairman of the Judiciary Committee, questioned John Roberts very closely on his view of congressional authority. Specter was offended that the Rehnquist Court had struck down a number of laws based on what it considered to be faulty congressional reasoning. Specter sought, with limited success, to get Roberts's admission that senators reasoned as well as judges. Roberts was confirmed, but Senator Specter made his point.

Second, Chief Justice Roberts and his colleagues well know that the budget of the federal courts is considered and approved, with increases and decreases each year, as Congress thinks appropriate. Third, the number of federal judges, the levels of their professional and clerical support, and their salaries are set by Congress. Fourth, the appellate jurisdiction of the courts is set by Congress and some have called for placing sensitive cultural and religious issues beyond the reach of the courts. Fifth, Congress can always pass new legislation or initiate constitutional amendments if it does not like the way the courts are interpreting existing law.

Popular Sentiment.   Popular noncompliance, although always a threat, has occurred irregularly. Respect for the Supreme Court and its decisions is sometimes stretched, as in the contemporary examples of school prayer, desegregation, and abortion, but for the most part, the Court enjoys a reservoir of latent support from the American people.

More commonly, the dynamic within the American political system has been for the Court to adjust its line of decisions to public sentiment rather than to challenge that sentiment directly. Robert McCloskey argues that "the Court, while sometimes checking or at any rate modifying the popular will, is itself in turn checked or modified. . . . In truth the Supreme Court has seldom, if ever, flatly and for very long resisted a really unmistakable wave of public sentiment. It has worked with the premise that constitutional law, like politics itself, is a science of the possible."[39]

JUDICIAL REFORM TODAY

Many consider that the federal judiciary is badly in need of reform. Three issues—selection, tenure, and compensation—are frequently mentioned. Many argue that judicial selection has turned into a media circus, that lifetime tenure is outmoded, and that top legal talent avoids the judiciary because salaries are too low.

The judicial nomination process has become highly politicized, especially when one party holds the presidency and the other holds the Senate. The states appoint judges differently and with less tumult. In two-thirds of the states, voters have a role in selecting Supreme Court justices. Many of these use a process called the Missouri System or merit selection, whereby an expert panel nominates prospective judges and the governor selects among them. Judges serve a term of six years or so and then have to stand in retention elections if they want to remain in office. Voters vote up or down, yes or no, whether to retain the judge. Would something like the Missouri System work at the federal level? Such changes would, of course, require a constitution amendment, so maybe just expert nomination of three or four potential judges, presidential selection from among them, and Senate confirmation would work better than what we have? What flaws do you see with this idea?

How about judicial tenure? Life expectancy today is about double what it was when the Constitution was written. Do federal judges need lifetime tenure to assure their independence from social and political pressure? Some say yes, others no. Those who say no call for elections, either initially or at a retention election at the end of a six- to ten-year term. Others call for one long term of eighteen to twenty or twenty-five years with no second term. Should federal judges be able to stay on the bench into their eighties or nineties if they wish?

Finally, graduates from top law schools command first-year salaries that are not far behind the salaries earned by federal judges. Top lawyers in mid-career make several times what federal judges make. Congress controls judicial salaries and has been reluctant to raise them above their own.[40]

WHAT DO YOU THINK?

- Would the Missouri system of judicial selection reduce the tension in modern judicial selection?
- To get good judges, do they have to be paid as much as top-flight private sector lawyers?
- Are federal judges ever really insulated from social and political considerations?

Chapter Summary

The Constitution prescribed a national judiciary composed of a Supreme Court and such inferior or lower courts as Congress, rather than the courts themselves, should think necessary. The Constitution included a "supremacy clause" declaring the national government supreme over the state governments within the area of national government responsibility and requiring state officers to swear allegiance to the U.S. Constitution and laws.

Nonetheless, the role and stature of the federal courts remained uncertain during the nation's early years. The Supreme Court began to come into its own during John Marshall's long service (1801–1835) as chief justice. No case did more to establish the role and future importance of the Court than *Marbury v. Madison,* for which Marshall wrote the opinion in 1803. *Marbury* made the point that one of the Court's primary roles is to safeguard and defend the Constitution. Judicial review is the power of the courts to declare unconstitutional, that is, incompatible with the Constitution, acts of Congress or the president, state or local governments, or the lower courts.

The broad history of the Supreme Court and of the U.S. federal courts in general has been a search for the proper balance between the rights of property and of persons when these conflict. For much of the nineteenth century, the Court advantaged property, sometimes very heavily, whereas in the twentieth century it has sought a better balance, although the pendulum has swung back and forth. It now seems to be swinging back in the direction of property.

The modern federal court system is organized on three levels. There are ninety-four district courts, thirteen courts of appeals, and one Supreme Court. Virtually all federal cases are tried in the district courts and are subject to review by the appropriate court of appeals. The Supreme Court has broad discretion to hear only the cases that raise important constitutional issues.

Judges who reach the federal bench have been nominated by the president and confirmed by a majority of the senators present and voting on the nomination. Federal judges hold their jobs "during good behavior," which really means for life; their salaries cannot be reduced and they can be removed only by impeachment by the House of Representatives and trial in the Senate. Presidents have the opportunity to replace with new appointments between one-third and two-thirds of the federal judiciary, and 90 percent of their appointments come from their own parties.

Finally, because the courts are so powerful, the role that they play in addressing major social issues is intensely debated. Some argue that elected politicians are often reluctant to tackle difficult issues and that judges, with their lifetime appointments, might be better positioned to take a leading role. Judicial activism has been a powerful force at some stages in our national history, as with the Marshall and Warren Courts, but judicial restraint is closer to the popular expectation.

Key Terms

affirm 400

amicus curiae brief 399

appellate jurisdiction 398

Bonham's Case 380

briefs 399

Brown v. Board of Education 403

Charles River Bridge v. Warren Bridge 388

civil code 379

civil law 380

common law 379

confirmation hearing 403

courts of appeals 396

criminal law 380

district courts 395

judicial activism 405

judicial restraint 405

judicial review 386

Judiciary Act of 1789 384

justiciability 381

law 378

opinion 399

oral argument 399

original jurisdiction 398

precedent 380

remand 400

reverse 400

Roe v. Wade 392

rule of four 399

Santa Clara County v. Southern Pacific Railroad 389

senatorial courtesy 402

Shelby County v. Holder 395

stare decisis 380

substantive due process 389

Supreme Court 397

United States v. Windsor 395

Webster v. Reproductive Health Services 392

writ of certiorari 398

Suggested Readings

Amar, Akhil Reed. *America's Unwritten Constitution: The Precedents and Principles We Live By.* New York: Basic Books, 2012. Amar argues that beyond the plain constitutional text lie traditions, legal principles, and interpretive theories that support the written constitution.

Baum, Lawrence. *American Courts: Process and Policy*, 7th ed. Boston: Houghton Mifflin, 2012. Leading textbook highlighting judicial process, policy, and reform.

Epstein, Lee and Jeffrey A. Segal. *Advice and Consent: The Politics of Judicial Appointments.* New York: Oxford University Press, 2005. Good empirical study of how the process of judicial appointments has evolved.

Friedman, Barry. *The Will of the People: How Public Opinion Has Influenced the Supreme Court and Shaped the Meaning of the Constitution.* New York: Farrar, Straus, and Giroux, 2009. Friedman argues that the court's legitimacy requires that it stay in touch with public opinion over time.

Geyh, Charles. *When Courts and Congress Collide.* Ann Arbor, Michigan: University of Michigan Press, 2006. Why there is increasing tension between the Congress and the courts and how those tensions might be resolved.

Rosen, Jeffrey. "The Most Democratic Branch," 2005. Rosen argues that the Supreme Court has nurtured its prestige and authority by regularly deferring to congressional and popular majorities.

Sunstein, Cass R. *A Constitution of Many Minds: Why the Founding Document Doesn't Mean What It Meant Before.* Princeton, NJ: Princeton University Press, 2009. Sunstein assesses three traditions of constitutional analysis and interpretation—traditionalism, populism, and cosmopolitanism—finding insights in each. He argues that a "many minds" perspective shows the strengths and limits of each.

Wilkinson III, J. Harvie. *Cosmic Constitutional Theory: Why Americans Are Losing Their Inalienable Right to Self-Governance.* New York: Oxford University Press, 2012. Wilkinson criticizes theorists of the right and left for encouraging judicial activism at the expense of the people's elected representatives.

Web Resources

For practice quizzes, key term flashcards, videos, links, and other study tools, visit the *American Government* website: www.routledge.com/cw/jillson

1. **www.findlaw.com/casecode/supreme.html**
   This is Findlaw's searchable database of the Supreme Court decisions since 1893 (U.S. Supreme Court Decisions: U.S. Reports 150–, 1893–). Students can browse by year or volume number.

2. **www.uscourts.gov**
   The official website of the federal judiciary, this site provides news, information, publications, and a list of frequently asked questions regarding the federal judiciary.

3. **www.commonlaw.com**
   The website provides an impressive array of excerpts, articles, and discussions concerning legal history and philosophy and contains excerpts from some of the most important legal thinkers in American history.

4. **www.loc.gov/law/guide/**
   This website contains links to U.S. judicial branch resources.

5. **library.lawschool.cornell.edu**
   The Law Library of Cornell Law School serves as a fantastic resource for Supreme Court decisions, hypertext versions of U.S. Code, U.S. Constitution, and Federal Rules of Evidence and Procedure, as well as other law-related sites.

Chapter 13

CIVIL LIBERTIES
Ordered Liberty in America

❝ *I conclude ... that it will be proper in itself, and highly politic, for the tranquility of the public mind, and the stability of the government, and that we should offer ... a declaration of the rights of the people.* ❞

JAMES MADISON,
June 8, 1789, First Congress

THE SECOND AMENDMENT AND
GUN RIGHTS IN AMERICA

The Constitution TODAY

Second Amendment: "A well regulated militia, being necessary to the security of a free state, the right of the people to keep and bear arms, shall not be infringed."

The Second Amendment is strangely phrased and, for most of American history, its meaning was thought to be somewhat murky. Legal analysts, political scientists, and historians long debated whether the first two clauses of the Second Amendment, "A well regulated militia, being necessary to the security of a free state," modified or limited the straightforward declaration of the last two phrases, "the right of the people to keep and bear arms, shall not be infringed." If the first two phrases do modify and limit the second two, then perhaps the people only have a constitutional right to keep and bear arms consequent to militia service. But if the first two clauses of the Second Amendment do not express limits, then the right to keep and bear arms is much more full and stark.

The debate appears to be over. In 2008, Justice Scalia declared for a Supreme Court divided 5 to 4 in a case called *District of Columbia v. Heller*, that "the Second Amendment protects an individual right to possess a firearm unconnected with service in a militia, and to use that arm for traditional lawful purposes, such as self-defense within the home." Heller was the Supreme Court's first unequivocal ruling that the Second Amendment right to bear arms was an individual right not connected to the collective responsibility of militia service. Moreover, hot on Heller's heels came *McDonald v. Chicago*, asking that the finding in Heller be applied in full against state and local gun laws. In 2010, in another 5–4 decision, with Justice Alito writing for the majority, the Supreme Court extended the Heller finding to a general protection against local, state, and federal intrusion on the individual right of citizens to keep and bear arms.

Two questions remain for us to ponder in light of the Supreme Court's decisions in *Heller* (2008) and *McDonald* (2010). First, was the Supreme Court correct in *Heller* to find that the Second Amendment right to bear arms was an individual right rather than a collective right related to militia service? It seems so, at least from an historical perspective. The Court and a number of scholars point out that several founding period state constitutions had a straightforward right to bear arms. Moreover, the first version of the Second Amendment submitted to Congress by James Madison on June 8, 1789 read; "The right of the people to keep and bear arms shall not be infringed; a well armed and well regulated militia being the best security of a free country. . . ." A second version, submitted on August 17, read; "A well regulated militia, composed of the body of the people, being the best security of a free state, the right of the people to keep and bear arms shall not be infringed." On either of these readings, an individual right to bear arms seems clear. In the first it is baldly stated before the semicolon and in the second it is clear that the militia is composed of the whole adult male population.

Second, was the Court right to apply the Second Amendment against states and localities? Until these two cases were decided, most gun ownership had been regulated by state constitutions and laws. For well over a century, in a series of cases including *U.S. v. Cruikshank* (1875), *Presser v. Illinois* (1886), *Miller v. Texas* (1894), and *U.S. v. Miller* (1939), the Court held, as they said in *Cruikshank*, that "the Second Amendment . . . has no other effect than to restrict the powers of the national government." The argument in *McDonald* was that the right to bear arms is among the "privileges and immunities of citizens of the United States" protected against state and local incursion by the Fourteenth Amendment. The Supreme Court has now agreed with that argument.

Cases raising gun control questions will be in the federal courts for years as cities and states defend their restrictions on gun ownership and use, and federal judges struggle to add detail and specificity to the broad but vague right declared by the nation's high court.

Focus Questions: from reading to thinking

Q1 How do civil liberties differ from civil rights?

Q2 Do our commitments to free speech and a free press conflict with our sense that flag burning should be prohibited or that pornography should be regulated?

Q3 Does our commitment to separation of church and state mean that no trace of religious sentiment or symbolism should emanate from government?

Q4 Should someone accused of a serious crime go free if police commit a procedural error during the investigation or during the arrest and questioning?

Q5 If we value civil liberties so highly, why do we keep so many people in prison?

WHAT DO YOU THINK?

- What role should states and municipalities have in deciding how to manage guns within their boundaries?
- Would James Madison, strolling down the streets of a major American city today, think that all citizens should be armed or that fewer guns on the street might be a good thing?

CIVIL LIBERTIES, CIVIL RIGHTS, AND MAJORITY RULE

human rights Fundamental rights to freedom and security that belong to all human beings.

Q1 How do civil liberties differ from civil rights?

We all believe in **human rights**—those fundamental rights to freedom and security that belong to every human being. In fact, our country was founded on the promise of human rights. Thomas Jefferson was very explicit in the Declaration of Independence: "We hold these truths to be self-evident, that all men are created equal, that they are endowed by their Creator with certain unalienable Rights, that among these are Life, Liberty and the pursuit of Happiness." Nor have we been alone in our attraction to the idea of human rights. One of the United Nations' most memorable early achievements was the passage of the Universal Declaration of Human Rights (1948). But declaring human rights is one thing; guaranteeing them is quite another. Guaranteeing individual rights and liberties is the difficult business of constitutions, law, politics, and policy.

Throughout American history we have used our political institutions to draw the line between those areas of social life where individuals generally will be free to do as they please and those areas of social life where certain sorts of individual choices will be required or prohibited. **Civil liberties** mark off areas of social life where we believe that government power should rarely intrude on the free choice of individuals. For example, our society has generally assumed that within the realm of religion, government should leave the individual alone—unless that individual believes that religion requires behavior like having several wives at once or treating controlled substances as sacraments. **Civil rights**, on the other hand, mark off areas of social life where we believe that government must act, must intrude upon what individuals might otherwise choose to do, to ensure that all citizens are treated fairly. For example, we promise each other that whatever our external characteristics of race, ethnicity, or gender, each of us will get a fair chance to compete, succeed, and enjoy the benefits of our society. What makes the broad question of individual rights fascinating and also troubling is that although civil liberties and civil rights reinforce and strengthen each other at one level, at another they clash directly. Civil liberties will be the focus of this chapter, civil rights of the next.

In this chapter, we ask how civil liberties were conceived early in U.S. history and how our understanding of them has changed and expanded over time. We first look at freedom of expression as it relates to both speech and press, then at freedom of religion and conscience, and then at the protections afforded to criminal suspects and defendants. In each case, we see that our sense of what these liberties entail is much broader and more comprehensive than it was formerly. We conclude the chapter by asking how our commitment to civil liberties squares with the fact that the U.S. holds more people in jails and prisons that any other country in the world.

civil liberties Areas of social life, including free speech, press, and religion, where the Constitution restricts or prohibits government intrusion on the free choice of individuals.

civil rights Areas of social life, such as the right to vote and to be free from racial discrimination, where the Constitution requires government to act to ensure that citizens are treated equally.

CIVIL LIBERTIES AND THE BILL OF RIGHTS

The men and women who colonized British North America fled Europe because the governments there would not permit them to pursue their religious, social, and economic lives as they saw fit. Not surprisingly, when these colonists turned to writing charters of government in America, they produced documents that explicitly defined the liberties of the people. Some of the most famous of these colonial charters were the Massachusetts Body of Liberties (1641), the New York Charter of Liberties (1683), and the Pennsylvania Charter of Privileges (1701).

As the conflict with England intensified after 1765, Americans came increasingly to believe that British tyranny threatened their cherished liberties. Freedoms of speech and the press were restricted; homes, businesses, and property were searched and sometimes seized without benefit of specific warrants; the right to trial by a jury of one's peers was denied; and other threats to the security and safety of persons and property seemed imminent.

Patrick Henry, perhaps the most famous American orator of the 1770s and 1780s, addresses the Virginia House of Burgesses. His most famous line, "Give me liberty, or give me death," helped bring on the American Revolution.

In the immediate wake of the Declaration of Independence, state after state produced new constitutions, many of which began with a preamble dedicated to enumerating and justifying the liberties of the people.[1] These charters were framed with recent British actions clearly in mind. They were, therefore, largely antigovernment documents aimed at limiting and defining government power.

The Origins of the Bill of Rights

Chapter 2 explained the movement in the late 1780s for a new constitution. Even in the Constitutional Convention's final days, after a powerful new national government had taken shape, the wish of some delegates to add a bill of rights was rejected by a unanimous vote of the states. The delegates badly miscalculated how their failure to include a bill of rights in the new Constitution would be received by the public at large.

The Anti-Federalists, led by Patrick Henry in Virginia, seized upon the absence of a bill of rights as the key reason for their opposition to ratification. The demand for a bill of rights gained momentum as the ratification process proceeded. By the time the Virginia convention met in June 1788, nine states had already approved the Constitution, though several had added lists of recommended amendments. Virginia's narrow 89–79 ratification was secured only by the Federalists' promise to support amendments in the first Congress. James Madison's Baptist constituents were particularly concerned that the Anglican majority in Virginia might deny them religious freedom.

When Madison reached New York, the site of the first Congress, he set about drafting amendments to the Constitution. He had before him several state bills of rights and more than two hundred proposed amendments that had come from the states during the ratification process. By late August of 1788, he had guided a set of seventeen proposed amendments through the House of Representatives. The House concurred in the Senate's proposal to narrow the list to twelve, and these were submitted to the states for ratification in late September. Two of the proposed twelve amendments failed to win approval from the required three-fourths of the state legislatures.

However, ten amendments to the Constitution, the Bill of Rights, were approved and went into effect on December 15, 1791. The first eight amendments contain broad guarantees of individual liberty: freedom of religion, speech, press, and assembly; the right to keep and bear arms; protection for the privacy of the home; assurance against double jeopardy and compulsory self-incrimination; the right to counsel and to trial by jury; and freedom from cruel and unusual punishment. The Ninth Amendment provided that rights not specifically enumerated in the first eight amendments or elsewhere in the Constitution were not thereby lost, and the tenth assured that all powers not delegated to the national government were retained by the people or by the state governments. Surveys show that Americans are far less familiar with these fundamental liberties than they should be. Study them well.

The explicit language of some of the amendments (e.g., "Congress shall make no law" in the First Amendment) made it clear that the Bill of Rights was to apply only against the national government. The Supreme Court reiterated this view in the famous case of **Barron v. Baltimore** (1833). Chief Justice Marshall held "that the Bill of Rights limited the actions only of the federal government and not the states, thus making those who claimed that their rights had been violated by the state and local governments dependent on appeals to state constitutions, state judges, and local juries."[2] In fact, the Supreme Court did not move to enforce the individual liberties of the Bill of Rights against state and local governments until well into the twentieth century.

Barron v. Baltimore The Court held that the Bill of Rights applied to the federal government, not the states. As a result, individuals whose rights had been violated by state and local governments had to appeal to state constitutions, state judges, and local juries.

As we shall see below, the Supreme Court held in the 1920s that the First Amendment freedoms of speech and press were protected against state action because they had been "incorporated" through the Fourteenth Amendment's "due process" clause. In the 1947 case of *Adamson v. California*, Justice Hugo Black wrote a dissenting opinion, in which he was joined by three other justices, arguing for the total **incorporation** of the Bill of Rights into the Fourteenth Amendment. Justice Black argued that "no state could deprive its citizens of the privileges and protections of the Bill of Rights." Though Black failed to win total incorporation, the process of "selective incorporation" continued, most recently in the cases discussed above on the right to bear arms, so that today most provisions of the Bill of Rights constrain both federal and state governments.

incorporation The idea that many of the protections of the Bill of Rights originally meant to apply only against the national government applied against the states as well because they were "incorporated" into the Fourteenth Amendment's guarantees of "due process" and "equal protection of the laws."

Freedom of Expression: Speech and the Press

Q2 Do our commitments to free speech and a free press conflict with our sense that flag burning should be prohibited or that pornography should be regulated?

Freedom of expression is absolutely fundamental to the idea of popular government. Political participation, the open debate of policies and programs, and majority rule all depend on freedom of speech, press, and assembly. Yet, society's leaders, including public officials, have been reluctant to see themselves and their activities criticized from the soapbox or in the press. Popular majorities have been similarly reluctant to see their mainstream values flouted.

Not surprisingly, political leaders confident of majority support often move to suppress unpopular minority opinions. Sometimes the courts have upheld their actions, sometimes not. Should political leaders or popular majorities be able to limit expression that they think ill advised or inconvenient? What circumstances might justify the government's limiting the right of citizens to express themselves as they see fit? These are fundamental questions in a free society and they have been center stage during the wars in Iraq and Afghanistan and in the broader war on terror.

Freedom of Speech.   As late as March 1919, in *Schenck v. United States*, the Supreme Court upheld the conviction of a prominent socialist for producing and mailing leaflets opposing U.S. involvement in World War I. Justice Oliver Wendell Holmes, writing for the Court's majority, argued that the right to free speech is never absolute and that Schenck's actions were punishable. Holmes's famous argument was that "the most stringent protection of free speech would not protect a man in falsely shouting fire in a theater." The distinction between protected and punishable speech, he wrote, is "whether the words used are used in such circumstances and are of such a nature as to create *a clear and present danger*." Critics argued that acts of protest such as Schenck's, which had only the most remote prospect of causing real disruption to society and government, should not be suppressed. Soon, Holmes came around to this view too.

Gitlow v. New York The Court accepted the argument that the First Amendment limited state as well as federal action, but then applied a relaxed version of the "clear and present danger" test that allowed speech to be punished if it created a "bad tendency" to produce turmoil, even at some point in the remote future.

The next major development in free speech law came in 1925 in the case of *Gitlow v. New York.* Benjamin Gitlow was a communist convicted under New York law for advocating the overthrow of democracy and capitalism in America. His lawyer contended that the New York law was unconstitutional because Gitlow's federal First Amendment right to free speech had been "incorporated" into the "due process" clause of the Fourteenth Amendment that applied to state actions. The Court accepted the defense's incorporation argument, declaring that "we may and do assume that freedom of speech and of the press—which are protected by the First Amendment from abridgement by Congress—are among the fundamental personal rights and 'liberties' protected by the due process clause of the Fourteenth Amendment from impairment by the States." Simultaneously, however, the Court relaxed Holmes's "clear and present danger" test to the more general "bad tendency" test. Any speech that had a "bad tendency," that might produce social or political turmoil even at some remote future point, could be punished.

Struggling Toward Democracy

Alexis de Tocqueville wrote in *Democracy in America*, "I know of no country in which there is so little independence of mind and real freedom of discussion as in America."

What do you think?
- What did Tocqueville mean by this?
- If it was true then, is it still true today?

Holmes and his colleague, Louis Brandeis, this time behind Brandeis's pen, responded in the 1927 case of *Whitney v. California*. Charlotte Whitney was convicted under California law of engaging in Communist Party organizational activities. Whitney lost when the Supreme Court upheld the California statute. Nonetheless, Brandeis argued in dissent that the danger that Whitney's actions represented was so distant that state action to suppress it was illegitimate. Brandeis wrote that "no danger flowing from speech can be deemed clear and present, unless . . . serious injury to the state . . . [is] so imminent that it may befall before there is opportunity for full discussion. . . . Only an emergency can justify repression."

Not until *Brandenburg v. Ohio* (1969) did the Court overrule *Whitney* to adopt the "clear, present, and imminent danger test" offered by Brandeis and Holmes forty years earlier. More recently, the Court has moved well beyond the standard conceptions of free speech to protect forms of **symbolic speech** or speech-related activities including demonstrations, picketing, and protests. In 1989, the Court found burning the American flag to be a speech-related act. In *Texas v. Johnson*, the Court held that, "If there is a bedrock principle underlying the First Amendment, it is that Government may not prohibit the expression of an idea simply because society finds the idea itself offensive or disagreeable."

Interestingly, one class of persons—students—have limited free speech rights. The controlling precedent on the free speech rights of students is *Tinker v. Des Moines School District* (1969). Tinker held that students have a presumptive

symbolic speech Speech-related acts, such as picketing or flag burning, that like actual speech are protected under the First Amendment because they involve the communication of ideas or opinions.

Texas v. Johnson This case upheld flag burning as protected expression or symbolic speech by applying the stringent clear and imminent danger test of *Brandenburg*.

Protesters burn an American flag and an effigy of both President Bush and Senator John Kerry on the last day of the 2004 Democratic National Convention. The U.S. Supreme Court has declared that symbolic speech, including flag burning, is protected by the Constitution.

right to engage in political speech so long as that speech does not unduly disrupt the basic educational mission of the school. In 2007, a case called *Morse v. Frederick* came before the Supreme Court. Joseph Frederick, a high school student in Juneau, Alaska, was released from school to see the Olympic torch pass through town. Frederick attended the event and stretched a 14-foot banner, reading "Bong Hits 4 Jesus," across the parade route. Was this a school-sponsored event, at which his speech rights could be limited, or a public event, at which he could say what he pleased? Chief Justice John Roberts, writing for the majority, took the former view in finding for the school and upholding its punishment of Mr. Frederick for what they deemed to be a pro-drug message.[3]

Unprotected Speech: The Cross Burning and Obscenity Examples.   Even expansive views of free speech do not hold that absolutely all speech is constitutionally protected. In 2003, the Supreme Court held, in ***Virginia v. Black***, that cross burning, a traditional form of racial intimidation, was not speech protected by the Fourteenth Amendment. Justice Sandra Day O'Connor, writing for the Court, noted that free speech rights "are not absolute. . . . [W]hen a cross burning is used to intimidate, few if any messages are more powerful." Another example of the limits of free expression involves the right of a community to protect its members from obscene materials. The difficulty, of course, is that in a community as varied as ours, people will disagree about what is obscene.

Obscenity, as a constitutional or legal issue, has always involved suppressing some expression, whether in speech, print, or art, in light of some community standard. The traditional test in American law followed a standard laid down in the nineteenth-century English case of *Regina v. Hicklin* (1868), in which the court asked "whether the *tendency* of the matter charged as **obscenity** is to *deprave and corrupt* those whose *minds are open* to such immoral influences."[4] This rule of law, that material could be found obscene on the basis of its "tendency" to "deprave and corrupt" those minds in the community most open to suggestion left great latitude to local community standards.

The modern standard in American law was established by a line of cases extending from *Roth v. United States* (1957) through ***Miller v. California*** (1973). *Miller* set out a three-part obscenity test: would the average person applying contemporary community standards find that the work taken as a whole (a) appeals to prurient interests; (b) depicts or describes sexual conduct in a patently offensive way; (c) and lacks serious literary, artistic, political, or scientific value? With the advent of the Internet, obscene materials became so pervasive that most prosecutors stopped bringing cases except in the area of child sexual exploitation. In 2007, the Supreme Court found the Protect Act of 2003, which outlawed trafficking in real or purported (i.e., computer-generated) child pornography, to be constitutional and not an infringement of First Amendment rights. Clearly, it is easier to say that obscenity is not protected speech than it is to define obscenity in a way that is both acceptable to the courts and understandable to most Americans.

Virginia v. Black The Court ruled that cross burning, due to its historical ties to racial fear and intimidation, is not protected speech.

obscenity Sexually explicit material, whether spoken, written, or visual, that "taken as a whole . . . lacks serious literary, artistic, political, or scientific value."

Miller v. California The Court allowed states and local communities greater latitude in defining and regulating obscenity.

Freedom of the Press. Freedom of speech and freedom of the press are closely related liberties. Yet, unaided speech can reach and potentially sway only a few people, whereas the same views expressed in print or distributed across the airwaves and the Internet can reach and potentially sway millions. Does government have a greater responsibility to screen and limit expression that can reach millions in seconds than it does speech that can reach only dozens or perhaps hundreds and never more than thousands? As we shall see, the answer is generally no.

No Prior Restraint versus Freedom to Publish. There are two views of freedom of the press, one much broader and richer than the other. One view is that the press should not be required to secure permission from the government before publication, that is, that there should be no **prior restraint** of the press, no censorship. The second and broader view of freedom of the press both prohibits prior restraint and severely limits the conditions under which one can seek legal redress after the fact for statements appearing in the press. The right to publish without "prior restraint" is of modest benefit if one has to worry about being punished after the fact.[5]

Two cases established the modern Court's position on these two key aspects of press freedom. The first case, ***Near v. Minnesota*** (1931), established an almost complete prohibition against prior restraint on publication by any agent or level of government. Jay M. Near was the editor of a newspaper called the *Saturday Press*, which regularly attacked Minnesota public officials. One such public official was Floyd B. Olson. Tired of being pilloried in Near's paper, Olson tried to use a Minnesota public nuisance law to force the closure of the *Saturday Press*. The Supreme Court held that closing the paper would be a form of prior restraint and therefore was unconstitutional. Since *Near*, American courts have rejected requests for prior restraint of the press virtually out of hand.

New York Times v. Sullivan arose out of the civil rights movement. Throughout the late 1950s blacks rallied, protested, and boycotted to end segregation and racial discrimination. On March 29, 1960, supporters of Dr. Martin Luther King Jr. took out a full-page advertisement in the *New York Times* claiming that Montgomery, Alabama, city officials had illegally harassed black protesters. L.B. Sullivan, the Montgomery city commissioner in charge of the police, sued the *New York Times* and others, claiming that the advertisement had libeled him with charges of "grave misconduct" and "improper actions and omissions as an official of the City of Montgomery."

Alabama courts, citing the potential damage done to Commissioner Sullivan's reputation, found against the *Times*. The *Times* appealed first to the Alabama Supreme Court, where it lost again, and then to the U.S. Supreme Court. Attorney Herbert Wechsler representing the *Times* argued that if Sullivan prevailed no newspaper would allow criticism of government policy or officials in its pages for fear that it might be sued if any aspect of the story offended a public official.

prior restraint Any limitation on publication requiring that permission be secured or approval be granted prior to publication. No prior restraint means no censorship or permission process that could hinder publication.

Near v. Minnesota This decision established an almost complete prohibition against prior restraint on publication by any agent or level of government.

New York Times v. Sullivan By concluding that a public official had to prove either "actual malice" or "reckless disregard for the truth" in order to be awarded damages in a libel case, the Court essentially constructed a right not to be punished after the fact for what has been published.

The Supreme Court found against Sullivan and for the *Times*. Justice Brennan, writing for the majority, echoed Madison in contending that, "free public discussion of the stewardship of public officials was . . . a fundamental principle of the American form of government." Brennan and his colleagues knew, as Madison had before them, that public officials able to intimidate their critics with the threat of legal action would be free from oversight and evaluation.

Most U.S. courts now recognize a "neutral report privilege" protecting journalists who report, without approval or disapproval, negative comments about politicians. However, knowingly publishing falsehoods with the intent to do harm, called "malicious intent," can produce criminal defamation charges in about half of the states. Such charges involving journalists are more common than they once were but are still fairly rare.[6]

Restrictions on Press Freedom: National Security and Fair Trial.   No freedom is without limits. Just as Justice Holmes noted that the right to free speech does not extend to falsely shouting "fire" in a crowded theater, others have noted that freedom of the press may be limited by national security concerns or by a criminal defendant's right to a fair trial. However, even these potential reasons for restricting press freedom have been very narrowly construed. For example, in the 1973 **Pentagon Papers Case**, the federal government went to court to constrain several newspapers including the *New York Times* and the *Washington Post* from publishing illegally obtained materials relating to the conduct of the Vietnam War. The Supreme Court declined to award the injunction, noting the heavy presumption against "prior restraint" of publication.

On the other hand, government officials often appeal to the press to withhold sensitive information, particularly in wartime. Oftentimes, the press will comply, at least for a time, if the government makes a plausible case. The Bush administration clashed repeatedly with the nation's leading newspapers, including the *New York Times*, *Los Angeles Times*, and *Washington Post* over stories about questionable intelligence, prisoner abuse, secret CIA prisons, surveillance of domestic communications, and international and domestic banking records. In each case, the administration claimed that publication would endanger national security and journalists pointed to the people's right to know what their government was doing.[7]

As a candidate, Barack Obama promised to roll back many of the Bush Administration's most aggressive claims to national security authority because they "undermined the Constitution." But as president, Barack Obama has been reluctant to disclaim these powers, especially in the area of domestic surveillance. Prior to 9/11 the FBI was required to secure approval, under the Foreign Intelligence Surveillance Act (FISA), for wiretapping or securing the phone records of Americans. After 9/11 the records of thousands of citizens were secured without warrants. In early 2010 the Obama Administration's Office of Legal Counsel supported the FBI's claim that the right to obtain phone records without court approval still obtained.[8]

Similarly, American courts have long sought to balance the public's right to know with a criminal defendant's right to a fair trial before an unbiased jury.

Pentagon Papers Case
Formally titled *New York Times Co. v. United States*. The Court found that prior restraint violated the First Amendment unless imminent danger could be proven.

The general rule is that "judges may *not* . . . forbid publication of information about criminal cases—even if, in the judge's opinion, such an order would help to assure the defendant a fair trial by preventing prejudicial publicity."[9] The courts have consistently seen the First Amendment as commanding a strong presumption against barring the press from judicial proceedings. The 1995 murder trial of O. J. Simpson highlighted Judge Lance Ito's struggle to control the effect of overwhelming media attention on Simpson's right to a fair trial before jurors not saturated by potentially prejudicial information derived from *People* magazine, *Hard Copy*, and *20/20*.

Freedom of Religion

Nine of the thirteen colonies had state-sanctioned churches as the revolution approached. Nonetheless, Jefferson's vision of a "wall of separation between Church and State" soon came to be the dominant image of church–state relations in American politics. Although this phrase has been repeated endlessly over the course of American political history, it has no obvious and decisive meaning.

There are three basic views about how the separation of church and state should be conceived and these are still hotly contested.[10] The first view calls for a strict separation in which government takes no notice of religion and permits no hint of religious sentiment or symbolism to attach to its actions. The second view holds that government may not favor one religion over another, and certainly not one over all of the others, but that it may provide general support and benefit to all religions. The third view contends that government should actively promote religion as beneficial to the nation's moral strength and health although once again, no religion or religions should be favored over others.

Occasionally a public official like Alabama Chief Justice Roy S. Moore will conclude that God's law underpins human law, perhaps even the U.S. Constitution, and that that fact needs to be more evident. In 2001, newly elected Chief Justice Moore had a two and one-half ton granite monument of the Ten Commandments placed in the foyer of the Alabama Supreme Court building. Every judicial authority in Alabama and every federal court up through and including the U.S. Supreme Court instructed Judge Moore to remove the monument. Moore refused. Although many citizens in Alabama and beyond rallied to his cause, Justice Moore was removed from office and his monument was wheeled away. After an absence of nearly a decade, Moore was again elected Chief Justice of the Alabama Supreme Court in 2012, though he assured voters that the monument was gone for good.

The Establishment Clause. The **establishment clause** of the First Amendment says "Congress shall make no law respecting an establishment of religion." This stark language has been taken to mean that the national government in general, and Congress in particular, may neither establish an official national religion nor favor one religion over the others. What is less clear

Q3 Does our commitment to separation of church and state mean that no trace of religious sentiment or symbolism should emanate from government?

establishment clause The First Amendment to the Constitution says that "Congress shall make no law respecting an establishment of religion." This clearly means that Congress may not establish a national religion. There is an ongoing debate over how much, if any, contact is allowed between religion and government.

Tami Chappell / Reuters / Landov

Justice Moore's monument being wheeled away.

is whether government, using tax dollars, public facilities, or moral suasion, may support, facilitate, or cooperate with religious groups even if government is equally supportive of all religious groups. The answer is yes, but carefully.

The Supreme Court's clearest attempt to draw the line between constitutional and unconstitutional government involvement with religion came in **Lemon v. Kurtzman** (1971). The Court developed a three-pronged test, widely known as the *Lemon* test, to determine the constitutionality of state aid to religious activities and institutions. The state program: (1) must have a secular purpose; (2) its principal effect must neither advance nor impede religion; and (3) it must not permit or encourage an "excessive entanglement" of church and state.

While various justices, including Sandra Day O'Connor before her retirement and Antonin Scalia more recently, have proposed refinements or alternatives to the Lemon test, it remains the foundation of court doctrine on the establishment clause. O'Connor proposed an endorsement test, that government may not endorse religion or non-religion, and Scalia proposed the coercion test, that the establishment clause is not violated unless individuals are coerced to support or participate in religious activities. The coercion test has not generated much support, but the endorsement test has been used by the courts to supplement, though not displace, the Lemon test.

Governments wishing to provide support to children attending religious schools have long argued that the support is going to the children rather than to the schools and that some children merely receive their state support in a religious school setting. Recent rulings have increased public aid to parochial

Lemon v. Kurtzman This case established the *Lemon* test for state support of religion. Such support must be secular in purpose, not unduly advance or impede religion, and not involve "excessive entanglement" of the state with religion.

schools by allowing federal funds to be used for transportation, lunch programs, textbooks, computers, and other instructional equipment in religious schools.[11]

Teaching intelligent design in the public schools is a hot-button issue that has recently been in the news and in the courts. Religious conservatives in Dover, Pennsylvania won a majority on the local school board and mandated that intelligent design (the idea that nature is too complex to have developed randomly and evinces signs of a creator) be taught as an alternative to evolution in biology classes. Judge John E. Jones III of the federal district court in Harrisburg presided over the six-week trial. He declared that intelligent design was religion, not science, and teaching it in public school science classes was a violation of the First Amendment establishment clause.

In 2005, the Supreme Court decided two cases involving display of the Ten Commandments in public spaces. The Court held that framed copies of the Ten Commandments on the walls of two Kentucky courthouses served as unconstitutional endorsements of religion, while a six-foot monument to the Ten Commandments on the grounds of the Texas state capitol among more than two dozen other statues was not an endorsement. Justice David Souter wrote that "the touchstone of our analysis is the principle that the First Amendment mandates government neutrality between religion and religion, and between religion and non-religion; . . . that liberty and social stability demand a religious tolerance that respects the religious views of all citizens."[12]

The Free Exercise Clause. If the establishment clause is essentially about how much support the state can give to institutionalized religion, the **free exercise clause** is about how completely free individuals must be to conduct their religious lives. The free exercise clause protects most, but not all, religious observances and practices from state interference.

free exercise clause The First Amendment to the Constitution, immediately after saying that Congress may not establish religion, says Congress may not prohibit the "free exercise" of religion. The intent of the free exercise clause is to protect a wide range of religious observance and practice from political interference.

Gary Brookins

The free exercise clause protects Americans in believing and asserting any religious principles they please. The Court has long held, however, that actions are not beliefs. In *Reynolds v. U.S.* (1879), the Court held that religiously inspired action, in this case the Mormon practice of plural marriage, is not protected by the free exercise privilege because it violates "otherwise valid law prohibiting conduct that the State is free to regulate" (i.e., marriage law). More recently, in *Employment Division v. Smith* (1990), a case in which two individuals were denied unemployment benefits after having been fired for sacramental peyote use, the Court affirmed that illegal action, even if religiously motivated, enjoys no exemption from "generally applicable criminal law."

In 1993 Congress sought to support free exercise of religion and limit government intrusion by passing the Religious Freedom Restoration Act. The act forbade any level of government to "substantially burden" religious observance without showing a "compelling" need to do so and without selecting the "least restrictive means available." The Supreme Court struck down the Religious Freedom Restoration Act in 1997, declaring that it gave religious activity more protection against normal law and regulation than the First Amendment required. Finally, Presidents Clinton and Bush issued

AP Photo / Bruce Newman

Prayer in public schools remains controversial. Here a Mississippi school official walks by placard-carrying opponents of school prayer at the opening of a March 1996 trial on this issue.

guidelines guaranteeing federal workers the right to express and reflect religious views at work.

Prayer in the Schools.   No issue in the broad area of separation of church and state has been as consistently contested as prayer in the schools. In 1962, the Supreme Court declared in *Engel v. Vitale* that "it is no part of the business of government to compose official prayers for any group of the American people to recite as part of a religious program carried on by government." *Engel* made clear that mandatory prayer in the public schools was unconstitutional. In 1982, the Supreme Court held that a Louisiana statute authorizing daily voluntary prayer in its public schools was unconstitutional. In 1994, the Ninth Circuit Court of Appeals in San Francisco declared a high school graduation prayer unconstitutional even though it was approved by a majority vote of the students. And in 2000, the Supreme Court held that organized, student-led prayers at high school football games constituted an unconstitutional establishment of religion.

On the other hand, no one in public schools was ever prohibited from praying privately. Private prayer—mostly before tests, to be sure—was always an option and much public prayer occurred among those who agreed and arranged to participate. Religious conservatives are, not surprisingly, always working to assure and even expand these rights. For example, in 2012, Florida passed a law allowing "inspirational messages" to be read during school assemblies and sporting events. And in 2013, Governor Phil Bryant (R-MS) signed a law instructing schools to develop policies allowing prayers over school intercoms and during ceremonies, like graduation, and sporting events. The governor suggested, "You might put on the program that this is not a state-sanctioned prayer if a prayer does break out at a football game or graduation."[13] Do you think judges will find this to be persuasive?

Both Presidents Clinton and Bush sought to clarify the complex and sensitive issue of prayer in public schools. Both issued statements through the Departments of Justice and Education, to ensure that school administrators were not unnecessarily and illegally discouraging religious activities in their schools. Basically, President Clinton made the point that student-initiated religious activity is subject to the same opportunities and limitations as are other nonacademic social and political activities. What students are permitted to do in support of their political or economic views, they may do in furtherance of their religious views, as long as other students are not coerced and school officials do not participate in the activity.

President Bush included provisions in the "No Child Left Behind Act" of 2001 requiring the Department of Education to ensure that schools were open to voluntary religious activity. Each state must declare that every school in the state is in compliance with national law and policy; failure to comply can trigger loss of federal funds.

Moreover, in recent decisions the Supreme Court and the Obama administration have moved to exempt religious institutions from some aspects of laws that others must obey. The Court declared in 2012 a "ministerial privilege" allowing churches to hire only within their own religion while other employers may not discriminate in hiring. Also in 2012, the Obama administration backed off, at least partially, when the Catholic Church and others complained that the new health care law required that they violate their religious principles by including birth control and abortion services in the health care plans they provided to employees.[14]

Nonetheless, one advocate of the separation of church and state, California's Michael Newdow, has been particularly active over the last decade. In 2000, Newdow filed a case, *Elk Grove Unified School District v. Newdow*, asking that the phrase "under God" be removed from the Pledge of Allegiance recited by public school students, including Newdow's daughter. In 2002, the U.S. Ninth Circuit Court of Appeals agreed with Newdow that the phrase "under God" in the pledge constituted a violation of the First Amendment "establishment clause." In 2004, the Supreme Court overturned the Ninth Circuit, not on the grounds that the case was wrongly decided, but on the ground that Newdow, as a non-custodial parent of his school-aged daughter, lacked the standing to bring the case. In 2005, Newdow brought an identical case, this time on behalf of other parents, and again the district court found the phrase "under God" in the pledge to be unconstitutional.

The case again came before the Ninth Circuit in late 2007. Newdow argued that supporters of the pledge "want to have their views espoused by government." This time the Ninth Circuit declared that the pledge was not an unconstitutional establishment of religion because students were not required to participate. Moreover, Judge Carlos Bea, for a court divided 2–1, held that "The Pledge of Allegiance serves to unite our vast nation through the proud recitation of some of the ideals upon which our republic was founded." In a separate 3–0 ruling, the court held that the phrase "In God We Trust" on U.S. coins and currency had a ceremonial and patriotic meaning rather than a strictly religious meaning.[15]

THE RIGHTS OF CRIMINAL DEFENDANTS

Q4 Should someone accused of a serious crime go free if police commit a procedural error during the investigation or during the arrest and questioning?

The fundamental question that arises in many people's minds over the rights of criminal defendants is why we should care about them? Why do we restrict our police and courts to a narrow range of specific procedures and methods for protecting us against those who would break the laws of our society? Fundamentally, we defend what we call "due process of law" even for the most heinous criminals because the treatment that we sanction for them might become the norm for the rest of us. We are protecting ourselves when we demand that no one be treated with cavalier brutality.

Judicial interest in the rights of the accused is more recent than one might imagine. Not until the 1960s did the Supreme Court move to regulate police, prosecutorial, and judicial conduct in the states. This was accomplished by incorporating Bill of Rights protections—for the right to counsel and a fair and speedy trial and against unreasonable searches and seizures, self-incrimination and double jeopardy, and cruel and unusual punishment—into the "due process" clause of the Fourteenth Amendment.

Something of a rollback has been underway since the mid-1980s and many new questions have been raised by government actions undertaken as part of the war on terror.

Searches, Seizures, and the Exclusionary Rule. The Fourth Amendment to the Constitution declares that "The right of the people to be secure in their persons, houses, papers, and effects, against **unreasonable searches and seizures**, shall not be violated, and no Warrants shall issue, but upon probable cause, supported by Oath or affirmation, and particularly describing the place to be searched, and the persons or things to be seized." Police cannot engage in general searches in the hope of uncovering wrongdoing. Traditionally, obtaining a search warrant required police to convince a judge that they have "probable cause" to believe that the search of a particular place would result in the seizure of particular items relevant to a specific crime.

To encourage police to abide by these stringent rules, American courts enforced the **exclusionary rule**. Developed first in *Weeks v. U.S.* (1914) at the federal level and then applied to state officials in *Mapp v. Ohio* (1961), the exclusionary rule says that evidence illegally obtained will be "excluded" from use against the defendant at trial. The pros and cons of the exclusionary rule have been clear from the beginning. Two prominent jurists, both future Supreme Court justices, laid them out during the discussion of *Weeks*. Louis Brandeis explained the necessity of the rule by saying, "If the government becomes a lawbreaker, it breeds contempt for law." New York Court of Appeals Judge Benjamin Cardozo responded incredulously, "the criminal is to go free because the constable blundered."

More recently, there has been some movement away from complete exclusion of tainted evidence. The Supreme Court held in 1984 that the exclusionary rule should be subject to a "good faith" exception. The government had long contended that officers acting on the "objectively reasonable" assumption that a warrant that they had obtained was good but was later found to be flawed somehow should not lose their evidence. Another 1984 case, *Nix v. Williams*, held that evidence should be admitted even if it first came to light in an illegal search "If the prosecution can establish by a preponderance of evidence that the information ultimately or inevitably would have been discovered by lawful means." The "good faith" and "inevitable discovery" exceptions significantly eroded the exclusionary rule and the deterrence that it provided to illegal police conduct.

In 2006, the Supreme Court declared in *Hudson v. Michigan* that although the police failed to observe the "knock and announce" rule (central to the common law since the thirteenth century), they could still use evidence obtained at trial. Police arriving at the home of Booker T. Hudson Jr., announced their presence but did not knock and waited only seconds before entering through an unlocked door. The police discovered drugs in the home. Justice Scalia, writing for a 5–4 majority, was dismissive of the exclusionary rule, weighing "the right not to be intruded upon in one's nightclothes" against the "grave adverse consequences that exclusion of relevant incriminating evidence always

unreasonable searches and seizures The Fourth Amendment to the Constitution guarantees that citizens will not be subject to unreasonable searches and seizures. A search must be authorized by a warrant secured on probable cause that specific, relevant evidence is to be found if a particular place is searched.

exclusionary rule The exclusionary rule holds that evidence illegally obtained by police cannot be used in court. The Supreme Court established the exclusionary rule in regard to the federal authorities in *Weeks v. U.S.* (1914) and in regard to state authorities in *Mapp v. Ohio* (1961).

entails."[16] Justice Kennedy, the swing vote in *Hudson*, signed the majority opinion, but he also wrote separately to declare that, "the continued operation of the 'exclusionary rule,' as settled and defined by our precedents, is not in doubt." Others were not so sure.

In 2009, Chief Justice Roberts, writing for a 5–4 court in *Herring v. U.S.*, struck another blow to the exclusionary rule. Bennie D. Herring went to the Coffee County, Alabama, Sheriff's office to check on an impounded truck. While inquiring into the truck, deputies asked the records clerk to check for outstanding warrants on Herring. The clerk reported an open felony warrant on Herring and he was arrested. Subsequent to the arrest, police found methamphetamine and an unloaded handgun on Herring. Almost immediately, the clerk corrected himself, reporting that the warrant on Herring had been recalled, but Herring was held anyway on the drug and weapons charges.

At trial, Herring's lawyer moved to have the case dismissed based on the "exclusionary rule." The trial court declined to dismiss the case and the appeals court agreed, citing the "good faith" exception to the exclusionary rule. Herring's appeal to the Supreme Court was decided in 2009. Chief Justice Roberts took the occasion to broaden exceptions to the exclusionary rule. Roberts wrote that, "To trigger the exclusionary rule, police misconduct must be sufficiently deliberate that exclusion can meaningfully deter it, and sufficiently culpable that such deterrence is worth the price paid by the justice system."[17] The Court's finding that police misconduct must be both "deliberate" and "culpable," meaning ill-intended, seems to envision a cost/benefit balancing test rather than an automatic exclusion of tainted evidence.

GPS--civil liberties case

In several recent cases the United States Supreme Court has held that a police-installed GPS device on a suspect's vehicle constitutes an illegal search.

Finally, in 2012 the Supreme Court decided a Fourth Amendment search and seizure case that brought this historic personal privacy right fully into the twenty-first century. Police suspected that Antoine Jones, a Washington D.C. nightclub owner, was involved in cocaine sales. As part of their investigation, the police secretly placed a GPS tracking device on Jones's Jeep Grand Cherokee to follow his movements. After a month of evidence gathering, Jones was arrested, convicted, and sentenced to life in prison. The U.S. Court of Appeals for the District of Columbia overturned the conviction and the U.S. Supreme Court agreed, declaring that police must secure a warrant because intensive tracking by GPS is a "search" within the meaning of the Fourth Amendment.[18]

Right to Counsel.   The Sixth Amendment provides for a federal **right to counsel**. The rights of criminal defendants in state courts to the assistance of legal counsel during trial were established in *Gideon v. Wainwright* (1963). Clarence Earl Gideon was a 51-year-old man charged with breaking into the Bar Harbor Poolroom in Panama City, Florida. Gideon denied having broken into the pool hall and requested the assistance of counsel at his trial. Assistance was denied, and Gideon was convicted. He appealed, claiming that it was a violation of the "due process" clause of the Fourteenth Amendment to confront an untrained citizen with the complexity of the legal and judicial systems. The Supreme Court agreed that persons charged with crimes should have the right to counsel at state expense if they cannot afford to provide it for themselves, saying "In our adversary system of criminal justice, any person haled into court, who is too poor to hire a lawyer, cannot be assured a fair trial unless counsel is provided for him."

States do comply with the requirement to provide counsel to indigent defendants, but their budgets are often meager and their performances spotty. Fully 80 percent of defendants are too poor to afford their own lawyer, so they must depend upon public defenders or legal aid lawyers. Some public defenders handle as many as 2,000 cases a year, so the amount of time they can spend preparing for each case, let alone doing independent investigation of the circumstances surrounding the case, is minimal. Hence, many public defenders are reduced to negotiating plea bargains and guilty verdicts.[19]

Self-Incrimination.   "Taking the Fifth" is the shorthand term for exercising one's Fifth Amendment right against **self-incrimination**. The Fifth Amendment reads in part, "nor shall any person . . . be compelled in any criminal case to be a witness against himself." As with the right to counsel, the Supreme Court has acted to ensure that the right against self-incrimination applies in state as well as federal courts, from the investigation stage of the legal process through arrest and trial. Since *Miranda v. Arizona* (1966), persons taken into custody must be specifically informed that they have the right to remain silent and that they cannot be questioned unless they waive that right. If the *Miranda* warning is not given, statements made by the accused cannot be used at trial.

The right against self-incrimination was strengthened in a 1986 case known as *Michigan v. Jackson*. *Michigan v. Jackson* held that police could not initiate

right to counsel *Gideon v. Wainwright* (1963) declared that a person accused of a crime has the right to the assistance of a lawyer in preparing his or her defense. The right to counsel is part of the meaning of the Fourteenth Amendment's guarantee of "due process of law."

self-incrimination The Fifth Amendment to the Constitution guarantees that one cannot be compelled "to be a witness against himself." Taking advantage of the right against self-incrimination is often called "taking the Fifth."

Pro & Con

Defending the USA Patriot Act (2001–Present)

Major Provisions of the USA Patriot Act

Improved Information Sharing

Allows greater information sharing between domestic law enforcement and the intelligence agencies.

Enhanced Surveillance Authority

Authorizes "sneak and peek" warrants with delayed notification to the target.

Authorizes "roving wiretaps" of all phones used by a target as opposed to tapping a specific phone number.

Expands FBI access to personal health, financial, and other records if agents certify foreign intelligence or antiterrorism activities.

Expands law enforcement's access to Internet routing, e-mail, and voice mail records and broadens Internet provider's responsibility to cooperate with authorities.

Strengthened Antiterrorism Laws

Expands the definition of domestic terrorism to include life-threatening activities designed to intimidate the public or to change government policy by threats, assassination, or mass destruction.

Expands the definition of what constitutes material support of terrorists and penalties attached.

Allows a federal judge to issue eavesdropping orders that can be executed anywhere in the country.

Following the Money

Gives intelligence agents access to financial records in international terrorism cases.

Permits expanded forfeiture in bulk-cash smuggling cases and cases against those planning or committing acts of terrorism in the United States.

The Debate over the Patriot Act

Passed only weeks after the 9/11 attacks, the USA Patriot Act has been controversial since its inception. The controversy was on stark display when Congress struggled over renewal of sixteen key provisions of the Patriot Act during 2005 and 2006. Its advocates, led by President Bush and Attorney General Alberto Gonzales, argue that the new powers were needed to defend the homeland and combat the threat of global terrorism. In April 2005, Attorney General Gonzales warned Congress that "Al Qaeda and other terrorist groups still pose a grave threat to the security of the American people, and now is not the time to relinquish some of our most effective tools in this fight."

questioning of a suspect who had a lawyer or who had asked for a lawyer until the lawyer was present. The Michigan case also held that defendants could not change their mind and agree to talk with police between the lawyer's appointment and arrival. But as with the search and seizure cases, the Supreme Court's recent rulings on self-incrimination represent a dialing back of the exclusionary rule to a more case-by-case "totality of the evidence" test.

The 2009 case of *Montejo v. Louisiana* began as an attempt to clarify whether a defendant had to affirmatively accept counsel for the Michigan prohibition on questioning to apply. Jesse Jay Montejo was convicted of murder in 2002. He had been appointed counsel, knew it, did not ask to consult with counsel, before leading the police to the murder weapon. On appeal, Montejo claimed

Critics on both the left and the right have expressed concerns about the Patriot Act and related national security laws and how these new powers have been used. These new powers of investigation, surveillance, and arrest press hard on the traditional rights and liberties that Americans have enjoyed. The point is frequently made that the terrorists have won if we become a more closed and fearful society. On the other hand, no one denies that the terrorists took advantage of our open society in wreaking the terrible destruction of 9/11. After a year-long debate, key provisions of the Patriot Act were renewed in March 2006.

Now more than a decade after 9/11, how should we be thinking about the relationship between security and liberty? Bush Attorney General Alberto Gonzales was right to point to the continuing terrorist threat but shouldn't we be at least a little bit surprised that Obama Attorney General Eric Holder takes much the same view. Scholars recall that every major war in our history—the Revolutionary War, the Civil War, World Wars I and II—produced restrictions on civil liberties that were later regretted and dismantled. But no president, conservative Republican or progressive Democrat can risk seeming to let down their guard against terrorist threats.[20]

This delicate balance between the liberty of individuals and the security of the nation returned to the front-burner with the 2013 revelations of National Security Agency (NSA) contractor Edward Snowden. Snowden released to the media and the public a vast array of secret documents showing a variety and scope of domestic and international surveillance not previously imagined. NSA, generally tasked with foreign surveillance and court-approved domestic surveillance related to its international responsibilities, was doing much more. The Snowden revelations showed NSA and related agencies to be sweeping up vast amounts of data, domestically and internationally, on phone, text, and Internet traffic. While most of this data was described as "metadata," not the full messages and not linked to individuals, the scope of the collection disturbed regular citizens as well as privacy advocates. The Obama administration responded with modest reforms, but a host of unanswered questions remain.

What do you think?
- Have we gone too far in sacrificing liberty to security in the Patriot Act?
- Or are the threats all too real and the sacrifices of personal liberty appropriately modest in your view?

PRO	CON
War on Terror demanded greater powers	National security challenges often elect over-reaction
Protecting Americans must be top priority	Individual rights must not be sacrificed
The War on Terror is on-going	Perpetual war gives government too much power

that the police should not have questioned him until his lawyer arrived. The Supreme Court declined simply to find that Montejo should have consulted with his lawyer before cooperating with the police. Instead, the Court asked the parties to brief the broader question of whether *Michigan v. Jackson* had been rightly decided. Should a defendant, in fact, be able to talk with police without a lawyer present if he chooses? Justice Scalia, writing for a 5–4 court, decided that the answer to this question was yes.

Justice Scalia declared in *Montejo* that, "It would be completely unjustified to presume that a defendant's consent to police-initiated interrogation was involuntary or coerced simply because he had previously been appointed a lawyer." Moreover, Scalia asserted that the benefits to police effectiveness far outweighed the cost to defendants' rights. "The considerable adverse effect of this (the *Michigan v. Jackson*) rule upon society's ability to solve crimes and bring criminals to justice far outweighs its capacity to prevent a genuinely coerced agreement to speak without counsel present."[21] In 2010, the Supreme Court limited Miranda rights a bit more by holding that suspects must explicitly invoke their right to remain silent and then follow through by remaining silent. Ambiguous invocations, as when a suspect initially declines to answer but later responds to some police questions, will be decided in favor of the police.[22]

Finally, much discussion of police and national security interrogation policy resolves around the famous "ticking time bomb" scenario. The question is posed—if you captured a terrorist, whether in the U.S. or outside, who was thought to have information about a bomb about to go off, do rules like Miranda rights and the Geneva Convention prohibitions on torture make sense? Aggressively questioning a terrorist, right up to and perhaps beyond torture, and perhaps saving many, or just a few, lives—is this a reasonable tradeoff? Something close to this hypothetical actually occurred in the wake of the Boston Marathon bombing in 2013. Four days after the bombing, Dzhokhar Tsarnaev, one of the two brothers who were the main perpetrators, was captured, seriously wounded, and questioned in his hospital bed without being read his Miranda rights. Federal authorities claimed a "public safety exemption" to the normal Miranda requirements. As in the "ticking time bomb" scenario, the claim is that there might be other plots afoot that the perpetrator—in this case Tsarnaev—might know about. There were not, but there might have been. What do you think of the "public safety exemption?" Too broad, or just common sense?[23]

Cruel and Unusual Punishment.   The Eighth Amendment to the Constitution forbids **cruel and unusual punishment**. This provision was not terribly controversial until the 1960s when the National Association for the Advancement of Colored People (NAACP) convincingly made the case that the death penalty in America was applied arbitrarily and more frequently against blacks than against whites. The Supreme Court suspended the death penalty in *Furman v. Georgia* (1972) until states could reconsider and refine their procedures. Georgia's rewritten death penalty procedures were approved by the Supreme Court in *Gregg v. Georgia* (1976).

Although the United States is one of the few advanced industrial countries to employ the death penalty, the Supreme Court has been adamant that the death penalty is constitutional if fairly and reasonably applied. Hence, until recently, the debate revolved around issues of age and mental development—how young is too young to be executed and how retarded is too retarded to be held responsible for your actions? In 1989, the Supreme Court held that executing young people at 16 or 17 was not "cruel and unusual." In 2005, in a case called *Roper v. Simmons*, the court reversed itself, citing evolving national and international standards, declaring that execution for crimes committed before age 18 was constitutionally prohibited. In 2012, the Court declared that sentences of life without the possibility of parole also are unconstitutional for those under 18.[24]

cruel and unusual punishment The Eighth Amendment to the U.S. Constitution prohibits "cruel and unusual punishment." Historically, this language prohibited torture and other abuses. Today the key question is whether the death penalty should be declared to be cruel and unusual punishment.

The issue of executing the mentally retarded and the mentally ill who are convicted of serious crimes has been particularly vexing. All recognize that at some level of mental incapacity, an individual lacks the ability to form criminal intent or to assist in his or own defense or both. In ***Atkins v. Virginia*** (2002) the Supreme Court agreed that it was unconstitutionally cruel to execute the severely mentally retarded (IQ below 70), but little guidance was given on how to deal with the more common cases of mild to moderate retardation. Courts also struggle with what it means to punish the mentally ill.

In 2007 and 2008, quite unexpectedly, a legal dispute erupted over whether the particular three-drug cocktail used to execute death row inmates in most states caused sufficient pain to be prohibited as "cruel and unusual." In 2007, the Supreme Court agreed to consider this question in a Kentucky case, *Baze v. Rees* (553 U.S. 35). By the end of the year an informal moratorium on executions was in place awaiting the court's determination. In 2008, the court declared that lethal injection using the three-drug cocktail was constitutionally permissible. While the result was no great surprise, a concurring opinion by Associate Justice William Brennan did create a stir. Brennan, the court's oldest and longest serving member, at 88 with 33 years of service on the court, declared that the time had come to reconsider "the justification for the death penalty itself."[25] While there is growing unease about the death penalty, change will come slowly.

Atkins v. Virginia The Supreme Court held that the execution of severely retarded persons violated the prohibition against "cruel and unusual punishment" in the Eighth Amendment.

Civil Liberties, Prisons, and the Death Penalty

Paradoxically, while the American commitment to civil liberties is strong, so is the commitment to prisons and punishment. The Bill of Rights was added to the Constitution by the first Congress because many were concerned that a powerful national government might threaten individual liberty. Yet, today the United States, with less than 5 percent of the world's population, holds one-quarter of the world's prisoners, the most of any nation in the world.[26]

It has not always been so. Alexis de Tocqueville commented in his famous *Democracy In America* (1835) on the moderate face of American justice; "In no country is criminal justice administered with more mildness than in the United States." The American justice system took on a harsher tone especially after the war on drugs picked up steam in the 1970s. Three things changed— more people were arrested, for a wider range of crimes, and sentenced to longer terms in prison, hence the burgeoning of the prison population. With increasing numbers came increasing expenses and many now wonder whether the system is broken or merely in need of reform.

Let's start with the number of state and federal prisoners held in the U.S. We have solid data going back nearly a century. In 1925, fewer than 92,000 prisoners were held by the federal and state governments. The numbers rose during the difficult depression years of the 1930, peaking at almost 180,000 in 1939, before falling back during the 1940s and early 1950s. The prison population stayed near 200,000 from the late 1950s through the early 1970s—and then it took off. In 1972, there were 196,092 federal and state prisoners in the U.S., by 1980 there were 316,000, by 1990 there were 740,000, by 2000 there

Q5 If we value civil liberties so highly, why do we keep so many people in prison?

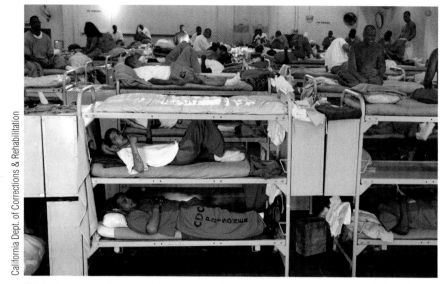

California prisons, like those in many other states, are overcrowded and increasingly expensive to administer.

Struggling Toward Democracy

Japan keeps 58 people per 100,000 of population in prison; Germany keeps 87, Canada 117, and the U.S. 497.

What do you think?

- As a free country, why do we keep so many people, especially so many minorities, in prison?
- What would need to change to lower incarceration rates—laws, sentencing practices, or behavior?

were 1.33 million, and by 2012 there were 1.6 million. China, with four times the U.S. population, holds 30 percent fewer prisoners.

Another way to think about the size of the federal and state prison population is in terms of prisoners per 100,000 of total population, also referred to as the incarceration rate (Figure 13.1). Population increases over time and so one would expect prison population to increase over time as well. If the prison population increased at the same rate as the general population, the incarceration rate would hold steady. It did not. In 1925, the incarceration rate was 79 per 100,000 of population. Again, the incarceration rate rose during the depression and then fell back during the 1940s and 1950s. The incarceration rate was 93 per 100,000 in 1972, 139 in 1980, 297 in 1990, 478 in 2000, and 480 in 2012. This is more than a six-fold increase in prisoners per 100,000 of population since 1925. The U.S. is number one in the world in incarceration rates. Russia is number two and the average for the world is about one-sixth the U.S. rate.[27]

Even more stunningly, when one adds those in local jails and on probation and parole to those in federal and state prisons, there are 7.1 million persons in the U.S. correctional system. This number has grown inexorably, increasing every year between 1982 and 2007. In 1982, the total corrections population was just under 2.2 million persons. By 1990 it was 4.35 million, by 2000 it was 6.45 million, and by 2007 it was 7.34 million. By 2012, the total number of persons in the U.S. corrections system had declined modestly to 6.9 million.[28] Just 1 in 89 women report to some element of the corrections system, while 1 in 18 men do. One in 11 blacks report to the corrections system, 1 in 27 Hispanics, and 1 in 45 whites report to some aspect of the corrections system.

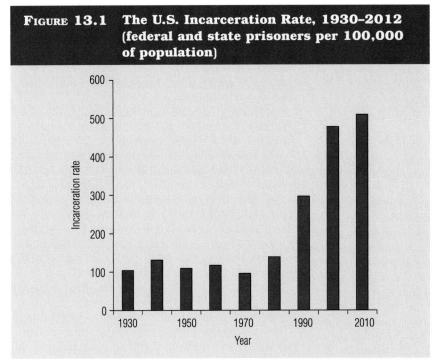

FIGURE 13.1   **The U.S. Incarceration Rate, 1930–2012 (federal and state prisoners per 100,000 of population)**

Source: U.S. Census, *Statistical Abstract of the United States, 2003*, Mini-Historical Series, HS-24, Federal and State Prisoners by Jurisdiction, 1925–2001 and Bureau of Justice Statistics, Number of Sentenced Inmates Incarcerated, see http://www.ojp.usdoj.gov/bjs/glance/tables/incrttab.htm.

Now, we come to the costs. In 2010, it cost the states $50 billion to control 1 in 31 Americans, 7.1 million people in prisons and jails and on probation and parole. Prisons are obviously the most expensive element of the corrections system. It costs an average of $29,000 annually to hold an inmate, $2,750 per parolee, and $1,250 per probationer.[29] Not surprisingly, the loss of state revenues produced by the economic downturn of 2007–2009 led a number of states to reduce prison populations by moving offenders onto probation and parole programs.

Interestingly, crime rates, incarceration rates, and corrections expenses all increased during the 1970s and 1980s, but for the last two decades, even as crime rates fell, prison populations and cost continued to rise. Both violent crime and property crime rates doubled between 1960 and 1970. Violent crime rates increased from 161 per 100,000 persons in 1960 to 364 in 1970 and property crime rates increased from 1,726 per 100,000 persons to 3,621. Congress and the states responded with "get tough on crime" campaigns, criminalizing more behavior and lengthening sentences, especially in drug cases. Crime continued to rise for two more decades, cresting at 758 violent crimes per 100,000 persons in 1991 and 5,140 property crimes. But crime has been trending steadily downward since. In 2012 there were 387 violent crimes per 100,000 and 2,859 property crimes, essentially back to the early to mid-1970s levels.

LET'S COMPARE

The Death Penalty in the U.S. and the World

In Chapter 4 we saw that Bianca Jagger has, for the past several years, been leading a European attempt to convince the U.S. that the day of the death penalty has passed. In much of the world it has, at least officially. Though war has by no means been banished from the earth, and in any given year a significant number of nations are wracked by civil wars, insurgencies, violent opposition movements, and deadly riots, most nations have given up the death penalty as a punishment for crime. Ninety-seven nations had officially abandoned the death penalty by the end of 2012.

Moreover, the list of nations that continue to employ the death penalty makes most Americans cringe. Fifty-eight nations retain the death penalty for at least some crimes, including China, the U.S., Iran, Iraq, Saudi Arabia, Thailand, Botswana, Sudan, Bangladesh, Japan, North Korea, Malaysia, Singapore, and Vietnam. And even on this list, most nations use the death penalty sparingly. A few use the death penalty regularly, and the U.S. is one of those. China uses the death penalty far more frequently than any other

nation—at least 1,718 times in 2009. Twenty-one nations in addition to China executed another 682 persons, probably more, in 2012.

Methods of execution are varied and grisly. The U.S. uses electrocution and lethal injection. China and Thailand also use lethal injection. Saudi Arabia uses public beheading and Iran uses stoning. Old-fashioned shooting is used in China, Libya, Syria, Vietnam, and Yemen. Hanging is favored in Bangladesh, Botswana, Egypt, Iran, Iraq, Japan, North Korea, Malaysia, Singapore, Sudan, and Syria. As the list shows, some nations use a number of execution techniques. During 2009, a total of 56 nations sentenced another 2,001 persons to death, bringing the world's death row total to 17,118 persons. The U.S. holds 3,279 inmates on death row.

In the U.S., 39 persons were executed in 2013: Texas (16), Florida (7), Oklahoma (6) Ohio (3), Arizona (2), Missouri (2), Virginia, Alabama and Georgia (1 each). On the other hand, nine inmates sentenced to death in the U.S. were exonerated and released in 2009 after serving a total of 121 years on death row. Six more men were exonerated between 2010 and 2013. Many find this latter fact deeply troubling. How likely is it, given these exonerations, that other innocent men are on death row or, worse, already wrongly executed?

State Sanctioned Executions in 2012							
China	1,718	United States	43	Gambia	9
Iran	314	Yemen	28	Taiwan	6
Iraq	129	Sudan	19	South Sudan	5
Saudi Arabia	79	Afghanistan	14	Belarus	3

Source: Amnesty International, Death Sentences and Executions, 2012, April 2013. In 2010, Amnesty International stopped publishing minimum execution numbers for China, so we include the 2009 number.

WHAT DO YOU THINK?

- Is there something in the American political culture that explains both the commitment to civil liberties and the proclivity to punish more types of behavior with longer prison terms than other nations, especially other advanced industrial nations?
- What explains our willingness to lock up so many people? Is it the focus on individualism, competition, personal responsibility, and property rights?
- Perhaps, but what explains the mildness de Tocqueville noted in the nineteenth century and the harshness we see today?

- And what explains the racial disparities—look at young men 18 and over, 1 in 15 blacks, 1 in 36 Hispanics, and 1 in 106 whites—in the corrections system?

Chapter Summary

Most of the delegates to the Constitutional Convention did not believe that the new constitution they drafted needed a Bill of Rights. They believed the limited powers granted to the national government and the institutional safeguards, including bicameralism, separation of powers, and checks and balances, would be sufficient protection for the liberties of the people. Yet, during ratification it became clear that many citizens disagreed and worried that their liberties were insecure. Fortunately, James Madison and other strong supporters of the Constitution listened to these concerns and responded to them in the first Congress by crafting and securing adoption by the states of the Bill of Rights.

The Bill of Rights codified a broad consensus, informed both by British history and colonial American experience, that certain individual rights and liberties were necessary for a people to be and remain free. Foremost among them are the rights of conscience; the right to speak, write, publish, think, and believe what one will. The justly famous First Amendment further claims the right of people to come together to debate their opinions, join with others who share their views, and to appeal to government on behalf of their opinions. The Second Amendment declares the right to bear arms. The Fourth through the Eighth Amendments secure basic procedural and legal rights, including rights against unreasonable search and seizure, double jeopardy, self-incrimination, excessive bail, and cruel and unusual punishment, and the rights to a speedy trial before a jury of one's peers. The Ninth Amendment, intriguingly, says this list of rights may not be complete and other rights may obtain, while the Tenth says powers not given to the national government remain with the states and the people.

Until the 1920s, the Bill of Rights acted as a limit only on the national government, though most state constitutions included bills of rights that applied within those states. Since the 1920s, a process of "partial incorporation" has applied the freedoms in Bill of Rights, beginning first with the freedoms of speech and the press, against the states through the "due process clause" of the Fourteenth Amendment. During the 1950s and 1960s, the Supreme Court, guided by Chief Justice Earl Warren, expanded freedoms of speech, press, assembly, and, more controversially, the rights of criminal defendants. More recently, the Rehnquist and Roberts counts have been trimming back the rights of criminal defendants in regard, for example, to search and seizure and the right against self-incrimination.

Finally, we asked why a country so dedicated to civil liberties would simultaneously have so many people in prison. The U.S. has 6.9 million people under the control of the corrections system, either incarcerated or on probation or parole. The U.S. has the largest prison population in the world. Moreover, though two-thirds of the nations in the world have abandoned capital punishment, the U.S. continues to employ the death penalty. The U.S. executed 39 people in 2013.

Key Terms

The following important cases have been referred to in this chapter and have been included in the Glossary of Cases for your convenience.

Suggested Readings

Fried, Charles. *Modern Liberty: And the Limits of Government.* New York: Norton, 2007. Fried, a libertarian, argues that modern liberty should be based on classic laissez-faire individualism.

Healy, Thomas. *The Great Dissent: How Oliver Wendell Holmes Changed His Mind—And Changed the History of Free Speech in America.* New York: Metropolitan Books, 2013. The story of how Holmes' famous dissent in *Abrams v. United States* signalled his shift from a defender of government power to control dissident speech to a defender of the "free trade in ideas."

Houppert, Karen. *Chasing Gideon: The Elusive Quest for Poor People's Justice.* New York: The New Press, 2013. Houppert argues that the promise of legal representation for the poor, made in *Gideon v. Wainwright* (1963), has gone largely unfulfilled.

Kasper, Eric T. *To Secure the Liberty of the People: James Madison's Bill of Rights and the Supreme Court's Interpretation.* DeKalb, IL: Northern Illinois University Press, 2010. Kasper analyzes Madison's goals in crafting the Bill of Rights and how the courts have followed or departed from those goals.

Madison, James. "Memorial and Remonstrance Against Religious Assessments," 1785. Madison makes the classic freedom of conscience case against government assessments or taxes in support of religion.

Lewis, Anthony. *Freedom for the Thought We Hate: A Biography of the First Amendment.* New York: Basic Books, 2008. Lewis, an author and longtime *New York Times* journalist, has written several important books on the First Amendment. This is the latest.

Mill, John Stuart. *On Liberty.* 1860. On Liberty is the classic nineteenth-century argument against political and social limits on intellectual freedom.

Web Resources

For practice quizzes, key term flashcards, videos, links, and other study tools, visit the *American Government* website: www.routledge.com/cw/jillson

1. **www.aclu.org**
   The official home page of the American Civil Liberties Union, an organization dedicated to issues surrounding civil liberties. This page provides up-to-date news as well as discussions of legal decisions and the rights of individuals.

2. **www.nationalgunrights.org**
   National Gun Rights organization whose webpage provides original and secondary material in favor of gun rights.

3. **www.deathpenaltyinfo.org**
   This is the key website maintained by opponents of the death penalty. It contains data on executions going back to colonial times, broken down by year, state, region, and race.

4. **bancroft.berkeley.edu/collections/meiklejohn/project.html**
   The Meiklejohn Civil Liberties Institute Archives contain briefs, transcripts, and opinions on major civil liberties cases since 1955.

5. **www.freedomforum.org**
   Freedom Forum maintains a Web page offering current coverage of censorship, speech, and the press, including links to archives, the Newseum, and a report on the First Amendment.

Chapter 14

CIVIL RIGHTS
Where Liberty and Equality Collide

It is of great importance in a republic not only to guard the society against the oppression of its rulers, but to guard one part of the society against the injustice of the other part.

JAMES MADISON,
Federalist Number 51

SEXUAL PRIVACY, THE NINTH AMENDMENT, AND UNENUMERATED RIGHTS

The Constitution TODAY

Ninth Amendment: "The enumeration in the Constitution, of certain rights, shall not be construed to deny or disparage others retained by the people."

The Ninth Amendment declares that we citizens have rights not explicitly enumerated in the U.S. Constitution. This seems like good news. But as you can imagine, the Ninth Amendment makes some people, including some Supreme Court justices, nervous. What rights do you want to claim under the Ninth Amendment?

Recall that the Constitution did not initially have a Bill of Rights. Federalist proponents of the Constitution argued that since the document gave only certain enumerated powers to the national government, no specific protections of rights and liberties were needed. For example, they argued that because Congress was not granted the power to legislate on religion, there could be no need for protection of religious liberty. Anti-Federalist opponents of the Constitution argued that broad phrases like "promote the general welfare," "necessary and proper," and "supreme law of the land," raised the specter of a dangerously powerful national government.

Proponents of the Constitution, led by James Madison in the first Congress, tried to assuage the concerns of opponents by adding a Bill of Rights. But adding a Bill of Rights raised the possibility that the list of rights specifically protected would be incomplete, one or more rights might be left off, or static, set once and for all. To address these concerns, Madison and the Congress added the Ninth Amendment (quoted above). OK, but what does it mean?

Most judges and scholars argue that the Ninth Amendment neither enhances nor limits other provisions of the Constitution. It acts principally as a rule of interpretation, saying that the absence in the Constitution of a claimed right cannot be taken by the court as proof that it does not exist. Still, judges and scholars are not of one mind about the Ninth Amendment. Justice Scalia, a conservative leader on the Supreme Court, says the Ninth Amendment's "refusal to 'deny or disparage' other rights is far removed from affirming any one of them, and even further removed from authorizing judges to identify what they might be."

Though the Ninth Amendment has been evoked relatively infrequently by the courts, it has done some heavy lifting in recent decades. It has arisen in cases regarding sexual privacy, abortion, and gay rights. In *Griswold v. Connecticut* (1965), a law prohibiting contraception was struck down as a violation of marital privacy. Justice William O. Douglas, writing for a 7–2 majority, argued that while no explicit "right to privacy" appeared in the Constitution, rights mentioned in the First, Third, Fourth, Fifth, and Ninth Amendments, "have penumbras, formed by emanations from those guarantees that help give them life and substance." The idea that provisions of the Constitution give off penumbras and emanations which sum to a right to sexual privacy has created some mirth among conservatives—but privacy is not a bad constitutional right to have.

In *Roe v. Wade* (1973), the U.S. District Court for the Northern District of Texas cited the "due process clause" of the Fourteenth Amendment and the Ninth Amendment in striking down Texas' abortion statute. Upon review, the Supreme Court declared that the Fourteenth Amendment was sufficient to protect a right to privacy encompassing abortion decisions during the early months of pregnancy. Justice Blackmun, writing for the majority, did not cite the Ninth Amendment but he did note the District Court's treatment of the Ninth Amendment respectfully. Finally, in *Lawrence v. Texas* (2003), in which the Supreme Court struck down sodomy laws in Texas and other states, Justice Kennedy cited Fourteenth Amendment protections to privacy, but Ninth Amendment claims were made as well.

Civil liberties and civil rights are the two brightest constellations in our constitutional firmament, and both have grown brighter over the more than 200 years of our national history. They are not, however, equally bright, and their relative glow has waxed and waned over the course of our national history. Initially, the idea of liberty was dominant. Liberty required only that white men should be free to think and behave as they wish in broad stretches of social and economic life. Equality seemed to demand no more than that all white, male property holders be free to compete. But when the Civil War raised the issue of interracial equality, tensions rose.

Focus Questions: from reading to thinking

Q1 Where does the energy that drives social movements come from?

Q2 What common theme or "frame" did the social movements of the 1960s and 1970s use to press their demands upon American society?

Q3 What role did the Supreme Court play in first limiting and then expanding civil rights for blacks?

Q4 Does affirmative action to assist minorities and women inevitably mean reverse discrimination against white men?

Q5 What were the similarities and differences between the movements for racial and gender equality?

WHAT DO YOU THINK?

- Is the Ninth Amendment an "inkblot," meaning anything or nothing at all, as the prominent conservative jurist Robert Bork has suggested?
- Or is it a valuable defense of new rights, perhaps well beyond the imagination of the Founders, that might come to be widely accepted as society develops and evolves?

Civil liberties restrict and control government power over individuals. Civil rights promise that government power will be used to ensure that individuals are treated equally and fairly by government and other individuals. Before the Civil War, civil liberties and civil rights seemed to be roughly the same thing and for white men they were very similar. The distinction became clearer after minorities and women began to claim the same liberties and rights available to white men.

Americans seldom stop to think that what made the struggle for minority and female rights so long and arduous was that the founding generation and several generations thereafter opposed them.[1] Moreover, law and policy governing relations between the races and genders, on slavery and marriage for example, were state matters, not national matters. Hence, even once attitudes about race and gender began to change for some people and in some regions of the country, the American federal structure meant that battles for equal rights had to be fought state by state and often on the most unfavorable terrain.[2]

In this chapter, we consider how the Civil War and its aftermath raised new issues of diversity, equality, and civil rights in America. First, we look at the stout resistance that white men put up even after the Civil War to claims by minorities and women for equal rights. Second, we explore the long struggle for minority and gender equality. Third, we follow the debate over whether attempts to redress historical disadvantages of minorities and women through "affirmative action" must inevitably involve "reverse discrimination" against white men. These are some of the most contentious issues in contemporary American politics. In both cases, broad social movements lasting centuries were required to break through existing privileges and bring fundamental change.

WHAT ARE SOCIAL MOVEMENTS?

Most politics are fairly predictable; the dominant party prevails, incumbents win, lobbyists have their way, and skeptical citizens turn their attention to

Debate over the role of immigrants, legal and illegal, in the American society stirs deep emotions, especially in difficult economic times. Here pro-immigration activists demonstrate outside the White House.

social movement A collective enterprise to change the way society is organized and operates in order to produce changes in the way opportunities and rewards are distributed.

family, work, and community. But sometimes political activity jumps the normal channels to cut new and broader channels for future politics. A **social movement** is a collective enterprise to change the organizational design or characteristic operating procedures of a society in order to produce changes in the way the society distributes opportunities and rewards. Genuine social movements aim to arouse large numbers of people alienated from the existing social order to force deep and permanent social change. The beneficiaries of the established order rarely give up without a fight, so social movements are always tumultuous.

Social movements do not arise over narrow issues like minimum wage, worker safety, or school funding. Rather, they arise in reaction to broad concerns over the place of religious values in society, war and peace, the right to life, racial justice, immigration or environmentalism. Social movements arise from dissatisfaction with the way that traditional political institutions have dealt with fundamental issues.

Social movements pose a twin threat to traditional political institutions like parties and interest groups and to the policies and programs they have developed for their constituents and supporters. The first threat is to policies, programs, and the existing flow of benefits. Movement supporters are dissatisfied with current policies and would change them. From the perspective of the status quo, change means that yesterday's insiders might become tomorrow's outsiders or at least that they might have to share benefits with a larger and more diverse group.

The second threat is potentially more serious. Social movements usually challenge not just policies but also the people, procedures, and institutions that produced them. Naturally, the people, groups, and institutions that have controlled and benefited from the existing system resist changes for as long as they are able, grant reforms when they must, and occasionally are swept away if they cannot move far enough or fast enough in the direction of popular demands.

Q1 Where does the energy that drives social movements come from?

The Origins of Social Movements.   For most of American history, popular uprisings were considered to be as natural and unpredictable as summer storms. Thomas Jefferson observed that popular upheavals, like summer showers with their accompanying thunder and lightning, broke the build-up of social heat and tension, cleansed the atmosphere, and refreshed the countryside.

Modern social science has developed several theories about the origins and nature of social movements. Each begins from the assumption that social movements reflect the social strain that develops and accumulates as society grows and evolves. Broad processes like westward expansion, immigration, industrialization, urbanization, and depressions introduce new actors and opportunities while simultaneously weakening traditional social controls. The success or failure of social movements lies in the resources that the aroused group can put toward pursuing its goals. Resources include money, office supplies, vans and buses, volunteer time, and the like. The sociologist Doug McAdam says that three factors, "expanding political opportunities; the mobilization of indigenous organizational resources; and the presence of certain shared cognitions" or values are necessary for a social movement to gain momentum.[3]

Movement Tactics and the Ambiguity of Violence.   For those who feel marginalized, if not completely closed out of the political system, protest may be the only form of influence that is available. Protesters seek to create sufficient cost to traditional actors and interests that they will grant concessions to get the protesters to stop the offensive behavior. The kind of protest behavior adopted by movement members—from sit-ins, pickets, boycotts, marches, and mass demonstrations to targeted violence and riots—involves predictable costs and benefits.[4]

The choice of movement tactics communicates a greater or lesser degree of threat to other actors, groups, and institutions in the political system and determines how they react to the movement, its leaders, and their demands. Sit-ins, pickets, and boycotts pursued over an extended period of time, even in the face of official violence, can force change. Marches and mass demonstrations may show such popular determination that reluctant officials have little choice but to respond positively to at least some movement demands. Targeted violence and riots may either force the entire community to confront the issues involved or trigger a backlash. One must always keep in mind that social movements involve many people with diverse agendas willing to employ a variety of means.[5]

Clearly, however, some forms of protest go so far beyond the bounds of democratic discourse that they elicit a near-unanimous condemnation from the society. For example, public reaction to the bombing of the Alfred P. Murrah Federal Building in Oklahoma City by Timothy McVeigh and others, almost

MCT via Getty Images

Some demonstrations spill over into violence as protesters seek to make their point and police seek to maintain order. The effectiveness of protest often depends more on the reaction of the general public than on the immediate reaction of public authorities.

universally seen as wildly beyond the pale of legitimate resistance to government authority, brought widespread condemnation down upon the entire militia movement.

Scholars disagree about whether movements that have captured public attention and even won an initial set of victories should seek to intensify protest behavior or try to build institutions that will protect and secure their gains. Francis Fox Piven and Richard Cloward argue that protest movements should push the system as far as they can while the moment is ripe. They complain that "during those brief periods in which people are roused to indignation, when they are prepared to defy the authorities to whom they ordinarily defer . . . leaders do not usually escalate the momentum of the people's protests."[6] Piven and Cloward suggest that movement leaders either believe that creating formal institutions is the best way to secure movement gains and build power for future battles or they seek benefits or positions for themselves.

Others point out that violent eruptions by social movements are usually short-lived. They flare up, perhaps force changes and reforms, and then die out. Unless movements leave institutions behind, there will be no one to monitor and protect the gains once the civil unrest dies away. For most movements, like the civil rights movement, the women's movement, the environmental movement, the gay rights movement, and the religious right, the need to have continuous institutional presence between movement peaks makes sense.

SOCIAL MOVEMENTS IN AMERICAN POLITICS

Q2 What common theme or "frame" did the social movements of the 1960s and 1970s use to press their demands upon American society?

Social movements arise from the effect that socioeconomic development has on prominent social divisions including ideology, race, ethnicity, gender, and lifestyle preference. Often, compatible movements cooperate and coalesce as a wave of collective action passes through society. The mid-nineteenth-century movements in favor of emancipation of the slaves, women's rights, and temperance often shared members, leaders, and resources. Similarly, the mid-twentieth century movements for civil rights, women's rights, nuclear disarmament, and environmentalism shared members, resources, and even protest strategies.

frame Dominant organizing frame or image, such as the equal rights image that motivated most of the movements of the 1960s and 1970s.

Students of social movements argue that both the surges in movement activity during particular periods and the similarities between movements that occur simultaneously are explained by the presence of a dominant **frame** or organizing theme. The frame of the mid-nineteenth century—free labor, entrepreneurship, and the right to contract—bound together the women's movement, the labor movement, and the abolition movement. The civil rights revolution of the mid-twentieth century, in which most racial and ethnic groups, women, gays, the disabled, the elderly, and many others joined, was built around the equal rights frame.[7]

Social movements designed to break through the barriers of race and gender have occurred throughout American history. Rather than offering brief sketches of several contemporary social movements, we treat just two, but we treat them in depth. We treat the civil rights movement and the movement for gender equality within American society. Neither movement was entirely successful. Social movements rarely achieve all of their aims. We will ask how and why the movement for black equality and women's rights movements arose, gained momentum, achieved their early success, and then declined before their final goals were reached.

SLAVERY AND ABOLITIONISM

Social change rearranges economic relationships and political opportunities in ways that make possible social movements that earlier seemed quite inconceivable. But broad social change is almost always the hard and systematic work of decades. The **abolitionist** movement of the mid-nineteenth century, which sought to abolish slavery in the United States, was part of a wave of social reform that also promoted temperance, peace, and women's rights.

abolitionist Advocates of slavery's abolition in the United States.

How did the movement to abolish slavery in America grow from just a few people scattered here and there to a movement that divided the nation and took it into Civil War? Abolitionism had its origins in the patriot debates over freedom and independence during the revolution. But very few American patriots thought that blacks were entitled to freedom and independence in the same way that they were.

From independence to the coming of the Civil War the internal structure and rhythms of American life changed dramatically. During these years the population of the United States grew from less than three million to more than thirty million, while the percentage of the population that was black and enslaved held steady at about 15 percent.

During the first decade of the nineteenth century settlers poured westward into the Ohio and Mississippi River valleys. The new white family farms of the upper Midwest fed the plantation South by shipping agricultural products downriver. The coming of the steamboat made the Ohio and Mississippi river systems into thriving trade routes by the 1830s and 1840s. Ties between the Midwest and the Atlantic coast were few because haulage back over the mountains was so difficult.

Because the nation's dominant patterns of trade and commerce were between the North and the South, political compromise on the place of slavery in American life seemed necessary. But by 1825 the ground upon which American politics rested began to shift. In that year the Erie Canal was completed, connecting the rich farm lands of the Midwest with New York and the Atlantic coast. Over the next decade the flow of trade shifted from north–south to east–west, and in the 1840s and 1850s the railroads, virtually all of which ran east–west, tied the Midwest to the East ever more securely. The shift of the nation's economic axis from north–south to east–west made possible an abolitionist, free-labor, antislavery majority coalition that had simply been impossible, at least in practical political terms, before. Political change soon followed.

An eloquent anti-slavery appeal from William Lloyd Garrison's abolitionist newspaper *The Liberator*, 1832.

Organization and Protest.   Blacks protested their circumstance throughout the period of their enslavement in America. Most of the early protests took the form of work slowdowns rather than rebellions, though violent rebellions like those of Denmark Vesey and Nat Turner were a constant threat. Free blacks in the North were allowed to organize and protest, but the economic, social, and political constraints on them were tight.[8] White protests, small at first, grew over time because, of course, whites were free to move around, organize, and employ their resources to advance the abolitionist cause.

The commitment of the Founders to freedom and independence led at least a few of them to dabble in emancipation after the revolution. John Jay, Alexander Hamilton, and Benjamin Franklin founded the Pennsylvania Society for the Abolition of Slavery in 1784 and the New York Manumission Society in 1785. Many others thought that slavery was dying out and that no great effort was needed to hasten its demise. However, by 1810 the invention of the cotton gin had rejuvenated slavery by increasing the value of slaves and of their labor.

In 1817 the American Colonization Society was founded to promote the transportation of emancipated slaves to Liberia, the society's colony on the west coast of Africa. Making emancipation more attractive to whites by linking it to the idea of sending freed slaves back to Africa had the support of prominent white Americans from Jefferson to Lincoln, including James Madison, James Monroe, John Marshall, and Henry Clay.[9] Each of these great leaders thought that slavery was morally wrong, but none thought that white

Americans would accept a biracial society in which blacks were treated as equal to whites. Few men, even few great men, think far beyond the parameters of the society they know.

The abolition movement took a more aggressive turn in the 1830s. In January 1831 William Lloyd Garrison published the first edition of *The Liberator* in Boston. In 1832 Garrison and eleven other white men founded the New England Anti-Slavery Society on a platform of immediate emancipation. In 1833 Garrison led his group into a coalition called the American Anti-Slavery Society (AASS).[10] By the middle of the 1830s the AASS claimed more than 200 local anti-slavery affiliates. In July 1835 more than 175,000 pamphlets were mailed from the New York post office into the southern states.

Reaction throughout the South, in Congress, and even in the North, was powerfully against the abolition movement. President Jackson and the Congress passed legislation to limit the movement of incendiary pamphlets through the mails and in 1836 Congress passed a "gag rule" against the debate of anti-slavery petitions on the floor of Congress. Tensions rose and fell over the next two decades until the *Dred Scott* decision and the election of Abraham Lincoln as president unleashed the furies.

CIVIL RIGHTS AND THE CIVIL WAR AMENDMENTS

The stark question of civil rights for blacks came powerfully to the fore in the famous case of *Dred Scott v. Sandford* (1857), in the Civil War amendments to the Constitution, and in the Civil Rights Act of 1875. Chief Justice Roger B. Taney, writing for the Court in the *Dred Scott* case, declared that white slave owners were at liberty to do as they wished with black slaves because blacks had "no rights which the white man was bound to respect." Dred Scott, a black slave from Virginia, was taken to Missouri and then by a new owner to the free state of Illinois and later into the free territory of Wisconsin. Taney declared not only that Scott was not free as a result of being carried into free territory, but also that no black, slave or free, was a citizen either of a state or of the United States. The Civil War amendments to the Constitution were designed to assure former slaves that they did, in fact, have "rights that the white man was bound to respect." And finally, the Civil Rights Act of 1875 was part of the national government's attempt to define and enforce civil rights in post-Civil War America. But white opinion in the nation and its courts proved too powerful.

The Civil War Amendments

President Abraham Lincoln described the Civil War as "essentially a people's contest. [A] struggle for maintaining in the world that form and substance of government whose leading object is to elevate the condition of man—to lift

Q3 What role did the Supreme Court play in first limiting and then expanding civil rights for blacks?

artificial weights from all shoulders; to clear paths of laudable pursuit for all; to afford all an unfettered start, and a fair chance in the race of life."[11] As the war raged on, Lincoln set the end of slavery in motion with the Emancipation Proclamation.

Not until after the war did the Republican Party in Congress begin to define the rights that the former slaves would enjoy and how those rights would be guaranteed and protected. The Civil War amendments and the Civil Rights Act of 1875 laid out a promise of full equality. However, within little more than a decade all of these promises had been broken. By the end of the century "separate but equal" was constitutional doctrine, and by 1910 an American apartheid, Jim Crow segregation, was in place across the land.

The Thirteenth Amendment: Freedom.   The Thirteenth Amendment completed the work of emancipation. It reads: "Neither slavery nor involuntary servitude, except as a punishment for crime whereof the party shall have been duly convicted, shall exist within the United States, or any place subject to their jurisdiction." The Thirteenth Amendment went into effect on December 18, 1865.

The Fourteenth Amendment: Equality.   The Fourteenth Amendment sought to define, without ever mentioning them directly, the position of former slaves within American society. The key section of the Fourteenth Amendment reads: "All persons born or naturalized in the United States, and subject to the jurisdiction thereof, are citizens of the United States and the State wherein they reside. No State shall make or enforce any law which shall abridge the privileges or immunities of citizens of the United States; nor shall any State deprive any person of life, liberty, or property, without due process of law; nor deny to any person within its jurisdiction the equal protection of the laws." This broad and generous language went into effect on July 28, 1868.

The Fifteenth Amendment: Voting.   The Fifteenth Amendment sought to ensure that black men would be able to defend their rights and liberties at the ballot box. The Fifteenth Amendment, which went into effect on March 30, 1870, read: "The right of citizens of the United States to vote shall not be denied or abridged by the United States or any State on account of race, color, or previous condition of servitude." The vote, it was hoped, would be a powerful weapon that could be wielded in defense of rights and privileges awarded in the previous two amendments. For a time it seemed that this would be so, but that time proved short.

Early Supreme Court Interpretations.   Almost before the ink was dry on the Civil War amendments, the Supreme Court interpreted them in the narrowest possible terms. Soon thereafter, the Civil Rights Act of 1875 met the same fate. Precisely how the words of the Civil War amendments and the Civil Rights Act of 1875 were made tools of continued oppression and exclusion of blacks rather than powerful tools for black equality can be shown by looking at several key Supreme Court decisions.

The first decision did not even involve blacks. Nonetheless, its implications for the place of the newly freed blacks in the American society were immense. The ***Slaughterhouse Cases*** (1873) were brought by a group of white New Orleans butchers who claimed that the creation of a slaughterhouse monopoly by the Louisiana state legislature denied them the equal protection of the laws that the Fourteenth Amendment promised them as citizens of the United States.

Justice Samuel F. Miller, writing for the majority of a Court divided 5–4, announced a strict dual-federalist view that saw national and state citizenships as essentially separate. Under Justice Miller's reading, national citizenship protected a citizen while traveling abroad, engaging in interstate or foreign commerce, or engaging in activities not within the jurisdiction of a single state. All other rights belonged to Americans as citizens of particular states. The *Slaughterhouse* decision meant that state governments would be allowed to define the domestic rights of their citizens, including their black citizens, as narrowly as they wished and the federal government would not interfere.

The first major test of the Civil Rights Act of 1875, which made most racial discrimination illegal, whether practiced by public institutions like governments or by private individuals, came in a set of cases known as the ***Civil Rights Cases*** (1883). In an 8–1 decision, Justice John Marshall Harlan I dissenting, the Supreme Court declared the Civil Rights Act of 1875 to be unconstitutional. Justice Joseph P. Bradley explained that in the view of the Court the Fourteenth Amendment prohibited discriminatory "state action" against blacks; it did not prohibit and could not reach the private discrimination of one individual against another. With this judgment, the federal government withdrew from the fight against private discrimination toward blacks.

Legal Segregation: *Plessy v. Ferguson.*

In 1890, the state of Louisiana passed a law requiring railroads to "provide equal but separate accommodations for the white and colored races" and requiring that "no person be permitted to occupy seats in coaches other than the ones assigned to his race." Homer Plessy, a citizen of Louisiana and one-eighth black, set out to test the law by boarding a train and occupying a seat in a car designated for white passengers. Following Plessy's arrest, his lawyer argued that the Louisiana statute violated the Thirteenth and Fourteenth Amendments, and most particularly the "equal protection" clause of the Fourteenth Amendment. The Court upheld the Louisiana statute and, by implication, most other segregation statutes, noting that "the action was not discriminatory since the whites were separated just as much from blacks as the blacks were separated from the whites."

Justice Harlan again rose in vehement dissent, pointing first to the obvious hypocrisy of the claim that segregation by race was no "badge of inferiority" for blacks subjected to it. Justice Harlan then went on to state the case for black equality that he believed was inherent in the Thirteenth and Fourteenth Amendments. He explained that "there is in this country no superior, dominant, ruling class of citizens .... Our Constitution is color blind, and neither knows nor tolerates classes among citizens. In respect of civil rights

Slaughterhouse Cases With this decision, the Supreme Court limited the impacts of the post-Civil War Amendments by defining U.S. citizenship narrowly and leaving the states to regulate domestic race relations.

Civil Rights Cases This decision struck down key parts of the Civil Rights Act of 1875. The Court held that Congress could only prohibit racial discrimination by state government and could not reach discrimination by individuals.

Plessy v. Ferguson The Court upheld a state law that segregated the races in transportation. According to the Court's analysis, the races could be confined to separate spheres within society as long as they were treated equally, thus originating the separate but equal doctrine.

all citizens are equal before the law. The humblest is the peer of the most powerful. The law regards man as man, and takes no account of his . . . color when his civil rights . . . are involved." It would be more than half a century before these powerful words would be accepted by a majority of the nation's highest court.

The Modern Civil Rights Movement

The early twentieth century was a bleak time for civil rights in America. Not until the 1930s did forces begin to build both domestically and internationally that put the country on the road to desegregation by mid-century. However, looking back on the successes and failures of the modern civil rights movement, many Americans, both blacks and whites, are struck both by how much has changed on the surface and by how little has changed beneath the surface.[12] Many are sobered by the backsliding toward segregation that has occurred over the past three decades.

Desegregation: The Coming of *Brown v. Board of Education*.   During the first decades of the twentieth century, Missouri, like several other border states and all of the states of the Deep South, ran a dual or segregated school system from kindergarten through college. However, as with most other segregated education systems, Missouri's did not provide a full range of advanced and professional degree programs at its black institutions. Therefore, upon graduation from Missouri's all-black Lincoln University in 1935, Lloyd Gaines sought admission to the University of Missouri's Law School. When Gaines was denied admission, he sued, claiming that his right to "equal protection of the laws" under the Fourteenth Amendment had been violated. The Supreme Court agreed in 1938 and informed the state of Missouri that it had to provide a separate law school or admit blacks to the University of Missouri Law School. The state responded by setting up a law school at Lincoln University.

Two landmark cases from 1950 raised the question of how equal separate facilities had to be. In *Sweatt v. Painter*, the Court held that a law school set up to avoid admitting blacks to the University of Texas Law School was unacceptable because it was inferior in facilities, books, faculty, and in general quality of legal education and opportunities. *McLaurin v. Oklahoma* struck down an attempt to admit blacks to a white program on a "segregated basis." McLaurin was admitted to the University of Oklahoma's School of Education to pursue graduate study because no black universities in the state offered similar programs. However, he was restricted to a seat in an anteroom adjacent to the classroom and to an assigned space in the library and the cafeteria. The Court supported McLaurin's contention that this treatment denied him "equal protection of the laws."[13]

Brown v. Board of Education This landmark case overturned *Plessy* and declared that separate was inherently unequal. Consequently, the segregation of public schools was unconstitutional.

The precedents established in *Gaines, Sweatt,* and *McLaurin* made the point that if facilities are to be separate, they must truly be equal. But could separate in fact be equal? In the landmark case of ***Brown v. Board of Education*** (1954), the U.S. Supreme Court was asked to take up precisely this question: Can separate be equal, or is separate inherently unequal and therefore discriminatory within the meaning of the "equal protection" clause of the Fourteenth Amendment? Arguing for the black complainants was Thurgood Marshall, chief counsel of the NAACP.

Brown v. Board of Education was before the Court when conservative Chief Justice Fred M. Vinson died and was replaced by the liberal Republican former governor of California, Earl Warren. Chief Justice Warren thought that segregation had to be dismantled and that *Brown* was the right case to begin that process. Writing on behalf of a unanimous Court, Warren reached back to resurrect Justice Harlan's dissent in *Plessy.* Warren wrote: "Segregation of white and colored children in public schools has a detrimental effect upon the colored children." Therefore, Warren concluded, "in the field of public education the doctrine of separate but equal has no place. Separate educational facilities are inherently unequal. . . . The plaintiffs . . . have been deprived of the equal protection of the laws guaranteed by the Fourteenth Amendment."

Thurgood Marshall, chief counsel of the NAACP, became the first black associate justice of the U.S. Supreme Court.

Before the decision in *Brown* was released to the public on May 17, 1954, seventeen states and the District of Columbia mandated segregation in their elementary and secondary schools. Although the District of Columbia and most of the border states complied with the instruction to desegregate their schools, the states of the Deep South dug in for a decade-long contest called "massive resistance."[14] As late as 1960, not a single black student attended a public school or university with whites in Alabama, Georgia, Louisiana, Mississippi, or South Carolina. Moreover, when John Kennedy took the oath of office as president of the United States early in 1961, fewer than 4 percent of voting-age blacks in Mississippi were registered to vote. The numbers were only slightly higher in the other southern states.

The Civil Rights Acts: 1964, 1965, and 1968. The Kennedy administration came under increasing pressure on the civil rights front during the "long, hot summer" of 1963 that culminated in the famous March on Washington in which 250,000 people participated. The highlight of the march was Martin Luther King Jr.'s "I Have a Dream" speech delivered from the steps of the Lincoln Memorial. The Kennedy administration responded to the demands of Dr. King and his followers by preparing legislation to supplement the Eisenhower administration's Civil Rights Act of 1957. That bill, the first major piece of civil rights legislation since Reconstruction, established the U.S. Civil Rights Commission and enhanced the Civil Rights Division of the Department of Justice.

In the wake of President Kennedy's assassination in November 1963, President Lyndon Johnson dramatically strengthened Kennedy's bill. The new bill came to be known as the Civil Rights Act of 1964. Its critical Title VI

Speaking from the steps of the Lincoln memorial, the Reverend Martin Luther King, Jr. rallied the nation's civil rights movement with his impassioned "I Have a Dream" speech on August 28, 1963.

held that "No person in the United States shall, on the ground of race, color, or national origin, be excluded from participation in, be denied the benefit of, or be subjected to discrimination under any program or activity receiving Federal financial assistance."

Title VII of the act prohibited discrimination on the basis of race, color, sex, religion, or national origin by employers or labor unions in businesses with one hundred or more employees; prohibited segregation or denial of service in any public accommodation, including motels, restaurants, movie theaters, and sports facilities; and permitted the U.S. attorney general to represent citizens attempting to desegregate state-owned, -operated, or -managed facilities including public schools. An even more far-reaching civil rights act was passed in 1965. Finally, in April 1968, only days after the assassination of Martin Luther King Jr., Congress passed a law that forbade discrimination based on race, color, religion, or national origin in the sale or rental of housing.

The Elementary and Secondary Education Act (ESEA) of 1965.   The ESEA provided federal education funds to school districts with large numbers of low-income students, provided that they were operating on a nondiscriminatory basis. The provision of federal money to support state and local programs, especially in education, seemed to break the back of segregation. Gerald Rosenberg noted that "financially strapped school districts found the lure of federal dollars irresistible . . . . And after federal money was received, the thought of losing it the next year, reducing budgets, slashing programs, firing staffs, was excruciating."[15] The most striking result of the movement of the Congress and the executive branch into the fray over desegregation was that the percentage of black school children attending school with whites in the South rose from 1.2 percent in 1964 to 91.3 percent in 1972.

The Voting Rights Act of 1965.   The foundation of **Jim Crow** had been the near-total exclusion of blacks from southern state and local electorates and their limited participation in northern elections. A complicated array of rules and practices including literacy tests, poll taxes, white primaries, and grandfather clauses kept blacks, other minorities, and the poor more generally, from registering and voting

Struggling Toward Democracy

In 2012, 39 percent of U.S. whites had a B.A. or better, compared to 21 percent of blacks and 14 percent of Hispanics.

What do you think?

- Is past racial discrimination the best way to understand these differences?
- Is affirmative action an appropriate or inappropriate way to try to address them?

in elections. The Voting Rights Act of 1965 prohibited these practices and sent federal marshals into southern states to assure that local election officials permitted all citizens to register to vote and to participate in elections. Ten million new black voters were on the rolls by 1970, and by 1984 black registration had passed white registration at 73 percent to 72 percent of those eligible. Large numbers of registered black voters simply could not be ignored by politicians expecting to remain in office.

Affirmative Action

Is government responsible for fighting discrimination now and in the future, or is it also responsible for making up for the effects of past discrimination? The civil rights agenda of the 1950s and 1960s demanded equality of opportunity and nondiscrimination. These ideas were embedded as promises and guarantees in the civil rights and voting rights acts of the mid-1960s. Affirmative action envisions making up for the effects of past discrimination suffered by specified racial and sexual groups by giving their members preference today in admission to training and educational programs and in decisions concerning hiring, promotion, and firing on the job. Not surprisingly, nondiscrimination is an easier sell than is **affirmative action**.

Confronting Direct Discrimination.   The Civil War amendments called for equality of rights and opportunities. Moreover, the Civil Rights Act of 1964 was carefully crafted to forbid both **direct discrimination** of one individual against another and racial preferences. Proponents of the Civil Rights Act of 1964 were very clear in assuring skeptical colleagues that the act offered redress only to specific individuals who could show that they had suffered direct discrimination as a result of racial bias. Numerous provisions of the Civil Rights Act of 1964 specifically prohibit racial quotas or hiring goals that might result in reverse discrimination against whites.

The Demand for Affirmative Action.   Proponents of affirmative action argue that nondiscrimination and equality of opportunity, although certainly important, are not enough to ensure the full and meaningful participation of blacks and other minorities in the American society and economy. They argue that the current unequal status of blacks in America, to take the prime example, is a stark reflection of two centuries of slavery in which the products of black labor went to white slave owners and another century in which segregation was used to deny blacks access to opportunity and wealth. As we shall see below, during the late 1970s and 1980s the Supreme Court seemed to agree that some measure of affirmative action was required to promote justice in America. Still, many disagreed.

Claims of Reverse Discrimination.   The first precedent-setting **reverse discrimination** case involved a man named Allan Bakke. Bakke was twice rejected for admission to the University of California at Davis Medical School even

Jim Crow Jim Crow is the generic name for all of the laws and practices that enforced segregation of the races in the American South and elsewhere from the end of the nineteenth century to the middle of the twentieth century.

Q4 Does affirmative action to assist minorities and women inevitably mean reverse discrimination against white men?

affirmative action Policies and actions designed to make up for the effects of past discrimination by giving preferences today to specified racial, ethnic, and sexual groups.

direct discrimination Discrimination practiced directly by one individual against another.

reverse discrimination The idea that the provision of affirmative action advantages to members of protected classes must necessarily result in an unfair denial of benefits or advantages to white males.

though on both occasions his academic credentials were superior to those of all of the minority students admitted under the school's affirmative action program. The medical school, like many other graduate and professional schools, set aside a number of seats, in this case sixteen out of about one hundred, for minorities and took the best minority candidates available. The remaining seats were awarded to the top candidates based on their academic credentials. Bakke sued the University of California at Davis Medical School and, in a case known as *Regents of the University of California v. Bakke* (1978), won—sort of.

Regents of the University of California v. Bakke This landmark affirmative action case stated that race could be taken into account in admissions decisions as long as the institution did not set aside a specific number of seats for which only minorities were eligible.

Justice Lewis Powell, writing for a badly divided Supreme Court, held that the university had violated Bakke's Fourteenth Amendment right to equal protection of the laws and that he should be admitted to the medical school. Specifically, the Court held in a narrow 5–4 decision that institutions could not set aside a specific number of seats for which only minorities were eligible. This stark denial of opportunity for whites to compete for these seats was unconstitutional. However, the Court further held that race could be used as a "plus factor" in admission decisions if it were not the sole factor.

Affirmative Action in the Workplace

One year after *Bakke* came *United Steelworkers of America v. Weber*. Kaiser Aluminum and the United Steelworkers had agreed that at least half of the thirteen slots in an on-the-job training program at Kaiser's Gramercy, Louisiana, plant would go to blacks. Brian Weber was denied a place in this training program on the basis of his race—he was white—so he sued the company and the union under Title VII of the Civil Rights Act of 1964. Title VII expressly prohibited discrimination in employment, forbidding any employer from granting "preferential treatment to any individual or to any group because of the race . . . of such individual or group."

Justice William Brennan, writing for the majority, upheld the affirmative action agreement reached by Kaiser and the United Steelworkers as a "voluntary" and "temporary" attempt by parties in the private economy to benefit black workers. Brennan argued that although the "letter" of the Civil Rights Act of 1964 required nondiscrimination, its "spirit" permitted voluntary agreements designed to improve the lot of blacks in the American economy. Then Associate Justice William Rehnquist, writing in dissent, accused the Court of rejecting race-blind in favor of race-conscious standards for government policymaking and private behavior.

Throughout the 1980s, although quotas continued to be illegal, racial preferences and set-asides were accepted tools of affirmative action. Nonetheless, with Ronald Reagan's election to the presidency in 1980, the tide of opinion in favor of affirmative action began to ebb. By the time Reagan left the presidency in 1989, he had appointed more than half of the federal judiciary and affirmative action was under increasing pressure. Within a few years, a new majority seemed to be taking shape that was hostile to affirmative action. But judicial change is almost always slow and incomplete.

Issues similar to the *Weber* case arose again recently in a case called *Ricci v. DeStefano* (2009). Frank Ricci, a white New Haven fire fighter, finished sixth among 77 candidates taking a promotion exam. None of the 19 African-American candidates taking the exam qualified for promotion, so the city, fearing a discrimination lawsuit, threw out the results. Ricci and 17 other white fire fighters, including one Hispanic, sued claiming that they had been discriminated against on the basis of their race.

The Supreme Court, seeking to balance two provisions of Title VII of the 1964 Civil Rights Act, ultimately ruled for the white fire fighters. Title VII requires both that employees not be treated differently on the basis of race and that promotion criteria and exams not have a "disparate impact" on members of one group. The white fire fighters, claiming differential treatment by race, prevailed. Justice Kennedy, writing for the Court's 5–4 conservative majority, observed that "the process was open and fair. The problem, of course, is that after the tests were completed, the raw racial results became the predominant rationale for the city's refusal to certify the results." As in other areas where race is involved, race can be a factor in the decision, but it cannot be the sole or driving factor.

Affirmative Action in Schools

A 2003 case dealing with undergraduate and law school admission criteria at the University of Michigan seemed to give affirmative action new life. At the undergraduate level, Michigan awarded 20 points to "underrepresented minorities" on a 150-point admissions index, while the law school used race as "one factor among many." As with the *Bakke* case 25 years earlier, white students with credentials superior to minority students who had been admitted sued, claiming that their Fourteenth Amendment right to equal protection of the laws and their 1964 Civil Rights Act promise of nondiscrimination had been violated.

The Michigan cases drew broad public attention. A long list of universities, major corporations, civic associations, military leaders, and others argued that programs like Michigan's to ensure a diverse student body were critical to their need for a diverse workforce, cadre of social leaders, and officer corps. More than three hundred organizations joined in 64 briefs filed in support of the university's affirmative action efforts. Fifteen briefs were filed on behalf of the plaintiffs, including one from the Bush administration, most claiming that affirmative action unconstitutionally harms whites and that diversity can be ensured by other, less objectionable means.

In the Michigan cases, the Court narrowly upheld affirmative action while striking down the specific point system used in the undergraduate admissions process. Justice Sandra Day O'Connor, writing for a narrow 5–4 majority in ***Grutter v. Bollinger***, upheld the *Bakke* ruling that race can be a "plus factor" in admissions, but that firm quotas are unconstitutional. She particularly approved the law school admissions process as a "highly individualized, holistic review of each applicant's file," allowing race to play a role, but not in a "mechanical way." Justice O'Connor observed that "in a society like our own . . . race unfortunately still matters." Justice Thomas dissented, saying, "every time the government places citizens on racial registers and makes race relevant to the provision of burdens or benefits, it demeans us all."

Grutter v. Bollinger The Court upheld Bakke, allowing affirmative action that takes race into account as one factor among many, but not in a rigid or mechanical way.

Yet, contentious issues like affirmative action remain perpetually open in American politics. While courts respect precedent, no one doubts that the Supreme Court can overturn earlier decisions with which its majority has come to disagree. *Grutter v. Bollinger* was a 5–4 case and Justice Sandra Day O'Connor, the deciding vote and author of the majority opinion, is now gone from the Court. Two new members, Chief Justice Roberts and Justice Alito, expressed discomfort with affirmative action and moved quickly to limit it. By 2007, they were part of a narrow 5–4 majority declaring that public elementary and secondary school districts may not use race in assigning students to schools even if the purpose is to maintain racial integration.

This dramatic reversal of more than 50 years of desegregation policy in regard to public schools occurred in two cases. School boards in Louisville, Kentucky (*Meredith v. Jefferson County Board of Education*), and Seattle, Washington, sought to maintain racial balance within schools by managing transfer requests to produce integrated schools. Writing for the majority, Chief Justice Roberts declared the use of race in assigning students to school to be unconstitutional. He famously declared that "The way to stop discrimination on the basis of race is to stop discriminating on the basis of race." The court's proponents of affirmative action were stunned. In the principal dissenting opinion, Justice Breyer observed, speaking of the court's

University of Texas President William Powers defends the university's use of race as one factor among many in UT's undergraduate admissions process. Abigail Fisher, a UT applicant denied admission to the university, had challenged the university's admissions process before the United States Supreme Court.

new members, Roberts and Alito, "It is not often in the law that so few have so quickly changed so much."

Nonetheless, the full impact of this opinion will have to play out over time. Though Justice Anthony Kennedy, the court's most frequent swing vote, joined the majority, he wrote a separate opinion, declaring that while he thought the Louisville and Seattle plans unconstitutional, he questioned the majority opinion's "all-too-unyielding insistence that race cannot be a factor in instances when, in my view, it may be taken into account."[16]

In 2006, the voters of Michigan approved a constitutional amendment prohibiting recognition of race in university admissions and state government hiring, but a federal appeals court struck it down as unconstitutionally burdensome to racial minorities.[17] The relief of advocates of affirmative action was short-lived because in 2011 Abigail Fisher, a white student denied admission to the University of Texas Law School, sued (*Fisher v. Texas*, No. 11–345) claiming reverse discrimination.

Fisher lost in the federal district court in Austin and in the generally conservative Fifth Circuit Court of Appeals, but observers immediately noted that turnover on the Supreme Court, most importantly Justice O'Connor's retirement and replacement by Justice Samuel Alito, had turned the 5–4 majority in *Grutter* in favor of affirmative action into a likely 5–4 majority against. Though Justice O'Connor's opinion in *Grutter* suggested that affirmative action might only be needed for another twenty-five years, the Supreme Court's acceptance

Pro & Con

Recognizing Gay Marriage

To many Americans, it seemed as if gay marriage came out of nowhere over the past decade or so. In a sense, it did. Gay marriage statutes existed only in a few states as late as 2010 and all had been enacted since 2003. Advocates of gay rights, calling for full equality, contend that loving gay couples should be able to enjoy all the rights and privileges of marriage, just as loving heterosexual couples do. Opponents of gay marriage contend that marriage is the bedrock of human society and has always been understood to be between a man and a woman.

U.S. policy had, until recently, been to discourage but not forbid gay marriage. In 1996, Congress passed and President Clinton signed the "Defense of Marriage Act" (DOMA) that defined marriage for the purposes of federal law as being between a man and a woman. The act further provided that, despite the Constitution's "full faith and credit clause," no state would be required to honor another state's same-sex marriages. In 2011, President Obama ordered the Justice Department not to enforce DOMA, but the law remained on the books. In May 2012 Vice President Biden and President Obama both declared, for the first time, that they supported gay marriage, and in 2014 Attorney General Eric Holder announced that a basket of federal benefits would be available to all married couples, gay and straight, in all states, whatever their state marriage laws might say. More than 30 states, including California (2013), Connecticut (2008), Delaware (2013), Hawaii (2013), Illinois (2014), Iowa (2009), Maine (2012), Maryland (2013), Massachusetts (2004), Minnesota (2013), New Hampshire (2010), New Jersey (2013), New Mexico (2013), New York (2011), Oregon (2014), Pennsylvania (2014), Rhode Island (2013), Vermont (2009), Washington (2012), and the District of Columbia (2010) permit gay marriage.

While change toward gay marriage has been picking up speed at the state level, the pace of change in the federal courts has been slower. The federal courts were instrumental in expanding civil rights for blacks, but less so for women. Will the courts find a constitutional right for gays to marry? In 2008 the California Supreme Court ruled on "due process" and "equal protection" grounds that gay marriage was legal in the state. Later that year an amendment to the California Constitution was approved by referendum prohibiting gay marriage. Some proponents of gay marriage brought a case in federal court in an attempt to overturn the California prohibition. Others worried that the case was premature.

Adding to the visibility of this case is the unusual legal team arguing the case for gay marriage. David Boies and Ted Olson were the top lawyers on opposite

of the Fisher case early in 2012 suggested that the pages of the calendar might be turning more quickly.[18] In fact, the Supreme Court did not use the Fisher case to overturn affirmative action. Instead, accepting the continued viability of Bakke and Grutter, the Supreme Court simply sent the case back to the appellate court with instructions that it required the university "to prove that its admissions program is narrowly tailored to obtain the educational benefit of diversity." In 2015, the Fifth Circuit Court found that the University of Texas's use of race in its admissions process was narrowly tailored and, therefore, constitutional.

While the American society has made a great deal of progress on civil rights in the past half century, many worry that progress has stalled and perhaps even slid back. In 2013, only a little more than 1 percent of Fortune 500 companies were headed by blacks. Blacks constitute about 6 percent of the STEM (science, technology, engineering, and mathematics) fields, 5 percent of doctors and sides of the legal battle over Florida's electoral votes in 2000. Boies represented Democrat Al Gore while Ted Olson represented Republican George W. Bush. Olson prevailed when the conservative U.S. Supreme Court decided *Bush v. Gore* (2000) in favor of Bush. Boies and Olson have joined forces to argue that gay marriage is required by the "equal protection" and "due process" clauses of the Fourteenth Amendment to the U.S. Constitution.

Olson and Boies, on behalf of two gay couples and some proponents of gay marriage, were confident. They pointed to a string of Supreme Court decisions, stretching back to *Loving v. Virginia* (1967), which struck down state laws against interracial marriage, defining marriage as "one of the most vital personal rights" of free persons.

In the June 2013 case of *United States v. Windsor*, the United States Supreme Court struck down the parts of DOMA denying federal benefits but stopped short of approving same sex marriage nationally. Gay rights advocates argue that this leaves a nation divided in which gay couples in more than 30 states recognizing gay marriage have many rights still denied to gay couples in about 20 states still refusing recognition to gay marriage. In January 2015, the U.S. Supreme Court agreed to hear a set of four cases starkly posing two questions. Must all 50 states permit marriage between same-sex couples, and, if not, must states that do not allow gay marriages respect legal marriages from other states. Arguments were held in April 2015 and a decision was expected soon thereafter. Advocates and opponents were on high alert. As with other contested issues, like abortion and school prayer, a Supreme Court decision may not, likely will not, end the fight.

What do you think?

- Should civil rights, rights to "due process" and "equal protection," be subject to majority vote?
- Should gay marriage be a constitutional right?
- If so, as a tactical matter, is this the right time to put this issue before this Supreme Court?

PRO	CON
Marriage is a human right	Marriage has always been heterosexual
The Constitution requires equal rights	States have always defined marriage
Public opinion is moving in favor	Red states are still strongly opposed

dentists, 4 percent of lawyers, and 3 percent of architects. Blacks comprise 11 percent of the total workforce.[19]

The Women's Rights Movement

Social change, the evolution of the American society from rural to urban, from the dependence on strong backs to the need for strong minds, opened the door to enhanced rights for women. From colonization throughout the nineteenth century, the place of women within the American society was defined by the legal concept of "coverture." **Coverture** was the rule of law whereby at marriage the husband and the wife became, in the phrase of the famous English jurist William Blackstone, "one person, and that person the husband." Coverture entailed the legal guardianship of women by men, their fathers before marriage and their husbands after marriage. During the first half of the nineteenth century, married women could not own or inherit property, control their own wages, sue or be sued in court, divorce drunk or abusive

Coverture A legal concept, transferred to America as part of English common law, holding that upon marriage the husband and the wife become "one person, and that person the husband."

Q5 What were the
similarities and differences
between the movements
for racial and gender
equality?

husbands, or have custody of their children if their husbands divorced them. Single women over 21, widows, and divorcees had more autonomy, but being alone generally meant poverty and exclusion.

Throughout the nineteenth century and into the 1970s, progress was slow because women were split on how best to frame their demands for change. Society has always socialized men and women to somewhat different roles. In the nineteenth century, men and women were seen as fitted for "separate spheres," men for the workplace and women for the home. More conservative women accepted broad gender differences and simply called for incremental changes—better education, fairer property and inheritance rights, and more protection against abusive husbands. These "difference feminists" were often scandalized by "equality feminists" who demanded full equality with men in society, the economy, and politics.

Sometimes difference feminists and equality feminists could work together and sometimes they could not. They joined forces to win suffrage by 1920, but equality feminists did not dominate the movement until the 1960s. While Congress and the president eventually joined to support suffrage, the Supreme Court did not abandon its separate spheres perspective until the 1970s.[20] This ground is still contested.

Organization and Protest. If any great social movement can be said to have begun at a specific place and time, the woman's movement in America began at Seneca Falls, New York, in 1848. The Seneca Falls Convention on women's rights produced two great products: one a statement of principles and demands, entitled a "Declaration of Sentiments," and the other a political alliance between Elizabeth Cady Stanton and Susan B. Anthony and their allies and associates, including Lucretia Mott, Lucy Stone, and Sojourner Truth.

Throughout American history women learned skills and techniques in other social movements that they have then put to work on behalf of women's interests. Women in the abolitionist movement learned how to run a meeting, get out a newsletter, and plan a speaker's itinerary. Soon they moved from behind the scenes to roles of visible public leadership. Susan B. Anthony was an organizer, particularly adept at networking, lobbying, and public speaking, and Elizabeth Cady Stanton was a consummate writer and strategist.

In the decade prior to the Civil War Stanton and Anthony worked to improve the legal status of women. They succeeded in winning greater economic rights for women in New York state, assuring that married women could own property and control their wages if they worked outside the home. They failed, however, to win the right to vote. After the war progress came slowly. The federal courts were consistent in upholding state and federal laws that barred women from the practice of law (*Bradwell v. Illinois*, 1872), voting (*U.S. v. Anthony*, 1873), and jury service (*Strauder v. West Virginia*, 1880).

During the second half of the nineteenth century, competing women's groups pursuing different strategies fought for a wide range of social, economic, and political rights. Women slowly gained the right to own and inherit property, control their wages, make contracts, sue in their own names, and have joint custody of children following divorce. Yet even as the end of the nineteenth century approached, women rarely had the right to vote, serve on juries, or attend professional schools. Moreover, some issues including sex outside marriage, birth control, and divorce, all seen as threats to the traditional family, were too controversial for most women's groups to touch.[21]

The final push for suffrage began in 1890. The women's movement narrowed its focus and expanded its alliances. First, Stanton's broad equal rights agenda was set aside in favor of a more singular focus on female suffrage. Second, two rival organizations, the National Woman Suffrage Association (NWSA), led by Stanton and Anthony, and the more conservative American Woman Suffrage Association (AWSA), led by Lucy Stone, merged in 1890 to become the National American Woman Suffrage Association (NAWSA). NAWSA convinced other important groups, like Frances Willard's Women's Christian Temperance Union, Jane Addams's settlement house movement, Consumers' Leagues, and the General Federation of Women's Clubs, that they could more readily accomplish their goals if women had the vote.

The suffrage bandwagon began to roll as Washington state approved female suffrage in 1910, California in 1911, and Arizona, Kansas, and Oregon in 1912. By the end of the decade half of the states allowed women to vote, but Congress and the Wilson administration remained ambivalent. Alice Paul laid siege to the powers that be in Washington, D.C., leading direct action confrontations including demonstrations, picketing of the White House, arrests, and starvation strikes. Finally, in June of 1919, at President Wilson's explicit urging, the Senate approved the Nineteenth Amendment. Thirty-six states ratified the amendment, and it went into effect on August 26, 1920. It reads: "The right of citizens of the United States to vote shall not be denied or abridged by the United States or by any State on account of sex."

Once suffrage was achieved in 1920, the women's movement lost much of its focus and direction until the 1960s. Nonetheless, broad-scale social and economic change including urbanization, expanded educational opportunities, and the steady growth of the service sector of the economy opened new opportunities for women. Still, in 1950, only about one-third of adult women worked for wages and they made less than half, about 48 percent, of what men made.[22]

By the early 1960s, women playing secondary roles in the civil rights and antiwar movements arrived at two conclusions: that they knew how to organize a protest and that they had a great deal to protest about. Women drew on the themes of individual rights and equal opportunity that were so central to the civil rights movement to understand their own oppression. President John F. Kennedy's Commission on the Status of Women provided detailed evidence of social and economic discrimination against women in its 1963 annual report. Almost simultaneously, Betty Friedan's *The Feminine Mystique* named the psychological impact that having few social or economic opportunities had on talented and well-educated women as "the problem with no name." Women's church groups, civic and service groups, and book clubs became forums for political discussion, networking, and consciousness raising.

When the Commission on the Status of Women proved unable or unwilling to press equal rights for women, several of the commission's leaders formed the National Organization for Women (NOW). NOW's charter promised "To take action to bring women into full participation in the mainstream of American society now, assuming all of the privileges and responsibilities thereof in truly equal partnership with men." NOW won important victories in the 1970s, fought to protect them throughout the 1980s and 1990s, and remains the focal point of the women's movement today.

Equal Rights and Personal Control.   NOW held its first annual convention in 1967. The convention produced a Women's Bill of Rights, which among many other things, called for an Equal Rights Amendment (ERA) to the Constitution and for women's control over family planning and procreation issues. The ERA was first introduced into the Congress in 1923 and was consistently reintroduced and largely ignored for most of the next fifty years. Slowly, the equal rights arguments of the civil rights and women's rights movements began to change the political consciousness of America. In 1970, the House of Representatives held hearings on the ERA, with many women members of the House speaking passionately in its favor, and in August 1970 the House voted in favor of the ERA by a margin of 350 to 15. Although the Senate moved more slowly, on March 22, 1972, it approved the ERA by a vote of 84 to 8. The ERA read: "Equality of rights under the law shall not be denied or abridged by the United States or by any State on account of sex." Within days of Senate approval, half a dozen states unanimously ratified the ERA, and within a year twenty-four states had ratified. Most observers believed that eventually thirty-eight states would ratify and the ERA would be added to the Constitution.

NOW's 1967 Women's Bill of Rights also called for removal of restrictive abortion laws. The National Abortion Rights Action League (NARAL) was formed in 1969 to focus exclusively on securing women's access to abortion services. Abortion law was the preserve of the states, so initially both NOW and NARAL focused their efforts at the state level. But state-by-state reform efforts had always been slow and uncertain. NOW and NARAL activists sought a Supreme Court judgment in favor of a woman's right to choose that would apply throughout the United States.

In 1973 the justices of the U.S. Supreme Court declared in *Roe v. Wade* that the Constitution guarantees a "right to privacy" that includes a woman's right to choose abortion. Justice Harry Blackmun, writing for a Court divided 7–2, described a broad right to privacy residing in the "Fourteenth Amendment's concept of personal liberty and restrictions upon state action" that included a woman's right to choose abortion. Although Blackmun did not deny that states have a legitimate interest in regulating some aspects of the provision of abortion services, the decision in *Roe v. Wade* invalidated, in whole or in part, the abortion laws in forty-six states and the District of Columbia.

Passage of the ERA by Congress and announcement of *Roe v. Wade* by the Supreme Court, both in 1973, marked the high point of the twentieth century tide in favor of women's rights. However, as with most social movements, successful mobilization bred counter-mobilization.

Counter-mobilization, Conflict, and Stalemate.   Liberal women's successful activism sparked a counter-mobilization among conservative women. Building on the organizational base of conservative religious and political groups, Phyllis Schlafly founded STOP ERA in 1972 and then the more broad-based Eagle Forum in 1975. Aided by Beverly LeHaye's Concerned Women of America (CWA), Schlafly's Eagle Forum warned that the traditional roles of wife and mother as well as the health of the traditional family were endangered by the ERA. Ronald Reagan's presidential campaign in 1980 affirmed and broadened conservative opposition to the ERA. Jane Mansbridge, a leading student of the effort to pass the ERA, concluded that "The campaign against the ERA succeeded because it shifted debate away from equal rights and focused it on the possibility that the ERA might bring . . . changes in women's roles and behavior."[23] The ERA died in 1982, three states short of the thirty-eight needed to ratify.

The attempts of conservative women and their allies to roll back abortion rights have been firm and steady. Within months of the *Roe v. Wade* decision, state legislatures were swamped with demands that limitations including counseling mandates, waiting periods, spousal and parental notification requirements, and doctor reporting requirements be placed on a woman's right to choose. Throughout the 1980s and 1990s state legislatures passed restrictions and limitations on women's access to abortion services. Conservative Reagan appointees on the federal bench threatened not just to let stand state restrictions, but to overturn *Roe v. Wade* in its entirety. Moreover, both pro-choice and pro-life advocates took to the streets to press their respective cases.

Feminists march in New York City on August 26, 1970, on the 50th anniversary of the passing of the Nineteenth Amendment granting American women full suffrage. On that day, the National Organization for Women (NOW) called upon women nationwide to "strike for equality."

Tension peaked in 1992 when the administration of the first President Bush joined the state of Pennsylvania and dozens of pro-life groups including the Eagle Forum, the U.S. Catholic Conference, and the National Right to Life Committee to support a highly restrictive set of regulations designed to make

Twelve years after the first, a second March for Women's Lives rallied half a million abortion rights supporters to the National Mall on April 25, 2004. As the sea of signs shows, abortion rights remain a very contentious issue.

LET'S COMPARE

The Gender Wage Gap in Twenty-Seven Countries

Women earn less than men the world over, but in some countries women make just a little less and in some they make a lot less. Among the twenty-eight wealthy nations that make up the Organization for Economic Cooperation and Development (OECD), the gender pay gap ranges from 4 percent in Hungary to 39 percent in South Korea. The gender wage gap shows the percent by which the median wages for women employed full-time trail the median wages for men employed full-time for each OECD country.

The two Asian nations in the OECD, with their more traditional gender roles, have the largest gender pay gaps. South Korean women make 39 percent less than their male counterparts and Japanese women make 28 percent less than Japanese men. German women make 22 percent less than German men and the women in six nations, including the U.S., U.K., and Canada, make 20 percent less than the men in those nations. Not surprisingly, the more egalitarian societies of northern Europe, including Sweden, Denmark, and Norway, have gender wage gaps of 15 percent and less.

Some cultures encourage women to focus on home and children while others encourage women to take an equal role, or nearly equal role, with men in the broader society and economy.

What do you think?
- Are you surprised to see the U.S., UK, and Canada with some of the larger gender wage gaps?
- Is the U.S. gender wage gap simply a function of the life choices that women make or is it evidence of illegal discrimination against women in the workplace and in the broader economy?

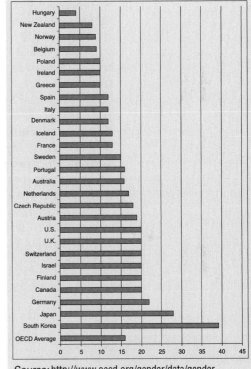

Source: http://www.oecd.org/gender/data/gender wagegap.htm.

abortions in Pennsylvania more difficult. Pro-choice groups, led by NOW, NARAL, and the National Women's Political Caucus, called women into the streets and nearly 700,000 women joined the March for Women's Lives in Washington on April 5, 1992. The case at issue was called *Planned Parenthood of Southeastern Pennsylvania v. Casey*. The court allowed Pennsylvania restrictive regulations to stand but refused to overturn *Roe*.

For more than a decade, the abortion battle focused on a specific technique, called "partial birth abortion," that opponents considered particularly objectionable. It is a late-term procedure used to abort a nearly fully formed fetus. During the 1990s, Congress twice voted to ban the procedure, but President Clinton blocked Congress both times. Meanwhile, thirty-one states adopted partial birth abortion bans between 1995 and 2000, before the Supreme Court struck them down as "an undue burden" on a woman's right to abortion services. In response, Congress passed a slightly revised ban and President Bush signed it into law. In 2007, the Supreme Court reversed field and upheld the Partial Birth Abortion Act by a narrow 5–4 margin.

Justice Anthony Kennedy wrote the majority opinion in *Gonzales v. Carhart* (2007), declaring that the "act expresses respect for the dignity of human life." Justice Kennedy's opinion emphasized the "ethical and moral concerns" surrounding abortion in general and partial birth abortion in particular. Some women were particularly dismayed by the majority opinion's declaration that banning partial birth abortion saved women from making a choice that they might later come to regret. Justice Ruth Bader Ginsberg, writing in opposition, said, "This way of thinking reflects ancient notions of women's place in the family and under the Constitution—ideas that have long since been discredited."[24] The battle over abortion is not over.

Women in Schools and Colleges. The Education Act of 1972, in its now-famous Title IX, forbade discrimination based on gender in any education program receiving federal funds. Title IX had its greatest direct impact by advancing equality in the funding of college sports programs, but women have experienced rapid progress toward educational equality. In the early 1980s, women reached parity with men in college attendance. In 2011 women received fully 57 percent of college bachelor's degrees and 60 percent of master's degrees. Similar progress is apparent at the level of professional and doctoral education. Women now receive 49 percent of professional (law, medicine, accounting, etc.) and 51 percent of Ph.D. degrees.[25] These important trends in women's educational achievement have begun to translate into enhanced career options and increased earnings.

Struggling Toward Democracy

In 2012, U.S. men, employed full-time, year round, made an average of $49,398 while women made 76.5 percent of that, or $37,791.

What do you think?

- Is this evidence of discrimination or of different choices freely made by men and women?

Women in the Workplace. Today women still lag behind men once they leave school and enter the workplace, but the gap is narrowing. Many occupations remain gender-specific. As late as 2012, women still comprised 98 percent of all kindergarten teachers and dental assistants, 95 percent of all secretaries and 98 percent of all child care workers, 93 percent of dieticians, 88 percent of all maids and cleaners. At the other end of the economic status and income spectrum, women comprised 5 percent of airline pilots, 15 percent of engineers, 34 percent of physicians, and 31 percent of lawyers.[26] Moreover, the jobs that men hold tend much more commonly to include retirement benefits and those retirement benefits tend to pay out at much higher rates.

Progress is evident for women in the workforce and seems to be picking up speed. In 1970 43 percent of women worked for wages, they made an average of 52 percent of what men made, and just 4 percent of married women earned more than their husbands. By 2012, 58 percent of adult women and 62 percent of married women worked for wages and made 82 percent of what men made. Moreover, almost one-third, 29 percent, of working women make more than do their husbands.[27]

The deep recession of late 2007 through much of 2009 highlighted the role of education in the changing place of women in the American economy. Education gains among women over the last several decades largely shielded women from the worst impact of the recession. Women's employment held up while men's employment fell. Three-quarters of the job losses during the recession were experienced by men and during several months in 2009 and 2010 women held more payroll jobs than men for the first time in U.S. history.[28] Still, gains are not equality. There is still a "glass ceiling" that blocks most women from rising to the level of the executive suite. In 2013, just 21 Fortune 500 companies were headed by women and only 17 percent of board seats were held by women. Many in the women's rights movement doubt that opportunity in the absence of affirmative action will produce true equality within an acceptable time frame.

Chapter Summary

Social movements are collective enterprises to change the structure of society in order to produce changes in the way the society distributes opportunities and rewards. Social movements arise in response to dissatisfaction with some broad dimension of social life, like the place, role, and prospects of women or minorities or the treatment of fundamental substantive issues like peace or the environment. Social movements usually require financial and material resources, some measure of political receptivity, and a shared sense of rightful purpose if members are to shake off their habits of sullen obedience and confront authorities with demands that they do better or go.

Social movements rarely achieve their goals quickly or completely. They wax and wane, rise and fall, rush forward and then are pushed back, over the course of decades, even centuries. Early demands for more equal treatment are made meekly and at first ignored. Initial failure leads to better organization, a broader search for allies, larger demonstrations, and greater public awareness of the issues and arguments involved. As society divides, the vague and shifting outlines of possible new majority coalitions come into view, and established groups and parties assess their implications. Reforms are promised, new access is granted, early victories are savored. However, early victories satisfy some and growing opposition intimidates others, setting off an exit spiral before the broader goals of the movement can be secured. Dissatisfaction builds, new leaders emerge, and the process begins anew.

Not until well into the twentieth century did the U.S. Supreme Court, at first only very selectively and tentatively, begin to draw civil liberties and later civil rights up to the national level and apply them uniformly throughout the country. Since the 1960s Americans have seen a vast expansion of both their individual liberties and their civil rights. Although most Americans look with pleasure on guarantees of equal opportunity for minorities and women, many also worry that equal opportunity has slipped beyond affirmative action to reverse discrimination. Others wonder whether the guarantees of civil rights to blacks and women change when they are extended to gays and lesbians, the disabled, and the elderly.

Key Terms

abolitionist 449

affirmative action 457

Brown v. Board of Education 454

Civil Rights Cases 453

coverture 463

direct discrimination 457

frame 448

Grutter v. Bollinger 460

Jim Crow 457

Plessy v. Ferguson 453

*Regents of the University
  of California v. Bakke* 458

reverse discrimination 457

Slaughterhouse Cases 453

social movement 446

The following important cases have been referred to in this chapter and have been included in the Glossary of Cases for your convenience.

Bradwell v. Illinois   464

Bush v. Gore 463

Dred Scott v. Sandford 451

Fisher v. Texas 461

Lawrence v. Texas 444

Loving v. Virginia 463

McLaurin v. Oklahoma 454

*Meredith v. Jefferson County Board of
  Education* 460

Ricci v. DeStefano 459

Roe v. Wade 444

Strauder v. West Virginia 464

Sweatt v. Painter 454

*United Steelworkers of America
  v. Weber* 458

U.S. v. Anthony 464

U.S. v. Windsor 463

Suggested Readings

Abraham, Henry J., and Barbara A. Perry. *Freedom and the Court: Civil Rights and Liberties in the United States,* 8th ed. Lawrence: University Press of Kansas, 2003. An excellent legal history of the judicial definition and elaboration of civil liberties and civil rights in America.

Chemerinsky, Erwin. *The Conservative Assault on the Constitution.* New York: Simon & Schuster, 2011. Chemerinsky argues that the Supreme Court has shifted dramatically to the right, limiting the scope of constitutional protections to all Americans.

Davis, Theodore J., Jr. *Black Politics Today: The Era of Socioeconomic Transition.* New York: Routledge, 2012. Davis traces black politics from the civil rights movement of the 1950s and 1960s to the more complicated contemporary period in which economic success and failure threaten to divide the black community.

Hewett, Sylvia Ann. *Off-Ramps and On-Ramps*. Cambridge, MA: Harvard Business School Press, 2007. Hewett argues that most women have "nonlinear careers" and employers should recognize the value of accommodating their needs.

King, Desmond and Rogers Smith, "Racial Orders in American Political Development," 2005. King and Smith contend that American political development is best understood as an interaction between an egalitarian order and a white supremacist order.

Piven, Francis Fox, and Richard A. Cloward. *Poor People's Movements: Why They Succeed, How They Fail*. New York: Vintage Books, 1979. This classic study argues that movement leaders would do better to ride the early surge of movement energy as far as it will go rather than leave the streets prematurely to build institutions.

Valelly, Richard M. "Institutions and Enfranchisement," 2004. Valelly describes how institutions affect political outcomes by comparing the first reconstruction, in the immediate wake of the Civil War, with the second reconstruction, following *Brown v. Board*.

Web Resources

For practice quizzes, key term flashcards, videos, links, and other study tools, visit the *American Government* website: www.routledge.com/cw/jillson

1. **www.womhist.alexanderstreet.com**
   This interesting page provides text to primary documents relating to women's and other social movements between 1600 and the present.

2. **www.usdoj.gov/crt/**
   The federal government has passed a number of statutes barring discrimination by employers and established the Civil Rights Division of the Justice Department to enforce these antidiscrimination statutes. This page provides a mission statement, a listing of cases, and a discussion of discrimination.

3. **www.naacp.org**
   This is the website of the nation's premier civil rights organization.

4. **www.now.org**
   This is the website of the nation's premier women's rights organization. The website includes discussion of key issues, including reproductive rights, economic justice, violence against women, and events.

5. **www.eagleforum.org**
   Eagle Forum is a conservative interest group supporting family values, small government, low taxes, and a strong national defense. It was founded by Phyllis Schlafly in 1967 as a counterweight to the National Organization for Women.

Chapter 15

GOVERNMENT, THE ECONOMY,
AND DOMESTIC POLICY

Democratic institutions awaken and foster a passion for equality which they can never entirely satisfy.

ALEXIS DE TOCQUEVILLE,
Democracy in America, 1835

CAN CONGRESS MANDATE THAT ALL AMERICANS BUY HEALTH INSURANCE?

The Constitution TODAY

> Article I, section 8 (in part): "The Congress shall have power to lay and collect taxes, . . . to pay the debts and pay for the common defense and general welfare of the United States; . . . .To regulate commerce . . . among the several states . . . . To make all laws which shall be necessary and proper for carrying into execution the foregoing powers."

When the Democrats' health care reform bill was signed into law in March 2010, Republicans in Congress remained uniformly opposed and polls showed that more people opposed the law than favored it. Democrats argued that health care reform was the law of the land and that citizens would soon see the benefits of insurance reform. But even after the law was signed, Republicans had one more arrow in their quiver. They contended that the health care bill passed by the Democrats in Congress was unconstitutional.

Democrats pointed to three main clauses of Article I, section 8, as the constitutional foundation for health care reform. As quoted above, the first is the power "to regulate commerce among the states," the second is the power to "collect taxes," and the third is the power to do what is "necessary and proper for carrying the foregoing powers into execution." Proponents pointed to a long series of commerce clause cases going back to *Wickard v. Filburn* (1942) allowing regulation of economic activity that touches even fairly modestly on interstate commerce. Proponents also argued that the "individual mandate" to buy health insurance or to pay tax penalties for non-compliance was an appropriate use of the power to tax, just like the mandatory payroll taxes on workers to fund social security and medicare.

Within hours of Obama signing health care reform, Florida Attorney General Bill McCollom, joined by a dozen other Republican Attorneys General and one Democrat, filed to challenge the bill in court. The Attorneys General and other opponents pointed to *U.S. v. Lopez* (1995) and *U.S. v. Morrison* (2000), in which the Supreme Court struck down congressional attempts to regulate carrying handguns near schools and domestic violence against women under the commerce power. The Court declared that neither had a sufficiently direct relation to commerce to stand. Opponents of health care reform argued that refusing to buy health insurance is not commerce at all, it is refusing to engage in commerce and so not subject to regulation. Former Judge Andrew Napolitano, a Fox News legal analyst, made this point in a September 15, 2009, *Wall Street Journal* opinion piece, that medical services were not in interstate commerce. He reasoned that, "In almost all instances, the delivery of medical services occurs in one place and does not move across interstate lines. One goes to a physician not to engage in commercial activity, . . . but to improve one's health."

Oral arguments took place before the Supreme Court in March 2012. The Obama administration's advocate was Solicitor General Donald Verrilli.

He argued that the health care law was clearly constitutional on commerce clause grounds, and, secondarily, under the taxing power as the penalties for non-compliance were to be collected by the IRS. Democrats were shaken by the skeptical, even hostile, questions thrown at Verrilli by members of the court. Republican hopes rose.

On June 28, 2012, conservative Chief Justice John Roberts announced the court's narrow 5–4 decision. Both sides were stunned and many Republicans were outraged when Roberts announced that the law would stand in most of its major parts, based not on the commerce clause, which he declared did not reach the inactivity of declining to buy health insurance, but on the federal government's taxing power. Democrats were elated; President Obama's signature first term policy achievement had survived, on Chief Justice Roberts casting vote. Republicans were so furious that they did not recognize for a time that Roberts had given them a victory too, limiting the range of the commerce power to economic activity—still a broad sweep—but not inactivity.

As this debate suggests, there is no more critical question in American politics than the following: should the Constitution be read narrowly (show me where it says anything about national health insurance) or broadly (it says general welfare and having health care promotes the general welfare).

Focus Questions: from reading to thinking

Q1 How has the role of government in relation to the economy changed over the course of American political history?

Q2 What roles do fiscal, monetary, and regulatory policy play in economic policymaking?

Q3 What are the key institutions of economic management at the national level, and what are their respective roles?

Q4 What roles do the president and Congress play in producing the federal budget each year?

Q5 What problems afflict the social security program and what reforms have been proposed?

WHAT DO YOU THINK?

- Should the Constitution be read narrowly (show me where it says anything about national health insurance) or broadly (it says general welfare and having health care promotes the general welfare)?
- Who gets to decide this—Congress, the courts, political parties?

◆◆◆◆◆

GOVERNMENT AND THE ECONOMY

What role should government play in the organization, management, and performance of the U.S. economy? Or better yet, is there really any meaningful sense in which the government organizes the economy? Should government try to manage the economy? And finally, should citizens hold government responsible for the strength and performance of the economy, for the unemployment and inflation rates, and for the pace at which new jobs are created?

These questions have long been at the center of American politics. Some argue that markets are naturally self-regulating and perform best when the hand of government rests lightly on them. But others, including the political-economist Marc Allen Eisner, make the more fundamental point that, "Markets are institutions for the exchange of property, and property rights are defined by public policy and defended by state institutions. . . . [Therefore,] rather than assuming some autonomous logic of economic activity, it is far more accurate to view the economy as being embedded in a dense network of laws and institutions."[1] Nonetheless, as we shall see below, the network of economic laws, regulations, and institutions has become notably denser over the course of our nation's history.

In this chapter, we discuss the history of the government's relationship to the economy and how that relationship has changed over time. We describe the tools that government has to manage the economy and how various schools of thought argue that those tools should be used. We then turn to the key government institutions charged to monitor the performance of the economy and how they attempt to do that. We analyze the great changes that have taken place in domestic spending priorities in recent decades and the problems these may pose for the future. Finally, we ask what public priorities are evident in the taxing, spending, deficit, and debt decisions of the national government and how democratic politics affects the character and structure of those priorities.

HISTORY OF ECONOMIC MANAGEMENT

Though the Constitution gave the national government the power to tax, to regulate foreign and interstate commerce, and protect contracts and patents, "the Constitution gave the states the power to govern most aspects of American markets."[2] Hence, the national government busied itself during the early decades of the nineteenth century with foreign relations, distribution of western lands, delivering the mail, and overseeing a modest administrative establishment.

Q1 How has the role of government in relation to the economy changed over the course of American political history?

The balance between federal and state authority over markets and commerce changed with President Franklin Roosevelt's response to the Depression of the 1930s. One of the lasting effects of FDR's New Deal was broad public expectation that the federal government should do more to promote economic growth and stability. So entrenched are these ideas today that politicians, especially presidents, live or die by the numbers on economic growth, productivity, employment, inflation, and trade. But Americans remain resolutely anti-tax, meaning that most expect more from government than they are willing to pay for. As a result, the U.S. faces significant problems with deficits and debt that neither the public nor our politicians seem to have the courage to confront.

Building the Economic Infrastructure

The earliest American colonies were organized as joint stock companies and were intended to be viable economic enterprises. Initially, most economic

The Granger Collection, New York

Alexander Hamilton, the first Secretary of the Treasury, is often called the father of the U.S. economy.

activities required government approval, assistance, and support. Colonial governments sold land, licensed businesses, constructed roads, harbors, and schools, and provided currency and credit.

Economic development policy during the early national period focused on the creation of financial, monetary, and transportation systems. Alexander Hamilton, the first secretary of the treasury, was the prime architect of the American economy. Hamilton was adamant that the public debt incurred in the revolution be repaid in order to establish the new nation's credit. Hamilton supported a tariff on imported goods to raise revenue and to protect American industry from foreign competition, and he established the first Bank of the United States to manage the currency and facilitate commercial transactions. Early in the nineteenth century, state governments invested heavily in roads and canals. Later in the century, they facilitated the development of railroads and the telegraph and encouraged the establishment of banks to hold deposits and to stimulate the credit required for economic development.[3] State governments were key actors in economic development because most economic activity was local or, at most, regional.

The Rise of Economic Regulation

The Civil War presented both the North and the South with massive problems of supply and distribution. The North solved its supply problems with innovative new techniques of mass production and its distribution problems with rapid expansion of telegraph and rail lines. The South was much less industrially developed and largely failed to solve these problems.

Northern capitalists also developed new forms of business organization. The modern **corporation** was a post-Civil War invention. Corporations, compared to earlier businesses, were huge, often employing thousands of people in facilities throughout the country. The first new corporate monopolies were the railroads. By the early 1880s, John D. Rockefeller had established **monopoly** control of the emerging oil industry. Soon monopolies arose in many lines of economic activity, from commodities like steel, lead, whiskey, and sugar to services like railroads, shipping, banking, and insurance. Rockefeller, Vanderbilt, Morgan, Carnegie, Stanford, and others accumulated vast fortunes.

As corporations grew larger and the economy became more complex, the national government moved to develop new tools for economic management. Complaints by farmers and shippers led Congress to create the Interstate Commerce Commission (ICC) in 1887 to set fair and equitable freight rates and to monitor railroad compliance. The Sherman Antitrust Act (1890) declared that "every . . . combination in restraint of trade or commerce" or

corporation A legal rather than a physical person. A corporation can do anything a person can do, including buying and selling property, loaning and borrowing money, but the liability of the shareholders is limited to the amounts of their investments in the corporation.

monopoly Circumstance in which one producer has exclusive control of a market, thus enabling market manipulation and discretionary pricing.

"attempt to monopolize" was illegal. The Clayton Act (1914) sought to protect consumers and the marketplace from corporate mergers that reduced competition. The Federal Reserve Act (1913) rationalized the national banking system, mandated rules to make banks safer and more stable, and established a uniform paper currency for the country. Government became increasingly involved in shaping and regulating the private economy.

The Growth of the Welfare State and Macroeconomic Regulation

Until well into the twentieth century, although government might seek to ensure that the marketplace operated fairly, individual success or failure was to be determined through competition. What today we call the "social safety net" of government assistance programs did not yet exist. The needy had to look to family and to churches and private charities for help.

The Great Depression, the worst economic downturn in American history, lasting twelve long years (1929–1941), changed how Americans thought about poverty, unemployment, and the performance of the economy. Four thousand banks and seventy thousand factories closed. The gross national product (GNP), the value of goods and services produced by the nation in a year, fell by 30 percent between 1929 and 1933. The unemployment rate rose from

Children labor at the Falls River, Massachusetts, spinning mill around 1900. Child labor standards varied by state, stronger in the north and weaker in the south, until federal standards were enacted in 1938.

about 3 percent in 1929 to nearly 15 percent throughout the 1930s, reaching a high of 25 percent in 1933. Farm income, already depressed in the 1920s, fell from an average of $900 in 1929 to $300 in 1932 and remained low for the remainder of the decade.[4]

New Deal The name given to President Franklin Roosevelt's policies and programs intended to address the Great Depression.

The **New Deal** is the name given to the set of programs developed by President Franklin Roosevelt and his advisers to address the Depression. In the famous "first hundred days" of his administration, FDR sought to reassure the nation and to begin putting people back to work. The Public Works Administration (PWA) was created to employ workers on large construction projects. Later, the Civil Works Administration (CWA) and the Works Progress Administration (WPA) hired workers to build public works like courthouses and post offices. The Civilian Conservation Corps (CCC) hired young people to work on public lands and parks.

A second wave of economic policymaking included the beginnings of an American welfare state designed both to help individuals in need and to stabilize the general performance of the economy. The Social Security Act of 1935 established the retirement system, to which 90 percent of working Americans contribute, and the unemployment compensation system. Related programs provided support to the needy blind, disabled, elderly, and dependent children. These programs were designed to support demand in the economy by providing funds to the retired, the temporarily unemployed, and those who due to age or infirmity could not be expected to take care of themselves.[5]

Despite the efforts of the Roosevelt administration, the economy did not fully recover until World War II. During the war years, 1941–1945, the federal government spent $320 billion but raised only $130 billion in taxes and other revenues. The resulting $190 billion in additional stimulus spurred demand sufficiently to return the economy to robust full employment. Nonetheless, policymakers were concerned that after the war was over and government demand for goods and labor declined, the economy might fall back into depression.

The Employment Act of 1946 formalized Washington's responsibility for maintaining the health of the American economy. This act stated that "it is the continuing policy and responsibility of the Federal Government . . . to promote maximum employment, production, and purchasing power." The Employment Act of 1946 also established the Council of Economic Advisers (CEA) in the Executive Office of the President and the Joint Economic Committee in Congress. Finally, it made the president responsible for submitting an economic report to the Congress each year.

PERSPECTIVES ON MODERN ECONOMIC MANAGEMENT

Q2 What roles do fiscal, monetary, and regulatory policy play in economic policymaking?

What policy tools do the president and Congress have to use in fulfilling their responsibility of economic management, and how are these tools employed? Fiscal policy, monetary policy, and regulatory policy are the principal tools that government uses in managing the economy. Precisely how these tools should be wielded to best effect has been subject to ongoing and continuous dispute.

Fiscal policy refers to government decisions about revenues and expenditures and about the relationship between the two. The president and Congress set taxes and spending levels through the annual preparation of the federal budget. If government raises more money than it spends, it is said to have a **surplus,** and if it spends more money than it raises it is said to have a **deficit**.

Government can alter its taxing and spending policies in ways intended to have a particular effect on the general performance of the economy. As during World War II, government can stimulate demand in the economy by running a deficit. On the other hand, it can restrict or limit demand in the economy by running a surplus. Governments can create deficits by decreasing taxes or increasing spending and can create surpluses by increasing taxes or decreasing spending.[6]

Monetary policy refers to government decisions about the money supply and interest rates. Whereas fiscal policy is largely the responsibility of the president and Congress, monetary policy is largely the responsibility of the Federal Reserve Board, an independent regulatory agency commonly called "the Fed." As we shall see more fully below, the Fed can expand or contract the nation's money supply and the availability of credit through its oversight of the banking industry.

Regulatory policy refers to the effects that legislation and bureaucratic rule making have on the performance of individual businesses and the economy in general. Regulations encompass a broad range of topics from business structure and practices, to workplace safety and environmental impact, to the distribution of basic services like telephones. Complying with government regulations costs businesses an eye-popping $1.75 trillion annually.[7] Scholars and policymakers differ about how government can best use fiscal, monetary, and regulatory policy to promote a healthy economy.

Traditional Conservatism

Traditional conservatives draw their economic insights from the tradition of classical economics that began with Adam Smith (1723–1790) and David Ricardo (1772–1823). They favor limited government, low taxes, modest regulation, and balanced budgets. Oftentimes, traditional conservatives draw an analogy between government budgets and family budgets. No family could spend more than it earned year after year without going bankrupt. On the other hand, a family might borrow to finance a home, car, or college education so long as it was willing to exercise restraint elsewhere to pay back the debt. Governments, traditional conservatives argue, should behave that way too. In truth, there are precious few traditional conservatives in either major party today.

Keynesianism

John Maynard Keynes (1883–1946) was the most influential economist of the twentieth century. Keynes rejected the traditional conservative view that

fiscal policy Government policies about taxing, spending, budgets, deficits, and debt.

surplus If government takes in more money than it spends in a given year, the amount left over is called the surplus.

deficit If government spends more than it collects in a given year, the amount that has to be borrowed to make up the shortfall is called the deficit.

monetary policy Monetary policy refers to government decisions about the money supply and interest rates.

regulatory policy Regulatory policy refers to the legislation and bureaucratic rules that affect the performance of individual businesses and the economy in general.

traditional conservatives Traditional conservatives believe in low taxes, limited government regulation, and balanced budgets.

John Maynard Keynes was the most prominent liberal economist in the first half of the twentieth century.

Milton Friedman was the most prominent conservative economist in the second half of the twentieth century.

Keynesianism Economic ideas associated with British economist John Maynard Keynes advocating countercyclical spending by government to manage demand in the private economy.

government should tighten its belt during bad economic times in order to maintain a balanced budget. **Keynesianism** holds just the opposite, that government spending should be countercyclical. Keynes argued that economic downturns are caused by inadequate demand for goods and services in the economy. Hence, government should buttress demand during bad economic times, when private consumption and business investment turn down, by reducing taxes or increasing spending even if that means running a deficit. Keynes also argued that government should be alert during good economic times. Excess demand, often described as too much money chasing too few goods, brings inflation and higher interest rates. Government should limit aggregate demand by raising taxes or cutting spending. Over a period of years government budgets should be in balance, although any given year might see a surplus intended to limit inflation or a deficit intended to combat recession. Again, in truth, politicians of both parties find it much easier to spend money and run deficits than they do to save money and run surpluses.

Supply-Side Economics

supply-side economics Supply-siders argue that lower taxes and lighter regulation improve the business climate, encourage new investment, and expand output.

Supply-siders, most of whom are Republicans, argue that the focus of economic policy should not be on managing demand but on enhancing supplies of goods and services to the economy. The centerpiece of **supply-side economics** is the argument that lower taxes and lighter regulation improve the business climate, encourage new business investment, and expand output. Supply-siders argue that an improved business climate and expanded production mean more jobs at higher wages. More people working and paying taxes means that government revenues go up and that the cost of government programs for welfare, job training, and the like go down. Some supply-siders also acknowledge that even if tax cuts produce deficits, those deficits have the desirable consequence of holding down new government spending.[8]

Monetarism

The economist Milton Friedman (1912–2006) is often called the father of modern monetarism. **Monetarists** contend that slow and steady growth in the money supply facilitates smooth economic growth and stable prices. Second, they argue that monetary policy can be adjusted throughout the year as circumstances change, whereas fiscal policy is set annually with adoption of the budget. Finally, changes in fiscal policy raise or lower someone's taxes and raise or lower someone's benefits or services. Changes in monetary policy increase or decrease the aggregate supply of money and credit in the economy, but the market decides how to distribute available money and credit.

monetarists Monetarists contend that slow and steady growth in the money supply facilitates smooth economic growth and stable prices.

The Rhetorical Economy

Although politicians and their economic advisers generally adopt one of these economic perspectives over the others, they also know that they must sell their economic prescriptions to an inattentive public. Though conservatives resisted, Keynesian ideas dominated official thinking from the 1930s through the 1970s. Democrats passed Social Security (1935) and Medicare and Medicaid (1965) at least partially by touting their stimulative effects. Since 1980, Republican supply-side and monetarist ideas have had the upper hand.

One of the more humorous causes of the shift in rhetorical advantage from Democrats to Republicans on economic issues was an influential 1976 essay by *Wall Street Journal* editorial writer Jude Wanniski. Wanniski decried the Democrats Santa Claus advantage—Democrats had for decades offered voters brightly wrapped gifts labeled "social security" and "medicare," while Republicans had played Scrooge, complaining that the gifts were too expensive. Wanniski proposed a "Two Santa Claus Theory" of party competition in which Democrats offered their entitlement gifts and Republicans offered tax cuts.[9] His bet—that higher income voters who turn out in greater numbers in elections would prefer tax cuts to more government spending—has been born out in large measure. Economic policymaking is important business, but communicating your ideas sharply, often at bumper sticker length, is part of conducting that business well.

While debate will undoubtedly continue over the best mix of fiscal, monetary, and regulatory policy, there is little doubt that government policies have, at least until recently, improved the performance of the economy. Political scientists John Frendreis and Raymond Tatalovich report that between 1854 and 1945 the economy was expanding about 60 percent of the time and contracting about 40 percent of the time. Between 1945 and the present the economy has expanded about 85 percent of the time and contracted about 15 percent of the time.[10]

INSTITUTIONS OF ECONOMIC POLICYMAKING

Q3 What are the key institutions of economic management at the national level, and what are their respective roles?

Congress had the dominant influence over economic policymaking throughout the nineteenth century. At times the departments of the executive branch submitted their annual budget requests directly to the Congress. At other times departmental budget requests were collected by the secretary of the treasury, but neither he nor the president had the clear authority to change or even coordinate these requests.

During the twentieth century, in response to the emergencies of war and economic crisis and to the activist leadership of presidents like Woodrow Wilson and Franklin Roosevelt, the initiative in economic policymaking shifted to the executive branch. The five agencies that make up the president's economic policymaking apparatus are the Department of the Treasury, the Federal Reserve Board, the Office of Management and Budget, the Council of Economic Advisers, and the National Economic Council.

Treasury Department

The Treasury Department was one of the original departments of the national government. The secretary of the Treasury is the administration's chief spokesman on economic issues. The tasks of the modern Treasury Department are to collect the government's revenues, pay its bills, and secure its credit. The Treasury Department also is active in the nation's financial markets, regularly selling government securities to raise cash to cover budget deficits. The Treasury Department also has the lead in managing the nation's interaction with the world economy and international agencies such as the International Monetary Fund.

Federal Reserve Board

The Federal Reserve Board is an independent regulatory commission that was created in 1913 and substantially strengthened in the 1930s. The Fed has principal responsibility for managing the nation's money supply and, through management of the money supply, for managing interest rates and inflation. All of the nation's depository institutions (commercial banks, savings banks, savings and loan associations, and credit unions) are subject to Fed rules. Following the economic collapse and "credit crunch" of late 2007 through 2009, some called for expansion of the Fed's mandate to cover investment banks and new actors like hedge funds. Others, charging that the Fed had failed to see the crisis coming, called for limits on the Fed's authority.

The Federal Reserve System is managed by a seven-member Board of Governors. Fed governors are nominated by the president and confirmed by the

Senate. However, to assure their independence from the president, Congress, and politics in general, their terms are very long, fourteen years, and they cannot be removed from office by the president. The chair and vice chair of the Board of Governors are nominated by the president and confirmed by the Senate to four-year terms. Janet Yellen, the current chairwomen of the Federal Reserve Board, began her first four-year term in 2014.

The Federal Reserve Board manages the nation's money supply by setting reserve requirements and discount rates for banks. **Reserve requirements** define the proportion of an institution's total deposits that must be held as cash. Lowering the reserve requirement gives banks more money to lend, and raising it gives them less. More money to lend usually means falling interest rates, whereas less means rising interest rates. The **discount rate** is the interest rate that the Fed charges banks for loans. A higher discount rate discourages borrowing from the Fed, thereby contracting the money supply and increasing interest rates. A lower discount rate encourages borrowing from the Fed, thus expanding the money supply and driving down interest rates.

In addition to the Federal Reserve Board, the other principal components of the Federal Reserve System are the Federal Open Market Committee (FOMC) and the twelve Federal Reserve Banks. The FOMC is composed of the seven members of the Federal Reserve Board and five of the twelve presidents of the Federal Reserve Banks. The FOMC directly affects the money supply and, hence, interest rates, by buying or selling U.S. government securities. Finally, the twelve Federal Reserve Banks make reserve loans to private banks and hold reserves for them, collect and clear checks from private banks, and supply currency.

Landov

Paul Volcker, Fed chairman from 1979 to 1987, is still a prominent figure in the U.S. economic community, and a top advisor to President Obama.

reserve requirements Requirements that define the portion of a financial institution's total deposits that the Fed says must be held in cash.

discount rate The interest rate that the Fed charges banks for loans.

Office of Management and Budget

The **Budget and Accounting Act of 1921** created the Bureau of the Budget (BOB) in the Treasury Department to assist in the preparation of a unified executive branch budget. When the Executive Office of the President was created in 1939, the BOB was moved there. In 1970 President Nixon renamed the BOB the Office of Management and Budget (OMB), and its director was given cabinet status.

The OMB is a powerful tool of presidential authority over economic policy because it prepares and administers the federal budget. Two other tasks enhance the power and influence of the OMB. In 1950, President Harry Truman assigned the task of legislative clearance and in the 1980s, President Reagan assigned the task of regulatory clearance to the OMB. This means that

Budget and Accounting Act of 1921 This act created the Bureau of the Budget (BOB) in the Treasury Department and enhanced presidential control over the budgetary process in the executive branch. BOB became the Office of Management and Budget in 1970.

all proposed legislation and regulations coming from the executive branch must go through OMB so that they can be analyzed both for their budgetary implications and for their compatibility with the president's policy goals.

Council of Economic Advisers

The Employment Act of 1946 established the Council of Economic Advisers (CEA). The three members of the CEA are appointed by the president subject to Senate confirmation. They are usually academic economists and they oversee a professional staff of about two dozen. Jason Furman, the current chair of the council, is a government economist and economic policy adviser with relatively little academic experience.

The mandate of the CEA is to provide expert advice to the president on the health and performance of the economy. The CEA also assists the president in the preparation of his annual economic report to Congress. The fact that the CEA's role is strictly advisory makes its position precarious in relation to Treasury, the Fed, and OMB.

National Economic Council

The National Economic Council (NEC) was established in 1993 to coordinate and centralize control of economic policy in the White House. The NEC was intended to play the same integrative role in economic policy that the National Security Council (NSC) plays in national security policy. Structurally, the NEC is an interagency body chaired by the president and includes the vice president, eight cabinet secretaries (Agriculture, Commerce, Energy, HUD, Labor, State, Transportation, Treasury), and several other high-level administrators. Former Clinton NEC director Gene Sperling has returned to head the Obama NEC.

The executive order by which the NEC was established defined four major tasks for the council: "(1) to coordinate the economic policy-making process with regard to domestic and international economic issues, (2) to coordinate economic advice to the president, (3) to insure that economic policy-making decisions and programs are consistent with the president's stated goals and to see that those goals are being effectively pursued, and (4) to monitor implementation of the president's economic policy agenda." Like the CEA, the NEC has trouble standing up to the weightier economic policy players at the Treasury, OMB, and the Fed.

FISCAL DECISION MAKING: BUDGETS, TAXES, AND SPENDING

Q4 What roles do the president and Congress play in producing the federal budget each year?

The federal government, once small and unobtrusive, now touches on almost every aspect of social, political, and economic life. The budget for the 2016 fiscal year authorized a record $4 trillion. Not surprisingly, extended battles occur each year between the president and Congress over how the necessary revenue will be raised and how it will be distributed across the government's various programs, obligations, and responsibilities.

Fundamentally, the budgetary process sets the government's priorities by making explicit decisions about revenues and expenditures. On the revenue side, the basic questions are how much money is to be raised, through what kinds of taxes and fees, and on whom will they be levied? On the expenditure side, the basic questions are how much money will be spent, on which programs, and for whose benefit? And finally, revenues must be matched to expenditures to see whether more money is to be raised than spent (leaving a surplus in government coffers) or more money is to be spent than raised (leaving a deficit that borrowing will need to fill). The president and Congress must bargain to agreement on all of these issues before a budget can go into effect. Big deficits going forward promise to make these discussions highly conflictual.

Budget Preparation

As shown in Table 15.1, the federal budget is prepared in two major phases; the first occurs in the executive branch, the second in the legislative branch. Preparation of the fiscal year (FY) 2016 budget began in the executive branch in the spring of 2014 so that it could be delivered to Congress for consideration early in 2015. Congress's consideration of the budget is supposed to be finished by summer 2015 so that FY 2016 can begin on October 1, 2015. The process seldom runs smoothly and frequently produces great conflict between the president and Congress.[11]

The process of budget preparation within the executive branch occurs as a set of structured discussions and negotiations among the president, the OMB, and the departments of the executive branch. The process begins in April each year. OMB presents the president with an analysis of the state of the economy and projections of economic performance for the coming year. On the basis of broad presidential guidance, the OMB formulates guidelines to the agencies, and the agencies respond by analyzing their current programs and outlining their budgetary needs for the coming year. The OMB analyzes the agency input and advises the president on how to respond to it, and the president establishes more detailed guidelines and targets for the agencies to follow.

YURI GRIPAS / UPI / Landov

Jim Wallis, a leader of Sojourners, a Christian social justice group, opposes spending cuts, arguing that "budgets are moral documents."

TABLE 15.1	Major Steps in Preparation of the Fiscal Year 2016 Budget
Executive Branch Preparation	
2014	
April–May	Budgetary framework set. The president and the OMB set broad budgetary parameters and communicate them to the agencies.
June–August	Agency budget preparation. Agencies build their budgets in light of presidential and OMB instructions.
September–November	OMB review. OMB reviews agency budgets, holds hearings, and makes recommendations to the president. The president makes final decisions on agency budgets.
December–January	Final budget preparation. Final economic reviews are conducted and adjustments are made, and the final budget is prepared for submission to Congress.
Congressional Preparation	
2015	
First Monday in February	Congress receives the president's budget.
February 15	CBO reports to the Budget Committee on the fiscal outlook, budget priorities, and how they relate to the president's budget.
February 25	Congressional committees submit to the Budget Committee estimates on revenues and spending.
April 1	Budget Committee reports concurrent resolution on the budget to each house.
April 15	Both houses complete action on the concurrent resolution.
May 15–June 10	House Appropriations Committee must complete consideration on all thirteen appropriations bills.
June 15	Congress must pass a reconciliation bill, which brings budget totals in line with approved ceilings.
June 30	House completes action on all appropriations bills.
October 1	Fiscal year 2016 begins.

During the summer, agencies refine their budgetary requests. In the fall, agencies submit their formal budget proposals along with analysis and arguments required to support budget allocations beyond those initially proposed by the president and OMB. OMB reviews the requests, holds hearings on each agency's request, and makes recommendations to the president who then sets each agency's budget allocation. OMB informs the agencies of the president's decisions.

During the winter OMB prepares the president's budget message to Congress and the budget document itself. The president reviews the latest economic data and projections, makes final adjustments in the budget and the budget message to Congress, and submits both to Congress by the first Monday in February.

During the entire time that the president's budget is in preparation, the Congressional Budget Office (CBO) is anticipating it, analyzing what it thinks will be in it, and developing a congressional alternative if that seems necessary. The CBO is required to submit an analysis of the president's budget to the House and Senate Budget Committees by February 15, and by February 25 the standing committees of both houses must submit their projections on revenues and expenditures to their respective budget committees.

On the basis of this information, the Budget Committees must produce a concurrent resolution on the budget by April 1. The concurrent resolution sets overall expenditure levels, estimates outlays for major budgetary categories, and makes a recommendation on revenue levels. Congress must complete action on the concurrent resolution and adopt it by April 15.

Between April 15 and June 10, the House Appropriations Committee produces thirteen appropriations bills that authorize spending in major budgetary categories for the coming fiscal year. If the spending totals in the appropriations bills breach the spending targets in the concurrent resolution, a process called **reconciliation** occurs to bring budgetary totals into conformity with mandated ceilings. Reconciliation is to be complete by June 15, and work on the budget as a whole is to be complete by June 30. Assuming that agreement by the Senate and the president is secured, the budget goes into effect on October 1. Difficulties abound, and the process is rarely completed on time.

reconciliation Congressional process to resolve differences if appropriations bills approve more spending than the spending targets permit.

Taxing

The United States was born in a tax revolt, so it should not be surprising that keeping taxes low has been a national obsession. The Constitution prohibited the national government from imposing direct taxes, such as those on income or property, but did authorize imposts and excises. Imposts are taxes on goods imported into the country, and excises are taxes on the sale within the country of specific goods, most often liquor and tobacco. The Constitution authorized the power to borrow and incur debt and to coin money and regulate the currency.

Taxes on imports formed the foundation for national revenues through the first half of the nineteenth century. Import fees comprised about 90 percent of national revenues between 1789 and 1815.[12] Excise taxes began to play a larger role after 1815, but import fees remained a major source of revenue throughout the nineteenth century. Nonetheless, the fiscal demands of the Civil War (1861–1865) and the growth

Struggling Toward Democracy

The Founders prohibited a tax on incomes; but the Sixteenth Amendment, ratified and implemented in 1913, permitted an income tax.

What do you think?

- Was this a mistake, one alternative source of revenue among others, or a necessity in the modern world?

Pro & Con

Debating the Income Tax

Oliver Wendell Holmes (1841–1935), associate justice of the United States Supreme Court from 1902 to 1932, famously said that "taxes are the price that we pay for a civilized society." If that is true, and in a sense it certainly is, many Americans are getting more civilization than they want. Most Americans recognize the need for taxation, but they differ over how much revenue is needed, what kinds of taxes should supply them, and who should pay.

Today, federal revenues come from three main sources. Forty-six percent comes from individual income taxes, 34 percent from payroll taxes levied on workers and employers to pay for Social Security and Medicare, and about 11 percent from corporate income taxes. The remaining 9 percent comes from a mix of imposts, excises, and estate taxes. Tax fairness is usually discussed in terms of whether a particular tax is regressive, progressive, or flat. A **regressive tax**, like the payroll tax, takes a higher proportion of the income of low-wage earners than of high-wage earners. A **progressive tax**, like the income tax, takes a higher proportion from the high-wage earners than from the low-wage earners. Critics of both regressive and progressive taxes sometimes argue for a **flat tax**— one that takes the same proportion of income irrespective of the level or amount of income.

The Medicare tax is a modest 2.9 percent on all income; hence, it is a flat tax. The Social Security tax is a more appreciable 12.4 percent and it is regressive.

The Social Security tax falls on the first \$118,500 of income. Most workers make under \$118,500, so they pay the Social Security tax on their whole incomes, whereas the wealthy pay only on the first \$118,500 of their incomes. In fact, 80 percent of workers pay more in payroll taxes than they pay in income taxes.

The wealthy usually pay much more in income taxes than in payroll taxes. Not surprisingly, then, the debate over tax fairness focuses on the income tax. The data below, from an analysis of 2006 income tax payments by the Congressional Budget Office, show that the top 1 percent of income earners paid 39 percent of all income taxes and 24 percent of all federal taxes. The top 10 percent paid 77 percent of income taxes and 53 percent of all federal taxes. Remarkably, the bottom 80 percent of income earners paid just 7 percent of income taxes and 31 percent of all federal taxes (because they pay a lot of payroll taxes).

The wealthy obviously pay a disproportionate share of income taxes. On the other hand, tax rates on high incomes have been steadily lowered in recent decades (from 90 percent as late as the early 1960s to 39.6 percent today), and the proportion of all income going to top earners has increased steadily since the early 1980s.

What do you think?
- Where does fairness lie?
- Is equality better captured by ability to pay or equal shares?

PRO	CON
Recognizes ability to pay	Taking a higher proportion from some is unjust
The income tax is highly efficient	It suppresses willingness to work
Federal courts have upheld it	Tax resistors claim it is unconstitutional

of government activity and responsibility late in the nineteenth century encouraged experimentation with a tax on incomes. The first federal income tax, adopted as a Civil War measure, was a tax of 3 percent on income above

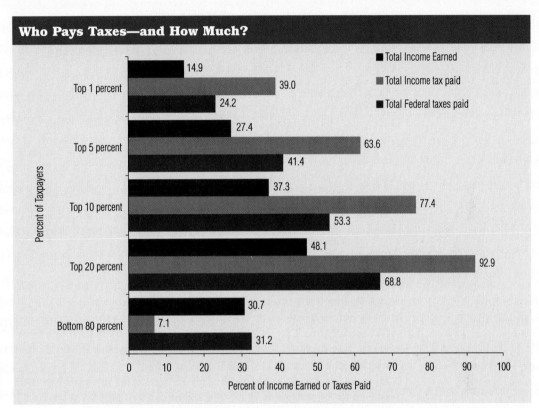

Who Pays Taxes—and How Much?

Legend:
- Total Income Earned
- Total Income tax paid
- Total Federal taxes paid

Top 1 percent:
- 14.9
- 39.0
- 24.2

Top 5 percent:
- 27.4
- 63.6
- 41.4

Top 10 percent:
- 37.3
- 77.4
- 53.3

Top 20 percent:
- 48.1
- 92.9
- 68.8

Bottom 80 percent:
- 30.7
- 7.1
- 31.2

Y-axis: Percent of Taxpayers
X-axis: Percent of Income Earned or Taxes Paid (0–100)

Source: Congressional Budget Office, "The Distribution of Household Income and Federal Taxes," see tables 1 and 3. http://www.cbo.gov/sites/default/files/cbofiles/attachments/440604-AverageTaxRates.pdf

a personal exemption of $800.[13] The income tax was discontinued after the Civil War and was not tried again until 1894. The Supreme Court promptly declared it unconstitutional.

By 1910, taxes on tobacco and alcohol provided nearly half of federal revenues and slightly more than import duties. However, impost and excise taxes both had natural limitations. Although rates could be raised a little to increase revenues, they could not be raised too much or else imports and consumption of the taxed items would be depressed. With government clearly outgrowing its revenues, the Sixteenth Amendment to the Constitution,

regressive tax A tax that takes a greater proportion of the income or wealth of the poor than of the wealthy.

progressive tax A tax that takes a higher proportion of the income or wealth of the wealthy than of the poor.

flat tax A tax that takes the same proportion of income or wealth from the wealthy as from the poor.

TABLE 15.2 History of Federal Income Tax Rates	
Years	**Tax Rates**
1861–1864	Flat 3% on incomes above $800
1864–1870	5%–15% with the top rate beginning at $10,000
1894	Flat 2% on incomes over $1,000
1913	Flat 1% on incomes over $3,000, 6% surcharge on wealthy
1916	2%–15%, top raised to 77% by 1918
1943–1964	20%–91%
1964–1981	14%–70%
1981–1986	11%–50%
1986–1990	15%, 28%, and 31%
1992–2000	36% and 39.6% brackets added
2001–2012	New 10% bracket created, 15% capped; in 2003 the 28%, 31%, 36%, and 39.6% rates were reduced to 25%, 28%, 33%, and 35%
2013	39.6% top rate was restored

Source: Derived from James W. Lindeen, *Governing America's Economy* (Englewood Cliffs, NJ: Prentice-Hall, 1994), 151. Updated by the author.

permitting a direct tax on incomes, was adopted in 1913. Soon thereafter the Congress adopted a modest tax of 1 percent on incomes over $3,000 with a surcharge of an additional six percent on very high incomes. Average income in 1913 was only $621, so the vast majority of wage earners paid no tax on their incomes. In fact, only 2 percent of adults paid an income tax in the first year (see Table 15.2).

However, as World War I pushed up demands for revenue, top rates were increased to 15 percent in 1916, 67 percent in 1917, and 77 percent in 1918.[14] Reductions in the amount of income required to make one liable for the tax meant that 20 percent of citizens were paying the income tax by the end of the war in 1918. New taxes on corporate income and on estates of the deceased were also added or expanded. Between World War I and World War II, the income tax and excise taxes each provided 35–40 percent of federal revenues, whereas tariffs provided somewhat less.

The Revenue Act of 1942 provided the basis for the modern U.S. tax system. The new system had at its center a broadly based and steeply progressive personal income tax. The tax was applied directly to middle-class wages and salaries and included a wartime surcharge that by 1944 was 23 percent on the first $2,000 to 94 percent on incomes over $200,000.[15] The revenue needs of the war made the federal income tax a mass tax, and after the war economic expansion brought unprecedented new revenues to government.

During the last half of the twentieth century the four principal sources of federal revenue were the personal income tax, the corporate income tax, the payroll taxes supporting Social Security, Medicare, and the various federal retirement programs, and excise taxes. However, Figure 15.1 clearly shows

FIGURE 15.1   Percent of Federal Revenue from Various Sources, Comparing FY 1955 and 2015

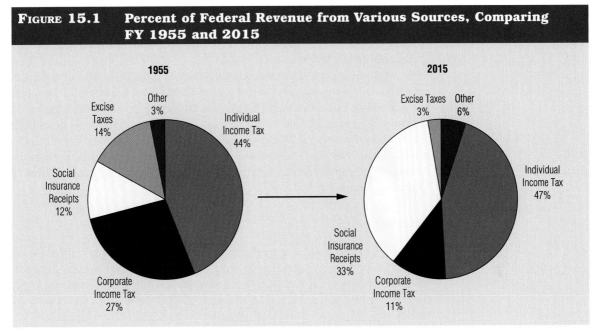

Source: *Budget of the United States Government, Fiscal Year 2014*, Historical Tables (Washington, D.C.: U.S. Government Printing Office, 2014), Table 2.2, 34–35. Figures for 2015 are official estimates.

that while the proportion of total revenues from personal income taxes has remained steady, revenues from the corporate income tax and excise taxes have declined markedly, while the revenues from payroll taxes have increased markedly.[16] The personal income tax and payroll taxes accounted for more than half of all federal revenues by the mid-1970s and 80 percent today.

Republican presidents have also sought to limit personal income taxes. The Economic Recovery Tax Act (ERTA) that President Reagan initiated in 1981 sought to stimulate economic growth by cutting the tax rate on personal income by 25 percent over three years and by providing additional tax breaks and incentives to businesses. The Tax Reform Act of 1986 collapsed tax rates on income into three broad bands. The top tax rate was brought down to 31 percent, and 6 million low-income taxpayers were removed from the rolls.[17] Finally, in the mid-1990s President Clinton raised taxes, especially on top earners, to reduce burgeoning budget deficits. Tax reform is never off the political agenda for long.

Advocates of reform charge that the existing tax system is too complex, collects too much money from the wrong places, and possibly limits economic growth.[18] President Bush pushed large tax cuts through Congress in 2001 and 2003, including across-the-board reductions in income tax rates, as well as adjustments in child tax credits, the marriage penalty, capital gains, and estate tax rates. In the immediate wake of President Obama's 2012 reelection victory, he forced congressional Republicans to accept modest increases in personal income and capital gains tax rates. Federal tax receipts for 2011, at 15.1 percent of GDP, were the lowest since 1950 when Harry Truman was president. Tax receipts at 18.6 percent were just slightly above the average of the last six decades.

In addition to tax rates and whether they should be raised or lowered, advocates of tax reform also point to the myriad tax exemptions, benefits, and exclusions buried in the U.S. tax code. These tax breaks, including broad deductions for interest paid on home loans and narrow deductions benefiting particular businesses and types of investments, are often called tax expenditures because they cost the treasury just as much and an equivalent expenditure would. Revenue lost through tax expenditures cost the U.S. approximately $1.2 trillion annually.[19]

Spending

The federal government during the nineteenth century was small, its revenues were modest, and its spending generally stayed within its means. Between 1800 and 1860, per capita federal government expenditures did not rise at all; they were $2.03 per person in 1800 and $2.00 per person in 1860. The Civil War changed the level of federal spending very sharply. After the war, federal spending per capita settled back to a new and higher level but then remained there for fifty years. In 1870 per capita federal expenditures were $7.76 per person, and in 1910 they were only $7.51.[20] The twentieth century, however, brought industrialization, urbanization, two world wars, the Depression, and massive increases in federal government spending.

The federal government in the twentieth century added to its traditional responsibilities (national defense, justice, and land management) broad new tasks such as managing the economy and providing social welfare. In 1940, just prior to the U.S. entry into World War II, federal spending consumed 9.8 percent of gross domestic product (GDP). Federal spending as a percentage of GDP rose steadily through the latter half of the twentieth century, reaching 23.5 percent in 1983. During the 1990s GDP grew faster than federal spending. Hence, by 2000 federal spending had declined to only 18.2 percent, the lowest since 1966. In the wake of 9/11 and the subsequent wars in Afghanistan and Iraq, spending as a percentage of GDP increased to 25.2 percent in 2009, its highest level since World War II. By 2015, it declined to 21.8 percent.

Analysts often distinguish between mandatory and discretionary spending. Mandatory spending, such as that on Social Security and Medicare, is spending required by law—when someone reaches retirement age and has established eligibility to begin drawing Social Security, government must, by law, pay. Discretionary programs, like military spending or spending on highways and national parks, are funded each year at levels the president and Congress think appropriate.

One of the most dramatic budgetary developments of the second half of the twentieth century was the relative decline of defense expenditures compared to social welfare expenditures. In 1960 defense spending accounted

TABLE 15.3 Federal Budget Priorities, 1960–2015							
(Percentage of Total Outlays)							
Function	1960	1970	1980	1990	2000	2010	2015[a]
Discretionary Spending							
National Defense	52.2	41.8	22.7	23.9	16.5	19.3	15.7
Domestic Discretionary	19.6	21.1	24.3	17.5	13.9	15.6	13.5
Mandatory Spending							
Social Security	12.6	15.5	20.1	19.8	23.2	19.4	23.5
Income Security[b]	8.0	8.0	14.6	11.7	14.2	18.4	13.7
Health Programs[c]	0.1	6.2	9.4	12.4	19.7	22.3	27.1
Interest on Debt	7.5	7.4	8.9	14.7	12.5	5.0	6.5
Total	100.0	100.0	100.0	100.0	100.0	100.0	100.0

[a] Figures for 2015 are estimates.
[b] Includes public assistance, food stamps, unemployment compensation, and related programs.
[c] Includes Medicare, Medicaid, and related health programs and research.
Source: Budget of the United States Government, Fiscal Year 2014, Historical Tables (Washington, D.C.: U.S. Government Printing Office, 2014), Table 3.1.

for about 10 percent of GDP and half of the federal budget. By 2015 defense spending was 3.4 percent of GDP and 15.7 percent of federal expenditures (see Table 15.3).

As defense spending fell, spending on social welfare and other entitlement programs rose. In 1960 entitlement programs, other mandatory expenditures, and interest payments on the federal debt accounted for just over 6 percent of GDP and about 36 percent of federal spending. By 2015 they accounted for almost 17 percent of GDP and 77 percent of federal spending.[21] As we shall see, there is a great deal of concern that the growth of mandatory domestic spending programs will be unsustainable in coming decades. How do U.S. spending levels, which strike many Americans as high, compare to spending levels in other advanced industrial nations? (See the Let's Compare box.)

DOMESTIC SOCIAL PROGRAMS
AND THEIR CHALLENGES

One frequently hears the argument that in a country as wealthy as ours it is unconscionable that millions live in poverty, or do not have health insurance, or cannot afford to go to college. Other wealthy nations tax their citizens at higher rates and do more to assure income, medical care, and education to all. The U.S. has lower taxes and fewer services and an ongoing debate about whether we should do more. What is the responsibility of government in an

Q5 What problems afflict the social security program and what reforms have been proposed?

Government Sector Spending in Twenty-Seven Countries

Americans hold as an article of faith that much government spending is wasteful. Citizens complain vehemently about high taxes, and our politicians promise solemnly prior to each election to lower taxes and control spending.

Is government spending out of control? The following data suggest that it is not. In fact, the United States spends a smaller proportion of the nation's income than do most of the world's advanced industrial nations.

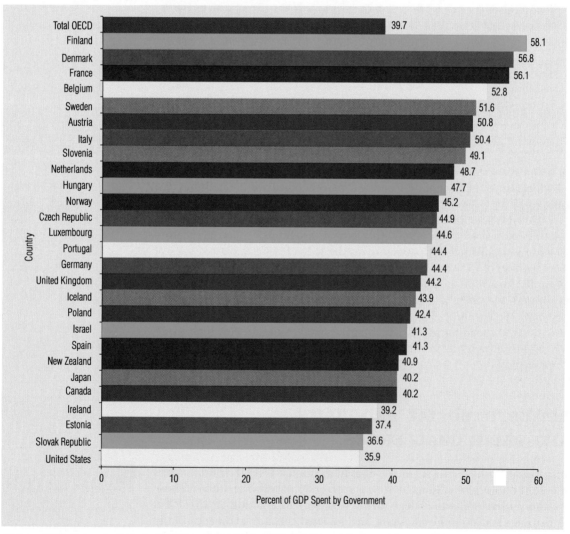

Country	Percent of GDP Spent by Government
Total OECD	39.7
Finland	58.1
Denmark	56.8
France	56.1
Belgium	52.8
Sweden	51.6
Austria	50.8
Italy	50.4
Slovenia	49.1
Netherlands	48.7
Hungary	47.7
Norway	45.2
Czech Republic	44.9
Luxembourg	44.6
Portugal	44.4
Germany	44.4
United Kingdom	44.2
Iceland	43.9
Poland	42.4
Israel	41.3
Spain	41.3
New Zealand	40.9
Japan	40.2
Canada	40.2
Ireland	39.2
Estonia	37.4
Slovak Republic	36.6
United States	35.9

Source: OECD Economic Outlook, November 2013, Annex Table 25, General Government Total Outlays. Data refer to general government outlays of central, state, and local government for 2015.

open, competitive, democratic, capitalist society like ours to alleviate need by providing social services?

Social welfare programs are of two general types. Programs of the first type, which include Social Security and Medicare, are called **social insurance programs**. Workers and their employers pay premiums in the form of payroll taxes so that the workers will be entitled to draw off of the programs when they become eligible. Programs of the second type, which include Medicaid, food stamps, and public housing assistance, are called **means-tested programs**. Such programs distribute money or other goods including food, housing, and medical care to those whose income falls below a certain level. Each of these programs is large, serving tens of millions of people; expensive, costing tens and even hundreds of billions of dollars each year; and under increasing pressure as the impending retirement of the baby boomers threatens to drive costs even higher.

social insurance programs
Social programs, such as Social Security and Medicare in which prior payments into the program establish eligibility to draw money out upon meeting program requirements.

means-tested programs
Social programs in which eligibility is established by low income and limited assets. Medicaid is a means-tested program.

Social Security

Social Security was enacted in 1935 as part of Franklin Roosevelt's "New Deal" response to the depression. Historically, the elderly, once beyond their working years and dependent on savings, family, or charity, frequently found themselves impoverished. FDR reasoned that a social insurance program, wherein workers and employers were required to pay into Social Security so that they would be eligible to draw benefits—to have a continuing income—after retirement would improve the security of the elderly.

Social Security is one of the most popular programs run by the federal government. However, Social Security faces difficulties that are easy to understand but not so easy to resolve. When Social Security began paying out monthly benefits in 1940, there were forty-two workers paying in for every retiree drawing out. By 1945, the ratio had fallen to twenty to one, by 1955 to nine to one, and the numbers have continued to fall. Basically, Americans are living longer and having fewer children. In 1955, there were 14 million Americans over age 65; today there are 43 million. Childbirth rates have dropped by half since 1955, from an average of 3.5 children per family to 1.70 children per family today. From 1975 to today, the proportion of workers to retirees hovered around three to one. It is dropping again and is expected to reach two to one by 2035. Fewer workers paying in and more retirees drawing out for longer has led to a heated debate over how to "save" Social Security.

In 2014, about 161 million workers paid into Social Security and 58 million retired and disabled persons were drawing out. Social Security is the main source of income for more than half of retired couples and nearly three-quarters of retired singles.[22] The average monthly benefit is about $1,328 for an individual and $2,100 for the average couple. The average disabled person draws about $1,165 a month. Social Security paid out a total of $853 billion in 2014.

Social Security has been modified or reformed several times, most recently in the mid-1980s, to keep revenues in line with expenditures. From the mid-1980s through 2009, Social Security ran budget surpluses totaling $2.5

trillion. Though these surpluses, rather than being saved, were spent to fund current operations of other government programs, they remain as assets on Social Security's books. Due to the recession of 2008–2009, Social Security ran a deficit in 2010 and forecasts suggest that it will have run through its accumulated paper surpluses by 2033.

The problems confronting Social Security, while large, are not overwhelming. Most reform proposals involve some combination of extending the retirement age, lowering benefits, raising taxes, and privatizing some or all of Social Security by allowing individuals, especially younger workers, to invest parts of their retirement contributions in private accounts. Democrats tend to call for increasing the proportion of income subject to payroll taxes, slowly walking up the retirement age, and adjusting the formula for cost-of-living increases private accounts. Republicans call for more thoroughgoing reform, sometimes including private accounts.

Opponents make three key arguments against private accounts. One, markets sometimes go down and investors lose their money. Two, private accounts undercut the universal nature of Social Security's promise. And three, allowing diversion of payroll taxes into private accounts will further weaken a system for which deficits already loom only a decade out. The stock market swoon of 2008–2009 chilled the discussion of private accounts.

Medicare and Medicaid[23]

Americans spend more on health care than any other people in the world. Health care costs consumed about 5 percent of GDP in 1960. In 2013, Americans spent over $9,255 per person or a total of $2.9 trillion on health care. That was 17.2 percent of GDP. Other wealthy nations spend about half that; Canada, France, and Britain, for example, spend less than 10 percent of their GDP on health care.[24]

Access to health care has traditionally been more limited in the United States than in most other wealthy nations. Canada and most European nations have long had some form of national health insurance, while the United States left citizens to find and pay for their own health insurance, whether through their employers or privately. As health care and insurance for it have become increasingly expensive, employers have dropped health coverage and employees have been unable to pay for it on their own. Thirty-five million Americans were without health insurance in 2013.[25]

For more than half a century, the mainstays of the federal government health care system were Medicare and Medicaid. Medicare and Medicaid were established in 1965 as major components of LBJ's "Great Society." Medicare, like Social Security, is a social insurance principle program funded by payroll taxes and open to all eligible retirees, irrespective of income or wealth. Medicare has dramatically improved access of the elderly to medical care, but it is increasingly expensive.

Medicare serves about 50 million beneficiaries at a cost of almost $551 billion annually. The ongoing retirement of 76 million baby boomers, which began in 2008, hangs over both Social Security and Medicare. Medicare, like Social Security, is running a surplus today, but it is moving quickly toward deficit. Medicare is expected to serve 65 million beneficiaries and to double in cost by 2021. Moreover, in late 2003 President Bush signed into law a new Medicare prescription drug benefit that took effect in 2006. This benefit, long demanded by seniors, will add significantly to the cost of Medicare in coming decades. Forty-one million seniors enrolled for the prescription drug benefit in 2009. The drug benefit alone is expected to cost $385 billion in the first five years and $1 trillion in the first decade.

Medicaid, on the other hand, is a means-tested program, a welfare program, administered jointly by the federal and state governments to cover the health care needs of the poor. When the economy went into decline in 2007, more people lost jobs, ran through their assets, and applied for Medicaid. Medicaid served about 68.5 million citizens in 2013 at a cost of more than $432 billion, $248 billion of which was federal funds. State governments, most of which are constitutionally forbidden to run deficits, have been especially hard-pressed. Tennessee dropped 300,000 from its Medicaid rolls in 2005 and Missouri dropped 90,000. Both the National Association of Governors and the National Conference of State Legislatures are actively working with Congress to limit costs without denying service to the most needy.[26]

President Obama made health care reform the top domestic priority of his first year in office. Congressional Democrats labored throughout 2009 and into 2010 to produce a comprehensive health reform bill, covering more than 30 million of the previously uninsured, providing subsidies to make the insurance affordable, and requiring insurance companies to cover everyone irrespective of pre-existing conditions. Democrats argued that the growth in health care costs could be moderated while coverage was being expanded by getting everyone in the system, improving health care delivery, and making strategic cuts to Medicare. Republicans argued that the Democratic program constituted an unnecessary government take-over of the American health care system. Democrats succeeded in passing health care reform, but many analysts remain unconvinced that it will both expand coverage and bring down costs. The new law proposes to expand Medicaid to cover 16 million more people and squeeze nearly half a trillion in costs out of Medicare. Cutting Medicare is particularly perilous for politicians because the elderly vote in large numbers and are tenacious defenders of their benefits.

The Federal Role in Education

Through most of American history, education was a state and local responsibility, and in many ways it remains so today. In

Associated Press

Many older Americans depend on Social Security and Medicare for retirement income and health care. Whether Democrat or Republican, they tend to oppose cuts in these programs.

the post-World War II period, the federal government provided the GI Bill to support the education of returning servicemen; in the 1950s the Eisenhower administration moved to buttress math and science education; and then in 1965 the Johnson administration enacted the Elementary and Secondary Education Act as part of its antipoverty, civil rights, and Great Society initiatives. These programs accounted for about 7 percent of total government spending on education in 2000.

As with health care, despite spending more on education than most advanced industrial nations, educational achievement compared with other wealthy nations has been mediocre. Piecemeal reforms and experiments have been attempted, and some states have improved education performance among their students. Hence, Texas Governor George W. Bush campaigned for president in 2000 on a platform of education reform. His "No Child Left Behind" program, passed in 2001 by large bipartisan majorities, required annual testing of students in grades 3 through 8, an end to social promotions, upgrading teacher skills, and new services and options for parents of students in failing schools.

Federal spending on elementary and secondary education nearly doubled between 2001 and 2006, before contracting in 2007 and 2008 (see Figure 15.2). Nonetheless, state and local governments continue to provide 90 percent of public funds for education, and they chafe under the strict "No Child Left Behind" guidelines and requirements. Critics point out that although federal funding has increased, Congress provided only about two-thirds of the funds authorized ($13 billion instead of $22.75 billion in 2006) for No Child Left

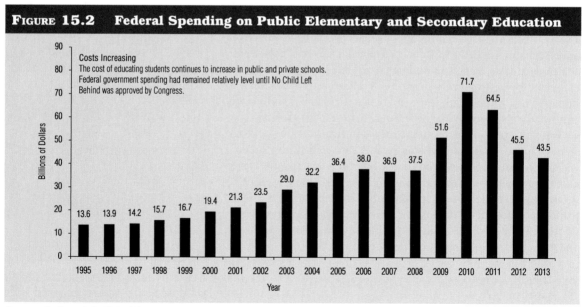

FIGURE 15.2   Federal Spending on Public Elementary and Secondary Education

Costs Increasing
The cost of educating students continues to increase in public and private schools. Federal government spending had remained relatively level until No Child Left Behind was approved by Congress.

Source: Budget of the United States Government, Fiscal Year 2014, Historical Tables (Washington, D.C.: U.S. Government Printing Office, 2014), Table 9.9.

Behind's critical Title 1 program to improve educational performance among poor students. President Obama has moved to reform No Child Left Behind and he included large, if only temporary, increases in federal funding of public schools in his 2009 stimulus program. Though stimulus funding is expected to fall in 2011 and cease thereafter, states are also competing for $4 billion in new "Race to the Top" funds intended to spur school improvement. While support for increased federal participation in education funding remains high, calls for less intrusive regulation and more local flexibility have been widespread.

The rising cost of federal retirement, health care, and education programs are made more worrisome by the general state of the nation's accounts. The collapse of the 1990s tech boom, the terrorist attacks of 9/11, the Bush tax cuts of 2001 and 2003, the wars in Afghanistan and Iraq, and the recession of late 2007 through 2009 have reduced the revenues and increased the expenses of the federal government. The budget surpluses of the late 1990s have become burgeoning deficits, and analysts worry that the national debt will be a burden on economic growth and the security of future generations. Unfortunately, discussions of fiscal responsibility and debt reduction, to which we turn next, always come down to hard decisions about what to cut.

THE DILEMMA OF DEFICITS AND DEBT

Unlike most state governments, the federal Constitution allows deficits and debt. The Constitution recognizes that the federal government will sometimes need to spend more money than it takes in during a year. Hence, Article I, section 8, of the Constitution authorizes the federal government both to "lay and collect Taxes" and to "borrow Money on the credit of the United States." A deficit occurs when government spends more money than it takes in during a year. The accumulation of annual deficits over the years is referred to as the **national debt.**

national debt The accumulation of annual deficits over the years is referred to as the national debt.

Not surprisingly, deficits and debt have been controversial topics from the country's earliest history. Alexander Hamilton and Thomas Jefferson clashed over the role and consequences of a national debt in the first Washington administration. Nonetheless, until well into the twentieth century, deficits were reasonably uncommon and generally associated with war. From 1800 through 1930, there were ninety years in which the federal budget was in surplus and only forty in which it was in deficit.[27] From 1931 through 1998, the federal budget was in surplus only eight times and was in deficit fully sixty times. After a brief flirtation with surpluses from 1998 through 2001, we are back into a pattern of persistent deficits (see Figure 15.3).

The annual deficits translated into a larger and larger national debt. In 1945, at the end of World War II, the national debt stood at $260 billion. It took thirty years, from 1945 to 1975, for it to double. It doubled again between 1975 and 1982 and then nearly quadrupled between 1982 and 1993.

President Clinton's election in 1992, followed by the election of a Republican Congress in 1994, motivated both to focus on budget deficits that seemed to be truly threatening. By 1994 both the annual deficits and the total debt

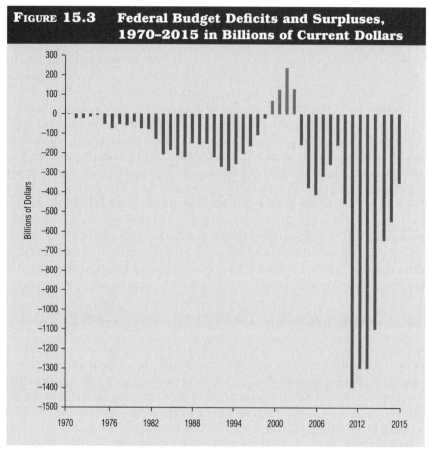

FIGURE 15.3   Federal Budget Deficits and Surpluses, 1970–2015 in Billions of Current Dollars

Source: Budget of the United States Government, Fiscal Year 2014, Historical Tables (Washington, D.C.: U.S. Government Printing Office, 2014), Table 1.3. Figures for 2014 and 2015 are official budget estimates.

as a proportion of GDP were trending sharply downward for the first time in decades. In 1997 there was a minuscule deficit, and 1998 saw the first budget surplus since 1969. In late 2000, as President Clinton prepared to leave office, OMB projected a $5.6 trillion surplus over the next decade and the possibility of paying off the national debt in a little more than a decade.

In a stunningly short period of time, a slowing economy, tax cuts, and the economic fallout from 9/11 turned large surpluses into larger deficits. The fiscal 2003 and 2004 deficits soared to $378 billion and $413 billion, respectively. Deficits fell to $318 billion in 2005, $248 billion in 2006, and $161 billion in 2007, before rebounding to $459 billion in 2008. The 2009 deficit was expected to be about $482 billion until the economic crisis that began in late 2008 drove it to 1.4 trillion dollars. The 2010 and 2011 deficits were a slightly smaller $1.3 trillion. It declined to $1.1 trillion in 2012 and is expected to be under $400 billion in 2015. However, the national debt now exceeds $16 trillion.

Getty Images

Young America's Foundation spokesperson Ashley Pratte spoke at the National Press Club in Washington, D.C., on the "Youth Misery Index." The Youth Misery Index adds together youth unemployment, average graduating student debt (in thousands), and national debt per capita (in thousands). Pratte said that at 98.6 the Youth Misery Index was as high as it had ever been.

During 2014 and 2015, both the Obama administration and the Yellen Fed will have to keep these critical issues surrounding deficits and debt in mind as they wean the economy from government fiscal stimulus. The Obama administration must, virtually all analysts agree, continue to bring down annual budget deficits, but not so fast that by withdrawing stimulus they tip the economy back into recession. Simultaneously, the Fed, which has kept interest rates near zero since late 2008, must draw down the money supply and raise interest rates before inflation picks up but not so soon that the recovery stalls.

These delicate economic policy moves will require close coordination between the Obama administration and Congress, who control fiscal policy, meaning taxing and spending, and the Fed, which controls money supply and interest rates. The executive and legislative branches of the federal government are the explicitly political branches of the government—and remember 2012 was an election year—while the Fed is an independent (meaning independent of the political branches) regulatory agency. Close coordination will be tricky, but the health and productivity of our economy—in which you will soon be looking for a job—is at stake.

Large budget deficits and the rapid increase of the total debt pose many problems. Let's look just briefly at one short-term, one medium-term, and one long-term problem. In the short term, deficits means that government is competing with the private sector for funds available to be borrowed, thereby threatening to push interest rates up. In the medium term, the proportion of each year's budget required for debt service—that is, to pay the interest on the national debt—will increase. And in the long term, a larger national debt means that this generation is leaving a more burdensome debt for the next generation. Today's economic policy decisions have consequences far into the future. Let's look more closely at those consequences now.

THE CONSEQUENCES OF ECONOMIC POLICYMAKING

Throughout this chapter we have seen that political decisions affect economic opportunity and performance. Government policies on taxes, spending, deficits, and debt affect the performance of the economy, how much wealth it creates, and how that wealth is distributed within the society and across generations. What goals should government try to achieve through its economic policymaking in regard to economic growth and wealth distribution?

Growth

Can the government, in fact, manage economic growth? That depends, of course, on what we mean by "manage economic growth." As we have seen in recent years, the government cannot simply pick a high growth rate and then use economic policy to achieve it without other complications arising. But government certainly can and does work through fiscal, monetary, and regulatory policies to affect the performance of the economy with an eye toward achieving a good, steady rate of economic growth.

What would knowledgeable economists and policymakers consider a "good, steady rate of economic growth"? History provides some interesting perspective on this question but little real guidance. The best information we have suggests that real GNP grew at an average annual rate of 4.5 percent for the century between 1830 and 1930. A 4.5 percent growth rate means a doubling of the size of the economy every sixteen years and (because population is growing at the same time) a doubling in GNP per capita (wealth per person) every forty-five years.[28]

However, the period from 1830 to 1930 may not be a good guide to our expectations for current growth rates. During this period we were a developing economy, much as Asia has been for the last fifty years, and developing economies can experience high growth because they can import and apply both technology and capital from societies with more advanced economies. By 1930, the United States was the most advanced industrial economy in the world, twice the size of the British and German economies, producing nearly 40 percent of the world's goods and services. The 1930s were the years of the Great Depression. The U.S. economy shrank by 30 percent between and 1929 and 1933 and did not regain its 1929 size until 1939.

War preparation beginning in 1939 and actual war through the first half of the 1940s spurred the U.S. economy rapidly forward. Average annual growth rates during the 1950s and 1960s, when the U.S. economy produced literally half of the goods and services produced in the world, remained near 4 percent.

However, as England, France, Germany, and Japan recovered from the devastation of World War II and began to compete with U.S. firms, growth rates in the United States declined to about 3 percent in the 1970s, 2.5 percent in the 1980s, and 2 percent in the early 1990s, before rebounding to 2.7 percent between 1995 and 2003.[29] The economy grew at just 1.7 percent from 2004 through 2007. GDP growth slipped to .4 percent in 2008 and to –2.4 in 2009, before rebounding to 1.3 percent between 2010 and 2013.

Slowing growth and high inflation in the 1970s convinced most economists that economic growth in an advanced industrial economy like ours cannot exceed about 2.5 percent without stressing the labor markets and igniting inflation. Nonetheless, as recently as the late 1990s annual growth rates of 3.5 to 4.5 percent were achieved, and inflation did not increase. Figure 15.4 shows that the economic growth rates are incredibly important. It presents the real growth of the U.S. economy from 1980 to 2012 and then projects average real growth rates of 2.5, 3.5, and 4.5 percent over the next twenty years, 2013 to 2030.[30] If annual GDP growth averaged 4.5 percent over the next twenty years, the U.S. economy would be more than 50 percent larger than if growth averaged only 2.5 percent per year.

Clearly, growth rates make a tremendous difference in the total amount of wealth that will be created by the American economy in the future. But, if total wealth increases and wages do not, or rise only slowly, who gets the lion's share of the new wealth? Does it matter that top U.S. executives made 270 times the average salary ($40,500) of U.S. workers?[31]

Fairness

If government policy affects the performance of the economy, and we know that it does, then it seems entirely reasonable to inquire into the fairness of

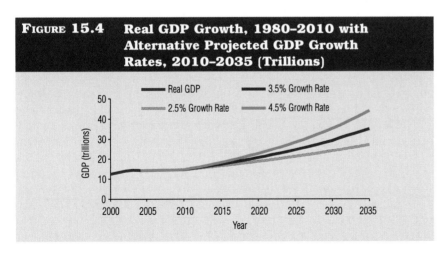

FIGURE 15.4   Real GDP Growth, 1980–2010 with Alternative Projected GDP Growth Rates, 2010–2035 (Trillions)

Source: *Budget of the United States Government, Fiscal Year 2014*, Historical Tables (Washington, D.C.: U.S. Government Printing Office, 2014), Table 10.1. Projections for 2013 through 2035 calculated by the author.

those effects. As we have seen throughout this chapter, there are intense disputes about what economic results government policy should be designed to achieve and how just or fair various outcomes would be.[32] Naturally we cannot resolve these disputes, but we can highlight two obvious examples of results produced by the U.S. economy over which discussions of fairness can, do, and should occur.

First, we will look at the distribution by class of the wealth created by the U.S. economy. What proportion of the wealth created by the U.S. economy annually goes to the more or less wealthy, and what proportion goes to the more or less poor? Second, we will ask how annual income and family wealth vary by race and ethnicity.

The federal government makes many decisions, including most prominently those on patterns of taxing and spending, that affect the distribution of income and wealth holding within the American society. What has been the effect of the taxing and spending policies of the federal government on the distribution of income by class in the United States during the post-World War II period? Look at Figure 15.5. Although the distribution of income by social class clearly does respond to broad shifts in national policy—note the steady rise in the share of income enjoyed by the top 20 percent over the past two decades—it is also clear that there is a broad stability in these numbers. The second wealthiest 20 percent has enjoyed a very steady 23 percent of income, whereas the

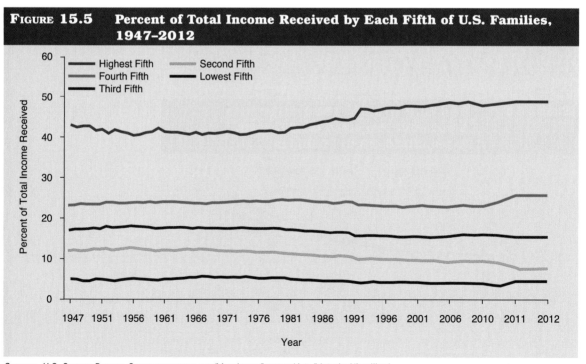

FIGURE 15.5   Percent of Total Income Received by Each Fifth of U.S. Families, 1947–2012

Source: U.S. Census Bureau. See www.census.gov/hhes/www/income/data/historical/families/

third and fourth quintiles (roughly the lower middle class and working poor) have seen their shares slowly deteriorate to 15 and 10 percent, respectively. The bottom 20 percent has over this same time period received only about 5 percent of total income. The Great Society programs pushed the bottom 20 percent's income up toward 6 percent in the late 1960s and 1970s, though since the 1980s it has fallen steadily, dipping under 4 percent in 2009.

Professor Emmanuel Saez, a Berkeley economist and a leading expert on the distribution of income through society, noted that, "If the economy is growing but only a few are enjoying the benefits, it goes to our sense of fairness. It can have important political consequences."[33] On the other hand, we all know that ours is a competitive, capitalist economy in which some do much better than others. Should we be concerned about the data in Figure 15.5, or do they seem natural and appropriate to a free market economy?

Perhaps even more striking is the relative stability of the distribution of income by race and ethnicity in the United States during the post-World War II period (see Figure 15.6). Although the categories used to describe nonwhites change over time, we can still get a pretty clear picture of the distribution of income by race and ethnicity over the past half century. Black and Hispanic income ran at about 55 percent of white income through the early 1960s, jumped to about 60 percent in the mid-1960s, and has remained in a very tight range around 60 percent ever since.[34]

Interestingly, Hispanic income ran slightly ahead of black income from the time such reports began to be kept in the early 1970s until the late 1980s.

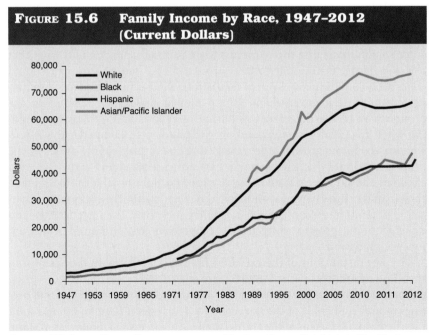

FIGURE 15.6   Family Income by Race, 1947–2012 (Current Dollars)

Source: U.S. Census Bureau. See www.census.gov/hhes/www/income/data/historical/families/

Immigration patterns led to a plateau in Hispanic income in the mid-1990s and the two were virtually identical until Hispanics pulled slightly ahead in 2005. Family income for Asians and Pacific Islanders has exceeded the average income of white families since such records began to be kept, in the mid-1980s. Ominously, median household income in the U.S. fell over the past decade after accounting for inflation; it was $67,643 in 2000 and $62,241 in 2010.[35]

Chapter Summary

Governments shape the structure and performance of the economy by the decisions they make on taxing, spending, deficits, and debt. During the first century of the nation's independent political history, the national government dealt principally with conducting foreign policy, providing national defense, distributing the western lands, and delivering the mail. The modest revenues required to fund the national government came almost exclusively from tariff fees and excise taxes on liquor and tobacco.

Economic regulation expanded late in the nineteenth century when the need to regulate the new corporate monopolies in such key economic activities as banking, railroads, steel, and oil became evident. Further expansion occurred during the 1930s as Franklin Roosevelt and the Democratic Congress sought to pull the economy out of the most severe depression in the nation's history. Government took responsibility for creating jobs, restarting the economy, and developing a social safety net centered on Social Security and unemployment compensation. The Employment Act of 1946 confirmed the national government's responsibility for managing the economy.

Although most observers agree that the national government should have some role in managing the economy, there is disagreement about what that role should be. Traditional conservatives contend that government should concentrate on low taxes, limited regulation, and balanced budgets. Keynesians contend that government should manage aggregate demand in the economy by increasing spending during recessions and decreasing spending when the economy is expanding. Monetarists contend that the key to smooth economic growth is to ensure that the money supply grows at the same general rate that the economy expands. Supply-siders argue that government should concentrate on low taxes and light regulation to improve the business climate even if short-term deficits result. New economy advocates contend that responsible fiscal policy promotes low interest rates and rapid economic growth while global competition and enhanced productivity check inflation.

Five key institutions of the executive branch, together with the taxing and spending committees in the Congress, are most directly responsible for setting national economic policy. The Treasury Department collects revenue and borrows money on behalf of the government. The Federal Reserve Board monitors the banking system of the United States and affects the money supply and interest rates through its reserve requirements and discount rate decisions.

The OMB assists in preparation of the president's budget, whereas the Council of Economic Advisers provides general advice on the economic outlook and assists in preparing the president's annual economic message to Congress. The National Economic Council coordinates national economic policy much like the National Security Council coordinates foreign policy.

During the nineteenth century and the first half of the twentieth century, nearly half of federal revenues went to national defense. After 1960 defense spending as a proportion of total spending began to decline, and spending on social programs began to rise. Today, spending on social programs exceeds 70 percent of the budget, and defense spending had fallen below 20 percent. Spiraling costs in mandatory domestic social programs, especially Social Security and Medicare, threaten to drive already large deficits to unsustainable levels.

Finally, we explored the implications of the government's role in managing the economy for the amount of wealth produced by the economy, how that wealth is distributed within the economy, and what those patterns mean for future generations. Government affects the economy, but politics affects how it does so.

Key Terms

Budget and Accounting Act of 1921   485

corporation   478

deficit   481

discount rate   485

fiscal policy   481

flat tax   491

Keynesianism   482

means-tested programs   497

monetarists   483

monetary policy   481

monopoly   478

national debt   501

New Deal   480

progressive tax   491

reconciliation   489

regressive tax   491

regulatory policy   481

reserve requirements   485

social insurance programs   497

supply-side economics   482

surplus   481

traditional conservatives   481

Suggested Readings

Bartlett, Bruce. *The Benefit and the Burden: Tax Reform—Why We Need It and What It Will Take.* New York: Simon & Schuster, 2012. Bartlett is a supply-sider who worked in the Reagan White House. He proposes to lower rates and cancel exemptions on the way to broader tax reform.

Blumenthal, David and James Morone. *The Heart of Power: Health and Politics in the Oval Office.* Berkeley, CA: University of California Press, 2009. History of U.S. health care politics and reform from FDR through George W. Bush.

Eisner, Mark Allen. *The American Political Economy: Institutional Evolution of Market and State.* New York: Routledge, 2011. Eisner traces and explains the evolution of federal and state policymaking on economic issues.

Kingdon, John W. "American Public Policy in Comparative Perspective," 1999. Kingdon asks why the U.S. provides less than other advanced nations in domestic policy and more than others in areas like defense and criminal justice.

Mettler, Suzanne. *The Submerged State: How Invisible Government Policies Undermine American Democracy.* Chicago: University of Chicago Press, 2011. Mettler highlights the fact that Americans deride government while approving many key government programs like Social Security.

Noah, Timothy. *The Great Divergence: America's Growing Inequality Crisis and What We Can Do About It.* New York: Bloomsbury Press, 2012. Noah explores the causes and consequences of growing inequality in the U.S.

Wessel, David. *In Fed We Trust: Ben Bernanke's War on the Great Panic.* New York: Crown Publishing Group, 2009. An analysis of how the leading figures at the Fed, Treasury, and regulatory agencies battled the Great Recession of 2008–2009.

Web Resources

For practice quizzes, key term flashcards, videos, links, and other study tools, visit the *American Government* website: www.routledge.com/cw/jillson

1. **www.federalreserve.gov**
   The Federal Reserve System is responsible for monetary policy in the United States. This agency is an independent executive agency and as such is insulated from many of the political pressures found at other agencies.

2. **www.whitehouse.gov/omb/index.html**
   This page links to the Office of Management and Budget, which provides information on proposed budgets and the budget process, as well as a complete copy of the federal budget.

3. **www.ustreas.gov**
   The U.S. Department of Treasury is a large federal agency with economic responsibilities. The Treasury is also responsible for maintaining the federal government accounts.

4. **www.cbo.gov**
   The Congressional Budget Office boasts professional nonpartisan analyses for economic and budget decisions. This site gives further insight into the budget process.

5. **www.brook.edu**
   The Brookings Institution offers scholarly analyses of public policy. This is a great resource for studies concerning the government and economy.

Chapter 16

AMERICA'S PLACE IN A DANGEROUS WORLD

"I have not undertaken to see differently than others, but to look further, and while they are busied for the morrow only, I have turned my thoughts to the whole future."

ALEXIS DE TOCQUEVILLE,
Democracy in America, 1835

The
Constitution
TODAY

CAN THE COMMANDER IN CHIEF ORDER TORTURE?

Article II, sections 1,2,3 (in part): "The executive power shall be vested in the President of the United States of America. . . . The President shall be commander in chief of the Army and Navy of the United States, and . . . he shall take care that the laws be faithfully executed."

On the morning of January 22, 2009, less than 48 hours after being sworn in as president, Barack Obama issued an executive order banning torture by members of the CIA and other government agencies. Obama's executive order, entitled "Ensuring Lawful Interrogations," rescinded President Bush's executive order 13440, interpreting the Geneva Conventions on the conduct of war as permitting enhanced interrogation techniques that many later concluded were torture. Stunningly, President Obama's executive order prohibited reliance on any legal advice on what constitutes torture issued by the Bush administration between September 11, 2001 (9/11) and the day they left office on January 20, 2009. What was that all about?

In the wake of 9/11, President George W. Bush, Vice President Cheney, and their national security team, including Secretaries Rumsfeld and Powell, CIA Director Tenet, and National Security Council Director Condoleezza Rice, decided to defend the nation by taking it to the enemy. President Bush and his team sought advice on how aggressively they might prosecute the "war on terror," especially in regard to interrogating captured "enemy combatants." Vice President Cheney was already committed to the unitary executive theory of independent presidential authority, especially in wartime. A number of White House and executive branch lawyers, led by Jay Bybee and John Yoo, concluded that presidents in wartime had unlimited and unchecked power to act in defense of the nation.

The lawyers argued that the president as commander in chief has complete authority to conduct war including the interrogation of captured enemy combatants. Congress and the courts, they argued, have no more authority in planning and conducting interrogations in wartime than they do in planning battlefield operations. Captured combatants may know something that if extracted immediately could save lives. This is the ticking time bomb scenario that asks—if you had a terrorist in custody who knew where a ticking time bomb was that might kill thousands, or millions, wouldn't it be right to torture him? Would it?

Throughout 2004 and 2005, the Bush administration assured everyone that the memos were simply advisory and had never driven actual policy. President Bush said many times that "the United States does not torture," but evidence accumulated that that was only true if you accepted the administration's new definition of torture. A 2002 memo authored by Jay Bybee declared that torture applied only to suffering "equivalent in intensity to the pain accompanying serious physical injury, such as organ failure, impairment of bodily function, or even death." Hence, on this logic, waterboarding, which is simulated drowning, is not torture despite the fact that the U.S. had considered it torture for more than a century.

As the sense of emergency surrounding 9/11 began to fade from some memories, Congress and the courts began to reassert their roles in checking executive power. Senator John McCain, a POW tortured during the Vietnam War, offered legislation outlawing torture. The Bush administration lobbied against McCain's legislation, arguing that the CIA needed flexibility. The legislation eventually passed and President Bush, with McCain present, signed the bill on December 30, 2005. On January 4, 2006, the Bush administration issued a "signing statement," intended to give the administration's sense of the bill, saying "The executive branch shall construe [the law] in a manner consistent with the constitutional authority of the President . . . as Commander in Chief." Opponents of torture were outraged because the Bush administration had spent years arguing that presidential power in wartime was unchecked.

Hence, President Obama's executive order setting aside all Bush administration interrogation policies was welcomed by many. But before long, doubt began to creep in. President Obama's January 22, 2009, executive order prohibited torture of all persons captured in "armed conflicts" to which the U.S. was a party. How about terrorism operations short of armed conflict? One assumed that the Obama administration meant the torture ban to apply there too. On the other hand, no president, should an emergency like 9/11 arise again, wants to look into his commander in chief toolbox and find empty compartments.

WHAT DO YOU THINK?

- Is torture ever justified? Never justified?
- What about the ticking time bomb scenario?

Focus Questions: from reading to thinking

Q1 Is it fair to say that the United States has been an expansionist power throughout its history?

Q2 What were our post-World War II political, economic, and military strategies in relation to western Europe, the Soviet Union, and Japan?

Q3 How does the United States wield its overwhelming economic and military power in the world today?

Q4 What responsibilities, if any, do the wealthy nations of the world have to the poorer nations?

Q5 In light of our cultural, economic, and military resources, what place should the United States seek to create for itself in the world of the twenty-first century?

AMERICA IN THE WORLD

Few would deny that the global military and economic leadership of the United States has been shaken in recent years. Yet, fewer still would argue that another nation or group of nations has stepped, or even could step, into America's leadership role. If changes in U.S. attitude and policy are necessary, what should they be?

For the United States to maintain its global leadership, U.S. leaders and citizens will have to better understand the challenges and opportunities that the future will lay before them. Americans will need to understand in a deep and fundamental way that the sources of both security and insecurity have changed.

Traditionally, a nation's security derived from the size of its territory, population, and economy. In the eighteenth century, these translated directly into the ability to raise and supply armies composed mostly of infantry troops. In the nineteenth and early twentieth centuries, these natural and physical resources remained important if they were tied together by telegraph and railway networks that allowed rapid mobilization and movement of troops and equipment. Once the post–World War II confrontation of superpowers concluded in America's favor, it appeared that an era of democratic peace might be at hand. But 9/11 taught that failed states and global terrorism are the modern faces of insecurity.

When the second plane went into the second tower on the morning of September 11, 2001 and word came that the Pentagon had also been struck, much changed about the way Americans thought about the world and their place in it. The blow had not been delivered by another great power, but by a stateless renegade, Osama bin Laden, and his diffuse band of al-Qaeda terrorists. A universal determination to strike back slowly matured into a broad debate, in academe, government, and the public, about the goals of American foreign policy and the best means to achieve them.

How should the United States act and what should the nation seek to achieve in the twenty-first-century world? What strengths, what resources or assets, does the United States have to draw on as it seeks to shape the course of world affairs? Scholars have identified two broad ways to think about how the United States (or any nation) should pursue its interests in the world. **Realists** contend that the United States should focus its attention and resources on protecting and expanding its national security and prosperity while other nations do the same. **Idealists** contend that the United States should act to promote its ideals of freedom, democracy, and opportunity in the world because we are most secure when others are safe, free, and prosperous. The Obama administration, led by the president, of course, Vice President Biden, Secretary Kerry at the State Department, and Secretary Panetta at Defense, like to think of themselves as realists with a strong idealistic streak. A third group, **neoconservatives**, prominent in the Bush administration, contend that American power should be used to promote American ideals and interests.

Realists, idealists, and neoconservatives agree that America has a certain set of assets to draw upon in pursuing its global interests, but they disagree on how those assets should be used. Realists and neoconservatives depend on America's **hard power** assets, especially military and economic powers, that allow the nation to insist on its preferences. Idealists agree that hard power,

---

Struggling Toward Democracy

The great nineteenth-century Prussian military strategist Karl von Clausewitz famously said: "War is the continuation of politics by other means."

What do you think?

- Even if true in some sense, can a modern democracy act on this insight?
- If not, does this give Putin and advantage over Obama?

---

realists Realists contend that the United States should focus its attention and resources on protecting and expanding its own security and prosperity.

idealists Idealists contend that nation-states should act to promote the ideals of freedom, democracy, and opportunity in the world.

neoconservatives Neoconservatives argue that military and economic power should be used to promote American ideals and interests.

hard power Assets, especially military and economic power, that allow a nation to insist on its preferences.

GEOFF GREEN / Landov

Debris rained down as the second plane went into the second of the Twin Towers on the morning of September 11, 2001. America's sense of the kinds of dangers that exist in the world changed on this day.

assets are important, but insist that **soft power** assets, especially attractive values, culture, and prosperity, as well as a willingness to act generously through supporting international organizations and awarding foreign aid, can make others want to follow and emulate the United States. Realists, idealists, and neoconservatives agree on the importance of hard and soft power, but they emphasize and weight them differently.[1]

In this final chapter, we describe the United States on the world stage. First, we look at the slow gathering of American power from colonial times to World War II. During this period, the United States went from being an inconsequential series of colonial outposts to an economic powerhouse, but not yet a world power. Second, we look at the post-World War II world and the Cold War confrontation that defined it. The United States emerged from World War II as the dominant economic power in the world and the leader of a political and military coalition that confronted the Soviet Union and its allies around the world. Finally, we look at America's place in the contemporary world. Following the collapse of the Soviet empire in the late 1980s, the United States has been the world's only superpower, but problems, ranging from AIDS to al-Qaeda, abound.

soft power Assets, such as attractive values, culture, and prosperity, that encourage others to emulate and cooperate with a nation.

THE UNITED STATES IN THE OLD WORLD ORDER

As the seventeenth century opened, the major powers of Europe—including England, France, Spain, Portugal, and the Netherlands—were in a constant state of economic and military competition that often led to war. Each European power scrambled to establish worldwide networks of colonies to ensure that the goods and raw materials that they might need could be secured on advantageous terms from their colonies. Colonies also provided a market for the finished products of the controlling European power. Colonies, including Britain's colonies in North America, struggled to take root in a dangerous world of kings and empires fighting for global dominance.

Early Experiences and Precedents

Britain's colonies in North America were prizes over which the great powers fought from the first landing of the Jamestown colonists in 1607 to American independence in 1776. For most of that time, the colonies were too weak to have independent weight in the European balance of power. Even as late as 1765 the British and French empires fought a world war in which India, Canada, the sugar islands of the Caribbean, and the colonies from Maine to Georgia hung in the balance. Britain's victory netted it India and Canada and secured, for a time, its North American colonies.

European politics also played a major role in the American Revolution. American independence might not have been achieved without loans from Europe and the timely aid of a French fleet in helping General Washington defeat British General Cornwallis at Yorktown to effectively end the war. However, after independence was achieved, it became increasingly clear that no European nation would favor American interests when its own were in play.

Independence and Its Dangers. Independence complicated America's position in the world. England remained hostile while nations such as France and Spain that provided assistance during the fight for independence made clear that they had interests of their own in North America.[2] Just as America seemed to find solid ground with the adoption of the federal Constitution, war erupted in Europe. The French Revolution began in 1789 as an effort to throw off monarchy in favor of a moderate republic. As political reform in France turned into social revolution, the conservative monarchies in Europe led by Britain counterattacked and all of Europe was soon at war. President Washington declared American neutrality, worked tirelessly to keep the new nation out of war, and used his farewell address to warn his fellow citizens against entanglement in the diplomatic and military affairs of Europe. This injunction remained at the core of American foreign policy for more than a century.

Sometimes, though, it was possible to benefit from the wars in Europe. The most remarkable instance of such benefit was President Jefferson's purchase of the Louisiana Territory from Napoleon in 1803. With a resumption

YORKTOWN—THE ENGAGEMENT BETWEEN THE FRENCH AND ENGLISH FLEETS OFF CAPE HENRY, SEPTEMBER 5, 1781.

Near the end of the Revolutionary War, as Washington's army maneuvered to trap British General Cornwallis' army at Yorktown, a French fleet held a British fleet at bay in the Battle of the Capes.

of war in Europe looming, Napoleon agreed to sell the territory between the Mississippi River and the Rocky Mountains, including the port at New Orleans, to the United States for $15 million. This purchase of 828,000 square miles of territory effectively doubled the size of the United States.

Generally, France and England both sought to forbid any U.S. activity that might benefit their opponents. Eventually, ongoing British violations of American commercial rights provoked President Madison to request, on June 1, 1812, that Congress issue a declaration of war against Britain. Although Britain had its main force committed to the wars in Europe, it generally managed to best the United States in Canada and on the Great Lakes. Napoleon's defeat in April 1814 allowed the British to concentrate on the Americans. In June, 4,000 seasoned British troops sailed for America. In August this force entered the Chesapeake, routed ill-equipped American militia near Bladensberg, Maryland, and burned the new American capital at Washington.

Meanwhile, American and British diplomats in Europe had been attempting to negotiate an end to hostilities. By October they agreed to terms and the Treaty of Ghent was signed on December 24, 1814. Fully two weeks after the war officially ended, but before word reached the United States, General Andrew Jackson won the greatest land victory of the war at New Orleans. This victory provided a powerful boost to American spirits, still smarting from the burning of the capital, and set General Jackson on the road to the presidency. The treaty finally reached New York on February 11, 1815, and was approved in the U.S. Senate four days later.

Monroe Doctrine.   The great powers of Europe came together at the Congress of Vienna in 1815 not only to hammer out a post-Napoleonic European order, but also to establish a "Concert of Europe" that would maintain a "balance of power" in Europe. The fledgling United States played no part in the calculations of the great powers in regard to Europe. Nonetheless, the issue of the role of European nations in the Americas arose when a series of revolts in Spain's and Portugal's Latin American colonies led to the establishment of several independent republics.

Even as Europe's grip on Latin America began to slip, American statesmen recognized their inability to shape events. John Quincy Adams, son of a president, future president, and one of the leading American diplomats of the nineteenth century, rose in the House on July 4, 1821, to declare that America "goes not abroad, in search of monsters [kings and emperors] to destroy. She is the well-wisher to the freedom and independence of all. She is the champion and vindicator only of her own." The United States formally recognized the independence of Colombia and Mexico in 1822, Chile and Argentina in 1823, Brazil and the Federation of Central American States in 1824, and Peru in 1826, but did nothing to assist in the birth of these new republics.

A bolder statement of the U.S. position on European involvement in the Americas came from President James Monroe in an address to the Congress on December 2, 1823. The **Monroe Doctrine** declared that although the remaining European colonies in the Americas would not be disturbed, further efforts at colonization would be viewed as hostile to U.S. interests in the region. Monroe knew that the British Navy would defend open access to the newly independent Central and South American markets. Hence, the cost of enforcing the Monroe Doctrine would be borne by the British Admiralty, not the much weaker American Navy.[3] Still, the Monroe Doctrine announced America's role as the region's dominant power, even if it could not yet defend that role against great powers from outside the region.

Manifest Destiny.   As westward migration filled the Ohio and Mississippi River valleys from the Canadian border to the Gulf of Mexico, American authorities moved to make good their claims to regional dominance. Attention turned increasingly to Texas and then to the Pacific coast. **Manifest destiny** was the claim that the United States had the right and the duty to secure the continent on behalf of democracy and free enterprise.

Texas declared its independence from Mexico on March 2, 1836. President Jackson recognized Texas as a free republic in March 1837, but it was not until 1845 that Texas was admitted to the Union and President Polk sent troops to secure disputed territory along the Rio Grande. The ensuing war with Mexico resulted not only in the acquisition of Texas but also in the conquest of what is now the southwestern United States and California. Almost simultaneously, Polk negotiated an end to the joint administration of the Oregon Territory by the United States and Britain, establishing American sovereignty. The acquisitions of Texas and all of the territory west of the Rocky Mountains to the Pacific by 1848 filled out the United States to its current continental boundaries.

Monroe Doctrine U.S. policy announced by President James Monroe in 1823 stating that attempts by European powers to establish new colonies anywhere in the Americas would be considered unfriendly to U.S. interests in the area.

Q1 Is it fair to say that the United States has been an expansionist power throughout its history?

manifest destiny Americans in the latter half of the nineteenth century commonly held the view that it was the "manifest destiny" of the United States to expand across the continent from the Atlantic to the Pacific.

Northern victory in the Civil War guaranteed that the country's economic development would proceed on the basis of free labor and competitive capitalism. Within a decade of the end of the Civil War, only a single century after independence, a national marketplace was coming into existence as both the telegraph and the railroads connected the Atlantic coast to the Pacific coast. Over the next two decades, an industrial boom carried the United States to a position of economic equality with and then dominance over the great powers of Europe. For many Americans this new-found strength was exhilarating. How exactly to employ it in the world was the subject of debate.

The Open Door Policy.   As the nineteenth century drew to a close, industry displaced agriculture as the most productive sector of the American economy. Soon American industry outgrew its domestic markets and looked for commercial opportunities abroad. Where these were not initially available, American policy was to convince local political authorities that they should be and, where diplomacy was insufficient, to install a new government. Between 1885 and 1900 military force was used to secure American economic interests in Panama, Chile, Peru, Hawaii, Samoa, Cuba, and the Philippines.

However, it was the conflict between the United States and Britain in China in 1899 and 1900 that brought forth the full articulation of America's **Open Door Policy.** China was very weak and subject to extensive foreign economic and military intervention. As American power grew, the United States became an increasingly staunch advocate of free trade while Britain sought to hold her advantages. Britain favored clear "spheres of influence" for the great powers, while U.S. policy called for equal treatment of American commerce throughout China. Commercial access was the goal of the U.S. policy throughout the developing world as the nineteenth century gave way to the twentieth.

Many assumed that participation in World War I signaled the emergence of the United States as a military and political equal of the great powers of Europe. President Woodrow Wilson hoped that the United States would step out of its political isolation in North America and participate in building the postwar world around the ideas of democratic politics and market economics. Despite President Wilson's leading role in creating postwar international institutions, particularly the League of Nations, the Senate and the American people declined the leadership role that he envisioned for them. America had business to conduct—surely Europe could set its house in order. It could not. Within fifteen years, Hitler came to power in Germany and war again threatened.

Open Door Policy U.S. policy at the end of the nineteenth century and beginning of the twentieth stating that China should remain open to free trade rather than be under the exclusive control of one or more colonial powers.

Q2   What were our post-World War II political, economic, and military strategies in relation to western Europe, the Soviet Union, and Japan?

World War II and World Power Status

At the end of World War II most of the advanced industrial nations of the world, both our allies like Britain, France, and the Soviet Union, and our enemies like Italy, Germany, and Japan, lay in ruins. The United States was the world's leading power. Militarily, the United States had unveiled the awesome power of the atomic bomb at Hiroshima and Nagasaki. Economically, the United States accounted for fully half of the industrial production of the world. What kind of world did the United States seek to build after World War II, and what kind of world did we actually get?

At home, U.S. leaders reorganized the national defense and security bureaucracies to play a broader global role. In 1947, Congress passed the National Security Act which created the Department of Defense (DOD), the National Security Council (NSC), the Central Intelligence Agency (CIA), and the Joint Chiefs of Staff (JCS). The DOD pulled together the old War and Navy Departments, with the newly created Department of the Air Force, under the Secretary of Defense. The Joint Chiefs report to the Secretary of Defense. The CIA replaced the wartime Office of Strategic Services and a number of smaller intelligence offices. Finally, the NSC began as a small White House office charged to coordinate for the president foreign policy materials from around the government. In 1953, President Eisenhower named an Assistant for National Security Affairs, often called the National Security Adviser, to head the NSC. Over the decades, the NSC has grown in importance and influence.

Internationally, the first instinct of U.S. policymakers was to recapture Woodrow Wilson's dream of a world made safe for democracy by collective security and widespread prosperity. But even before the war was over, Soviet communism challenged the U.S. vision of the postwar world. American and allied policymakers responded by building a set of international institutions that both embodied democratic and free market principles and guaranteed the United States a leadership position within them.

"Containment" of the Soviet Menace.   As the postwar chill between the western democracies and the Soviet Union became an increasingly **Cold War,** U.S. strategists looked for ways to strengthen potential friends and weaken potential enemies. This **bipolar** vision spawned the Marshall Plan (1947) and the North Atlantic Treaty Organization (1949). Much of the political and intellectual vision behind America's evolving postwar strategy came from George Kennan. In a 1947 article in *Foreign Affairs,* Kennan wrote that "the main element of any United States policy toward the Soviet Union must be that of a long-term patient but firm and vigilant **containment** of Russian expansive tendencies." Secretary of State George C. Marshall laid out the new containment policy in a speech delivered at Harvard University on June 5, 1947, and President Harry Truman followed up with a broader statement that came to be known as the **Truman Doctrine.** President Truman declared it to be "the policy of the United States to support free peoples who are resisting attempted subjugation by armed minorities or by outside pressures."[4] American policymakers believed that denying communism the opportunity to grow and expand would eventually lead to its decay and collapse.

U.S. policy in Europe was to reestablish political and economic stability so that the Europeans could reassume responsibility for their own security. Between 1947 and 1953, the United States provided to the nations of Europe through its European Recovery Program, popularly known as the **Marshall Plan,** a total of more than $15 billion. Each recipient nation had to sign an agreement with the United States "promising to balance its budget, free prices, . . . halt inflation, stabilize its exchange rate and devise a plan for removing

Cold War The period of continuous hostility short of actual warfare that existed between the United States and the Soviet Union from the end of World War II through the mid-1980s.

bipolar An international system organized around two dominant powers.

containment U.S. policy developed by Marshall, Kennan, and Truman after World War II to contain Soviet power by strengthening U.S. allies on the periphery of the Soviet empire.

Truman Doctrine Post-World War II policy of supporting noncommunist forces around the world as they struggled against communist pressure from domestic or foreign sources.

Marshall Plan Part of the containment strategy, the Marshall Plan provided $15 billion in economic aid to help in rebuilding Europe between 1947 and 1953.

most trade controls."⁵ U.S. policy was designed to ensure that European economies were rebuilt along open, stable, capitalist, free trade lines. The United States wanted a strong and wealthy Europe to help balance Soviet power and to provide a market for U.S. goods.

Cold War Security: NATO, the Warsaw Pact, and Deterrence. U.S. policymakers also negotiated and signed an array of multilateral defense pacts with more than four dozen nations between 1947 and 1960. These included the Inter-American Treaty of Reciprocal Assistance (Rio Pact, 1947), the North Atlantic Treaty Organization (NATO, 1949), the Australia, New Zealand, United States Pact (ANZUS, 1951), the Southeast Asia Treaty Organization (SEATO, 1955), and the Central Treaty Organization (CENTO, 1959). This alliance network was designed to encircle and contain the Soviet empire. Bilateral relationships such as those with Israel and Saudi Arabia were formed to give the United States additional leverage in the world's most sensitive regions.

Central to the United States' post-World War II alliance structure was the **North Atlantic Treaty Organization (NATO)**. NATO was formed in 1949 to protect against Soviet aggression in western Europe. Originally composed of twelve nations (Canada, United States, Britain, France, Italy, Portugal, Belgium, Luxembourg, Netherlands, Denmark, Norway, Iceland), it added Greece and Turkey in 1951, West Germany in 1954, and Spain in 1982. The Soviets responded by forming an alliance of their own, the Warsaw Pact, composed of the communist states of eastern Europe. Each side claimed to be pursuing a policy of **deterrence**. The idea was that each side would deter the other's aggression by building up such a huge arsenal of nuclear and conventional weapons that conflict would be too dangerous for either to permit.

The collapse of the Soviet Union and the end of the Cold War left NATO in an unfamiliar position. NATO responded in two ways. First, the alliance sought to integrate former members of the Warsaw Pact into NATO while reassuring Russia that the expanded alliance was not directed against her. Former Warsaw Pact nations sought NATO membership both to insure themselves against future Russian domination and to demonstrate political commitment to the West. In 1999, the Czech Republic, Poland, and Hungary formally entered NATO, in 2004, Romania, Bulgaria, Slovakia, Lithuania, Slovenia, Latvia, and Estonia joined and in 2008 Albania and Croatia joined them. These ten countries brought NATO's membership to twenty-eight. Second, as the Russian threat seemed to fade, NATO tried to develop a more flexible military structure to respond to trouble beyond the core of Europe.⁶ This broader military role led to a successful deployment of NATO forces in the Balkans beginning in 1999, but NATO struggled in Afghanistan since entering that fight in 2003 and in the brief Libyan mission in 2011. The U.S. accounts for fully three-fourths of NATO's military spending.

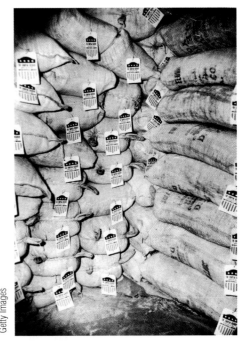

Getty Images

This shipment of flour was on its way to Austria from New York in October 1948. The tags read "For European Recovery supplied by the U.S.A," as part of the Marshall Plan.

North Atlantic Treaty Organization (NATO) A collective security pact formed in 1949 between the United States, Canada, and their western European allies to oppose further Soviet expansion in Europe.

deterrence The military doctrine and strategy that seeks to amass sufficient power to prevent or deter an opponent from resorting to force.

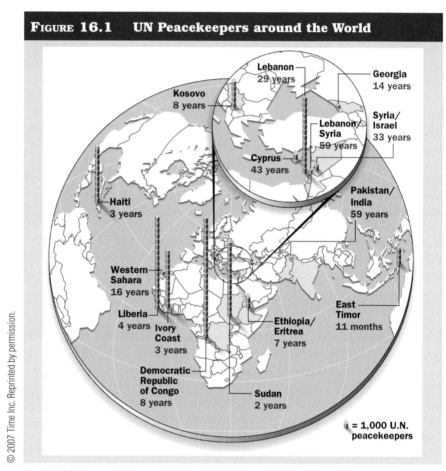

FIGURE 16.1   UN Peacekeepers around the World

Lebanon
29 years

Georgia
14 years

Kosovo
8 years

Syria/
Israel
33 years

Lebanon/
Syria
59 years

Cyprus
43 years

Pakistan/
India
59 years

Haiti
3 years

Western
Sahara
16 years

East
Timor
11 months

Liberia
4 years   Ivory
Coast
3 years

Ethiopia/
Eritrea
7 years

Democratic
Republic
of Congo
8 years

Sudan
2 years

= 1,000 U.N.
peacekeepers

The United Nations maintains peacekeeping forces in many of the world's trouble spots.

United Nations (UN) Formed in 1945 and open to all the nations of the world, the UN provides a forum for discussing the full range of international issues and has major peacekeeping responsibilities.

United Nations: International Order versus Terrorism.   The **United Nations (UN)** was formed in 1945 "to maintain international peace and security." The principal components of its institutional structure are the General Assembly and the Security Council. Currently, 193 nations are represented in the General Assembly. Each has a single vote, but their powers are limited to debate and recommendation. The fifteen-member Security Council can initiate action including the use of force. Within the Security Council, five nations—the victors of World War II—the United States, Russia, Britain, France, and China—hold permanent seats and have the right to veto any council action. The remaining ten are elected to two-year terms and do not have veto power.

During the Cold War, superpower conflict kept the UN and its Security Council tied in knots. Because the United States and the Soviet Union were at odds around the world, proposed UN actions frequently were vetoed by one or the other of them. The replacement of bipolar confrontation with American predominance has not kept Russia and China from opposing some U.S. Security Council initiatives. Like NATO, the UN has been forced to rethink its role in a world defined by American power.

Bush administration disdain for the UN, deepened by a series of scandals including charges of mismanagement and corruption in the Iraqi oil-for-food program, sexual exploitation of girls by UN peacekeepers in Africa, and a broad sense of staff malaise and management inefficiency throughout the UN made reform a major issue in 2005 and 2006. UN Secretary-General Kofi Annan proposed to expand the Security Council, create a new human rights panel, and new personnel, budget, and management practices, but in the end little came of it. In late 2006, Ban Ki-moon, a former South Korean foreign minister, replaced Annan as Secretary-General and within weeks he was mired in a debate over reform.[7] The United States was a founding member of the UN and remains the largest contributor to its budget to this day. The UN operates on a two-year, or biennial, budget. The U.S. pays 22 percent of the UN's $5 billion operating budget and 27 percent of its $8 billion peacekeeping budget. The Obama administration has worked hard to rebuild relations with the UN. Despite its troubles, the UN is engaged in absolutely irreplaceable relief and peacekeeping work throughout the world.[8]

IMF, World Bank, and GATT.   The Bretton Woods Conference of July 1944 led by the United States and Britain was called to design the postwar world economy. The delegates hoped to encourage international trade and enhance economic development among the nations of the world.

The first pillar of the postwar economic structure was the **International Monetary Fund (IMF).** The IMF was established to monitor a system of fixed exchange rates between the currencies of the signatory nations, provide short-term loans to nations adjusting their domestic policies to buttress their currencies, and ensure that any adjustments in the exchange rates among currencies were fair and in the general interest of the world economy. The IMF responded to the debt problems and currency devaluations that swept Asia in the late 1990s by arranging massive loan packages for nations including Indonesia, Malaysia, and South Korea. In exchange, the recipient nations agreed to adopt and implement extensive economic reforms. The IMF traditionally has been headed by a European, though there is pressure to reduce European clout in the IMF to allow more weight to rapidly developing countries like India and Brazil.

International Monetary Fund (IMF) A key part of the post-World War II international financial system, the IMF was responsible for monitoring the system of fixed currency exchange rates and now seeks to assist nations in managing debt.

The second pillar of the postwar economic structure was the **World Bank.** Formally named the International Bank for Reconstruction and Development, the World Bank was to provide capital to member nations, predominantly western European nations in the beginning, to finance their post-World War II reconstruction and development. Recipient nations were required to pursue domestic policies designed to stabilize their currencies, keep interest rates low, and open their economies to free trade as soon as possible. The World Bank continues to finance large-scale development programs although its focus has shifted to the developing world and it has added support for social and

World Bank A key part of the post-World War II international financial system, the World Bank provided capital to finance reconstruction and development, first in Western Europe and then in the Third World.

smaller-scale economic development programs. The Bank traditionally has been headed by an American.

The third pillar of the postwar economic structure was specifically intended to promote and enhance free trade. The **General Agreement on Tariffs and Trade (GATT)** lowered tariffs and other trade barriers so that international trade could flow more freely. Seven rounds of GATT talks have been completed since the first in 1947. Each round brought new products and services into the agreement. The last round of GATT talks, known as the Uruguay Round, began in 1986 and was not completed until 1994. The Uruguay Round extended GATT rules to initiate coverage of such traditionally sensitive areas as textiles, agricultural products, banking and brokerage services, and patents and copyrights on items ranging from pop songs to computer software. In 1995, the GATT was replaced by the World Trade Organization (WTO). The WTO has 160 member states and is headed by Roberto Carvalho de Azevêdo, a Brazilian.

These three pillars of postwar economic structure—the IMF, the World Bank, and the GATT—along with the Marshall Plan in Europe and the Dodge Plan in Japan, succeeded in providing the resources necessary to rebuild economies devastated by World War II. Moreover, they did so through policies and institutions that were consonant with the long-term interests of the United States in an increasingly open system of international politics and trade. Now that the uncertainties of the Cold War have been replaced by those of the War on Terror, some argue that the IMF, the World Bank, and the WTO have lost their relevance.[9] How should the United States position itself in the world to protect its own interests and to join with others in addressing the world's most pressing problems? As we shall see, opinions differ.

THE UNITED STATES IN THE NEW WORLD ORDER

Q3 How does the United States wield its overwhelming economic and military power in the world today?

The United States has been an economic superpower for more than a century and a military superpower for seventy years. Nonetheless, we feel keenly in the wake of 9/11 and the recent global economic crisis that the world is a dangerous place and that we may need to conceive and apply power and influence in new ways. How should we think about the use of American economic and military power in the world?[10]

To answer this critically important question, we must have a clear sense of how the world is likely to evolve in the twenty-first century. The broad outlines already seem clear. First, the United States, western Europe, and Japan will continue to be important centers of economic activity, probably as the engines of regional trading blocs in North America, Europe, and Asia. Second, the global economy will have to adjust to the presence of powerful new actors—most obviously, China, India, Russia, and Brazil—while aiding the slow rise of the world's poorest peoples and nations. Third, America will remain, at least for

Getty Images

On the night that U.S. helicopters secretly swooped deep into Pakistan to kill Osama Bin Laden, President Obama, Vice President Biden, and their national security team watched apprehensively in the White House Situation Room.

the foreseeable future, the dominant military power in the world. That military power, supplemented by subtle use of softer forms of power—trade, diplomacy, and culture—will have to be employed to bring stability to dangerous places. And finally, the civilized world will have to find the practical and moral means for shining light in the world's dark corners, shrinking the domain of ignorance, poverty, and hopelessness where violence and terror breed.

What is the status of American economic and military power in the world today? In brief, the answer is that both are substantial, but neither is unchallenged. Moreover, when one compares U.S. economic and military power with those of others, one finds that different dynamics have been at work. In recent decades, the gap between the United States and other wealthy nations has narrowed while the gap between the United States and other military powers has widened. Let's review the facts and then their implications.

The Global Economy

In the years immediately following the end of World War II, the late 1940s and early 1950s, the United States was in the extraordinary position of not simply being the strongest and wealthiest nation in the world, but being stronger and wealthier than the rest of the nations in the world *combined*.

Post-World War II Economic Dominance.   The U.S. economy grew by 50 percent during World War II, whereas the Europeans, Soviets, and Japanese lost a quarter or more of their economies. In 1945, at the end of World War II, the United States accounted for about half of the value of goods and services produced in the world, more than 60 percent of the value of manufactured goods, and dominated virtually all of the leading-edge technologies of the mid-century.

U.S. economic dominance at the end of World War II allowed the nation to take a leading role in shaping the global economic order of the postwar world. As these institutions, including the IMF, the World Bank, GATT, and Marshall Plan, did their work and the nations of the world recovered from the devastation of the war, the dominance of the U.S. economy receded. In fact, the recovery of western Europe and Japan was a critical part of the broad American strategy to "contain" the Soviet Union. By 1960, the U.S. share of gross world product had slipped to 28 percent, by 1970 to 25 percent, by 1980 to 23 percent, and was 18.75 percent in 2013.

U.S. policymakers knew that America's exaggerated share of global power resources after World War II was not sustainable. Nonetheless, Americans were nervous, especially during the 1970s and 1980s, because they were uncertain whether the decline in the U.S. share of global production was a controlled return to a more natural position within the world economy or an uncontrolled slide toward economic marginality. The 1990s brought renewed confidence as the American economy led the world in productivity, growth, and innovation. Yet, as America slowly emerges from the global recession of 2008–2009, China, India, and Brazil have resumed more rapid growth, so the future remains to be won.[11] Now let's look at the structure of the modern world economy and at the competitiveness of the United States within it.

The Growth of a Multipolar World Economy. The last quarter of the twentieth century saw three supereconomies emerge in Europe, North America, and Asia. The next quarter-century will determine whether these three super-economies become closed and competitive trading blocs or whether the GATT (now WTO) process of steadily lowering international trade barriers integrates nations into a growing and increasingly efficient world economy.[12]

Trading blocs usually form among nations with similar political and economic regimes that are in close proximity to, often contiguous with, each other.[13] The oldest and most developed major trading bloc is the European Community (now the European Union). The European Community was established in 1957 by the Treaty of Rome with six founding members—Belgium, France, Germany, Italy, Luxembourg, and the Netherlands. Soon thereafter, in 1960, Austria, Finland, Iceland, Liechtenstein, Norway, Sweden, and Switzerland formed an alternative trade organization called the European Free Trade Association (EFTA). In 1991, the EC and the EFTA agreed to form a common market (the EU) among their fifteen members. In 2004, the EU admitted ten new members—Cyprus, the Czech Republic, Estonia, Hungary, Latvia, Lithuania, Malta, Poland, Slovakia, and Slovenia. Bulgaria and Romania joined in 2007, while others, including Turkey, wait in the wings.

The economic crisis in Europe that began in 2009 led to enhanced powers for the EU over budgets of member states.[14] The expanded EU has 28 members encompassing 506 million people and more than $16.5 trillion in economic activity annually.

A second major regional trading bloc is the North American Free Trade Agreement (NAFTA). Approved in 1994, NAFTA ratified and expanded trade liberalization that had been occurring for some time among the United States, Canada, and Mexico. In 2004, U.S. trade officials inked a new Central American Free Trade Agreement (CAFTA) with five Central American nations. But work has stalled among thirty-four North, Central, and South American nations on the Free Trade Area of the Americas (FTAA) initiative.[15] Congress and the American public have become increasingly skeptical about the balance of costs and benefits from international trade. Critics cite loss of U.S. manufacturing jobs, rising trade deficits, and lack of labor and environmental protections as critical objections to free trade. The EU has sought to exploit these doubts by proposing closer trade ties between Europe and Latin America.

The East Asian bloc (a loose group including China, Japan, Indonesia, Malaysia, and the so-called Asian Tigers—Hong Kong, Singapore, South Korea, and Taiwan) was, until recently, a trading region rather than an integrated regional economy. Although East Asia experienced serious economic turmoil in the late 1990s, it had been the fastest-growing region in the world economy for half a century. Trade within the region accounts for only about one-third of the group's foreign trade, whereas several of these nations send more than half of their foreign trade to the United States. However, Southeast Asia has begun to integrate. In 2004, China and the ten-nation Association of Southeast Asian Nations (ASEAN) signed a free trade pact that went into full effect in 2010.[16]

It is likely that these regional economies will continue to integrate and strengthen. Moreover, the forces of global free trade are in some disarray. The Doha round of global trade talks initiated in late 2001 and scheduled for completion in early 2005 was intended to focus on the economic prospects of the world's poor. WTO officials hoped that the rich countries would reduce farm and textile subsidies in exchange for poor countries lowering tariff and trade barriers. Neither side was willing to move first, and talks finally collapsed in July 2008.[17]

Two other important problems stand in the way of continued global trade liberalization. The first is the existence of important national economies that have succeeded to this point by exporting aggressively while keeping domestic markets closed. China and Japan are the two biggest offenders. The second is the need to deal explicitly with the concerns of labor, environmental, and human rights activists, about the impact of globalization on the planet and its people.[18]

Global Competition and U.S. Competitiveness.   Prior to World War II, the American economy was almost wholly made up of American businesses and corporations producing for and selling in an American market (see Table 16.1).

TABLE 16.1 World's Largest Economies	
Country	**Gross Domestic Product, 2013**
WORLD	$87.25 trillion
United States	$16.72 trillion
China	$13.39 trillion
India	$4.99 trillion
Japan	$4.73 trillion
Germany	$3.23 trillion
Russia	$2.55 trillion
Brazil	$2.42 trillion
United Kingdom	$2.39 trillion
France	$2.28 trillion
Mexico	$1.85 trillion
Italy	$1.81 trillion
South Korea	$1.67 trillion
Canada	$1.52 trillion

Source: Central Intelligence Agency, *World Factbook 2014* (Washington, D.C.: U.S. Government Printing Office, 2014).

Neither exports nor imports as a percentage of GNP reached 5 percent. Economic activity, from ownership of firms to patterns of cooperation and joint ventures between firms to the composition of individual products is much more complex than it was even a few decades ago.[19]

Global exports now exceed $18.3 trillion in goods and services and constitute 19 percent of world economic output annually. U.S. exports run at about 14 percent of GDP, while imports run at about 17 percent of GDP. American firms and workers must compete with firms and workers around the globe. Global competition refers to producers from many nations competing with each other for sales within their own and each other's markets. U.S. competitiveness refers to the extent to which U.S. producers are successful in the global competition within their own and other markets. Competitiveness is a general term describing that combination of quality and price that makes one product more attractive (i.e., more competitive) than a similar product.

Joseph Nye pointed out that "Improving American competitiveness will require, among other things, greater attention to productivity, research and development, education, and savings."[20] Consider for a moment the first of these issues—productivity. Increased productivity, or increased output per worker per hour, enhances competitiveness by allowing reductions in the unit price to make the item more attractive against alternatives, or it allows increased profits and wages while price remains stable. The key to our country's economic future is the productive potential of our citizens. What proportion of our citizens—20 percent, 50 percent, 80 percent—will be creative, productive members of the information class of the new world economy? The answer to this question will determine the kind of nation that we will be only a few short years from now.

The Role of U.S. Military Power: Hegemony or Empire

Now we turn from issues of American prosperity to issues of American security. Although the pursuit of collective security and containment guided American national security and foreign policy during the second half of the twentieth century, some realists always argued that the United States should exercise its great power in its own interests, unbound by international institutions and coalitions, while some idealists and, more recently, neoconservatives, argued that U.S. power should be used to advance peace, prosperity, and human rights throughout the world. As technological developments in travel and communication made the world seem an ever smaller place, realists worried that American sovereignty was being compromised from above by international institutions like the UN and the WTO and from below by nongovernmental organizations (NGOs) like Greenpeace and the International Campaign to Ban Land Mines. Idealists believed that U.S. power was amplified and made more acceptable to others by working through such institutions.

In this section, we describe and assess the nature and disposition of American power in the world. First, we describe the scope of American power and compare it to the powers of other major nations. Second, we describe the debate over how American military power should be employed in the world.

AFP / Getty Images

NATO assisted Libyan rebels in overthrowing the dictator Muammar Gaddafi in one of the most successful uprisings of the Arab Spring.

Third, we describe the military and national security strategy pursued by the Obama administration and the policies that they have promised to pursue.

The Scope of U.S. Military Power

All nations seek to stabilize their strategic environment. Most nations seek security not through their raw power, but through allying with more powerful nations and seeking membership in international organizations. Only a very few nations in history have had the power to shape, if never completely control, their international environment. Today and for the foreseeable future, the United States enjoys a military predominance unequalled in world history. Yet, raw power is rarely sufficient to permit a nation to bend other nations to its will.

Most Americans know that the United States is, in the oft-repeated phrase, "the world's only remaining superpower," but few Americans appreciate the full scope of U.S. military power. Consider this: In 2013, the world's 192 nations spent a total of $1.75 trillion on defense. Thirty-seven percent of that total, $640 billion, was spent by the United States. U.S. military spending increased 67 percent between 2001 and 2012. The United States spends more on its military than do the next nine most powerful nations in the world *combined*.[21]

U.S. military expenditures buy both quantity and quality, but spiraling costs for new weapons systems are threatening the future plans of all of the services. For example, the U.S. Navy has ten "super-carrier" battle groups. No other nation in the world has even one, although a few nations—Great Britain, France, India, China, and Russia—have older, smaller carriers. The U.S. has more advanced fighters and bombers than all other nations combined. No other nation even has a stealth aircraft in its arsenal.[22] The U.S. Army enjoys technological advantages that not only make it the most effective fighting force in the world, but make it so far superior that allied forces have difficulty keeping up, let alone making significant battlefield contributions. Finally, the United States is the only nation in the world with a global basing structure, the air and sealift capability to move heavy forces in large numbers, and the computing and telecommunications technology to integrate and co-ordinate air, sea, and ground forces in combat anywhere in the world.

Nonetheless, critics contend that the nation's global commitments and the cost of new weapons systems are stretching the U.S. military beyond its capabilities and threatening its future effectiveness.[23] In more than a dozen years of war following 9/11, the troops, their equipment, and public support frayed. Civilian and military analysts warn of a "broken force." President Bush made permanent the 30,000 troops added to the Army and Marines after 9/11 and proposed to add 30,000 more troops by 2012. President Obama worked to end the wars in Iraq and Afghanistan and tight budgets required reductions in military spending. But some costs are both large and hard to reduce.

The first new CVN-21-class carrier due in 2015 will have a price tag of $15 billion, twice the cost of the last Nimitz-class carrier delivered in 2008.[24] Moreover, the Air Force's new Joint Strike Fighter program, roughly $300 billion to build 2,456 planes, is the largest defense contract in U.S. history. These are only two of the eighty new weapons systems that the Pentagon has under development at a projected cost of $1.5 trillion. President Obama immediately moved to check defense costs and had some success in 2009, though his attempts to reduce costs in the Joint Strike Fighter program were repulsed.[25]

Military Hegemony and the Bush Doctrine

The collapse of the Soviet Union and the end of the Cold War highlighted the question of how the United States should use its military predominance. The Clinton administration believed it could reap a "peace dividend" of reduced military spending and increased domestic spending and still manage global security and growth. The Bush administration believed that hegemony allowed more attention to U.S. national interests and less attention to the interests, assumptions, and preferences of others. Hence, the Bush administration walked away from several international agreements including the Kyoto Treaty on global climate change, a biological weapons convention, the International Court of Justice, the convention on land mines, and the Anti-Ballistic Missile Treaty with Russia. Each was seen as limiting U.S. policy options and hence limiting U.S. sovereignty. The terrorist attacks of September 11, 2001,

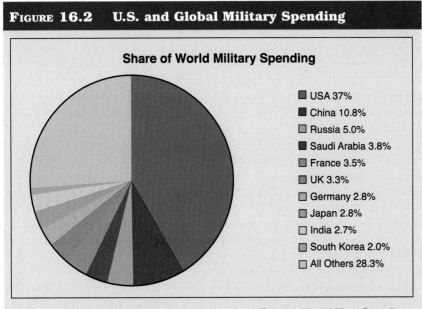

FIGURE 16.2   U.S. and Global Military Spending

Share of World Military Spending

- USA 37%
- China 10.8%
- Russia 5.0%
- Saudi Arabia 3.8%
- France 3.5%
- UK 3.3%
- Germany 2.8%
- Japan 2.8%
- India 2.7%
- South Korea 2.0%
- All Others 28.3%

Notes: Stockholm International Peace Research Institute, "Trends in World Military Expenditure, 2013," released April, 2014.

deepened the Bush administration's sense that the nation must be free to act in defense of its critical national interests.

The **Bush Doctrine**, the broadest reassessment of the U.S. security posture since the Truman administration, was announced in an October 2002 document entitled "The National Security Strategy of the United States."[26] Although no element of the Bush Doctrine was entirely new, its several key elements had never been as boldly, even baldly, stated. The key elements of postwar American foreign policy were multilateralism, collective security, deterrence, and containment. The key elements of the Bush Doctrine were sovereignty, national security, preemption, and supremacy. Let us examine the key principles of the "National Security Strategy" in turn.

The Bush Doctrine contended that the classic Cold War doctrines of multilateralism, containment, and deterrence would not work against the twenty-first-century dangers of terrorists, rogue states, and weapons of mass destruction. Although President Bush frequently cited the importance of multilateral institutions including the UN, NATO, and the WTO to American foreign and national security policy, he just as frequently made the point that "the U.S. cannot remain idle while dangers gather" and will not ask others for permission to defend itself.

Moreover, some threats may be so pressing, so imminent, that unilateral action is required. Hence, the National Security Strategy declared: "The United States has long maintained the option of preemptive actions to counter a sufficient threat to our national security." As the strategy noted, preemption is a classic doctrine of international law, which "international jurists often conditioned . . . on the existence of an immediate threat . . . most often a visible mobilization of armies . . . preparing to attack." The world has changed and new dangers have arisen. Hence, the document stated, "We must adapt the concept of imminent threat" to the new era. "As a matter of common sense and self-defense, America will act against such emerging threats before they are fully formed." Acting against gathering, as opposed to imminent, threats moves beyond preemption to preventive war. The distinction between preemption and preventive war is often expressed as the difference between a war of necessity and a war of choice.

Finally, the Bush Doctrine declared an intent to maintain and dissuade others from challenging American military supremacy. "We must build and maintain our defenses beyond challenge. . . . The United States must and will maintain the capability to defeat any . . . enemy." Few would object to maintaining unchallengable defensive and offensive military capability. Many were, however, perplexed by the declaration that "our forces will be strong enough to dissuade potential adversaries from pursuing a military build-up in hopes of surpassing, or equaling, the power of the United States." Declaring American military superiority to be permanent seemed an unnecessary provocation.[27]

The Bush Doctrine embedded in the National Security Strategy of 2002 was thoroughly revised in March 2006.[28] Though some of the aggressive posturing of the 2002 national security strategy was still present, the substance of the 2006 document represented a return to the traditional principles of American foreign policy. The twin pillars of the new strategy were, first, human rights, freedom, and democracy, and second, working with friends and allies to advance these goals. The new strategy moved away from unilateral use of force and military predominance toward multilateral diplomacy and international cooperation. The ascendancy of Secretary of State Condoleezza Rice and her more traditional diplomatic agenda was critical to producing changes in both tone and substance from the first Bush administration to the second.

President Obama's first national security team was built around Secretary of State Hillary Clinton, former Marine Commandant and NATO commander General James Jones as National Security Adviser, and Bush holdover Robert Gates at Defense. The term most frequently used to describe this team was pragmatic (as opposed to ideological). President Obama charged them to set a new national security course to rebuild U.S. ties to international organizations like the UN and traditional allies like NATO. When the Obama administration produced its equivalent of President Bush's "National Security Strategy of the United States" it sought to rebalance the elements of national power. It stressed, but put less stress on, the "hard power" elements of military and economic influence and more stress on the "soft power" influences of multilateralism, collective security, and diplomacy.

President Obama laid out his national security principles in his Nobel Peace Prize acceptance speech in Oslo, Norway, in December 2009 and, more formally, in his "National Security Strategy" in May 2010.[29] The key principles that have guided the Obama administration's foreign policy are: (1) lead

Getty Images

Joint Chiefs of Staff Chairman General Martin Dempsey (right) and Secretary of Defense Chuck Hagel speak to the press about the ongoing bombing campaign against militants in Iraq and Syria during a news conference at the Pentagon in September 2014.

Pro & Con

Should the U.S. Take the Lead on Global Climate Change?

For more than twenty years the nations of the world have been meeting under the auspices of the UN at least annually to discuss what to do about global climate change. Despite growing evidence that climate change is real and threatening, these meetings had failed to produce a comprehensive climate change treaty that everyone could get behind. Though a "breakthrough" agreement was achieved at a 2011 meeting in Durban, South Africa, reasons for skepticism remain. Why?

The U.S. has been a reluctant participant in these meetings, always arguing for a go-slow approach, modest rather than aggressive targets, voluntary rather than mandatory agreements, in which all nations, rich and poor, are similarily bound. This hesitant approach has characterized both Democratic and Republican administrations. The closest thing to a comprehensive climate change agreement that the world had achieved prior to Durban was the Kyoto Protocol of 1997. The Kyoto Protocol set firm targets for industrialized nations to meet in reducing greenhouse gases. Even before the Protocol was completed, the U.S. Senate passed a resolution, 95–0, that the U.S. should not accede to the Protocol until greenhouse gas reductions numbers were established for developing nations, especially China and India, as well as for developed nations. Despite the fact that 187 nations ratified Kyoto, neither President Clinton nor President Bush even bothered to formally submit the Protocol to the Senate for ratification.

Three main reasons have long explained the U.S. position on global climate change. First, until China passed the U.S. in 2006, the U.S. had for more than a century been the world's largest emitter of greenhouse gases. Second, presidents Clinton and Bush worried that retrofitting U.S. plants with new technology to reduce greenhouse gas emissions would be very expensive and might slow economic growth and cost jobs. Finally, President Bush argued that the science behind global climate change concerns was shaky and more research was needed before expensive fixes would be economically justified.

Despite some continuing questions about the science behind global climate change, most experts believe that global warming must be addressed. Climate change scholars point to rapid melting of mountain glaciers worldwide, retreating ice shelves in Greenland and Antarctica, and new sea passages through melted summer ice in the Arctic. Moreover, the Associated Press wrote in 2009 that "the world's power plants, automobiles, burning forests and

with diplomacy whether dealing with traditional friends or adversaries, (2) strengthen international institutions like the UN and traditional alliances like NATO as instruments of cooperative problem-solving, (3) recognize global development as advancing U.S. peace and security, (4) enhance the civilian elements of U.S. nation-building capabilities as a complement to military forces, and (5) promote U.S. political and economic success, democracy and free markets, as examples that others might emulate.

During the first six years of the Obama presidency, the nation withdrew from Iraq, before dipping a toe back in in 2015, and moved to largely withdraw from Afghanistan by the end of 2016. President Obama showed deep reluctance to engage the military in new conflicts. He pushed NATO to take the lead in the Libyan conflict and held out against involvement in Ukraine and in the Syrian civil war even after chemical weapons were used. President Obama and most Americans, after more than a decade of war, are reluctant to enter new long-term conflicts.

other sources are producing 29 percent more carbon dioxide than in 2000."[30]

U.S. leaders claim to be in favor of limiting greenhouse gases and point out that most of the increase in emissions since Kyoto has come from newly industrializing nations, principally India and China. U.S. leaders contend that developing and developed nations must agree to verifiable emissions reductions if global limits are to work. Leaders of the industrializing nations contend that climate change stems from the industrial pollution produced by the West over the past two centuries. The West grew rich on this industrial activity and now should pay for the clean-up. Late industrializing nations like India and China, though they are now large emitters of greenhouse gases, argue that they need unrestricted economic growth to bring their populations closer to western standards of living. Today, per capita GDP in India is $3,700, in China it is $9,300, and in the U.S. it is $50,700. Moreover, each Indian produces 1.2 tons of carbon emissions, each Chinese produces 6 tons, and each American produces 19 tons.

The breakthrough at Durban came late in the meetings when poor nations agreed to take on the same legal commitments to reduce pollution as the wealthy nations and the wealthy nations agreed to provide tens of billions of dollars to help them meet those commitments.[31] Momentum built slowly until in late 2014 President Obama and Chinese President Xi announced a dramatic carbon reduction agreement and just a month later 200 nations agreed to put their own national carbon reduction plans in place. Both agreements were intended to jumpstart a global agreement when the nations of the world gather in Paris in December 2015. Good news, right! Maybe, skepticism abounds because the U.S. Congress failed to ratify Kyoto and may not ratify the agreement that ultimately emerges from the Paris meetings.

What do you think?
- Should the U.S. lead on climate change?
- Or should it hang back to see that our economy is not disadvantaged in relation to developing countries?

PRO	CON
Industrial nations created the problem	All nations must fight climate change
Wealthy nations must aid poor nations	Others must learn to pay their share
The U.S. is the indispensable nation	U.S. economic interests will suffer

President Obama's second national security blueprint, released in 2015, confirmed many of his long-held views on America's role in the world. He affirmed that the U.S., as the world's indispensable nation, must lead, but must also avoid hyper-active involvement, hubris, and "overreach."[32] Clearly, Obama is more comfortable working to solve complex problems diplomatically than through use of force. Whether these decades-old problems will permit of peaceful resolution remains to be seen.

THE BURDEN OF THE OLD ORDER ON THE NEW

Clearly, the United States is the wealthiest and most powerful nation in the world today. Most of the nations of Europe and a few in Asia enjoy comparable levels of wealth, if not of military power, but many nations continue to be

Q4 What responsibilities, if any, do the wealthy nations of the world have to the poorer nations?

wracked by poverty, disease, hunger, and violence. What responsibility does strength have to succor weakness in a world in which danger threatens even the strong?

While we cannot provide a definitive answer to this question, we can suggest how large and complex are the issues involved. Let's look briefly at three interrelated issues—income, energy, and population. The first issue, income, is quite simple and constrains the other two. There are vast differences in wealth between the U.S. at $50,700 per capita, Germany at $39,700, Mexico at $15,600, China at $9,300, and the truly desperate, such as Uganda at $1,400. The wealthiest 20 percent of the world's population enjoy two-thirds of its wealth, while the bottom 80 percent subsist on the remaining one-third.

The position of the developing world is—in a nutshell—we must have more! Therefore, the fundamental question that the people of the world face is this: Will nations be able to find a set of policies that permit increased levels of energy use, address pressing environmental problems like the destruction of the rain forests and the depletion of the ozone layer, and control population growth so that the people of the world can live better lives? These issues, although not absolutely intractable, will be difficult to resolve to the mutual satisfaction of the developed and the developing nations.[33]

Energy

Energy, in its various forms, powers the economic engines of the world. The key questions in regard to energy in the world economy are (1) who has it? (2) who gets it? and (3) at what price? These questions are particularly critical to the United States because we are the world's second largest consumer of energy. The U.S. uses one-quarter of the world's oil and one-third of its gasoline (recall that we are less than 5 percent of the world's population) and we import one-sixth of the energy that we use, down from 30 percent less than a decade ago. Increases in U.S. production have reduced, but not eliminated, dependence on foreign energy supplies. Close U.S. ties to Saudi Arabia, Qatar, Oman, and other oil-rich Persian Gulf states, to say nothing of two wars with Iraq, and ongoing tensions with Iran were intended to assure dependable access to the region's huge oil reserves. On the other hand, current trends suggest that future increases in world energy use will come not from the developed nations, but from the developing nations. Access to energy at affordable prices will determine whether the developing nations grow at a rate that will satisfy the rising aspirations of their people.

For most of the twentieth century, access to cheap and plentiful energy was not a problem for the United States. Even into the early 1970s, eight multinational oil companies, five of them American, controlled the production and price of world oil. These companies were Exxon, Gulf, Mobil, Standard, Texaco, British Petroleum, Royal Dutch Shell, and Compagnie Francaise des Petroles. The situation began to change in the early 1970s when the oil-producing nations (through the **Organization of Petroleum Exporting Countries (OPEC)**) seized effective control of world oil markets from

Organization of Petroleum Exporting Countries (OPEC) The commodity cartel of mostly Middle Eastern oil-producing nations. OPEC exercises more control than any other organization on both the volume and price of oil in the international economy.

the large Western oil companies and their governments. The answers to the questions posed above quickly became: Who has it? OPEC. Who gets it? Whoever OPEC says. At what price? Dramatically higher.

It took a decade and two major oil shocks—the first in 1973–1974 and the second in 1979–1980, during which prices rose from $3 a barrel to more than $40 a barrel—for the nations of the world to adjust to dramatically more expensive energy. Adjustments in both supply and demand allowed prices to settle back into the $15 to $25 range for most of the 1980s and 1990s. Prices pushed into a $25 to $35 range after 2000, $50 oil became the norm by 2005, and prices broke through $100 a barrel early in 2008, reaching $147 in July before falling back below $35 a barrel as the recession of late 2008 and 2009 took hold. It again advanced to the $100 range, before falling below $50 a barrel in 2014. OPEC provides about 35 percent of world oil demand, about 33 of the 92 million barrels consumed daily in the world, but it sits on 73 percent of the world's known oil reserves.

How does oil fit into the general pattern of energy use in the world? Estimates suggest that more than 75 percent of world energy and 86 percent of U.S. energy in 2030 will be from oil, coal, and natural gas, much as it is now. Although proven oil reserves are large, extracting the oil will become increasingly expensive as the most accessible reserves are depleted and less accessible reserves are tapped.[34] Renewable energy sources like wind, tides, biomass, and thermals supply only a small portion of energy needs.

Coal, natural gas, nuclear power, and renewables like hydropower and wind are the major alternatives to oil (see Figure 16.3). Coal is abundant, but it burns "dirty," producing acid rain and carbons that contribute to global warming. Sixty percent of known coal reserves are in the United States, Russia, and China. Natural gas is cleaner than either coal or oil but is concentrated in the United States and Russia. Hydropower, biomass, and wind are cleaner still

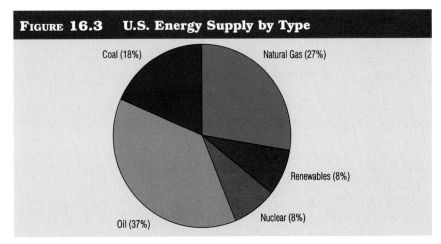

FIGURE 16.3   U.S. Energy Supply by Type

Coal (18%) Natural Gas (27%) Renewables (8%) Nuclear (8%) Oil (37%)

Source: Department of Energy, Annual Energy Outlook 2014, available online at http://www.eia.doe.gov/oiaf/aeo/pdf/overview.pdf.

LET'S COMPARE

Income, Energy, and Population Growth: Development versus Underdevelopment, or Rolling Rocks Uphill

These figures show how clearly wealth, energy consumption, and population growth are related. People can survive by gathering what they need to live directly from nature without the use of labor-saving and labor-enhancing help like fuel and factories. Such people create little wealth and often seek to assure survival in lean years and old age by having large families. Greater wealth per person allows savings and accumulation, which reduce the sense of vulnerability and permit families to have fewer children. Children are no longer seen as extra hands to do the work or to care for aging parents but rather as persons who will require extensive nurturing to reach their full potential.

On the other hand, producing more wealth almost always involves using greater amounts of energy, and energy must be severed from nature and often creates pollution when used. Wealthy countries, although their populations may be more sensitive to environmental issues, are in no position to tell poorer countries and people that they must limit their growth in order to protect the environment. Poor countries wishing to become wealthier fast are unlikely to divert precious resources to environmental protection.[35]

Country	GDP Per Capita in 2012 (U.S. Dollars)	Per Capita Electric Consumption (kWh)	Percent Increase in Population
United States	50,700	13,246	0.90
Switzerland	46,200	7,928	0.85
Sweden	41,900	14,030	0.18
Canada	43,400	16,406	0.77
Germany	39,700	7,081	−0.19
United Kingdom	37,500	5,516	0.55
Japan	36,900	7,848	−0.10
South Korea	32,800	10,162	0.18
Spain	31,100	5,598	0.73
Italy	30,600	5,393	0.34
Mexico	15,600	2,092	1.07
Brazil	12,100	2,438	0.83
China	9,300	3,298	0.46
Algeria	7,600	1,091	1.90
Egypt	6,700	1,743	1.88
India	3,600	684	1.28
Ghana	3,400	344	2.19
Uganda	1,400	55	3.32
Niger	800	37	3.32
Burundi	600	26	3.08

Source: Central Intelligence Agency, *World Factbook 2014* (Washington, D.C.: U.S. Government Printing Office, 2013). Electric consumption from http://data.worldbank.org/indicator/EG.USE.ELEC.KH.PC

but comprise only 8 percent of U.S. energy use. Their principal costs arise both from construction and also from water use and land management. Nuclear power, 8 percent of U.S. energy use, poses dangers both from accidents and in the disposal of waste.

Beyond the issue of the kinds of energy we use is the question of how much energy we use. The developing nations are intensely aware that the relationship between rising energy use and rising incomes is very close. The more energy per capita the citizens of a nation use, the more wealth they create. Therefore, even though energy consumption is expected to hold steady or increase only modestly in the developed nations, energy consumption in the developing countries is expected to continue growing rapidly. Moreover, these increases are taking place in some of the largest nations on earth. One analyst summed up the problem by saying, "China and India together are a third of humanity, and they don't want to ride bicycles anymore."[36]

Phenomenally, energy consumption in China doubled each decade between 1950 and 2000. In 2010, for the first time in modern history, China used more total energy than did the U.S.[37] In India, energy use more than tripled between 1970 and 2000 and is expected to more than double again by 2020, and similar increases are common throughout the developing world. Nonetheless, energy consumption per capita in China and India is still only 25 and 5 percent, respectively, of consumption in the United States. Shockingly, the U.S., China, and India are all holdouts in attempts to limit global pollution and its consequence, global warming. While President Obama seems more amenable to global cooperation on pollution control than President Bush was, nothing much has yet been done. A top Chinese official recently declared, "the ball is not in China's court," and India's planning minister, Singh Alluwalliah, said that "every country should have the same per capita rights to pollution."[38] Despite the Durban framework, managing global energy use, pollution, and global warming is still a long way off.

World Population

The world's population has been growing at an astounding rate. Improvements in food stocks and medical care—both good things, to be sure—have led to improved survival rates for the world's children and longer life spans for the world's adults. Nonetheless, this progress has been uneven. The world now is home to about 7.2 billion people, though the UN reports that fully 1 billion of them suffer from hunger.[39] One can get a sense of the rate of population growth by asking how long it has taken for each new billion to be added to the world's population.

It took from the beginning of time until about 1804 for the world's population to reach 1 billion. It took another 123 years, from 1804 to 1927, for it to reach 2 billion, and each new billion has come ever more quickly. The population of the world reached 3 billion by 1960, 4 billion by 1974 (only 14 years), 5 billion by 1987 (only 13 years), and 6 billion by 1999 (only 12 years). Global population reached 7 billion in 2011 (12 years). Although

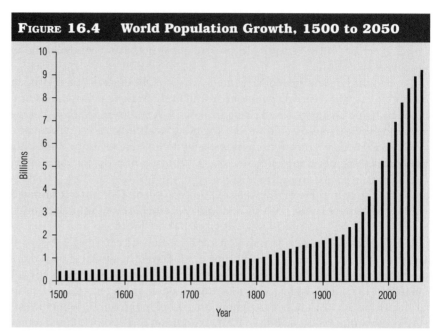

Source: United Nations Population Division, Department of Economic and Social Affairs, World Population Prospects: The 2010 Revision. http://esa.un.org/unpd/wpp/Excel-Data/population.htm

the rates of growth have begun to level off, current estimates suggest that the world will have to support 9.6 billion people by 2050.

After economic growth, population growth is probably the biggest issue dividing the developed from the developing nations. Both sides see population and development issues as closely related but they see the relationships differently. Developed nations focus on total world population and worry that it is too large. Developing nations focus on the fact that no matter how many people there are in the world, those in the developed nations consume most of the world's resources. The fact that both perspectives are valid means that the differences between them are hard to resolve.

WHAT SHOULD AMERICA BE IN THE WORLD?

Q5 In light of our cultural, economic, and military resources, what place should the United States seek to create for itself in the world of the twenty-first century?

As the leading military and economic power, how should the United States deploy its assets in the world? In the 1990s, it seemed that the United States could decline the role of "policeman to the world," reduce military spending, and concentrate all of its attention on enhancing its position within the global economy. Since 9/11, it has seemed that the United States, as the world's lone superpower, must act as the ultimate guarantor of democracy, free trade, and human rights in the world. If we do not, who will? The integration of the world economy, the rise of global terror, threats to the environment, and population growth will present the United States with complex and difficult choices both in domestic and foreign policy.

No other nation approaches the United States either in size of economy or available military power. On the other hand, Europe enjoys comparable living standards and parts of Asia are economic powerhouses whose growth trajectory has been equal to or steeper than that of the United States for most of the past fifty years. The full inclusion of China, India, Russia, and Brazil in the global economy will cause dislocations. Nonetheless, we can be reasonably confident that strong growth and productivity will make this country one center of wealth creation in the twenty-first-century world economy, even if not its runaway leader.

The terrorist attacks of 9/11 and the Afghan and Iraqi wars that followed are the problems that give pause. Osama bin Laden's al-Qaeda terrorists struck a heavy blow against the preeminent symbols of American economic and military power—the Twin Towers and the Pentagon. The United States, with the mostly modest help of others, pressed al-Qaeda throughout the world, overthrew their Taliban supporters in Afghanistan, and broadened the War on Terror to include the toppling of Saddam Hussein in Iraq. Major combat operations in the Afghan and Iraq wars left no doubt that U.S. military might was incomparably superior to any other military force in the world. No other nation in the world, not the British, French, Germans, Japanese, or Russians, could have played the central role of projecting massive conventional force over great distance.

On the other hand, the cost of maintaining overwhelming force is quite high, and occasions for employing it are not often as clear as was use of U.S. force against al-Qaeda and the Taliban. Despite the demonstrable evil of Saddam Hussein, many wonder whether the cost in U.S. blood and treasure in Iraq has been warranted. Others argue that no matter how powerful the U.S. military, it is simply not the right tool for the nation-building operations that come after combat operations. Still others suggest that the starvation, ethnic strife, and genocide of Somalia, South Sudan and Syria are closer to what we will see in the future.

Successive U.S. administrations will have to decide whether the United States should work to maintain global military supremacy into the twenty-first century, as the Bush Doctrine held or reduce military spending and concentrate on maintaining and even enhancing its ability to foster and spread economic development in the new century. Americans, both citizens and political leaders, hope to do both.[40]

The challenge facing the Obama administration is to continue the work of restoring global confidence in American leadership. The U.S. is still the most powerful nation in the world, but others are rising and the gap between them and us is closing, so the goal must be to make as many nations as possible want to follow where we lead.

Chapter Summary

All nations exist in an international context. Within that context, each nation plays a particular role, depending on its relative power and influence. At most points in history, one or a few nations held sway, and the rest had to find their places in relation to the major powers. Only a few—Rome, Britain, the United States—have gained general dominance and were able to hold it for any period of time. Inevitably, new political, economic, and military developments lead to change in regional and global balances of power—the strong grow weak and the weak strong. The United States' role in the world has gone from vulnerable in its early years to one of military and economic dominance (see Table 16.2).

The initial experience of the British colonies in North America with the world order was exploitation. Colonies were expected to produce profit to the empire by providing raw materials and controlled markets. Independence did not end the vulnerability of the United States to the military and economic coercion of the European great powers. It took the Louisiana Purchase in 1803 to remove the Spanish and French threats from the south and a second war with England, the War of 1812, to remove the British threat from the north and from the high seas.

TABLE 16.2　The Emergance of a Global Superpower

International Role	Global Events and Institutional Responses
Early Vulnerability	French aid American independence (1776)
	War of 1812 (Britain dominates U.S.) (1812–15)
	Monroe Doctrine (1823)
National Consolidation	Annexation of Texas (1845)
	Annexation of American Southwest, California, and the Oregon Territory (1848)
	American Civil War (1861–65)
	Open Door Policy (1899)
	World War I; U.S. refuses to join League of Nations (1914–20)
Global Military Dominance	World War II (1941–45)
	World Bank; International Monetary Fund (1944)
	United Nations (1945)
	Marshall Plan; Truman Doctrine (1947)
	North Atlantic Treaty Organization (NATO) (1949)
	Height of U.S. economic dominance (1950s)
	Cold War (1950–90)
	Oil shock; economic stagnation (1970s)
	Collapse of the Soviet Union (1989)
Global Economic Competition	Emergence of the global economy (1990s)
	Al-Qaeda strikes the U.S. (2001)
	Wars in Iraq and Afghanistan (2001–14)

The United States then set about establishing its regional dominance. The Monroe Doctrine declared that the United States would consider further efforts by the European powers to establish colonies in the Americas to be hostile acts. Nations in the Americas would develop according to the republican example of the United States rather than the monarchical examples of Europe. Although less formal than the Monroe Doctrine in foreign affairs, the domestic economic and social policy of the United States was set for the nineteenth century by the doctrine of manifest destiny that envisioned the United States as a continental power stretching from the Atlantic to the Pacific.

After the Civil War decided the issue of slave versus free labor, the northern United States went on a ragged cycle of boom and bust that by century's end had made the United States the world's leading economy. With large agricultural and manufacturing surpluses to export, the United States strongly favored free trade, most pointedly in its turn-of-the-century Open Door Policy in China. It was, however, unwilling to assume the international stance of leading world power. Instead, the United States withdrew from international politics after World War I to continue tending its domestic economic machine. Conflict soon engulfed Europe once again.

World War II devastated every advanced economy in the world except that of the United States. The United States pursued a two-pronged postwar foreign policy. First, the United States took the leading role in financing and guiding European recovery through the Marshall Plan and in organizing global political and financial systems through the UN, IMF, World Bank, and GATT. Second, the United States established a series of collective security and alliance arrangements centered on NATO to contain Soviet expansionism.

As the rest of the world recovered, the world's two superpowers, the United States and the Soviet Union, faced off globally. They engaged in an arms race that proved to be terribly expensive, both in raw dollars and rubles, and in its impact on the structure, dynamism, and health of their national economies. Ultimately, the Soviet Union collapsed. After the dust had cleared, the United States looked around to find that, although it was the only military superpower remaining in the world, it had a long list of economic competitors.

The collapse of the Soviet Union seemed to offer the United States a "peace dividend." A reduced threat seemed to justify smaller military and foreign intelligence expenditures and greater attention to economic and domestic policy. Those assumptions collapsed with the Twin Towers on September 11, 2001. Americans were awakened to two facts: one was that the world remained a dangerous place, and the other was that only the United States had the moral and military stature to serve as "the world's policeman." Achieving a sustainable balance between global economic competitiveness and the military capability to project overwhelming force around the globe is a singularly American dilemma. No one else is called upon even to consider it.

Key Terms

bipolar   520

Bush Doctrine   532

Cold War   520

containment   520

deterrence   521

General Agreement on Tariffs and
   Trade (GATT)   524

hard power   514

idealists   514

International Monetary Fund
   (IMF)   523

manifest destiny   518

Marshall Plan   520

Monroe Doctrine   518

neoconservatives   514

North Atlantic Treaty Organization
   (NATO)   521

Open Door Policy   519

Organization of Petroleum Exporting
   Countries (OPEC)   536

realists   514

soft power   515

Truman Doctrine   520

United Nations (UN)   522

World Bank   523

Suggested Readings

Gelb, Leslie H. *Power Rules: How Common Sense Can Rescue American Foreign Policy.* New York: Harper Collins Publishers, 2009. Gelb argues that the most successful presidents have a coherent foreign policy that can be convincingly communicated to the public.

Hendrickson, David C. *Union, Nation, or Empire: The American Debate Over International Relations, 1789–1941.* Lawrence, KS: University of Kansas Press, 2009. Americans were interested in and engaged in impassioned debates of international relations from the nation's earliest days.

Herring, George C. *From Colony to Superpower: U.S. Foreign Relations Since 1776.* New York: Oxford University press, 2008. Masterful overview of U.S. foreign policy from independence to the modern era.

Kagan, Robert. *The World America Made.* New York: Knopf, 2012. Denies that the U.S. is in decline and argues that it is the indispensable guarantor of the liberal democratic order internationally.

Kegley, Charles W., Jr., and Gregory A. Raymond. *The Global Future: A Brief Introduction to World Politics,* 2nd ed. New York: Wadsworth, 2007. This leading textbook presents contemporary international politics in terms of continuities with the past and transitions into an indefinite future in which the United States' economic performance will be as important as military power.

Murphy, Cullen. *Are We Rome? The Fall of an Empire and the Fate of America.* New York: Houghton Mifflin, 2007. Do the same elements of imperial overreach that preceded the fall of Rome afflict America today?

Turbowitz, Peter. *Politics and Strategy: Partisan Ambition and American Statecraft.* Princeton, NJ: Princeton University Press, 2011. Turbowitz asks why some American Presidents pursue aggressive foreign policies and some do not. He finds that domestic politics from a large part of the explanation.

Web Resources

For practice quizzes, key term flashcards, videos, links, and other study tools, visit the *American Government* website: www.routledge.com/cw/jillson

1. **www.cdi.org**
   The Center for Defense Information page includes access to its monthly publication, *Defense Monitor,* and to an arms trade database, military spending clock, and links to related sites.

2. **www.nato.int**
   North Atlantic Treaty Organization (NATO) has a site where students can learn the history of the organization. The page also looks at NATO's role in the post-Cold War era.

3. **www.un.org**
   The official Web page of the United Nations offers news, information, activities, and events of the UN around the world. It also includes links to divisions and committees within the UN.

4. **www.imf.org**
   The International Monetary Fund is a voluntary association of nations designed to create a stable system of buying and selling currency. The IMF lends money to member states during economic crises under the condition that the country follow certain fiscal reform policies.

5. **www.cfr.org**
   The Council on Foreign Relations (CFR) is a nonpartisan organization dedicated to the study of international affairs. This site also links to its magazine, *Foreign Affairs.*

Appendix A

THE DECLARATION OF INDEPENDENCE

IN CONGRESS, July 4, 1776.

The unanimous Declaration of the thirteen united States of America, When in the Course of human events, it becomes necessary for one people to dissolve the political bands which have connected them with another, and to assume among the powers of the earth, the separate and equal station to which the Laws of Nature and of Nature's God entitle them, a decent respect to the opinions of mankind requires that they should declare the causes which impel them to the separation.

We hold these truths to be self-evident, that all men are created equal, that they are endowed by their Creator with certain unalienable Rights, that among these are Life, Liberty and the pursuit of Happiness.—That to secure these rights, Governments are instituted among Men, deriving their just powers from the consent of the governed.—That whenever any Form of Government becomes destructive of these ends, it is the Right of the People to alter or to abolish it, and to institute new Government, laying its foundation on such principles and organizing its powers in such form, as to them shall seem most likely to effect their Safety and Happiness. Prudence, indeed, will dictate that Governments long established should not be changed for light and transient causes; and accordingly all experience hath shewn, that mankind are more disposed to suffer, while evils are sufferable, than to right themselves by abolishing the forms to which they are accustomed. But when a long train of abuses and usurpations, pursuing invariably the same Object evinces a design to reduce them under absolute Despotism, it is their right, it is their duty, to throw off such Government, and to provide new Guards for their future security.—Such has been the patient sufferance of these Colonies; and such is now the necessity which constrains them to alter their former Systems of Government. The history of the present King of Great Britain is a history of repeated injuries and usurpations, all having in direct object the establishment of an absolute Tyranny over these States. To prove this, let Facts be submitted to a candid world.

He has refused his Assent to Laws, the most wholesome and necessary for the public good.

He has forbidden his Governors to pass Laws of immediate and pressing importance, unless suspended in their operation till his Assent should be obtained; and when so suspended, he has utterly neglected to attend to them.

He has refused to pass other Laws for the accommodation of large districts of people, unless those people would relinquish the right of Representation in the Legislature, a right inestimable to them and formidable to tyrants only.

He has called together legislative bodies at places unusual, uncomfortable, and distant from the depository of their public Records, for the sole purpose of fatiguing them into compliance with his measures.

He has dissolved Representative Houses repeatedly, for opposing with manly firmness his invasions on the rights of the people.

He has refused for a long time, after such dissolutions, to cause others to be elected; whereby the Legislative powers, incapable of Annihilation, have returned to the People at large for their exercise; the State remaining in the mean time exposed to all the dangers of invasion from without, and convulsions within.

He has endeavoured to prevent the population of these States; for that purpose obstructing the Laws for Naturalization of Foreigners; refusing to pass others to encourage their migrations hither, and raising the conditions of new Appropriations of Lands.

He has obstructed the Administration of Justice, by refusing his Assent to Laws for establishing Judiciary powers.

He has made Judges dependent on his Will alone, for the tenure of their offices, and the amount and payment of their salaries.

He has erected a multitude of New Offices, and sent hither swarms of Officers to harrass our people, and eat out their substance.

He has kept among us, in times of peace, Standing Armies without the Consent of our legislatures.

He has affected to render the Military independent of and superior to the Civil power.

He has combined with others to subject us to a jurisdiction foreign to our constitution, and unacknowledged by our laws; giving his Assent to their Acts of pretended Legislation:

For Quartering large bodies of armed troops among us:

For protecting them, by a mock Trial, from punishment for any Murders which they should commit on the Inhabitants of these States:

For cutting off our Trade with all parts of the world:

For imposing Taxes on us without our Consent:

For depriving us in many cases, of the benefits of Trial by Jury:

For transporting us beyond Seas to be tried for pretended offences:

For abolishing the free System of English Laws in a neighbouring Province, establishing therein an Arbitrary government, and enlarging its Boundaries so as to render it at once an example and fit instrument for introducing the same absolute rule into these Colonies:

For taking away our Charters, abolishing our most valuable Laws, and altering fundamentally the Forms of our Governments:

For suspending our own Legislatures, and declaring themselves invested with power to legislate for us in all cases whatsoever.

He has abdicated Government here, by declaring us out of his Protection and waging War against us.

He has plundered our seas, ravaged our Coasts, burnt our towns, and destroyed the lives of our people.

He is at this time transporting large Armies of foreign Mercenaries to compleat the works of death, desolation and tyranny, already begun with circumstances of Cruelty & perfidy scarcely parallel'd in the most barbarous ages, and totally unworthy of the Head of a civilized nation.

He has constrained our fellow Citizens taken Captive on the high Seas to bear Arms against their Country, to become the executioners of their friends and Brethren, or to fall themselves by their Hands.

He has excited domestic insurrections amongst us, and has endeavoured to bring on the inhabitants of our frontiers, the merciless Indian Savages, whose known rule of warfare, is an undistinguished destruction of all ages, sexes and conditions.

In every stage of these Oppressions We have Petitioned for Redress in the most humble terms: Our repeated Petitions have been answered only by repeated injury. A Prince whose character is thus marked by every act which may define a Tyrant, is unfit to be the ruler of a free people.

Nor have We been wanting in attentions to our British brethren. We have warned them from time to time of attempts by their legislature to extend an unwarrantable jurisdiction over us. We have reminded them of the circumstances of our emigration and settlement here. We have appealed to their native justice and magnanimity, and we have conjured them by the ties of our common kindred to disavow these usurpations, which, would inevitably interrupt our connections and correspondence. They too have been deaf to the voice of justice and of consanguinity. We must, therefore, acquiesce in the necessity, which denounces our Separation, and hold them, as we hold the rest of mankind, Enemies in War, in Peace Friends.

We, therefore, the Representatives of the united States of America, in General Congress, Assembled, appealing to the Supreme Judge of the world for the rectitude of our intentions, do, in the Name, and by Authority of the good People of these Colonies, solemnly publish and declare, That these United Colonies are, and of Right ought to be Free and Independent States; that they are Absolved from all Allegiance to the British Crown, and that all political connection between them and the State of Great Britain, is and ought to be totally dissolved; and that as Free and Independent States, they have full Power to levy War, conclude Peace, contract Alliances, establish Commerce, and to do all other Acts and Things which Independent States may of right do. And for the support of this Declaration, with a firm reliance on the protection of divine Providence, we mutually pledge to each other our Lives, our Fortunes and our sacred Honor.

Georgia:
Button Gwinnett
Lyman Hall
George Walton
North Carolina:
William Hooper
Joseph Hewes
John Penn
South Carolina:
Edward Rutledge
Thomas Heyward, Jr.
Thomas Lynch, Jr.
Arthur Middleton
Maryland:
Samuel Chase
William Paca
Thomas Stone
Charles Carroll of Carrollton

Virginia:
George Wythe
Richard Henry Lee
Thomas Jefferson
Benjamin Harrison
Thomas Nelson, Jr.
Francis Lightfoot Lee
Carter Braxton
Pennsylvania:
Robert Morris
Benjamin Rush
Benjamin Franklin
John Morton
George Clymer
James Smith
George Taylor
James Wilson
George Ross

Delaware:
Caesar Rodney
George Read
Thomas McKean
New York:
William Floyd
Philip Livingston
Francis Lewis
Lewis Morris
New Jersey:
Richard Stockton
John Witherspoon
Francis Hopkinson
John Hart
Abraham Clark
Rhode Island:
Stephen Hopkins
William Ellery

New Hampshire:
Josiah Bartlett
William Whipple
Matthew Thornton
Massachusetts:
John Hancock
Samuel Adams
John Adams
Robert Treat Paine
Elbridge Gerry
Connecticut:
Roger Sherman
Samuel Huntington
William Williams
Oliver Wolcott

Appendix B

The Articles of the Confederation (1781)

TO ALL TO WHOM these Presents shall come, we the undersigned Delegates of the States affixed to our Names send greeting. Whereas the Delegates of the United States of America in Congress assembled did on the fifteenth day of November in the Year of our Lord One Thousand Seven Hundred and Seventy seven, and in the Second Year of the Independence of America agree to certain articles of Confederation and perpetual Union between the States of New Hampshire, Massachusetts bay, Rhode Island and Providence Plantations, Connecticut, New York, New Jersey, Pennsylvania, Delaware, Maryland, Virginia, North Carolina, South Carolina and Georgia in the Words following, viz. "Articles of Confederation and perpetual Union between the states of New Hampshire, Massachusetts bay, Rhode Island and Providence Plantations, Connecticut, New York, New Jersey, Pennsylvania, Delaware, Maryland, Virginia, North Carolina, South Carolina and Georgia.

Article I.

The Style of this confederacy shall be "The United States of America."

Article II.

Each state retains its sovereignty, freedom and independence, and every Power, Jurisdiction and right, which is not by this confederation expressly delegated to the United States, in Congress assembled.

Article III.

The said states hereby severally enter into a firm league of friendship with each other, for their common defence, the security of their Liberties, and their mutual and general welfare, binding themselves to assist each other, against all force offered to, or attacks made upon them, or any of them, on account of religion, sovereignty, trade, or any other pretence whatever.

Article IV.

The better to secure and perpetuate mutual friendship and intercourse among the people of the different states in this union, the free inhabitants of each of these states, paupers, vagabonds and fugitives from Justice excepted, shall be entitled to all privileges and immunities of free citizens in the several states; and the people of each state shall have free ingress and regress to and from any other state, and shall enjoy therein all the privileges of trade and commerce, subject to the same duties, impositions and restrictions as the inhabitants thereof respectively, provided that such restriction shall not extend so far as to prevent the removal of property imported into any state, to any other state of which the Owner is an inhabitant; provided also that no imposition, duties or restriction shall be laid by any state, on the property of the united states, or either of them.

If any Person guilty of, or charged with treason, felony, or other high misdemeanor in any state, shall flee from Justice, and be found in any of the united states, he shall upon demand of the Governor or executive power, of the state from which he fled, be delivered up and removed to the state having jurisdiction of his offence.

Full faith and credit shall be given in each of these states to the records, acts and judicial proceedings of the courts and magistrates of every other state.

Article V.

For the more convenient management of the general interests of the united states, delegates shall be annually appointed in such manner as the legislature of each state shall direct, to meet in Congress on the first Monday in November, in every year, with a power reserved to each state, to recall its delegates, or any of them, at any time within the year, and to send others in their stead, for the remainder of the Year.

No state shall be represented in Congress by less than two, nor by more than seven Members; and no person shall be capable of being a delegate for more than three years in any term of six years; nor shall any person, being a delegate, be capable of holding any office under the united states, for which he, or another for his benefit receives any salary, fees or emolument of any kind.

Each state shall maintain its own delegates in a meeting of the states, and while they act as members of the committee of the states.

In determining questions in the united states, in Congress assembled, each state shall have one vote.

Freedom of speech and debate in Congress shall not be impeached or questioned in any Court, or place out of Congress, and the members of congress shall be protected in their persons from arrests and imprisonments, during the time of their going to and from, and attendance on congress, except for treason, felony, or breach of the peace.

Article VI.

No state without the Consent of the united states in congress assembled, shall send any embassy to, or receive any embassy from, or enter into any conference, agreement, or alliance or treaty with any King prince or state; nor shall any person holding any office of profit or trust under the united states, or any of them, accept of any present, emolument, office or title of any kind

whatever from any king, prince or foreign state; nor shall the united states in congress assembled, or any of them, grant any title of nobility.

No two or more states shall enter into any treaty, confederation or alliance whatever between them, without the consent of the united states in congress assembled, specifying accurately the purposes for which the same is to be entered into, and how long it shall continue.

No state shall lay any imposts or duties, which may interfere with any stipulations in treaties, entered into by the united states in congress assembled, with any king, prince or state, in pursuance of any treaties already proposed by congress, to the courts of France and Spain.

No vessels of war shall be kept up in time of peace by any state, except such number only, as shall be deemed necessary by the united states in congress assembled, for the defence of such state, or its trade; nor shall any body of forces be kept up by any state, in time of peace, except such number only, as in the judgment of the united states, in congress assembled, shall be deemed requisite to garrison the forts necessary for the defence of such state; but every state shall always keep up a well regulated and disciplined militia, sufficiently armed and accoutered, and shall provide and constantly have ready for use, in public stores, a due number of field pieces and tents, and a proper quantity of arms, ammunition and camp equipage.

No state shall engage in any war without the consent of the united states in congress assembled, unless such state be actually invaded by enemies, or shall have received certain advice of a resolution being formed by some nation of Indians to invade such state, and the danger is so imminent as not to admit of a delay, till the united states in congress assembled can be consulted: nor shall any state grant commissions to any ships or vessels of war, nor letters of marque or reprisal, except it be after a declaration of war by the united states in congress assembled, and then only against the kingdom or state and the subjects thereof, against which war has been so declared, and under such regulations as shall be established by the united states in congress assembled, unless such state be infested by pirates, in which case vessels of war may be fitted out for that occasion, and kept so long as the danger shall continue, or until the united states in congress assembled shall determine otherwise.

Article VII.

When land-forces are raised by any state for the common defence, all officers of or under the rank of colonel, shall be appointed by the legislature of each state respectively by whom such forces shall be raised, or in such manner as such state shall direct, and all vacancies shall be filled up by the state which first made the appointment.

Article VIII.

All charges of war, and all other expenses that shall be incurred for the common defence or general welfare, and allowed by the united states in congress assembled, shall be defrayed out of a common treasury, which shall be supplied by the several states, in proportion to the value of all land within each state, granted to or surveyed for any Person, as such land and the buildings and improvements thereon shall be estimated according to such mode as the united states in congress assembled, shall from time to time direct and appoint. The taxes for paying that proportion shall be laid and levied by the authority and direction of the legislatures of the several states within the time agreed upon by the united states in congress assembled.

Article IX.

The united states in congress assembled, shall have the sole and exclusive right and power of determining on peace and war, except in the cases mentioned in the sixth article—of sending and receiving ambassadors—entering into treaties and alliances, provided that no treaty of commerce shall be made whereby the legislative power of the respective states shall be restrained from imposing such imposts and duties on foreigners, as their own people are subjected to, or from prohibiting the exportation or importation of any species of goods or commodities whatsoever—of establishing rules for deciding in all cases, what captures on land or water shall be legal, and in what manner prizes taken by land or naval forces in the service of the united states shall be divided or appropriated—of granting letters of marque and reprisal in times of peace—appointing courts for the trial of piracies and felonies committed on the high seas and establishing courts for receiving and determining finally appeals in all cases of cap-

tures, provided that no member of congress shall be appointed a judge of any of the said courts.

The united states in congress assembled shall also be the last resort on appeal in all disputes and differences now subsisting or that hereafter may arise between two or more states concerning boundary, jurisdiction or any other cause whatever; which authority shall always be exercised in the manner following. Whenever the legislative or executive authority or lawful agent state in controversy with another shall present a petition to congress, stating the matter in question and praying for a hearing, notice thereof shall be given by order of congress to the legislative or executive authority of the other state in controversy, and a day assigned for the appearance of the parties by their lawful agents, who shall then be directed to appoint by joint consent, commissioners or judges to constitute a court for hearing and determining the matter in question; but if they cannot agree, congress shall name three persons out of each of the united states, and from the list of such persons each party shall alternately strike out one, the petitioners beginning, until the number shall be reduced to thirteen; and from that number not less than seven, nor more than nine names as congress shall direct, shall in the presence of congress be drawn out by lot, and the persons whose names shall be so drawn or any five of them, shall be commissioners or judges, to hear and finally determine the controversy, so always as a major part of the judges who shall hear the cause shall agree in the determination: and if either party shall neglect to attend at the day appointed, without showing reasons, which congress shall judge sufficient, or being present shall refuse to strike, the congress shall proceed to nominate three persons out of each state, and the secretary of congress shall strike in behalf of such party absent or refusing; and the judgment and sentence of the court to be appointed, in the manner before prescribed, shall be final and conclusive; and if any of the parties shall refuse to submit to the authority of such court, or to appear to defend their claim or cause, the court shall nevertheless proceed to pronounce sentence, or judgment, which shall in like manner be final and decisive, the judgment or sentence and other proceedings being in either case transmitted to congress, and lodged among the acts of congress for the security of the parties concerned: provided that every commissioner, before he sits in judgment, shall take an oath to be administered by one of the judges of the supreme or superior court of the state, where the cause shall be tried, "well and truly to hear and determine the matter in question, according to the best of his judgment, without favor, affection or hope of reward"; provided also that no state shall be deprived of territory for the benefit of the united states.

All controversies concerning the private right of soil claimed under different grants of two or more states, whose jurisdictions as they may respect such lands, and the states which passed such grants are adjusted, the said grants or either of them being at the same time claimed to have originated antecedent to such settlement of jurisdiction, shall on the petition of either party to the congress of the united states, be finally determined as near as may be in the same manner as is before prescribed for deciding disputes respecting territorial jurisdiction between different states.

The united states in congress assembled shall also have the sole and exclusive right and power of regulating the alloy and value of coin struck by their own authority, or by that of the respective states—fixing the standard of weights and measures throughout the united states—regulating the trade and managing all affairs with the Indians, not members of any of the states, provided that the legislative right of any state within its own limits be not infringed or violated—establishing and regulating post offices from one state to another, throughout all the united states, and exacting such postage on the papers passing through the same as may be requisite to defray the expenses of the said office—appointing all officers of the land forces, in the service of the united states, excepting regimental officers—appointing all the officers of the naval forces, and commissioning all officers whatever in the service of the united states—making rules for the government and regulation of the said land and naval forces, and directing their operations.

The united states in congress assembled shall have authority to appoint a committee, to sit in the recess of congress, to be denominated "A Committee of the States," and to consist of one delegate from each state; and to appoint such other committees and civil officers as may be necessary for managing the general affairs of the united states under their direction—to appoint one of their number to preside, provided that no per-

son be allowed to serve in the office of president more than one year in any term of three years; to ascertain the necessary sums of Money to be raised for the service of the united states, and to appropriate and apply the same for defraying the public expenses—to borrow money, or emit bills on the credit of the united states, transmitting every half year to the respective states an account of the sums of money so borrowed or emitted,—to build and equip a navy—to agree upon the number of land forces, and to make requisitions from each state for its quota, in proportion to the number of white inhabitants in such state; which requisition shall be binding, and thereupon the legislature of each state shall appoint the regimental officers, raise the men and clothe, arm and equip them in a soldier like manner, at the expense of the united states, and the officers and men so clothed, armed and equipped shall march to the place appointed, and within the time agreed on by the united states in congress assembled. But if the united states in congress assembled shall, on consideration of circumstances judge proper that any state should not raise men, or should raise a smaller number than its quota, and that any other state should raise a greater number of men than the quota thereof, such extra number shall be raised, officered, clothed, armed and equipped in the same manner as the quota of such state, unless the legislature of such state shall judge that such extra number cannot be safely spared out of the same, in which case they shall raise officer, clothe, arm and equip as many of such extra number as they judge can be safely spared. And the officers and men so clothed, armed and equipped, shall march to the place appointed, and within the time agreed on by the united states in congress assembled.

The united states in congress assembled shall never engage in a war, nor grant letters of marque and reprisal in time of peace, nor enter into any treaties or alliances, nor coin money, nor regulate the value thereof, nor ascertain the sums and expenses necessary for the defence and welfare of the united states, or any of them, nor emit bills, nor borrow money on the credit of the united states, nor appropriate money, nor agree upon the number of vessels of war, to be built or purchased, or the number of land or sea forces to be raised, nor appoint a commander in chief of the army or navy, unless nine states assent to the same: nor shall a question on any other point, except for adjourning from day to day be determined, unless by the votes of a majority of the united states in congress assembled.

The congress of the united states shall have power to adjourn to any time within the year, and to any place within the united states, so that no period of adjournment be for a longer duration than the space of six Months, and shall publish the Journal of their proceedings monthly, except such parts thereof relating to treaties, alliances or military operations as in their judgment require secrecy; and the yeas and nays of the delegates of each state on any question shall be entered on the Journal, when it is desired by any delegate; and the delegates of a state, or any of them, at his or their request shall be furnished with a transcript of the said Journal, except such parts as are above excepted, to lay before the legislatures of the several states.

Article X.

The committee of the states, or any nine of them, shall be authorized to execute, in the recess of congress, such of the powers of congress as the united states in congress assembled, by the consent of nine states, shall from time to time think expedient to vest them with; provided that no power be delegated to the said committee, for the exercise of which, by the articles of confederation, the voice of nine states in the congress of the united states assembled is requisite.

Article XI.

Canada acceding to this confederation, and joining in the measures of the united states, shall be admitted into, and entitled to all the advantages of this union: but no other colony shall be admitted into the same, unless such admission be agreed to by nine states.

Article XII.

All bills of credit emitted, monies borrowed and debts contracted by, or under the authority of congress, before the assembling of the united states, in pursuance of the present confederation, shall be deemed and considered as a charge against the united states, for payment and satisfaction whereof the said united states, and the public faith are hereby solemnly pledged.

Article XIII.

Every state shall abide by the determinations of the united states in congress assembled, on all questions which by this confederation are submitted to them. And the Articles of this confederation shall be inviolably observed by every state, and the union shall be perpetual; nor shall any alteration at any time hereafter be made in any of them; unless such alteration be agreed to in a congress of the united states, and be afterwards confirmed by the legislatures of every state.

AND WHEREAS it hath pleased the Great Governor of the World to incline the hearts of the legislatures we respectively represent in congress, to approve of, and to authorize us to ratify the said articles of confederation and perpetual union. KNOW YE that we the undersigned delegates, by virtue of the power and authority to us given for that purpose, do by these presents, in the name and in behalf of our respective constituents, fully and entirely ratify and confirm each and every of the said articles of confederation and perpetual union, and all and singular the matters and things therein contained: And we do further solemnly plight and engage the faith of our respective constituents, that they shall abide by the determinations of the united states in congress assembled, on all questions, which by the said confederation are submitted to them. And that the articles thereof shall be inviolably observed by the states we respectively represent, and that the union shall be perpetual. In Witness whereof we have hereunto set our hands in Congress. Done at Philadelphia in the state of Pennsylvania the ninth Day of July in the Year of our Lord one Thousand seven Hundred and Seventy-eight, and in the third year of the independence of America.

On the part and behalf of the State of New Hampshire:
JOSIAH BARTLETT
JOHN WENTWORTH JUNR.
August 8th 1778

On the part and behalf of The State of Massachusetts Bay:
JOHN HANCOCK
SAMUEL ADAMS
ELBRIDGE GERRY
FRANCIS DANA
JAMES LOVELL
SAMUEL HOLTEN

On the part and behalf of the State of Rhode Island and Providence Plantations:
WILLIAM ELLERY
HENRY MARCHANT
JOHN COLLINS

On the part and behalf of the State of Connecticut:
ROGER SHERMAN
SAMUEL HUNTINGTON
OLIVER WOLCOTT
TITUS HOSMER ANDREW ADAMS

On the part and behalf of the State of New York:
JAMES DUANE
FRANCIS LEWIS
WM DUER
GOUV MORRIS

On the part and in behalf of the State of New Jersey:
JNO WITHERSPOON
NATHANIEL SCUDDER
November 26, 1778

On the part and behalf of the State of Pennsylvania:
ROBT MORRIS
DANIEL ROBERDEAU
JOHN BAYARD SMITH
WILLIAM CLINGAN
JOSEPH REED
22nd July 1778

On the part and behalf of the State of Delaware:
THO McKEAN
February 12, 1779
JOHN DICKINSON
May 5th 1779
NICHOLAS VAN DYKE

On the part and behalf of the State of Maryland:
JOHN HANSON
March 1 1781
DANIEL CARROLL

On the part and behalf of the State of Virginia:
RICHARD HENRY LEE
JOHN BANISTER
THOMAS ADAMS
JNo HARVIE
FRANCIS LIGHTFOOT LEE

On the part and behalf of the State of North Carolina:
JOHN PENN
July 21st 1778
CORNs HARNETT
JNo WILLIAMS

On the part & behalf of the State of South Carolina:
HENRY LAURENS
WILLIAM HENRY DRAYTON
JNo MATHEWS
RICHD HUTSON
THOs HEYWARD Junr

On the part and behalf of the State of Georgia:
JNo WALTON
24th July 1778
EDWD TELFAIR
EDWD LANGWORTHY

Appendix C

Constitution of the United States

WE THE PEOPLE of the United States, in order to form a more perfect union, establish justice, insure domestic tranquility, provide for the common defense, promote the general welfare, and secure the blessings of liberty to ourselves and our posterity, do ordain and establish this Constitution for the United States of America.

Article I

Section 1.   All legislative powers herein granted shall be vested in a Congress of the United States, which shall consist of a Senate and House of Representatives.

Section 2.   The House of Representatives shall be composed of members chosen every second year by the people of the several states, and the electors in each state shall have the qualifications requisite for electors of the most numerous branch of the state legislature.

No person shall be a Representative who shall not have attained to the age of twenty five years, and been seven years a citizen of the United States, and who shall not, when elected, be an inhabitant of that state in which he shall be chosen.

Representatives and direct taxes shall be apportioned among the several states which may be included within this union, according to their respective numbers, which shall be determined by adding to the whole number of free persons, including those bound to service for a term of years, and excluding Indians not taxed, three fifths of all other persons. The actual enumeration shall be made within three years after the first meeting of the Congress of the United States, and within every subsequent term of ten years, in such manner as they shall by law direct. The number of Representatives shall not exceed one for every thirty thousand, but each state shall have at least one Representative; and until such enumeration shall be made, the state of New Hampshire shall be entitled to choose three, Massachusetts eight, Rhode Island and Providence Plantations one, Connecticut five, New York six, New Jersey four, Pennsylvania eight, Delaware one, Maryland six, Virginia ten, North Carolina five, South Carolina five, and Georgia three.

When vacancies happen in the representation from any state, the executive authority thereof shall issue writs of election to fill such vacancies.

The House of Representatives shall choose their speaker and other officers; and shall have the sole power of impeachment.

Section 3.   The Senate of the United States shall be composed of two Senators from each state, chosen by the legislature thereof, for six years; and each Senator shall have one vote.

Immediately after they shall be assembled in consequence of the first election, they shall be divided as equally as may be into three classes. The seats of the Senators of the first class shall be vacated at the expiration of the second year, of the second class at the expiration of the fourth year, and the third class at the expiration of the sixth year, so that one third may be chosen every second year; and if vacancies happen by resignation, or otherwise, during the recess of the legislature of any state, the executive thereof may make temporary appointments until the next meeting of the legislature, which shall then fill such vacancies.

No person shall be a Senator who shall not have attained to the age of thirty years, and been nine years a citizen of the United States and who shall not, when elected, be an inhabitant of that state for which he shall be chosen.

The Vice President of the United States shall be President of the Senate, but shall have no vote, unless they be equally divided.

The Senate shall choose their other officers, and also a President pro tempore, in the absence of the Vice President, or when he shall exercise the office of President of the United States.

The Senate shall have the sole power to try all impeachments. When sitting for that purpose, they shall be on oath or affirmation. When the President of the United States is tried, the Chief Justice shall preside: And no person shall be convicted without the concurrence of two thirds of the members present.

Judgment in cases of impeachment shall not extend further than to removal from office, and disqualification to hold and enjoy any office of honor, trust or profit under the United States: but the party convicted shall nevertheless be liable and subject to indictment, trial, judgment and punishment, according to law.

Section 4.   The times, places and manner of holding elections for Senators and Representatives, shall be prescribed in each state by the legislature thereof; but the Congress may at any time by law make or alter such regulations, except as to the places of choosing Senators.

The Congress shall assemble at least once in every year, and such meeting shall be on the first Monday in December, unless they shall by law appoint a different day.

Section 5.   Each House shall be the judge of the elections, returns and qualifications of its own members, and a majority of each shall constitute a quorum to do business; but a smaller number may adjourn from day to day, and may be authorized to compel the attendance of absent members, in such manner, and under such penalties as each House may provide.

Each House may determine the rules of its proceedings, punish its members for disorderly behavior, and, with the concurrence of two thirds, expel a member.

Each House shall keep a journal of its proceedings, and from time to time publish the same, excepting such parts as may in their judgment require secrecy; and the yeas and nays of the members of either House on any question shall, at the desire of one fifth of those present, be entered on the journal.

Neither House, during the session of Congress, shall, without the consent of the other, adjourn for more than three days, nor to any other place than that in which the two Houses shall be sitting.

Section 6.   The Senators and Representatives shall receive a compensation for their services, to be ascertained by law, and paid out of the treasury of the United States. They shall in all cases, except treason, felony and breach of the peace, be privileged from arrest during their attendance at the session of their respective houses, and in going to and returning from the same; and for any speech or debate in either house, they shall not be questioned in any other place.

No Senator or Representative shall, during the time for which he was elected, be appointed to any civil office under the authority of the United States, which shall have been created, or the emoluments whereof shall have been increased during such time: and no person holding any office under the United States, shall be a member of either House during his continuance in office.

Section 7.   All bills for raising revenue shall originate in the House of Representatives; but the Senate may propose or concur with amendments as on other Bills.

Every bill which shall have passed the House of Representatives and the Senate, shall, before it become a law, be presented to the President of the United States; if he approve he shall sign it, but if not he shall return it, with his objections to that house in which it shall have originated, who shall enter the objections at large on their journal, and proceed to reconsider it. If after such reconsideration two thirds of that house shall agree to pass the bill, it shall be sent, together with the objections, to the other house, by which it shall likewise be reconsidered, and if approved by two thirds of that house, it shall become a law. But in all such cases the votes of both houses shall be determined by yeas and nays, and the names of the persons voting for and against the bill shall be entered on the journal of each house respectively. If any bill shall not be returned by the President within ten days (Sundays excepted) after it shall have been presented to him, the same shall be a law, in like manner as if he had signed it, unless the Congress by their adjournment prevent its return, in which case it shall not be a law.

Every order, resolution, or vote to which the concurrence of the Senate and House of Representatives may be necessary (except on a question of adjournment) shall be presented to the President of the United States; and before the same shall take effect, shall be approved by him, or being disapproved by him, shall be repassed by two thirds of the Senate and House of Representatives, according to the rules and limitations prescribed in the case of a bill.

Section 8.   The Congress shall have power to lay and collect taxes, duties, imposts and excises, to pay the debts and provide for the common defense and general welfare of the United States; but all duties, imposts and excises shall be uniform throughout the United States;

To borrow money on the credit of the United States;

To regulate commerce with foreign nations, and among the several states, and with the Indian tribes;

To establish a uniform rule of naturalization, and uniform laws on the subject of bankruptcies throughout the United States;

To coin money, regulate the value thereof, and of foreign coin, and fix the standard of weights and measures;

To provide for the punishment of counterfeiting the securities and current coin of the United States;

To establish post offices and post roads;

To promote the progress of science and useful arts, by securing for limited times to authors and inventors the exclusive right to their respective writings and discoveries;

To constitute tribunals inferior to the Supreme Court;

To define and punish piracies and felonies committed on the high seas, and offenses against the law of nations;

To declare war, grant letters of marque and reprisal, and make rules concerning captures on land and water;

To raise and support armies, but no appropriation of money to that use shall be for a longer term than two years;

To provide and maintain a navy;

To make rules for the government and regulation of the land and naval forces;

To provide for calling forth the militia to execute the laws of the union, suppress insurrections and repel invasions;

To provide for organizing, arming, and disciplining, the militia, and for governing such part of them as may be employed in the service of the United States, reserving to the states respectively, the appointment of the officers, and the authority of training the militia according to the discipline prescribed by Congress;

To exercise exclusive legislation in all cases whatsoever, over such District (not exceeding ten miles square) as may, by cession of particular states, and the acceptance of Congress, become the seat of the government of the United States, and to exercise like authority over all places purchased by the consent of the legislature of the state in which the same shall be, for the erection of forts, magazines, arsenals, dockyards, and other needful buildings;—and

To make all laws which shall be necessary and proper for carrying into execution the foregoing powers, and all other powers vested by this Constitution in the government of the United States, or in any department or officer thereof.

Section 9.   The migration or importation of such persons as any of the states now existing shall think proper to admit, shall not be prohibited by the Congress prior to the year one thousand eight hundred and eight, but a tax or duty may be imposed on such importation, not exceeding ten dollars for each person.

The privilege of the writ of habeas corpus shall not be suspended, unless when in cases of rebellion or invasion the public safety may require it.

No bill of attainder or ex post facto Law shall be passed.

No capitation, or other direct, tax shall be laid, unless in proportion to the census or enumeration herein before directed to be taken.

No tax or duty shall be laid on articles exported from any state.

No preference shall be given by any regulation of commerce or revenue to the ports of one state over those of another: nor shall vessels bound to, or from, one state, be obliged to enter, clear or pay duties in another.

No money shall be drawn from the treasury, but in consequence of appropriations made by law; and a regular statement and account of receipts and expenditures of all public money shall be published from time to time.

No title of nobility shall be granted by the United States: and no person holding any office of profit or trust under them, shall, without the consent of the Congress, accept of any present, emolument, office, or title, of any kind whatever, from any king, prince, or foreign state.

Section 10.   No state shall enter into any treaty, alliance, or confederation; grant letters of marque and reprisal; coin money; emit bills of credit; make anything but gold and silver coin a tender in payment of debts; pass any bill of attainder, ex post facto law, or law impairing the obligation of contracts, or grant any title of nobility.

No state shall, without the consent of the Congress, lay any imposts or duties on imports or exports, except what may be absolutely necessary for executing its inspection laws: and the net produce of all duties and imposts, laid by any state on imports or exports, shall be for the use of the treasury of the United States; and all such laws shall be subject to the revision and control of the Congress.

No state shall, without the consent of Congress, lay any duty of tonnage, keep troops, or ships of war in time of peace, enter into any agreement or compact with another state, or with a foreign power, or engage in war, unless actually invaded, or in such imminent danger as will not admit of delay.

Article II

Section 1.   The executive power shall be vested in a President of the United States of America. He shall hold his office during the term of four years, and, together with the Vice President, chosen for the same term, be elected, as follows:

Each state shall appoint, in such manner as the Legislature thereof may direct, a number of electors, equal to the whole number of Senators and Representatives to which the state may be entitled in the Congress: but no Senator or Representative, or person holding an office of trust or profit under the United States, shall be appointed an elector.

The electors shall meet in their respective states, and vote by ballot for two persons, of whom one at least shall not be an inhabitant of the same state with themselves. And they shall make a list of all the persons voted for, and of the number of votes for each; which list they shall sign and certify, and transmit sealed to the seat of the government of the United States, directed to the President of the Senate. The President of the Senate shall, in the presence of the Senate and House of Representatives, open all the certificates, and the votes shall then be counted. The person having the greatest number of votes shall be the President, if such number be a majority of the whole number of electors appointed; and if there be more than one who have such majority, and have an equal number of votes, then the House of Representatives shall immediately choose by ballot one of them for President; and if no person have a majority, then from the five highest on the list the said House shall in like manner choose the President. But in choosing the President, the votes shall be taken by States, the representation from each state having one vote; a quorum for this purpose shall consist of a member or members from two thirds of the states, and a majority of all the states shall be necessary to a choice. In every case, after the choice of the President, the person having the greatest number of votes of the electors shall be the Vice President. But if there should remain two or more who have equal votes, the Senate shall choose from them by ballot the Vice President.

The Congress may determine the time of choosing the electors, and the day on which they shall give their votes; which day shall be the same throughout the United States.

No person except a natural-born citizen, or a citizen of the United States, at the time of the adoption of this Constitution, shall be eligible to the office of President;

neither shall any person be eligible to that office who shall not have attained to the age of thirty five years, and been fourteen Years a resident within the United States.

In case of the removal of the President from office, or of his death, resignation, or inability to discharge the powers and duties of the said office, the same shall devolve on the Vice President, and the Congress may by law provide for the case of removal, death, resignation or inability, both of the President and Vice President, declaring what officer shall then act as President, and such officer shall act accordingly, until the disability be removed, or a President shall be elected.

The President shall, at stated times, receive for his services, a compensation, which shall neither be increased nor diminished during the period for which he shall have been elected, and he shall not receive within that period any other emolument from the United States, or any of them.

Before he enter on the execution of his office, he shall take the following oath or affirmation:—"I do solemnly swear (or affirm) that I will faithfully execute the office of President of the United States, and will to the best of my ability, preserve, protect and defend the Constitution of the United States."

Section 2. The President shall be commander in chief of the Army and Navy of the United States, and of the militia of the several states, when called into the actual service of the United States; he may require the opinion, in writing, of the principal officer in each of the executive departments, upon any subject relating to the duties of their respective offices, and he shall have power to grant reprieves and pardons for offenses against the United States, except in cases of impeachment.

He shall have power, by and with the advice and consent of the Senate, to make treaties, provided two thirds of the Senators present concur; and he shall nominate, and by and with the advice and consent of the Senate, shall appoint ambassadors, other public ministers and consuls, judges of the Supreme Court, and all other officers of the United States, whose appointments are not herein otherwise provided for, and which shall be by law: but the Congress may by law vest the appointment of such inferior officers, as they think proper, in

the President alone, in the courts of law, or in the heads of departments.

The President shall have power to fill up all vacancies that may happen during the recess of the Senate, by granting commissions which shall expire at the end of their next session.

Section 3. He shall from time to time give to the Congress information of the state of the union, and recommend to their consideration such measures as he shall judge necessary and expedient; he may, on extraordinary occasions, convene both Houses, or either of them, and in case of disagreement between them, with respect to the time of adjournment, he may adjourn them to such time as he shall think proper; he shall receive ambassadors and other public ministers; he shall take care that the laws be faithfully executed, and shall commission all the officers of the United States.

Section 4. The President, Vice President and all civil officers of the United States, shall be removed from office on impeachment for, and conviction of, treason, bribery, or other high crimes and misdemeanors.

Article III

Section 1. The judicial power of the United States, shall be vested in one Supreme Court, and in such inferior courts as the Congress may from time to time ordain and establish. The judges, both of the supreme and inferior courts, shall hold their offices during good behaviour, and shall, at stated times, receive for their services, a compensation, which shall not be diminished during their continuance in office.

Section 2. The judicial power shall extend to all cases, in law and equity, arising under this Constitution, the laws of the United States, and treaties made, or which shall be made, under their authority;—to all cases affecting ambassadors, other public ministers and consuls;—to all cases of admiralty and maritime jurisdiction;—to controversies to which the United States shall be a party;—to controversies between two or more states;—between a state and citizens of another state;— between citizens of different states;—between citizens of the same state claiming lands under grants of different states, and between a state, or the citizens thereof, and foreign states, citizens or subjects.

In all cases affecting ambassadors, other public ministers and consuls, and those in which a state shall be party, the Supreme Court shall have original jurisdiction. In all the other cases before mentioned, the Supreme Court shall have appellate jurisdiction, both as to law and fact, with such exceptions, and under such regulations as the Congress shall make.

The trial of all crimes, except in cases of impeachment, shall be by jury; and such trial shall be held in the state where the said crimes shall have been committed; but when not committed within any state, the trial shall be at such place or places as the Congress may by law have directed.

Section 3.   Treason against the United States, shall consist only in levying war against them, or in adhering to their enemies, giving them aid and comfort. No person shall be convicted of treason unless on the testimony of two witnesses to the same overt act, or on confession in open court.

The Congress shall have power to declare the punishment of treason, but no attainder of treason shall work corruption of blood, or forfeiture except during the life of the person attainted.

Article IV

Section 1.   Full faith and credit shall be given in each state to the public acts, records, and judicial proceedings of every other state. And the Congress may by general laws prescribe the manner in which such acts, records, and proceedings shall be proved, and the effect thereof.

Section 2.   The citizens of each state shall be entitled to all privileges and immunities of citizens in the several states.

A person charged in any state with treason, felony, or other crime, who shall flee from justice, and be found in another state, shall on demand of the executive authority of the state from which he fled, be delivered up, to be removed to the state having jurisdiction of the crime.

No person held to service or labor in one state, under the laws thereof, escaping into another, shall, in consequence of any law or regulation therein, be discharged from such service or labor, but shall be delivered up on claim of the party to whom such service or labor may be due.

Section 3.   New states may be admitted by the Congress into this union; but no new states shall be formed or erected within the jurisdiction of any other state; nor any state be formed by the junction of two or more states, or parts of states, without the consent of the legislatures of the states concerned as well as of the Congress.

The Congress shall have power to dispose of and make all needful rules and regulations respecting the territory or other property belonging to the United States; and nothing in this Constitution shall be so construed as to prejudice any claims of the United States, or of any particular state.

Section 4.   The United States shall guarantee to every state in this union a republican form of government, and shall protect each of them against invasion; and on application of the legislature, or of the executive (when the legislature cannot be convened) against domestic violence.

Article V

The Congress, whenever two thirds of both houses shall deem it necessary, shall propose amendments to this Constitution, or, on the application of the legislatures of two thirds of the several states, shall call a convention for proposing amendments, which, in either case, shall be valid to all intents and purposes, as part of this Constitution, when ratified by the legislatures of three fourths of the several states, or by conventions in three fourths thereof, as the one or the other mode of ratification may be proposed by the Congress; provided that no amendment which may be made prior to the year one thousand eight hundred and eight shall in any manner affect the first and fourth clauses in the ninth section of the first article; and that no state, without its consent, shall be deprived of its equal suffrage in the Senate.

Article VI

All debts contracted and engagements entered into, before the adoption of this Constitution, shall be as valid against the United States under this Constitution, as under the Confederation.

This Constitution, and the laws of the United States which shall be made in pursuance thereof; and all treaties made, or which shall be made, under the authority of the United States, shall be the supreme law of the land; and the judges in every state shall be bound thereby, anything in the Constitution or laws of any State to the contrary notwithstanding.

The Senators and Representatives before mentioned, and the members of the several state legislatures, and all executive and judicial officers, both of the United States and of the several states, shall be bound by oath or affirmation, to support this Constitution; but no religious test shall ever be required as a qualification to any office or public trust under the United States.

Article VII

The ratification of the conventions of nine states, shall be sufficient for the establishment of this Constitution between the states so ratifying the same.

Done in convention by the unanimous consent of the states present the seventeenth day of September in the year of our Lord one thousand seven hundred and eighty seven and of the independence of the United States of America the twelfth. In witness whereof we have hereunto subscribed our Names,

---

Virginia
G. Washington—Presidt. and deputy from Virginia
New Hampshire
John Langdon, Nicholas Gilman
Massachusetts
Nathaniel Gorham, Rufus King
Connecticut
Wm. Saml. Johnson, Roger Sherman
New York
Alexander Hamilton
New Jersey
Wil. Livingston, David Brearly, Wm. Paterson, Jona. Dayton
Pennsylvania
B. Franklin, Thomas Mifflin, Robt. Morris, Geo. Clymer, Thos. FitzSimons, Jared Ingersoll, James Wilson, Gouv Morris

Delaware
Geo. Read, Gunning Bedford jun, John Dickinson, Richard Bassett, Jaco. Broom
Maryland
James McHenry, Dan of St Thos. Jenifer, Danl Carroll
Virginia
John Blair—, James Madison Jr.
North Carolina
Wm. Blount, Richd. Dobbs Spaight, Hu Williamson
South Carolina
J. Rutledge, Charles Cotesworth Pinckney, Charles Pinckney, Pierce Butler
Georgia
William Few, Abr Baldwin

Bill of Rights

Amendments I through X of the Constitution

Amendment I

Congress shall make no law respecting an establishment of religion, or prohibiting the free exercise thereof; or abridging the freedom of speech, or of the press; or the right of the people peaceably to assemble, and to petition the government for a redress of grievances.

Amendment II

A well regulated militia, being necessary to the security of a free state, the right of the people to keep and bear arms, shall not be infringed.

Amendment III

No soldier shall, in time of peace be quartered in any house, without the consent of the owner, nor in time of war, but in a manner to be prescribed by law.

Amendment IV

The right of the people to be secure in their persons, houses, papers, and effects, against unreasonable searches and seizures, shall not be violated, and no warrants shall issue, but upon probable cause, supported by oath or affirmation, and particularly describing the place to be searched, and the persons or things to be seized.

Amendment V

No person shall be held to answer for a capital, or otherwise infamous crime, unless on a presentment or indictment of a grand jury, except in cases arising in the land or naval forces, or in the militia, when in actual service in time of war or public danger; nor shall any person be subject for the same offense to be twice put in jeopardy of life or limb; nor shall be compelled in any criminal case to be a witness against himself, nor be deprived of life, liberty, or property, without due process of law; nor shall private property be taken for public use, without just compensation.

Amendment VI

In all criminal prosecutions, the accused shall enjoy the right to a speedy and public trial, by an impartial jury of the state and district wherein the crime shall have been committed, which district shall have been previously ascertained by law, and to be informed of the nature and cause of the accusation; to be confronted with the witnesses against him; to have compulsory process for obtaining witnesses in his favor, and to have the assistance of counsel for his defense.

Amendment VII

In suits at common law, where the value in controversy shall exceed twenty dollars, the right of trial by jury shall be preserved, and no fact tried by a jury, shall be otherwise reexamined in any court of the United States, than according to the rules of the common law.

Amendment VIII

Excessive bail shall not be required, nor excessive fines imposed, nor cruel and unusual punishments inflicted.

Amendment IX

The enumeration in the Constitution, of certain rights, shall not be construed to deny or disparage others retained by the people.

Amendment X

The powers not delegated to the United States by the Constitution, nor prohibited by it to the states, are reserved to the states respectively, or to the people.

Additional Amendments

Amendment XI

(1798)

The judicial power of the United States shall not be construed to extend to any suit in law or equity, commenced or prosecuted against one of the United States by citizens of another state, or by citizens or subjects of any foreign state.

Amendment XII

(1804)

The electors shall meet in their respective states and vote by ballot for President and Vice President, one of whom, at least, shall not be an inhabitant of the same state with themselves; they shall name in their ballots the person voted for as President, and in distinct ballots the person voted for as Vice President, and they shall make distinct lists of all persons voted for as President, and of all persons voted for as Vice President, and of the number of votes for each, which lists they shall sign and certify, and transmit sealed to the seat of the government of the United States, directed to the President of the Senate;—The President of the Senate shall, in the presence of the Senate and House of Representatives, open all the certificates and the votes shall then be counted;—the person having the greatest number of votes for President, shall be the President, if such number be a majority of the whole number of electors appointed; and if no person have such majority, then from the persons having the highest numbers not exceeding three on the list of those voted for as President, the House of Representatives shall choose immediately, by ballot, the President. But in choosing the President, the votes shall be taken by states, the representation from each state having one vote; a quorum for this purpose shall consist of a member or members from two-thirds of the states, and a majority of all the states shall be necessary to a choice. And if the House of Representatives shall not choose a President whenever the right of choice shall devolve upon them, before the fourth day of March next following, then the Vice President shall act as President, as in the case of the death or other constitutional disability of the President. The person having the greatest number of votes as Vice President, shall be the Vice President, if such number be a majority of the whole number of electors appointed, and if no person have a majority, then from the two highest numbers on the list, the Senate shall choose the Vice President; a quorum for the purpose shall consist of two-thirds of the whole number of Senators, and a majority of the whole number shall be necessary to a choice. But no person constitutionally ineligible to the office of President shall be eligible to that of Vice President of the United States.

Amendment XIII

(1865)

Section 1.   Neither slavery nor involuntary servitude, except as a punishment for crime whereof the party shall have been duly convicted, shall exist within the United States, or any place subject to their jurisdiction.

Section 2.   Congress shall have power to enforce this article by appropriate legislation.

Amendment XIV

(1868)

Section 1.   All persons born or naturalized in the United States, and subject to the jurisdiction thereof, are citizens of the United States and of the state wherein they reside. No state shall make or enforce any law which shall abridge the privileges or immunities of citizens of the United States; nor shall any state deprive any person of life, liberty, or property, without due process of law; nor deny to any person within its jurisdiction the equal protection of the laws.

Section 2.   Representatives shall be apportioned among the several states according to their respective numbers, counting the whole number of persons in each state, excluding Indians not taxed. But when the right to vote at any election for the choice of electors for President and Vice President of the United States, Representatives in Congress, the executive and judicial officers of a state, or the members of the legislature thereof, is denied to any of the male inhabitants of such state, being twenty-one years of age, and citizens of the United States, or in any way abridged, except for participation in rebellion, or other crime, the basis of representation therein shall be reduced in the proportion which the number of such male citizens shall bear to the whole number of male citizens twenty-one years of age in such state.

Section 3.   No person shall be a Senator or Representative in Congress, or elector of President and Vice President, or hold any office, civil or military, under the United States, or under any state, who, having previously taken an oath, as a member of Congress, or as an officer of the United States, or as a member of any state legislature, or as an executive or judicial officer of any state, to support the Constitution of the United States, shall have engaged in insurrection or rebellion against the same, or given aid or comfort to the enemies thereof. But Congress may by a vote of two-thirds of each House, remove such disability.

Section 4.   The validity of the public debt of the United States, authorized by law, including debts incurred for payment of pensions and bounties for services in suppressing insurrection or rebellion, shall not be questioned. But neither the United States nor any state shall assume or pay any debt or obligation incurred in aid of insurrection or rebellion against the United States, or any claim for the loss or emancipation of any slave; but all such debts, obligations and claims shall be held illegal and void.

Section 5.   The Congress shall have power to enforce, by appropriate legislation, the provisions of this article.

Amendment XV

(1870)

Section 1.   The right of citizens of the United States to vote shall not be denied or abridged by the United States or by any state on account of race, color, or previous condition of servitude.

Section 2.   The Congress shall have power to enforce this article by appropriate legislation.

Amendment XVI

(1913)

The Congress shall have power to lay and collect taxes on incomes, from whatever source derived, without apportionment among the several states, and without regard to any census of enumeration.

Amendment XVII

(1913)

The Senate of the United States shall be composed of two Senators from each state, elected by the people thereof, for six years; and each Senator shall have one vote. The electors in each state shall have the qualifications requisite for electors of the most numerous branch of the state legislatures.

When vacancies happen in the representation of any state in the Senate, the executive authority of such state shall issue writs of election to fill such vacancies: Provided, that the legislature of any state may empower the executive thereof to make temporary appointments until the people fill the vacancies by election as the legislature may direct.

This amendment shall not be so construed as to affect the election or term of any Senator chosen before it becomes valid as part of the Constitution.

Amendment XVIII

(1919)

Section 1.   After one year from the ratification of this article the manufacture, sale, or transportation of intoxicating liquors within, the importation thereof into, or the exportation thereof from the United States and all territory subject to the jurisdiction thereof for beverage purposes is hereby prohibited.

Section 2.   The Congress and the several states shall have concurrent power to enforce this article by appropriate legislation.

Section 3.   This article shall be inoperative unless it shall have been ratified as an amendment to the Constitution by the legislatures of the several states, as provided in the Constitution, within seven years from the date of the submission hereof to the states by the Congress.

Amendment XIX

(1920)

The right of citizens of the United States to vote shall not be denied or abridged by the United States or by any state on account of sex.

Congress shall have power to enforce this article by appropriate legislation.

Amendment XX

(1933)

Section 1.   The terms of the President and Vice President shall end at noon on the 20th day of January, and the terms of Senators and Representatives at noon on the 3d day of January, of the years in which such terms would have ended if this article had not been ratified; and the terms of their successors shall then begin.

Section 2.   The Congress shall assemble at least once in every year, and such meeting shall begin at noon on the 3d day of January, unless they shall by law appoint a different day.

Section 3.   If, at the time fixed for the beginning of the term of the President, the President-elect shall have died, the Vice President-elect shall become President. If a President shall not have been chosen before the time fixed for the beginning of his term, or if the President-elect shall have failed to qualify, then the Vice President-elect shall act as President until a President shall have qualified; and the Congress may by law provide for the case wherein neither a President elect nor a Vice President-elect shall have qualified, declaring who shall then act as President, or the manner in which one who is to act shall be selected, and such person shall act accordingly until a President or Vice President shall have qualified.

Section 4.   The Congress may by law provide for the case of the death of any of the persons from whom the House of Representatives may choose a President whenever the right of choice shall have devolved upon them, and for the case of the death of any of the persons from whom the Senate may choose a Vice President whenever the right of choice shall have devolved upon them.

Section 5.   Sections 1 and 2 shall take effect on the 15th day of October following the ratification of this article.

Section 6.   This article shall be inoperative unless it shall have been ratified as an amendment to the Constitution by the legislatures of three-fourths of the several states within seven years from the date of its submission.

Amendment XXI

(1933)

Section 1.   The eighteenth article of amendment to the Constitution of the United States is hereby repealed.

Section 2.   The transportation or importation into any state, territory, or possession of the United States for delivery or use therein of intoxicating liquors, in violation of the laws thereof, is hereby prohibited.

Section 3.   This article shall be inoperative unless it shall have been ratified as an amendment to the Constitution by conventions in the several states, as provided in the Constitution, within seven years from the date of the submission hereof to the states by the Congress.

Amendment XXII

(1951)

Section 1.   No person shall be elected to the office of the President more than twice, and no person who has held the office of President, or acted as President, for more than two years of a term to which some other person was elected President shall be elected to the office of the President more than once. But this article shall not apply to any person holding the office of President when this article was proposed by the Congress, and shall not prevent any person who may be holding the office of President, or acting as President, during the term within which this article becomes operative from holding the office of President or acting as President during the remainder of such term.

Section 2.   This article shall be inoperative unless it shall have been ratified as an amendment to the Constitution by the legislatures of three-fourths of the several states within seven years from the date of its submission to the states by the Congress.

Amendment XXIII

(1961)

Section 1.   The District constituting the seat of government of the United States shall appoint in such manner as the Congress may direct:

A number of electors of President and Vice President equal to the whole number of Senators and Representatives in Congress to which the District would be entitled if it were a state, but in no event more than the least populous state; they shall be in addition to those appointed by the states, but they shall be considered, for the purposes of the election of President and Vice President, to be electors appointed by a state; and they shall meet in the District and perform such duties as provided by the twelfth article of amendment.

Section 2.   The Congress shall have power to enforce this article by appropriate legislation.

Amendment XXIV

(1964)

Section 1. The right of citizens of the United States to vote in any primary or other election for President or Vice President, for electors for President or Vice President, or for Senator or Representative in Congress, shall not be denied or abridged by the United States or any state by reason of failure to pay any poll tax or other tax.

Section 2. The Congress shall have power to enforce this article by appropriate legislation.

Amendment XXV

(1967)

Section 1. In case of the removal of the President from office or of his death or resignation, the Vice President shall become President.

Section 2. Whenever there is a vacancy in the office of the Vice President, the President shall nominate a Vice President who shall take office upon confirmation by a majority vote of both Houses of Congress.

Section 3. Whenever the President transmits to the President pro tempore of the Senate and the Speaker of the House of Representatives his written declaration that he is unable to discharge the powers and duties of his office, and until he transmits to them a written declaration to the contrary, such powers and duties shall be discharged by the Vice President as Acting President.

Section 4. Whenever the Vice President and a majority of either the principal officers of the executive departments or of such other body as Congress may by law provide, transmit to the President pro tempore of the Senate and the Speaker of the House of Representatives their written declaration that the President is unable to discharge the powers and duties of his office, the Vice President shall immediately assume the powers and duties of the office as Acting President.

Thereafter, when the President transmits to the President pro tempore of the Senate and the Speaker of the House of Representatives his written declaration that no inability exists, he shall resume the powers and duties of his office unless the Vice President and a majority of either the principal officers of the executive department or of such other body as Congress may by law provide, transmit within four days to the President pro tempore of the Senate and the Speaker of the House of Representatives their written declaration that the President is unable to discharge the powers and duties of his office. Thereupon Congress shall decide the issue, assembling within forty-eight hours for that purpose if not in session. If the Congress, within twenty-one days after receipt of the latter written declaration, or, if Congress is not in session, within twenty-one days after Congress is required to assemble, determines by two-thirds vote of both Houses that the President is unable to discharge the powers and duties of his office, the Vice President shall continue to discharge the same as Acting President; otherwise, the President shall resume the powers and duties of his office.

Amendment XXVI

(1971)

Section 1. The right of citizens of the United States, who are 18 years of age or older, to vote, shall not be denied or abridged by the United States or any state on account of age.

Section 2. The Congress shall have the power to enforce this article by appropriate legislation.

Amendment XXVII

(1992)

No law varying the compensation for the services of the Senators and Representatives shall take effect until an election of Representatives shall have intervened.

Appendix D

Federalist Number 10

The Union as a Safeguard Against Domestic Faction and Insurrection

Author: James Madison

To the People of the State of New York:

AMONG the numerous advantages promised by a well-constructed Union, none deserves to be more accurately developed than its tendency to break and control the violence of faction. The friend of popular governments never finds himself so much alarmed for their character and fate, as when he contemplates their propensity to this dangerous vice. He will not fail, therefore, to set a due value on any plan which, without violating the principles to which he is attached, provides a proper cure for it. The instability, injustice, and confusion introduced into the public councils, have, in truth, been the mortal diseases under which popular governments have everywhere perished; as they continue to be the favorite and fruitful topics from which the adversaries to liberty derive their most specious declamations. The valuable improvements made by the American constitutions on the popular models, both ancient and modern, cannot certainly be too much admired; but it would be an unwarrantable partiality, to contend that they have as effectually obviated the danger on this side, as was wished and expected. Complaints are everywhere heard from our most considerate and virtuous citizens, equally the friends of public and private faith, and of public and personal liberty, that our governments are too unstable, that the public good is disregarded in the conflicts of rival parties, and that measures are too often decided, not according to the rules of justice and the rights of the minor party, but by the superior force of an interested and overbearing majority. However anxiously we may wish that these complaints had no foundation, the evidence, of known facts will not permit us to deny that they are in some degree true. It will be found, indeed, on a candid review of our situation, that some of the distresses under which we labor have been erroneously charged on the operation of our governments; but it will be found, at the same time, that other causes will not alone account for many of our heaviest misfortunes; and, particularly, for that prevailing and increasing distrust of public engagements, and alarm for private rights, which are echoed from one end of the continent to the other. These must be chiefly, if not wholly, effects of the unsteadiness and injustice with which a factious spirit has tainted our public administrations.

By a faction, I understand a number of citizens, whether amounting to a majority or a minority of the whole, who are united and actuated by some common impulse of passion, or of interest, adverse to the rights of other citizens, or to the permanent and aggregate interests of the community.

There are two methods of curing the mischiefs of faction: the one, by removing its causes; the other, by controlling its effects.

There are again two methods of removing the causes of faction: the one, by destroying the liberty which is essential to its existence; the other, by giving to every citizen the same opinions, the same passions, and the same interests.

It could never be more truly said than of the first remedy, that it was worse than the disease. Liberty is to faction what air is to fire, an aliment without which it instantly expires. But it could not be less folly to abolish liberty, which is essential to political life, because it nourishes faction, than it would be to wish the annihilation of air, which is essential to animal life, because it imparts to fire its destructive agency.

The second expedient is as impracticable as the first would be unwise. As long as the reason of man continues fallible, and he is at liberty to exercise it, different opinions will be formed. As long as the connection subsists between his reason and his self-love, his opinions and his passions will have a reciprocal influence on each other; and the former will be objects to which the latter will attach themselves. The diversity in the faculties of men, from which the rights of property originate, is not less an insuperable obstacle to a uniformity of interests. The protection of these faculties is the first object of government. From the protection of different and unequal faculties of acquiring property, the possession of different degrees and kinds of property immediately results; and from the influence of these on the sentiments and views of the respective proprietors, ensues a division of the society into different interests and parties.

The latent causes of faction are thus sown in the nature of man; and we see them everywhere brought into different degrees of activity, according to the different circumstances of civil society. A zeal for different opinions concerning religion, concerning government, and many other points, as well of speculation as of practice; an attachment to different leaders ambitiously contending for pre-eminence and power; or to persons of other descriptions whose fortunes have been interesting to the human passions, have, in turn, divided mankind into parties, inflamed them with mutual animosity, and rendered them much more disposed to vex and oppress each other than to co-operate for their common good. So strong is this propensity of mankind to fall into mutual animosities, that where no substantial occasion presents itself, the most frivolous and fanciful distinctions have been sufficient to kindle their unfriendly passions and excite their most violent conflicts. But the most common and durable source of factions has been the various and unequal distribution of property. Those who hold and those who are without property have ever formed distinct interests in society. Those who are creditors, and those who are debtors, fall under a like discrimination. A landed interest, a manufacturing interest, a mercantile interest, a moneyed interest, with many lesser interests, grow up of necessity in civilized nations, and divide them into different classes, actuated by different sentiments and views. The regulation of these various and interfering interests forms the principal task of modern legislation, and involves the spirit of party and faction in the necessary and ordinary operations of the government.

No man is allowed to be a judge in his own cause, because his interest would certainly bias his judgment, and, not improbably, corrupt his integrity. With equal, nay with greater reason, a body of men are unfit to be both judges and parties at the same time; yet what are many of the most important acts of legislation, but so many judicial determinations, not indeed concerning the rights of single persons, but concerning the rights of large bodies of citizens? And what are the different classes of legislators but advocates and parties to the causes which they determine? Is a law proposed concerning private debts? It is a question to which the creditors are parties on one side and the debtors on the other. Justice ought to hold the balance between them. Yet the parties are, and must be, themselves the judges; and the most numerous party, or, in other words, the most powerful faction must be expected to prevail. Shall domestic manufactures be encouraged, and in what degree, by restrictions on foreign manufactures? are questions which would be differently decided by the landed and the manufacturing classes, and probably by neither with a sole regard to justice and the public good. The apportionment of taxes on the various descriptions of property is an act which seems to require the most exact impartiality; yet there is, perhaps, no legislative act in which greater opportunity and temptation are given to a predominant party to trample on the rules of justice. Every shilling with which they overburden the inferior number, is a shilling saved to their own pockets.

It is in vain to say that enlightened statesmen will be able to adjust these clashing interests, and render them all subservient to the public good. Enlightened statesmen will not always be at the helm. Nor, in many cases, can such an adjustment be made at all without taking into view indirect and remote considerations, which will rarely prevail over the immediate interest which one party may find in disregarding the rights of another or the good of the whole.

The inference to which we are brought is, that the CAUSES of faction cannot be removed, and that relief is only to be sought in the means of controlling its EFFECTS.

If a faction consists of less than a majority, relief is supplied by the republican principle, which enables the majority to defeat its sinister views by regular vote. It may clog the administration, it may convulse the society; but it will be unable to execute and mask its violence under the forms of the Constitution. When a majority is included in a faction, the form of popular government, on the other hand, enables it to sacrifice to its ruling passion or interest both the public good and the rights of other citizens. To secure the public good and private rights against the danger of such a faction, and at the same time to preserve the spirit and the form of popular government, is then the great object to which our inquiries are directed. Let me add that it is the great desideratum by which this form of government can be rescued from the opprobrium under which it has so long labored, and be recommended to the esteem and adoption of mankind.

By what means is this object attainable? Evidently by one of two only. Either the existence of the same passion or interest in a majority at the same time must be prevented, or the majority, having such coexistent passion or interest, must be rendered, by their number and local situation, unable to concert and carry into effect schemes of oppression. If the impulse and the opportunity be suffered to coincide, we well know that neither moral nor religious motives can be relied on as an adequate control. They are not found to be such on the injustice and violence of individuals, and lose their efficacy in proportion to the number combined together, that is, in proportion as their efficacy becomes needful.

From this view of the subject it may be concluded that a pure democracy, by which I mean a society consisting of a small number of citizens, who assemble and administer the government in person, can admit of no cure for the mischiefs of faction. A common passion or interest will, in almost every case, be felt by a majority of the whole; a communication and concert result from the form of government itself; and there is nothing to check the inducements to sacrifice the weaker party or an obnoxious individual. Hence it is that such democracies have ever been spectacles of turbulence and contention; have ever been found incompatible with personal security or the rights of property; and

have in general been as short in their lives as they have been violent in their deaths. Theoretic politicians, who have patronized this species of government, have erroneously supposed that by reducing mankind to a perfect equality in their political rights, they would, at the same time, be perfectly equalized and assimilated in their possessions, their opinions, and their passions.

A republic, by which I mean a government in which the scheme of representation takes place, opens a different prospect, and promises the cure for which we are seeking. Let us examine the points in which it varies from pure democracy, and we shall comprehend both the nature of the cure and the efficacy which it must derive from the Union.

The two great points of difference between a democracy and a republic are: first, the delegation of the government, in the latter, to a small number of citizens elected by the rest; secondly, the greater number of citizens, and greater sphere of country, over which the latter may be extended.

The effect of the first difference is, on the one hand, to refine and enlarge the public views, by passing them through the medium of a chosen body of citizens, whose wisdom may best discern the true interest of their country, and whose patriotism and love of justice will be least likely to sacrifice it to temporary or partial considerations. Under such a regulation, it may well happen that the public voice, pronounced by the representatives of the people, will be more consonant to the public good than if pronounced by the people themselves, convened for the purpose. On the other hand, the effect may be inverted. Men of factious tempers, of local prejudices, or of sinister designs, may, by intrigue, by corruption, or by other means, first obtain the suffrages, and then betray the interests, of the people. The question resulting is, whether small or extensive republics are more favorable to the election of proper guardians of the public weal; and it is clearly decided in favor of the latter by two obvious considerations:

In the first place, it is to be remarked that, however small the republic may be, the representatives must be raised to a certain number, in order to guard against the cabals of a few; and that, however large it may be, they must be limited to a certain number, in order to guard against the confusion of a multitude. Hence, the number of representatives in the two cases not being in proportion to that of the two constituents, and being proportionally greater in the small republic, it follows that, if the proportion of fit characters be not less in the large than in the small republic, the former will present a greater option, and consequently a greater probability of a fit choice.

In the next place, as each representative will be chosen by a greater number of citizens in the large than in the small republic, it will be more difficult for unworthy candidates to practice with success the vicious arts by which elections are too often carried; and the suffrages of the people being more free, will be more likely to centre in men who possess the most attractive merit and the most diffusive and established characters.

It must be confessed that in this, as in most other cases, there is a mean, on both sides of which inconveniences will be found to lie. By enlarging too much the number of electors, you render the representatives too little acquainted with all their local circumstances and lesser interests; as by reducing it too much, you render him unduly attached to these, and too little fit to comprehend and pursue great and national objects. The federal Constitution forms a happy combination in this respect; the great and aggregate interests being referred to the national, the local and particular to the State legislatures.

The other point of difference is, the greater number of citizens and extent of territory which may be brought within the compass of republican than of democratic government; and it is this circumstance principally which renders factious combinations less to be dreaded in the former than in the latter. The smaller the society, the fewer probably will be the distinct parties and interests composing it; the fewer the distinct parties and interests, the more frequently will a majority be found of the same party; and the smaller the number of individuals composing a majority, and the smaller the compass within which they are placed, the more easily will they concert and execute their plans of oppression. Extend the sphere, and you take in a greater variety of parties and interests; you make it less probable that a majority of the whole will have a common motive to invade the rights of other citizens; or if such a common motive exists, it will be more difficult for all who feel it to discover their own strength, and to act in unison with each other. Besides other impediments, it may be remarked that, where there is a consciousness of unjust or dishonorable purposes, communication is always checked by distrust in proportion to the number whose concurrence is necessary.

Hence, it clearly appears, that the same advantage which a republic has over a democracy, in controlling the effects of faction, is enjoyed by a large over a small republic,—is enjoyed by the Union over the States composing it. Does the advantage consist in the substitution of representatives whose enlightened views and virtuous sentiments render them superior to local prejudices and schemes of injustice? It will not be denied that the representation of the Union will be most likely to possess these requisite endowments. Does it consist in the greater security afforded by a greater variety of parties, against the event of any one party being able to outnumber and oppress the rest? In an equal degree does the increased variety of parties comprised within the Union, increase this security. Does it, in fine, consist in the greater obstacles opposed to the concert and accomplishment of the secret wishes of an unjust and interested majority? Here, again, the extent of the Union gives it the most palpable advantage.

The influence of factious leaders may kindle a flame within their particular States, but will be unable to spread a general conflagration through the other States. A religious sect may degenerate into a political faction in a part of the Confederacy; but the variety of sects dispersed over the entire face of it must secure the national councils against any danger from that source. A rage for paper money, for an abolition of debts, for an equal division of property, or for any other improper or wicked project, will be less apt to pervade the whole body of the Union than a particular member of it; in the same proportion as such a malady is more likely to taint a particular county or district, than an entire State.

In the extent and proper structure of the Union, therefore, we behold a republican remedy for the diseases most incident to republican government. And according to the degree of pleasure and pride we feel in being republicans, ought to be our zeal in cherishing the spirit and supporting the character of Federalists.

PUBLIUS.

FEDERALIST NUMBER 51

The Structure of the Government Must Furnish the Proper Checks and Balances Between the Different Departments

Author: James Madison

To the People of the State of New York:

TO WHAT expedient, then, shall we finally resort, for maintaining in practice the necessary partition of power among the several departments, as laid down in the Constitution? The only answer that can be given is, that as all these exterior provisions are found to be inadequate, the defect must be supplied, by so contriving the interior structure of the government as that its several constituent parts may, by their mutual relations, be the means of keeping each other in their proper places. Without presuming to undertake a full development of this important idea, I will hazard a few general observations, which may perhaps place it in a clearer light, and enable us to form a more correct judgment of the principles and structure of the government planned by the convention.

In order to lay a due foundation for that separate and distinct exercise of the different powers of government, which to a certain extent is admitted on all hands to be essential to the preservation of liberty, it is evident that each department should have a will of its own; and consequently should be so constituted that the members of each should have as little agency as possible in the appointment of the members of the others. Were this principle rigorously adhered to, it would require that all the appointments for the supreme executive, legislative, and judiciary magistracies should be drawn from the same fountain of authority, the people, through channels having no communication whatever with one another. Perhaps such a plan of constructing the several departments would be less difficult in practice than it may in contemplation appear. Some difficulties, however, and some additional expense would attend the execution of it. Some deviations, therefore, from the principle must be admitted. In the constitution of the judiciary department in particular, it might be inexpedient to insist rigorously on the principle: first, because peculiar qualifications being essential in the members, the primary consider-ation ought to be to select that mode of choice which best secures these qualifications; secondly, because the permanent tenure by which the appointments are held in that department, must soon destroy all sense of dependence on the authority conferring them.

It is equally evident, that the members of each department should be as little dependent as possible on those of the others, for the emoluments annexed to their offices. Were the executive magistrate, or the judges, not independent of the legislature in this particular, their independence in every other would be merely nominal.

But the great security against a gradual concentration of the several powers in the same department, consists in giving to those who administer each department the necessary constitutional means and personal motives to resist encroachments of the others. The provision for defense must in this, as in all other cases, be made commensurate to the danger of attack. Ambition must be made to counteract ambition. The interest of the man must be connected with the constitutional rights of the place. It may be a reflection on human nature, that such devices should be necessary to control the abuses of government. But what is government itself, but the greatest of all reflections on human nature? If men were angels, no government would be necessary. If angels were to govern men, neither external nor internal controls on government would be necessary. In framing a government which is to be administered by men over men, the great difficulty lies in this: you must first enable the government to control the governed; and in the next place oblige it to control itself. A dependence on the people is, no doubt, the primary control on the government; but experience has taught mankind the necessity of auxiliary precautions.

This policy of supplying, by opposite and rival interests, the defect of better motives, might be traced through the whole system of human affairs, private as well as public. We see it particularly displayed in all the subordinate distributions of power, where the constant aim is to divide and arrange the several offices in such a manner as that each may be a check on the other that the private interest of every individual may be a sentinel over the public rights. These inventions of prudence cannot be less requisite in the distribution of the supreme powers of the State.

But it is not possible to give to each department an equal power of self-defense. In republican government, the legislative authority necessarily predominates. The remedy for this inconveniency is to divide the legislature into different branches; and to render them, by different modes of election and different principles of action, as little connected with each other as the nature of their common functions and their common dependence on the society will admit. It may even be necessary to guard against dangerous encroachments by still further precautions. As the weight of the legislative authority requires that it should be thus divided, the weakness of the executive may require, on the other hand, that it should be fortified. An absolute negative on the legislature appears, at first view, to be the natural defense with which the executive magistrate should be armed. But perhaps it would be neither altogether safe nor alone sufficient. On ordinary occasions it might not be exerted with the requisite firmness, and on extraordinary occasions it might be perfidiously abused. May not this defect of an absolute negative be supplied by some qualified connection between this weaker department and the weaker branch of the stronger department, by which the latter may be led to support the constitutional rights of the former, without being too much detached from the rights of its own department?

If the principles on which these observations are founded be just, as I persuade myself they are, and they be applied as a criterion to the several State constitutions, and to the federal Constitution it will be found that if the latter does not perfectly correspond with them, the former are infinitely less able to bear such a test. There are, moreover, two considerations particularly applicable to the federal system of America, which place that system in a very interesting point of view.

First. In a single republic, all the power surrendered by the people is submitted to the administration of a single government; and the usurpations are guarded against by a division of the government into distinct and separate departments. In the compound republic of America, the power surrendered by the people is first divided between two distinct governments, and then the portion allotted to each subdivided among distinct and separate departments. Hence a double security arises to the rights of the people. The different governments will control each other, at the same time that each will be controlled by itself.

Second. It is of great importance in a republic not only to guard the society against the oppression of its rulers, but to guard one part of the society against the injustice of the other part. Different interests necessarily exist in different classes of citizens. If a majority be united by a common interest, the rights of the minority will be insecure. There are but two methods of providing against this evil: the one by creating a will in the community independent of the majority that is, of the society itself; the other, by comprehending in the society so many separate descriptions of citizens as will render an unjust combination of a majority of the whole very improbable, if not impracticable. The first method prevails in all governments possessing an hereditary or self-appointed authority. This, at best, is but a precarious security; because a power independent of the society may as well espouse the unjust views of the major, as the rightful interests of the minor party, and may possibly be turned against both parties. The second method will be exemplified in the federal republic of the United States. Whilst all authority in it will be derived from and dependent on the society, the society itself will be broken into so many parts, interests, and classes of citizens, that the rights of individuals, or of the minority, will be in little danger from interested combinations of the majority. In a free government the security for civil rights must be the same as that for religious rights. It consists in the one case in the multiplicity of interests, and in the other in the multiplicity of sects. The degree of security in both cases will depend on the number of interests and sects; and this may be presumed to depend on the extent of country and number of people comprehended under the same government. This view of the subject must particularly recommend a proper federal system to all the sincere and considerate friends of republican government, since it shows that in exact proportion as the territory of the Union may be formed into more circumscribed Confederacies, or States oppressive combinations of a majority will be facilitated: the best security, under the republican forms, for the rights of every class of citizens, will be diminished: and consequently the stability and independence of some member of the government, the only other security, must be proportionately increased. Justice is the end of government. It is the end of civil society. It ever has been and ever will be pursued until it be obtained, or until liberty be lost in the pursuit. In a society under the forms of which the stronger faction can readily unite and oppress the weaker, anarchy may as truly be said to reign as in a state of nature, where the weaker individual is not secured against the violence of the stronger; and as, in the latter state, even the stronger individuals are prompted, by the uncertainty of their condition, to submit to a government which may protect the weak as well as themselves; so, in the former state, will the more powerful factions or parties be gradually induced, by a like motive, to wish for a government which will protect all parties, the weaker as well as the more powerful. It can be little doubted that if the State of Rhode Island was separated from the Confederacy and left to itself, the insecurity of rights under the popular form of government within such narrow limits would be displayed by such reiterated oppressions of factious majorities that some power altogether independent of the people would soon be called for by the voice of the very factions whose misrule had proved the necessity of it. In the extended republic of the United States, and among the great variety of interests, parties, and sects which it embraces, a coalition of a majority of the whole society could seldom take place on any other principles than those of justice and the general good; whilst there being thus less danger to a minor from the will of a major party, there must be less pretext, also, to provide for the security of the former, by introducing into the government a will not dependent on the latter, or, in other words, a will independent of the society itself. It is no less certain than it is important, notwithstanding the contrary opinions which have been entertained, that the larger the society, provided it lie within a practical sphere, the more duly capable it will be of self-government. And happily for the REPUBLICAN CAUSE, the practicable sphere may be carried to a very great extent, by a judicious modification and mixture of the FEDERAL PRINCIPLE.

PUBLIUS.

FEDERALIST NUMBER 78

The Judiciary Department

Author: Alexander Hamilton

To the People of the State of New York:

WE PROCEED now to an examination of the judiciary department of the proposed government.

In unfolding the defects of the existing Confederation, the utility and necessity of a federal judicature have been clearly pointed out. It is the less necessary to recapitulate the considerations there urged, as the propriety of the institution in the abstract is not disputed; the only questions which have been raised being relative to the manner of constituting it, and to its extent. To these points, therefore, our observations shall be confined.

The manner of constituting it seems to embrace these several objects: 1st. The mode of appointing the judges. 2d. The tenure by which they are to hold their places. 3d. The partition of the judiciary authority between different courts, and their relations to each other.

First. As to the mode of appointing the judges; this is the same with that of appointing the officers of the Union in general, and has been so fully discussed in the two last numbers, that nothing can be said here which would not be useless repetition.

Second. As to the tenure by which the judges are to hold their places; this chiefly concerns their duration in office; the provisions for their support; the precautions for their responsibility.

According to the plan of the convention, all judges who may be appointed by the United States are to hold their offices DURING GOOD BEHAVIOR; which is conformable to the most approved of the State constitutions and among the rest, to that of this State. Its propriety having been drawn into question by the adversaries of that plan, is no light symptom of the rage for objection, which disorders their imaginations and judgments. The standard of good behavior for the continuance in office of the judicial magistracy, is certainly one of the most valuable of the modern improvements in the practice of government. In a monarchy it is an excellent barrier to the despotism of the prince; in a republic it is a no less excellent barrier to the encroachments and oppressions of the representative body. And it is the best expedient which can be devised in any government, to secure a steady, upright, and impartial administration of the laws.

Whoever attentively considers the different departments of power must perceive, that, in a government in which they are separated from each other, the judiciary, from the nature of its functions, will always be the least dangerous to the political rights of the Constitution; because it will be least in a capacity to annoy or injure them. The Executive not only dispenses the honors, but holds the sword of the community. The legislature not only commands the purse, but prescribes the rules by which the duties and rights of every citizen are to be regulated. The judiciary, on the contrary, has no influence over either the sword or the purse; no direction either of the strength or of the wealth of the society; and can take no active resolution whatever. It may truly be said to have neither FORCE nor WILL, but merely judgment; and must ultimately depend upon the aid of the executive arm even for the efficacy of its judgments.

This simple view of the matter suggests several important consequences. It proves incontestably, that the judiciary is beyond comparison the weakest of the three departments of power [1]; that it can never attack with success either of the other two; and that all possible care is requisite to enable it to defend itself against their attacks. It equally proves, that though individual oppression may now and then proceed from the courts of justice, the general liberty of the people can never be endangered from that quarter; I mean so long as the judiciary remains truly distinct from both the legislature and the Executive. For I agree, that "there is no

liberty, if the power of judging be not separated from the legislative and executive powers." [2] And it proves, in the last place, that as liberty can have nothing to fear from the judiciary alone, but would have every thing to fear from its union with either of the other departments; that as all the effects of such a union must ensue from a dependence of the former on the latter, notwithstanding a nominal and apparent separation; that as, from the natural feebleness of the judiciary, it is in continual jeopardy of being overpowered, awed, or influenced by its co-ordinate branches; and that as nothing can contribute so much to its firmness and independence as permanency in office, this quality may therefore be justly regarded as an indispensable ingredient in its constitution, and, in a great measure, as the citadel of the public justice and the public security.

The complete independence of the courts of justice is peculiarly essential in a limited Constitution. By a limited Constitution, I understand one which contains certain specified exceptions to the legislative authority; such, for instance, as that it shall pass no bills of attainder, no ex-post-facto laws, and the like. Limitations of this kind can be preserved in practice no other way than through the medium of courts of justice, whose duty it must be to declare all acts contrary to the manifest tenor of the Constitution void. Without this, all the reservations of particular rights or privileges would amount to nothing.

Some perplexity respecting the rights of the courts to pronounce legislative acts void, because contrary to the Constitution, has arisen from an imagination that the doctrine would imply a superiority of the judiciary to the legislative power. It is urged that the authority which can declare the acts of another void, must necessarily be superior to the one whose acts may be declared void. As this doctrine is of great importance in all the American constitutions, a brief discussion of the ground on which it rests cannot be unacceptable.

There is no position which depends on clearer principles, than that every act of a delegated authority, contrary to the tenor of the commission under which it is exercised, is void. No legislative act, therefore, contrary to the Constitution, can be valid. To deny this, would be to affirm, that the deputy is greater than his principal; that the servant is above his master; that the representatives of the people are superior to the people themselves; that men acting by virtue of powers, may do not only what their powers do not authorize, but what they forbid.

If it be said that the legislative body are themselves the constitutional judges of their own powers, and that the construction they put upon them is conclusive upon the other departments, it may be answered, that this cannot be the natural presumption, where it is not to be collected from any particular provisions in the Constitution. It is not otherwise to be supposed, that the Constitution could intend to enable the representatives of the people to substitute their WILL to that of their constituents. It is far more rational to suppose, that the courts were designed to be an intermediate body between the people and the legislature, in order, among other things, to keep the latter within the limits assigned to their authority. The interpretation of the laws is the proper and peculiar province of the courts. A constitution is, in fact, and must be regarded by the judges, as a fundamental law. It therefore belongs to them to ascertain its meaning, as well as the meaning of any particular act proceeding from the legislative body. If there should happen to be an irreconcilable variance between the two, that which has the superior obligation and validity ought, of course, to be preferred; or, in other words, the Constitution ought to be preferred to the statute, the intention of the people to the intention of their agents.

Nor does this conclusion by any means suppose a superiority of the judicial to the legislative power. It only supposes that the power of the people is superior to both; and that where the will of the legislature, declared in its statutes, stands in opposition to that of the people, declared in the Constitution, the judges ought to be governed by the latter rather than the former. They ought to regulate their decisions by the fundamental laws, rather than by those which are not fundamental.

This exercise of judicial discretion, in determining between two contradictory laws, is exemplified in a familiar instance. It not uncommonly happens, that there are two statutes existing at one time, clashing in whole or in part with each other, and neither of them containing any repealing clause or expression. In such a case, it is the province of the courts to liquidate and fix their meaning and operation. So far as they can,

by any fair construction, be reconciled to each other, reason and law conspire to dictate that this should be done; where this is impracticable, it becomes a matter of necessity to give effect to one, in exclusion of the other. The rule which has obtained in the courts for determining their relative validity is, that the last in order of time shall be preferred to the first. But this is a mere rule of construction, not derived from any positive law, but from the nature and reason of the thing. It is a rule not enjoined upon the courts by legislative provision, but adopted by themselves, as consonant to truth and propriety, for the direction of their conduct as interpreters of the law. They thought it reasonable, that between the interfering acts of an EQUAL authority, that which was the last indication of its will should have the preference.

But in regard to the interfering acts of a superior and subordinate authority, of an original and derivative power, the nature and reason of the thing indicate the converse of that rule as proper to be followed. They teach us that the prior act of a superior ought to be preferred to the subsequent act of an inferior and subordinate authority; and that accordingly, whenever a particular statute contravenes the Constitution, it will be the duty of the judicial tribunals to adhere to the latter and disregard the former.

It can be of no weight to say that the courts, on the pretense of a repugnancy, may substitute their own pleasure to the constitutional intentions of the legislature. This might as well happen in the case of two contradictory statutes; or it might as well happen in every adjudication upon any single statute. The courts must declare the sense of the law; and if they should be disposed to exercise WILL instead of JUDGMENT, the consequence would equally be the substitution of their pleasure to that of the legislative body. The observation, if it prove any thing, would prove that there ought to be no judges distinct from that body.

If, then, the courts of justice are to be considered as the bulwarks of a limited Constitution against legislative encroachments, this consideration will afford a strong argument for the permanent tenure of judicial offices, since nothing will contribute so much as this to that independent spirit in the judges which must be essential to the faithful performance of so arduous a duty.

This independence of the judges is equally requisite to guard the Constitution and the rights of individuals from the effects of those ill humors, which the arts of designing men, or the influence of particular conjunctures, sometimes disseminate among the people themselves, and which, though they speedily give place to better information, and more deliberate reflection, have a tendency, in the meantime, to occasion dangerous innovations in the government, and serious oppressions of the minor party in the community. Though I trust the friends of the proposed Constitution will never concur with its enemies, [3] in questioning that fundamental principle of republican government, which admits the right of the people to alter or abolish the established Constitution, whenever they find it inconsistent with their happiness, yet it is not to be inferred from this principle, that the representatives of the people, whenever a momentary inclination happens to lay hold of a majority of their constituents, incompatible with the provisions in the existing Constitution, would, on that account, be justifiable in a violation of those provisions; or that the courts would be under a greater obligation to connive at infractions in this shape, than when they had proceeded wholly from the cabals of the representative body. Until the people have, by some solemn and authoritative act, annulled or changed the established form, it is binding upon themselves collectively, as well as individually; and no presumption, or even knowledge, of their sentiments, can warrant their representatives in a departure from it, prior to such an act. But it is easy to see, that it would require an uncommon portion of fortitude in the judges to do their duty as faithful guardians of the Constitution, where legislative invasions of it had been instigated by the major voice of the community.

But it is not with a view to infractions of the Constitution only, that the independence of the judges may be an essential safeguard against the effects of occasional ill humors in the society. These sometimes extend no farther than to the injury of the private rights of particular classes of citizens, by unjust and partial laws. Here also the firmness of the judicial magistracy is of vast importance in mitigating the severity and confining the operation of such laws. It not only serves to moderate the immediate mischiefs of those which may have been passed, but it operates as a check upon the legislative body in passing them; who, perceiving that obstacles to the success of iniquitous intention are to be expected from the scruples of the courts, are in a manner compelled, by the very motives of the injustice they meditate, to qualify their attempts. This is a circumstance calculated to have more influence upon the character of our governments, than but few may be aware of. The benefits of the integrity and moderation of the judiciary have already been felt in more States than one; and though they may have displeased those whose sinister expectations they may have disappointed, they must have commanded the esteem and applause of all the virtuous and disinterested. Considerate men, of every description, ought to prize whatever will tend to beget or fortify that temper in the courts: as no man can be sure that he may not be to-morrow the victim of a spirit of injustice, by which he may be a gainer to-day. And every man must now feel, that the inevitable tendency of such a spirit is to sap the foundations of public and private confidence, and to introduce in its stead universal distrust and distress.

That inflexible and uniform adherence to the rights of the Constitution, and of individuals, which we perceive to be indispensable in the courts of justice, can certainly not be expected from judges who hold their offices by a temporary commission. Periodical appointments, however regulated, or by whomsoever made, would, in some way or other, be fatal to their necessary independence. If the power of making them was committed either to the Executive or legislature, there would be danger of an improper complaisance to the branch which possessed it; if to both, there would be an unwillingness to hazard the displeasure of either; if to the people, or to persons chosen by them for the special purpose, there would be too great a disposition to consult popularity, to justify a reliance that nothing would be consulted but the Constitution and the laws.

There is yet a further and a weightier reason for the permanency of the judicial offices, which is deducible from the nature of the qualifications they require. It has been frequently remarked, with great propriety, that a voluminous code of laws is one of the inconveniences necessarily connected with the advantages of a free government. To avoid an arbitrary discretion in the courts, it is indispensable that they should be bound down by strict rules and precedents, which serve to define and point out their duty in every particular case that comes before them; and it will readily be conceived from the variety of controversies which grow out of the folly and wickedness of mankind, that the records of those precedents must unavoidably swell to a very considerable bulk, and must demand long and laborious study to acquire a competent knowledge of them. Hence it is, that there can be but few men in the society who will have sufficient skill in the laws to qualify them for the stations of judges. And making the proper deductions for the ordinary depravity of human nature, the number must be still smaller of those who unite the requisite integrity with the requisite knowledge. These considerations apprise us, that the government can have no great option between fit character; and that a temporary duration in office, which would naturally discourage such characters from quitting a lucrative line of practice to accept a seat on the bench, would have a tendency to throw the administration of justice into hands less able, and less well qualified, to conduct it with utility and dignity. In the present circumstances of this country, and in those in which it is likely to be for a long time to come, the disadvantages on this score would be greater than they may at first sight appear; but it must be confessed, that they are far inferior to those which present themselves under the other aspects of the subject.

Upon the whole, there can be no room to doubt that the convention acted wisely in copying from the models of those constitutions which have established GOOD BEHAVIOR as the tenure of their judicial offices, in point of duration; and that so far from being blamable on this account, their plan would have been inexcusably defective, if it had wanted this important feature of good government. The experience of Great Britain affords an illustrious comment on the excellence of the institution.

PUBLIUS.

1 The celebrated Montesquieu, speaking of them, says: "Of the three powers above mentioned, the judiciary is next to nothing." "Spirit of Laws." vol. i., page 186.

2 Idem, page 181.

3 Vide "Protest of the Minority of the Convention of Pennsylvania," Martin's Speech, etc.

Appendix E

Partisan Control of the Presidency, Congress, and the Supreme Court

Term	President	Party	Congress	Majority Party		Party of Appt. President	
				House	Senate	Supreme Court	
1789–1797	George Washington	Federalist	1st	(N/A)	(N/A)	6F	
			2nd	(N/A)	(N/A)		
			3rd	(N/A)	(N/A)		
			4th	(N/A)	(N/A)		
1797–1801	John Adams	Federalist	5th	(N/A)	(N/A)	6F	
			6th	Fed	Fed		
1801–1809	Thomas Jefferson	Democratic-	7th	Dem-Rep	Dem-Rep	5F	1DR
		Republican	8th	Dem-Rep	Dem-Rep		
			9th	Dem-Rep	Dem-Rep		
			10th	Dem-Rep	Dem-Rep		
1809–1817	James Madison	Democratic-	11th	Dem-Rep	Dem-Rep	3F	4DR
		Republican	12th	Dem-Rep	Dem-Rep		
			13th	Dem-Rep	Dem-Rep		
			14th	Dem-Rep	Dem-Rep		
1817–1825	James Monroe	Democratic-	15th	Dem-Rep	Dem-Rep	2F	5DR
		Republican	16th	Dem-Rep	Dem-Rep		
			17th	Dem-Rep	Dem-Rep		
			18th	Dem-Rep	Dem-Rep		
1825–1829	John Quincy Adams	Democratic-	19th	Admin	Admin	2F	5DR
		Republican	20th	Jack	Jack		
1829–1837	Andrew Jackson	Democrat	21st	Dem	Dem	2D 1F	4DR
			22nd	Dem	Dem		
			23rd	Dem	Dem		
			24th	Dem	Dem		

Term	President	Party	Congress	Majority Party		Party of Appt. President	
				House	Senate	Supreme Court	
1837–1841	Martin Van Buren	Democrat	25th	Dem	Dem	7D	2DR
			26th	Dem	Dem		
1841–1841	William Henry Harrison	Whig	27th	Whig	Whig	7D	2DR
1841–1845	John Tyler	Whig	27th	Whig	Whig	7D	2DR
			28th	Dem	Whig		
1845–1849	James K. Polk	Democrat	29th	Dem	Dem	8D	1W
			30th	Whig	Dem		
1849–1850	Zachary Taylor	Whig	31st	Dem	Dem	8D	1W
1850–1853	Millard Fillmore	Whig	32nd	Dem	Dem	7D	2W
1853–1857	Franklin Pierce	Democrat	33rd	Dem	Dem	7D	2W
			34th	Rep	Dem		
1857–1861	James Buchanan	Democrat	35th	Dem	Dem	8D	1W
			36th	Rep	Dem		
1861–1865	Abraham Lincoln	Republican	37th	Rep	Rep	5D 1W	3R
			38th	Rep	Rep		
1865–1869	Andrew Johnson	Republican	39th	Union	Union	2D 1W	6R
			40th	Rep	Rep		
1869–1877	Ulysses S. Grant	Republican	41st	Rep	Rep	2D	7R
			42nd	Rep	Rep		
			43rd	Rep	Rep		
			44th	Dem	Rep		
1877–1881	Rutherford B. Hayes	Republican	45th	Dem	Rep	1D	8R
1881	James A. Garfield	Republican	47th	Rep	Rep	1D	8R
1881–1885	Chester A. Arthur	Republican	48th	Dem	Rep		9R
1885–1889	Grover Cleveland	Democrat	49th	Dem	Rep		9R
			50th	Dem	Rep		
1889–1893	Benjamin Harrison	Republican	51st	Rep	Rep	2D	7R
			52nd	Dem	Rep		
1893–1897	Grover Cleveland	Democrat	53rd	Dem	Dem	2D	7R
			54th	Rep	Rep		
1897–1901	William McKinley	Republican	55th	Rep	Rep	3D	6R
			56th	Rep	Rep		
1901–1909	Theodore Roosevelt	Republican	57th	Rep	Rep	3D	6R
			58th	Rep	Rep		
			59th	Rep	Rep		
			60th	Rep	Rep		

Term	President	Party	Congress	Majority Party		Party of Appt. President	
				House	Senate	Supreme Court	
1909–1913	William Howard Taft	Republican	61st	Rep	Rep	1D	8R
			62nd	Dem	Rep		
1913–1921	Woodrow Wilson	Democrat	63rd	Dem	Dem	2D	7R
			64th	Dem	Dem		
			65th	Dem	Dem		
			66th	Rep	Rep		
1921–1923	Warren G. Harding	Republican	67th	Rep	Rep	3D	6R
1923–1929	Calvin Coolidge	Republican	68th	Rep	Rep	2D	7R
			69th	Rep	Rep		
			70th	Rep	Rep		
1929–1933	Herbert Hoover	Republican	71st	Rep	Rep	2D	7R
			72nd	Dem	Rep		
1933–1945	Franklin D. Roosevelt	Democrat	73rd	Dem	Dem	5D	4R
			74th	Dem	Dem		
			75th	Dem	Dem		
			76th	Dem	Dem		
			77th	Dem	Dem		
			78th	Dem	Dem		
1945–1953	Harry S. Truman	Democrat	79th	Dem	Dem	9D	
			80th	Rep	Rep		
			81st	Dem	Dem		
			82nd	Dem	Dem		
1953–1961	Dwight D. Eisenhower	Republican	83rd	Rep	Rep	6D	3R
			84th	Dem	Dem		
			85th	Dem	Dem		
			86th	Dem	Dem		
1961–1963	John F. Kennedy	Democrat	87th	Dem	Dem	4D	5R
1963–1969	Lyndon B. Johnson	Democrat	88th	Dem	Dem	5D	4R
			89th	Dem	Dem		
			90th	Dem	Dem		
1969–1974	Richard M. Nixon	Republican	91st	Dem	Dem	4D	5R
			92nd	Dem	Dem		
1974–1977	Gerald R. Ford	Republican	93rd	Dem	Dem	2D	7R
			94th	Dem	Dem		

Term	President	Party	Congress	Majority Party		Party of Appt. President	
				House	Senate	Supreme Court	
1977–1981	Jimmy Carter	Democrat	95th	Dem	Dem	2D	7R
			96th	Dem	Dem		
1981–1989	Ronald Reagan	Republican	97th	Dem	Rep	2D	7R
			98th	Dem	Rep		
			99th	Dem	Rep		
			100th	Dem	Dem		
1989–1993	George Bush	Republican	101st	Dem	Dem	1D	8R
			102nd	Dem	Dem		
1993–2001	William Clinton	Democrat	103rd	Dem	Dem	2D	7R
			104th	Rep	Rep		
			105th	Rep	Rep		
			106th	Rep	Rep		
2001–2009	George W. Bush	Republican	107th	Rep	Dem	2D	7R
			108th	Rep	Rep		
			109th	Rep	Rep		
			110th	Dem	Dem		
2009–2017	Barack Obama	Democrat	111th	Dem	Dem	2D	7R
			112th	Rep	Dem	4D	5R
			113th	Rep	Dem		
			114th	Rep	Rep		

ENDNOTES

Chapter 1 The Origins of American Political Principles

1. Seymour Martin Lipset, *The First New Nation: The United States in Historical and Comparative Perspective* (New York: Basic Books, 1963).
2. Samuel H. Beer, *To Make a Nation: The Rediscovery of American Federalism* (Cambridge, MA: Harvard University Press, 1993), 31.
3. Plato describes types of government and patterns of governmental change in the *Republic*, Francis MacDonald Cornford, ed. (New York: Oxford University Press, 1941), 267–292.
4. Aristotle describes types of government and patterns of governmental change in the *Politics*, Ernest Barker, ed. (New York: Oxford University Press, 1970), 110–184. See especially page 156.
5. Aristotle, *Politics*, 115–116.
6. Aristotle, *Politics*, 123, 125.
7. Marcus Tullius Cicero, *On the Commonwealth*, George Holland Sabine and Stanley Barney Smith, eds. (New York: Liberal Arts Press, 1929), 129–134.
8. Andrew Lintott, *The Constitution of the Roman Republic* (New York: Oxford University Press, 1999).
9. St. Augustine, *On the Two Cities: Selections from The City of God*, E.W. Strothmann, ed. (New York: Frederick Ungar, 1957), 11.
10. St. Augustine, *On the Two Cities*, 101.
11. Talcott Parsons, "Christianity," in *International Encyclopedia of the Social Sciences*, David L. Silk, ed. (New York: Crowell Collier and Macmillan, 1968), vol. 2, 434–435.
12. Beer, *To Make a Nation*, 42–45.
13. Beer, *To Make a Nation*, 64–65.
14. Niccolo Machiavelli: *The Prince* and *The Discourses*, ed. Max Lerner (New York: Modern Library, 1950), 56.
15. Robert C. Schultz, ed., *Luther's Works: The Christian in Society*, vol. 46 (Philadelphia: Fortress Press, 1967), 39.
16. Thomas Hobbes, *Leviathan*, Michael Oakeshott, ed. (London: Collier Books, 1962), 100.
17. John Locke, *Two Treatises of Government*, Peter Laslett, ed. (New York: Cambridge University Press, 1960), 374–375.
18. Mark Hulliung, *The Social Contract in America: From the Revolution to the Current Age* (Lawrence, KS: University of Kansas Press, 2007).
19. Joyce Appleby, *Economic Thought and Ideology in Seventeenth-Century England* (Princeton, NJ: Princeton University Press, 1978), 80, 93.
20. J. G. A. Pocock, The *Machiavellian Moment: Florentine Political Thought and the Atlantic Political Tradition* (Princeton, NJ: Princeton University Press, 1976).

21. Clinton Rossiter, *The First American Revolution* (New York: Harcourt Brace, 1956), 90.

22. Sean Wilentz, *The Rise of American Democracy* (New York: Norton, 2005), 6.

23. Daniel Boorstin, *The Genius of American Politics* (Chicago: University of Chicago Press, 1953), 53.

24. Rossiter, *American Revolution*, 69.

25. Rossiter, *American Revolution*, 52, 56.

26. David Hackett Fischer, *Albions Seed: Four British Folkways in America* (New York: Oxford University Press, 1989), 429.

27. These percentages were derived from Rossiter, *American Revolution*, 18. See also Gordon S. Wood, *Empire of Liberty: A History of the Early Republic, 1789–1815* (New York: Oxford University Press, 2009), 39 for similar figures from the 1790 census.

28. Arthur M. Schlesinger, *The Birth of the Nation: A Portrait of the American People on the Eve of Independence* (New York: Knopf, 1969), 10.

29. Rossiter, *American Revolution*, 68.

30. Desmond S. King and Rogers S. Smith, "Racial Orders in American Political Development," *American Political Science Review*, vol. 99, no. 1 (February 2005): 75–92.

Chapter 2 The Revolution and the Constitution

1. J. Franklin Jameson, *The American Revolution Considered as a Social Movement* (Princeton, NJ: Princeton University Press, 1925), 9. See also Theda Skocpol, *States and Social Revolutions* (New York: Cambridge University Press, 1979).

2. Joseph F. Zimmerman, *Contemporary American Federalism: The Growth of National Power*, 2nd ed. (Albany, NY: State University of New York Press, 2008), 13.

3. See Jackson Turner Main, *The Sovereign States, 1775–1783* (New York: New Viewpoints, a division of Franklin Watts, 1973), 99–142, for a thorough treatment of the general structure and powers of American colonial political institutions.

4. Marc Egnal, "The Economic Development of the Thirteen Continental Colonies 1720 to 1775," *William and Mary Quarterly*, vol. 32, no. 2 (April 1975): 221; see also Gordon S. Wood, *The American Revolution* (New York: Modern Library, 2002), 12–16.

5. Thomas Jefferson quoted in Bernard Bailyn, *The Ideological Origins of the American Revolution* (Cambridge, MA: Harvard University Press, 1967), 118–143.

6. J. Franklin Jameson, *The American Revolution Considered as a Social Movement* (Princeton, NJ: Princeton University Press, 1925), 9.

7. *Journals of the Continental Congress, 1774–1789*, Worthington C. Ford, ed. (Washington, D.C.: U.S. Government Printing Office), 2: 22.

8. Thomas Jefferson to Henry Lee, May 8, 1825, in Paul Leicester Ford, ed., *The Works of Thomas Jefferson*. Vol. 10 (New York: G.P. Putnam's Sons, 1904–05), 342–343.

9. Donald S. Lutz, *Popular Consent and Popular Control: Whig Political Theory in the Early State Constitutions* (Baton Rouge, LA: Louisiana State University Press, 1980).

10. Leonard L. Richards, *Shays's Rebellion: The American Revolution's Last Battle* (Philadelphia, PA: University of Pennsylvania Press, 2003).

11. Richard Beeman, *Plain, Honest Men: The Making of the American Constitution* (New York: Random House, 2009).

12. David Robertson, *The Constitution and America's Destiny* (New York: Cambridge University Press, 2005).

13. Martin Diamond, *The Founding of the Democratic Republic* (Itasca, IL: Peacock, 1981), 16–18. See also Charles A. Beard, *An Economic Interpretation of the Constitution of the United States* (New York: Macmillan, 1913), 73–151.

14. Alan Gibson, *Understanding the Constitution: The Critical Questions* (Lawrence, KS:

University of Kansas Press, 2007), especially Chapter 4, 130–164.

15. Mark Tushnet, *Why the Constitution Matters* (New Haven, CT: Yale University Press, 2010), 1.

16. Calvin C. Jillson, *Constitution-Making: Conflict and Consensus in the Federal Convention of 1787* (New York: Agathon, 1988), 1–17.

17. Gaillard Hunt, *The Writings of James Madison* (New York: Putnam, 1901), 2: 43, 134.

18. Max Farrand, *The Records of the Federal Convention of 1787* (New Haven, CT: Yale University Press, 1937), 1: 225–228.

19. Thornton Anderson, *Creating the Constitution: The Convention of 1787 and the First Congress* (University Park: PA, Pennsylvania State University Press, 1993).

20. Sean Wilentz, *Rise of American Democracy* (New York: Norton, 2005).

21. Larry Diamond, *The Spirit of Democracy: The Struggle to Build Free Societies Throughout the World* (New York: Times Books, 2008).

22. Zimmerman, *Contemporary American Federalism*, 29.

23. Jack N. Rakove, *Original Meanings: Politics and Ideas in the Making of the Constitution* (New York: Random House, 1996), 106.

24. Farrand, *Records*, 2: 665.

25. Ralph Ketcham, *Framed for Posterity: The Enduring Philosophy of the Constitution* (Lawrence, KS: University of Kansas Press, 1993), 75.

26. David J. Siemers, *The Anti-Federalists: Men of Great Faith and Forbearance* (New York: Rowman and Littlefield, 2003).

27. Joseph J. Ellis, *Founding Brothers: The Revolutionary Generation* (New York: Alfred A. Knopf, 2001), 1–19.

28. John Nichols and Robert W. McChesney, *Dollarocracy: How the Money and Media Election Complex Is Destroying America* (New York: Nation Books, 2013), 260.

29. Robert A. Dahl, *How Democratic Is the American Constitution?* (New Haven, CT: Yale University Press, 2002), 15–20, 141–157.

30. Sanford Levinson, *Our Undemocratic Constitution* (New York: Oxford University Press, 2006), 12, 171–176.

31. Ketcham, *Framed for Posterity*, 40.

Chapter 3   Federalism and American Political Development

1. G. Ross Stephens and Nelson Wikstrom, *American Intergovernmental Relations: A Fragmented Federal Polity* (New York: Oxford University Press, 2007), 2–6.

2. Department of Commerce and Bureau of the Budget, *Statistical Abstract of the United States, 2012* (Washington, D.C.: U.S. Government Printing Office, 2012), table 428, 267. See also "Government Organization Summary Reports" 2012, http://www2.census.qov/govs/cog/g12_org.pdf.

3. Samuel H. Beer, *To Make a Nation: The Rediscovery of American Federalism* (Cambridge, MA: Harvard University Press, 1993), 223–224. Beer quotes briefly from Patrick Riley, "The Origins of Federal Theory in International Relations Ideas," *Polity*, vol. 6, no. 1 (Fall 1973): 97–98.

4. Joseph F. Zimmerman, *Contemporary American Federalism: The Growth of National Power*, 2nd ed. (Albany, NY: State University of New York Press, 2008), 2–4. See also Raymond A. Smith, *The American Anomaly: U.S. Politics and Government in Comparative Perspective*, 2nd ed. (New York: Routledge, 2011), 34–37.

5. Vincent Ostrom, *The Meaning of American Federalism: Constituting a Self-Governing Society* (San Francisco, CA: ICS Press, 1991), 45.

6. David Brian Robertson, *Federalism and the Making of America* (New York: Routledge, 2012), 31–33.

7. Edward Meade Earle, ed., *The Federalist* (New York: Modern Library, 1937), no. 51, 339, no. 31, 193.

8. Edward A. Purcell, Jr., *Originalism, Federalism, and the American Constitutional Enterprise: A Historical Inquiry* (New Haven, CT: Yale University Press, 2007), 3–10.

9. Earle, ed., *The Federalist*, no. 39, 249.

10. Joseph E. Zimmerman, *Contemporary American Federalism: The Growth of National Power* (New York: Praeger, 1992), 35.

11. Zimmerman, *Contemporary American Federalism*, 146.

12. Robertson, *Federalism and the Making of America*, 34.

13. Bruce Ackerman, *We the People: Foundations* (Cambridge, MA: Harvard University Press, 1991), 40.

14. Edward S. Corwin, "The Passing of Dual Federalism," *Virginia Law Review*, vol. 36, no. 1 (February 1950): 4.

15. David B. Walker, *Toward a Functioning Federalism* (Cambridge, MA: Winthrop, 1981), 66.

16. David Brian Robertson, *Federalism and the Making of America* (New York: Routledge. 2012), 40, 151, 155, 171.

17. Woodrow Wilson, *Constitutional Government in the United States* (New York: Columbia University Press, 1908), 173.

18. Walker, *Functioning Federalism*, 68.

19. Theodore J. Lowi, *The Personal President: Power Invested, Promise Unfulfilled* (Ithaca, NY: Cornell University Press, 1985), 49–50. See also Adam Liptak, "At Heart of Health Law Clash, a 1942 Case of a Farmer's Wheat," *New York Times*, March 20, 2012, A1, A14.

20. Ross Sandler and David Schoenbrod, *Democracy by Decree: What Happens When Courts Run Government* (New Haven, CT: Yale University Press, 2003), 13–34.

21. Roberton Williams, "Federal, State, and Local Government Revenues," Tax Policy Center, July 2, 2007.

22. Joseph F. Zimmerman, *Congressional Preemption: Regulatory Federalism* (Albany, NY: State University of New York Press, 2005), 1–9; see also Zimmerman, "Congressional Preemption Trends," *The Book of the States*, 2012, vol. 44, 51–55.

23. Timothy Conlan, *New Federalism: Intergovernmental Reform from Nixon to Reagan* (Washington, D.C.: Brookings Institution, 1988), 153–154.

24. Jackie Calmes, "States Confront Fiscal Crisis," *Wall Street Journal*, December 18, 2003.

25. Linda Greenhouse, "Justices Say U.S. May Prohibit the Use of Medical Marijuana," *New York Times*, June 7, 2006, A15.

26. Linda Greenhouse, "States Are Given New Legal Shield by the Supreme Court," *New York Times*, June 24, 1999, Al. See also Anthony Lewis, "No Limit But the Sky," *New York Times*, January 15, 2000, A19.

27. Donald F. Kettl, *System Under Stress: Homeland Security and American Politics*, 2nd ed. (Washington, D.C.: CQ Press, 2007), 102.

28. William T. Pound, "Federalism at the Crossroads," *State Legislatures*, June 2006, 18–20.

29. Roberton Williams and Yuri Shadunsky, "State and Local Tax Policy: What Are the Sources of Revenue for State Government," Tax Policy Center, May 7, 2013.

Chapter 4   Political Socialization and Public Opinion

1. See, for example, Donald J. Devine, *Political Culture of the United States* (Boston, MA: Little, Brown, 1972); and Herbert McClosky and John Zaller, *The American Ethos: Public Attitudes Toward Capitalism and Democracy* (Cambridge, MA: Harvard University Press, 1984), 17.

2. Fred I. Greenstein, *Children and Politics*, rev. ed. (New Haven, CT: Yale University Press, 1969), 157–158. See also David Easton and Jack Dennis, *Children in the Political System* (New York: McGraw-Hill, 1969).

3. Louis Hartz, *The Founding of New Societies* (New York: Harcourt, Brace & World, 1964).

4. Gunnar Myrdal, *An American Dilemma: The Negro Problem and Modern Democracy* (New York: Harper and Brothers, 1944), I: 4, 8.

5. Samuel P. Huntington, *American Politics: The Politics of Disharmony* (Cambridge,

MA: Harvard University Press, 1981), 14–15; Seymour Martin Lipset, *American Exceptionalism: A Double-Edged Sword* (New York: Norton, 1996), 19.

6. Greenstein, *Children and Politics*, 12.

7. Lawrence R. Jacobs, Fay Lomax Cook and Michael X. Delli Carpini, *Talking Together: Public Deliberation and Public Participation in America* (Chicago: University of Chicago Press, 2009).

8. Douglas B. Sosnik, Matthew J. Dowd, and Ron Fournier, *Applebee's America: How Successful Political, Business, and Religious Leaders Connect With the New American Community* (New York: Simon & Schuster, 2006).

9. Frank J. Sorauf, *Party Politics in America*, 2nd ed. (Boston, MA: Little, Brown, 1972), 144. See also M. Kent Jennings and Richard G. Niemi, *Generations and Politics: A Panel Study of Young Adults and Their Parents* (Princeton, NJ: Princeton University Press, 1981), especially chapter 4. More recently, see M. Kent Jennings, Laura Stoker, and Jake Bowers, "Politics Across Generations: Family Transmission Reexamined," *Journal of Politics*, vol. 71, No. 3, July 2009, 782–799.

10. Robert S. Erikson and Kent L. Tedin, *American Public Opinion*, 8th ed. (New York: Longman, 2011), 140.

11. Erikson and Tedin. *American Public Opinion*, 125–129.

12. Jan E. Leighley and Jonathan Nagler, *Who Votes Now? Demographics, Issues, Inequality and Turnout in the United States* (Princeton, NJ: Princeton University Press, 2014), 128, 135. Michele Lamont and Mario Small, *Culture and Inequality* (New York: W.W. Norton, 2008).

13. Deborah J. Schildkraut, "Defining American Identity in the Twenty-First Century: How Much 'There' Is There?" *Journal of Politics*, vol. 69, no. 3 (August 2007): 597–615.

14. Amy Fried, *Pathways to Polling: Crisis, Cooperation, and the Making of Public Opinion Professions* (New York: Routledge, 2012), 9, 30.

15. Fried, *Pathways to Polling*, 89–97.

16. Erikson and Tedin, *American Public Opinion*, 28–30.

17. Jack Rosenthal, "Precisely False vs. Approximately False: A Reader's Guide to Polls," *New York Times*, August 7, 2006, Wk 10.

18. Nate Silver, "Spin and Bias Are the Norm in Campaigns' Internal Polling," *New York Times*, December 3, 2012, A17.

19. Brian F. Schaffner, "Polling: Innovations in Survey Research," in Stephen K. Medvic, ed., *New Directions in Campaigns and Elections* (New York: Routledge, 2011), 39.

20. F. Chris Garcia and Gabriel R. Sanchez, *Hispanics and the U.S. Political System: Moving into the Mainstream* (Upper Saddle River, NJ: Pearson, 2008), 107.

21. Theodore J. Davis, Jr., *Black Politics Today: The Era of Socioeconomic Transition* (New York: Routledge, 2012), 35, 40, 72. See also Andrew Romano and Allison Samuels, "Is Obama Making It Worse," *Newsweek*, April 16, 2012, 40–42.

22. Garcia and Sanchez, *Hispanics and the U.S. Political System*, 104–106.

23. Mark Hugo Lopez, Rich Morin, and Paul Taylor, "Illegal Immigration Backlash Worries, Divides Latinos," Pew Hispanic Center, October 28, 2010.

24. Simon Romero and Janet Elder, "Hispanics Optimistic About Life, Poll Finds," *Dallas Morning News*, March 6, 2003, 9A. Adam Nagourney and Janet Elder, "Hispanics Back Big Government and Bush, Too," *New York Times*, August 3, 2003, Yt 1, 14.

25. See the 2008 National Asian-American Survey at http://www.naasurvey.com. See also Zoltan L. Hajnal and Taeku Lee, *Why Americans Don't Join the Party: Race, Immigration and the Failure (of Political Parties) to Engage the Electorate* (Princeton, NJ: Princeton University Press, 2011), 151, 168.

26. Adam J. Berinsky, *In Time of War: Understanding American Public Opinion from World War II to Iraq* (Chicago: University of Chicago Press, 2009).

27. Pew Research Center for the People and the Press and the Council on Foreign Relations, Calendar and Correspondence, December 2001, 14. New York Times/CBS News poll, *New York Times*, February 23, 2003, Wk 5.

28. CNN/ORC Poll, October 28, 2011, Question 15 at http://iz.cdn.turner.com/cnn/2011/images/10/28/rel17h.pdf.

29. James A. Stimson, *Tides of Consent: How Opinion Movements Shape American Politics* (New York: Cambridge University Press, 2004).

30. Erikson and Tedin, *American Public Opinion*, 61.

31. Marcus Prior and Arthur Lupia, "Money, Time, and Political Knowledge," *American Journal of Political Science*, vol. 52, no. 1 (January 2008): 169–183.

32. Erikson and Tedin, *American Public Opinion*, 63.

33. James M. Prothro and Charles M. Grigg, "Fundamental Principles of Democracy: Bases of Agreement and Disagreement," *Journal of Politics*, vol. 22, no. 2 (May 1960): 276–294.

34. Darren Davis and Brian Silver, "Civil Liberties Versus Security," *American Journal of Political Science*, 48: 47–61.

35. Richard J. Niemi, John Mueller, and Tom W. Smith, *Trends in Public Opinion: A Compendium of Survey Data* (New York: Greenwood Press, 1989), 22–23, 180.

36. The Gallup Organization, "Some Americans Reluctant to Vote for Mormon, 72-Year-Old Presidential Candidate," February 20, 2007.

37. Lydia Saad, "In U.S., 22% Are Hesitant to Support a Mormon in 2012," Gallup poll at http://www.gallup.com/poll/148100/Hesitant-Support-Mormon-2012.aspx.

38. http:www.pollingreport.com/abortion.htm. See also the poll archive at http://www.youdebate.com/abortion.htm.

39. Erikson and Tedin, *American Public Opinion*, 43–44.

40. John R. Zaller, *The Nature and Origins of Mass Opinion* (New York: Cambridge University Press, 1992).

41. Philip E. Converse, "The Nature of Belief Systems in Mass Publics," in David E. Apter, ed., *Ideology and Discontent* (New York: Free Press, 1964), 215–218.

42. Michael S. Lewis-Beck, William G. Jacoby, Helmut Norpoth, and Herbert F. Weisberg, *The American Voter Revisited* (Ann Arbor, MI: University of Michigan Press, 2008), 241–247, 258–291.

43. Tom Raum, "Study: We Talk of Austerity, Want New Spending," *Dallas Morning News*, March 9, 2013, A11.

44. Christopher Ellis and James A. Stimson, *Ideology in America* (New York: Cambridge University Press, 2012). See also Robert S. Erikson, Michael B. Mackuen, and James A. Stimson, *The Macro Polity* (New York: Cambridge University Press, 2002), 223–230.

45. William S. Maddox and Stuart A. Lilie, *Beyond Liberal and Conservative: Reassessing the Political Spectrum* (Washington, D.C.: Cato Institute, 1984), 59.

Chapter 5   The Mass Media and the Political Agenda

1. Shanto Ayengar, *Media Politics: A Citizens' Guide* (New York: W.W. Norton, 2011), 2.

2. Pew Research Center for the People and the Press, "Internet Gains on Television as Public's Main News Source," January 4, 2011, http://www.people-press.org/2011/01/04/internet-gains-on-television.

3. Sean Wilentz, *The Rise of American Democracy* (New York: Norton, 2005), 49–50.

4. Thomas C. Leonard, *The Power of the Press: The Birth of American Political Reporting* (New York: Oxford University Press, 1986), 193–213.

5. Meg Spratt, "When Police Dogs Attacked: Iconic News Photographs and Construction of History, Mythology, and Political Discourse," *American Journalism Review*, Spring 2008, 25: 2, 85–105.

6. Pew Research Center, " In Changing News Landscape, Even Television Is Vulnerable," October 1, 2012. See http://www.people-press.org/2012/09/27.

7. Audit Bureau of Circulations, "The Top U.S. Newspapers for September 2012. http://accessabc.wordpress.com.

8. Jose Antonio Vargas, "For Candidates, Web is Power and Poison," *Washington Post*, November 8, 2007, A1.

9. Robert W. McChesney, *The Problem of the Media: U.S. Communication Politics in the Twenty-First Century* (New York: Monthly Review Press, 2004).

10. Ben H. Bagdikian, *The New Media Monopoly*, 7th ed. (Boston, MA: Beacon Press, 2004), 4–16.

11. Daniel Lyons, "Why Comcast Bought NBC," *Newsweek*, December 21, 2009, 38.

12. Brian Stetler, "F.C.C. Seeks to Ease Media Ownership Rule," *New York Times*, December 23, 2011, B3.

13. "Scrubbing the Airwaves: The Media Industry and Decency," *The Economist*, July 23, 2005, 55–56

14. http://www.emarketer.com/Article/US-Total-Media-Ad-Spend.

15. Bartholomew H. Sparrow, *Uncertain Guardians: The News Media as a Political Institution* (Baltimore, MD: Johns Hopkins University Press, 1999).

16. Gadi Wolfsfeld, *Making Sense of the Media and Politics* (New York: Routledge, 2011), 2. See also Murray Edelman, *Constructing the Political Spectacle* (Chicago: University of Chicago Press, 1988), 91.

17. Elizabeth Bumiller, "Trying to Bypass the Good News Filter," *New York Times*, October 20, 2003, A12.

18 http://www.gallup.com/poll/167412/July 8, 2013.

19. Wolfsfeld, *Making Sense of the Media and Politics*, 19, 61–62.

20. Matthew Hindman, *Myth of Digital Democracy* (Princeton, NJ: Princeton University Press, 2009), 98.

21. "Most Online News Readers Use 5 Sites or Fewer, Study Says," *New York Times*, March 15, 2010, B2.

22. Matthew J. Kerbel, *Netroots: Online Progressives and the Transformation of American Politics* (Boulder, CO: Paradigm Publishers, 2009), 17. See also Hindman, *Myth of Digital Democracy*, 23, 25, 128.

23. John Nichols and Robert W. McChesney, *Dollarocracy: How the Money and Media Election Complex Is Destroying America* (New York: Nation Books, 2013), 228.

24. Marion R. Just, Anne N. Crigler, Dean E. Alger, Timothy E. Cook, Montague Kern, and Darrell M. West, *Crosstalk: Citizens, Candidates, and the Media in a Presidential Campaign* (Chicago: University of Chicago Press, 1996).

25. See the Center for Responsive Politics, OpenSecrets.org.http://www.opensecrets.org/overview/topraces.php.

26. Project for Excellence in Journalism, "How the Media Covered the 2012 Primary Campaign." See http://www.journalism.org/analysis-report/romney-report.

27. Larry J. Sabato, *Feeding Frenzy: How Attack Journalism Has Transformed American Politics* (New York: Free Press, 1991).

28. Iyengar, *Media Politics*, 176–7, 196.

29. Bernard C. Cohen, *The Press and Foreign Policy* (Princeton, NJ: Princeton University Press, 1963), 13.

30. Shanto Iyengar and Donald R. Kinder, *News That Matters: Television and American Opinion* (Chicago, University of Chicago Press, 1987), 117, 124–125.

31. Shanto Iyengar, *Is Anyone Responsible? How Television Frames Potitical Issues* (Chicago: University of Chicago Press, 1991), 124–125.

32. *The Daily Oklahoman*, 16 March 1982, quoted in Iyengar and Kinder, *News That Matters*, 34.

33. Pew Research Center, Project for Excellence in Journalism, http://www.journalism.org/2012/11/02. See also Diane J. Heath,

"The Presidency and Public Opinion," 73, in Lori Cox Han, *New Directions in the American Presidency* (New York: Routledge, 2011).

34. http://www.gallup.com/poll/146567.

35. Darrell M. West, *Air Wars: Television Advertising in Election Campaigns, 1952–1996* (Washington, D.C.: Congressional Quarterly Press, 1997).

36. Jacques Sternberg, "To Grab Young Readers, Newspapers Print Free, Jazzy Journals," *New York Times*, December 1, 2003, C23.

37. Thomas E. Patterson, *The Vanishing Voter: Public Involvement in an Age of Uncertainty* (New York: Alfred A. Knopf, 2002).

38. Project for Excellence in Journalism, "Winning the Media Campaign," October 22, 2008. See http://www.journalism.org/node/13307.

39. Shanto Iyengar, *Is Anyone Responsible? How Television Frames Political Issues* (Chicago: University of Chicago Press, 1991), 67–68.

Chapter 6   Interest Groups

1. James Madison, *The Federalist* (New York: Modern College Library Edition, 1937), no. 10, 54.

2. David B. Truman, *The Governmental Process: Political Interests and Public Opinion* (New York: Knopf, 1958), 33.

3. Graham Wilson, *Interest Groups* (Cambridge, MA: Blackwell, 1990), 1.

4. Mancur Olson, *The Logic of Collective Action* (Cambridge, MA: Harvard University Press, 1965); Jack L. Walker, *Mobilizing Interest Groups in America* (Ann Arbor, MI: University of Michigan Press, 1991).

5. David Brian Robertson, *Federalism and the Making of America* (New York: Routledge, 2012), 167. See also Raymond A. Smith, *The American Anomaly*, 2nd ed. (New York: Routledge, 2011), 106.

6. James Sterling Young, *The Washington Community, 1800–1828* (New York: Columbia University Press, 1966), 25, see also 161.

7. Daniel Walker Howe, *What God Hath Wrought: The Transformation of America, 1815–1848* (New York: Oxford University Press, 2007).

8. David J. Rothman, *Politics and Power: The United States Senate, 1869–1901* (Cambridge MA: Harvard University Press, 1966), 191–220.

9. Theda Skocpol, *Protecting Soldiers and Mothers* (Cambridge, MA: Harvard University Press, 1992), 111–112.

10. Dorothy Ross, *The Origins of American Social Science* (New York: Cambridge University Press, 1991).

11. Sidney Verba, Kay L. Schlozman, and Henry E. Brady, *Voice and Equality: Civic Volunteerism in American Politics* (Cambridge, MA: Harvard University Press, 1995), 83–84.

12. Salisbury, "Interest Representation," 64.

13. Jay Newton-Small, Time-Swampland, "Don't Cry For K-Street," August 8, 2013.

14. Frank L. Baumgartner, "The Growth and Diversity of U.S. Associations, 1956–2004," March 29, 2005. See http://www.personal.psu.edu/frb1/EA_Data_Source.pdf.

15. Charles E. Lindblom, *Politics and Markets* (New York: Basic Books, 1977), 170–188.

16. Sheryl Gay Stolberg, "The Pugnacious Builder of the Business Lobby," *New York Times*, June 21, 2013, BU1, BU6.

17. Steven Greenhouse, "Union Growth in 2008 was Largest in 25 Years," *New York Times*, January 28, 2009, A16.

18. Ronald J. Hrebenar, *Interest Group Politics in America*, 3rd ed. (Armonk, NY: Sharpe, 1997), 315.

19. Lawrence S. Rothenberg, *Linking Citizens to Government: Interest Group Politics at Common Cause* (New York: Cambridge University Press, 1992), 32.

20. Hrebenar, *Interest Group Politics in America*, 72.

21. http://www.opensecrets.org/lobbyists/overview.asp.

22. Marie Hojnacki, "Interest Groups' Decisions to Join Alliances or Work Alone," *American Journal of Political Science*, vol. 41, no. 1 (January 1997): 61–88.

23. Robert Pear, "A Million Faxes Later, A Little Known Group Claims a Victory on Immigration," *New York Times*, July 15, 2007, A13.

24. David D. Kirkpatrick, "Tougher Rules Change Game for Lobbyist," *New York Times*, August 7, 2007, A1, A12.

25. Mark Leibovich, "Eric Cantor Is on the Market," *New York Times Magazine*, July 20, 2014, 12–13.

26. David Kirkpatrick, "For Lobbyists, No Downturn, Just a Turnover," *New York Times*, November 25, 2008, A1, A16.

27. Public Citizen study cited in a *New York Times* editorial, "A Richer Life Beckons Congress," August 8, 2005, A18. See also Lawrence Lessig, *Republic Lost: How Money Corrupts Congress—and a Plan to Stop It* (New York: Twelve, 2011), 99, 123.

28. John Soloman, "Lawmakers' Lobbying Spouses Avoid Hill Reforms," *Washington Post*, January 17, 2007, A1.

29. Matthew Leising, "ICE Hires House Committee's Roberson as Lobbyist," Bloomberg.com, March 29, 2010.

30. Ken Kollman, *Outside Lobbying* (Princeton, NJ: Princeton University Press, 1998).

31. Katharine Q. Seelye, "Pro and Con: Lobbying Thrived," *New York Times*, January 31, 2009, A21.

32. Greg Hitt and Janet Adamy, "House Passes Historic Health Bill," *Wall Street Journal*, March 22, 2010, A1, A4. Karen Tumulty, Kate Pickert with Alice Park, "America: The Doctor Will See You Now," *Time*, April 15, 2010, 24–32.

33. Dan Eggen, "Interest Groups' Work Has Just Begun," *Washington Post*, March 24, 2010, A1.

34. http://www.nytimes.com/pages/health/index.html. Search on "Health Care Reform". Read Times Topic: Health Care Reform.

Chapter 7   Political Parties

1. John F. Bibby and L. Sandy Maisel, *Two Parties—or More: The American Party System* (Boulder, CO: Westview Press, 2003), 5.

2. Austin Ranney, *Curing the Mischiefs of Faction* (Berkeley, CA: University of California Press, 1975), 202.

3. James MacGregor Burns, *The Deadlock of Democracy* (Englewood Cliffs, NJ: Prentice-Hall, 1963), chapters 9 and 10.

4. Barbara Norrander, *The Imperfect Primary: Oddities, Biases, and Strengths of U.S. Presidential Nomination Politics* (New York: Routledge, 2010), 125–126.

5. Cal Jillson, *Pursuing the American Dream: Opportunity and Exclusion over Four Centuries* (Lawrence, KS: University of Kansas Press, 2004), chapter 1.

6. Andrew Gelman, *Red State, Blue State, Rich State, Poor State: Why Americans Vote the Way They Do* (Princeton, NJ: Princeton University Press, 2008), 13–14.

7. David R. Mayhew, *Electoral Realignment: A Critique of an American Genre* (New Haven, CT: Yale University Press, 2004); and Jeffrey M. Stonecash, *Political Parties Matter: Realignment and the Return of Partisan Voting* (Boulder, CO: Lynne Rienner Publishers, 2006).

8. John Aldrich, *Why Parties? The Origin and Transformation of Party Politics in America* (Chicago: University of Chicago Press, 1995), 68–95.

9. Sean Wilentz, *The Rise of American Democracy: Jefferson to Lincoln* (New York: Norton, 2005), 49–62.

10. Richard P. McCormick, *The Second American Party System: Party Formation in the Jacksonian Era* (New York: Norton, 1966), 28–30, 343–344.

11. Richard Hofstadter, *The Idea of a Party System: The Rise of a Legitimate Opposition in the United States* (Berkeley, CA: University of California Press, 1969).

12. Michael Holt, *The Rise and Fall of the American Whig Party* (New York: Oxford University Press, 2003).

13. Charles W. Calhoun, *Conceiving a New Republic: The Republican Party and the Southern Question, 1869–1900* (Lawrence, KS: University Press of Kansas, 2006).

14. Michael McGeer, *A Fierce Discontent: The Rise and Fall of the Progressive Movement in America, 1870–1920* (New York: Free Press, 2003).

15. Sidney M. Milkis, *The President and the Parties: The Transformation of the American Party System Since the New Deal* (New York: Oxford University Press, 1993).

16. A. James Reichley, *The Life of the Parties: A History of American Political Parties* (New York: Rowman and Littlefield, 2000), 248.

17. Stanley B. Greenberg, *The Two Americas: Our Current Political Deadlock and How to Break It* (New York: Thomas Dunne Books, 2005).

18. Marjorie R. Hershey, *Party Politics in America*, 13th ed. (New York: Pearson Longman, 2009), 6–10.

19. Arthur M. Schlesinger Jr., *The Cycles of American History* (Boston, MA: Houghton Mifflin, 1986), 272.

20. Hershey, *Party Politics in America*, 29–220.

21. Robert S. Erikson and Kent L. Tedin, *American Public Opinion*, 8th ed. (New York: Longman, 2011), 84.

22. Erikson and Tedin, *America Public Opinion*, 112–114. See also Michael S. Lewis-Beck, William G. Jacoby, Helmut Norpoth, and Herbert F. Wersberg, *The American Voter Revisited* (Ann Arbor, MI: University of Michigan Press, 2008), 126–130.

23. William H. Flanigan and Nancy H. Zingale, *Political Behavior of the American Electorate*, 12th ed. (Washington, D.C.: CQ Press, 2010), 95–99. See also Dan Balz and Jon Cohen, "A Political Force with Many Philosophies: A Survey of Independents," *Washington Post*, July 1, 2007, A1.

24. Pew Research Center Publications, "Obama's 2010 Challenge: Wake Up Liberals, Calm Down Independents," December 17, 2009.

25. Erikson and Tedin, *American Public Opinion*, 151–152, 264.

26. Zoltan L. Hajnal and Taeku Lee, *Why Americans Don't Join The Party: Race, Immigration, and the Failure (of Political Parties) to Engage the Electorate* (Princeton, NJ: Princeton University Press, 2011), 2–3.

27. Hajnal and Lee, *Why Americans Don't Join the Party*, 148, 168.

28. David R. Mayhew, *Placing Parties in American Politics* (Princeton, NJ: Princeton University Press, 1986), 73.

29. Andrew Stern, "Chicago Mayor Daley Won't Run for Re-election," Reuters, September 7, 2010.

30. Reichley, *The Life of the Parties*, 321.

31. Scot Schraufnagel, *Third Party Blues: The Truth and Consequences of Two-Party Dominance* (New York: Routledge, 2011), 7.

32. Maurice Duverger, *Political Parties: Their Organization and Activity in the Modern State* (New York: Wiley, 1954).

33. Raymond A. Smith, *The American Anomaly: U.S. Politics and Government in Comparative Perspective* (New York: Routledge, 2011), 138–151.

34. Christopher J. Anderson and Christine Guillory, "Political Institutions and Satisfaction with Democracy: A Cross-National Analysis of Consensus and Majoritarian Systems," *American Political Science Review*, March 1997, 91: 66–81.

35. J. David Gillespie, *Politics at the Periphery: Third Parties in Two-Party America* (Columbia, SC: University of South Carolina Press, 1993), 6–40.

36. Bibby and Maisel, *Two Parties—or More*, 55–78.

37. John Kenneth White and Daniel M. Shea, *New Party Politics: From Jefferson and Hamilton to the Information Age* (Boston, MA: Bedford/St. Martin's Press, 2001), 291–296.

Chapter 8   Voting, Campaigns, and Elections

1. M. Margaret Conway, *Political Participation in the United States*, 3rd ed. (Washington, D.C.: Congressional Quarterly Press, 2000), 3.

2. John Aldrich, *Why Parties: A Second Look* (Chicago: University of Chicago Press, 2011), 109–110.

3. Alexander Keyssar, *The Right to Vote: The Contested History of Democracy in the United States* (New York: Basic Books, 2000).

4. Akhil Reed Amar, "How Women Won the Vote," *Wilson Quarterly*, vol. 30 (Summer 2005): 30–34.

5. Damien Cave and Christine Jordan Sexton, "New Florida Rules Return More Than 115,000 Ex-Offenders to Voting Rolls," *New York Times*, June 18, 2008, A17.

6. U.S. Bureau of the Census, *Statistical Abstract of the United States, 2010*, table 406, 254. See also U.S. Census Bureau, "Voting and Registration in the Election of November 2008," 1.

7. Matthew J. Streb, *Rethinking American Electoral Democracy* (New York: Routledge, 2008), 17–25.

8. Ian Urbina, "Hurdles to Voting Persisted in 2008," *New York Times*, March 11, 2009, A14.

9. Michael S. Lewis-Beck, William G. Jacoby, Helmut Norpoth, and Herbert F. Weisberg, *The American Voter Revisited* (Ann Arbor, MI: University of Michigan Press, 2008), 293–414.

10. Andrew Gelman, *Red State, Blue State, Rich State, Poor State* (Princeton, NJ: Princeton University Press, 2008), 144.

11. William H. Flanigan and Nancy H. Zingale, *Political Behavior of the American Electorate*, 12th ed. (Washington, D.C.: Congressional Quarterly Press, 2010), 57; Conway, *Political Participation in the United States*, 32–35.

12. Jan E. Leighley and Jonathan Nagler, *Who Votes Now? Demographics, Issues, Inequality and Turnout in the United States* (Princeton, NJ: Princeton University Press, 2014).

13. Richard R. Lau and David P. Redlawsk, *How Voters Decide: Information Processing in Electoral Campaigns* (New York: Cambridge University Press, 2006). See also Daniel Kahneman, *Thinking, Fast and Slow* (New York: Farrar, Straus, and Giroux, 2011), 90–91.

14. Stephen Ansolabehere and Shanto Iyengar, *Going Negative: How Political Advertisements Shrink and Polarize the Electorate* (New York: Free Press, 1995), 65–66.

15. Nelson W. Polsby, Aaron Wildavsky, Steven Schier, and David Hopkins, *Presidential Elections*, 13th ed. (Lanham, MD: Rowman and Littlefield, 2012), 16.

16. Samuel L. Popkin, *The Reasoning Voter: Communication and Persuasion in Presidential Campaigns* (Chicago: University of Chicago Press, 1991), 41, 57.

17. Gary C. Jacobson, *The Electoral Origins of Divided Government* (Boulder, CO: Westview Press, 1990), 112.

18. Ryan Lizza, "Battle Plans: How Obama Won," *The New Yorker*, November 17, 2008, 46–56.

19. W. Lance Bennett, *The Governing Crisis: Media, Money, and Marketing in American Elections* (New York: St. Martin's Press, 1996), 66, 126.

20. Alan Ehrenhalt, *United States of Ambition: Politicians, Power, and the Pursuit of Office* (New York: Times Books, 1992), 9.

21. http://www.opensecrets.org/news/2012 10/2012-election-spending-will-reach-6.html.

22. Jacobson, *The Electoral Origins of Divided Government*, 51.

23. Walter J. Stone, et al., "Candidate Entry, Voter Response and Partisan Tides in the 2002 and 2006 Elections," in Jeffrey J. Mondak and Donna-Gene Mitchell (eds.), *Fault Lines: Why the Republicans Lost Congress* (New York: Routledge, 2008).

24. David R. Mayhew, *Parties and Policies: How the American Government Works* (New Haven, CT: Yale University Press, 2008), 26.

25. Steven V. Roberts, "Politicking Goes High-Tech," in Allan J. Cigler and Burdett A. Loomis (eds.), *American Politics: Classic and Contemporary Readings*, 3rd ed. (Princeton, NJ: Houghton Mifflin, 1995), 212–221.

26. Dan Gilgoff, "Everyone Is a Special Interest: Microtargeters Study Who You Are and What You Like," *U.S. News and World Report*, September 25, 2006, 30–32.

27. Bennett, *The Governing Crisis*, 145.

28. David W. Nickerson and Todd Rogers, "Political Campaigns and Big Data," Faculty Research Working Paper Series, Harvard Kennedy School, November 2013, RWD 13–045. See also John Nichols and Robert W. McChesney, *Dollarocracy: How The Money and Media Complex Is Destroying America* (New York: Norton Books, 2013), 238–239.

29. Barbara Norrander, The *Imperfect Primary* (New York: Routledge, 2010), 9–14.

30. Polsby and Wildavsky, *Presidential Elections*, 99–102.

31. Wayne, *Road to the White House 2012*, 134.

32. Polsby, et al., 13th ed., 148–152.

33. Matthew R. Kerbel, *Netroots: Online Progressives and the Transformation of American Politics* (New York: Routledge, 2009), 9.

34. Wayne, *Road to the White House 2008*, 37.

35. Michael Luo and Griff Palmer, "For Democrats, Financial Edge in Campaigns," *New York Times*, October 27, 2010, A1, A14.

36. Nicholas Confessore, "Compaigns Plan Maximum Push To Raise Money," *New York Times*, April 13, 2012, A1, A15.

37. Linda Greenhouse, "Justices Hear Vigorous Attacks on New Campaign Finance Law," *New York Times*, September 9, 2003, A1, A19.

38. Linda Greenhouse, "Justices, In a 5 to 4 Decision, Back Campaign Finance Law That Curbs Contribution," *New York Times*, September 11, 2003.

39. Robert Barnes and Dan Eggan, "Supreme Court Rejects Limits on Corporate Spending on Political Campaigns," *Washington Post*, January 22, 2010, A1.

40. http://www.opensecrets.org/news/2012/10/2012-election-spending-will-reach-6.html.

Chapter 9   Congress

1. John R. Hibbing and Elizabeth Theiss-Morse, *Congress and Public Enemy: Public Attitudes Toward American Political Institutions* (New York: Cambridge University Press, 1995). See also Gallup's Rating Congress website at http://www.gallup.com/poll/ratecong.html.

2. Barbara Sinclair, *Unorthodox Lawmaking: New Legislative Processes in the U.S. Congress*, 4th ed. (Washington, D.C.: Congressional Quarterly Press, 2011).

3. John Locke, *Second Treatise*, chap. 13, no. 150 (New York: Cambridge University Press, 1960), 413–414.

4. Calvin C. Jillson and Rick K. Wilson, *Congressional Dynamics: Structure, Coordination, and Choice in the First American Congress, 1774–1789* (Stanford, CA: Stanford University Press, 1994).

5. Raymond A. Smith, *The American Anomaly*, 2nd ed. (New York: Routledge, 2011), 76, 84.

6. Roger H. Davidson, Walter J. Oleszek, Frances E. Lee, and Eric Schickler, *Congress and Its Members*, 14th ed. (Washington, D.C.: Congressional Quarterly Press, 2014), 6.

7. Andrew Katz, "Congress Now Mostly a Millionaire's Club," *Time*, January 9, 2014.

8. John R. Hibbing, *Congressional Careers: Contours of Life in the U.S. House of Representatives* (Chapel Hill, NC: University of North Carolina Press, 1991), 2.

9. Davidson, et al., *Congress and Its Members*, 60.

10. Walter J. Oleszek, *Congressional Procedures and the Policy Process.* 9th ed. (Washington, D.C.: CQ Press, 2014), 27.

11. Randall B. Ripley, *Party Leaders in the House of Representatives* (Washington, D.C.:

Brookings Institution, 1967), 54; David-son, Oleszek, and Lee, *Congress and Its Members*, 157–159, 170–173.

12. Ripley, *Party Leaders in the House of Representatives*, 6–8.

13. Ronald M. Peters Jr., *The American Speakership: The Office in Historical Perspective* (Baltimore, MD: Johns Hopkins University Press, 1990), 92–93.

14. David W. Rohde, *Parties and Leaders in the Postreform House* (Chicago: University of Chicago Press, 1991), 83–88.

15. Phil Duncan, "Senate Leader's Role a Recent One," *Congressional Quarterly Weekly Report*, May 18, 1996, 1368–1369.

16. Christopher J. Deering and Steven S. Smith, *Committees in Congress*, 3rd ed. (Washington, D.C.: Congressional Quarterly Press, 1997), 26.

17. Davidson, et al., *Congress and Its Members*, 198–200; Steven S. Smith, Jason M. Roberts, and Ryan J. Vander Wielen, *The American Congress*, 4th ed. (New York: Cambridge University Press, 2006), 198, 216.

18. John Hibbing, *Congressional Careers*, 126.

19. Richard E. Fenno, *Congressmen in Committees* (Boston, MA: Little, Brown, 1973), 1.

20. David R. Mayhew, *Congress: The Electoral Connection* (New Haven, CT: Yale University Press, 1974), 16.

21. Barbara Sinclair, *The Transformation of the United States Senate* (Baltimore, MD: Johns Hopkins University Press, 1989), 145. See also Sinclair, *Unorthodox Lawmaking*, 82–86.

22. Evans and Oleszek, *Congress under Fire*, 91–92.

23. Ida R. Brudnick, "Congressional Salaries and Allowances," Congressional Research Service, January 7, 2014.

24. Sinclair, *The Transformation of the U.S. Senate*, 131.

25. Jennifer Steinhauer, "New House Speaker Enters, Bringing Rewritten Rule Book With Him," *New York Times*, January 5, 2011, A14.

26. Sinclair, *Unorthodox Lawmaking*, 18, 54, 147.

27. Sinclair, *Unorthodox Lawmaking*, 21.

28. Gerald F. Seib, "Senate Woes Flag Wider Disease," *Wall Street Journal*, February 15, 2010, A2.

29. Jeremy W. Peters, "Senate Vote Curbs Filibuster Power to Stall Nominees," *New York Times*, November 22, 2013, A1, A16.

30. Edward Epstein, "Dusting Off Deliberation," *CQ Weekly*, June 14, 2010, 1437–1442.

31. Rohde, *Parties and Leaders in the Post-reform House*, 41; Davidson, Oleszek, and Lee, *Congress and Its Members*, 271–299.

32. Richard Fenno, *Home Style: House Members in Their Districts* (Boston, MA: Little, Brown, 1978), 1–30.

33. Morris P. Fiorina, *Congress: Keystone of the Washington Establishment* (New Haven, CT: Yale University Press, 1977), 42–43.

34. Ron Nixon, "Special Funds in Budget Called Earmarks," *New York Times*, February 6, 2012, A13.

35. Janie Velencia, "Members Get Personal on Instagram, Tumblr and Pinterest," *Roll Call*, January, 22, 2014.

36. Steven S. Smith, *Party Influence in Congress* (New York: Cambridge University Press, 2007).

37. Steven Brill, "On Sale: Your Government," *Time*, July 12, 2012, 28–35.

Chapter 10 The President

1. Charles O. Jones, *The Presidency in a Separated System*, 2nd ed. (Washington, D.C.: Brookings Institution, 2005), 1–3.

2. Stephen Skowronek, *The Politics Presidents Make: Leadership from John Adams to George Bush* (Cambridge, MA: Harvard University Press, 1993), 20.

3. Edward S. Corwin, *The President: Office and Powers, 1787–1957* (New York: New York University Press, 1957, originally published, 1940), 3, 171.

4. Donald L. Robinson, *To the Best of My Ability: The Presidency and the Constitution* (New York: Norton, 1987), 22–24.

5. Calvin Jillson, "The Executive in Republican Government: The Case of the American Founding," *Presidential Studies Quarterly* (Fall 1979): 386–402.

6. Charles C. Thach Jr., *The Creation of the Presidency, 1775–1789* (Baltimore, MD: Johns Hopkins University Press, 1923), reprinted in 1969 with an introduction by Herbert J. Storing, 132–133.

7. Michael Isikoff and Mark Hosenball, "Pardon Me? Don't Bet On It," *Newsweek,* November 24, 2008, 9.

8. Louis Fisher, *Presidential War Power,* 2nd ed. (Lawrence, KS: University Press of Kansas, 2004), 3–16.

9. Mark Rozell, *Executive Privilege: Presidential Power, Secrecy, and Accountability,* 2nd ed., revised (Lawrence, KS: University Press of Kansas, 2002).

10. Stephen Skowronek, *Building a New American State: The Expansion of National Administrative Capacities, 1877–1920* (New York: Cambridge University Press, 1982).

11. Lewis W. Koenig, *The Chief Executive,* 6th ed. (New York: Harcourt Brace, 1996), 214.

12. Joseph Cooper, *The Origins of the Standing Committees and the Development of the Modern House,* Rice University Studies, vol. 56, no. 3, Summer 1970, 3–5. For an alternative view, see Bruce Ackerman, *Failure of the Founding Fathers: Jefferson, Marshall, and the Rise of Presidential Democracy* (Cambridge, MA: Harvard University Press, 2005).

13. John Hart, *The Presidential Branch: Executive Office of the President from Washington to Clinton,* 2nd ed. (Chatham, NJ: Chatham House, 1995), 4.

14. Robert E. DiClerico, *The American President,* 5th ed. (Upper Saddle River, NJ: Prentice-Hall, 2005), 34.

15. Arthur Schlesinger Jr., *The Imperial Presidency* (Boston, MA: Houghton Mifflin, 1973).

16. Matthew Crenson and Benjamin Ginsberg, *Presidential Power: Unchecked and Unbalanced* (New York: W.W. Norton, 2007).

17. Richard E. Neustadt, *Presidential Power and the Modern Presidents* (New York: Free Press, 1990), Chapter 3.

18. Aaron Wildavsky, "The Two Presidencies," in Aaron Wildavsky, *The Presidency* (Boston, MA: Little Brown, 1969), 230–243. More recently, see Bryan W. Marshall and Richard L. Pacelle, "Revisiting the Two Presidencies," *American Politics Review,* vol. 33, no. 1 (January 2005): 81–105.

19. Davidson, et al., *Congress and Its Members,* 287.

20. Stephanie Condan, "Marijuana Dominates Questions for Obama's YouTube Q&A," CBS News, January 27, 2011.

21. Jones, *The Presidency in a Separated System,* 133–145. See also, Peter Baker, "Few News Conferences, But Still Taking Questions," *New York Times,* February 4, 2010, A18.

22. Robert S. Erikson and Kent L. Tedin, *American Public Opinion,* 9th ed. (New York: Longman, 2011), 118–122.

23. Charlie Savage, "Provisions in Budget Bill Are Challenged by Obama," *New York Times,* December 24, 2011, A13.

24. Paul Light, *The President's Agenda,* 3rd ed. (Baltimore, MD: Johns Hopkins University Press, 1999), 45. See also, Jeffrey S. Peake, "Presidential Agenda-Setting in Foreign Policy," *Political Research Quarterly,* vol. 54, no. 1 (March 2001): 69–86.

25. John T. Woolley and Gerhard Peters, *The American Presidency Project,* University of California, Santa Barbara, see http://www.presidency.vcsb.edu/signingstatements.php

26. Charlie Savage, "Obama's Embrace of Bush Tactic Criticized by Lawmakers of Both Parties," *New York Times,* August 9, 2009, Y18.

27. Michael Abramowitz, "Bush's Tactic of Refusing Laws is Probed," *Washington Post,* July 24, 2006, A5.

28. Fisher, *Presidential War Power,* 69, 75, 81.

29. Quoted in Anthony Lewis, "License to Torture," *New York Times,* October 15, 2005, A35.

30. Linda Greenhouse, "Justices, 5–3, Broadly Reject Bush Plan to Try Detainees," *New York Times*, June 30, 2006, A1, A18.

31. Richard A. Smith, " Make the Cabinet More Effective," *New York Times*, Op-Ed, January 11, 2013, A21.

32. Helene Cooper, Mark Landler, and Jeff Zebeny, "In Shifting Staff Duties, Obama Seeks More Cohesive White House," *New York Times*, November 9, 2011, A18.

33. Mark Landler, "Obama's Growing Trust in Biden Is Reflected in His Call on Troops," *New York Times*, June 25, 2011, A4, A9.

Chapter 11   Bureaucracy

1. Joel D. Aberbach, *Keeping a Watchful Eye: The Politics of Congressional Oversight* (Washington, D.C.: Brookings Institution, 1990), 3 (both quotations).

2. Sean M. Theriault, "Patronage, the Pendleton Act, and the Power of the People," *Journal of Politics*, vol. 65, no. 1 (February 2003): 50–68.

3. Allan W. Lerner and John Wanat, *Public Administration* (Englewood Cliffs, NJ: Prentice-Hall, 1992), 13.

4. Scott Shane, "The Beast that Feeds on Boxes," *New York Times*, April 10, 2005, WK3.

5. H.H. Gerth and C. Wright Mills, eds., *From Max Weber: Essays in Sociology* (New York: Oxford University Press, 1946), 228–229, 232–233.

6. Census Bureau, *Statistical Abstract of the United States, 2014*, Table 512, http://www.census.gov/compendia/statab.

7. Ron Nixon, "Government Pays More in Contracts, Study Finds," *New York Times*, September 12, 2011, A1. See also Paul C. Light, *A Government Ill-Executed* (Cambridge, MA: Harvard University Press, 2008), 189–211, especially Table 7.1 at 197.

8. Noble E. Cunningham, Jr., *The Process of Government Under Jefferson* (Princeton, NJ: Princeton University Press, 1978).

9. Richard Bensel, *Yankee Leviathan: The Origins of Central State Authority in America, 1859–1877* (New York: Cambridge University Press, 1990).

10. Richard Bensel, *The Political Economy of American Industrialization, 1877–1900* (New York: Cambridge University Press, 2000).

11. William F. West, *Controlling the Bureaucracy: Institutional Constraints in Theory and Practice* (Armonk, NY: Sharpe, 1995), 64.

12. Binyamin Appelbaum, "On Finance Bill, Lobbying Shifts to Regulations," *New York Times*, June 27, 2010, A1, A14.

13. Damien Paletta, "Disability Claims Judge Has Trouble Saying 'No'," *New York Times*, May 19, 2011.

14. Greg Winter, "College Aid Rules Change, and Families Pay More," *New York Times*, June 6, 2005, A1, A15.

15. Tim Padgett, "Are Minorities Being Fleeced In The Stimulus?" *Time*, November 23, 2009.

16. James Q. Wilson, *Bureaucracy: What Government Agencies Do and Why They Do It* (New York: Basic Books, 1989), 131–133.

17. Charles T. Goodsell, *The Case for Bureaucracy: A Public Administration Polemic*, 4th ed. (Washington, D.C.: CQ Press, 2004), 60.

18. Gardiner Harris, "Potentially Incompatible Goals at FDA," *New York Times*, June 11, 2007, A16.

19. Davidson, et al., *Congress and Its Members* 195.

20. Matthew J. Dickinson, "The Presidency and the Executive Branch," in Lori Cox Han, ed., *New Directions in the American Presidency* (New York: Routledge, 2011), 145.

21. Martha Derthick, *Agency under Stress: The Social Security Administration in American Government* (Washington, D.C.: Brookings Institution, 1990), 192.

22. Kettl, *System Under Stress*, 40.

23. Francis E. Rourke, "Whose Bureaucracy Is This Anyway? Congress, the President

and Public Administration," the 1993 John Gaus Lecture, *PS: Political Science & Politics*, December 1993, 687–691.

24. B. Dan Wood and Richard W. Waterman, *Bureaucratic Dynamics: The Role of Bureaucracy in a Democracy* (Boulder, CO: Westview Press, 1994), 1.

25. Light, *A Government Ill-Executed*, 163–188.

26. West, *Controlling the Bureaucracy*, 67.

27. Oleszek, *Congressional Procedures and the Policy Process*, 386.

Chapter 12 The Federal Courts

1. Herbert Jacob, *Law and Politics in the United States* (Boston, MA: Little, Brown, 1986), 6–7.

2. Henry J. Abraham, *The Judicial Process*, 7th ed. (New York: Oxford University Press, 1998), 147.

3. Geoffrey C. Hazard Jr. and Michele Taruffo, *American Civil Procedure: An Introduction* (New Haven, CT: Yale University Press, 1993), 11.

4. Bernard Schwartz, *A History of the Supreme Court* (New York: Oxford University Press, 1993), 3–4.

5. Abraham, *Judicial Process*, 147.

6. Barry Friedman, *The Will of the People* (New York: Farrar, Straus, and Giroux, 2009), 94.

7. Richard A. Smith, The *American Anomaly: U.S. Politics and Government in Comparative Perspective*, 2nd ed. (New York: Routledge, 2011), 21.

8. Lawrence Baum, *The Supreme Court*, 11th ed. (Washington, D.C.: CQ Press, 2013), 93.

9. Quoted in Arthur Schlesinger Jr., *The Age of Jackson* (Boston, MA: Little, Brown, 1945), 312.

10. Schwartz, *A History of the Supreme Court*, 180.

11. Davidson, et al., *Congress and Its Members*, 342.

12. Quoted in Schwartz, *A History of the Supreme Court*, 232.

13. Lawrence Baum, *The Supreme Court*, 11th ed. (Washington, D.C.: Congressional Quarterly Press, 2012), 23.

14. Mark Silverstein, *Judicious Choices: The New Politics of Supreme Court Confirmations* (New York: Norton, 1994), 49.

15. Charles Lane, "Chief Justice Dies at 80," *Washington Post*, September 4, 2005, A1, A4.

16. Schwartz, *A History of the Supreme Court*, 374.

17. Warren Richey, Rehnquist's Unfinished Agenda," *Christian Science Monitor*, September 6, 2005, 1–2.

18. Adam Liptak, "Justices Offer a Receptive Ear to Business Interests," *New York Times*, December 19, 2010, A1, A32.

19. Linda Greenhouse, "Justices 5–4, Limit Use of Race For School Integration Plans," *New York Times*, June 29, 2007, A1, A20. See also Greenhouse, "In Steps Big and Small, Supreme Court Moved Right," *New York Times*, July 1, 2007, A1, A18.

20. David G. Savage, "Justices Affirm Gun Rights," *Los Angeles Times*, June 27, 2008, A1.

21. Adam Liptak, "Stevens' Era, Nearing End, Takes on Edge," *New York Times*, January 26, 2010, A12.

22. Adam Liptak, "Friend of the Corporation," *New York Times*, May 5, 2013, BU1, BU5.

23. Baum, *The Supreme Court*, 5–6.

24. Chief Justice John Roberts, "2014 Year-End Report on the Federal Judiciary," December 3, 2014. See http://www.supremecourtus.gov.

25. Steven G. Calabresi and Lames Lindgren, "Term Limits for the Supreme Court: Life Tenure Reconsidered," *Harvard Journal of Law and Public Policy*, vol. 29, no. 3 (2006): 768–877.

26. Mark V. Tushnet, *Why the Constitution Matters* (New Haven, CT: Yale University Press, 2010), 175.

27. Deborah Barrow, Gary Zuk, and Gerald Gryski, *The Federal Judiciary and Institutional*

Change (Ann Arbor, MI: University of Michigan Press, 1996), 12.

28. Alliance For Justice, "Judicial Selection During the Bush Administration," October 6, 2008, 2. www.allianceforjustice.org.

29. Baum, *American Courts*, 6th ed., 2008, 96–99.26.

30. Richard Davis, *Electing Justice: Fixing the Supreme Court Nomination Process* (New York: Oxford University Press, 2005), 19.

31. Carl Hulse, "Bipartisan Group in Senate Averts Judge Showdown," *New York Times*, May 24, 2005, A1, A16.

32. http://www.senate.gov/pagelayout/reference/nominations/Nominations.htm.

33. Silverstein, *Judicious Choices*, 71.

34. "Who Died and Made You Supreme Court Justice?" *Newsweek*, July 20, 2009, 68.

35. Tom Raum, AP, "Court Asserting Its Own Power," *Dallas Morning News*, June 30, 2006, A24.

36. Jeffrey Rosen, *The Most Democratic Branch: How the Courts Serve America* (New York: Oxford University Press, 2006), xii–xiii, 4.

37. Abraham, *Judicial Process*, 364.

38. David S. Broder, "It Is the Judges Who Set the South on a New Course," *Dallas Morning News*, December 8, 1993, A17.

39. Robert G. McCloskey and Sanford Levinson, *The American Supreme Court*, 4th ed. (Chicago: University of Chicago Press, 1960, 2005), 14.

40. Tushnet, *Why the Constitution Matters*, 164. See also Roger C. Cramton and Paul D. Carrington, ed., *Reforming the Court: Team Limits for Supreme Court Justices* (Durham, NC: Carolina Academic Press, 2006.)

Chapter 13 Civil Liberties

1. James MacGregor Burns and Stewart Burns, *The People's Charter: The Pursuit of Rights in America* (New York: Vintage Books, 1993), 44.

2. Burns and Burns, *The People's Charter*, 199. See also Henry J. Abraham and Barbara A. Perry, *Freedom and the Court: Civil Rights and Liberties in the United States*, 7th ed. (New York: Oxford University Press, 1998), 30–31.

3. Linda Greenhouse, "Court Hears Whether a Drug Statement is Protected Free Speech," *New York Times*, March 20, 2007, A16.

4. Abraham and Perry, *Freedom and the Court*, 206.

5. Anthony Lewis, *Make No Law: The Sullivan Case and the First Amendment* (New York: Vintage Books, 1991), 68.

6. Katharine Q. Seeyle, "Clash of a Judge and a Small Paper Underlies the Tangled History of Defamation," *New York Times*, November 20, 2006, C4.

7. Dean Baquet and Bill Keller, editors of the *New York Times* and *Los Angeles Times* respectively, "When Do We Publish a Secret?" *New York Times*, Op-Ed, July 1, 2006. See also Richard Stengel, managing editor of *Time*, July 10, 2006, 6.

8. Marisa Taylor, McClatchy Newspapers, "Administration Backing FBI Phone Policy," *Dallas Morning News*, January 23, 2010, A16.

9. Abraham and Perry, *Freedom and the Court*, 180.

10. The key debate is to be found in Michael J. Malbin, *Religion and Politics: The Intentions of the Authors of the First Amendment* (Washington, D.C.: American Enterprise Institute, 1978), and in Leonard W. Levy, *The Establishment Clause: Religion and the First Amendment* (New York: Macmillan, 1986).

11. Linda Greenhouse, "Justices Approve U.S. Financing of Religious Schools' Equipment," *New York Times*, National Edition, June 29, 2000, A21.

12. Linda Greenhouse, "Justices Allow a Commandment Display, Bar Others," *New York Times*, June 28, 2005, A1, A17.

13. Kim Severson, "Mississippi Tells Public Schools to Develop Policies Allowing Prayers," *New York Times*, March 15, 2013, A12.

14. Adam Liptak, "Religious Groups Given Freer Hand on Employment," *New York Times*, January 12, 2012, A1, A3.

15. Terrence Chan, AP, "Appeals Court Backs God References," *Dallas Morning News*, March 12, 2010, A16.

16. Linda Greenhouse, "Court Limits Protection Against Improper Entry," *New York Times*, June 16, 2006, A24.

17. Adam Liptak, "Supreme Court Edging Closer to Repeal of Evidence Rule," *New York Times*, January 31, 2009, A13.

18. Adam Liptak, "Justices Reject GPS Tracking in a Drug Case," *New York Times*, January 24, 2012, A1, A3.

19. Karen Houppert, *Chasing Gideon: The Elusive Quest for Poor People's Justice* (New York: The New Press, 2013).

20. Kettl, *System Under Stress*, Chap. 6, "Balancing Liberty with Protection," 104–107, 112–117.

21. Jesse J. Holland, AP, "Suspect Questioning Ruling is Overturned," *Dallas Morning News*, May 27, 2009, A8.

22. Jess Bravin, "Justices Narrow Miranda Rule," *Wall Street Journal*, June 2, 2010, A2.

23. Ethan Bronner and Michael S. Schmidt, "In Questions at First, No Miranda for Suspect," *New York Times*, April 23, 2013, A13.

24. Adam Liptak and Ethan Bronner, "Mandatory Life Terms Barred for Juveniles in Murder Cases," *New York Times*, June 26, 2012, A1, A14.

25. Linda Greenhouse, "After a 32-Year Journey, Justice Stevens Renounces Capital Punishment," *New York Times*, April 18, 2008, A20.

26. Pew Center for the States, "One in 31: The Long Reach of America's Corrections," March 2009.

27. E. Ann Carson and Daniela Golinelli, "Prisoners in 2012—Advance Counts," U.S. Department of Justice, Bureau of Justice Standards, July 2013.

28. Lauren E. Glaze and Erinn J. Herberman, "Correctional Population in the United States, 2012," U.S. Department of Justice, December 2013.

29. Solomon Moore, "Study Shows High Cost of Criminal Corrections," *New York Times*, March 3, 2009, A13.

Chapter 14   Civil Rights

1. Dorothy E. McBride and Janine A. Parry, *Women's Rights in the U.S.A.*, 4th ed. (New York: Routledge, 2011), 19.

2. David Brian Robertson, *Federalism and the Making of America* (New York: Routledge, 2012), 57–58.

3. Doug McAdam, *Political Process and the Development of Black Insurgency, 1930–1970* (Chicago: University of Chicago Press, 1982), 60–61.

4. Sidney Tarrow, *Power in Movement: Social Movements, Collective Action and Politics* (New York: Cambridge University Press, 1994), 4.

5. Associated Press, "Domestic Extremists Concern Researchers," *Dallas Morning News*, February 18, 2008, 4A.

6. Francis Fox Piven and Richard A. Cloward, *Poor People's Movements: Why They Succeed, How They Fail* (New York: Vintage Books, 1979), xxi–xxii.

7. Tarrow, *Power in Movement*, 153–157. See also F. Chris Garcia and Gabriel R. Sanchez, Hispanics and the U.S. Political System: Moving into the Mainstream (Upper Saddle River, NJ: Pearson, 2008), 49.

8. Bruce C. Levine, *Half Slave and Half Free: The Roots of the Civil War* (New York: Hill and Wang, 1992), 153.

9. Robert William Fogel, *Without Consent or Contract* (New York: W.W. Norton, 1989), 303–304.

10. Eric Foner, *Politics and Ideology in the Age of the Civil War* (New York: Oxford University Press, 1980), 62.

11. Speech by Abraham Lincoln delivered to the Congress on July 4, 1861.

12. Derrick Bell, *Faces at the Bottom of the Well* (New York: Basic Books, 1992), 12.

13. Alfred H. Kelly, Winfred A. Harbison, and Herman Belz, *The American Constitution:*

Its Origins and Development, 7th ed. (New York: Norton, 1991), 2: 586.

14. Michael Janofsky, "A New Hope For Dreams Suspended by Segregation," *New York Times,* July 31, 2005, A1, A14.

15. Gerald N. Rosenberg, *The Hollow Hope: Can Courts Bring about Social Change?* (Chicago: University of Chicago Press, 1991), 99, and related tables, 98–100.

16. Linda Greenhouse, "Justices, 5–4, Limit Use of Race for School Integration Plans," *New York Times,* June 29, 2007, A1, A20.

17. Tamar Lewin, "Michigan Rule on Admission to University Overturned," *New York Times,* July 2, 2012, A9.

18. Adam Liptak, "Justices Take Up Race as a Factor in College Entry," *New York Times,* February 22, 2012, A1, A13.

19. U.S. Census Bureau, *Statistical Abstract of the United States, 2014* (Washington, D.C.: Government Printing Office, 2014), table 642, 415–418.

20. Dorothy E. McBride and Janine A. Perry, *Women's Rights in the USA: Policy Debates and Gender Roles,* 4th ed. (New York: Routledge, 2011), 47–48.

21. Sara M. Evans, *Born for Liberty: A History of Women in America,* 2nd ed. (New York: Free Press, 1997), 93–143.

22. Nancy E. McGlen and Karen O'Connor, *Women, Politics, and American Society,* 2nd ed. (Upper Saddle River, NJ: Prentice-Hall, 1998), 11, 117, 177–181; Evans, *Born for Liberty,* 301–303.

23. Jane J. Mansbridge, *Why We Lost the ERA* (Chicago: University of Chicago Press, 1986), 20.

24. Linda Greenhouse, "In Reversal of Course, Justices 5–4, Back Ban on Abortion Method," *New York Times,* April 19, 2007, A1.

25. U.S. Census Bureau, *Statistical Abstract of the United States, 2014* (Washington, D.C.: U.S. Government Printing Office, 2014), table 303, 197.

26. U.S. Census Bureau, *Statistical Abstract, 2014,* table 642, 416–418.

27. U.S. Census Bureau, *Statistical Abstract, 2014,* table 625, and 626, 406–407 and 384. See also "Women in the Labor Force: A Databook," 2011. U.S. Department of Labor, Bureau of Labor Statistics, December 2011, Report 1034, Table 25, 78.

28. M.P. McQueen, "Education Gains Shield Woman From Worst of Job Woes," *Wall Street Journal,* February 12, 2010, A4.

Chapter 15   Government, the Economy, and Domestic Policy

1. Marc Allen Eisner, *The American Political Economy: Institutional Evolution of Market and State* (New York: Routledge, 2011), 19, 119.

2. David Brain Robertson, *Federalism and the Making of America* (New York: Routledge, 2012), 74.

3. John P. Frendreis and Raymond Tatalovich, *The Modern Presidency and Economic Policy* (Itasca, IL: Peacock, 1994), 116, 20; see also Lisa A. Keister, *Wealth in America: Trends in Wealth Inequality* (New York: Cambridge University Press, 2000).

4. Ballard C. Campbell, *The Growth of American Government: Governance from the Cleveland Era to the Present* (Bloomington, IN: Indiana University Press, 1995), 83–84.

5. James T. Patterson, *America's Struggle against Poverty in the Twentieth Century* (Cambridge, MA: Harvard University Press, 2000), 60.

6. Jeffrey E. Cohen, *Politics and Economic Policy in the United States* (New York: Houghton Mifflin, 2000), 228.

7. Nicole V. Crain and W. Mark Crain, "The Impact of Regulatory Costs on Small Firms," Small Business Administration, Office of Advocacy, September 2010.

8. John Cassidy, "After the Blowup: Laissez-Faire Economists Do Some Soul-Searching—And Finger-Pointing," *The New Yorker,* January 11, 2010, 28–33.

9. Catharine Rampell, "Tax Pledge May Scuttle a Deal on Deficits," *New York Times,* November 19, 2011, B1, B2.

10. Frendreis and Tatalovich, *The Modern Presidency and Economic Policy*, 170. James Pethokoulis, "America's Bull Run: Can We Keep It Going?," *U.S. News & World Report*, January 14, 2008, 14.

11. Martha Coven and Richard Kogan, "Introduction to the Federal Budget Process," Center on Budget and Policy Priorities, December 17, 2008. See http://www.cbpp.org/cms/Index.cfm.

12. W. Elliot Brownlee, *Federal Taxation in America: A Short History* (New York: Cambridge University Press, 1996), 19.

13. Brownlee, *Federal Taxation in America*, 26–28.

14. Carolyn Webber and Aaron Wildavsky, *A History of Taxation and Expenditure in the Western World* (New York: Simon and Schuster, 1986), 421–422.

15. Department of Commerce, Bureau of the Census, *Historical Statistics of the United States, Colonial Times to 1957* (Washington, D.C.: U.S. Government Printing Office, 1960), 703.

16. Edmund L. Andrews, "Why U.S. Companies Shouldn't Whine About Taxes," *New York Times*, July 9, 2006, Bu3.

17. Campbell, *The Growth of American Government*, 227–228; Brownlee, *Federal Taxation in America*, 1.

18. Richard W. Stevenson, "Itching to Rebuild the Tax Law," *New York Times*, November 24, 2002, B1, B11.

19. Congressional Budget Office, "The Distribution of Major Tax Expenditures," http://www.cbo.gov/sites/default/files/cbofiles/attachments/437.

20. U.S. Bureau of the Census, *Historical Statistics of the United States, Colonial Times to 1957* (Washington, D.C.: 1960), Series A 1–3, 7, and Series Y 254–257, 711.

21. Edmund L. Andrews, "80% of Budget Effectively Off Limits to Cuts," *New York Times*, April 6, 2006, A18.

22. Benjamin Bridges and Sharmila Choudhury, "Social Security as a Retirement Resource, by Race and Ethnicity," Social Security Administration, ORES Working Paper No. 109. See http://www.socialsecurity.gov/policy.

23. Christian J. Wolfe, Barbara S. Klees, and Catharine A. Curtis, "Brief Summaries of Medicare and Medicaid," Office of the Actuary, Centers for Medicare and Medicaid Services, November 1, 2009. See http://www.cms.hhs.gov/Medicare ProgramRatesStats/Downloads/Medicare-MedicaidSummaries 2009.pdf.

24. Robert Pear, "Another Modest Rise for Health Costs," *New York Times*, January 7, 2014, A10.

25. Robert Pear, "Trustees Say Medicare Finances Worsened Because of Sluggish Economy," *New York Times*, May 14, 2011, A12.

26. Robert Pear, "States Proposing Sweeping Changes to Trim Medicaid," *New York Times*, May 9, 2005, A14.

27. U.S. Bureau of the Census, *Historical Statistics of the United States*, Series Y 254–257, 711.

28. U.S. Census Bureau, *Historical Statistics of the United States, Colonial Times to 1957* (Washington, D.C.: U.S. Government Printing Office, 1960), Series F 1–5, 139. See also Jonathan Hughes, *American Economic History*, 3rd ed. (New York: HarperCollins, 1990), 332.

29. *Historical Statistics of the United States*, Series F 1–5, 139; Hughes, *American Economic History*, 530, 582; *Economic Indicators*, September 1997, prepared for the Joint Economic Committee by the Council of Economic Advisers (Washington, D.C.: U.S. Government Printing Office, 1997), 2.

30. Tyler Cowan, "For Much of the World, A Fruitful Decade," *New York Times*, January 3, 2010, BU4.

31. James Surowiecki, "Open Season," *The New Yorker*, October 21, 2013, 31.

32. Timothy Noah, *The Great Divergence: America's Growing Inequality Crisis and What We*

Can Do About It (New York: Bloomsbury Press, 2012).

33. David Kay Johnson, "Income Gap is Widening, Data Shows," *New York Times*, March 29, 2007, C1.

34. Julia B. Isaacs, Pew Charitable Trusts, has offered a number of studies on economic mobility by generation, race, and gender. See www.econmicmobility.org.

35. Ronald Brownstein, "Closing the Book on the Bush Legacy," TheAtlantic.com, September 11, 2009.

Chapter 16   America's Place in a Dangerous World

1. Joseph S. Nye Jr., *The Paradox of American Power* (New York: Oxford University Press, 2002), 4–12. See also Walter Isaacson, "The Return of the Realists," *Time*, November 20, 2006, 39.

2. Frederick W. Marks III, *Independence on Trial: Foreign Affairs and the Making of the Constitution* (Baton Rouge, LA: Louisiana State University Press, 1973), 24.

3. Robert O. Keohane and Joseph S. Nye, Jr. *Power and Interdependence*, 4th ed. (New York: Longman, 2012), 78.

4. Quoted in G. John Eikenberry, 'Rethinking the Origins of American Hegemony," 24, 26, in Theodore Reuter (ed.), *The United States in the World Political Economy* (New York: McGraw-Hill, 1994).

5. "Bretton Woods Revisited," *The Economist*, July 9, 1994, 69–75.

6. Robert Burns, "Gates: NATO Cannot Be Afraid to Use Force," *Associated Press*, February 24, 2010.

7. Warren Hoge, "U.N. Envoys See Loss of Steam for Expanding Security Council," *New York Times*, November 11, 2005, A8.

8. Neil MacFarquhar, "In Peacekeeping, A Muddling of the Mission," *New York Times*, February 11, 2009, A6.

9. Steven R. Weisman, "Cracks in the Foundation: Three Institutions' Roles in a Chang-

ing Global Economy Questioned," *New York Times*, May 23, 2007, C1. C8.

10. Fareed Zakaria, "The Future of American Power," *Foreign Affairs*, vol. 87, no. 3, May/June 2008, 18–43.

11. Justin LaHart, "U.S. Keeps Science Lead, But Other Countries Gain," *Wall Street Journal*, January 16–17, 2010, A5.

12. John Agnew, *The United States in the World Economy: A Regional Geography* (New York: Cambridge University Press, 1987), 48–49.

13. James H. Mittelman, *The Globalization Syndrome: Transformation and Resistance* (Princeton, NJ: Princeton University Press, 2000), 111–146.

14. Steven Erlanger and Stephen Castle, "German Vision Prevails As European Leaders Agree on Fiscal Treaty," *New York Times*, December 10, 2011, A1, A8.

15. G. Robert Hillman, "Bush Leaves Argentina Without Free Trade Deal," *Dallas Morning News*, November 6, 2005, A26.

16. AP, "China Nets Landmark Free Trade Agreement," *Dallas Morning News*, November 30, 2004, D14.

17. Stephen Castle and Mark Landner, "After 7 Years, Talks Collapse on World Trade," *New York Times*, July 30, 2008, A1, A7.

18. Brian Knowlton, "Global Support for Trade Mixed with Some Doubts," *New York Times*, October 5, 2007, A10.

19. Michael Mandel, "How Pigs Saved Our Bacon," *BusinessWeek*, March 17, 2008, 26.

20. Joseph S. Nye, *Bound to Lead: The Changing Nature of American Power* (New York: Basic Books, 1990), 209.

21. http://www.sipri.org/databases/milex

22. Elizabeth Bomiller, "U.S. Will Counter U.S. Arms Build-up," *New York Times*, January 9, 2011, A6.

23. Ellen Nakashima, "New Post Proposed at Pentagon: Director Would Review Spending on U.S. Weapons Systems," *Washington Post*, March 4, 2009.

24. Todd Spangler, "The Ford Will Ushar in the Navy's First New Class of Carriers in 40 Years," *Detroit Free Press*, November 7, 2013.

25. Mark Thompson, "How To Save A Billion Dollars," *Time*, April 25, 2011, 23–29.

26. The National Security Strategy of the United States of America. See http://www.whitehouse.gov/nsc/nss.html.

27. Judith Miller, "Keeping U.S. No. 1: Is It Wise? Is It New? The Bush Doctrine of Preemption Plucks a Sensitive Nerve," *New York Times*, October 26, 2003, A19.

28. Robert Kagan, "A Tougher War for U.S. Is One of Legitimacy," *New York Times*, January 24, 2004, A17, A19.

29. White House, "National Security Strategy." May 2010, http://www.whitehouse.gov . . . national_security_strategy.gov.pdf.

30. Jan M. Olsen, AP, "Agreement May Be Elusive at Denmark Climate Change Conference," *Dallas Morning News*, December 6, 2009, A26.

31. John Broder, "U.S. Climate Envoy Seems to Shift Stance on Timetable for New Talks," *New York Times*, December 9, 2011, A13. See also AP, "Delegates Reach Deal on Climate Program," *Dallas Morning News*, December 11, 2011, 16A.

32. White House, "National Security Strategy," February 2015, http://www.whitehouse.gov . . . 2015_national_security_strategy.pdf.

33. "How Many Planets?: A Survey of Global Environment," *The Economist*, July 6, 2002, 1–18.

34. "Increasing Oil Reserves," *Time*, July 9, 2007, 7.

35. Keith Bradsher and David Barbosa, "Pollution from Chinese Coal Casts Shadow Around Globe," *New York Times*, June 11, 2006, A1, A14–15.

36. Sudeep Reddy and Brendan M. Case, "Oil Supply Enters New Era of Demand," *Dallas Morning News*, August 11, 2005, D1, D8.

37. Liam Denning, "China's Dubious Accolade," *Wall Street Journal*, July 20, 2010, C10.

38. Fareed Zakaria, "Preview of a Post-U.S. World," *Newsweek*, February 5, 2007, 47.

39. Tom Maliti and Ariel David, "UN Report: More Than 1 Billion Suffer Hunger," AP to *Dallas Morning News*, October 15, 2009, A10.

40. Jack A. Goldstone, "The New Population Bomb: The Four Megatrends that Will Change the World," *Foreign Affairs*, January/February 2010, 31–43.

GLOSSARY OF KEY TERMS

abolitionist Advocates of slavery's abolition in the United States (Chapter 14).

administrative adjudication Procedures designed to allow resolution of complex issues based on specific facts rather than general rules (Chapter 11).

Administrative Procedures Act (APA) Passed in 1946, the APA remains the single most important attempt by Congress to define the nature and process of bureaucratic decision making (Chapter 11).

advice and consent Article II, section 2, of the Constitution requires the president to seek the advice and consent of the Senate in appointing Supreme Court justices, senior officials of the executive branch, and ambassadors, and in ratifying treaties with foreign nations (Chapter 2).

affirm Action of a higher court supporting the decision of a lower court (Chapter 12).

affirmative action Policies and actions designed to make up for the effects of past discrimination by giving preferences today to specified racial, ethnic, and sexual groups (Chapter 14).

AFL-CIO Formed in 1955 when the American Federation of Labor joined with the Congress of Industrial Organizations, the nine million-member AFL-CIO is the largest labor organization in the United States (Chapter 6).

agenda-setting effect The extent to which the amount of media coverage of an issue affects the public's attention to and interest in that issue (Chapter 5).

agents of socialization The persons, such as parents and teachers, and settings, such as families and schools, that carry out the political socialization process (Chapter 4).

American Political Development (APD) The study of development and change in American political processes, institutions, and policies (Chapter 1).

amicus curiae briefs Arguments filed with the court by parties interested in a case but not directly involved in it as contending parties. *Amicus curiae* is Latin meaning "friend of the court." (Chapter 12).

Annapolis Convention Held in Annapolis, Maryland, in September 1786 to discuss problems arising from state restrictions on interstate commerce, it was a precursor to the Constitutional Convention (Chapter 2).

Anti-Federalists Opponents of a stronger national government who generally opposed ratification of the U.S. Constitution (Chapter 2).

appellate jurisdiction Substantive area in which a higher court may hear cases appealed from a lower court (Chapter 12).

appointment power Article II, section 2, of the Constitution empowers the president, often with the advice and consent of the Senate, to appoint many senior government officials (Chapter 10).

appropriations committees House and Senate committees that appropriate or allocate specific funding levels to each government program or activity (Chapter 9).

aristocracy For the ancients, aristocracy meant rule by the few, who were usually also wealthy, in the interest of the entire community. More broadly, *aristocracy* denotes the class of titled nobility within a society (Chapter 1).

Articles of Confederation Written in the Continental Congress in 1776 and 1777, the Articles outlining America's first national government were finally adopted on March 1, 1781. The Articles were replaced by the United States Constitution on March 4, 1789 (Chapter 2).

authorizing committees House and Senate committees that develop or authorize particular policies or programs through legislation (Chapter 9).

benchmark poll A poll conducted early in a campaign to gauge the name recognition, public image, and electoral prospects of a candidate (Chapter 4).

bicameralism A two-house, as opposed to a unicameral or one-house, legislature (Chapter 2).

Bill of Rights The first ten amendments to the U.S. Constitution, proposed by the first Federal Congress and ratified by the states in 1791, were intended to protect individual rights and liberties from action by the new national government (Chapter 2).

Bipartisan Campaign Reform Act (BCRA) Commonly known as McCain-Feingold, the 2002 BCRA was the first major revision of campaign finance laws since the early 1970s (Chapter 8).

bipolar An international system organized around two dominant powers (Chapter 16).

block grants Federal funds made available to states or communities in which they have discretion over how the money is spent within the broad substantive area covered by the block grant (Chapter 3).

Boston Massacre A clash on March 5, 1770, between British troops and a Boston mob that left five colonists dead and eight wounded (Chapter 2).

Boston Tea Party Boston patriots oppose British attempts to tax the colonies by dumping tea into Boston Harbor rather than pay the required taxes.

briefs Written arguments prepared by lawyers in a case outlining their views of the relevant law and the decision that should be rendered based on the law (Chapter 12).

Budget and Accounting Act of 1921 This act created the Bureau of the Budget (BOB) in the Treasury Department and enhanced presidential control over the budgetary process in the executive branch. BOB became the Office of Management and Budget in 1970 (Chapter 15).

bureaucracy A hierarchical organization in which offices have specified missions and employees are assigned responsibilities based on merit, knowledge, and experience (Chapter 11).

Bush Doctrine Highlighted in the National Security Strategy of October 2002, the Bush Doctrine put sovereignty, national security, preemption, and supremacy at the core of American foreign policy (Chapter 16).

cabinet The secretaries of the fifteen executive departments and other officials designated by the president.

The cabinet is available to consult with the president (Chapter 10).

casework Casework refers to the direct assistance that members of Congress or their staff provide to their constituents who need something from a federal agency or department (Chapter 9).

categorical grant A program making federal funds available to states and communities for a specific, often narrow, purpose and usually requiring a distinct application, implementation, and reporting procedure (Chapter 3).

caucus Face-to-face meeting in which rank-and-file party members discuss and vote on candidates to stand for election to offices under the party label at a later general election (Chapter 8).

checks and balances The idea that governmental powers should be distributed to permit each branch of government to check and balance the other branches (Chapter 2).

civil code Legal tradition that envisions a complete and fully articulated legal system based on clear statutes that lay out legal principles and commands in plain language that citizens can understand and obey (Chapter 12).

civil law Law dealing primarily with relations between individuals and organizations, as in marriage and family law, contracts, and property. Violations result more in judgments and fines than punishment as such (Chapter 12).

civil liberties Areas of social life, including free speech, press, and religion, where the Constitution restricts or prohibits government intrusion on the free choices of individuals (Chapter 13).

civil rights Areas of social life, such as the right to vote and to be free from racial discrimination, where the Constitution requires government to act to ensure that citizens are treated equally (Chapter 13).

civil service system Rules governing the hiring, advancement, pay, and discipline of civilian federal employees (Chapter 11).

classical liberalism Doctrine identified with Hobbes, Locke, and Smith favoring limited government and individual rights. The dominant American political and social ideology in the nineteenth and early twentieth centuries (Chapter 1).

classical republicanism Doctrine identified with Montesquieu and Hume that highlights concern for the common good over the self-interest of individuals (Chapter 1).

cloture A cloture vote, requiring a 60-vote majority, is the only way to half a filibuster in the Senate (Chapter 9).

coercive federalism A pejorative term to describe the federalism of the 1960s and 1970s suggesting that the national government was using its financial muscle to coerce states into following national dictates as opposed to serving local needs (Chapter 3).

Cold War The period of continuous hostility short of actual warfare that existed between the United States and the Soviet Union from the end of World War II through the mid-1980s (Chapter 16).

Committee of the Whole House convened under a set of rules that allows limitations on debate and amendment and lowers the quorum required to do business from 218 to 100 to facilitate speedier action (Chapter 9).

common law Judge-made law, as opposed to a fully integrated legal code, developed over time as judges consider particular legal disputes and then future judges cite earlier decisions in resolving similar issues (Chapter 12).

Communications Act of 1934 Established the Federal Communications Commission (FCC) as the federal agency responsible for regulating the media (Chapter 5).

concurrent majority South Carolina Senator John C. Calhoun's idea for restoring balance between the North and South by giving each region the right to reject national legislation thought harmful to the region (Chapter 3).

concurrent powers Powers, such as the power to tax, that are available to both levels of the federal system and may be exercised by both in relation to the same body of citizens (Chapter 3).

confederation Loose governing arrangement in which separate republics or nations join together to coordinate foreign policy and defense but retain full control over their domestic affairs (Chapter 3).

Confederation Congress The Congress served under the Articles of Confederation from its adoption on March 1, 1781, until it was superseded by the new Federal Congress when the U.S. Constitution went into effect on March 4, 1789 (Chapter 2).

conference committees Committees composed of members of the House and Senate charged to resolve differences between the House and Senate versions of a bill (Chapter 9).

confirmation hearing Setting in which nominees for federal judicial posts appear before the Senate Judiciary Committee to respond to questions from the members (Chapter 12).

conservative A conservative generally favors small government, low taxes, deregulation, and the use of market incentives where possible (Chapter 4).

Constitutional Convention Met in Philadelphia between May 25 and September 17 and produced the U.S. Constitution. It is sometimes referred to as the Federal Convention or the Philadelphia Convention (Chapter 2).

containment U.S. policy, developed by Marshall, Kennan, and Truman, after World War II to contain Soviet power by strengthening U.S. allies on the periphery of the Soviet empire (Chapter 16).

Continental Congress Met in September 1774 and from May 1775 forward to coordinate protests against British policy and then revolution. The Continental Congress was superseded by the Confederation Congress when the Articles of Confederation went into effect on March 1, 1781 (Chapter 2).

cooperative federalism Mid-twentieth century view of federalism in which national, state, and local governments share responsibility for virtually all functions (Chapter 3).

corporation A legal rather than a physical person. A corporation can do anything a person can do, including buying and selling property, loaning and borrowing money, but the liability of the shareholders is limited to the amount of their investment in the corporation (Chapter 15).

courts of appeals Thirteen courts that form the intermediate level of the federal judicial system and hear appeals of cases tried in the federal district courts (Chapter 12).

coverture A legal concept, transferred to America as part of the Common Law, holding that upon marriage the husband and the wife became "one person, and that person the husband." (Chapter 14).

creative federalism 1960s view of federalism that refers to LBJ's willingness to expand the range of federal programs to support state and local activities and to bring new, even nongovernmental, actors into the process (Chapter 3).

criminal law Criminal law prohibits certain actions and prescribes penalties for those who engage in the prohibited conduct (Chapter 12).

cruel and unusual punishment The Eighth Amendment to the U.S. Constitution prohibits "cruel and unusual punishment." Historically, this language prohibited torture and other abuses. Today the key question is whether the death penalty should be declared to be cruel and unusual punishment (Chapter 13).

Declaration of Independence The document adopted in the Continental Congress on July 4, 1776, to explain and justify the decision of the American colonies to declare their independence from Britain (Chapter 2).

Declaratory Act An act passed in Parliament in March 1766 declaring that the British king and Parliament had the right to pass laws binding on the colonies in America "in all cases whatsoever." (Chapter 2).

deficit If government spends more than it collects in a given year, the amount that has to be borrowed to make up the shortfall is called the deficit (Chapter 15).

delegate A view of representation that sees the representative's principal role as reflecting the views and protecting the interests of his or her own constituents (Chapter 9).

democracy Rule by the people. For the ancients, democracy meant popular rule, where the people came together in one place, in the interest of the community. More broadly, democracy denotes political systems in which free elections select public officials and affect the course of public policy (Chapter 1).

deterrence The military doctrine and strategy that seeks to amass sufficient power to prevent or deter an opponent from resorting to force (Chapter 16).

devolution The return of political authority from the national government to the states beginning in the 1970s and continuing today (Chapter 3).

direct discrimination Discrimination practiced directly by one individual against another (Chapter 13).

discount rate The interest rate that the Fed charges banks for loans (Chapter 15).

district courts The ninety-four general trial courts of the federal judicial system (Chapter 12).

dual federalism Nineteenth-century view of federalism envisioning a federal system in which the two levels were sovereign in fairly distinct areas of responsibility with little overlap or sharing of authority (Chapter 3).

Duverger's law Political scientist Maurice Duverger was the first to note that electoral rules influence party systems. Majoritarian systems usually produce two-party systems, and proportional representation systems usually produce multiparty systems (Chapter 7).

educational effect The public learns from what it sees discussed in the media and cannot learn, obviously, about issues that are not taken up by the media (Chapter 5).

Electoral College An institution created by the Federal Convention of 1787 to select the president. Each state has a number of votes equal to the number of its seats in the U.S. House of Representatives plus its two senators (Chapter 10).

elitism The belief that the interest group structure of American politics is skewed toward the interest of the wealthy (Chapter 6).

enumerated powers The specifically listed or enumerated powers of the Congress found in Article I, section 8, of the Constitution (Chapter 2).

establishment clause The First Amendment to the Constitution says that "Congress shall make no law respecting an establishment of religion." This clearly means that Congress may not establish a national religion. There is an ongoing debate over how much, if any, contact is allowed between religion and government (Chapter 13).

exclusionary rule The exclusionary rule holds that evidence illegally obtained by police cannot be used in court. The Supreme Court established the exclusionary rule in regard to the federal authorities in *Weeks v. U.S.* (1914) and in regard to state authorities in *Mapp v. Ohio* (1961) (Chapter 13).

executive agreements Agreements negotiated between the president and foreign governments. Executive agreements have the same legal force as treaties but do not require confirmation by the Senate (Chapter 10).

Executive Office of the President (EOP) Established in 1939, the EOP houses the professional support personnel working for the president (Chapter 10).

executive privilege The right of presidents, recognized by the Supreme Court, to keep conversations and communications with their advisers confidential (Chapter 10).

exit poll A poll taken after voters have cast their ballots to get an early sense of who won and why (Chapter 4).

extradition Provision of Article IV, section 2, of the U.S. Constitution providing that persons accused of a crime in one state fleeing into another state shall be returned to the state in which the crime was committed (Chapter 3).

Federal Communications Commission (FCC) Established in the Communications Act of 1934, the FCC is a five-member commission empowered to regulate the media in the public interest (Chapter 5).

Federal Election Campaign Act (FECA) Campaign reform legislation passed in 1971, with major amendments in 1974 and later, that required disclosure and set limits on campaign contributions, and provided public funding of presidential elections (Chapter 8).

federalism A form of government in which some powers are assigned to the national government, some to lower levels of government, and some, such as the power to tax, overlap or are exercised concurrently (Chapter 2).

Federalists Supporters of a stronger national government who favored ratification of the U.S. Constitution (Chapter 2).

filibuster Senators enjoy the right of unlimited debate. Use of unlimited debate by a senator to stall or block passage of legislation is called a filibuster (Chapter 9).

fiscal policy Government policies about taxing, spending, budgets, deficits, and debt (Chapter 15).

flat tax A tax that takes the same proportion of income or wealth from the wealthy as from the poor (Chapter 15).

focus group A small but carefully selected group of ten to fifteen persons led through an in-depth discussion of a political issue or campaign to delve behind opinions in search of their root causes (Chapter 4).

frame Dominant organizing frame or image, such as the equal rights image that motivated most of the movements of the 1960s and 1970s (Chapter 6).

framing effect The way an issue is framed or presented in the media, either episodically or thematically, suggests to the public where the praise or blame should be laid (Chapter 5).

free exercise clause The First Amendment to the Constitution, immediately after saying that Congress may not establish religion, says Congress may not prohibit the "free exercise" of religion. The intent of the free exercise clause is to protect a wide range of religious observance and practice from political interference (Chapter 13).

Freedom of Information Act (FOIA) Passed in 1966, FOIA requires government agencies to provide citizens, including the press, with most kinds of information in their possession (Chapter 5).

frontloading The crowding of presidential primaries and caucuses into the early weeks of the nomination period (Chapter 8).

full faith and credit Article IV, section 1, of the Constitution requires that each state give "full faith and credit" to the legal acts of the other states (Chapter 2).

General Agreement on Tariffs and Trade (GATT) A series of international treaties, the first completed in 1947, the most recent in 1994, designed to rationalize and reduce tariff and nontariff barriers to international trade. In January 1995 the GATT gave way to the World Trade Organization (WTO) (Chapter 16).

general election A final or definitive election in which candidates representing their respective parties contend for election to office (Chapter 8).

general revenue sharing Program enacted in 1974, discontinued in 1986, that provided basically unrestricted federal funds to states and localities to support activities that they judged to be of highest priority (Chapter 3).

gerrymander Refers to the strange shape of some congressional districts that result when parties draw districts intended to maximize their political advantage (Chapter 9).

hard power Assets, especially military and economic power, that allow a nation to insist on its preferences (Chapter 16).

human rights Fundamental rights to freedom and security that belong to all human beings (Chapter 14).

idealists Idealists contend that nation-states should act to promote the ideals of freedom, democracy, and opportunity in the world (Chapter 16).

impeachment The process of removing national government officials from office. The House votes a statement of particulars or charges, and a trial is conducted in the Senate (Chapter 10).

implementation The process of making a program or policy actually work day-to-day in the real world (Chapter 11).

implied powers Congressional powers not specifically mentioned among the enumerated powers, but which are reasonable and necessary to accomplish an enumerated end or activity (Chapter 3).

incorporation Incorporation is the idea that many of the protections of the Bill of Rights, originally meant to apply only against the national government, applied against the states as well because they were "incorporated" into the Fourteenth Amendment's guarantees of "due process" and "equal protection of the laws." (Chapter 13).

individualism The idea that the people are the legitimate source of political authority and that they have rights which government must respect (Chapter 1).

inherent powers Powers accruing to all sovereign nations, whether or not specified in the Constitution, allowing executives to take all actions required to defend the nation and protect its interests (Chapters 3 and 10).

initiative Legal or constitutional process common in the states that allows citizens to place questions on the ballot to be decided directly by the voters (Chapter 7).

inside strategy Lobbying strategies usually involving direct contact with elected or appointed officials or their staff to shape their view of issues (Chapter 6).

institution A custom, practice, or organization, usually embedded in rules and law, that define and structure social and political activity (Chapter 1).

interest groups Organizations based on shared interests that attempt to influence society and government to act in ways consonant with the organization's interests (Chapter 6).

International Monetary Fund (IMF) A key part of the post-World War II international financial system, the IMF was responsible for monitoring the system of fixed currency exchange rates and now seeks to assist nations in managing debt (Chapter 16).

Interstate Commerce Commission (ICC) First independent regulatory commission, established in 1887, to develop, implement, and adjudicate fair and reasonable freight rates (Chapter 11).

Intolerable Acts Acts passed in Parliament during the spring of 1774, in response to the Boston Tea Party and similar events, to strengthen British administration of the colonies (Chapter 2).

inverted pyramid model The idea that newspaper stories should put the most important facts in the opening paragraph, followed by less important supporting facts and details as the story goes on (Chapter 5).

Jim Crow The generic name for all of the laws and practices that enforced segregation of the races in the American South and elsewhere from the end of the nineteenth century to the middle of the twentieth century (Chapter 14).

joint committees Congressional committees made up of members of both the House and the Senate and assigned to study a particular topic (Chapter 9).

judicial activism Active policymaking by courts, especially in sensitive cases such as desegregation and abortion (Chapter 12).

judicial restraint The idea that courts should avoid policymaking and limit themselves to implementing legislative and executive intent (Chapter 12).

judicial review Power of any federal court to hold any law or official act based on law to be unenforceable because it is in conflict with the Constitution (Chapter 12).

Judiciary Act of 1789 Originating act for the federal judiciary passed by the first Congress (Chapter 12).

justiciability Legal term indicating that an issue or dispute is appropriate for or subject to judicial resolution (Chapter 12).

Keynesianism Economic ideas associated with British economist John Maynard Keynes advocating countercyclical spending by government to manage demand in the private economy (Chapter 15).

law Authoritative rules made by government and backed by the organized force of the community (Chapter 12).

legislative supremacy The idea that the lawmaking authority in government should be supreme over the executive and judicial powers (Chapter 9).

liberal A liberal generally favors government involvement in economic activity and social life to assure equal opportunity and assistance to those in need (Chapter 4).

libertarian A libertarian generally favors minimal government involvement in the social and economic lives of individuals and believes that government should be limited mostly to defense and public safety (Chapter 4).

litigation Bringing a case in court for the purpose of demanding a beneficial policy change or avoiding an adverse change (Chapter 6).

lobbyists Hired agents who seek to influence government decision making in ways that benefit or limit harm to their clients (Chapter 6).

manifest destiny Americans in the latter half of the nineteenth century commonly held the view that it was the "manifest destiny" of the United States to expand across the continent from the Atlantic to the Pacific (Chapter 16).

Marshall Plan Part of the containment strategy, the Marshall Plan provided $15 billion in economic aid to help rebuild Europe between 1947 and 1953 (Chapter 16).

means-tested programs Social programs in which eligibility is established by low income and limited assets. Medicaid is a means-tested program (Chapter 15).

micro targeting Campaign consultants analyze dozens of pieces of demographic, political, and consumer data to determine what issues, themes, and arguments are likely to move a voter or group of similar voters toward a candidate (Chapter 8).

minor party A party that raises issues and offers candidates but has little chance of winning and organizing the government (Chapter 7).

monarchy For the ancients, monarchy meant the rule of one man in the interest of the entire community. More broadly, monarchy denotes kingship or the hereditary claim to rule in a given society (Chapter 1).

monetarists Monetarists contend that slow and steady growth in the money supply facilitates smooth economic growth and stable prices (Chapter 15).

monetary policy Monetary policy refers to government decisions about the money supply and interest rates (Chapter 15).

monopoly Circumstance in which one producer has exclusive control of a market, thus enabling market manipulation and discretionary pricing (Chapter 15).

Monroe Doctrine U.S. policy announced by President James Monroe in 1823 stating that attempts by European powers to establish new colonies anywhere in the Americas would be considered unfriendly to U.S. interests in the area (Chapter 16).

Motor Voter Popular name for the National Voter Registration Act of 1993. The act permits people to register to vote while they are doing other common tasks like getting or renewing their driver's licenses (Chapter 8).

muckraking tradition Progressive journalism of the late nineteenth and early twentieth centuries that dedicated much of its attention to uncovering political and corporate corruption (Chapter 5).

national debt The accumulation of annual deficits over the years is referred to as the national debt (Chapter 15).

national party convention The Democratic and Republican parties meet in national convention every four years, in the summer just prior to the presidential election, to choose a presidential candidate and adopt a party platform (Chapter 8).

National Security Council (NSC) Part of the Executive Office of the President, established in 1947, that coordinates advice and policy for the president on national security issues (Chapter 10).

Natural Law God's act of creation entailed a just and proper end or purpose for the natural world, including man. God's purpose for man, the Natural Law, is imprinted on the mind and heart of man.

"necessary and proper" clause The last paragraph of Article I, section 8, of the Constitution, which states that Congress may make all laws deemed necessary and proper to carry into execution the powers specifically enumerated in Article I, section 8 (Chapter 2).

neoconservatives Neoconservatives argue that military and economic power should be used to promote American ideals and interests (Chapter 16).

New Deal The name given to President Franklin Roosevelt's policies and programs intended to address the Great Depression (Chapter 15).

New Jersey Plan A plan to add a limited number of new powers to the Articles, supported by most of the delegates from the small states, introduced into the Constitutional Convention as an alternative to the Virginia Plan (Chapter 2).

North Atlantic Treaty Organization (NATO) A collective security pact formed in 1949 between the United States, Canada, and their western European allies to oppose further Soviet expansion in Europe (Chapter 16).

nullification The claim prominent in the first half of the nineteenth century that states have the right to nullify or reject national acts that they believe to be beyond national constitutional authority (Chapter 3).

objectivity The demand for objectivity in journalism required that reports present readers with facts and information rather than opinion and interpretation (Chapter 5).

obscenity Sexually explicit material, whether spoken, written, or visual, that "taken as a whole . . . lacks serious literary, artistic, political, or scientific value." (Chapter 13).

Office of Management and Budget (OMB) Part of the Executive Office of the President that provides budgetary expertise, central legislative clearance, and management assistance to the president (Chapter 10).

oligarchy For the ancients and more generally, oligarchy denotes the rule of the few, usually an economic elite, in their own interest (Chapter 1).

Open Door Policy U.S. policy at the end of the nineteenth century and beginning of the twentieth that China should remain open to free trade rather than be under the exclusive control of one or more colonial powers (Chapter 16).

opinion Written finding or decision of a court (Chapter 12).

opinion survey Poll or survey used by political campaigns, the media, civic organizations, and marketers to gauge opinion on particular questions and issues (Chapter 4).

oral argument The opportunity in a case before the Supreme Court for the opposing lawyers orally to present their legal arguments (Chapter 12).

Organization of Petroleum Exporting Countries (OPEC) The commodity cartel of mostly Middle Eastern oil-producing nations. OPEC exercises more control than any other organization on both the volume and price of oil in the international economy (Chapter 16).

original jurisdiction Mandatory jurisdiction of the Supreme Court as laid out in Article III of the Constitution (Chapter 12).

outside strategy Lobbying strategies intended to inform and shape public opinion as an indirect way of influencing policymakers.

pardon A pardon makes the recipient a new person in the eyes of the law as if no offense had ever been committed (Chapter 10).

partisan press Most papers in the nineteenth century were identified with a political party and served to rally the party faithful rather than to objectively inform the entire public (Chapter 5).

party identification The emotional and intellectual commitment of a voter to his or her preferred party (Chapter 7).

party in government The officeholders, both elected and partisan-appointed officials, who ran under or have been associated with the party label (Chapter 7).

party in the electorate The voters who identify more or less directly and consistently with a political party (Chapter 7).

party organization The permanent structure of party offices and officials who administer the party apparatus on a day-to-day basis (Chapter 7).

party primary An election in which voters identified with a political party select the candidates who will stand for election under the party label in a subsequent general election (Chapter 7).

party unity Each year *Congressional Quarterly* reports the proportion of votes in the House and Senate on which a majority of one party lines up against a majority of the other party (Chapter 7).

patronage The awarding of political jobs or contracts based on partisan ties instead of merit or expertise (Chapter 11).

peak associations Peak associations, like the U.S. Chamber of Commerce, represent the general interests of business (Chapter 6).

Pendleton Act The Pendleton Act of 1883 was the original legislation establishing the civil service system (Chapter 11).

penny press Popular newspapers of the early nineteenth century that sold on the street for a penny and oriented their coverage toward the common man (Chapter 5).

persuasion effect The way an issue is presented by the media can sometimes change the substance of what people think about the issue (Chapter 5).

philosopher-king A term, closely identified with Plato, denoting ideal political leadership. The philosopher-king would know the true nature of justice and what it required in every instance (Chapter 1).

pluralism The belief that the interest group structure of American politics produces a reasonable policy balance (Chapter 6).

polis Greek term for a political community on the scale of a city (Chapter 1).

political culture Patterns of thought and behavior that are widely held in a society and that refer to the relationship of citizens to their government and to each other in matters affecting politics and public affairs (Chapter 4).

political ideology An organized and coherent set of ideas that form a perspective on the political world and how it works (Chapter 4).

political party An organization designed to elect government officeholders under a given label (Chapter 7).

political socialization The process by which the central tenets of the political culture are transmitted from those immersed in it to those, such as children and immigrants, who are not (Chapter 4).

politico A view of representation that sees representatives following constituent opinion when that is clear and his or her own judgment or political interest when constituency opinion is amorphous or divided (Chapter 9).

polity The general meaning of polity is political community. Aristotle used it to denote a political community in which the institutions of oligarchy and democracy were mixed to produce political stability (Chapter 1).

popular sovereignty The idea that all legitimate governmental authority comes from the people and can be reclaimed by them if government becomes neglectful or abusive (Chapter 9).

populist A populist generally favors government involvement in the economy to assure growth and opportunity but opposes government protection of individual liberties that seem to threaten traditional values (Chapter 4).

pork barrel politics Pork barrel politics usually refers to spending for specially targeted local projects, acquired by a congressman or senator outside the regular appropriations process (Chapter 9).

precedent A judicial decision that serves as a rule or guide for deciding later cases of a similar nature (Chapter 12).

preemption The Article VI declaration that national statutes are "the supreme law of the land" allows Congress to preempt or displace state authority in areas where they choose to legislate (Chapter 3).

preference poll A poll that offers respondents a list of candidates for a particular office and asks which is preferred (Chapter 4).

presidential support Each year *Congressional Quarterly* reports the proportion of votes in Congress on which the president took a clear position and Congress supported him (Chapter 7).

primary A preliminary election in which voters select candidates to stand under their party label in a later and definitive general election (Chapter 8).

primary groups Face-to-face groups, such as families and friends, with whom an individual has regular, often continuous, contact (Chapter 4).

prior restraint Any limitation on publication requiring that permission be secured or approval be granted prior to publication. No prior restraint means no censorship or permission process that could hinder publication (Chapter 13).

privileges and immunities clause Article IV, section 2, of the Constitution guarantees to the citizens of each state the "privileges and immunities" of citizens of the several states (Chapter 2).

probability sampling A sampling model in which every person in the target population has an identical chance of being selected for the sample to be polled.

progressive tax A tax that takes a higher proportion of the income or wealth of the wealthy than of the poor (Chapter 15).

public opinion The distribution of citizen opinion on matters of public concern or interest (Chapter 4).

push poll A push poll is not a real poll, instead it is designed to influence voters by providing negative and often false information (Chapter 4).

ready response team A group within a campaign staff that is assigned to respond immediately to any charge or negative comment made by the opposition or the media (Chapter 8).

realists Realists contend that the United States should focus its attention and resources on protecting and expanding its own security and prosperity (Chapter 16).

recall A legal or constitutional device that allows voters to remove an offensive officeholder before the normal end of his or her term (Chapter 7).

reciprocity norm Congressional norm promising that if members respect the views and expertise of members of other committees, their committee expertise will be respected as well (Chapter 9).

reconciliation Congressional process to resolve differences if appropriations bills that approve more spending than the spending targets permit (Chapter 15).

redistricting The redrawing of congressional boundaries after each census (Chapter 9).

referendum A legal or constitutional device that allows state and local governments to put questions directly to the voters for determination (Chapter 7).

referral The process by which a bill is referred or assigned to a standing committee for initial consideration (Chapter 9).

regressive tax A tax that takes a greater proportion of the income or wealth of the poor than of the wealthy (Chapter 15).

regulatory commissions Commissions headed by bipartisan boards charged with developing, implementing, and adjudicating policy in their area of responsibility (Chapter 11).

regulatory policy Regulatory policy refers to the legislation and bureaucratic rules that affect the performance of individual businesses and the economy in general (Chapter 15).

remand To send a case back to a lower court for further consideration (Chapter 12).

representative government A form of government in which elected representatives of the people, rather than the people acting directly, conduct the business of government (Chapter 2).

reprieve A temporary postponement of the effect of a judicial decision to give the executive time to consider a request for a pardon (Chapter 10).

republic A limited government in which power is widely though not necessarily equally, vested in the people either directly or through their elected representatives. (Chapter 1).

republican government Mixed or balanced government that is based on the people but may retain residual elements of monarchical or aristocratic privilege. Americans of the colonial period were particularly impressed with the example of republican Rome (Chapter 2).

reserved powers The Tenth Amendment to the U.S. Constitution declares that powers not explicitly granted to the national government are reserved to the states or to the people (Chapter 3).

reserve requirements Requirements that define the portion of a financial institution's total deposits that the Federal Reserve says must be held in cash (Chapter 15).

resource mobilization theory Suggests that since social strain is always present, the key to movement success or failure is the kind and quality of resources that the aroused group can put toward pursuing their rights (Chapter 6).

reverse Action by a higher court to overturn the decision of a lower court (Chapter 12).

reverse discrimination The idea that the provision of affirmative action advantages to members of protected classes must necessarily result in an unfair denial of benefits or advantages to white males (Chapter 14).

right to counsel *Gideon v. Wainwright* (1963) declared that a person accused of a crime has the right to assistance of a lawyer in preparing his or her defense. The right to counsel is part of the meaning of the Fourteenth Amendment's guarantee of "due process of law." (Chapter 13).

rule of four Four justices must approve a writ of certiorari before a case will be heard on appeal before the Supreme Court (Chapter 12).

rule making Process of defining rules or standards that apply uniformly to classes of individuals, events, or activities (Chapter 11).

Rules Committee Committee that writes rules or special orders that set the conditions for debate and amendment of legislation on the floor of the House (Chapter 9).

secession The claim that states have the right to withdraw from the Union (Chapter 3).

secondary groups Broader and more diffuse than primary groups, secondary groups often serve a particular role or purpose in the life of the member, and often do not meet together as a full membership (Chapter 4).

secular The nonreligious, this-worldly, everyday aspects of life (Chapter 1).

seditious libel English legal principle influential in America into the twentieth century, that criticism of government officials and policy that reduced the prestige and influence of government was punishable (Chapter 5).

select committees Temporary committees of the Congress that go out of business once they complete their work or at the end of each Congress unless specifically renewed (Chapter 9).

self-incrimination The Fifth Amendment to the Constitution guarantees that one cannot be compelled "to be a witness against himself." Taking advantage of the right against self-incrimination is often called "taking the Fifth." (Chapter 13).

senatorial courtesy Expectation that the president will clear federal district court judgeship appointments with senators of his party from the state in which the judge will serve (Chapter 12).

seniority norm The norm that holds that the member of a congressional committee with the longest continuous service on the committee shall be its chair (Chapter 9).

separation of powers The idea that distinctive types of governmental power, most obviously the legislative and the executive powers, and later the judicial power, should be placed in separate hands (Chapter 2).

Shays's Rebellion An uprising of Massachusetts farmers during the winter of 1786–87 convinced many Americans that political instability in the states required a stronger national government (Chapter 2).

social contract theory Argument identified with Hobbes and Locke that the legitimate origin of government is in the agreement of a free people (Chapter 1).

social insurance programs Social programs, such as Social Security and Medicare, where prior payments into the program establish eligibility to draw money out upon meeting program requirements (Chapter 15).

social movement A collective enterprise to change the way society is organized and operates in order to produce changes in the way opportunities and rewards are distributed (Chapter 6).

soft money Amendments to the FECA passed in 1979 allowed unlimited contribution to political parties, called soft money, for party building, voter registration, and voter turnout (Chapter 8).

soft power Assets, such as attractive values, culture, and prosperity, that encourage others to emulate and cooperate with a nation (Chapter 16).

special revenue sharing The Nixon administration developed block grants which bundled related categorical grants into a single block grant to enhance state and local discretion over how the money was spent (Chapter 3).

specialization norm The norm that encourages Congress members to specialize and develop expertise in the subject matter covered by their committee assignments (Chapter 9).

spoils system Patronage system prominent between 1830 and 1880 in which strong political parties struggled for control of Congress and the presidency with the winner taking the bureaucracy and its jobs as a prize (Chapter 11).

Stamp Act Congress Delegates from nine colonies met in New York City in October 1765 to coordinate their resistance to Parliament's attempt to tax the colonies directly. They argued that only colonial legislatures could levy taxes in the colonies (Chapter 2).

standing committees Permanent committees of the Congress enjoying fixed jurisdiction and continuing automatically from one Congress to the next (Chapter 9).

stare decisis The judicial principle of relying on past decisions or precedents to devise rulings in later cases (Chapter 12).

substantive due process Late nineteenth-century Supreme Court doctrine that held that most attempts to regulate property were violations of due process (Chapter 12).

suffrage Another term for the legal right to vote (Chapter 8).

supply-side economics Supply-siders argue that lower taxes and lighter regulation improve the business climate, encourage new investment, and expand output (Chapter 15).

supremacy clause Article VI of the U.S. Constitution declares that the acts of the national government within its areas of legitimate authority will be supreme over the state constitutions and laws (Chapter 3).

Supreme Court The high court or court of last resort in the American judicial system (Chapter 12).

surplus If government takes in more money than it spends in a given year, the amount left over is called the surplus (Chapter 15).

symbolic speech Speech-related acts, such as picketing or flag burning, that like actual speech are protected under the First Amendment because they involve the communication of ideas or opinions (Chapter 13).

"take care" clause Article II, section 3, of the Constitution requires that the president "take care that the laws be faithfully executed." (Chapter 2).

tracking poll Frequent polling using overlapping samples to provide daily updates of the status of a race (Chapter 4).

trade associations Associations formed by businesses and related interests involved in the same commercial, trade, or industrial sector (Chapter 6).

traditional conservatives Traditional conservatives believe in low taxes, limited government regulation, and balanced budgets (Chapter 15).

treaty-making power Article II, section 2, of the Constitution gives the president, with the advice and consent of the Senate, the power to make treaties with foreign nations (Chapters 2 and 10).

Truman Doctrine Post–World War II policy of supporting noncommunist forces around the world as they struggled against communist pressure from domestic or foreign sources (Chapter 16).

trustee A view of representation that says representatives should listen to their constituents but use their own expertise and judgment to make decisions about public issues (Chapter 9).

unanimous consent Legislative device by which the Senate sets aside its standard rules for a negotiated agreement on the order and conduct of business on the floor. Plays roughly the same role as rules or special orders in the House (Chapter 9).

unitary executive theory Strong presidency theory holding that the president embodies executive authority and is the sole judge, particularly in wartime, of what is required to protect the nation and its people (Chapter 10).

unitary government Centralized government subject to one authority as opposed to a federal system that divides power across national and subnational (state) governments (Chapter 3).

United Nations (UN) Formed in 1945 and open to all the nations of the world, the UN provides a forum for discussing the full range of international issues and has major peacekeeping responsibilities (Chapter 16).

unreasonable searches and seizures The Fourth Amendment to the Constitution guarantees that citizens will not be subject to unreasonable searches and seizures. Searches must be authorized by a warrant secured on probable cause that specific, relevant evidence is to be found if a particular place is searched (Chapter 13).

veto power The president has the right to veto acts of Congress. The act can still become law if both houses pass the bill again by a two-thirds vote (Chapter 10).

Virginia Plan Outline of a strong national government, written by Virginia's James Madison and supported by most of the delegates from the large states, that guided early discussion in the Constitutional Convention (Chapter 2).

voter registration The process by which members of the voting-age population sign up, or register, to establish their right to cast a ballot on election day (Chapter 8).

voter turnout That portion of the voting-age population that actually turns up to vote on election day (Chapter 8).

voting-age population Total population over the age of eighteen (Chapter 8).

War Powers Resolution Passed in Congress in 1973 requiring the president to consult with Congress on the use of force and to withdraw U.S. forces from conflict should congressional approval not be forthcoming (Chapter 10).

World Bank A key part of the post–WW II international financial system, the World Bank provided capital to finance reconstruction and development, first in Western Europe and then in the Third World (Chapter 16).

writ of certiorari Judicial instrument that makes a formal request that a case be submitted for review by a higher court (Chapter 12).

GLOSSARY OF CASES

Adamson v. California 332 U.S. 46 (1947) Justice Hugo Black argued for total incorporation of First Amendment liberties through the Fourteenth Amendment. He lost 5 to 4 (Chapter 13).

Atkins v. Virginia 536 U.S. 304 (2002) The Supreme Court held that execution of severely retarded persons violated the prohibition against "cruel and unusual punishment" in the Eighth Amendment (Chapter 13).

Barron v. Baltimore 7 Pet. 243 (1833) The Court held that the Bill of Rights applied to the federal government, not the states. As a result, individuals whose rights had been violated by state and local governments had to appeal to state constitutions, state judges, and local juries (Chapter 13).

Bonham's Case (1610) British case in which Sir Edward Coke, chief justice of the King's Bench, laid the foundation for judicial review (Chapter 12).

Bradwell v. Illinois 83 U.S. 130 (1873) The Supreme Court concluded that the federal government had no power to oversee state bar standards; therefore, the Illinois bar could exclude women from the practice of law (Chapter 14).

Brandenburg v. Ohio (1969) This decision overruled *Whitney v. California* to apply a more stringent version of the clear and present danger test. In order to warrant a legitimate suppression of speech, the state had to prove that danger resulting from such speech was imminent (Chapter 13).

Brown v. Board of Education 347 U.S. 483 (1954) This landmark case overturned *Plessy v. Ferguson* and declared that separate was inherently unequal. Consequently, the segregation of public schools was unconstitutional (Chapters 12 and 14).

Buckley v. Valeo 424 U.S. 1 (1976) This decision declared provisions of the 1974 Federal Election Campaign Act (FECA) limiting the amount that a candidate could contribute to his or her campaign to be an unconstitutional limitation on free speech (Chapter 8).

Bush v. Gore 531 U.S. 98 (2000) The U.S. Supreme Court held that the Florida Supreme Court's order to proceed with a hand count of disputed ballots was an unfair electoral practice in violation of the equal protection and due process clauses of the Constitution. The effect of the ruling was to award the presidency to George W. Bush (Chapter 14).

Charles River Bridge v. Warren Bridge 11 Pet. 420 (1837) The Court limited the more expansive property rights precedents of the Marshall Court and concluded that any ambiguity within a contract should be interpreted to benefit the public interest, asserting the rights of the community without fundamentally damaging property rights (Chapter 12).

Civil Rights Cases 100 U.S. 3 (1883) This decision struck down key parts of the Civil Rights Act of 1875. The Court held that Congress could only prohibit racial discrimination by state government and not reach discrimination by individuals (Chapter 14).

Dred Scott v. Sandford 60 U.S. 393 (1857) The Court declared that African Americans, whether free or slave, were not citizens of the U.S. Moreover, slaves were property and could be carried into any state of the union (Chapter 3).

Elk Grove Unified School District v. Newdow 542 U.S. 1 (2004) Michael Newdow, an atheist, sued to have the phrase 'Under God' removed from the Pledge of Allegiance. Newdow's initial victory was set aside by the Supreme Court (Chapter 13).

Employment Division v. Smith 494 U.S. 872 **(1990)** Oregon "free exercise" case, upheld *Reynolds v. United States*, that religious practices are controlled by otherwise valid law (Chapter 13).

Engel v. Vitale 370 U.S. 421 **(1962)** The Supreme Court declared that official prayers, drafted and sponsored by government, for recitation in the public schools were unconstitutional (Chapter 13).

Fisher v. Texas 11–345 **(2012)** This case challenged the Court's findings in Grotter (2003) and Bakke (1978) that universities could consider race as one among many factors in admissions decisions.

Furman v. Georgia 408 U.S. 238 **(1972)** Suspended use of the death penalty in the United States pending state development of jury guidelines to ensure imposition was not arbitrary or racially biased (Chapter 13).

Gibbons v. Ogden 9 Wheat. 1 **(1824)** This decision employed an expansive reading of the commerce clause, the doctrine of the "continuous journey," to allow Congress to regulate commercial activity if any element of it crossed a state boundary (Chapter 3).

Gideon v. Wainwright 372 U.S. 335 **(1963)** This case announced that criminal defendants in state courts were entitled to counsel during their trials unless they had waived their rights (Chapter 13).

Gitlow v. New York 268 U.S. 652 **(1925)** The Court accepted the argument that the First Amendment limited state as well as federal action, but then applied a relaxed version of the clear and present danger test that allowed speech to be punished if it created a "bad tendency" to produce turmoil, even at some point in the remote future (Chapter 13).

Gregg v. Georgia 428 U.S. 153 **(1976)** Following suspension of the death penalty in *Furman v. Georgia* (1972), thirty-five states, including Georgia, rewrote their death penalty statutes to better guide juries. The Supreme Court approved the guidelines and reinstituted the death penalty (Chapter 13).

Grutter v. Bollinger 539 U.S. 306 **(2003)** The Court upheld *Bakke*, allowing affirmative action that takes race into account as one factor among many, but not in a rigid or mechanical way (Chapter 14).

Hudson v. Michigan No. 04–1360 **(2006)** The Court declared that although police had failed to observe the "knock and announce" rule, evidence gained could still be used at trial (Chapter 13).

Lawrence v. Texas 539 U.S. 558 **(2003)** The Supreme Court found that the Texas statute making it a crime for two people of the same sex to engage in certain intimate sexual conduct violates the Due Process Clause (Chapter 14).

Lemon v. Kurtzman 403 U.S. 602 **(1971)** This case established the "lemon test" for state support of religion. Such support must be secular in purpose, not unduly advance or impede religion, and not involve "excessive entanglement" of the state with religion (Chapter 13).

Loving v. Virginia 388 U.S. 1 **(1967)** The Supreme Court unanimously held that Virginia's antimiscegenation law, barring interracial marriage, violated the equal protection clause of the Constitution (Chapter 14).

Mapp v. Ohio 367 U.S. 643 **(1961)** The Court extended the exclusionary rule of *Weeks v. United States* so that it limited state action as well (Chapter 13).

Marbury v. Madison 1 Cr. 137 **(1803)** Chief Justice John Marshall derived the power of judicial review from the Constitution by reasoning that the document was supreme and therefore the Court should invalidate legislative acts that run counter to it (Chapter 3).

McConnell v. F.E.C. 540 U.S. 93 **(2003)** The Supreme Court upheld all major elements of the Bipartisan Campaign Reform Act (BCRA) of 2002, including those permitting regulation of "soft money" and "issue ads." (Chapter 8).

McCulloch v. Maryland 4 Wheat. 316 **(1819)** The Court announced an expansive reading of the necessary and proper clause, holding that Congress's Article I, section 8, enumerated powers imply unspecified but appropriate powers to carry them out (Chapter 3).

McDonald v. Chicago No. 08–1521 **(2010)** The Court expanded the Heller case (2008) to cover state and local governments as well as the federal government. Citizens have an individual right to bear arms which no local of government can infringe.

McLaurin v. Oklahoma 339 U.S. 637 **(1950)** The Court began to chip away at the separate but equal doctrine of *Plessy v. Ferguson* by examining intangible dimensions of equality in higher education. Although this case did not overrule *Plessy*, the Court found that the segregation in question denied the African American student the "equal protection of the laws." (Chapter 14).

Meredith v. Jefferson County Board of Education 551 U.S. _ **(2007)** The Supreme Court held that using race as the sole criterion for assigning students to schools was an unconstitutional violation of the equal protection clause of the Fourteenth Amendment (Chapter 14).

Michigan v. Jackson 475 U.S. 625 **(1986)** The Supreme Court declared that police could not initiate questioning of a defendant who had a lawyer or had asked for a lawyer until that lawyer was present (Chapter 13).

Miller v. California 413 U.S. 15 (1973) The Court allowed states and local communities greater latitude in defining and regulating obscenity (Chapter 13).

Miranda v. Arizona 384 U.S. 436 (1966) The Court concluded that the right against self-incrimination applied during even the initial stages of the legal process. The *Miranda* warnings, outlined to protect these rights, became a standard part of police procedure following this decision (Chapter 13).

Montejo v. Louisiana 556 U.S. _ (2009) Overturned *Michigan v. Jackson* to say that a defendant who had a lawyer might still choose to talk to police without the lawyer present (Chapter 13).

Morse v. Frederick 551 U.S. 393 (2007) Students released from school to attend a public event, in this case the Olympic torch passing through Juneau, Alaska, can still be punished for messages unacceptable to the school (Chapter 13).

Near v. Minnesota 283 U.S. 697 (1931) This decision established an almost complete prohibition against prior restraint on publication by any agent or level of government (Chapter 13).

New York Times Co. v. Sullivan 376 U.S. 254 (1964) By concluding that a public official had to prove either "actual malice" or "reckless disregard for the truth" in order to be awarded damages in a libel case, the Court essentially constructed a right not to be punished after the fact for what has been published (Chapter 13).

Nix v. Williams 467 U.S. 431 (1984) This decision constructed the "ultimate and inevitable discovery exception" for the exclusionary rule so that a prosecutor could admit information into trial if he demonstrated by a preponderance of the evidence that the information obtained illegally would have been discovered eventually by lawful means (Chapter 13).

Paul v. Virginia 75 U.S. 168 (1869) This decision declared that the privileges and immunities clause of the U.S. Constitution guarantees citizens visiting, working, or conducting business in another state the same freedoms and legal protections that would be afforded to citizens of that state (Chapter 3).

Pentagon Papers Case (1971) see *New York Times Co. v. United States* (Chapter 13).

Plessy v. Ferguson 163 U.S. 537 (1896) The Court upheld a state law that segregated the races in transportation. According to the Court's analysis, the races could be confined to separate spheres within society as long as they were treated equally, thus originating the separate but equal doctrine (Chapter 14).

Regents of the University of California v. Bakke 438 U.S. 265 (1978) This landmark affirmative action case stated that race could be taken into account in admissions decisions as long as the institution did not set aside a specific number of seats for which only minorities were eligible (Chapter 13).

Regina v. Hicklin (1868) British case holding that the test of obscenity is whether the material tends to "deprave and corrupt those whose minds are open to such immoral influences, such as children and the mentally depraved." (Chapter 13).

Reynolds v. United States. 98 U.S. 145 (1878) In regard to the Mormon practice of plural marriage, the Court held that "free exercise" of religion claims must give way to "otherwise valid law" governing conduct (Chapter 13).

Ricci v. De Stefano 557 U.S. _ (2009) The Supreme Court held that Frank Ricci, a white fire fighter, had been denied equal protection of the laws when results of a promotion exam were set aside because no blacks had scored high enough to be eligible for promotion (Chapter 14).

Roe v. Wade 410 U.S. 113 (1973) With this landmark decision, the Court struck down a Texas law regulating access to abortion as a violation of a woman's fundamental right to privacy. It recognized two state interests in prescribing abortion and determined that the compelling nature of these interests would depend on the trimester of the pregnancy and present medical knowledge (Chapter 12).

Roper v. Simmons 543 U.S. 551 (2005) The Court reversed earlier decisions to hold that execution for crimes committed before the age of 18 was cruel and unusual (Chapter 13).

Roth v. United States 354 U.S. 476 (1957) Because the Court determined that obscenity was not protected under the First Amendment, it reasoned that material was obscene and therefore unprotected if the "average person, applying contemporary community standards" found the dominant theme of the material "appeals to prurient interests" of society or was "utterly without redeeming social importance." (Chapter 13).

Santa Clara County v. Southern Pacific Railroad (1886) The Court interpreted the word "persons" in the Fourteenth Amendment to apply equally to corporations. The substantive right of persons to enter into contracts was used subsequently as a justification for striking down government regulation of business (Chapter 12).

Schenck v. United States 249 U.S. 47 (1919) This decision announced that speech was not absolutely protected by the First Amendment and could be regulated if it created a "clear and present danger." In this case, a socialist mailer urging draft dodging was deemed punishable (Chapter 13).

Shelby County v. Holder No. 12-96 (2013) The Court struck down elements of the 1965 Voting Rights Act including the critical "preclearance" provisions. The Court argued that the data used to decide which states were covered by the preclearance provisions were outdated (Chapter 12).

Slaughterhouse Cases 83 U.S. 36 (1873) With this decision, the Supreme Court limited the impact of the post-Civil War Amendments by defining U.S. citizenship narrowly and leaving the states to regulate domestic race relations (Chapter 14).

Strauder v. West Virginia 100 U.S. 303 (1880) The Supreme Court concluded that states had the right to limit jury service to men only (Chapter 14).

Sweatt v. Painter 339 U.S. 629 (1950) The Court examined tangible and intangible aspects of equality (facilities, books, and quality of education) to conclude that a law school constructed so that the University of Texas Law School could remain segregated was unconstitutional (Chapter 14).

Texas v. Johnson 491 U.S. 397 (1989) This case upheld flag burning as protected expression or "symbolic speech" by applying the stringent clear and imminent danger test of *Brandenburg v. Ohio* (Chapter 14).

Tinker v. Des Moines School District 393 U.S. 503 (1969) Students have a right to engage in free speech so long as it does not disrupt the basic educational mission of the school (Chapter 13).

United States v. Anthony 24 F. Cas. 829 (1873) The Supreme Court held that laws denying women the right to vote were constitutional (Chapter 14).

United States v. E.C. Knight 156 U.S. I (1895) The Court held that Congress's power to regulate interstate commerce extended only to transportation of goods across state lines, not to manufacturing or production (Chapter 3).

United States v. Lopez 514 U.S. 549 (1995) The Court found that Congress's desire to forbid carrying handguns near schools was too loosely related to its power to regulate interstate commerce to stand. The police powers of the states cover such matters (Chapter 3).

United States v. Morrison 529 U.S. 598 (2000) Citing *U.S. v. Lopez*, the Court found that the Violence Against Women Act was too loosely related to Congress's power to regulate interstate commerce to stand (Chapter 3).

United States v. Windsor No. 12–307 (2013) The Court declared that the Defense of Marriage Act, defining marriage as between one man and one women, was an unconstitutional denial of gay persons 5th Amendment protection of equal liberty (Chapter 12).

United Steelworkers of America v. Weber 443 U.S. 193 (1979) One year after the *Bakke* decision, the Court declared that a private, "voluntary" affirmative action program could be adopted as a temporary measure to benefit African American workers (Chapter 14).

Virginia v. Black 538 U.S. 343 (2003) The Court ruled that cross burning, due to its historical ties to racial fear and intimidation, is not protected speech (Chapter 14).

Webster v. Reproductive Health Services 492 U.S. 490 (1989) The Court upheld all abortion regulations in question and concluded that such regulations did not prohibit a woman from having an abortion, but reasonably furthered the state's interest in encouraging childbirth. The trimester analysis was rejected; *Roe*, however, was not overturned (Chapter 12).

Weeks v. United States 232 U.S. 383 (1914) This decision developed the exclusionary rule in relation to the federal government by holding that information obtained through an illegal search or seizure could not be admitted into evidence at a federal trial (Chapter 13).

Whitney v. California 274 U.S. 357 (1927) This decision applied the "bad tendency" reasoning of *Gitlow v. New York* and upheld the California law that prohibited people from engaging in activities supporting the Communist Party (Chapter 13).

Wickard v. Filburn 317 U.S. 111 (1942) The Court rejected the narrow reading of the commerce power in *U.S. v. E.C. Knight*, to return to the broader reading in *Gibbons v. Ogden* where Congress could regulate virtually all commercial activity (Chapter 3).

INDEX